20¢

American Sea Power
Since 1775

Above, *Fleet Admiral Chester W. Nimitz signs the surrender instrument aboard the* U. S. S. Missouri *in Tokyo Bay on September 2, 1945.*

Below, *Vice Admiral Marc A. Mitscher, U. S. N., awaits results of the Battle of the Philippine Sea on the bridge of his carrier-flagship.*

American SEA POWER SINCE 1775

BY

MEMBERS OF THE DEPARTMENT OF ENGLISH, HISTORY, AND
GOVERNMENT, UNITED STATES NAVAL ACADEMY

Assistant Professor J. ROGER FREDLAND, U.S.N.A.
Lieutenant Commander WILLIAM W. JEFFRIES, U.S.N.R.
Lieutenant Commander NEVILLE T. KIRK, U.S.N.R.
Lieutenant Commander THOMAS F. McMANUS, U.S.N.R.
Commander ELMER B. POTTER, U.S.N.R.
Associate Professor RICHARD S. WEST, JR., U.S.N.A.
Senior Professor ALLAN WESTCOTT, U.S.N.A.

EDITED BY

ALLAN WESTCOTT
Senior Professor, United States Naval Academy

CHICAGO

J. B. LIPPINCOTT COMPANY

PHILADELPHIA   NEW YORK

Preface

Preface

THE PRESENT VOLUME is primarily an operational history of the
Navy, covering its work in peace and war, from the beginnings to
the present, in protection and promotion of our national interests. Inevitably such a treatment calls for a new proportion and a new perspective in view of the great scope and achievements of American sea
power in recent times. Yet amid epoch-making changes, certain con-
stants remain. The achievements just mentioned were built on the
spirit and traditions of the past, and it is highly desirable that not only
professional students but all Americans should have an understanding
of the part played by sea power throughout our history, its relation to
our foreign policies, and its continued importance in any scheme of
national defense.

Without neglecting the narrative interest of the operations themselves and their value as a basis for more advanced professional study,
the present treatment seeks to emphasize those aspects of our naval history of special significance today. In particular it stresses technological
advances and the impact of new weapons on tactical and strategical
concepts, a field in which the record has been one of striking changes,
from the advent of steam propulsion, armor, heavy rifled ordnance,
torpedoes, submarines, and aircraft, to the revolutionary applications
of science to warfare in our own time. The treatment stresses also the
many factors which enter into sea power, including command of trade
routes and communications, shipping, bases, supply of strategic materials, and similar elements which must be considered in any estimate
of national security in the close-knit world of today.

Emphasis, furthermore, has been placed on the close and ever increasing interdependence of sea, land, and air arms. In our military

history joint operations are no new development. Our first naval vessels were commissioned by General Washington to harass enemy communications by sea. In the Revolution and the War of 1812 the operations on Lake Champlain and on the Great Lakes had a vital bearing on the land campaigns. In the Civil War, both on the coast and on the Mississippi waterways, Army and Navy operations were closely interrelated. And in the conflicts of our own century the vast problem of securing the ocean highways for transport of troops and supplies overseas has further illustrated the close integration of all services in war. From both the successes and the failures of co-ordination in the past, there are highly significant lessons for today.

Working in collaboration, each in a selected field, the authors have sought to maintain community of purpose, but have not thought it necessary to avoid some individuality in treatment and style. In a general treatment of this nature, they have considered it needless to indicate fully their source material or their constant obligation to other workers in the naval field. A list of the more useful works of reference is given at the end of the book. To Captain Sherman R. Clark, Head of the Department of English, History, and Government at the United States Naval Academy, the authors owe a special debt for his share in the inception of their work and for his generous co-operation and encouragement in its completion. The authors are particularly grateful for expert criticism and helpful suggestions to their colleague Professor Charles Lee Lewis, to Mr. Louis H. Bolander, Librarian of the Naval Academy, and to Lieutenant R. I. Curts of the Far Eastern Section of the Office of Naval Intelligence. Assistance in research has been cheerfully given by the library staffs of the Naval Academy, the Navy Department, and the Library of Congress. Finally, to many officers of the Navy the authors are indebted for first-hand information and practical suggestions.

Contents

American Sea Power
Since 1775

☆   ☆   ☆   ☆   ☆

1

The American Revolution

THE WAR OF AMERICAN INDEPENDENCE," writes a British historian, "was in all its main features a maritime war."[1] For the British this was clearly true. They were wholly dependent on sea transport for the movement of troops, munitions, and supplies to the theater of war; and for the transit of their armies along the coast, to and from Boston, New York, Philadelphia, and Charleston, they took advantage of sea transport and sea control. Moreover, for the British the war in its later stages became primarily a naval conflict against a coalition of France, Spain, and the Netherlands, the three chief rival naval powers.

For the Americans, the maritime aspect of the war was perhaps less obvious. Much of the hard fighting they did was on shore, in defense of their native soil. Yet, as will be seen, control of water communications played a vital part in the campaigns ending at Saratoga and Yorktown, two decisive victories of the war. Almost equally with the British, the colonists were dependent on sea transport for the export of their products, for the sending of agents abroad, for highly essential reinforcements of troops and munitions from their French ally. Transportation within the colonies was also chiefly by sea. Roads were primitive and slow. Traffic moved along the coast and the broad rivers, the Connecticut, the Hudson, and the streams flowing into the Delaware and Chesapeake bays. Grain from Western Massachusetts, for example, went to Boston, not overland, but down the Connecticut River and thence by sea.

American interests were maritime to a far greater extent than in later years. With only a trickle of pioneers beyond the Alleghenies,

---

[1] Captain W. M. James, *The British Navy in Adversity: A Study of the War of American Independence*, Preface.

3

the colonists were spread along the coast and looked to the Old World for markets and essential imports. Tobacco, rice, and grain from the central and southern colonies sought the European market. New England fish, lumber, and cereals found their best sale in Southern Europe and in the sugar islands of the West Indies, a trade which was carried in New England ships and which also developed into a triangular traffic in African slaves, molasses, and New England rum. British restrictions on this trade, while conforming to the old mercantilist theory that colonies exist for the benefit of the mother country, were one of the potent causes of the Revolution.

Shipbuilding, seafaring, and the fisheries were important New England industries. From native oak and pine, ships could be constructed at half their European cost, with the result that in 1769 American-built ships constituted nearly a third of the British merchant marine. Fisheries and whaling supplemented the produce of the rocky New England farms. In 1750 there were over 300 Massachusetts whalers. "No sea," declared Burke in his stately periods, "but what is vexed by their fisheries; no climate but what is witness to their toils."[2]

The colonists, furthermore, were not without experience in fighting by sea. They had fitted out and transported expeditions against Port Royal, Nova Scotia, in 1690, 1709, and 1710, had shared in the capture of Louisburg in 1745, and had participated in numerous other expeditions of the colonial wars. Merchant ships of the period were usually armed with cannon, and in the Seven Years' War Massachusetts alone fitted out 300 to 400 privateers. All the colonies were familiar with commerce warfare, and when the Revolution came they well understood that by preying on British commerce they could both enrich themselves and draw away British naval pressure from their coasts and seaborne trade.

EARLY OPERATIONS

Figures for the British fleet in this period may give a somewhat exaggerated idea of its strength. In 1775 there were 270 of all classes, including 131 ships of the line, and in 1783 the number had grown to 468. Of these from 80 to 100, consisting largely of frigates and lighter craft, were usually kept on the American station, based at Halifax and Jamaica, though after the advent of France and Spain the

---

[2] *Speech on Conciliation with America.*

concentration was heavier in the West Indies and included more ships of the line. But from 1771 on, the British fleet suffered severely from graft and bad administration. Capable officers declined to serve. It was truly a period of naval adversity, and the incompetence of the government appeared also in the faulty strategic direction of the war.

On the American side, the need for naval forces appeared early in the conflict. In the autumn of 1775, during the siege of Boston, General Washington saw the advantage to be gained by capturing British supply ships entering the port. For this purpose he organized his own little squadron, which he officered and manned from the "amphibious" regiments of the Massachusetts coast. The schooner *Hannah,* under Captain Nicholson Broughton, commissioned by Washington on September 2, may be regarded as our first war vessel, and the ship *Unity,* laden with naval stores, was her first prize. Altogether there were six schooners and a brigantine in the squadron. The best of the skippers was John Manley of Marblehead, and the best of his prizes the *Nancy,* with a cargo of 2,000 muskets, 31 tons of musket shot, 3,000 round shot, several barrels of powder, and a 13-inch brass mortar, "the noblest piece of ordnance ever landed in America."[3] It would have taken the Americans 18 months to have manufactured a like quantity of ordnance.[4] In all, some 35 prizes were taken, estimated with their cargoes at over $600,000, but doubly valuable in that their capture transferred from the enemy to our own forces most useful munitions of war. After the evacuation of Boston in March, 1776, the squadron was less active, and it was disbanded in the next year.

Later in the autumn of 1775 Congress, at the instance of the Rhode Island delegation, appointed a "Naval Committee" of seven for "fitting out armed vessels." Ships were purchased, a Marine Corps of two battalions was established (November 10), and rules and regulations were drawn up by John Adams, largely a simplification of those for the British service. The administration of the Continental Navy throughout the war was in the hands of Congress and was delegated in various ways. An unwieldy "Marine Committee" of 13, one for each colony, controlled naval affairs from December 1775 to December 1779; then a "Board of Admiralty" was set up consisting of three private citizens and two members of Congress; and after 1781 the

---

[3] *N.E. Chronicle,* Dec. 7, 1775, cited in Gardner W. Allen, *Naval History of the American Revolution,* Vol. I, p. 68.

[4] C. O. Paullin, *The Navy of the American Revolution,* p. 68.

administration was centered more efficiently under a single official, Robert Morris, in addition to his duties as Director of Finance. There were subordinate boards in Boston and Philadelphia to direct operations and handle prizes, and ships and officers were also commissioned by American agents in France.

The first ships purchased and assembled at Philadelphia were the merchant vessels *Alfred* and *Columbus,* fitted out respectively as 24- and 20-gun frigates, and the brigs *Andrea Doria* and *Cabot* with fourteen 6-pounders, to which were added the smaller ships *Providence,* 12,[5] and *Hornet,* 10, and the 8-gun schooners *Wasp* and *Fly.* This was the little squadron of 110 guns which was to cope with the British force of 78 ships mounting over 2,000 guns then in American waters. Esek Hopkins, a 58-year-old Rhode Island skipper and ex-privateersman of the Seven Years' War, was made "commander-in-chief," and three of the four captains hailed from New England. The fourth captain, Nicholas Biddle of Philadelphia, who had served as a midshipman in the British Navy, was the able commander of the *Doria,* and Paul Jones, first lieutenant in the flagship *Alfred,* was senior among the officers from the South.

Hopkins' orders from the congressional committee were most sweeping: he was to "attack, take, or destroy" an enemy flotilla in the Chesapeake organized by Governor Dunmore of Virginia, next clear the British from the Carolina coasts, and then sail for Rhode Island and do the same! Fortunately there was a saving clause permitting him to follow such courses as his best judgment should suggest, and this Hopkins proceeded to do. Leaving the Delaware in February, 1776, he sailed for Nassau in the Bahamas, where he landed a force of Marines and seamen and with little or no opposition captured over 100 cannon and mortars and large quantities of military stores, which were to prove a godsend to Washington in his New York campaign. It is doubtful if Hopkins could have done better. Returning to the American coast, he took several prizes, but on the night of April 5–6 the *Glasgow,* 20, from a British division then lying at Newport, ran through his squadron and after a three-hour action escaped with less damage than she inflicted. Among Hopkins' heavily laden ships there was some confusion, and an over-consumption of liquor from prizes

---

[5] Here and later, figures following the names of ships indicate the number of guns carried. Frequently ships carried more guns than their regular rating, a frigate rating as a "44" often mounting 50 or more, but such discrepancies, if significant, are generally indicated.

taken the day before. Hopkins made New London, and later took his ships to Providence. He was not again at sea, and, certainly showing little energy, he was suspended in the next year and afterward dismissed.

COMMERCE WARFARE

From the time of Hopkins' cruise, commerce warfare, with some convoy work and communication service, became the main occupation of the Continental Navy. Supporting it were the "State Navies," which were fitted out by all the colonies except New Jersey and Delaware, but consisted chiefly of small vessels for coastal defense. To these must also be added great numbers of privateers. All shared in commerce destroying, and all may properly be regarded as naval forces engaged in the common cause. The extent of privateering is indicated by the 1,697 letters of marque issued by Congress, together with large numbers issued by the States. The privateers, probably more than 2,000 in all, operated off our own coast, in the West Indies, in British home waters, wherever along the Atlantic sea lanes enemy shipping was to be found. Merchants in every port joined in this grand adventure, which filled their pockets in a patriotic cause. Since the profits[6] were greater and discipline less strict, seamen flocked to the privateers, and national ships had hard work filling out their crews.

Admiral Mahan and other later historians have inclined to depreciate the service of the privateers, both in the Revolution and the War of 1812, and to argue that more could have been accomplished by concentrating upon a national fleet. Writing with an eye to conditions in his own time, and rightly advocating a strong navy, the Admiral had special reasons for minimizing the effects of earlier commerce warfare, but in the Revolution this "infallible method of humbling the British," as John Adams described it, accomplished results which could not have been attained by other means.

Its part in the winning of our independence deserves emphasis. For one thing, though commerce warfare did not directly protect our coasts and trade, it greatly decreased the pressure by forcing the British to scatter their fleet in escort work and trade protection all over the seas, a task in some degree comparable with the inordinate effort

[6] In the Continental service, officers and crew received at first only a third (later a half) share of merchant ship prizes, but full value for captures of privateers and men-of-war. According to an order of 1776, the captors' share was divided into 20 parts, of which eleven and a half went to the officers and eight and a half to the crew.

required in later times to cope with the German submarine. The raiders also slowed down the movement of trade to convoy speed, and sometimes even interfered with the land campaigns. Thus in 1776 the late arrival in Canada of reinforcements for Carleton, which were kept in slow convoys for fear of American raiders, greatly delayed the campaign of that year.[7]

The prizes, as already stated, shifted from enemy hands to our own great quantities of highly essential munitions and supplies. It is a typical instance that when the French fleet under D'Estaing entered Boston in 1778, his needs could not have been supplied save for the timely arrival of prizes taken by our cruisers. The value of these prizes can hardly be reckoned in money terms. Maclay in his *History of Privateering* mentions $18,000,000 as the value of the captures made by the privateers alone—probably a low estimate when it is noted that the privateer *Rattlesnake* in a single Baltic cruise took prizes worth over $1,000,000, and that the *Ranger, Providence,* and *Queen of France* (in this case Continental ships) stole into a Jamaica convoy off the Banks in 1779 and in a day's operations cut out 11 prizes valued at a like sum. It is true that American trade suffered from British privateering, but this would have happened in any event. The American ships taken were fewer and many of them were small vessels in the coastal trade. According to figures provided by Lloyd's, the British lost 2,980 merchant vessels and privateers during the war (excluding recaptures), and the Americans 1,351, of which 216 were privateers.[8] Accepting a value of $30,000 for each prize (a figure used by Maclay), the British total loss amounted to about $90,000,000, and the net loss to $50,000,000.

To an England with finances depleted, in mortal conflict with European enemies, and with a large party sympathetic toward the principles for which the Americans were fighting, the commercial losses were a strong argument for ending the American conflict. All the peace appeals to Parliament from the powerful British mercantile elements stressed the injuries to trade.

As for organizing a large national fleet for commerce warfare, or for any other purpose, this was quite beyond the capacity of the harried, impoverished Continental Congress. Naval affairs under the

---

[7] James, *The British Navy in Adversity,* p. 40. If they had arrived earlier, they might have cut off the American retreat from Quebec. Speaking of the American operations at sea, James remarks that "the power of a well handled mosquito fleet was never more clearly shown." *Ibid.,* p. 38.

[8] Clowes, *The Royal Navy,* Vol. III, p. 296.

Congress were none too well managed. Private interests were eager to take over, and the captures and profits in any case went into the war effort. A navy cannot be improvised. The officers of our Revolutionary fleet were many of them hard fighters and superb seamen, but they showed in general a lack of discipline, teamwork, and understanding of co-ordinated tactics, and sometimes a tendency to subordinate national to personal interests.

These weaknesses cropped out during Hopkins' cruise, and they may be suggested also in the following very brief account of some of the ships built later for the Continental service. In December, 1775, Congress ordered 13 frigates, five of 32, five of 28, and three of 24 guns. Of these, two built near New York and two at Philadelphia were destroyed in 1777 after the British occupation of these cities, and a fifth was captured during the fighting with Howe's fleet in the Delaware. Another Philadelphia-built frigate, the *Randolph,* under Captain Nicholas Biddle, cruised to France in '77 but was lost the next year in the West Indies in a gallant action with the 64-gun ship *Yarmouth.* Biddle had handled the British ship so roughly, according to an observer, that "shortly she must have struck," when, after 15 minutes' action, the *Randolph's* magazine blew up with a terrific explosion. Only four men adrift on wreckage survived.

In the next year the *Virginia,* built at Baltimore, ran aground in the Chesapeake and surrendered to superior force. The six other frigates, built in New England, made for the most part creditable cruises and captures before the heavy concentration against them ended their careers. The *Hancock,* 32, Captain John Manley, surrendered in 1777 to the *Rainbow,* 44. The *Raleigh,* 32, Captain John Barry, was beached on the Maine coast in September, 1778, after a two-day running fight with the *Experiment,* 50, and the frigate *Unicorn,* Barry escaping with part of his crew. The *Providence* and *Boston,* after successful work in commerce destroying, were among several ships rather tamely given up when a British fleet and army captured Charleston in May, 1780. The troops landed at this time were among those that surrendered at Yorktown in the next year. The *Trumbull,* 28, last survivor of the 13 frigates, did not get out of the Connecticut River until 1780. That year she outfought the privateer *Watt* in a fierce action off Bermuda, but in the next year she surrendered after a hard battle to the *Iris* (ex-Continental frigate *Hancock*) and a small consort. Altogether some 50 to 60 ships, ranging from 19 frigates to small sloops and schooners, were in the Continental service, but not more

than half that number were at sea in any one year. After 1777 the
force declined rapidly, both because of losses and because the naval
war was largely taken over by the fleets of France and Spain.

One of the New England frigates, the *Warren*, 32, has been left
for special mention because of her part in the ill-fated Penobscot Expedition in the summer of 1779. Organized at Boston to capture an
enemy outpost and raider's nest established at what is now Castine,
Maine, this expedition was on a large scale, with four state navy ships,
12 privateers, 3 Continental ships headed by the *Warren*, 20 transports, and about 3,000 men aboard the transports and naval vessels,
with Captain Dudley Saltonstall of the *Warren* in general naval command. The force arrived at Castine on July 25. Since the British
fleet at New York had been warned, speed was most essential, and the
big combined force should quickly have taken the three 20-gun sloops
at Castine and then concentrated on the shore defenses. But there were
inexplicable delays and lamentable lack of co-operation between the
ships and troops. When at last on August 13 a British squadron from
New York hove in sight headed by a 64-gun ship, the Americans in-
continently fled up the river and ran their ships ashore, with a loss of
nearly 500 men. The failure of the combined operation may be attributed partly to lack of experience and training, but chiefly to the
glaring incapacity of the naval command.

Arnold on Lake Champlain

More significant than the preceding actions in its direct relation to
land operations was the work of General Benedict Arnold's little
flotilla in 1776 on Lake Champlain. After their unsuccessful attack
on Quebec in the preceding winter, the forces of Montgomery and
Arnold had retreated to Crown Point, where the Americans were now
threatened by a British army of about 13,000 in Canada under Sir
Guy Carleton, the Governor General. The British plan was for an
invasion southward along the Richelieu-Champlain-Hudson line of
water communication, linking up with General Howe in New York,
and cutting off New England, which was considered the storm center
of rebellion, from the colonies to the south.

To block such an advance, General Arnold, who possessed some
sea experience as a commander of merchant vessels, had earlier urged
the building of a strong naval force on Lake Champlain. Construction
of a flotilla had started the winter before, and when Arnold was put in
command in July 1776, he had an odd collection consisting of a sloop,

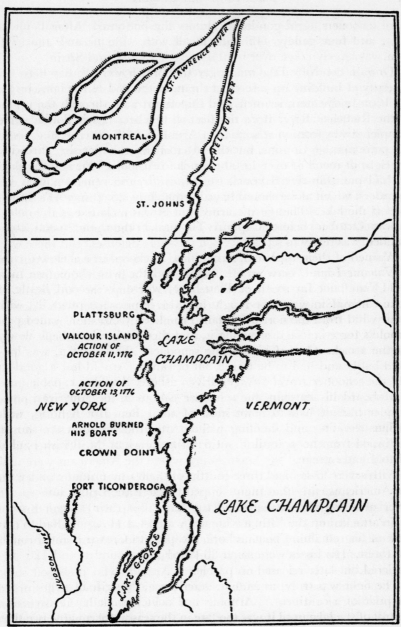

MONTREAL

ST. LAWRENCE RIVER

RICHELIEU RIVER

ST. JOHNS

PLATTSBURG

VALCOUR ISLAND
ACTION OF
OCTOBER 11, 1776

LAKE
CHAMPLAIN

ACTION OF
OCTOBER 13, 1776

NEW YORK

VERMONT

ARNOLD BURNED
HIS BOATS

CROWN POINT

FORT TICONDEROGA

LAKE CHAMPLAIN

HUDSON RIVER

LAKE GEORGE

From *The United States Navy: A History* by Alden and Westcott.

three schooners, eight gondolas (clumsy flat-bottomed gunboats under sail), and four galleys—15 units in all with 94 guns and some 700 men.

To gain control of the waterway the British were thus put to the necessity of building up a force at the northern end of the lake, bringing boats, carpenters, seamen, and ship timbers up through the rapids of the Richelieu River from the fleet at Quebec. Their flotilla when completed was somewhat similar to Arnold's, with 20 craft and about the same number of guns, but the latter of much larger size, throwing a weight of metal of over 1,000 pounds to Arnold's 605, and the British had one ship-rigged vessel, the *Inflexible,* mounting eighteen 12-pounders, which alone should have been able to sweep Arnold's squadron off the lake. Though the army and Sir Guy chafed at the delay, it was October before Captain Thomas Pringle, the naval commander, was ready to set sail.

Warned of their approach, Arnold had anchored in a sheltered cove of Valcour Island, between the island and the west shore (see map p. 11) and not far south of Plattsburg, where the second Battle of Lake Champlain was to be fought in 1814. Somewhat unwarily, with a fair wind from the north, Captain Pringle on October 11 sailed past Arnold's force before discovering it, and then had to beat back slowly for the attack. One of his leading schooners, the *Carleton,* was battered badly and had to be towed out of range. Arnold lost a gondola and the schooner *Royal Savage,* driven ashore. Lacking capable gunners aboard his flagship, the schooner *Congress,* the American commander himself had to point most of the guns. Hot fighting, with Indians shouting and shooting without much effect from the shores, continued from noon until about 5:00 P.M., when the British hauled off to greater range.

With severe losses, and three-fourths of their ammunition shot away, the Americans early that night slipped through the British lines under cover of a fog and retreated up the lake. But their stragglers were again attacked on the 13th, a schooner was lost, and Arnold had to run most of his remaining boats ashore, escaping to Crown Point through the forest. His losses were some 80 killed and wounded and 120 surrendered but later released on parole.

The fight was truly, as Mahan describes it, "a strife of pygmies for the prize of a continent." Arnold's real achievement lay in disputing control of the lake until it was too late in the season for an advance that year. Carleton returned to Canada. But in 1777 conditions were far less favorable than in 1776 for splitting the colonies and quite possibly bringing about an early end of the conflict. Through faulty directions from London, when Burgoyne advanced in 1777, Howe's army had shifted to Philadelphia. Loyalist support in Central New York was not forthcoming, and Burgoyne was finally faced with an overwhelming concentration. Thus Arnold's losing fight on Lake Champlain was an important link in the chain of events leading to the victory of Saratoga, which swung France into open alliance and marked a turning point in the war.

☆ ☆ ☆ ☆ ☆

2
The American Revolution

(CONTINUED)

THE SAILOR OF FORTUNE, John Paul Jones, short, muscular, sandy-haired, an expert seaman and devoted student of his profession, intensely aggressive and keen for glory, became the outstanding naval figure of the American Revolution and a founder of American naval traditions. With many faults of temper, he had the indomitable fighting spirit which spells success in war. Born in 1747 on the west coast of Scotland close to the English border, the son of a gardener and gamekeeper, he early went to sea and quickly rose to captain in the American and West Indies trade. In the colonies at the outbreak of the Revolution, he at once joined the Continental service, was first lieutenant in the flagship *Alfred* of Hopkins' squadron, as already noted, and in May, 1776, received the little sloop *Providence* as his first independent command.

JONES IN AMERICAN WATERS

In the *Providence,* after engaging in convoy work along the coast, he made in the autumn a commerce-destroying cruise to northward, raiding Canadian fishing bases and taking in all 16 prizes, of which about half were brought in. By clever seamanship he escaped the frigate *Solebay* and later the *Milford,* giving the latter "a wild goose chase to tempt him to throw away powder and shot," and posting a Marine with a musket on the afterdeck to return the *Milford's* broadsides fired at too great range. Jones had been promoted to captain, though much to his chagrin he found that, as a result of political pressure, he stood 18th, with 13 juniors passed over him, on the Congressional list published in October, 1776. Late that autumn he made another successful cruise, this time in the *Alfred,* bringing in among

JOHN PAUL JONES. From a bust by Jean Antoine Houdon in the crypt of the Chapel, United States Naval Academy.

other prizes the brig *Mellish,* laden with winter clothing for the British forces in Canada, and described as the most valuable capture thus far in the war. Again he eluded the *Milford,* drawing her away at night from his five prizes.

Long an advocate of carrying the war into British home waters, he sailed for France in November of the next year in the new 18-gun ship *Ranger.* The *Ranger* is thought to have been the first naval vessel to hoist the new flag of 13 stripes and stars, and at Quiberon Bay in February, 1778, Jones arranged with a French admiral for the first fully authorized foreign salute to the American flag. This was not long after the news of Saratoga, and the French secret alliance with America had been signed only the week before.

EARLY ACTIVITIES IN EUROPEAN WATERS

For a year or more preceding Jones's arrival, American raiders had been active in European waters, and American agents busy in the French Court. Silas Deane had arrived in France as representative of Congress early in 1776, and had found the French quite ready to aid the revolting colonies as a means of striking at the British and avenging their humiliations in the Seven Years' War. Through the Foreign Minister Vergennes and the secret agent Beaumarchais, arrangements were made for secret loans from France and Spain and for large shipments of munitions overseas. In the autumn of 1776 Franklin arrived in the Continental ship *Reprisal,* 18, Captain Lambert Wickes. Her prizes, taken during the voyage and brought into Nantes, were probably the first to enter a French port. Loud protests from the British ambassador to the French government over the disposal of these prizes were met by soft words and subterfuges. The enterprising Wickes was out again in the Bay of Biscay early in 1777, and sent into French ports five more prizes, including a Falmouth-Lisbon packet mounting 16 guns. It may be assumed that the American commissioners were not at all displeased by the hot Franco-British controversies which the sale of these prizes aroused.

In the spring Wickes was at sea once more with a squadron of three Continental ships, the *Reprisal,* the *Lexington,* newly in from America, and the *Dolphin,* a small craft purchased secretly at Dover, England, for the American service. With these fast cruisers Wickes ranged the Irish Sea and the Channel, taking 18 prizes. Off the French coast he was chased for eight hours by the British *Solebay,* ship of the line, but he hove his guns overboard, cut some of the ship's beams to give her more "spring," and got safely away. Returning to America that autumn, the *Reprisal* was lost off the Newfoundland Banks with all but one of her crew; and the *Lexington,* also on the way home, was captured by the British cutter *Alert,* after a hard fight in which the *Lexington* exhausted her ammunition.

The effect of these cruises in British waters, together with the activities of American privateers in the same area, was to create something like a panic along the British coasts. Insurance rates went up 23 per cent,[1] convoys became necessary, and shippers sought security for their cargoes by employing neutral French and Dutch bottoms.

Another of the daring American raiders out of French ports was Gustavus Conyngham, a Philadelphia skipper of Irish birth whom the American commissioners provided with the lugger *Surprise,* purchased at Dunkirk, and with a captain's commission sent out in blank by Congress. After a few days' cruise in the Channel in May, 1777, Conyngham was back at Dunkirk with two prizes, one of them a mail packet from Harwich. At British outcries, the *Surprise* and her captures were seized and her skipper was jailed, but the "Dunkirk pirate" was soon released and at sea again in July in the cutter *Revenge,* cruising in British home waters and later in the Bay of Biscay, and disposing of his prizes in the ports of Spain. Conyngham afterward sailed for the American coast and was captured there in April, 1779. He was sent to England in irons and placed in the Mill prison at Plymouth, but escaped with some 50 others in November, burrowing his way out, and thus, as he said, "committing treason through his Majesty's earth."

CRUISE OF THE RANGER

It was with these forerunners, and with the advantage now of open French support, that Jones began his operations in European waters. Sailing in April, 1778, in the *Ranger,* he took several prizes in the narrow seas between England and Ireland, and on April 22 made a bold attempt to bring the war home to the British by burning the 200 or more sailing craft congregated in the harbor of Whitehaven, England, close to his native home. Led by Jones himself, some thirty volunteers in two boats went in, captured the sentinels and spiked the guns in the two forts on the waterfront, and succeeded in setting fire to one of the largest vessels in the harbor. By this time, however, the

1 Clowes, *Royal Navy,* Vol. III, p. 296.

townspeople and garrison were roused, it was broad daylight, and the boats were forced to retreat, after an attack more successful in the alarm created than in actual damage.

Next day the *Ranger* crossed Solway Firth to touch at St. Mary's Isle, the estate of the Earl of Selkirk, where Jones's father had once been employed. Here the plan was to seize the Earl himself as a hostage for the better treatment of American seamen in British prisons. But the Earl was away in London, and Jones gave in to his crew's demand for a levy on the family silver, which he later bought from the men with his own funds and returned.

With alarm fires flaring all along the coasts, Jones next, on the 24th, crossed the North Channel to attack the sloop of war *Drake,* anchored in the Irish port of Carrickfergus. The *Drake,* rather hastily officered and manned, came out to meet the *Ranger,* and the ensuing action, in the words of Jones's report, was "warm, close, and obstinate." It lasted an hour and four minutes, when the enemy "called for quarter . . . her sails and rigging entirely cut to pieces, her masts and yards all wounded, and her hull also very much galled." The American loss was two killed and six wounded; that of the British, according to Jones's estimate, 42 killed and wounded. The *Drake* had a raw crew and her armament of twenty 4-pounders was a little inferior to the *Ranger's* eighteen 6-pounders. But the American commander also had had trouble with some of his officers, especially his first lieutenant Simpson, whom he later put under arrest. Early in May the *Ranger* reached Brest safely with the Stars and Stripes flying from the first British man-of-war taken as an American prize.

Thereafter Paul Jones was ashore in France for over a year, a year of hopes deferred, of endless correspondence with the French ministers and American commissioners, in quest of a promised command worthy of his proved abilities. At last in January, 1779, Jones saw possibilities in an old East Indies ship, the *Duras,* up for auction at L'Orient, and to make sure of her he hastened to Paris, following the advice of Franklin's *Poor Richard's Almanac,* "If a man wishes to have any business faithfully and expeditiously performed, let him do it himself, otherwise he may send."

He got his ship, which he renamed the *Bonhomme Richard* in honor of Franklin, but it was a six months' business to fit her out with guns and crew. For armament, finding a battery of 18-pounders too heavy for her old timbers, he put 28 secondhand 12's on her gundeck, with eight 9-pounders on her poop and forecastle, and as a supplement six old 18-pounders for which special ports had to be cut below the gun-deck aft, close to the water line. In his crew of about 250 there was a nucleus of 79 Americans, in part a contingent of exchanged officers and seamen from British prisons headed by an able officer, Richard Dale, who was made first lieutenant. The rest were of many nations, including 77 British-born. Besides the crew, there were 137 very capable French soldiers trained as Marines.

Jones in the Bonhomme Richard

As finally arranged, Jones in the *Richard* was to command a squadron under the American flag, in which the best, and also the only American ship, was the fine new frigate *Alliance*, 32. Unfortunately, Congress, on the foolish recommendation of some of our agents abroad, had seen fit to put this ship under the command of a half-mad Frenchman, Pierre Landais, formerly discharged from the French service, whom John Adams charitably described as a "jealous . . . absent, bewildered man" with "an embarrassed mind." To the *Richard* and *Alliance* were added the French ships *Pallas,* 32, *Cerf,* 18, and *Vengeance,* 12. Before they sailed from L'Orient on August 17, 1779, the captains of this mixed command were required by the French authorities to sign a concordat, chiefly relating to prizes. Reading of the concordat[2] hardly supports the common assumption that it greatly weakened Jones's authority as commander-in-chief. But it may be admitted, perhaps, that winning the loyalty of disgruntled subordinates was not his strongest point of leadership; and that to achieve unity in this patched-up, bi-national squadron would have required something beyond human power.

Some of this disaffection appeared early in the cruise. Off the west coast of Ireland several prizes were captured, but a boat's crew from the *Richard* seized an opportunity to desert, another boat sent in pursuit was captured, and the *Cerf* at this time separated and returned to France. Landais was insubordinate, and his ship as well as others often disappeared for several days. Around the Orkneys and on the east coast of Scotland, Jones conceived a daring project for an attack on the port of Leith, near Edinburgh, but was frustrated by long delays for persuading his fellow captains into the enterprise, and then by an off-shore gale, September 17, just as the boats were ready to go ashore.

---

[2] Printed in Allen, *Navy History of the American Revolution,* Appendix VIII.

CRUISES OF JOHN PAUL JONES
IN BRITISH WATERS

RANGER
BON HOMME RICHARD
SERAPIS
AFTER SEPTEMBER 25
ALLIANCE
AFTER DECEMBER 27

SCOTLAND

NORTH SEA

LEITH
EDINBURGH

ST. MARY'S ISLE
CARRICKFERGUS
WHITEHAVEN

IRELAND

FLAMBOROUGH
HEAD

TEXEL

ENGLAND

HOLLAND

LONDON

SPANISH
NETHER-
LANDS

ENGLISH CHANNEL

ATLANTIC OCEAN

PARIS

BREST

TO SPAIN

L'ORIENT

FRANCE

From *The United States Navy: A History* by Alden and Westcott.

Prizes, however, were now plentiful, and the four ships were kept busy as they edged southward. This was the area for one of the main objects of the cruise, the interception of a big British convoy from the Baltic, laden with naval stores; and the commander's heart must have leaped with delight when, about 2 P.M. on September 23, 41 sail of such a convoy appeared to northward on the English coast, off Flamborough Head. As Jones's ships were sighted, the convoy scurried to leeward for protection under the coast defenses of Scarborough, while their escort, the fine new frigate *Serapis,* mounting 50 guns, and the *Countess of Scarborough,* 20, beat up to windward to meet the attack.

With light breezes from the southwest, the *Richard* was not up with the *Serapis* until about 7 that night, coming in on her port or weather side as she stood toward shore. During the ensuing action the *Alliance* and *Vengeance* remained for the most part with topsails aback and safely to windward, while the *Pallas* somewhat later engaged and captured the lighter *Countess of Scarborough.*

After brief hails between the *Serapis* and *Richard,* broadsides were exchanged, and this most famous of all frigate battles was joined. At their first discharge two of the *Richard's* 18-pounders exploded, blowing out the deck above and killing most of their crews, with the result that none of the guns in this lower battery were later used. In view of his inferior speed and armament—not counting the 18-pounders, the *Richard's* weight of broadside was 204 to the *Serapis'* 300—Jones fully realized that his best hope was to bring the two ships close aboard, and his early maneuvers had this aim. In a first attempt, his bow reached only to the enemy's quarter, and he backed his sails to wrench clear. As Captain Pearson of the *Serapis* also checked speed to keep abreast, Jones now filled his sails and succeeded in laying the *Richard* athwart the enemy's bow. The American commander himself aided in lashing the *Serapis'* jibboom to his mizzenmast, and wind and tide combined to bring the two ships alongside, locked bow to stern, for the rest of the battle.

The rammers of the guns, as Dale describes it, were "run into the respective ships to enable the men to load." Shooting through the port-shutters, still closed on her hitherto unengaged starboard side, the *Serapis'* heavy 18's tore apart the *Richard's* rotten timbers, which, in Jones's words, "were mangled beyond my powers of description." Most of the lower-deck guns were put out of action. "I had only two pieces of cannon, 9-pounders on the quarterdeck," continues the commander in his report, "that were not silenced." Taking the place of a wounded officer at these guns, and bringing a third 9-pounder from the port side, Jones used grape-shot in two of these to clear the enemy's decks, and directed the third at the *Serapis'* mainmast, which fell just as the battle closed.

Between 9 and 10 P.M., when the *Richard* was aflame in a dozen places and leaking badly, a gunner rushed on deck, seeking to lower the colors and crying loudly for quarter. Jones, according to the legend, felled the man with his boarding pistols, and to Pearson's queries as to whether the *Richard* had struck, he shouted back the memorable reply that has become a naval watchword, "I have not yet begun to fight."[3]

The master-at-arms, no less terrified than the gunner, about this time released some 200 British prisoners, who swarmed on deck; but Dale, with great promptitude, set them to working for dear life at the pumps. One, wilier than the rest, slipped through a port to the *Serapis,* and told Pearson that he would win if he held on.

But the British themselves were heavily beset. From the *Richard's* tops Marines with muskets and sailors with baskets of hand grenades, to the number of over 40, had worked through the tangled rigging of both ships, and with the help of the 9-pounders, had practically cleared the enemy's upper deck. One of the grenades, hurled through a hatchway, fell among loose cartridges on the deck below and set off a tremendous explosion which from the mainmast aft put guns and gun crews out of action. This was a definite turning point in the battle, though it continued for perhaps another hour.

Earlier in the engagement, shortly after the main contestants had grappled, Landais in the *Alliance* had approached, and from a position to windward had fired ill directed volleys of cross-bar and grape shot which, according to the general testimony, did more injury to friend than to foe. Much the same maneuver was repeated a little after 10 P.M. Whatever may have been in the mind of the half-crazed Landais, the presence of this fresh ship, the *Alliance,* no doubt influenced Pearson's decision to surrender.

His flag came down at 10:30 P.M. after a conflict lasting three and a half hours. Casualties in the main frigate action ran to over 100 on each side. "The victory," in the words of Captain A. S. Mackenzie, "was wholly and solely due to the immovable courage of Paul

---

[3] So given by Dale, and certainly the purport if not the precise wording of his reply.

Jones. The *Richard* was beaten more than once; but the spirit of Jones could not be overcome."[4]

Though her crew worked hard to save the battered *Richard,* she had to be abandoned, and sank on the morning of the 26th, Jones shifting his command to the *Serapis.* With the British now in hot search, the squadron left the scene of battle none too soon, but on October 3 arrived safely at Texel Island, outside the Zuyder Zee, with the two captured men-of-war.

To avoid complications, in view of British insistence that Holland surrender the prisoners and prizes taken by the "American pirate," all the ships except the *Alliance* were later placed under the French flag. On December 27 the *Alliance,* now under Jones's command, sailed boldly out of the Texel, eluding the British blockading squadrons, and passing through the Channel in plain view of British ships anchored in the Downs. After a cruise in Spanish waters, she put in at L'Orient for overhaul.

Only brief mention may be made of the events of Jones's later career—his honors in France, where the King bestowed on him a gold-hilted sword and the Cross of the Order of Military Merit, with the title of chevalier, his return to America, his later service in the Russian Navy, and his last years in Paris, where he died in 1792 at the age of 45. On his return to America in 1781 he was greeted first by "47 questions" propounded by the Board of Admiralty at the instance of Congress, which, when satisfactorily answered, were followed by a Congressional letter of thanks for "services by which he has added lustre to his character and to the American arms."

He was later given command of the ship of the line *America,* 74, building at Portsmouth, but, since the war was then near an end, she was presented to France in August 1782, to take the place of a French ship wrecked off Boston harbor. After the peace, Jones returned to Paris as agent for the collection of money due on prizes taken during the war.

Just prior to this assignment, in the spring of 1783, Jones had joined the French fleet in a cruise to the West Indies, as a means of increasing his knowledge of fleet operations. Throughout his mature years he had made naval tactics and strategy his constant study, and his frequent written comments on these subjects indicate a remarkable grasp of the principles of aggressive naval war. Thus, in discussing

---

[4] *Life of Paul Jones,* 1844, Vol. I, p. 205.

the Yorktown campaign, while he admitted that the ulterior objects of grand strategy were accomplished by the "skillful maneuver, the inspiring demonstration, the distant cannonade practiced by the Count de Grasse," he added that, had he been in the shoes of de Grasse, "there would have been disaster to some one off the Capes of the Chesapeake; disaster of more lasting significance than an orderly retreat of a beaten fleet to a safe port. . . ." He continued:

It would have cost more men and perhaps a ship or two; but, in my opinion, success in naval warfare is measured more perfectly by the extent to which you can capture or sink the ships and kill the seamen of the enemy than by the promptness with which you can force him, by skillful manoeuvre or distant cannonade, to sheer off and thereby, with your consent, avoid a conflict that could hardly result otherwise than in conquest for you and destruction to him.

Views such as these reveal his disapproval of French defensive tactics, and add point to the remark ascribed to Napoleon in 1805 after Trafalgar, that "had Jones lived to this day, France might have had an admiral."

The Alliance Under John Barry

The frigate *Alliance*, last mentioned when Jones left her at L'Orient, was brought to America under the command once more of the impossible Landais; but his aberrations necessitated his removal on the voyage across, and he was later discharged from the service. Early in 1781 the *Alliance*, now under Captain John Barry, brought representatives of General Washington to Paris, strongly urging the co-operation of a French fleet on the American coast—a co-operation which later that year resulted in the successful Yorktown campaign. On his return voyage, Barry, in May, 1781, fought a brilliant four-hour action with the ship *Atalanta*, 16, and brig *Trepassy*, 14, off Nova Scotia. Using their sweeps in the prevailing calm, the smaller British ships for a time had the advantage, but when the wind rose they were quickly brought to terms. Early in 1783, while bringing specie home from Cuba and convoying a smaller vessel, Barry in the *Alliance* was engaged by two British frigates in the last notable action fought by American ships in the war. Interposing the *Alliance* between his consort and one of the British frigates in pursuit, Barry saved his smaller vessel and after a sharp 45-minute action forced his opponent, the *Sybil*, to withdraw.

The Yorktown Campaign

Though American naval forces played no important part, the York-town campaign of 1781 is noteworthy both as a highly successful com-bined operation and as a deciding factor in the struggle for independ-ence. Ever since the French alliance two years earlier, General Wash-ington had seen the strategic advantages that might be gained by the co-operation of a strong French fleet on the American coast, and he had conserved his own forces with this end in view. Even a temporary wresting of sea control from the British would cut their supply lines, halt the movement of their troops by sea and prevent a concentration of their land forces, especially when, as in 1781, these forces were divided between New York and the South. As Washington repeatedly insisted, naval superiority would prove decisive; "the navy must have the casting vote."[5]

Since in the preliminary communications of 1781 the French Ad-miral de Grasse had indicated a preference for the Chesapeake as the area for such a combined operation, Washington late in August began quietly moving his army southward from the New York area toward Yorktown, where Cornwallis's army of 7,000 was held in check by forces under Lafayette. The last stage of the journey, from the head of the Chesapeake, was hastened by water transport down the bay.

Moving with promptitude according to plan, de Grasse had already denuded the West Indies stations of naval protection, left homeward-bound convoys to await his return, and sailed north with his entire fleet of 28 of the line, reaching Norfolk on August 30. Admiral Hood, anticipating the northward move but not in such strength, followed with his 14 ships available, passed de Grasse en route, and seeing no signs of the French at Norfolk, went on to join Admiral Graves at New York. On their return to the Chesapeake with a combined force of 19 ships, under Graves as senior officer, the British on September 11 found 24[6] of de Grasse's force at anchor in the mouth of the bay.

Missing an opportunity to concentrate as the French fleet came out, Graves made his ensuing attack on the conventional parallel lines. There was a confusion of signals, failure to bring all the British ships into action, and indecisive results, but with injuries to the British which deterred them from aggressive action during the maneuvering of the

---

[5] Washington to de Grasse, October 28, 1781. *Writings of Washington* (Ed. by W. C. Ford), Vol. IX, p. 399.

[6] Four ships had been detached for service within the bay.

next four days. Meantime de Grasse's purpose had been accomplished, for he had maintained control, and a French squadron of eight ships from Newport with siege artillery had got safely into the bay. With retreat and reinforcements cut off, and besieged by an overwhelming concentration, Cornwallis's army surrendered October 17, after a limited defense.

This was the culminating blow which led ultimately to the fall of Lord North's ministry and negotiations for ending the unpopular American war. Their finances depleted, their shipping and trade heavily injured, and their fleet faced by a strong European coalition, the British were now heartily in favor of letting the colonies go free.

The little Continental navy, ill administered and ill disciplined, dwindling inevitably as the conflict continued, had perhaps only a limited part in winning the war. But it had shared in commerce destruction, kept lines of communication open, aided in the supply of our armies from enemy captures and from abroad, and in the Lake Champlain operations it had vitally influenced the course of the land campaign. Both the Continental ships and the privateers provided a training school for men such as John Barry, Thomas Truxtun, Richard Dale, Joshua Barney, and others who a decade or more later were to aid in organizing a new national navy.

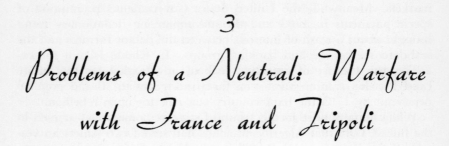

3

Problems of a Neutral: Warfare with France and Tripoli

SINCE THE CONTINENTAL NAVY during the Revolution had faced superior force in home waters, it had been unable to interrupt enemy communications along the seaboard or even to restrain the inshore depredations of British warships. The resulting disruption of American coastwise trade, an important artery of the American economy before the railroad era, had produced widespread commercial distress. Clearly the command of the sea for a distance beyond the coasts was a first requisite of American defense. There were some leaders in the new American republic who held that the only proper naval policy was to build a capital-ship Navy.

After the war, however, the Congress of the Confederation had to grapple with the formidable economic depression which followed demobilization. Without power to tax, and hard pressed to maintain any armed forces at all, the government felt impelled to disband even the skeleton organization of its Navy. In 1785 its surviving vessels were sold or given to France. However thoroughly some Americans were convinced of the need for a naval force to command our offshore waters, this long-range demand of strategy was ruled out at the dictate of immediate financial necessity. In so ruling, Americans were willing to gamble on the continuing usefulness to their new state of the political balance of power in Europe. On future occasions, as in their War of Independence just ended, America might well profit by Europe's distresses.

MARITIME REVIVAL AND A NEW NAVY

Established pre-war channels of American trade were broken up with the coming of peace. England and France, in conformity with

26

the mercantilist principles which continued to govern the administration of colonies, excluded American vessels from the West Indies markets. Meanwhile the United States Government's resumption of specie payments in 1783 and the accompanying deflationary trend brought about a clash of interests between the debtor farmers and the seaboard mercantile and banking groups. In Rhode Island, for example, the scarcity of cash and lack of any market for real estate caused a rise of interest rates on farm mortgages to 30 and even 60 per cent. By 1785 the back country was ripe for open rebellion.

While matters were in this troubled state at home, news arrived in the fall of 1785 that Algerine warships had seized two American vessels off the Portuguese coast. Algiers had already, on the appearance of the United States as an independent nation, solicited treaty relations and the payment of "protection" money exacted of all small-navy maritime states. To give point to the demand, Algerine corsairs[1] now resorted to positive action. Suffering financial chaos at home and without naval strength, the United States could neither resist successfully nor comply with the stipulation of the Barbary state. So Congress temporized, while 21 American crew members and passengers remained captive in Algiers.

After 1783 America urgently needed new overseas markets. The triangular trade of Europe, the West Indies, and New England was not regained after the Revolution and commerce with the West Indies did not greatly increase. An act of Parliament and orders in council had indeed permitted American trade with Britain in goods that did not compete with British manufactures, and after 1784 American vessels of less than 60 tons[2] were admitted to the French West Indies. American trade in the Mediterranean also increased steadily. But it was the opening of the China trade that did most to restore stability to American maritime industry. In 1784 the New York ship *Empress of China,* six months out, reached Canton via the Cape of Good Hope and the Sunda Straits. Two years after this pioneer voyage the first American commercial house was set up in Canton, and by 1792 the "Boston-Pacific Northwest-Canton-Boston" route was well established.

---

[1] The word "corsair" did not necessarily imply connection with piracy. It meant "cruiser," and in that sense was occasionally applied to American warships of the 1812 period. The Barbary corsairs were warships of the Barbary governments—Morocco, Algiers, Tunis, and Tripoli.

[2] It must be noted that the bulk of coastwise traffic employed sloops and schooners averaging less than 70 tons, and that the French restriction was designed to confine American ships to direct trade, reserving the trans-Atlantic carriage to French vessels.

The adoption of the Constitution in 1789 marked a new era of American maritime trade. In its earliest legislation the new government gave protection to American shipping by excluding foreign vessels from the coastwise trade and by imposing harbor dues that discriminated in favor of American ships. After the outbreak of war between England and France in 1793 American shippers gained further advantages. Faced with the destruction of its ocean traffic and striving to maintain the flow of trade to and from its West Indian colonies, the French government opened its ports, both home and colonial, and called in neutral carriers to redress the balance of British sea power. Ten years after the establishment of the new government the United States was the foremost maritime carrier among the neutrals.

The growth of our shipping, however, brought to a head the envious dissatisfaction of the Barbary powers. When the war between Portugal and Algiers came to an end in 1793, the ocean beyond Gibraltar was opened to the latter's corsairs. As the Dey's demands for a treaty settlement with the United States were still unsatisfied, his warships again fell on American commerce, and, in October and November, 11 merchantmen were seized and their complements, numbering 113 American citizens, taken prisoner to Algiers. But this time the United States was better able to deal with the situation. The Constitution empowered Congress to provide for the common defense and also to levy and collect taxes. Hamilton's financial measures had restored the public finances and made ample credit available. American representatives abroad urged positive action and Congress moved to meet the crisis. As our Minister to Spain wrote to Secretary of State Pickering in December, 1793, "If we mean to have a commerce, we must have a naval force to defend it."[3]

A resolution was passed in January, 1794, recommending the establishment of a naval force, and the committee appointed to draw up a program reported in favor of building six frigates. The naval bill, however, was carried through Congress only after acrimonious debate. Members from the back country of the Middle and South Atlantic States reflected in their views the scarcity of cash in the frontier and farming regions. Naval construction was opposed by them as favoring privileged mercantile groups on the seaboard. National defense, in their opinion, should properly be limited to a small standing army for

[3] C. E. Goldsborough, *The United States Naval Chronicle,* p. 51.

the protection of the border against the Indians. Congress finally approved the committee's recommendation by a vote of 43 to 41. So close was the margin that, to placate the opposition, the Naval Act of 1794 was amended to provide that there should be "no further proceeding" with the program if peace with Algiers should be made.

Since there was yet no naval shore establishment, the Cabinet officer responsible for national defense, Secretary of War Henry Knox, was directed to carry out the construction of the frigates. In order that the Navy's needs should contribute wherever possible to the development of domestic industry, construction and procurement operations were deliberately spread. Knox had the ships laid down immediately.[4] New England timber crews were dispatched to North Carolina and Georgia to cut the required live oak, cedar, and pine. Ordnance contracts were let in Connecticut, New Jersey, Pennsylvania, and Maryland. A Boston firm supplied the sails.

Secretary Knox directed the Philadelphia shipbuilder Joshua Humphreys to prepare designs for the frigates and to transmit them to the construction yards. Humphreys had given much thought to the country's naval needs, and a year before Congress authorized construction he had written to Knox:

Ships that comprise the European navies are generally distinguished by their rates; but as the situation and depth of water of our coasts and harbors are different in some degree from those of Europe, and as our Navy for a considerable time will be inferior in numbers, we are to consider what size ships will be most formidable, and be an overmatch for those of an enemy; such frigates as in blowing weather would be an overmatch for double-deck ships, and in light winds evade coming into action. . . . These ships should have the scantlings equal to 74's.

Humphreys worked with the young shipwright Josiah Fox and the Philadelphia draughtsman William Doughty to produce designs for five of the six ships. To carry out Humphreys' concepts of speed and fire-power the associates gave the frigates greater displacement than any existing types. In these vessels the United States Navy in reality introduced a new type of warship. The American "44-gun" frigates, which usually carried over 50 guns, were the heaviest armed frigates afloat. Their 24-pounder main deck guns revolutionized the arma-

---

[4] They were: The *Constitution*, 44 guns, laid down at Boston; *President*, 44, at New York; *United States*, 44, at Philadelphia;; *Congress*, 36, at Portsmouth; *Constellation*, 36, at Baltimore; *Chesapeake*, 36, at Norfolk.

ment of ships of their class. Guns of that caliber had previously been
carried only by ships of the line. The extra length which Humphreys
gave his ships made them as speedy as the fast frigates of foreign
navies. They could outfight anything they could not outrun.

The War Department chartered shipyards and shortly afterwards
detailed to each ship a captain, a naval constructor, and a naval agent
to procure construction materials. Work was well under way when,
early in 1796, news arrived that the American representative in Algiers had negotiated a treaty with the Dey, engaging the United States
to pay $642,000 ransom for prisoners and to send each year a gift of
naval stores worth $21,000. The Senate considered the terms a par-
ticularly obnoxious form of marine insurance, yet cheaper than war,
and so ratified the treaty. Under the Naval Act the settlement with
Algiers threatened to bring construction of the frigates to a standstill.
Another heated debate ensued in Congress and another compromise
was arrived at, directing the President to continue the construction of
three ships. The *Constitution, United States,* and *Constellation* were
selected for completion.

Neutral Rights and European Sea Power

Concern with the trend of war in Europe underlay the decision to
continue naval building. Within a decade of their struggle for independence, the people of the United States found themselves threatened
with involvement in another conflict, waged on an unprecedented
scale and with an intensity unknown to earlier European dynastic and
colonial wars. As neutral traders selling to belligerents, American
shippers gained ill will and came to feel the hand of all the fighting
nations which possessed the tools of sea power.

In its first stage the war that grew out of the French Revolution was
fought with all the bitterness of class conflict, as the neighboring mon-
archs closed on France to make Europe safe for hereditary privilege.
Later, the conflict resolved itself into a battle of men versus machines,
as Napoleon Bonaparte, deprived of sea power, mobilized the armies
of France and her satellites to extend his control over all the coasts
of Europe in an effort to exclude British manufactures. Mass conscription and mass propaganda, first used in war at this time, gave
the struggle some aspects of modern total war. In the final phases,
British fleets blockaded the coasts of France and her allies in the Low
Countries, but throughout the 20 years of war the prime function of
Britain's "far-distant, storm-beaten ships" was the protection of the

power looms and the forges which supplied the world with manufactures and provided England with her principal sinew of war—gold. The Treasury in London financed successive coalitions of continental allies and these eventually brought Napoleon's empire to disaster. Ocean trade became the decisive factor with which each side tried to destroy the other. In this contest between Britain's blockade fleets lying off the shores of Europe and Napoleon's "ring of steel" in all the major continental ports, it soon became evident that the measure of a neutral's rights was the neutral's naval strength.

On the outbreak of war between France and Great Britain, President Washington issued a proclamation of neutrality prohibiting the use of American ports to the privateers and warships of all belligerents. This neutrality policy, since it operated to the advantage of the dominant sea power, was immediately protested by the French government as contravening the terms of the 1778 treaties of alliance. Protests from within the United States were hardly less vigorous. The small farmer-artisan groups, now becoming organized politically under the leadership of Jefferson, espoused the cause of France and denounced the Neutrality Proclamation as partial to Great Britain. The Federalists, deriving their chief strength from the seaboard commercial interests, supported the British and viewed them as defenders of social stability and property rights. Moreover, financial relations with London were important to the American economy. As James Truslow Adams writes,[5]

Not only did the imports from England after independence continue greatly to exceed those from any other country, but the credit extended by English bankers to New England merchants was absolutely essential to the carrying on of their business with almost any part of the world, even the newly developing Northwest Coast-China trade. Bills on London were good virtually anywhere, whereas those on American banks were not. Supercargoes could sell at any port where a favorable market offered, receive London bills, and use them elsewhere to purchase other goods wherever most desirable. Business relations with France had grown closer than before independence was won, but after 1792 these became dangerously speculative, and the more conservative merchants were driven to almost complete dependence upon their London connections.

All attempts of the Federalist administration to create a standing Navy were attacked by their opponents as deliberate attempts to involve the

[5] *New England and the Republic, 1776–1850,* p. 209.

United States in war on Britain's behalf. Before the war was many years old, however, breaches at home were closed by the pressure of external events.

The British government countered the opening of French ports to neutrals with an order in council issued in November, 1793, directing British warships to seize all ships laden with the produce of hostile colonies or carrying supplies to them. Issued without warning and effective immediately, the order resulted in the taking up of 300 American merchant vessels. From the earliest days of independence the United States government had insisted that noncontraband enemy property carried in neutral bottoms was immune from capture. Lacking naval strength, however, the only recourse of the Washington administration was vigorous protest. Partly as a result of American objections, the British shortly afterward revoked the drastic order and replaced it with a decree making effective the "Rule of 1756," which in time of war closed to neutrals hostile colonial ports to which they had not been admitted in peace. The United States in turn protested this order, inasmuch as American vessels of limited tonnage had been permitted to trade with five West Indian ports before the war and were now excluded. The British also made a unilateral extension of the contraband list by seizing grain cargoes consigned to France in neutral carriers, though here their offense was somewhat mitigated by payment for seized cargoes.

John Jay was sent to London in 1794 to press American claims and to secure redress for the seizures. The treaty he concluded the following year, though unpopular in this country, did much to settle outstanding issues and defined the wartime relationship between the countries. The United States consented to the seizure of enemy property and by its silence acquiesced in the Rule of 1756. The seizure of grains was sanctioned if payment was made. The British, in turn, agreed to regard the broken voyage as "purging the origin of commodities." That is, neutrals would be permitted to ship the produce of hostile colonies to enemy home ports if the voyage were broken by call at a neutral home port and payment of duties. By thus controlling the marketing of enemy commodities, Great Britain improved the competitive position of her own products, especially the sugar and coffee of the British West Indies, and strengthened her own war economy.

While the Jay Treaty stabilized Anglo-American relations for more than ten years, it had an opposite effect on our relations with France.

When the terms of the treaty were learned in Paris in 1796 they caused a fresh outburst of resentment. The government of the French Republic had earlier protested against Washington's Neutrality Proclamation and had embargoed 100 American merchantmen for more than a year at Bordeaux without indemnity to the owners. It now charged the United States with violation of the alliance treaties of 1778 by its acceptance of the enemy property and grain contraband provisions. The French government was particularly concerned with the last because a series of bad harvests in western Europe had made France dependent on grain shipments from the Middle Atlantic States. In actual fact, the treaties with France were binding on the United States as a belligerent, not as a neutral, and, in any case, France had already vitiated them by numerous violations in her dealings with American commerce.

THE QUASI-WAR WITH FRANCE

In July of 1796 the French Directory recalled its minister to the United States and shortly after, by its refusal to receive a successor to Minister Monroe at Paris, brought diplomatic relations to an open break. By a series of decrees in 1796 and 1797 French cruisers and privateers were turned loose on American shipping, and though there was not even the pretense of a blockade of the areas specified, neutrals bound to and from British ports or French ports captured by Great Britain were declared good prize. According to Secretary of State Pickering, 316 vessels under the American flag were captured between July, 1796, and June 21, 1797. Augmenting their unlawful seizures, the Directory in January, 1798, ordered French warships and privateers to seize neutral vessels carrying goods of English manufacture or origin.[6] A French legislator commented, "If a handkerchief of English origin is found on board a neutral ship, both the rest of the cargo and the ship itself are subject to condemnation."

The naval strength of the United States meanwhile consisted of three frigates under construction, three more on the stocks with all work suspended, and ten revenue cutters.[7] But as the seizures by

---

[6] Seizure of enemy property and condemnation of the neutral carrying it had been authorized under the decree of March 2, 1797. The old rule of war had held vessel and other cargo immune if enemy property were seized. Under the 1798 decree the fact of British manufacture, regardless of ownership, was declared sufficient for condemnation of the carrier and other cargo.

[7] The Revenue Cutter Service, now the United States Coast Guard, was organized in 1790 under the Treasury Department.

French privateers increased, with one impudent capture actually within the Capes of the Delaware, Congress and public sentiment were thoroughly aroused. In the following months of 1798 a series of measures created the Navy Department (April 30), put into effect the Navy Regulations of 1775 (July 1), and organized the Marine Corps (July 11). Other acts appropriated funds to complete the six original frigates and to provide for the construction and purchase of 24 additional warships mounting from 18 to 32 guns. To expedite the increases, patriotic citizens of New York, Philadelphia, Boston, Baltimore, Richmond, and Salem advanced money on the credit of the United States Government and at local yards began construction of some of the authorized vessels. Captains, lieutenants, and masters, as well as midshipmen and other warrant officers, were appointed. In each principal port of the Atlantic seaboard recruiting of seamen went on vigorously.

Heading the Navy List were the six captains appointed in 1794 to the six frigates. They were, with one exception, veterans of the Revolutionary Navy or privateers, and included John Barry, senior on the List, who had commanded the *Alliance,* and Richard Dale, who had been first lieutenant in the *Bonhomme Richard.* Most conspicuous, perhaps, for professional ability, was stocky Thomas Truxtun, recently a master in the merchant service and a privateersman during the War of Independence. Truxtun was a consummate seaman; he had devised an improved system of masting and rigging and had published a work on it. His manual of celestial navigation was one of the earliest to come from an American press. Prior to his entry in the Navy he had commanded one of the first vessels in the China trade. In 1797 Truxtun wrote the first signal book used in the United States Navy, and his ship organization bills were models for the rest of the Service. He was a tireless drillmaster in matters of ship routine and a rigid disciplinarian. Above all, he possessed a qualification which was not common in the days of sail when seamanship was held the hallmark of the good officer. He believed that, while maintenance of the ship was the first requirement for battle efficiency, knowledge of the use of a ship or a fleet in action was equally important. Accordingly, he was emphatic in urging on his officers and midshipmen the constant study of naval tactics.

Benjamin Stoddert, the first to fill the newly created office of Secretary of the Navy, was an energetic Maryland merchant who combined executive ability with a real talent for war strategy. More than any of his successors before the Civil War, Stoddert appreciated the naval requirements of expanding American foreign trade, and advocated a capital ship policy which was a century in advance of his time.

The purchased vessel *Ganges,* 24, Captain Dale, was the first unit of the Navy to get to sea to protect American shipping against the French. She sailed from Philadelphia on May 24 to cruise between Long Island and the Chesapeake. Four days afterwards Congress authorized the capture of French armed vessels "hovering on the coast of the United States" for the purpose of seizing American ships, and the scope of the act was soon broadened to include French armed raiders "elsewhere on the high seas." To supplement the strength of the Navy the President was authorized to issue letters of marque.[8] Under this act 365 merchant vessels were duly licensed, but, inasmuch as their operations were limited by the law to capture of enemy armed ships having hostile intent and in view of the entire absence of a French merchant marine, privateering cannot be said to have existed. At no time during the French conflict did Congress sanction the capture of private vessels, and for this, as well as other reasons, the operations which followed have been termed a "quasi-war."

Immediately after Congress sanctioned widespread offensive activities, Secretary Stoddert despatched Captain Barry with the *United States,* 44, and the *Delaware,* 20, to the West Indies with instructions to attack French bases and destroy provisions and naval stores. Stoddert accepted the hazards of the hurricane season in order to act promptly and take the enemy by surprise; "The American Navy," he wrote, "should be taught to disregard problematic dangers."[9] Barry, however, found that his force was inadequate to assault fortified places, and returned home two months later, having accomplished little except the capture of two French privateers.

The Navy Department now despatched several squadrons to the West Indies to contain or capture enemy ships in their bases and hideouts, while detailing other ships to patrol the Atlantic coast or convoy merchantmen. As winter weather approached and the danger of raiders on the coast diminished, the bulk of American naval forces was shifted to the West Indies, the home areas of the enemy. Four squad-

---

[8] A merchant vessel was authorized under a letter of marque to capture enemy warships, armed ships, and merchantmen. The term "privateer" was applied to a vessel commissioned under a letter of marque which engaged primarily in the capture of prizes. If a commissioned vessel maintained its normal commercial activity, capturing only such prizes as were necessary to permit the continuance of its voyage, the ship itself was known as a "letter of marque."

[9] Quoted in G. W. Allen, *Our Naval War with France,* p. 68.

rons consisting of 21 frigates, brigs, sloops, and schooners were disposed around the arc of the Antilles from Cuba to Curaçao and thence to Cayenne, French Guiana. A squadron under Stephen Decatur, Sr., patrolled the north coast of Cuba and covered the Florida Straits. Another under Captain Tingey watched the Windward Passage and the northern coast of Hayti. A third under Thomas Truxtun, including the *Constellation* and four other warships, covered the Mona Passage and the Leeward Islands to St. Kitts. The fourth and strongest squadron, commanded by Barry and consisting of the *United States, Constitution,* and eight smaller vessels, patrolled the Windward Islands and kept special watch on Guadaloupe, which had become the principal resort of enemy cruisers and privateers.

In thus concentrating naval strength to hunt down the French raiders in their base areas rather than at large over the ocean, the Navy Department employed its available forces to best advantage. Except for occasional concentrations off Puerto Rico and San Domingo, these dispositions were maintained throughout 1799 and 1800 to the conclusion of peace. The resulting reduction of French spoliations restored the confidence of American shippers, and ocean-borne commerce increased steadily. It was estimated that marine insurance premiums were cut by at least $8,500,000 in the first year of the war, as against appropriations for the Navy in 1799 totaling $2,000,000.

THE NAVAL ACTS OF 1799

Secretary Stoddert now took the view that the satisfactory progress of naval operations in the West Indies had created a favorable opportunity to put forward the program of capital ship construction which he considered essential to the security of the United States in a time of world-wide warfare. This program he embodied in his estimates and defended in his celebrated Secretary's Report of December 29, 1798, in which he analyzed the strategic situation of the United States and the need of commanding American coastal waters against strong European powers. Stoddert asked for twelve 74-gun ships, 12 frigates, and "20 or 30 smaller vessels," with a proportionate shore establishment of docks and stores. Nor did he fail to point out that a large navy would promote the development of domestic manufactures, especially the production of iron, copper, hemp, and canvas.

The anti-Federalist opposition to the 74-gun ships, headed by young Albert Gallatin of Pennsylvania, argued for inshore coast defense based on floating batteries, coastal fortifications, and mobile batteries, all to

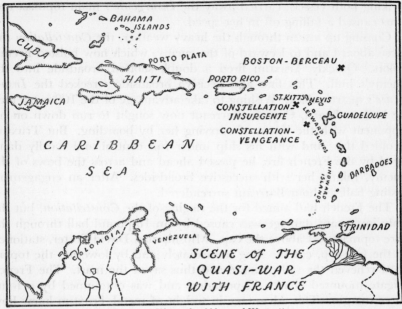

From *The United States Navy: A History* by Alden and Westcott.

be manned by local militia. It was pointed out that the geographic isolation of the United States diminished the need for a navy, that a capital ship fleet capable of operating in distant areas would inevitably involve the nation in difficulties in those areas, and that even without a battle line of 74's American shipping had steadily increased in volume. Congress finally compromised by authorizing six 74's and providing funds for a timber supply and the building of two dry docks.

THE CONSTELLATION CAPTURES THE INSURGENTE

Our squadrons were not adequate to prevent all French cruisers and privateers from slipping to sea. Many sharply fought actions occurred between light units, and there were two notable frigate engagements. Cruising off Nevis at noon, February 5, 1799, the *Constellation* under Truxtun sighted a sail to leeward and altered to a converging course. As the vessels approached on opposite tacks, the stranger, which proved to be the French 36-gun frigate *Insurgente*, went about to a course parallel to that of the *Constellation*. His recognition signals not being answered, Truxtun ordered a chase, in the course of which a squall, striking both vessels, carried away the *Insurgente's* main topmast and thus caused a falling off in her speed.

Coming up astern through the heavy weather, the *Constellation* ran close aboard and to leeward of the enemy, which now hoisted French colors. Quickly Truxtun fired a double-shotted broadside into the enemy's hull. This first and decisive broadside wrecked the *Insurgente's* quarter-deck. Wishing to take advantage of the 100 extra men he had on board, Captain Barreaut now sought to run down on his opponent with the intent of carrying her by boarding. But Truxtun avoided this, and with his ship under full control and hardly damaged by the French fire, he passed ahead and across the bows of the enemy, raking her with successive broadsides. After an engagement lasting half an hour Barreaut surrendered.

The French had aimed for the rigging of the *Constellation,* but the only important damage was caused by an 18-pound ball through the fore topmast just above the cap. Midshipman David Porter, stationed in the fore-top, cut the sling immediately and by lowering the topsail yard relieved the sail pressure and thus saved the mast. The French frigate mounted chiefly 12-pounders and was outgunned by a four-three margin. This advantage in weight of metal Truxtun knew how to use most effectively. His seamanship was superior and he got in the first broadside. American markmanship in the heavy weather fore-shadowed the gunnery prowess that was to distinguish our Navy in the War of 1812. The *Insurgente* suffered 71 casualties including 29 killed; the *Constellation* had two dead and two wounded. Lieutenant John Rodgers and Midshipman Porter, with a handful of men, were put on the *Insurgente* as prize crew. In the heavy weather that developed the ships became separated, and before rejoining the *Constellation* at St. Kitts the Americans spent three sleepless nights and two days handling the injured frigate and keeping 173 prisoners below-decks.

THE CONSTELLATION AND THE VENGEANCE

A year after the capture of the *Insurgente,* the *Constellation* was on station near Basse Terre Rocks when, on the morning of February 1, 1800, a strange sail was observed bearing southeast on course west. Now commodore commanding the Guadaloupe station, Truxtun hoisted English colors to induce the other to come up and hail him. The ruse was not successful and Truxtun bore down to make a closer examination. He shortly found himself overhauling the French 54-gun

Vengeance which possessed at least a three-two superiority of fire-power. Not till eight that evening did he bring the enemy within hailing distance, when he hoisted the American ensign, lighted candles in all battle lanterns, and demanded surrender. At the reply of a round of fire from the enemy's stern and quarter guns, the American commander enjoined his division officers "not to throw away a single charge of powder and shot, but to take good aim and to fire directly into the hull of the enemy . . . to encourage the men at their quarters and to cause or suffer no noise or confusion whatever, but to load and fire as fast as possible when it could be done with certain effect."[10]

From a position on the *Vengeance's* weather quarter, the *Constellation* then engaged in "as close and as sharp an action as ever was fought between two frigates," which continued until nearly 1:00 A.M., "when the enemy's fire was completely silenced and he was again sheering off." But as Truxtun was about to come alongside, his mainmast went by the board, carrying with it the top men and their commander, Midshipman James Jarvis, who had refused to leave his post without orders.

The resultant delay enabled the *Vengeance* to escape. Four days later she ran ashore at Curaçao, with only her fore and mizzen lower masts standing, and five feet of water in her shattered hull. The *Constellation*, with "not a spar or fathom of rigging abaft the foremast," came to anchor at Port Royal, Jamaica, a week after the battle. She had suffered 25 dead and 14 wounded.

Commodore Truxtun fulfilled his mission of protecting commerce and acted in accord with the highest standards of the naval profession when he engaged his superior enemy. While the *Constellation* had a single gun in action she had opportunity to incapacitate her opponent from further commerce raiding and render her liable to capture by another American warship. As it was, Truxtun inflicted three times the number of casualties he had himself suffered and he put his opponent out of action for the remainder of the war. Congress voted him a gold medal and in a formal resolution commemorated the conduct of Midshipman Jarvis.

The overthrow of the French Directory in November, 1799, provided an opportunity for the new executive, Napoleon Bonaparte, to open negotiations for peace, which the French government now earnestly desired. The American Navy had demonstrated unexpected

---

[10] From Truxtun's official report as quoted in G. W. Allen, *Our Naval War with France,* p. 173.

strength in the Caribbean, and France had no wish to force it into a working alliance with British sea power. The American peace mission which arrived in Paris in March, 1800, was thus able to reach a satisfactory settlement, concluded in September of that year.

While Truxtun's victories in the quasi-war with France gained the Navy its first popularity with the American people, it must be noted that the conflict in Europe had helped the slender American forces to hold their ground in the West Indies. Nelson's victory at the Nile in August of 1798 had reduced the strength of the French Navy and dealt a serious blow at French morale, and the French ships of the line had been contained in European waters by the blockading fleets of Britain.

Despite the difficulties of one-year enlistments, inexperienced personnel, inexperienced civil administration, and the political opposition of a considerable part of the population, the Navy accomplished its mission with signal success. During the period of hostilities its 51 vessels took 85 prizes. President Adams in his speech to Congress in November, 1800, voiced the opinion of most Americans: "The present Navy of the United States, called suddenly into existence by a great national emergency, has raised us in our own esteem; and by the protection afforded to our commerce has effected to the extent of our expectations the objects for which it was created."

WAR WITH TRIPOLI

The commerce protection spoken of by President Adams was accomplished economically. By a naval expenditure for the French hostilities estimated at about $6,000,000, protection had been given to an export trade during the war period of over $200,000,000, and to an import trade on which the tariff returns alone amounted to over $22,000,000. The peace establishment brought serious cuts in personnel and a reduction of the fleet to 14 ships, which included the six original frigates, seven smaller frigates and sloops of war, and of the lighter vessels only the little clipper schooner *Enterprise* of 12 guns. The retention of the heavier units was fortunate, for within the year commerce protection in the Mediterranean demanded renewed activity of the naval arm.

Although threats and demands for increased tribute were common practice with all the Barbary potentates, those of the Dey of Tripoli were most insistent, for he had made a treaty in 1796 for only $57,000, and later bitterly envied the far better terms extorted by Algiers. On

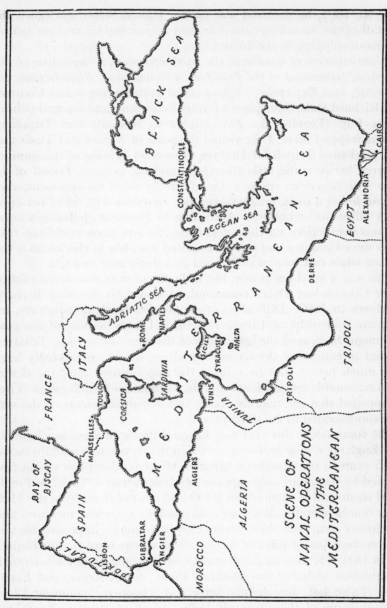

SCENE OF
NAVAL OPERATIONS
IN THE
MEDITERRANEAN

From *The United States Navy: A History* by Alden and Westcott.

May 10, 1801, he declared war on the United States, cut down the flagstaff of the American consulate, and despatched his cruisers against American shipping in the Inland Sea.

In anticipation of trouble in the Mediterranean, a "squadron of observation," consisting of the *President,* 44 (flagship), *Philadelphia,* 36, *Essex,* 32, and *Enterprise,* 12, had sailed in the spring under Commodore Richard Dale, Paul Jones's former lieutenant, and reached Gibraltar in July. Leaving the *Philadelphia* to blockade two Tripolitan cruisers trapped there, Dale visited the ports of Algiers and Tunis and then blockaded Tripoli for 18 days. The chief fighting of the summer occurred between the little *Enterprise* and the polacca *Tripoli* of 14 guns. The American commander repeatedly raked his opponent, and, without losing a man, finally forced her surrender with 50 of her crew of 84 killed and wounded. According to President Jefferson's overcautious instructions on their departure, the squadron could not take prizes since Congress had not yet declared war, but in this instance the polacca when cast loose was stripped to a single spar and sail.

This was a good beginning, but little else of note was accomplished under Commodore Dale's command, or under his successor Richard V. Morris in 1802. Difficulties of supply, lax blockade measures, inadequate leadership, and frequent return of ships because of one-year enlistments hampered the operations of these first two years. Truxtun, selected to command the second squadron, would undoubtedly have done much better,, but he refused the appointment after the denial of his reasonable request for a captain to command his flagship. Thus it happened that the notable events and accomplishments of the war were concentrated in the third year.

The commodore this year was Edward Preble, a vigorous, irascible New Englander, who had seen service in the Revolution and afterward for 15 years in the Merchant Marine. His strict discipline was at first resented by the young ship captains of his squadron—"boys" as Preble called them—all of them under thirty and most of them from the Middle or Southern states. But their commander's aggressive measures and firm justice soon won their devoted loyalty, and he impressed his virtues on these junior officers, nearly all of whom were to win distinction in 1812–15. Besides the *Constitution* (flagship) and *Philadelphia,* his squadron included the *Nautilus, Vixen, Siren, Argus,* and *Enterprise.* These last were lighter brigs and schooners, mounting 12 to 16 guns, some of them recently built and all of them well adapted for work inshore.

Top left, BENJAMIN J. STODDERT, FIRST SECRETARY OF THE NAVY. *Top right,* COMMODORE OLIVER HAZARD PERRY. *Center,* COMMODORE STEPHEN DECATUR. *Bottom left,* COMMODORE THOMAS MACDONOUGH. *Bottom right,* COMMODORE DAVID PORTER.

On his arrival at Gibraltar in September, 1803, Preble found that the *Philadelphia,* coming earlier, had already captured and brought into port the Moroccan corsair *Mirboka,* caught red-handed with an American schooner which she had taken as a prize. In view of this breach of treaty, Preble entered the port of Tangier with a concentration of force, including some ships about to leave the station, and soon secured from the Moroccan ruler a disavowal of the capture and a renewal of the 1786 treaty without further payments.

Meanwhile the *Philadelphia* and the *Vixen* had proceeded ahead to blockade Tripoli, and on Oct. 31, while chasing a small craft to eastward of the harbor, the *Philadelphia* had struck hard on an uncharted shoal. Her commander, William Bainbridge, made every effort to work her loose, backing the sails, starting the pumps, heaving the forward guns overboard, and even cutting away the foremast, while running guns out of the stern ports to bear on the swarm of enemy gunboats which gathered round. Finally, when the frigate listed so that no guns could be brought to bear, he was forced to surrender, with his 22 officers and 315 men. With lighters, on a flood tide, the Tripolitans later got her off and brought her in triumph into the inner harbor, a prize which deprived Preble of at least a fourth of his squadron strength.

The subsequent destruction of the *Philadelphia* by a boat expedition under Lieutenant Stephen Decatur was an outstanding exploit of the war, described in words attributed to Nelson (then blockading Toulon) as "the boldest act of the age."

In a captured 60-ton ketch of Mediterranean rig, the *Mastico,* renamed *Intrepid,* Decatur with 83 picked men, all told, entered the harbor on the night of Feb. 16, 1804. Most of the crew lay hidden or below-decks, while only Decatur, a Maltese pilot named Catalano, and a few sailors in Maltese garb remained above. In response to a hail from the *Philadelphia* as they drifted close, Catalano replied in his own tongue that they had lost their anchors and wished to moor to the frigate. A line was passed, and in a matter of moments, despite a sudden alarmed cry of "Americanos" as they came alongside, the boarders swarmed up the main chains and over the bulwarks. The enemy on deck were put to the sword or driven overboard, combustibles were placed and ignited, and within 20 minutes Decatur and his band were back in the ketch and using their sweeps to pull out of the harbor, now lighted by the blazing frigate, while ill-directed shots from the batteries on shore spattered about them. When news of this

gallant action reached America, Decatur, on Preble's warm recommendation, was promoted to captain, though he was then just over 25.

In the following summer, with the help of six gunboats and two
bomb vessels procured from Sicily, Preble undertook a series of vigorous bombardments of the Tripoli shipping and shore defenses, despite
the fact that the 42 long guns mounted in the *Constitution,* and one
each on the gunboats, were opposed by 115 guns on shore. The first
attack, on August 3, was marked by hard fighting between American
and Tripolitan gunboats at the harbor mouth. Decatur, commanding
one gunboat division, brought his craft alongside an enemy and captured it in a desperate melee with pistols, boarding pikes, and sabers.
As he was towing out his prize, he learned that his brother James had
just been treacherously killed while attempting to board an enemy
boat which had raised the white flag. Overtaking this opponent, now
in flight, Decatur and his crew leaped aboard and overcame opposition, though the leader at one time was thrown to the deck and narrowly escaped death. To quote Preble's report of another encounter:

Lieutenant Trippe, of the *Vixen,* in No. 6, ran alongside one of the
enemy's large boats, which he boarded with only Midshipman Henly and
nine men—his boat falling off before any more could get on board; thus
was he left to conquer or to perish, with the odds of 36 to 11. The
Turks, however, could not withstand the ardor of this brave officer and
his assistants—in a few minutes the decks were cleared and her colors
hauled down.

During the ensuing month there were four further bombardments,
though the enemy boats now stayed cautiously under the batteries,
after being worsted in a style of combat at which they were supposedly
adept. In the second attack one of the former Tripolitan gunboats,
now in American service, blew up, killing or wounding 18 of her men.

As a further means of injuring the enemy, the ketch *Intrepid* was
loaded with 100 barrels of gunpowder and other combustibles, in the
hope that her explosion inside the harbor might destroy shipping and
even shatter the forts. On the evening of September 4 Lieutenant
Richard Somers of the *Nautilus,* with Lieutenants Wadsworth and
Israel and ten volunteers, took the ketch in, moving slowly shoreward
on a light easterly breeze. Shortly before 10:00 P.M., when the *Intrepid* was invisible to the anxious watchers in the ships outside, but
apparently before she had reached her desired destination, the silence
was broken by a terrific explosion. Since there were no survivors, what

happened that night was never fully known. Next day little damage was evident in the harbor; it was believed that Somers' approach had been discovered, and that to prevent capture he had been forced prematurely to fire the magazines.

Decisive results by naval action alone were difficult, for the larger ships were kept at long range by the shoal water and the strength of the shore defenses. Yet it was thought at the time that if Preble had had the help of the heavy frigates which came later, he might have brought the Bey quickly to terms. Additional frigates arrived in September, and since all but two of the captains on the Navy List were senior to Preble, one of these, Samuel Barron, now took over the squadron. Barron, who was ailing, died on the station and was succeeded by John Rodgers. Little further was accomplished until the negotiation of peace terms in the following June. These called for no further tribute, but a payment of $60,000 ransom for the *Philadelphia's* officers and crew.

Prior to the peace, our consul at Tunis, a militant veteran of the Revolution named William Eaton, had formed a league with the Dey of Tripoli's deposed elder brother Hamet, the plan being to stir up a revolt and threaten the Dey by land attack. With a motley army of some 1,200 Arabs, adventurers, and a sturdy handful of American Marines under Lieutenant O'Bannon, Eaton struggled across the desert from Alexandria, invaded Tripoli, and on April 27, 1805, aided by the batteries of the *Nautilus* and *Hornet* off-shore, captured the coastal town of Derne. The fighting in this area undoubtedly helped the peace negotiations, though by the terms of the settlement Eaton and Hamet, with their officers, were later forced to abandon their native followers and go aboard the squadron.

Both the French conflict and the Tripolitan war, thus ended in 1805, helped to gain recognition among the European powers for the new nation overseas. The fighting under Truxtun and Preble had given the reborn Navy useful practical training, and established standards and traditions which could scarcely lapse in the brief years of tension before 1812. American naval practice and organization naturally stemmed from the parent British service. But there were distinctive native contributions from the American merchant service and from American life in the New World—notably a sense of good markmanship, expert seamanship, and, along with something of the frontiersman's impatience of subordination and discipline, something also of his ready initiative and aggressive fighting spirit.

☆ ☆ ☆ ☆ ☆

4
War of 1812: Victories at Sea

A S ONE of the chief neutral maritime nations, greatly dependent on its trade with both Europe and the West Indies, the United States could scarcely hope to escape involvement in the long period of European warfare which extended with but one short break from 1793 to 1815. With France, as already related, we were actually engaged for two and a half years in hostilities at sea. With England, we were very nearly embroiled before the ratification of the Jay treaty, and again after the sharpening of British impressments and trade restraints in 1805–07, when we were saved from war only by the Embargo and Non-Intercourse acts which nearly ruined our trade.

Familiar as later experience has made us with the trials of the neutral trader, we need hardly dwell at length on the specific grievances which finally led to our declaration of war against England, June 26, 1812. The declaration itself stressed (1) impressment of our seamen, and (2) trade restraints, including improper blockades and illegal seizures, carried out often by British ships hovering close to our shores. But other factors will later appear.

Impressment was a grievance of long standing. It grew out of the greatly increased wartime need for men in the British Navy, the poor pay and evil conditions existing within that service, and the flocking of British seamen, with or without steps toward naturalization, into the rapidly expanding American merchant marine. The British denied the right of expatriation—"Once an Englishman always an Englishman." But in seizing men from American merchant vessels they were not only stretching their rights under international law, but none too careful in their tests of the nationality of the men seized. A tough British lieutenant, with his eye on a likely foretopman, was seldom to be deterred by papers (which might be fraudulent) showing the man was an American, either naturalized or native born. Before the war the files of our State Department were filled with complaints of such seizures, and in 1811 a British list showed over 3,000 Americans in His Majesty's Navy.

The offense became almost unendurable when, as in the *Chesa-peake-Leopard* affair of June 1807, men were seized from one of our national ships of war. In this instance the men sought had joined the *Chesapeake* after quitting British naval vessels at Norfolk, Va., but two of them at least were known to be Americans. On the *Chesapeake's* departure for the Mediterranean her commander, James Barron, made no preparation for trouble, and when he was overtaken by H.M.S. *Leopard,* he could offer little resistance. Upon Barron's refusal to permit search, the *Leopard* fired several broadsides, killing or wounding 21 of the *Chesapeake's* crew. Four men were then seized. One of them was hanged, but two survivors were returned in 1811 when the British Government finally disavowed the action. For his negligence in preparation, Captain Barron was suspended for five years.

A more alert spirit of resistance was shown in another pre-war clash, the *President-Little Belt* affair of May, 1811. At the time of this encounter the *President* under Captain John Rodgers had put to sea after a number of flagrant impressment offenses committed by H.M.S. *Guerrière* off New York. When the American frigate met H.M. Sloop *Little Belt,* near the Virginia Capes, there was some confusion of identity, and after an unsatisfactory exchange of signals in the growing darkness, both ships opened fire. The sloop suffered 31 casualties, but sailed away at dawn after refusing proffered assistance. Though diplomacy dropped the affair, it well revealed the increasing tension at sea.

Trade difficulties with England first became serious when the so-called "Rule of 1756" was revived to bar American vessels from the carrying trade between France and her West Indies islands, on the ground that this trade had been restricted to French ships in time of peace. For some years American vessels evaded the rule by taking the goods first to America, transshipping them there, receiving a drawback on duties paid, and thus establishing a "broken voyage." But in the famous *Essex* Case (1805) the British prize court held that, unless there were no drawback on duties and the goods actually became part of the stock of the country, then despite the interruption the voyage was "continuous," and ship and cargo were liable to seizure. England's later policy, in the intensified conflict brought on after 1806 by Napoleon's Continental System, was "No trade except through England." American ships were required to enter British ports, pay duties and port charges, and put their cargoes at British disposition, thus enabling the British to share largely in the profits involved. French policy, on the other hand, as manifested in the Berlin and numerous later decrees, was to penalize American trade if it observed British rules, and this policy was carried out by wholesale seizures of American ships and cargoes in European ports. After the American Non-Intercourse Act, Napoleon still continued the seizures, in order, so he professed, to help the Americans enforce their own law. Obviously the only effective answer to such coercion from both sides would have been an American fleet strong enough to command respect—"the best diplomats in Europe," as Nelson had once described his own ships of the line.

Despite these restrictions, American trade had flourished, and our maritime states were opposed to a war which would sweep their profits away. Furthermore, even in 1812 there were signs that the preoccupations of England in the European conflict might not continue indefinitely, and signs also that England was in a mood for immediate concessions. Actually the obnoxious orders in Council were suspended on June 16, two days before the American war declaration, though it took a month or more for the news to come overseas.

In truth, the War of 1812 was unusual in two striking respects, first, that in both nations there were powerful elements opposed to the conflict, and second, that peace negotiations were under way almost from the time it began. Both these circumstances affected the conduct of the war. The anti-war sentiment in this country was shown by the close vote on the war declaration—79 to 49 in the House and 19 to 12 in the Senate, a majority of the congressman in every maritime state north of Virginia, except Pennsylvania, standing opposed.

The tide was turned by the militant young "War Hawks" from the West and South who had entered Congress after the elections of 1810, men who were in revolt against Jeffersonian pacifism, smarted at the long record of maritime injuries, and above all burned with a zeal to end British aid for the Indians and to open the way for expansion west and north. "Canada, Canada," as John Randolph said, was their whippoorwill refrain. "Extinguish the torch that lights up savage warfare . . . acquire the entire fur trade," was the cry of their able leader Henry Clay. There has been some dispute as to how much the maritime grievances influenced these western leaders. Certainly they did not worry greatly over the stoppage of trade and blockade which were almost certain to ensue. Nor did they take even the first steps toward strengthening the Navy for war.

It may, in fact, be taken as only too typical of military policy in the republic that, though war had long threatened, there was little or no preparation by either land or sea. The regular army was well under 10,000, only a small part of which could be drawn from scattered posts in the West. It was to be increased by 25,000 regulars and 50,000 volunteers, but there was only a trickle of recruits, while the levies of militia were of dubious value and rarely served beyond their state lines. With a white population of over 6,000,000, a draft of men on the scale of World War II would have created an army of some 400,000, but actually hardly a fortieth of this strength was engaged in any one campaign. No doubt the slack war preparations were due not only to anti-war sentiment but to a feeling that the conquest of Canada would be easy—a mere matter, as Jefferson had once said, of "marching to Quebec." Canada had a population of only a half million, largely French, and was garrisoned by only about 7,000 regular troops, with an equal force of militia. But, as will be seen, the hopeful prospect for Canadian operations was soon altered by energetic British defense measures, and by the complete ineptitude of American strategy and leadership in the opening campaigns.

For the Navy the only notable increases in the preceding decade had been 100 more Jeffersonian gunboats, bringing the total to about 250. Their uselessness even for defense must have been realized long before the war, as suggested by the satirical comment, when one of them was washed ashore into a cornfield, that it was "the best gunboat on earth." Of the seagoing navy there were some 16 ships, the best of which were the frigates *Constitution, United States,* and *President* of 44 guns, the *Chesapeake, Congress,* and *Constellation* of 38, and the *Essex,* 32. The rest were sloops of war, schooners, and brigs mounting from 10 to 18 guns. Against this, the great British Navy had in active service over 600 ships, including 124 of the line and 116 frigates. Only one of the line and seven frigates were immediately available at Halifax, but counting squadrons off Newfoundland and in the West Indies, there were nearly 100 in the western Atlantic.

One probable reason for our naval unpreparedness was the assumption that the British fleet would be kept busy in European waters. But in the critical years preceding hostilities, it might have been realized that, while there could be no question of building to rival the

British Navy, an effective American force, available either for commerce protection or commerce destruction, would have guarded American interests and would have been regarded by the British as a strong deterrent to war.

Opening operations. At the outbreak of hostilities, there was no well-settled plan for operations at sea. Decatur and Bainbridge had favored dispersing our ships, singly or in small groups, for commerce raiding. But, in accord rather with the views of Commodore John Rodgers, most of the ships in readiness, including the *President, United States, Congress,* sloop *Hornet,* and brig *Argus,* were assembled at New York, and on June 21 put to sea as a squadron under his command. Rodgers' hope was to encounter a big Jamaica convoy, then homeward bound; but he lost time in a futile stern chase of the British frigate *Belvidera,* and missed the convoy after following it nearly to the English coast. Better luck attended Captain David Porter in the *Essex,* who while cruising in the same period captured the British sloop of war *Alert* and ten merchant prizes. The best justification for the concentration of Rodgers' ships was that it forced the British to adopt a similar concentration, preventing their dispersion all along our coast, and thus facilitating the return of great numbers of American merchant ships, which in anticipation of hostilities had rushed cargoes to Europe in the spring.

Escape of the Constitution. When the *Belvidera* brought the first news of hostilities to Halifax, the admiral on that station despatched the *Africa,* 64, and four frigates, under Captain P. B. V. Broke as senior officer, to operate off our coast. On July 17 this force made contact with the U.S.S. *Constitution,* under Master Commandant Isaac Hull, en route from the Chesapeake to New York. The escape of the American frigate, after a three-day chase extending till the morning of the 20th, has long been celebrated in our naval annals. It was achieved primarily by the masterly seamanship of her commander, one of the ablest ship handlers of his time.

In the calm weather, both sides resorted to towing, at which the British had the advantage in number of boats, but were exposed to fire whenever the boats drew in range. Hull also—and the enemy following his example—made use of kedging, accomplished by bending all the ship's cables together, attaching them to a light anchor dropped nearly a mile ahead, and then heaving away with all hands. On the 19th, the *Constitution* made the most of light breezes, picking up her boats without shortening sail. Then that evening, a little to windward, she was hit by a passing wind squall, and, as the story goes, Hull "let everything go by the run apparently in the utmost confusion, as if unable to show a yard of canvas. . . . The enemy, perceiving this, hastened to get everything snug, before the gust should reach them; but no sooner had they got their sails furled than Captain Hull had his courses and topsails set and the *Constitution* was darting ahead with great rapidity,"[1] By dawn the pursuers were nearly out of sight, and soon abandoned the chase. In view of his persistence and admirable seamanship in this affair, as well as his subsequent victory over one of his pursuers, the *Guerrière,* Hull is ranked by Theodore Roosevelt as "above any single ship captain of the war."

DEFEAT OF THE GUERRIÈRE

Hull put in at Boston but was soon again at sea, without waiting for orders which, had they reached him, would have detained his ship in port. His cruise into Canadian waters and then again southward brought about a meeting on August 17, some 750 miles east of Boston, with H.M.S. *Guerrière,* 44, then Halifax-bound for supplies. Her commander, Captain Dacres, had unbounded faith in his ship's fighting qualities, and only a few days earlier had written in a merchant ship's log that he would be happy to meet the U.S.S. *President,* "or any other frigate of equal force . . . for a few minutes tête-à-tête." In fact British officers of the time, having swept opposition from the seas in the European war with a record of something like 200 victories to five defeats, had grown both over-confident and lax in gunnery.

To windward in a brisk northwester, Hull bore down under easy sail. The *Guerrière* wore two or three times to fire broadsides at long range, but Hull yawed to prevent raking and for the most part held his fire. Finally, as he came within 50 yards' range on the *Guerrière's* port beam, he gave the enemy everything he had. (See diagram, 3.) This was shortly before 6 P.M. In the ensuing cannonade the British firing was wild, for the *Constitution* was injured only in the rigging, whereas the *Guerrière* received in all over 30 hits in the hull, five of them below the water line.

At 6:20 P.M. the British ship's mizzenmast went by the board, acting as a rudder to throw her bow to windward. From this time on she was a beaten ship. Hull crossed her bow for a raking fire and then wore to rake again. In the maneuver the *Guerrière's* bowsprit fouled

---

[1] *Naval Monument,* pp. 8–9.

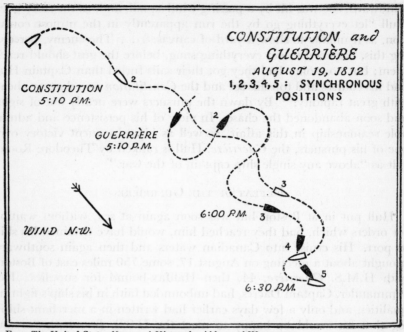

CONSTITUTION and
GUERRIÈRE
AUGUST 19, 1812
1, 2, 3, 4, 5 : SYNCHRONOUS
POSITIONS

CONSTITUTION
5:10 P.M.

GUERRIÈRE
5:10 P.M.

WIND N.W.

6:00 P.M.

6:30 P.M.

From *The United States Navy: A History* by Alden and Westcott.

the *Constitution's* mizzen rigging (position 5), and there were cries on both sides of "Boarders away." The chief losses on each ship were suffered at this time. The American sailing master and the captain of Marines were killed, and Lieutenant Morris was wounded as he leaped to the taffrail to lead his men. The *Guerrière* wrenched away in the seas, and as she did so her weakened fore and mainmasts both fell. She was now rolling her main deck guns under, and surrendered at 7 P.M, when the *Constitution* returned after drawing off briefly for repairs. Badly shot to pieces, the *Guerrière* sank the next day. Aboard the American ship with his crew, Captain Dacres later spoke warmly of the attention shown him by "a brave and generous enemy," in keeping with the chivalrous courtesy of the time.

The figures which follow show that the *Constitution* was the heavier ship, with an advantage in broadside of about ten to seven. But there could be no sounder principle in ship construction than that observed in building the American frigates to outmatch any of their type. And the disparity of five to one in losses, as well as the damage to the British ship, indicate American superiority not only in weight of metal but in the handling of the guns. On the other hand, the *Guerrière*, like the *Macedonian* in the next frigate action, was, as a British naval officer said, "just such a ship as the British have achieved all their single ship victories in . . . such a ship as the British prefer to all others, and have, till the *Guerrière's* loss, always thought a match for any single-decked ship afloat."[2]

Ship	Guns	Weight of Metal	Crew	Killed	Wounded	Total
Constitution*	55	736	468	7	7	14
Guerrière	49	570	263	15	63	78

* There is some variation in the figures for weight of broadside, crew, losses, etc., in this and other actions of the war. Roosevelt deducts about seven per cent from the American weight of broadside, because American shots were lighter than British of the same size.

Cheers from roof, wharf, and street greeted the *Constitution* when on September 12 she drew into Boston harbor, leading Rodgers' squadron which had joined her a day or so earlier in the outer roads. There was a great dinner in Faneuil Hall, and Congress voted Hull a gold medal and $50,000 in lieu of prize money for his officers and crew. It might be said of this, as of the two frigate victories which followed within the year, that they gained little strategic advantage, and were mere pinpricks to the great British Navy, waking it to a realization that it was in for a real war. But the battles worked wonders for American morale. Even New Englanders, lukewarm to the war and cast down by news within the week of the surrender of Detroit by the aged General Hull, uncle of the naval officer, could shout over this Boston-built frigate's victory at sea.

The United States and the Macedonian

In the autumn of 1812, with most of the available naval vessels at Boston, and commerce destruction now definitely the chief objective, it was planned that the ships, either in pairs or singly, should spread fan-wise over the central Atlantic trade routes, from the West Indies and South America to the Canaries and Cape Verdes. Early in October Rodgers with the *President* and *Congress* headed toward the Canaries on a cruise, relatively slight in accomplishment, which lasted till the year-end and covered 11,000 miles. Bainbridge in the *Constitution*, with the sloop *Hornet* under Master Commandant James Lawrence,

[2] Lord Howard Douglass in *Naval Gunnery*, quoted by Roosevelt, p. 115.

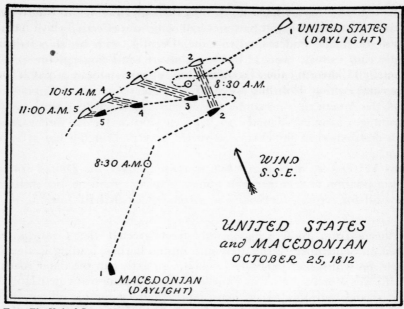

UNITED STATES
(DAYLIGHT)

8:30 A.M.

10:15 A.M.

11:00 A.M.

8:30 A.M.

WIND
S.S.E.

UNITED STATES
and MACEDONIAN
OCTOBER 25, 1812

MACEDONIAN
(DAYLIGHT)

From *The United States Navy: A History* by Alden and Westcott.

sailed for South American waters, where they were to be joined later by Captain David Porter in the *Essex*. Decatur in the *United States*, together with the brig *Argus*, left Boston with Rodgers, but soon separated on a course somewhat more to southward, and, in keeping with his preference for single ship cruising, despatched the *Argus* also to operate alone. On October 25, about 600 miles west of the Canaries, the *United States* encountered the British frigate *Macedonian*, 38, in the second frigate battle of the year.

Though lighter in broadside than the *Guerrière*, the *Macedonian* was a "crack ship," fresh from overhaul, faster than the *United States*, and with an aggressive commander, Captain Carden, whose one purpose was to engage. At the time, it is true, he had no news of the fate of the *Guerrière*, and he also at first took his opponent to be the smaller frigate *Essex*, which had been reported in the vicinity and which was armed chiefly with carronades. It was this error, as Carden testified later in his court martial, which led him during the first of the action to keep at some distance to windward, whereas against the heavier long guns of the *United States* his best hope would have been to press quickly to close range.

As indicated in the diagram, the *Macedonian* held well to windward till her opponent's heavier batteries had come into effective play. Then when she finally endeavored to close, Decatur, with his ship steady under easy canvas, brought to bear a severe semi-diagonal fire (diagram, 2, 3), shooting away the *Macedonian's* mizzen topmast and other spars and cutting down her speed. Unlike the daredevil of Tripolitan days, the American commander fought this action warily, seizing every advantage, avoiding damage to his own ship and even forebearing such destruction of the enemy as would prevent bringing her in as a prize.

By 11:00 A.M., after nearly two hours in contact, the *United States* took a position to rake her now almost helpless opponent, but instead drew off for repairs, receiving the surrender a half hour later.

Ship	Commander	Guns	Weight of Metal	Crew	Casualties
United States	Decatur	54	786	478	12
Macedonian	Carden	49	547	301	104

Contemporary sources are full of details of the harsh discipline aboard the British ship, of the carnage in this battle, and the fighting spirit that prevailed to the end. Eight Americans in her crew, who objected to fighting against their flag, were peremptorily ordered to their stations and at least one of them was slain. The total British casualties were 104, as compared with an American list of 12.

After nearly two weeks spent in repairing the prize, the *United States* brought her safely to Newport and later to New London, though, to temper American pride in the outcome, it may be added that the ships stayed bottled up in Long Island Sound for the rest of the war.

THE CONSTITUTION AND THE JAVA

As already mentioned, the *Constitution* and the *Hornet* under Bainbridge were to have been joined by the *Essex,* but the *Essex* was delayed in reaching an appointed rendezvous off the South American coast, and later set out on her famous cruise against British whalers in the Pacific. In December of 1812 Bainbridge in his two ships spent some time blockading the sloop of war *Bonne Citoyenne* at Bahia. Lawrence in the *Hornet* even challenged the British commander to a single-ship duel, which the latter declined on the proper enough grounds that he had

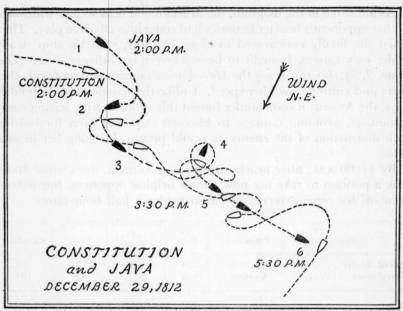

JAVA
2:00 P.M.
1

CONSTITUTION
2:00 P.M.

WIND
N.E.

2

4

3

3:30 P.M. 5

CONSTITUTION
and JAVA
DECEMBER 29, 1812

6
5:30 P.M.

From *The United States Navy: A History* by Alden and Westcott.

large quantities of specie aboard and, furthermore, could not be assured
that the *Constitution* would not intervene. On December 26 Bainbridge left the *Hornet* alone on the blockade, and three days later,
cruising somewhat to southward, made out the British frigate *Java*, 44,
approaching Bahia in company with an American prize.

Though the complicated maneuvering of the battle which followed
can hardly be described in brief space, a glance at the diagram will
suggest the freedom of movement, the skillful jockeying for weather
gage, raking position, or other advantage, which marked this well-
fought action, covering more than three hours. As Mahan describes it:

The battle was not merely an artillery duel, like those of the *Constitution* and the *Guerrière,* the *Wasp* and the *Frolic,* nor yet one in
which a principal manuever, by its effect upon the use of artillery, played
the determining part, as was the case with the *United States* and the
Macedonian. Here it was a combination of the two factors, a succession
of evolutions resembling the changes of position, the retreats and advances, of a fencing or boxing match, in which the opponents work round
the ring, accompanied by a continual play of the guns, answering to the
thrusts and blows of individual encounter.

Top, VICTORY OF THE U.S.S CONSTITUTION OVER H.M.S. JAVA. *Center*, FRIGATE CONSTITUTION BOMBING THE FORTS OF TRIPOLI. Two of the four panels by Gordon Grant in the commodore's cabin of the *Constitution*. *Bottom*, VICTORY OF THE U.S.S. UNITED STATES OVER H.M.S. MACEDONIAN. From a painting by Thomas Birch. Engraving in the Beverly R. Robinson Collection United States Naval Academy Museum.

At 2:30 P.M., some 20 minutes after the opening fire, the *Constitution* was somewhat handicapped by having her wheel shot away, which necessitated steering by relieving tackles rigged two decks below. A turning point came about an hour afterward, when the *Java*, as a result of loss of head sails, was caught temporarily in stays. Then and later, the *Constitution* poured in a deadly raking fire. For a short time (position 5) the *Java's* bowsprit was fouled in the *Constitution's* mizzen rigging, and it was during this contact that American Marines, firing from the main top, gave Captain Lambert of the *Java* a mortal wound. By 4:30 P.M. the British ceased fire, their decks a tangle of fallen spars and rigging, though their colors flew till an hour later, when the *Constitution* returned after a brief withdrawal for repairs.

The casualties given in the table below indicate the severity of the fighting. The table shows also that, though the *Constitution* carried three fewer guns than in the *Guerrière* action, she still had about 13 per cent superiority of broadside. Furthermore, according to a British authority, the *Java's* crew since leaving England had had only one day's practice in firing their guns.

Ship	Commander	Guns	Weight of Metal	Crew	Casualties
Constitution	Bainbridge	52	654	475	34
Java	Lambert	49	576	426	122

By his victory Captain Bainbridge retrieved a long record of ill fortune. In the French war, his ship, surrendering to superior forces, had been the only American man-of-war to strike to the tricolor; he had been subjected to severe humiliation by the Dey of Algiers; and the loss of the *Philadelphia*, under his command, was the greatest disaster of the Tripolitan War. His military character was now redeemed. Following the battle, the *Java* was sunk at sea, and the *Constitution* put back to Boston for overhaul.

The *Hornet*, left on the Bahia blockade, was soon after driven off by a British 74. On her way northward, February 24, 1813, off British Guiana, she won a quick, decisive victory over the British brig *Peacock*, 20 guns. Carrying a main battery of 32's as compared with the *Peacock's* 24-pounders, the *Hornet* closed on her opponent's starboard quarter and reduced her to a sinking condition in less than 15 minutes. The brig actually sank shortly after her surrender, carrying down three of the *Hornet's* prize crew along with six of her own men. The *Peacock*, fitting her name, was a "spit and polish" ship, but her loss, according to the British historian James, could be attributed to "neglect to exercise the ship's company at the guns"—a fault, he added, which "prevailed then over two-thirds of the British Navy."[3]

This was the second of eight sloop and brig actions during the war, in most of which the opponents were equally matched, and in all but one of which the American ship gained the advantage. The earlier sloop action had been a brisk running fight in the preceding October between the *Hornet's* sister ship *Wasp*, 18, under Master Commandant Jacob Jones, and the *Frolic*, 19, in a heavy sea, some 500 miles east of the Chesapeake. Firing as she rolled down in the seas, whereas the *Frolic* fired on the crests, the *Wasp* swept the enemy's decks and injured her hull. When the *Wasp's* men boarded, they found only four alive on the *Frolic's* decks. But both the American sloop and her prize, while engaged in repairs, were captured that same day by a British ship of the line.

THE CHESAPEAKE AND THE SHANNON

James Lawrence, who had come home in the spring of 1813 with four prizes after his victory over the *Peacock*, was now promoted to captain at the age of 32 and added to the "galaxy of naval heroes" whom the nation delighted to honor. He was given command of the *Chesapeake*, 38, then at Boston refitting. Though Lawrence reported her ready for sea by the close of May, she was actually far from "shaken down" or fit for action, for she had numerous raw recruits, a new captain and a new first lieutenant, and all but one of the other lieutenants newly promoted. At Boston, the conditions at Bahia were reversed, for Captain Broke, blockading with the *Shannon* and *Tenedos* off the port, ordered the *Tenedos* to sea and sent in a sharp challenge to single-ship combat. "Only by repeated triumphs," taunted Broke, "can your little navy now hope to console your country for the loss of that trade it cannot protect."

Lawrence had seen the *Shannon* alone outside, and before the challenge reached him he was on his way out to attack. No doubt he should have considered that by so doing he was playing into the Britisher's hands, with much to lose and little to gain. His proper mission was preying on commerce, especially supply ships for Canada, and he could have accomplished it by stealing past the blockaders, as the *Congress* and *President* had done shortly before. Furthermore, in

---

[3] Quoted in Mahan, *Sea Power in Its Relations to the War of 1812*, Vol. II, p. 8.

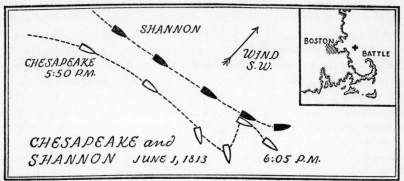

From *The United States Navy: A History* by Alden and Westcott.

fighting the *Shannon* he was opposing a skilled officer who had commanded his ship for the past seven years. Twice a day, five days in the week, Broke had drilled his men at the guns in actual fire at a target, and he had adopted quadrants, circles with degrees marked on them in the deck behind each gun, and other devices to gain accuracy of fire.

In these circumstances, if he were to fight at all on that afternoon of June 1, Lawrence adopted the best tactics for his relatively green ship and crew—a straightaway broadside duel, without complicated maneuvers, at close range. This suited Broke also. He was under easy sail on a southeasterly course as Lawrence about 5:50 P.M. came up on his weather side. Both ships fired as their guns bore, in what for perhaps five minutes was a fairly even exchange. But coming in with a little more headway, the *Chesapeake* slowly forged ahead, while at the same time injury to her foresails threw her bow toward the wind. To add to her misfortunes, it was just at this point that the sailing master and other officers on deck were killed, and Lawrence himself was fatally wounded and carried below.

Meantime the *Chesapeake* had gathered sternway and drifted down on the *Shannon*. At the call for boarders on both sides, the *Chesapeake's* third officer, leading his men on deck, stopped to aid his beloved commander down the steerage ladder. Before he returned, the British were aboard and the hatches battened down. The American Marines fought hard around the mainmast, suffering 32 killed and wounded out of 44. The ships had drifted apart, and there was a brief, fierce struggle on the *Chesapeake's* forecastle, in which Broke himself was severely wounded, but in which there were no officers to rally the American crew. The whole action was over in 15 minutes' time.

The American loss was 48 killed and 97 wounded as compared with a British loss of 43 killed and 29 wounded—a combined casualty list which, as Admiral Gleaves in his *Life of Lawrence* points out, was only 45 less than the loss of the 42 Spanish and British ships in the famous Battle of Cape Vincent. Lawrence died on the way to Halifax, still, it is said, muttering the words "Don't give up the ship," which have become a watchword of our Navy.

Ship	Commander	Guns	Weight of Metal	Crew	Casualties
Chesapeake	Lawrence	50	542	379	145
Shannon	Broke	52	550	330	72

To explain the defeat, the American press were put to it for excuses. It was true that the *Chesapeake's* officers and crew were new to each other, but not true that the men were drunk, or mutinous over delays in pay, or chiefly foreign-born. Undoubtedly the victory should be attributed to the superior training of the British ship, combined with the fortunes of war as manifested in the loss of most of the *Chesapeake's* officers at a crucial time.

It has already been pointed out that these early sloop and frigate battles, glorious as they were, accomplished little toward attaining American aims in the war. The British ships followed a sound policy in engaging, even when they were inferior, for it was their mission to protect commerce and drive American raiders from the seas, and it may be noted that even though they were defeated, they usually brought their American opponents' cruises to an end.

However, the American victories had at least the excellent effect of bolstering popular morale and establishing respect for our fleet and country abroad. And we can hardly blame the young American nation, bullied as it had been for years by the European belligerents, for its state dinners to the naval heroes, its toasts, medals, and huzzas. The Navy had established golden standards of skill, valor, and fighting spirit, which were to endure through the years, and which we may do well to cherish today.

At the outset of the war the British had been found negligent in gunnery, and with frigates of inferior type. Throughout the conflict, in truth, whether in naval vessels, privateers, or merchant craft, the British failed to match American skill in ship handling and ship design.

Loud were the outcries in the British press when the first losses became known. "A national disgrace!" cried old "Thunderer," the *London Times,* after the capture of the *Macedonian.* And again later, "In the name of God, what was done with this immense disparity of force?" [4] The strength was indeed there, though it had been caught napping, and already a blockade of the American coast was closing down. The story is not so glowing for the later years of the war at sea.

[4] *London Times,* Dec. 26, 29, 1812. Quoted in Maclay, *History of the Navy,* Vol. I, p. 416.

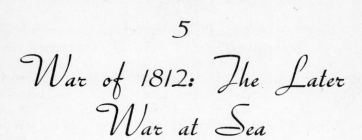

5

War of 1812: The Later War at Sea

The Cruise of the Essex

As noted in the preceding chapter, the frigate *Essex,* 32, under Captain David Porter, was to have joined the *Constitution* and the *Hornet* in the South Atlantic. Missing these ships at several appointed meeting-places, Porter in December of 1812 set out upon his famous cruise against British whalers in the Pacific, which was ended finally by his engagement with the *Phoebe* and *Cherub* in March of 1814. As the *Essex* in 1800 had been the first American naval vessel to round the Cape of Good Hope, so she was now the first to double Cape Horn.

After a stormy passage on short rations, she put in at Valparaiso, Chile, in March, 1813, and thence proceeded northward in pursuit of the 20 or more British whaling vessels operating chiefly in the vicinity of the Galapagos Islands. Of this number, the American frigate captured 12 in all in the six-month period between April and October, and the effect of her cruise was not only to ruin the British industry but to protect American whalers in these waters. Prizes were so numerous that even Porter's youngest midshipman, his foster son David Glasgow Farragut, then not quite 12 years old, was put with a prize crew in charge of one of the captured vessels. Two of the prizes were sent home, one was used as a store ship, and another, renamed the *Essex Junior,* was fitted as an auxiliary cruiser, with 20 light guns. To quote from Porter's *Journal* of the cruise (Vol. II, p. 161):

I had completely broken up the British navigation in the Pacific. . . . The valuable whale fishery there is entirely destroyed, and the actual

From *The United States Navy: A History* by Alden and Westcott.

injury we have done them may be estimated at two and a half million dollars, independent of the expenses of the vessels sent in search of me. They have supplied me amply with sails, cordage, cables, anchors, provisions, medicines, and stores of every description—and the slops aboard them have furnished clothing for the seamen. We have in fact lived on the enemy since I have been in that sea; every prize having proved a well-found store ship for me. . . .

Hearing reports of British cruisers sent in pursuit, Porter in preparation for them sailed 3,000 miles westward to the Marquesas Islands, where he gave his ships a thorough overhauling, made friends with one of the native tribes, and even joined briefly in one of their tribal wars.[1]

With the *Essex* and *Essex Junior* he returned to Valparaiso in February, 1814, and shortly thereafter his expectation of meeting British pursuers was borne out by the arrival in the port of H.M. frigate *Phoebe,* mounting 30 long 18's and sixteen 32-pounder carronades, together with the sloop of war *Cherub* of 28 guns. The *Essex* herself mounted 46 guns, though these were chiefly carronades (forty 32-pound carronades and six long 12's), and at close quarters she might well have proved a match for the *Phoebe* alone, but hardly for the *Phoebe* and her consort combined. In such an encounter, the support of the *Essex Junior* could be discounted, since she was neither armed nor timbered as a man-of-war.

At the first coming of the British, the two frigates were close to a conflict, under conditions very favorable for the American arms. Hearing from a British merchant vessel as he entered the port that most of the *Essex* men were ashore, Captain Hillyar of the *Phoebe* hoped to catch Porter by surprise and luffed his ship close under the *Essex's* bow. But Porter had called all shore parties aboard and was in complete readiness for action, all hands at quarters, "the powder-boys stationed with slow matches ready to discharge the guns, the boarders, cutlass in hand, standing by to board in the smoke." [2] Noting this, Hillyar hailed courteously, and Porter replied in kind, but with the added warning, "You have no business where you are. If you touch a rope-yarn of this ship, I shall board instantly."

The *Phoebe* drew slowly past, her yards almost touching, and the tenuous neutrality of the port was thus preserved.

Fearing the arrival of other enemy ships, Porter in a heavy gale on March 28 sought to slip out to sea to windward of the British blockaders lying near the mouth of the bay. He had almost succeeded when a gust carried away his main-topmast and he was forced to anchor in a cove, near a Chilean battery and about a quarter-mile off shore.

Regardless of neutral waters, the British now closed in, shortly before 4:00 P.M., the *Phoebe* under the *Essex's* stern and the *Cherub* on her bow. Though few of her guns would bear, the *Essex* managed to bring an effective fire against the *Phoebe* with three long 12's run

---

[1] On his departure, Porter left four prizes in the islands, with Lieutenant Gamble of the Marines, three midshipmen, and 26 men to serve as a guard. After a mutiny, Gamble and a small party of loyal followers escaped in one of the prizes and sailed to the Hawaiian Islands, where they were taken later by the *Cherub.*

[2] See Loyall Farragut, *Life of David Glasgow Farragut,* p. 32 ff.

out of her stern-ports. After 30 minutes the British ships hauled off for repairs, but soon re-engaged, both now on the port quarter out of carronade range.

From this point on, with his ship leaking badly and sails shot to ribbons, Porter still tried every expedient for defense. First he cut his cable in a vain attempt to close; then he sought unsuccessfully to run his ship ashore. According to his report,

The enemy from the smoothness of the water [the squall had blown over], the impossibility of our reaching him with our carronades, and the little apprehension that was excited by our fire that had now become much slackened, was enabled to aim at us as at a target . . . and my ship was cut up in a manner which was perhaps never before witnessed: in fine I saw no hopes of saving her and at 20 minutes after 6:00 P.M. gave the painful orders to strike the colors.

Of the *Essex's* crew of 255, there were 58 killed, 66 wounded, and 31 missing. The British on their two ships lost five killed and ten wounded. Aside from the violation of neutrality, a practice common enough in those times and later, Hillyar's attack was expertly handled, taking full advantage of the American injuries and faulty armament. Porter's defense under adverse conditions was perhaps the most stubborn in the whole war. Returning with the survivors of his crew in the *Essex Junior* as a cartel ship, he was received in New York with acclaim, for his ship, before her capture, had struck one branch of British seafaring a highly effective blow.

BLOCKADE OF THE AMERICAN COAST

Even had the *Essex* escaped into the Atlantic, she would have been faced by the British blockade on the American coast, which shut down with increasing severity in the later years of the war. With a view to fostering antiwar sentiment in New England, and also securing foodstuffs for their continental armies, the British in their first blockade order of December, 1812, had closed only the exits from the Delaware and Chesapeake. In May following, the blockade was extended from Long Island to the Mississippi, while still excluding New England. But in May of 1814, when the peace with France released both British naval forces and troops, it was further expanded to "all the ports, harbors, bays . . . and seacoasts of the United States."

Mahan and other advocates of a strong national navy have properly stressed the ruinous effect of this blockade on American shipping and trade. Though rich in natural resources, the nation was dependent for prosperity on the sale of its foodstuffs and tobacco abroad, and dependent also on imports of sugar, tea, and all manner of manufactured goods. Our exports, which had risen to a peak of $138,000,000 in 1807 and were valued at $45,000,000 in 1811, fell to only $7,000,-000 in 1814. Prices of imports sky-rocketed, as evidenced by the fact that on the announcement of peace, sugar dropped over night from $26 to $2.50 a puncheon, and tea from $2.25 to $1.00 a pound. Internal trade was also disrupted, since land communications were slow and poor, and traffic up and down the coast moved largely by sea. A wagon-load of goods from Philadelphia to South Carolina took 46 days, and from Philadelphia to Boston, 17. The stagnation of trade affected tariff revenues and the collection of taxes, with the result that public credit was lowered, the currency depreciated, and the government finally at its wit's end for funds to carry on the war. Conditions as early as the year 1813 are pictured in a contemporary journal: "Our harbors blockaded; our shipping destroyed or rotting at the docks; silence and stillness in our cities; the grass growing upon the public wharves." [3]

The burning of Washington. In both 1813 and 1814 British squadrons lay within the Delaware and the Chesapeake, and in the latter year the arrival in the Chesapeake of 3,400 seasoned troops under General Ross, released from the European war, made possible considerable activities on shore, including the capture and burning of the national capital. These operations, through described as partly "punitive," in retaliation for minor excesses committeed by the Americans on the border, were intended primarily as a diversion to draw attention from the aggressive campaign already planned on the northern frontier.

The British force, augmented from the fleet to about 4,000, landed on August 18 near the mouth of the Patuxent River and began its march toward Washington. Some dozen or more American barges and gunboats under Commodore Joshua Barney, which had been annoying the British from a base in the Patuxent, were driven up the river, Barney burning his boats and joining his 400 or more men to the Washington defense forces under General Winder. Winder had been promised 15,000 troops, but on August 24, the date of his first

[3] *Columbian Centinel,* July 28, 1813. This reference and the sources for other figures above may be found in Mahan, *Sea Power in its Relations to the War of 1812,* Vol. II, ch. XIII.

and only encounter with the enemy, he had less than half that number, mostly raw militia. Though well placed to defend the bridge crossing the East Branch of the Potomac at Bladensburg, just north of Washington, the militia took to their heels as the British steadily advanced.[4] Only the Marines and seamen under Barney kept hammering away with their five artillery pieces until outflanked and left without support.

The British, after burning the Capitol, the White House, and other public buildings, and throwing the government into panic-stricken flight, began on the evening of the 25th their unmolested return to the fleet. Threatened also by a squadron which had worked up the Potomac to Alexandria, the American authorities themselves had burned a frigate and a sloop on the stocks in the Washington Navy Yard. At Baltimore, in a subsequent attack in September, the British ships were kept below the city by the defenses of Fort McHenry, and the landing forces, seeing stiff resistance ahead, soon re-embarked.

DESTRUCTION OF BRITISH COMMERCE

In bright contrast to the stifling effects of the blockade and the breakdown of our coastal defense, were the achievements of our naval cruisers and privateers. The big American frigates, it is true, were carefully watched and shut in port, but the fast, lighter-draft sloops of war could still slip past the blockaders; and American shippers and seamen, deprived of their ordinary livelihood, found an outlet for their energies—and violent animosities—in the fitting out and operating of swift, heavily-armed privateers. As British defense measures tightened, both the sloops and the privately owned raiders pushed their commerce destroying into distant waters, and set up almost a counter-blockade around Britain's home shores.

In this commerce warfare, the heavy frigates, for reasons just given, were less effective than the lighter sloops, and in the later years of the war they were relatively inactive. Throughout the conflict the *Constellation* remained bottled up at Norfolk, defending herself successfully against boat attacks in June of 1813 but never getting out to sea. The *United States* and the captured *Macedonian,* after refitting at New London, failed in several later efforts to escape from Long Island Sound. After 1813 the *Congress* was shut up at Portsmouth, N.H.,

---

[4] Primitive rocket missiles of the period were used here by the British, and also later in the attack on Fort McHenry, as described in "The Star Spangled Banner," "The rockets' red glare, the bombs bursting in air."

and the *President* at New York. Only the lucky *Constitution* managed to elude the Boston blockaders in January of 1814 for a three-months' cruise, and once again in the final stage of the war.

Sloop actions. In effect, however, the British preoccupation with the big frigates facilitated the escape and freedom of action of the smaller naval vessels and privateers. In the West Indies, along the Atlantic sailing routes, and in British home waters, the speedy, clean-lined, skillfully handled American sloops of the *Wasp* type preyed on British shipping. Nor did they hesitate to engage vessels of their own class, the slower, more heavily built British brigs, on which the burden of commerce protection chiefly fell.

As stated in a previous chapter, there were eight of these actions in the course of the war, in seven of which victory rested with the American arms. Two have already been recounted, the victory of the *Wasp* over the *Frolic* and of the *Hornet* over the *Peacock*. The one American defeat was that of the brig *Argus,* 20, Master Commandant W. H. Allen, which in the summer of 1813 extended her raiding into the Channel and the Irish Sea, capturing or destroying a score of merchant vessels in a month's time. She was defeated by the brig *Pelican,* of somewhat heavier broadside, in an engagement in which the American commander was severely wounded and his crew, according to his successor's report, showed a drop in morale resulting from a "very rapid succession of prizes."

A mere roll call of these sloop actions—and little more is here possible—brings up names again made famous when borne by aircraft carriers of World War II. In September of 1813 the "lucky little *Enterprise,*" 14, won a sharp engagement with H.M. brig *Boxer* off the Maine coast. Both commanders, killed in action, were buried side by side in a Portland cemetery overlooking the sea.[5] It was in connection with this battle that the London *Times* (October 22, 1813) made its often-quoted comment, "The fact seems to be but too clearly established that the Americans have some superior mode of firing."

Early in 1814 three of the six new sloops ordered by Congress were ready for action—a second *Wasp,* armed like all these later sloops with 20 short 32's and two long 12's, the *Frolic,* and the *Peacock,* the last two with names commemorating the victories of Jacob Jones and Lawrence. Off the Florida coast the *Peacock* in April won a one-sided gunnery duel with the lighter *Epervier,* and after the action she suc-

---

[5] This was the "sea fight far away" mentioned in Longfellow's poem "My Lost Youth."

ceeded in eluding two British frigates and getting into Savannah with her prize, which carried £25,000 in gold. Under her able commander, Lewis Warrington, the *Peacock* was soon off again for a destructive cruise on the European coast. The *Wasp* also, during the summer of 1814, operated in the British Channel, capturing fourteen prizes, and winning two battles, about two months apart, with the British brigs *Reindeer* and *Avon*. Driven from her second prize by the approach of several enemy vessels, the *Wasp* cruised southward and was later lost at sea. Last spoken in mid-October west of the Cape Verde Islands, she was never heard of again.

The *Peacock* and the *Hornet* escaped from New York in January of 1815, and the latter sloop, under Captain James Biddle, fought on March 23 the last notable naval action of the war. This was with the brig *Penguin*, near the remote island of Tristan da Cunha in the South Atlantic. Though but one gun superior, the *Hornet* made a "perfect wreck" of the *Penguin* in 22 minutes' time, and, with not a shot in her hull, soon rejoined the *Peacock* for an East Indies cruise.

Privateers. The privateers of the 1813–1814 vintage, often specially built for commerce destroying in distant waters, were heavier, faster, and better armed than the improvised craft of 1812. Though individually less successful than the naval vessels, they steadily increased in numbers and effectiveness during the later stages of the war. Mahan gives figures showing that of 22 vessels in the naval service, 18 were engaged in commerce warfare and took 165 prizes. Of the 526 registered privateers, only about 200 engaged in extended operations, taking a total of 1,344 prizes. Of these 1,054 were captured in the last 18 months of the war—an average loss to the enemy of nearly two ships a day which put even the great British merchant marine under a severe strain. Spreading out for their prey to the Caribbean, the North Sea, the Channel and Biscay waters, the South Atlantic, and even the East Indies, these raiders infested every trade route to the British Isles.

They had their share of hard fighting, too, not only with armed enemy merchant vessels but with lighter ships of war. To cite only a few typical examples of their activities, the *Rattlesnake* of Philadelphia and the *Scourge* of New York scoured through the North Sea, the first ship taking 18 prizes valued at a million dollars, and the second in a year's time taking 27. *Lion* took 14 ships off the Spanish coast and sold their cargoes at L'Orient for $400,000. *Kemp* of Baltimore drew off the frigate watchdog from a convoy of eight West Indies

ships, and then, doubling back, boarded six of them and got away
with four. The *Chasseur,* another famous Baltimore raider, under
Captain Tom Boyle, operated in the Channel during the winter of
1814–1815, sending ashore a not-too-fantastic mock proclamation putting "the seacoast of the United Kingdom . . . in a state of strict and
rigorous blockade." [6] Boyle later in the West Indies boarded and captured a 15-gun naval schooner, the *St. Lawrence,* apologizing afterward to his owners for "having sought a contest with a king's ship,
knowing that is not our object." [7] The *Yankee* of Bristol, R.I., said to
have been one of the most successful privateers, took 40 prizes during
the war, valued at $3,000,000.

Best instance of the fighting spirit of the privateersmen is afforded
by the defense of the *General Armstrong,* 14, in September, 1814,
when pinned down by three British men-of-war at Fayal in the Azores.
The British attacked first with boats and barges and finally by a long-
range bombardment, but before the American commander scuttled
his ship and escaped with his crew ashore he had inflicted the extraordinary loss on the enemy of 65 killed and 117 wounded. Since the
British were carrying troops and guns for the Louisiana expedition,
the three weeks' delay caused by the *Armstrong* greatly aided Jackson's preparations at New Orleans.

Not only did this commerce warfare bring to American shipowners
and seamen a very solid recoupment for their losses by the blockade;
it had the sound strategic effect of creating among the powerful British
merchant classes a strong opposition to the war. The files of the Admiralty were filled with their protests. Most violent was the declaration
of the Glasgow merchants in September of 1814:

At a time when we are at peace with all the world . . . it is equally
disheartening and mortifying that our ships cannot, with safety, traverse
our channels; that insurance cannot be effected but at an excessive premium; that a horde of American cruisers should be allowed, unheeded,
unrestricted, and unmolested, to take, burn, or sink, our own vessels in our
own inlets, and almost in sight of our own harbors.[8]

As the merchants state, insurance rate went sky-high, that from
England to Ireland rising at one time from a rate of 16 shillings, nine

[6] George Coggeshall, *History of the American Privateers,* p. 361.
[7] *Ibid.,* p. 365.
[8] *Ibid.,* pp. 301–302.

pence to five guineas.[9] American commerce destroyers, if they could not win the war, could at least create a strong sentiment for a peace on reasonable terms.

LATER FRIGATE ACTIONS

Just before the escape of the *Hornet* and *Peacock*, mentioned earlier, the frigate *President*, now under Captain Stephen Decatur, also attempted to break through the New York blockade. On the night of January 14, 1815, in a howling northwester, the *President* nosed through the Narrows, but struck the bar and pounded there heavily for over an hour, starting a leak and cutting down her speed.

Then sailing eastward, she was sighted at dawn by the blockading squadron—the razee *Majestic,* 56, and the 38-gun frigates *Endymion, Pomone,* and *Tenedos.* At nightfall, when the fastest of the pursuers, the *Endymion,* had drawn in range, Decatur turned on her and in a running action stripped her of sails and rigging. But the *President* had also suffered, and when at about 11:00 P.M. the *Tenedos* overtook him, Decatur struck without firing another shot.

Later critics have viewed unfavorably this rather tame surrender, when Decatur, if resolved on a last-ditch fight, might perhaps have wrecked the light *Tenedos* before the other British ships came in range. But Decatur himself was wounded, and in his later report he pointed out other circumstances justifying his course—"one-fifth of my crew killed and wounded, my ship crippled, and a more than fourfold force opposed." When Decatur returned in a cartel from Bermuda, the court of inquiry on the battle made no unfavorable comment, and he continued a popular idol as in the past.

Somewhat earlier, during a storm in December, 1814, the *Constitution* under the able command of Charles Stewart got out of Boston, and as she swung across the Atlantic she soon had every available ship of the British Navy in alarmed pursuit. On the afternoon of February 20, not far from the Madeiras, "Old Ironsides" encountered the light frigate *Cyane,* 34, and the sloop *Levant* of 20 guns, an example of the pairs of ships now used by the British to cope with the big American 44's. In his report of the ensuing action Stewart speaks of the enemy's advantage in "a divided, more active force" and a heavier combined broadside of 804 to 704 lbs. As the *Constitution* was maneuvered, however, the real advantage lay in her concentrated strength.

---

[9] *Niles' Register,* VII, p. 175.

Engaging the enemy in line ahead, Stewart first weakened the *Cyane* with several broadsides and then, throwing his sails quickly aback, pounded the *Levant*. When the two ships turned to run before the wind, by equally swift maneuvers he raked both in succession. The *Cyane* struck at 6:50 P.M. An hour later the *Constitution* met the little *Levant* pluckily returning to the attack. The sloop made off after another broadside or two but was soon overtaken and captured. The *Constitution's* loss of three killed and 12 wounded was only one-fifth that of the two enemy ships. Surprisingly enough, though the *Levant* was recaptured, both the *Constitution* and her larger prize safely entered American ports. The news of the peace, reaching the United States on February 11, had by this time ended naval operations, save those of ships already at sea.

In a recapitulation of the conflict at sea, it will be seen that after the first year it was limited almost wholly to commerce warfare. American trade, both foreign and coastwise, was paralyzed by the British blockade, and though in most foodstuffs the nation was amply self-sufficient, its business and public revenues suffered severely. On the other hand, the injuries inflicted on British commerce by American raiders were felt keenly by a nation which in a quarter-century of fighting had counted on its mastery at sea. Long before the peace was signed, there was strong sentiment on both sides to bring this war of limited—and largely lost—objectives to an end.

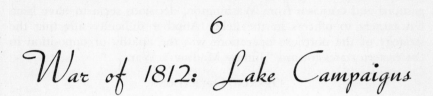

6

War of 1812: Lake Campaigns

As COMPARED with the conflict at sea, which in its later stages became largely a matter of commerce warfare and blockade, there is relatively greater interest in the campaigns of the War of 1812 on our northern frontier. Here there was a definite objective—the conquest of Canada, and no such disparity of naval forces. For both sides the St. Lawrence and Great Lakes were the vital line of communications, and the joint operations thus called for have significant lessons for later times. The campaigns were marked by striking and decisive naval victories, and also by much bungling—the latter illustrating defects long inherent in American military policy.

Defects of preparation have already been shown. Defects of leadership were more conspicuous in the army than in the naval commands. In the Navy, thanks partly to its complete nonexistence for a period after the Revolution, the command of ships and squadrons went to younger officers, for the most part well under forty, who had seen active service in the French and Tripolitan wars and whose professional interest had since been kept keen by the constant threat of naval conflict. Perry and Macdonough, victors on Erie and Champlain, were both under thirty; Chauncey, when he assumed general command on the Great Lakes, was only forty-three. In contrast, the army leaders were at first old veterans of the Revolution like Dearborn and Hull, aged respectively fifty-nine and sixty, who had been conspicuous chiefly in politics, or like the unsavory Wilkinson, aged fifty-five, who had shown neither character nor ability in his military career. Colonel Winfield Scott described his superiors succinctly as "very generally sunk into either sloth, ignorance, or habits of intemperate drinking."[1]

[1] See Henry Adams, *History of the United States*, 1801–1817, from which this quotation is taken.

Even more serious, especially for joint operations where unity of purpose is essential, was the lack of any central direction or well-thought-out planning of campaigns. Though there were plenty of suggestions and criticism from Washington, decisions seem to have been left largely to officers in the field. Another difficulty affecting the strategy of the northern operations was the apathy or opposition in the eastern states toward "Jimmy Madison's War."

OPENING OPERATIONS

In the northern campaigns, as already noted, water communications were vitally important. Roads were primitive and for a large part of the year impassable for heavy traffic. On the American side, naval and military stores had first to be brought north from the coast, but even for this purpose water transport was largely used. To the base established on Lake Ontario at Sackett's Harbor (see map p. 75) the route followed the Hudson and Mohawk, thence by portage to Oneida Lake and the Oswego River, and then over a stretch of Lake Ontario exposed to enemy attack. To the base at Presque Isle on Lake Erie, supplies after reaching Pittsburgh went up the Allegheny River and French Creek and then by portage to the lake. For transport from these bases east or west, the lakes themselves were the easiest available means.

For the British, the St. Lawrence and the Great Lakes were virtually the only route for the supply of all Upper Canada. Brought by ships under naval escort to Quebec or Montreal, all the countless stores necessary for naval and military operations had to be dragged up the six St. Lawrence rapids in bateaux, cross Lake Ontario in vessels from Kingston, and then portage round Niagara for Lake Erie and the West. It was said that a ship's anchor was worth its weight in silver by the time it had covered the full journey. The route, however, was long established, and had better facilities than those on the American side of the border.

This long British communications line has been compared to a great tree, with the base at its contact with salt water.[2] To attack the line at its western extremity might further be compared to cutting a tree by lopping off its top branches rather than striking at the trunk, whereas a decisive blow at Kingston or Montreal would bring the whole tree down. Of these two, Kingston would have been the better objective,

---

[2] This comparison was used by Chauncey during the war, and was afterward stressed by Mahan. See his *Sea Power in its Relation to the War of 1812*, Vol. II, p. 35, ff.

From *The United States Navy: A History* by Alden and Westcott.

for it was equally accessible to attack and equally vital to the control of Upper Canada, yet beyond the direct support of the British fleet.

But largely because forces were avaliable and the war sentiment was strongest in the West, the opening attack was made at Detroit. Here on July 12 General William Hull crossed the border and issued his magniloquent proclamation offering the Canadians a choice between "peace, liberty, and security . . . . or war, slavery, and destruction." The sequel is well known—the British General Brock's energetic transfer of troops to the West, the seizure of Mackinac before the little garrison there had been warned of hostilities, the rallying of Indians to the British side, the retreat of Hull to Detroit, and his surrender on August 16 without striking a blow.

Hull had earlier realized that naval control on Lake Erie was the key to success in the West, and measures were now tardily taken to gain such control. The two brigs put under construction that winter at Presque Isle (now Erie, Pa.) were to become the backbone of the squadron that would win victory in the next year.

OPERATIONS ON LAKE ONTARIO, 1812–14

On Lake Ontario, accepted by both sides as the main theater of naval operations, American preparations had begun as early as 1809. A base had been selected at Sackett's Harbor, some 60 miles across from the British station at Kingston, at the foot of the lake, and by 1812 the brig *Oneida,* 16, had been built and a number of light schooners had been purchased for naval use. In September of that year Captain Isaac Chauncey, a capable executive who had served under Preble in the Tripolitan war, assumed the general lakes command, bringing with him large numbers of shipwrights, rope and sail makers, ship fitters, and seamen from his former station at the Brooklyn Navy Yard. With the brig and schooners, Chauncey was on the lake in November, trying out the Kingston defenses and taking some small prizes. But cruising soon ended, and upon the approach of winter, the yard at Sackett's and the surrounding forests rang with the noise of axe, adz, and hammer in ship construction, the chief activity of the base for the next three years. Two vessels were started, the brig *Madison,* 24, which was finished early in the spring of 1813, and a ship of 28 guns completed later that summer.

The British already had several well built armed vessels on the lake, and were building two more, one at York (now Toronto) and one at Kingston, to be ready by spring. Their commander was to be Captain Sir James Yeo, who arrived in the following May with 36 officers and 450 men of the Royal Navy. In line with the British policy in Canada, Yeo's orders enjoined upon him a strict defensive; so far as possible, he was to maintain communications but take no avoidable risks with his fleet.

Chauncey's strategy, if the plans for an invasion of Canada were really serious, should evidently have been quite the opposite—a vigorous offensive to gain lake control. He was ready with his new brig *Madison,* and army forces under General Dearborn, by April of 1813. Unquestionably the objective should have been the ships and base at Kingston, the seizure and firm holding of which would have rendered unnecessary all the subsequent hard fighting on the Niagara frontier. But the defenses of Kingston were grossly exaggerated (though espionage should have been simple) and both Chauncey and Dearborn were men of the "no risks" type. In a letter written that same year to Perry on Lake Erie, Chauncey stressed the sage counsel, "Never despise your enemy,"[3] but he himself carried this precept to an extreme.

Instead of Kingston, the easier choice was made of a raid on York, with 13 ships and nearly 1,800 troops. The attack, April 27, was successful, though there were 288 casualties caused largely by the explo-

---

[3] Mackenzie, *Life of Perry,* p. 188.

sion of a magazine. A naval schooner in the harbor was captured and the ship of 30 guns under construction there was burned, together with large quantities of naval stores destined for the British forces on Lake Erie. The American expedition later moved on to attack Fort George at the mouth of the Niagara, May 27, the capture of which forced a temporary British withdrawal all along the Niagara line.

Still the problem of lake control remained unsolved. Yeo's squadron was soon at large, and Chauncey returned to his base to await the completion of his new ship, the *General Pike*. In fact, throughout the season the advantage shifted back and forth. Yeo's ships, though fewer, were more stoutly built and better in blowing weather. Chauncey had two excellent craft in the *Madison* and *Pike*, but the *Oneida* was sluggish and his schooners were both slow and cranky. Given these conditions, and the cautious policies and characters of the two leaders, the outcome may readily be foreseen. When one was ready to fight, the other was ready to withdraw. There were three inconclusive encounters, one on August 8–10 and the other two in September. In the August contact, two of Chauncey's schooners capsized the first night in a squall, and the next night two other schooners became separated from the rest and were captured, while Chauncey's only move to save them was to "edge away," as he said, in hope that the enemy would follow. In the next two actions the British suffered some damage, but since Chauncey would not fight without his slower units, they were able to get away.

The possibilities of a concentration against Kingston were demonstrated in the autumn of this year when about 8,000 troops, all told, were gathered at the foot of the lake. Dearborn had now retired, and that "tarnished warrior," Wilkinson[4], was brought up from the South to take command. The Secretary of War, General Armstrong, was also on the scene. Chauncey now favored the Kingston objective, but Wilkinson was opposed to this, or apparently to any other plan that involved immediate fighting. Finally, at the end of October, the Army set out in 300 bateaux, ostensibly for Montreal. They were harried by the British on their way down the river, defeated in a partial action (Chrysler's Field) near the Long Sault Rapids, and then went into winter quarters on the New York border north of the Adirondacks, where they were half frozen, half starved before spring. Thus a golden opportunity was frittered away.

---

[4] See the biography *Tarnished Warrior: Major General James Wilkinson,* by J. R. Jacobs, 1938.

The failure in this and other instances may be laid to faulty strategic direction and poor army leadership. But Chauncey's overcaution played a part, as well as his jealousy of military control. This last is well revealed in his reply to a letter of General Jacob Brown, a far abler leader than Wilkinson, begging his full co-operation in the Niagara operations of the next year. "For God's sake," wrote the General, "let me see you; Sir James [Yeo] will not fight." To which the Commodore replied stiffly, "We are intended to seek and fight the enemy's fleet, and I shall not be diverted from my efforts by any sinister attempt to render us subordinate to, or an appendage of the Army." The "sinister attempt," as Roosevelt remarks in citing the letters,[5] was simply "to make him co-operate intelligently in a really well-concerted plan of invasion."

Chauncey's defects are significant, for he was in many respects an excellent officer, highly capable in all matters of administration. His was the chief command in the main theater. But decisive battles were fought, and interest today centers, on Lake Erie and Lake Champlain, when junior officers bent on action attained victory and lasting fame.

Though little of naval significance occurred on Ontario in 1814, the building rivalry continued. At the end of the war the British had a ship of the line, the *St. Lawrence,* of 102 guns, and the Americans had two three-deckers on the stocks, one of which, named the *New Orleans,* was carried on the Navy List till after the Civil War.[6] The British historian James remarked that it was well the war ended when it did, else "the building mania would have continued until there was scarcely room on the lake for working the ships."[7]

OPERATIONS ON LAKE ERIE

In the autumn of 1812 Chauncey had sent Lieutenant Jesse D. Elliott to Lake Erie to purchase vessels and establish a naval base. On October 7, the very day of the arrival at Niagara of Elliott's first detachment of 51 seamen, two British armed brigs, the *Detroit* and *Caledonia,* were seen to anchor at Fort Erie, across the river from Black Rock. With commendable energy, Elliott that same night took his sailors and a somewhat larger number of army volunteers, pulled

---

[5] *Naval War of 1812,* pp. 563–564.

[6] She was left unfinished, for the Rush-Bagot Agreement of 1817 limited each nation to vessels mounting a single 18-pounder, one on Champlain, one on Ontario, and two on the upper lakes.

[7] W. James, *Naval History of Great Britain,* chap. VI, p. 246.

across in two boats, and captured both brigs with hardly a struggle. The *Detroit* grounded later on Squaw Island and had to be burned after removal of her guns, but the *Caledonia,* with a $200,000 cargo of furs, was brought in and joined to the four schooners purchased or under construction at Black Rock.

In the following winter the Lake Erie command was turned over to Master Commandant Oliver Hazard Perry, a Rhode Islander of 27, eager for more active service than his former charge of a dozen gunboats at Newport. Perry despatched 150 prime seamen from Narragansett to Sackett's Harbor, joined Chauncey there in March, and soon proceeded by boat and sleigh to Presque Isle, where, as already noted, two brigs were under construction.

Perry's task was not merely that of commanding his ships in action, but of completing them from the timber in the forest, and with infinite difficulty securing the transport to this remote frontier post of their equipment, armament, and crews. To this he applied himself with abounding confidence and drive. His first problem was to organize a militia defense against threatened enemy raids. Next he was in Pittsburgh hurrying up ordnance and stores. When Chauncey attacked Fort George in May, he was there to lead ashore the companies of sailors and Marines. Upon the consequent British evacuation of Fort Erie, at the head of the Niagara River, he was able to warp his brig and four schooners up the current from Black Rock, with the help of oxen and a company of soldiers; and by mid-June, escaping in a fog the British squadron out to intercept them, he had brought the vessels safely from Buffalo to Presque Isle.

The two brigs *Lawrence* and *Niagara* were completed by July. Each was of about 500 tons, with eighteen short 32's and two long 12's. In addition there was the brig *Caledonia,* with two long 24's and one short 32, and six small schooners and a sloop each mounting one or two long guns. The chief remaining task was to get the brigs (of 12-foot draft) over the shallow six-foot bar at the mouth of the bay, and to accomplish it in the face of the British squadron blockading outside. This force was commanded by an experienced officer, Barclay, a veteran of Trafalgar, who with some 160 officers and seamen had reached the lake in May.

Perry's opportunity came when on July 30 Barclay—for reasons unrevealed, though there were reports of a big dinner in his honor—lifted the blockade for a brief visit to Long Point across the lake. Immediately Perry was at work floating the brigs over the bar. Their guns were hoisted out, and specially fitted pontoons, filled with water until they just floated, were brought along the sides of each brig in turn, with timbers run through the gunports and resting on the pontoons. Then the pontoons were pumped out, lifting the brigs so that they scraped over the bar. On August 4, when only one of the brigs had her guns back aboard, Barclay reappeared on the scene. But, with a few shore batteries Perry had mounted, the array against him looked dangerous, and he sailed away to his base at Malden to complete the fitting out of a new ship, the *Detroit*.

Perry soon moved up the lake, blocking the British transport of supplies. At Malden the effects were keenly felt. Along with the garrison, some 14,000 Indians, counting squaws and papooses, were making heavy inroads on meat and flour. Within a month it became a question of starvation or a fight for naval control.

Upon the completion of the *Detroit*, armed with a very mixed battery of 19 guns, Barclay had six vessels in all, including the *Queen Charlotte*, 17, *Lady Prevost*, 13, *Hunter*, 10, and two smaller. The relative strength of the two squadrons is indicated in the table, the significant features being Perry's superiority of almost two to one in carronades and three to two in long guns. But his strength was divided among numerous small units difficult to maneuver and to bring into concerted attack. He had, in short, all the problems of a fleet action, even though his total broadside hardly equalled that of a single ship of the line. His plan of battle was well conceived. As at Trafalgar, which most officers of his day had studied, there was to be a diagonal approach, and the ships were to assume positions to match ships of similar strength in the enemy line. There was an additional order, paraphrasing Nelson's, that if the captains "laid their vessels alongside of the enemy they could not be out of the way."

	Number of Ships*	Tonnage	Men	Broadside (total lbs.)	Broadside (long guns)
American	9	1671	532	896	288
British	6	1460	440	459	195

* The figures are taken from Roosevelt's *Naval War of 1812*, pp. 260–261. They are based on careful study of divergent sources, and give a fair approximation.

At daylight of September 10, Barclay's squadron was in sight from the American temporary base in the Bass Islands, at Put-In Bay. On this bright morning of early autumn, with a light breeze veering to south-

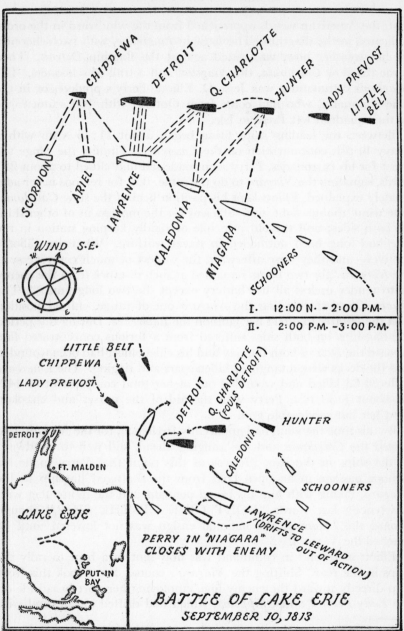

WIND S.E.

I. 12:00 N. – 2:00 P.M.
II. 2:00 P.M. – 3:00 P.M.

BATTLE OF LAKE ERIE
SEPTEMBER 10, 1813

From *The United States Navy: A History* by Alden and Westcott.

east, the American vessels approached from the windward in the order indicated in the diagram. The flagship *Lawrence,* with two schooners on her weather bow, was pitted against the flagship *Detroit.* Then came the slow *Caledonia,* the *Niagara,* and a trail of schooners. The *Niagara's* commander was Jesse D. Elliott, Perry's predecessor in the Erie command, who had come from Ontario with 100 seamen just as the squadron left Presque Isle.

Between the leading ships firing began about 11:45 A.M., with a heavy British concentration on the *Lawrence.* Finding the range too great for his carronades, Perry soon made sail and closed to about 250 yards, signaling the *Niagara* to do the same. But, for reasons never adequately explained, Elliott kept his position behind the slow *Caledonia.* The wind, though light, was sufficient for the movement of other ships on both sides; and the old principle of rigidly keeping station in the line had long been outmoded in naval warfare. Whatever Elliott's motives—and they were afterward the subject of much controversy— the *Niagara* "for two hours remained at such distance from the enemy as to render useless all her battery except the two long guns.[8]" The *Queen Charlotte,* finding the *Niagara* out of range, shifted position past the *Hunter* to direct her guns on the *Lawrence.* During this period the flagships on both sides suffered from a furious concentrated fire. Aboard the *Detroit* both Barclay and his chief officer had been wounded and the decks were a tangle of fallen spars and rigging. The *Lawrence* suffered 83 killed and wounded out of her total complement of 142. At about 1:30 P.M. Perry with the aid of the purser and chaplain fired her last serviceable gun.

By this time the wind had apparently freshened, for the *Niagara* had passed the *Caledonia* and was ranging ahead, still well to windward of the ships in the van. It was at this point that Perry made his famous passage in an open boat from the shattered flagship to the *Niagara,* taking with him his broad pennant and the motto flag with Lawrence's last words "DONT GIVE UP THE SHIP," though aboard the *Lawrence* the national ensign was not lowered until he reached the *Niagara.*

Elliott as second in command was now sent in a boat to rally the ships in the rear. Shifting the *Niagara's* course, Perry took this fresh ship directly toward the enemy line, employing her port broadside on the *Lady Prevost* and *Chippewa,* which had drifted ahead, and with

---

[8] Mahan, *Sea Power in Its Relations to the War of 1812,* chap. II, p. 88.

his starboard guns double-shotted raking the *Detroit* and *Charlotte* at half pistol shot range. In attempting to wear in order to shift broadsides, these ships had fouled each other and lay almost helpless under the guns of the *Niagara,* as well as those of some of the American schooners which had closed in.

At about 3:00 P.M. the flag of the *Detroit* and near-by ships went down, and the *Little Belt* and *Chippewa* were later overtaken as they attempted to escape. Through the action the major British ships were handled with coolness and skill, and they were close to victory before Perry's timely shift to the *Niagara.* The casualty lists of 123 for the Americans and 135 for the British indicate the closeness of the fight. To receive the final surrender Perry returned to the *Lawrence,* whose flag had again been raised. His laconic dispatch to General Harrison summarized the outcome: "We have met the enemy and they are ours; two ships, two brigs, one schooner, and one sloop."

The naval victory was decisive for the whole western campaign. Harrison's army was transported to the Canadian side and defeated the retreating British in the Battle of the Thames, October 5, in which the Indian leader Tecumseh was killed. In the peace negotiations of the next year there could no longer be serious question of setting up a neutral Indian state in Michigan territory, which was now firmly in American hands.

OPERATIONS ON LAKE CHAMPLAIN

Despite the results in the West, the next year, 1814, opened prospects threatening to the American cause. With the coming of a precarious peace in Europe the British were able to strengthen the blockade of our coasts, send troops for attacks in the Chesapeake area, and despatch 11,000 veterans of the Spanish Peninsular campaign for aggressive operations in Canada. Designs were under way also for the later formidable expedition against New Orleans. The plan for the Canadian forces was an advance southward over the old invasion route via Lake Champlain. Its objective was limited to the gaining of military advantages which would support British claims in the peace conference (already under way at Ghent in Belgium), particularly to the control of the Great Lakes as a military barrier and rectifications of the Maine frontier.

Against this menace, American military defense measures can only be described as singularly inept. Just five days before the British army of over 14,000 crossed the border, about 4,000 troops at Plattsburg, in accordance with earlier instructions from Washington, were sent to Sackett's Harbor for operations in the West. Only about 1,500 effectives, together with some volunteers and militia, were left to man the defenses of the Plattsburg base.

As in the Revolution, however, the British advance was conditioned upon command of Lake Champlain. The road skirting the west side of the lake was exposed to naval gunfire, and the lake itself was the only satisfactory means for quick transport of supplies. Hence the advance of the army was held up until an adequate naval force could be built up at the foot of the lake. Here the British already had the brig *Linnet,* 16, the schooners *Chubb* and *Finch* of 11 guns each which had been taken from the Americans the year before, and a dozen one-gun bateaux. In addition they were just completing the *Confiance,* 37, rated later in the American Navy as a full-sized frigate, which in favorable conditions might have coped with the whole American squadron.

In command of the American naval forces was Master Commandant Thomas Macdonough, only thirty years of age but with earlier fighting experience in the Mediterranean, an officer who rose ably to the responsibilities imposed. After operating freely on the lake during the summer, his fleet now assembled in Plattsburg Bay was composed of the flagship *Saratoga,* 26, the brig *Eagle,* 20, the converted steamboat *Ticonderoga,* 17, the little sloop *Preble,* and ten bateaux. In gun power, as indicated in the table, there was little to choose between the two squadrons, though the British had a concentration of strength in their frigate and some advantage in long guns.

	Number of Ships	Men	Number of Guns	Weight of Broadside	Long Guns
American	14	882	86	1194	480
British	16	937	92	1192	660

The American commodore's ability appears most clearly in his utilizing of every advantage of his defensive position. It will be recalled that, only 16 years earlier, Nelson at the battle of the Nile had almost annihilated a French fleet under very similar conditions by "doubling" on the head of the line. Macdonough guarded against this by placing his van ships well to the north of Cumberland Head (see diagram), so that the British, who needed a north wind to come up the lake, would have difficulty in tacking up to cap his column. In addition, his ships were anchored a mile and a half from Plattsburg,

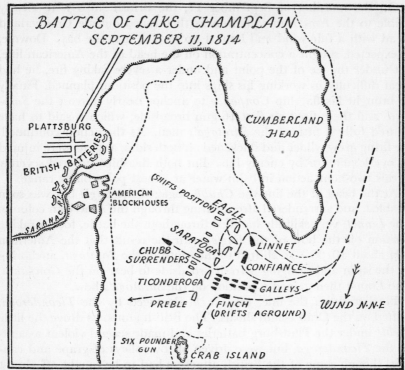

From *The United States Navy: A History* by Alden and Westcott.

out of effective range of shore batteries if they were taken by the enemy; and the foot of his line had some protection from the Crab Island shoals. His most effective measure was a thorough arrangement of anchors at bow and stern with springs attached to wind ship and bring fresh broadsides quickly to bear.

As it was already late in the season, the Governor General of Canada, Sir George Prevost, in command of the British forces, goaded the naval commander to hasten his preparations. Even before the *Confiance* was completely finished, or the seamen brought up from the fleet at Quebec were familiar with their new berth, the naval commander, Captain Downie, set sail with his squadron to protect the flank of the army on its march south. Prevost advanced as far as the Saranac River, which flows through Plattsburg; but there, though capture of the American shore fortifications would have been a serious blow, he settled down quietly to await the outcome of the naval attack.

On the morning of September 11, the British ships were clearly visible to the American squadron as they sailed outside Cumberland Head with a fair wind and hauled up to tack into the bay. Downie, as expected, sought a concentration on the head of the American line, but under the lee of the point and under a severe raking fire, he had great difficulty in working his ships into the positions planned. Finally he brought his flagship *Confiance* to anchor nearly abreast the *Saratoga,* and there fired his first 16-gun broadside, which is said to have injured fully a fifth of the *Saratoga's* men. As the action continued, the firing grew wilder and slackened on both sides, as guns were injured by overloading or by enemy hits. But both flagships suffered severely in this two-hour action in calm water at almost point-blank range.

At the head of the line the *Chubb* engaged the *Eagle* but was soon disabled, and surrendered after drifting through the American column. The *Linnet,* very skilfully handled throughout the battle, took a raking position off the bow of the *Eagle,* with the result that the American brig about 10:30 A.M. shifted to the south of the *Saratoga,* anchoring by the stern and bringing a fresh broadside to bear on the *Confiance.* The *Linnet* then gained a position on the *Saratoga's* bow.

Further down the line, the *Finch,* damaged by the *Ticonderoga,* drifted on the Crab Island shoals. The British gunboats drove the little *Preble* under the Plattsburg batteries and made several violent assaults on the *Ticonderoga,* but were driven off by volleys of grape and canister, though some of the British attackers had to be fought off almost from the ship's rail.

Shortly before 11:00 A.M. the *Saratoga,* under concentration from two enemy ships, had not a gun left on her engaged side. The *Confiance,* though she still had four guns firing, was in even worse case, her commander Captain Downie killed early in the battle, and the ship leaking so badly it was necessary to shift the guns to keep the shot holes above water. After the action it was found that the *Saratoga* had 55 hits in the hull and the *Confiance* 105. At this point, Macdonough was able to use his springs most opportunely to wind ship and bring his port broadside into play. The *Saratoga* tried to do likewise, but her progress halted when she was only partly swung around. Almost sinking and with no guns able to bear on the American ships, she surrendered at 11:00. Within 15 minutes, the *Linnet's* flag also went down.

Like the Erie action in its strategic importance, the battle of Lake Champlain ended the British invasion, and had a highly favorable effect on the peace negotiations at Ghent. The Duke of Wellington, who was now offered the American command, remarked truly that the success of military operations in Canada depended on control of the lakes, of which there was evidently little prospect, and he advised a peace settlement without territorial demands.

The later American victory at New Orleans in January 1815 was won after the peace terms had been signed. From the standpoint of naval interest, however, it may be noted that Commodore Patterson's gunboats on Lake Borgne delayed the British advance on New Orleans, and the naval batteries of the *Louisiana* and *Carolina* played an important part in the final defense.

It has often been remarked that the peace treaty of Ghent made no mention of the issues on which we had based our declaration of war. But with the end of the European conflict, the impressment and trade grievances had lost significance. In a measure, the real aims of the war had been accomplished. Our stiff resistance had won an increased respect for the American nation among the European powers, and, though the conquest of Canada remained a dream, we had established the security of the Northwest Territory and the lake frontier.

In later times the rigors of the British blockade, the raiding of our coasts and capital, the mismanagement of the military campaigns were easily forgotten, while popular memory treasured the frigate and sloop actions and the naval victories on the lakes. The Navy gained in popularity and its achievements contributed to the increased spirit of national unity and loyalty in the post-war years.

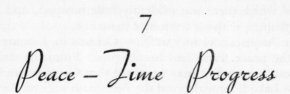

7
Peace – Time Progress

THOUGH THE LESSONS of the war of 1812 were not fully appreci-ated at the time, the rigors of the British blockade indicated clearly the need of capital ships capable of challenging and dispersing off-shore blockaders. Four ships of the line, in addition to six frigates and six sloops, had been authorized during the war, and a year after the peace nine more 74's were laid down, together with 12 frigates. Funds were also provided for three steam batteries, though on these the President was permitted to suspend construction.

NAVAL ADMINISTRATION

So modest had been the naval establishment prior to the War of 1812 that little thought had been given to the planning and direc-tion of naval operations. During the war itself, the Secretary of the Navy had attempted to exercise overall control, with the advice of officers who might be stationed in or visiting the capital. Func-tions of supply and operations were not differentiated within the Department, and Secretary Jones, an energetic merchant and former shipmaster, complained that procurement problems absorbed his time to the exclusion of war plans. He accordingly delegated purchasing and related problems of inspection and accounts to special clerks who supervised the Navy Agents at the various ports, while he himself gave his time wholly to the direction of operations. Even so, without a per-manent professional staff, he had been unable properly to co-ordinate the activities of the officers at sea. During the war, however, the prob-lem had soon solved itself, for after the first year the majority of our naval vessels were immobilized in port.

Jones's successor, Benjamin Crowninshield, took up the problem, and in 1815 induced Congress to create a Board of Navy Commissioners, to consist of three senior captains, who were to advise the Secretary, and, under his "superintendence," direct "the procurement of naval stores and materials, and the construction, armament, equipment, and employment of vessels of war," and also "furnish all the estimates of expenditure which the several branches of the service may require." Captains Porter, Bainbridge, and Decatur were early members. Continued until 1842, the Board represented the first attempt to solve the most important problem of naval administration, that of combining satisfactorily the expert knowledge of the professional officer with civilian control.

Naval Policy

The 1816 construction program, authorized while memories of the British blockade were still fresh in mind, gave promise of a capital-ship policy adequate to assure command of the sea off the coasts. The war lessons were soon forgotten, however, in the optimism which dominated a nation nerved to exploit the resources of a continent. The spirit of the age moved west. Railroads, canals, and land speculation captured the public eye as well as its pocketbook, and in the kaleidoscopic American scene only imminent armed conflict could hold public attention on naval matters for long. During the extended period of peace from 1815 to the Civil War the Navy's activities went relatively unnoticed. The security of geographic isolation was enhanced after 1830 by the balance of power in Europe which resulted from renewed Anglo-French rivalries. To the dominant group of agrarian congressmen representing the South and West, these facts were sufficient reasons for maintaining naval appropriations at an average of $7,000,000 annually, as against British and French appropriations each exceeding four times that amount. The Navy became, in effect, a patrol force, subject to short term and ill-co-ordinated construction programs. Its function was not to conduct offensive operations against hostile fleets of major maritime powers. The practice of squadron tactics was accordingly relegated to a minor place. Advances in naval technology were recognized and adopted but tardily. Naval officers who urged the application of steam propulsion met determined opposition in Congress and among their seniors, and it required conclusive demonstration of the steamer's war advantages, as provided by the naval operations against Mexico in 1846–47, to bring widespread adoption of that revolutionary technical development.

The Navy did, however, remain a most important defender and promoter of American maritime commerce. With the exception of the brief period of the war with Mexico, the Navy's story in the years between 1815 and 1860 is concerned chiefly with its activities of commercial importance. American warships displayed the flag wherever American merchantmen penetrated. In a day when the consular service was largely confined to Europe and to South America, and when telegraph and wireless were unknown, naval officers assumed the role of diplomats and opened up new markets for American trade. The Navy protected merchants from discriminating duties, and their ships from pirates.

Moreover, some of the most distinguished public servants of these years were naval officers such as Maury, Wilkes, Ringgold, and Kane, whose surveys and explorations contributed substantially to oceanography and made new trade routes available for safe navigation.

Naval policy, between 1815 and 1860, was determined by fundamental strategic concepts which had wide acceptance in Congress during these years. That strategy was based on defense against invasion of coastal waters, with an offensive component consisting of commerce raiding on the high seas. Leading naval officers and successive national administrations were both in full agreement with this view, and were much influenced by the series of reports on coast defense issued between 1815 and 1830 by the military engineers Barnard and Totten. These recommended elaborate coastal fortifications connected by lines of communication with rear supply bases. In this system the Army was to be the first line of defense. Abundant reserves of militia, it was expected, would spring to arms on the threat of war and repel invaders, as at New Orleans under Jackson. The Navy was to be used as a weapon of opportunity, raiding enemy commerce and cutting off such portions of hostile fleets as might be exposed to successful attack by bad weather or faulty disposition. Public men of the period, in their devotion to commerce raiding concepts, discounted the possibility of long continued blockade of American ports; the destruction of the enemy's merchant vessels would speedily bring him to sue for peace. American policy makers did not investigate the problem of cruiser raiding warfare in the face of strongly defended convoys, such as were instituted by the British Navy in the later stages of the War of 1812. In any case, it was held, the balance of power in Europe would prevent a major nation from detaching any considerable part of its strength for adventures overseas.

Andrew Jackson, alone of the pre-Civil War presidents, entered a vigorous dissent to these prevailing views. He perceived that the coast was too long for passive defense, and recommended an increased naval strength that would "enable you to reach and annoy the enemy, and . . . give to defense its greatest efficiency for meeting danger at a distance from home." But American warships up to the Civil War, and indeed for 30 years after, were determined by the concept of a small number of ships armed with the heaviest batteries and each supreme in its class. As in the Revolution and the War of 1812, privateering with fast merchantmen was to be a war auxiliary of major importance.

PROTECTION OF TRADE

American foreign trade received great impetus with the coming of peace, and its expansion continued, with occasional slight recessions, through the period 1815–1860. Whereas imports tripled in value (from $113,044,000 in 1815 to $362,166,000 in 1860), exports increased nearly eight-fold ($52,557,000 to $400,122,000). In that period, when there was "no law west of the Horn," as the seaman's saying had it, American shipmasters traded in distant, ill-charted waters made still more hazardous by widespread piracy. The protection and promotion of American commercial interests all over the globe taxed the capacity of the Navy.

Permanent foreign cruising stations were established, and all ships in commission were normally attached to the five principal squadrons abroad: the Mediterranean, the Pacific, the West Indies, the Brazil, and the East Indies. Somewhat later, in 1841, the Home Squadron was established, and in 1842 the regular slave patrol or African Squadron. Individual ship cruising comprised the normal routine on a station, and outside the Mediterranean, a squadron was hardly ever assembled in full strength.

The Mediterranean Squadron was reconstituted in 1815 to meet renewed threats of war by the Barbary states. For a decade previous the Dey of Algiers had complained that American protection payments under the treaty of 1796 had been met neither promptly nor in full. Beginning in 1807, Algerian cruisers seized American ships and held their crews until the Dey should receive satisfaction. Negotiations continued until 1812 when the United States broke off diplomatic relations with Algiers. After the treaty of Ghent the Madison administration decided to deal summarily with the Barbary state. There was now available a naval force of far different quality from the ill-equipped vessels of Preble in 1803.

In May, 1815, a mixed force of nine ships commanded by Commodore Stephen Decatur in the new *Guerrière,* 44, sailed for the Mediterranean. Off Cape de Gat, on June 16, the squadron encountered the Algerian 46-gun frigate *Meshuda,* carrying the Dey's admiral, Rais Hammida. In a running fight the *Constellation* headed the *Meshuda* off from the coast and brought her to with a crippling broadside. The *Ontario,* 18, *Guerrière,* and *Epervier,* 18, then engaged the enemy successively and reduced her to helplessness. When Rais Hammida, wounded and fighting his ship from a couch on deck, was killed by a cannon shot, his crew struck the flag. Picking up another prize, an Algerian 22-gun brig, Decatur proceeded with his formidable squadron to Algiers and presented the American grievances and demands. Thoroughly cowed, and with a good recollection of Dacatur's past record in the Mediterranean, the Dey accepted the terms and concluded a treaty on the "most favored nation" basis. Thus ended American tribute paying to Algiers.

Decatur then visited Tunis and Tripoli, where he immediately secured indemnity for American privateer prizes which, when taken into these ports during the War of 1812, had been turned over to the British. Meanwhile Commodore Bainbridge with the new *Independence,* 74, and eight other vessels put into Algiers, and later Tunis and Tripoli, to enforce Decatur's demands. A short while thereafter a British squadron of five of the heaviest sail of the line under Lord Exmouth bombarded the fortifications of Algiers and sank the Dey's Navy, thus ending the whole wretched system of tribute payments to the Barbary powers.

The Mediterranean Squadron was maintained continuously until the Civil War. The vessels usually wintered at Port Mahon, Minorca, and spent the fine weather months on patrol in Levantine waters, where the Greek War of Independence (1821–1831) had engendered extensive piracy.

Meanwhile the menace of piracy in the Caribbean engaged the Navy in one of its most arduous operations. In their efforts to break free from Spain, the revolutionary juntas of the new South American republics commissioned as privateers many of the lawless adventurers and sailors of fortune who had left Europe after the downfall of Napoleon and gathered under the standards of San Martin and Bolivar. Few of this gentry were likely to draw fine distinctions between merchant ships of the Spanish enemy and those flying neutral flags. Some resorted to outright piracy, gathering in the numerous passages of the Caribbean islands to prey on the rapidly growing commerce of the West Indies and Gulf. Nearly 3,000 piratical attacks there were reported between 1815 and 1823. As the principal carriers in these waters, American ships were particularly affected.

Since the first trans-Appalachian settlements, New Orleans had been the outlet to the Atlantic coast and Europe for the produce of the Mississippi valley. The city's exports increased most rapidly after 1815, with the more extensive taking up of western lands and greatly expanded cotton cultivation in the states along the Gulf. Britain and France had also gradually relaxed their mercantilist restrictions on trade with their West Indies colonies. New Orleans by 1828 thus grew to be the second largest port in the United States. The problem of piracy in the Caribbean therefore became of moment to the United States, and to deal with it, the West India Squadron was organized in 1822 and placed under Commodore James Biddle. It consisted at first of the frigates *Macedonian* and *Congress,* the sloops *Cyane, John Adams, Hornet,* and *Peacock,* two brigs, four schooners, and two gunboats. For the next six years Biddle and his successors, David Porter and Lewis Warrington, conducted vigorous operations against the buccaneers. The task of searching out pirate hiding places in uncharted bays and inlets involved the most arduous kind of tropical service. Boat expeditions and cutting out parties, chiefly in the waters of Cuba, Puerto Rico, and Haiti, cost the Navy many lives. An even greater toll was exacted by yellow fever and malaria.

To facilitate inshore work the squadron was reinforced, in 1823, with nine new schooners and five row barges. Equally important was the *Sea Gull,* a converted 100-ton ferryboat and the first steamer to engage in operations against an enemy. This vessel, despite her low speed and limited radius, proved her worth as a general utility ship during periods of calms and light airs. By 1829 over 60 piratical craft had been taken and the threat to commerce greatly reduced. Thereafter the West India squadron was maintained at decreased strength, but it was not until the period of the Civil War and the fast steam warship that maritime outlawry in the Antilles was finally extirpated.

While menaced by buccaneers in the Caribbean, American merchantmen were also threatened by the operations of belligerents on the west coast of South America. The revolutions there had been followed by friction between the victors, and in 1824 war broke out between Chile and Peru. The Chilean squadron under Lord Cochrane swept the coast and blockaded Peruvian ports. American whalers, only recently freed from the blockade during the War of 1812, found themselves hampered as they put into Peruvian harbors for provisions and water. This situation, together with the need for protecting a growing American trade with the South Seas, prompted the Navy Department, in 1821, to organize the Pacific Squadron, a unit which was maintained with few interruptions until 1921, when, as the Pacific Fleet, it was enlarged into the United States Fleet. To protect American interests in the area of the La Plata River, another standing unit, the Brazil Squadron, was established, and until the Civil War it displayed the flag with good effect between the Falkland Islands and Cape San Roque at the tip of Brazil.

Trade with the Far East also experienced revival and marked expansion after the Peace of Ghent. Its increase was facilitated by the work of naval officers who protected mercantile interests and opened up new areas to American trade. In 1819 the frigate *Congress,* the first man-of-war flying the Stars and Stripes to reach the East Indies, convoyed a large number of American merchant ships through the pirate-infested waters between the Sunda Straits and Macao. Ten years later the sloop *Vincennes,* Captain W. B. Finch, crossed the Pacific from Callao to China, where the display of the flag was welcomed by American merchants at Canton. After impressing Chinese officials with the need of according merchants full protection, Finch visited Manila, where grievances of American traders were redressed. The *Vincennes* returned via the Cape of Good Hope, reaching New York in June of 1830, the first American warship to cross the Pacific and circumnavigate the globe.

Trade with China proper, however, was limited to the port of Canton, and even there was not protected by treaty or by municipal law. In 1832 the government sent a special agent, Edmund Roberts, in the sloop of war *Peacock,* Commander David Geisinger, to secure treaty protection for American merchants who had penetrated into the lesser countries of the Orient as well as for those settled in Canton. Roberts and Geisinger, though they failed in negotiations with Cochin China, succeeded in establishing treaty relations with Siam and the Sultan of Muscat, whose domains extended from the Persian Gulf to Zanzibar.

At this time, also, the first eastward passage of an American warship around the world was undertaken by the frigate *Potomac,* Captain John Downes, in 1831. Downes was to obtain satisfaction for the treacherous slaughter, at Quallah Battoo, Sumatra, of American seamen from the pepper trader *Friendship* of Salem. Appearing off Quallah Battoo February 5, 1832, disguised as a Danish merchant ship, the *Potomac* next day put ashore 282 seamen and Marines. Attacking at dawn, the party rapidly stormed three forts guarding the town. Although a heavy fire was encountered, the quality of native arms was poor and American losses were limited to two killed and 11 wounded. The village was burned and Po Mohamet, the offending chieftain, met his end in the fighting. Downes then received promises of safety for American traders who should visit the region thereafter. The *Potomac,* after a stormy passage around Cape Horn, reached Boston in May of 1834.

To check the recurrence of similar outrages, a permanent East India Squadron was established in 1835. Another important duty of the squadron was to help enforce the Chinese Government's prohibition of opium imports by preventing smuggling in American ships. Commodore Lawrence Kearny, commanding the squadron from 1840 to 1842, through his fairness and tactful firmness so inspired the confidence of the Chinese authorities that he gained much for the United States. After the Treaty of Nanking, which secured for Britain the opening of six "treaty ports" in 1842, Viceroy Ke offered to instruct the Imperial Commissioners, who were shortly to visit Canton, to negotiate a treaty with Kearny placing the United States on a "most favored nation" footing. In the absence of specific instructions, the Commodore did not feel empowered to negotiate a formal treaty, but instead accepted assurances of equal treatment for American merchants. In thus establishing friendly relations with the authorities at Canton, Kearny laid the groundwork for the Treaty of Wanghia, concluded by Caleb Cushing two years later.

THE OPENING OF JAPAN

A more distinctively naval accomplishment in the diplomatic field was the opening of Japan by Commodore Matthew Calbraith Perry in 1853–54. Since the early seventeenth century Japan, save for limited trading privileges extended to the Dutch at Nagasaki, had held herself isolated from the western world. Now, as President Fillmore's letter to the Mikado pointedly stated, Commodore Perry was sent "with a powerful squadron" to seek protection for shipwrecked seamen, arrange for coaling and refitting stations on the route to China, and if possible open ports of Japan to American trade.

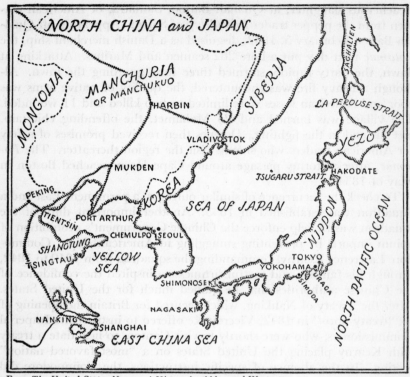

From *The United States Navy: A History* by Alden and Westcott.

Drawing lessons from rebuffs suffered by Commodores Biddle and Glynn in earlier visits, Perry thoroughly prepared for the expedition by purchasing Dutch charts and reading all the available literature on Japan. His policy, as he mapped it out for himself, was "to demand as a right, not to solicit as a favor, those acts of courtesy due from one civilized nation to another . . . and to practice a little of Japanese diplomacy by allowing no [Japanese] on board the ships except officers having business . . ."; in short, he would adopt a courteous yet stiff and ceremonious bearing, indicative not of a humble trader but the representative of a powerful nation overseas.

After a preliminary visit to the Ryukyu and Bonin Islands, Perry's "black ships," the big side-wheelers *Mississippi* and *Susquehanna* towing the sloops *Plymouth* and *Saratoga,* on July 8, 1853, steamed up Tokyo Bay and dropped anchor off Uraga, within 30 miles of the capital. Guard boats thronging alongside were forcibly fended off. When a local official posing as the "Vice-Governor" of Uraga came on board he was allowed to parley only with a lieutenant; and the "Governor," when he later appeared, was met by a committee of captains. The "Lord of the Forbidden Interior" remained in seclusion. The exclusive Commodore, bearer of the President's message to the Emperor, declined to appear until "Princes" of the realm had been appointed to receive him.

The pomp and pageantry of this meeting on July 14 was calculated to impress the Oriental mind. Partly for security, the big ships moved closer in, so that their guns commanded the pavilion set up by the Japanese on shore. Fifteen boats, each with a gun in the bow, halted midway to the beach as a salute of thirteen guns announced the Commodore's descent into his barge. In the procession on shore were 100 Marines, as many seamen, and two brass bands. With his staff of officers, stiff-necked "old Matt," as his sailors spoke of him, marched in full dress, flanked by a stalwart Negro guard on each side, and with two ship's boys ahead bearing the precious documents, inscribed on vellum and resting in a rosewood box with clasps of gold.

After the solemn delivery of the documents Perry withdrew, giving a parting assurance that he would return for an answer in the spring, probably with a "much larger squadron." In fact, hastened by fears that the French or Russians might forestall him, he was back in February, and penetrated still nearer Tokyo. Meantime Japanese policy had already been decided. The power of the Tokugawa Shogunate had greatly weakened after over two centuries of control, and in other ways the country was ripe for change. Since resistance was futile, Japan would sign the treaty, and set herself to master as soon as possible the arts and skills, the ships and weapons of the barbarians.

Further ceremonies and presentation of gifts marked the subsequent negotiations. Rich silks, lacquer work, porcelains, and carved ornaments of the Orient were exchanged for firearms, tools, telegraph instruments, clocks, and other symbols of western civilization, including a miniature railway on which Mandarins, their robes flying, whirled about "at 20 miles an hour."

The treaty signed March 31, 1854 contained a most-favored-nation clause, a promise of protection for shipwrecked seamen, and a meager provision of two ports, Hakodate and Shimoda (the latter with an American consul), where American ships could take coal and supplies. Trade privileges came later in the treaty negotiated by Consul Townsend Harris in 1858, and other nations were quick to secure similar concessions. For his role as august ambassador in this epoch-making first opening of Japan to Western influence, the imposing and indeed slightly pompous Commodore had shown himself admirably suited; his accomplishment was a triumph of skilful policy backed by a truly indomitable will.

Voyages of Exploration

Of the many voyages of exploration and survey undertaken by the Navy between the War of 1812 and the Mexican War, none was more widely known than the United States Exploring Expedition of 1838–1842, commanded by Lieutenant Charles Wilkes. Authorized by Congress for the purpose of obtaining navigational information relating to the Pacific and of adding to oceanographic and geographic knowledge generally, the expedition was elaborately equipped and included a group of scientists. To carry the expedition, the Navy Department detailed six vessels; the sloops of war *Vincennes and Peacock* of 700 tons each, a brig, two schooners, and a storeship.

Leaving Hampton Roads in August, 1838, the expedition prosecuted its investigations for four years. The ships pushed south from Cape Horn and touched Palmer Land, losing in these operations the schooner *Sea Gull* which failed to return from detached duty. After a preliminary survey of the Tuamotu and the Society Islands, Wilkes went to Australia and thence south again to the antarctic continent. There followed a 1,000-mile voyage along the ice barrier, attended with the most disagreeable features of sailing ship life—frequent gales accompanied by snowstorms, frozen rigging, and the discomforts of wet and unheated quarters. At several points the expedition observed the antarctic land mass. The party surveyed portions of the Fiji group and sailed to the northwest coast of America. Another series of surveys were run from Puget Sound to northern California and included the navigable portions of the Columbia, Willamette, and Sacramento rivers. The expedition crossed the Pacific again and reached New York in June of 1842, after stopping at Singapore, the Cape of Good Hope, and Brazil. Wilkes' well-written *Narrative* was republished in popular form and was widely read by the pre-Civil War generation. It was, in fact, the counterpart of Darwin's contemporary *Voyage of a Naturalist*.

Naval Construction and Technological Developments

Following the close of the War of 1812 and in consequence of the application of strategic concepts already described, the Navy declined relatively to the fleets of England and France, and for nearly a quarter of a century no more units other than light craft were authorized. Warship construction was confined to the seven ships of the line of the 1816 program. Three others, the 74-gun *Washington, Franklin,* and *Independence,* started during the war, had not been completed in time to participate. They were designed by William Doughty, formerly assistant to Joshua Humphreys, and they embodied to an extreme degree Humphreys' theory of warships supreme in their class. Carrying on a moderate displacement the heaviest batteries of any 74's, they were notoriously heavy rollers. To correct this in six of the seven later 74's, Doughty increased displacement to accommodate minimum designed batteries of 82 guns, although 102 were actually carried. Nominally rated as 74's, they were the most powerful of their class afloat. The *Pennsylvania* was still larger and mounted 130 guns. For some years after her commissioning in 1835 she was the largest warship in the world. But construction work was hampered by a long-continued naval policy which confined squadron operations to the dull routine of "showing the flag," and which did not envision the proper fleet function of a capital ship. Three of the 74's were still unfinished at the outbreak of the Civil War. More suitable for the duties of the period were the 12 sloops of war also authorized in the 1816 program.

Though these inter-war years might well be termed the doldrums of American naval development, scientists, investigators, and naval officers conducted technical experiments so revolutionary in character that their widespread application in the 40 years after 1860 was to transform the warship more than in the centuries since the oar had given way to sail, and to produce by 1900 a type basically similar in respect of construction, armament, and propulsion to the warship of today. Seven developments of these years constitute the basis of modern naval technology. They were the marine steam engine and boiler, the screw propeller, the iron hull, the built-up rifled gun, slow-burning powder, percussion fuse shells, and armor.

The first of these inventions of far-reaching significance was steam propulsion. As early as 1813 the engineering genius Robert Fulton had designed a steam floating battery and Congress had authorized its construction. The 2,475-ton *Demologos,* completed in 1815, was not available for use until after the war. Her twin hulls were arranged catamaran fashion, and gave her a length of 156 feet and breadth of 56 feet, with paddle wheel on the center line. The engines and boilers were placed below the water line and, as the sides were protected by five feet of timber, the *Demologos* was invulnerable to the fire of existing warships. On trials she developed a speed of five knots. With her battery of twenty 32-pounders the *Demologos* would have been a formidable opponent for the average British frigate on blockade off American ports. And if she had had an opportunity for wartime action, the value of steam propulsion for warships would probably have been so conclusively demonstrated that the long and acrimonious controversy over its adoption would have been modified and the progress of naval technology accelerated. The *Demologos,* renamed the *Fulton* after the death of her inventor in 1815, was subsequently equipped with a set of sails. After brief active duty she was immobilized as receiving ship at the Brooklyn Navy Yard, where she was destroyed by fire in 1829.

Paddle steam vessels were constructed after 1825 for the British and French navies, but their function was primarily as tugs to tow sailing ships of the line during adverse winds or calms. By 1835 there were over 700 steamers under American registry, most of them on inland waters. Secretary Mahlon Dickerson of Jackson's cabinet first recognized the value to the Navy of steam warships, at least for coastal operations. In June, 1835, drawing on funds authorized for steam batteries by the unrepealed act of 1816, he ordered the construction of a steamer, the second *Fulton.* The vessel was frankly experimental. Her engines were located on the spar deck and drove 22-foot paddle wheels. Although her copper boilers were below decks and safe from shot, their operation was attended with some danger, for the steam pipes, like most then in use, were of iron and many failures resulted from galvanic action set up by the salt make-up feed water. At 20 revolutions per minute she reached a speed of 12 knots, though defects of design rendered her unfit for deep-sea service.

To Captain Matthew C. Perry, as the first commanding officer of the second *Fulton,* fell the important task of first recruiting engineering personnel for the Navy and establishing a policy toward this new specialized group. A younger brother of Oliver Hazard Perry and a distinguished officer in his own right, M. C. Perry wielded considerable influence in the Navy. His recommendations were adopted by the Navy Commissioners as a sound basis for the organization of the new Engineer Corps, which continued until its amalgamation with the line in 1899. Perry fully comprehended the value of the steamer, and became its foremost advocate in the Navy. He was also tireless in his efforts to secure the adoption of the shell gun.

Top left, SECRETARY OF THE NAVY GEORGE BANCROFT. From a paint-ing by Gustav Richter. *Bottom left,* COMMODORE ANDREW H. FOOTE. *Right,* COMMODORE MATTHEW CALBRAITH PERRY.

In 1839 Congress authorized construction of three more steamers, the *Mississippi, Missouri,* and *Allegheny,* which were the earliest first-rate seagoing steam warships of the Navy. Each was 229 feet in length, 40 feet in breadth, with a 19-foot draft and 3,220 tons displacement. They were propelled by paddle wheels and each was armed with two 10-inch and eight 8-inch guns. Guns of this size were heavier than any carried previously on American warships. The guards of the paddles occupied so much space that the resultant loss in weight of broadside had to be compensated by mounting the heaviest possible ordnance in the space available. To avoid strain caused by excessive weights at the ends of the wooden ships, the guns were pivoted so that each could be used on either side.

The shell gun had been perfected independently by Major George Bomford of the Coast Artillery during the War of 1812 and by General Paixhans of the French Army in 1820. Paixhans' model was a larger gun and had greater range. In both types the shell fuse was ignited by the flame of the propellant.[1] In 1840 Whitworth of England invented the percussion fuse, but the improvement was not widely adopted until 20 years later, when rifled ordnance and elongated projectiles were first installed on shipboard. The shell gun, however, was particularly destructive against wooden ships, and the first armored warships were designed to protect personnel against shell, rather than the solid shot of greater penetrative capacity.

Iron hull construction was inaugurated in the Navy in 1842 when the 643-ton paddle steamer *Michigan* was laid down and launched on the Great Lakes. But the innovation was not exploited further and no more iron warships were constructed before the Civil War monitor types, save for the abortive and uncompleted Stevens Battery started in 1842. Iron shipbuilding was retarded in the United States for the same reason that its development was forced in Europe—the state of the timber reserves. While European stocks of ship timber were depleted by 1840, those of the United States appeared limitless. Low construction costs of wooden ships gave the American ship owner a competitive advantage over the first European steamers, and to maintain the advantage American builders developed ever faster sailing models as foreign steamship speeds increased. Donald Mackay, the Boston shipbuilder, brought the sailing merchant ship to its highest

---

[1] The spherical shell was steadied in the bore by sabots or grommets of equal diameter with the shell. The windage or clearance between the shell and the bore gave the flame access to the fuse.

development in point of speed. His clippers competed with many foreign steamers on the fast transatlantic run. American vessels in foreign trade increased to a total of over two and a half million tons in 1860, or at the rate of 50 per cent per decade for 40 years, and 67 per cent of all foreign trade passing through American ports was carried in American bottoms. But the advantage was shortlived, and iron construction definitely asserted its superiority over wood. By 1860 American shipbuilders were handicapped; their European rivals had gained a 20-year start.

The *Mississippi* was regarded as a satisfactory war steamer when she was first commissioned, but her exposed paddle wheels were especially vulnerable to enemy fire. This disadvantage led to experimentation with the screw propeller. The *Princeton,* a 954-ton screw-propelled warship, was commissioned in 1844. She was built under the direction of progressive-minded Captain Robert F. Stockton, with the assistance of John Ericsson, the famous Swedish engineer. Ericsson designed the screw propeller, a chief advantage of which was that not only the screw itself but the engines could be placed wholly below the water line. The boilers were fitted to burn anthracite coal, thereby avoiding the smoke that might betray the ship's presence. Steam-driven blowers were introduced into the *Princeton,* as well as a telescopic smokestack. Her battery, also revolutionary, consisted of twelve 42-pound carronades and two 12-inch wrought-iron chasers each firing a 225-pound shot. One of the 12-inch guns was constructed by Ericsson and was called the "Oregon," significant of the contemporary controversy with Great Britain. This piece was strengthened by hoops shrunk on the breach. In tests it penetrated four-and-a-half-inch iron plates. The other 12-inch gun, designed by Stockton, was named "Peacemaker." On Feb. 28, 1844, the *Princeton* ran a trial trip down the Potomac with President Tyler and his cabinet on board. During the practice firing which followed, the Peacemaker burst, wounding Stockton, and killing Secretary of State Abel P. Upshur and Secretary of the Navy Thomas W. Gilmer.

The *Princeton* accident clearly indicated the chief obstacle in the development of ordnance before the Civil War—the difficulty of producing iron and steel of uniform quality. Satisfactory gun metal was not available until the improved Bessemer process, after 1870, which permitted a high degree of carbon control. Prior to 1840 gun design had progressed little since the days of the Spanish Armada. The customary slight decrease in external diameter from breech to barrel bore no relation to the varying internal pressures along the length of the bore. The problem of gun design was then subjected to extended investigation by Captain Thomas J. Rodman of the Coast Artillery and Commander John A. Dahlgren, Superintendent of Ordnance at the Washington Navy Yard. Rodman devised a pressure gauge which could be inserted into holes drilled perpendicularly to the bore. He discovered that the standard .3-inch grain cannon powder created high pressures near the breech, the maximum rate of combustion taking place almost immediately. The pressure thereafter fell away rapidly, as the projectile traveled along the bore. Having determined this "curve of pressures," Rodman designed a gun that was tapered in conformity with it. After independent experiments Dahlgren also determined a pressure relationship and in 1850 constructed a bottle-shaped gun so efficient that it remained the Navy's standard smoothbore during the Civil War. The Rodman 15-inch gun was the heaviest naval weapon of its day.

Another advance in naval ordnance before the Civil War was made possible by Rodman's experiments with the elasticity of gun metals. Previously, in 1842, Professor Daniel Treadwell of Harvard College had patented the hooped built-up gun. The fabrication of this type, however, was costly, and Rodman introduced the principle in the cheaper cast-iron ordnance. Compression of the interior metal was accomplished by rapidly cooling the bore and permitting the exterior portions to cool more slowly and contract on the already solidified interior. Dahlgren's cast-iron gun was also "built-up" on this principle.

The limitations of metal strength had even greater effect in hampering the development of rifled ordnance. Small arms had been rifled since the sixteenth century, but heavy ordnance was unable to stand the excessive pressures developed by fast-burning powders augmented by the greater mass and hence greater inertia of the elongated projectile. Robert J. Parrott, a former captain of artillery, developed a cast-iron rifled gun banded at the breech with a welded coil hoop of wrought-iron. Although the Parrot rifle was adopted by the Army and Navy before the Civil War, it was not a trustworthy weapon, as the war was to demonstrate. As early as 1846 Rodman developed the first slow-burning powder in the form of "perforated cake" rather than the grain type then in use. Rodman's principle is employed today in the molding of smokeless powder. But good steel was also requisite before the rifling of cannon could be fully successful, and that was a development of the post-Civil War period.

Engineering progress before the Civil War was steady though not spectacular. The surface condenser replaced the jet condenser and made fresh water feed available. The standard propulsive unit was the horizontal back-acting simple engine, usually installed in tandem. In the field of engineering experiment before the Civil War, as in ordnance, attention was paid to problems which are generally considered as of far more recent date. The Martin boiler, installed in the steam frigates authorized in 1857, was an experimental type designed by the Engineer-in-Chief of the Navy and employing the principles of the water tube and the superheater—all subject to the limitation of a 20-pound working pressure. Progress in machinery design was retarded during the first half of the nineteenth century by primitive metallurgical processes and lack of alloy steels for machine tools.

The coming of steam propulsion and the opposition to it by some of the Navy Commissioners brought about a reorganization of the Navy Department in 1842. Five bureaus were set up in place of the old Board, and a form of organization was established which has continued as basic in the Department to the present. With the bureau system appeared the fundamental problem of naval administration thereafter, namely, the devising of means to co-ordinate the activities of the bureau chiefs, other than through the civilian—and frequently inexperienced—Secretary of the Navy.

Naval Education

The problem of naval officer training was sharply defined by a tragic incident which occurred in the brig *Somers* returning from the African coast in 1842. Midshipman Philip Spencer and two crew members were hanged for inciting the ship's company to mutiny. Spencer's troubled life before entering the Navy suggests a psychopathological explanation of his offense. Inasmuch as he was the son of the Secretary of War, the affair received nation-wide publicity. It also gave point to the demand for a naval academy which had been made by successive Secretaries of the Navy for the past 20 years.

Hitherto midshipmen had received in haphazard fashion the instruction preparatory to promotion. The schoolmasters carried by law on the cruising ships were too often incompetent and always ill paid. Naval schools which functioned irregularly at the navy yards were wholly un-co-ordinated. Furthermore, the application of steam to warships made some knowledge of engineering principles requisite for all officers. By 1845 the impending Oregon crisis and the threat of war with Mexico weakened Congressional opposition to an academy, and the new Secretary of the Navy in Polk's cabinet, George Bancroft, on his own initiative drew on the general funds of the Department to start the school. The United States Naval Academy, thus founded at Fort Severn, Annapolis, October 10, 1845, has remained the primary source of supply for the Navy's regular officers.

The Mexican War

The five years after 1840 were marked by a series of diplomatic crises which affected the organization of the Navy and eventually involved it in war. The Maine boundary question, friction over the African slave patrol, and the Oregon problem led to controversy with Great Britain attended with recurrent war scares. In 1841 Congress established the Home Squadron and ended the practice of keeping on foreign stations all ships in commission. American interest in preserving the independence of Texas caused even greater friction with Mexico, and the annexation of the Texas Republic in 1845 soon led to war. Since Mexico had no naval force whatever, there was no opposition to American naval movements save occasionally from weak batteries on shore. The Navy played no spectacular role in the leisurely two-year conflict, but its command of the sea gave American land forces superior mobility and enabled their commanders to select times and places for offensive operations. Sea power also permitted the free flow of supplies, and for this reason the American armies struck with overwhelming superiority in matériel at every stage of the war.

By early July of 1846, little more than a month after receiving news of the war declaration, Commodore John D. Sloat, commanding the Pacific Squadron, had captured the principal ports of California. He disposed his forces of five sloops so that descents on Monterey, the capital, and on San Francisco were made nearly simultaneously. Operations were conducted in conjunction with a handful of American troops from the Frémont exploring party, together with a small band of American settlers who had revolted and set up the "Bear Flag Republic." Commodore Stockton, succeeding Sloat on July 15, consolidated the results of Sloat's quick strike and, by supporting the improvised land forces in a series of minor operations, broke all resistance and completed the conquest of California in January, 1847.

On the east coast Commodore David Conner, commanding the Home Squadron, supported General Zachary Taylor's thrust into northern Mexico from the Rio Grande by securing his base of supplies at Point Isabel at the mouth of the river. At the same time a blockade was set up on the Mexican coast and supplies from Europe were effectively cut off. During the rest of 1846 expeditions against Alvaredo, Tabasco, and Tampico were undertaken by detachments of Conner's squadron. Perry's steamers at Tabasco achieved their objective of penetrating 75 miles upstream and destroying enemy shipping gathered in that port. The other expeditions were not fully successful because of the swift river currents and sand bars. The results, nevertheless, had great significance in demonstrating the value of the steamer in war.

Though in the winter months of 1846–1847 the frequent hard gales called "northers" limited the squadron to blockade duties, offensive operations were resumed with the coming of moderate weather in the spring. To force a decision it was now planned to strike directly at Mexico City from the east coast. General Winfield Scott, commanding the expedition, selected Vera Cruz as his base, and brought 12,000 troops to take the city. The army was landed on March 9, 1847, and prepared for a general assault. A three-day bombardment, supported on the land side by a naval battery on the siege lines and on the harbor side by a gunboat flotilla, caused the surrender of the garrison and opened the way to Mexico City. The Vera Cruz operation virtually ended the Navy's participation in the conflict.

☆ ☆ ☆ ☆ ☆

8
The Civil War: Opening Events

CIVIL CONFLICT, which for decades had hung like a cloud over the nation, became an imminent menace at the close of 1860. The North, with its large annual influx of immigrant laborers, was very rapidly developing into an industrialized community; whereas the South, with its more stable population, remained agrarian. Divergent economic interests underlay the bitter sectional quarrels over tariff, abolition, states' rights, and slavery in the territories. In the campaign oratory of 1860 each side bluntly accused the other of warping the federal Constitution to suit its own special purposes. Southern leaders apparently convinced themselves that the election of Lincoln would justify secession; at any rate after November they proceeded to carry out their pre-election threats.

South Carolina voted for secession on December 10, 1860, and by the following February six other states in the deep South had followed her example. Bands of militia, vaunting the shibboleth of states' rights, took possession of several United States military posts in Texas. Louisiana authorities seized Forts Jackson and St. Philip and ousted United States officials from the New Orleans mint and the Baton Rouge arsenal. Major Anderson and his garrison of loyal troops were driven from Fort Moultrie to a precarious refuge in the ancient stronghold of Fort Sumter in Charleston Harbor. At Pensacola, where the Florida state militia seized the United States Navy Yard, the loyal Unionist personnel of the yard escaped across the bay to barricade themselves in abandoned Fort Pickens on Santa Rosa Island. All these overt acts occurred before March 4, 1861, when Lincoln took the oath of office. Nevertheless at noon on March 4, Lincoln kissed a pretty girl from each state in the Union in a ceremony designed to symbolize that national unity which had already in fact disappeared.

For his Secretary of the Navy Lincoln chose Gideon Welles, a staunch Connecticut editor and politician who had once served as chief of a naval bureau. "Grandfather" Welles, as newspaper men called him because of his ample beard and henna-gray wig, had a youthful zest for reforming.[1] He was honest to a fault, he was an inveterate and canny analyzer of his fellowmen, and his chief passion was to be exorcising and driving out from the naval establishment those twin devils of waste and incompetence. For such a man the moribund Navy Department of 1861 offered a veritable paradise.

Welles's chief assistant in the Department was an intelligent and energetic ex-naval officer named Gustavus Vasa Fox. In 1856, after 18 years as a junior officer, Lieutenant Fox had resigned from the Navy to become a textile mill executive. The latter experience had brought him into touch with New England shipping interests and was to prove useful to the Department in wartime.

Soon after Lincoln's inauguration Fox's offer to lead a relief expedition to Fort Sumter was accepted. Fox planned to have a naval force engage the Confederate shore batteries while a fast supply steamer ran the gauntlet in to the beleaguered fort. Unfortunately while Fox's expedition was being prepared a cabal of well-intentioned persons, organizing behind Secretary Welles's back a similar and *secret* expedition to relieve Fort Pickens at Pensacola, obtained authorization from President Lincoln to employ the huge side-wheeler the U.S.S. *Powhatan*. Unknown to the cabal, which consisted of Secretary of State W. H. Seward, Lieutenant D. D. Porter, U.S.N., and Captain M. C. Meigs, U.S.A., the *Powhatan* had been earmarked by the Navy Department for Fox's mission. This extraordinary example of inter-departmental meddling led to Fox's discomfiture on April 12, 1861, when Fort Sumter was fired on by the Secessionists and Fox's expedition had no sufficient force with which to reply. In three ways the episode cleared the air. Fox himself was appeased by a job as Chief Clerk in the Navy Department, and the position of Assistant Secretary was soon created for him. Secretary Welles, his ideas of correct administration seriously affronted, went to the mat with the President on the issue of extra-departmental interference. Henceforth, both Lincoln and Seward agreed, there should be no wheels within wheels. The Navy Depart-

---

[1] See R. S. West, Jr., *Gideon Welles, Lincoln's Navy Department,* 1943, Ch. IV.

ment was to be run by its responsible head, the Secretary of the Navy. Thirdly, the episode at Sumter brought an end to six agonizing weeks of doubt and chaos. The war, which for years had seemed irrepressible, had now had its "official" opening.

THE GIANT BLOCKADE

Smarting from the blow at Fort Sumter and fearful lest the Confederate States carry out their threat to unleash privateers against American shipping, Lincoln on April 19 proclaimed a formal blockade of the Southern coast from South Carolina through Texas. A "competent force," he announced, would be so posted as to prevent the use of Southern ports. A neutral ship seeking to enter such ports would first be warned away by the commander of a blockading vessel, and the fact of the warning duly noted on her register, after which any further effort to violate the blockade would render the ship and her cargo liable to seizure and condemnation as naval prize.

Unhappily for the Union cause, Lincoln's grave proclamation carried less weight with border states than South Carolina's victory over Fort Sumter. Virginia and North Carolina within a week seceded and their writhing and folding coastlines were included in the blockade under Lincoln's supplementary proclamation of April 27. From Washington down the Potomac and south around the coast to the Rio Grande there were 3,549 miles of shore including 189 river mouths and harbors that would have to be given special attention.

Early in the war the Washington government recognized the paramount military importance of the blockade. The South had begun the war without a navy, and must not be permitted to obtain one from the outside world. The South lacked the heavy industries essential to building a navy, and must be cut off from access to the industrial resources of Europe. General Scott's term "the Anaconda policy" was an apt characterization of the Federal overall strategy. As a huge snake coils around its victim, denying him outside aid, ever tightening the dread grip, and finally smothering him, so must the Federal blockade stifle the Confederacy and destroy its will to resist.

Against this basic Federal strategy the South was destined to make a heroic resistance. For a time the Confederate government toyed with the idea of sending out privateers to prey on the fatted commerce of Yankeedom; but they soon abandoned the idea in favor of commerce raiding by nationally owned cruisers. In the first months of the war several Southern-owned ships were outfitted as raiders and sent out through the sparsely held picket line of Union blockaders. Later on, ships like the *Alabama,* built abroad, would be used. Commerce raiding by the South would more often make headlines in the press than the relatively dull incidents of the blockade; but the main objective of the Southerner throughout the war would be to break through the Union's starvation blockade. Mines, torpedoes, ironclad warships, and submarines would be invented and operated against the blockaders primarily with this aim in view. At times it would seem that nature herself was fighting on the side of the Confederacy. A "double" coastline along Virginia and North Carolina enclosed several navigable sounds. The chain of "sea islands" off South Carolina and Georgia afforded breakwaters to navigable channels skirting the mainland. All of the chief Southern harbors had more than one entrance, to multiply difficulties for the blockaders.

To begin the work of the blockade the habitually unprepared United States could neither rent naval ships as she had in her five-year war against the pirates of Tripoli, nor could she resort to the guerrilla tactics of privateering as in 1812 when she measured her puny naval strength against the mistress of the seas. Privateering had been outlawed by the civilized world in 1856 and in any case the South had no merchant marine to make such operations feasible. Of ships in commission at the outbreak of the war the Federal Navy had 19 sail-driven men-of-war of doubtful effectiveness and only 23 steam-driven warships. Had it been physically possible to station this handful of 42 heterogeneous craft at equal intervals around the hostile coast, each one would have had to patrol 84 miles of coastline with an average of three or four inlets per mile.

For the Navy Department in Washington the month ushered in by the humiliation of Fort Sumter was in some ways the blackest month of the war. High ranking Southern naval officers resigning from strategic positions included Captain Franklin Buchanan, Commandant of the Washington Navy Yard, Commander Matthew Fontaine Maury of the Naval Observatory, and Captain George A. Magruder, Chief of the Bureau of Ordnance and Hydrography. Each ship returning home from abroad brought to the Department a new sheaf of resignations. In Annapolis the situation was most critical, as indeed it was in Washington itself because of Maryland's threats to secede. In the third week of April Baltimoreans tore down rail bridges leading to the north and Virginia placed cannon along the Potomac to interrupt the essential water-borne freight line to the Capital. "Washington was severed from the northern states, without mail facilities or telegraphic intercourse," wrote Secretary Welles; "the troops which were on their way to the Capital were stopped and denied approach. . . . The few naval vessels on the Atlantic coast that were available had been sent to Charleston, and when they returned would be wholly inadequate for the immediate and indispensable wants of the government."

HOLOCAUST AT NORFOLK

At its inception the blockade suffered a staggering blow in the loss of the Norfolk Navy Yard. This largest of the navy yards contained valuable machine shops and had the only centrally located drydock in the country. Norfolk was the logical northern base for the block-aders, but more important still it was the chief arsenal for the U. S. Navy's reserve supply of naval guns. While many hundreds of cannon stacked in its yard were obsolete, there were some 300 pieces of mod-ern ordnance of the Dahlgren type, built on Commander John A. Dahlgren's principle of the curve of pressures. According to the best authorities there were at Norfolk about 50 of the largest and most powerful Dahlgren guns, having a nine-inch diameter of bore. In addition to several obsolete sailing sloops and brigs, there was at Nor-folk, decommissioned and unready to sail, one of the Navy's largest and best screw-propelled steam warships, the 50-gun U.S.S. *Merri-mack.*

Anxiety for the safety of Norfolk gripped Secretary Welles on the eve of Fort Sumter, partly because at this time the court-martial of the sixty-seven-year-old late commandant of the lost Pensacola Navy Yard was revealing behind closed doors a sorry tale of demoralization, in-competence, and senility. With Washington a hotbed of rumors and treasons, Welles on April 10 warned Commodore C. S. McCauley, the sixty-eight-year-old commandant at Norfolk, that "in view of the peculiar condition in the country . . . it becomes necessary that great vigilance should be exercised in guarding and protecting the public interests committed to your charge."

The *Merrimack's* guns were on shore and her engines and boilers had been opened up for repairs. Daily the yard workmen at Norfolk fell off in number and joined the growing band of Virginia militia and avowed secessionists assembling outside the walls. Four of the five naval officers of the rank of commander attached to the yard resigned, as well as four out of eight lieutenants—men whose advice was suffi-cient to paralyze the initiative of the aged commandant. A few marines and enlisted seamen deserted or refused to obey orders. On April 12 Engineer-in-chief Benjamin F. Isherwood was sent from Washington to put the *Merrimack's* engines together so that she could be taken to Philadelphia. The commandants at Philadelphia and New York were ordered to send crews to Norfolk at once to get the vessels out, but neither official was able to get men there in time. In defiance of a Federal Government order the Baltimore Steam Packet Company, which ran a bay steamer to Norfolk, refused to transport naval recruits to help save the Norfolk yard. On the 18th Isherwood returned to Washington in disgust and despair to report as follows: By 4 P.M. he had repaired the *Merrimack's* engines, and assembled a skeleton engine-room crew. McCauley, fearful of provoking the Virginia militia, told him to delay firing the boilers until the next morning. At 9 A.M. on the 18th the only thing wanting was the Commodore's order to cast loose and go. "He then, to my great surprise and dissatisfaction, informed me that he had not yet decided to send the vessel, but would let me know further in the course of a few hours." About 2 P.M. McCauley had directed him to draw the fires. When Isherwood finished his report, Secretary Welles dispatched Commodore Hiram Paulding posthaste to Norfolk "to take command of all the naval forces there afloat," and if necessary to "repel force by force." Paulding was to make use of any ships that he might find in the Hampton Roads area to accomplish his mission: the evacuation or destruction of the naval ships and material at Norfolk.

Paulding took with him on board the U.S.S. *Pawnee* 100 Marines 40 barrels of gunpowder, 11 tanks of turpentine, and 12 barrels of cotton waste, with which to destroy the establishment. He arrived after dusk on the 20th and superseded McCauley. The *Merrimack,* the *Germantown,* the *Plymouth,* and the *Dolphin,* their seacocks just opened by McCauley's order, Paulding found to be already settling fast at their anchorages. Quickly he divided his Marines into three groups and sent them out with combustibles to prepare the destruction of the drydock, the shops, barracks, and ship houses, and the as yet unsunk tophamper of the ships.

Paulding's second in command, Captain Charles Wilkes, distributed combustibles aboard the *Merrimack* and six other nearby ships and laid powder trains across their decks. "The ship *Delaware* was left out in consequence of the distance she lay off, and the frigate *United States* was in so decayed a condition that it was deemed unnecessary to waste the material of turpentine upon her." Commander John

Rodgers, U.S.N., with Captain H. G. Wright of the Army Engineers, laid mines under the gates of the drydock; Commanders James Alden and B. F. Sands prepared the shops, barracks, and ship houses. At 1:45 A.M. on Sunday, April 21, all the powder trains were laid. The troops from Fortress Monroe and Commodore Paulding's Marines, giving up their futile efforts to destroy the store of guns by sledging off their trunnions, were re-embarked. Paulding was all set to send up a rocket as signal to ignite the powder trains throughout the yard when the youngest son of Commodore McCauley, tears streaming down his cheeks, dashed up to report that his father refused to vacate his post. Commander Alden ran to the commandant's house and induced him, "with great reluctance, to remove to the *Cumberland*." The *Pawnee* and the sailing sloop *Cumberland,* the latter towed by the tug *Yankee,* moved out into the river and at 4:20 A.M. Paulding lighted his rocket. Torches everywhere were applied to powder trains, "and in a few minutes the whole area of the yard was one sheet of flame—the two ship houses and the whole line of stores, as well as the *Merrimack*." All save one of the firing crews escaped in rowboats to the ships. Commander Rodgers and Captain Wright, whose task had been to blow up the drydock, were caught behind "vast sheets of flames and dense smoke . . . impossible for anyone to pass through."

Large flakes of burning debris rained on the evacuation ships as they retreated down the river. Near Craney Island the *Cumberland* grounded on some hulks the Confederates had sunk to obstruct the channel, but the chartered ship *Key Stone State* helped the tug to pull her free. Virginia militiamen led by one of McCauley's former officers, rushing into the yard as the Federals retired, hurriedly flooded the drydock, drowned the 20 barrels of powder, and saved the drydock. Commander Rodgers and Captain Wright were arrested and detained a few days in Richmond as "guests" of Governor John Letcher.[2] In addition to one of the two best drydocks in the country, the Confederate Government obtained a quantity of naval ordnance which it could not itself have manufactured for many months. With these guns they were able to set up heavy batteries at strategic points around their long perimeter to threaten the blockaders, and ease the pressure from the giant Anaconda. "Had it not been for the guns captured at Norfolk and Pensacola," in Admiral Porter's opinion, "the Confederates would have found it a difficult matter to arm their fortifications

[2] J. T. Scharf, *History of the Confederate States Navy,* 1886, p. 132.

for at least a year. . . . Great as was, therefore, the loss of our ships, it was much less than the loss of our guns."[3]

CLEARING THE DECKS FOR ACTION

With Norfolk gone the inland navy yard at Washington gained a new importance, despite the fact that its communications down the Potomac were vulnerable. During the effort to save Norfolk the *Anacostia* was stationed a few miles below the Washington Navy Yard at Kettlebottom Shoals to frustrate Confederate attempts to block the Potomac channel by sinking hulks. The Virginia bank of the Potomac presented many fine sites for placement of artillery and the first Federal naval activity of the war occurred on May 31 when Commander J. H. Ward with a flotilla of light converted river boats attempted to knock out Confederate batteries near Aquia Creek. Throughout the first year of the war the Confederates held the south bank and menaced Union shipping. Union naval craft seldom hesitated to pass these batteries, and they did so in daytime as channel lights and buoys had been removed; but ordinary freighters were either deterred altogether or had to be furnished naval escort.

Two or three ships were left on the antislave patrol off West Africa, but aside from these all foreign stations were disbanded for the duration and all ships ordered home.

In the summer of 1861—the First Battle of Bull Run seemed to determine the atmosphere for this wretched summer—the Union Navy was so desperately short of ships and its task was so immense that need was felt for a scapegoat. Despite the economic depression of 1857 and the fact that America had never before been any better prepared when a war came, the Buchanan administration was excoriated for not having prepared the Navy to meet its present extreme emergency. Ex-Secretary Toucey of Connecticut was denounced as pro-Secessionist. Ex-Senator Jefferson Davis was said to have boasted that he had voted appropriations only for ships that were too heavy to enter Southern harbors. Northerners, recalling that ex-Senator Slidell had remained in Washington after his native Louisiana had seceded, now inferred that his ulterior motive had been to frustrate military preparations in the North. In an atmosphere thick with recrimination Lincoln's Cabinet split into two camps on the international implications of the blockade, as it had been proclaimed. It had been a mistake,

---

[3] D. D. Porter, *Naval History of the Civil War*, 1886, p. 32.

argued Secretary Welles who was Secretary Seward's bitterest critic, to proclaim a formal blockade, as that act by implication accorded belligerent rights to the South. All that was necessary, it was urged, was a simple closure of the ports in an insurrectionist region—a domestic matter with which diplomats had no concern. The dispute spread to Congress and a new law was passed which required the President to proclaim the closure of the Southern ports. Lincoln, observing that the new proclamation "would be like the Pope's bull to the comet, trade would go on in spite of law and the executive proclamation," issued the required new proclamation without specifically cancelling the previous formal proclamations of the blockade. The blockade therefore, in its international aspects remained unchanged, and the moribund pre-war Navy was gradually reconditioned and built up to meet its vast new wartime obligations.

The purchase of merchant craft and their outfitting as war vessels, begun early in April, had been speeded by the Secretary's granting to certain prominent businessmen of New York the power to act as proxies for the Secretary of the Navy. Further cutting red tape, the Department engaged a single broker to purchase ships and found him better skilled than the average naval officer in beating down prices. Keels for new ships were laid in the navy yards and contracts were let with commercial builders for a number of "90-day" gunboats. Old ships of any use at all were repaired and recommissioned. Early in August a Washington *Star* reporter wrote, "So effective a naval force was never improvised by any Government with so small means at hand."

The appointment of three naval boards in the summer of 1861 did much to clear the decks of the Navy for action. The first was the strategy board headed by Captain S. F. Du Pont. As a result of this board's analysis of Southern coastal geography, basic divisions were established for the squadrons that would eventually seal the blockade. After Congress in July passed the nation's first naval retirement law, the Secretary appointed Captain D. G. Farragut as a member of the Retirement Board. A corollary to the removal of aged and feeble officers from the active list was the Secretary's policy of selecting younger men, if necessary, for responsible higher commands. "Rank," Welles wrote to an ambitious older officer, with perhaps a note of warning, "has its merits, is to be respected, and in peaceable times may be recognized and regarded; but when difficulties like the present are impending, the Department can not permit its action to be restricted and the welfare of the country endangered by this consideration merely."[4] With Congressional sanction a third board headed by Commander Joseph Smith was appointed to consider and investigate the momentous possibility of ironclad warships.

HATTERAS INLET

On August 26, one month after Bull Run, the first combined military and naval expedition sailed south from Hampton Roads under Flag Officer Silas H. Stringham and Major General Benjamin F. Butler. Stringham's force consisted of two large steam frigates, a sailing sloop, two small steam gunboats, and two converted steamers. Butler had 860 troops. Their mission, comprising the first phase of operations down the coast as planned by Du Pont's strategy board, was to seize an advanced base suitable as headquarters for a blockading squadron.

The eastern boundary of North Carolina is a slim natural breakwater of sand which protects Pamlico and Albemarle Sounds. Here and there the tides of the ocean spilling across the low flat breakwater have washed out channel entrances into the sounds and cut the breakwater into island segments. Hatteras Inlet, the entrance into Pamlico Sound which cuts across the south end of Cape Hatteras Island, was Stringham's and Butler's objective. The naval commander considered it "the key to all the ports south of Hatteras."

Two log-sand fortifications, called Forts Hatteras and Clark, had recently been erected by the Confederates to guard this inlet. Together they mounted a heterogeneous assortment of 21 guns, chiefly old 32-pounder, muzzle-loading smoothbores, of limited range. Only a meager supply of ammunition was available, and none at all for their most effective gun, a 10-inch Columbiad of 15,000 pounds. For all their limitations, the log-sand forts were able to imperil any wooden ship that might try to force its way into Pamlico Sound. They were of course completely unprepared to cope with such an avalanche of strength as descended upon them on the morning of August 28.

Ironically from the point of view of the defenders the depth of water through the inlet was so shallow that Stringham was compelled to anchor his ships to seaward and well beyond the range of the guns from either of the forts. An unequal bombardment ensued, with Stringham's ships, *Minnesota,* 43 guns, *Wabash,* 44, *Cumberland,* 24, *Susquehanna,* 15, *Pawnee,* 10, pounding the forts and the woods be-

---

[4] The chief source for this chapter is *Official Records . . . Navies,* Series I, Vol. 4, 6, and 12. This reference is to Vol. 6, p. 233.

hind Fort Clark. Through a mounting surf some 300 of Butler's men were put ashore with a view to rushing Fort Clark from the rear, but even while the Federal troops were landing the Confederate garrison was being evacuated on board a bay steamer to fall back on Fort Hatteras. In the night the Federal armada was compelled by rough weather to stand off shore, a maneuver which offered the Confederates a brief opportunity for a counterblow against the 300 Union troops marooned on shore with scanty provisions. The weather cleared next day, however, and a renewal of the naval bombardment brought the surrender of the Confederate forces. On the afternoon of the first day the military commanders of the forts, when their two forces were combined, had requested Commodore Samuel Barron to assume the general command, and Barron in the face of hopeless odds had acceded. Thus Samuel Barron, who until the outbreak of secession had been a senior officer in the U. S. Navy, now struck his new flag in surrender to the naval and military commanders of the United States expeditionary force.

Far from being a "key" to ports south of it, Hatteras Inlet, a few miles from the tempestuous Cape, proved inadequate even as a coaling and supply base for the blockade, because of its shifting and shallow channel and an inner bulkhead or bar of quicksand that separated the "breakwater" from the deep waters of the sound.

Port Royal Sound

Hatteras Inlet was the curtain raiser for operations against larger Confederate forts at Port Royal Sound. This sound, strategically located between Charleston and Savannah, was geographically suitable for development as a coal and supply base for the blockade. Forts Walker and Beauregard, standing 2.2 miles apart on Hilton Head and St. Helena Island, formed a strong military barrier guarding the entrance to the sound. Unlike Hatteras Inlet, the channel at Port Royal was not only deep enough for the heaviest ships to pass through, but wide enough for them to maneuver in. In this case sea room was important, for reconnaissance by blockaders had indicated that Confederate preparations at Port Royal, near the fountainhead of secession, were more formidable than they had been at Hatteras. On August 3 Captain S. F. Du Pont of the Strategy Board was notified of his selection to lead the naval force in this major "expedition upon the flank of the enemy," and on September 18, when the Atlantic Squadron was split into two blockading squadrons, he was made Flag

Officer of the South Atlantic Blockading Squadron to cover the coasts of South Carolina and Georgia and the eastern shore of Florida.

Du Pont, enjoined by the Secretary "to lose no time in getting afloat," yet unwilling to risk a failure, insisted on waiting for the completion of the first group of "90-day" gunboats and assembled from various stations a number of pre-war screw sloops like the *Pawnee, Iroquois, Mohican,* and *Seminole,* which carried 11-inch guns. In the days of sail, naval experts had rated one gun on shore as the equivalent of four or five on a ship. The uncertain factor in Du Pont's mind seems to have been the new ratio of strength now that steam had supplanted sail. The scantlings of his wooden gunboats afforded almost no protection to the brittle and vulnerable machinery of motive power. Du Pont wanted, and got, a force whose superiority in guns was four or five times that of the two enemy forts combined. Even so he was uneasy. "We have considerable power to carry on an offensive warfare; that of endurance against forts is not commensurate," he reminded the Department a few hours before he set sail for Port Royal.[5]

The army force of about 13,000 men under Brigadier General Thomas W. Sherman embarked on transports at Annapolis. Du Pont dispatched a fleet of 25 coal and supply vessels under naval convoy on October 28 and on the 29th the joint expedition set out from Hampton Roads. Behind the flagship *Wabash* steamed ten warships in a double line. Back of these about three dozen transports, mostly chartered craft, steamed in three lines headed by the converted ocean liners *Vanderbilt, Atlantic,* and *Baltic.* Several smaller naval craft formed a rear guard.

Off Hatteras the unwieldly armada was so completely scattered by a gale that at one time Du Pont from the quarter-deck of the heaving *Wabash* could see only a single other sail on the horizon. Two supply steamers carrying horses and cattle were wrecked on the coast of North Carolina and their crews taken as prisoners to Raleigh. The chartered steamer *Governor* with Du Pont's entire battalion of 300 Marines on board was slowly broken up by the storm. Two small vessels whose crowded decks could not hold all the Marines, even though they jettisoned their guns, stood by her until the large blockader *Sabine,* providentially blown off her station, sighted the miserable little group and came to their rescue.

Du Pont with about 30 other ships and transports arrived off Port

---

[5] *Ibid.,* Vol. 12, p. 231.

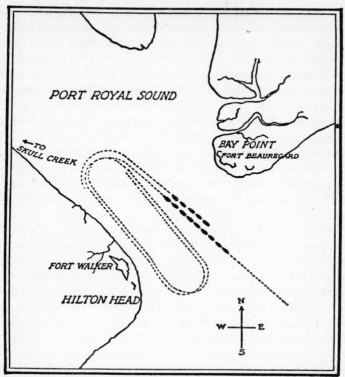

PORT ROYAL SOUND

BAY POINT
FORT BEAUREGARD

←TO
SKULL CREEK

FORT WALKER

HILTON HEAD

N
W — E
S

From *The United States Navy: A History* by Alden and Westcott.

Royal on November 4. Crossing the bar which lay ten miles out from the entrance, the ships anchored in the roadstead beyond range of the forts for several days while other ships straggled in and while the expedition's coast survey party sounded the channel and reset markers. Out from the sound to annoy the survey boat came five or six bay steamers, each mounting two guns, under command of Commodore Josiah Tattnall, until lately an officer of the U. S. Navy. One of Du Pont's ships chased this group inside the sound.

Loss of landing boats in the storm led Du Pont and General Sherman to set aside their original plan to land troops in rear of the forts, in favor of a simple naval bombardment. Du Pont's reconnaissance party confirmed the fact that Fort Walker was strongest on its sea and channel faces. On its inland wing toward the sound, from which quarter no attack was anticipated, there were only two antiquated guns, a 32- and a 42-pounder. This latter circumstance determined Du

Pont's tactics. He called his officers to a council, and a few minutes after 9 A.M. on November 7 he signalled for the fleet to get under way.

The ships entered the sound in two columns, one a battle squadron of 9 ships led by the flagship and the other a flanking squadron of 5 smaller gunboats. On this first run past the forts the two columns passed abreast up the middle of the channel, receiving and returning the fire of both forts.

A shot through her steam drum disabled the *Penguin's* engines, but in passing her the vessel next astern threw out a tow line and kept the crippled vessel's guns in action. The flanking squadron, led by Commander Charles Steedman in the *Bienville,* first chased away the Confederate mosquito fleet under Tattnall and then took up a position off the weak inner flank of Fort Walker to administer a punishing enfilading fire.

When the battleship column had passed about two miles beyond the forts, Du Pont turned southward to port and repassed Fort Walker at close range. As his ships were now breasting a flood tide, he was able to retard speed to an extremely slow pace though still sufficient to confuse enemy gunners. The flanking squadron continued to enfilade Fort Walker, first from ten-second, then five-second range; while the battle squadron completed two elliptical runs between the forts. At 1:15 P.M. the two leading battleships had delivered their fire for the third time when the *Ottawa* at the after end of the line signaled that Fort Walker had been abandoned.

Commander John Rodgers, Du Pont's aide, was sent ashore to verify this report and to hoist the Stars and Stripes. Fort Beauregard across the channel hauled down its flag before nightfall.

Casualties in the fleet totaled eight killed and 28 wounded, against 11 killed and 48 wounded in the forts. In a total of 13 guns on the channel face of Fort Walker ten had been dismounted and the gunners had used all but their last 500 pounds of powder. Commander Percival Drayton, U.S.N., whose snail-paced U.S.S. *Pocahontas* arrived late in the battle, was a South Carolinian whose secessionist brother Brigadier General Thomas F. Drayton commanded the Confederate defenders of Fort Walker. As to the psychological effect of the victory upon the people in the Port Royal area, Percival Drayton affirmed that "the demoralization can only be compared to that [of the Federals] after Bull Run." In honor of the victory national salutes were fired on all ships and stations of the U. S. Navy, and Du Pont was accorded a vote of thanks by Congress. On the material side the Navy had interposed to obtain an invaluable lodgment between the two great blockade-running ports of Savannah and Charleston. Port Royal's fine harbor, moreover, because the surrounding country was cut up into islands and partially drowned swamps, was easily defensible for a great supply base. Port Royal marked a very real advance for Union arms. Du Pont's handling of the campaign, as Captain Dudley W. Knox puts it, "marks him as one of the great leaders of the war."[6]

There were, however, two developments likely to disrupt the blockade, now that the Federal Navy was really prepared to tighten the squeeze. One of these was the evolution of the ironclad warship and another was the growing irritation of European states who depended upon the South for their supply of raw cotton.

---

[6] *A History of the United States Navy,* 1936, p. 203.

☆   ☆   ☆   ☆   ☆

9

The Monitor and the Virginia

Transforming the Merrimack

STEPHEN R. MALLORY, Secretary of the Confederate States Navy, was well informed on naval matters after having served for nearly ten years as chairman of the Naval Affairs Committee of the U. S. Senate. As Naval Secretary of a cotton-farming "nation" whose navy did not exist, and whose industrial facilities for building a navy were severely limited, Mallory at the outbreak of war made a clear-headed appraisal of the situation. The South could not hope to compete with the North in the construction of wooden ships, for in this category the North already was so well supplied that the South would have to out-build by two or three ships to one or fall an easy prey to superior numbers. But what the South lacked in numbers, he firmly believed, might be "compensated by invulnerability." On May 8, 1861, Mallory wrote the Confederate Naval Committee, "I regard the possession of an iron-armored ship as a matter of the first necessity." The ironclad was Mallory's answer to the Federal blockade. "Such a vessel at this time could traverse the entire coast of the United States, prevent all blockades, and encounter, with a fair prospect of success, their entire Navy." The Confederate Congress appropriated $2,000,000 to buy ironclads abroad, and Mallory at once dispatched an agent with the admonition that "We want a ship which can not be sunk or penetrated by the shell or shot of the U. S. Navy at a distance at which we could penetrate and sink ships of the enemy, and which can not be readily carried by boarders."[1]

While lack of credit and the active opposition of United States

---

[1] J. P. Baxter, *Introduction of the Ironclad Warship,* 1933, p. 225.

diplomacy delayed the construction of ironclads for the Confederacy abroad, the need at home for ironclads became pressing. In June Mallory ordered designs for an ironclad to be drawn, and eventually the ideas of several men were combined in the plan for transforming what remained of the wooden U. S. steam frigate *Merrimack* into the C. S. ironclad *Virginia*. The machine-age bottleneck that gave the Confederate Navy Department no choice as to building a completely new ship or reconstructing upon the wreckage of the *Merrimack* was a critical shortage of marine engines. In all the South there was no factory for building such engines, and the only engines available were those already installed in vessels or hulks under Southern control. After the *Merrimack* had been tugged into the undestroyed drydock at Norfolk Navy Yard and sluiced out, her engines were found to be salvageable, but as it was possible to install them only in a vessel of equal draft, it was decided to improvise an ironclad upon the hull of the old ship.

To three men, J. L. Porter, J. M. Brooke, and W. P. Williamson, the design and construction of the C. S. S. *Virginia* were chiefly due.

Naval Constructor John L. Porter supervised the removal of the charred upper works of the ship and cut her down to her old berth deck, which was now strengthened to become the new gundeck. He also built the thick-walled protective shield or casemate, 22 inches of wood, plus two layers of rolled iron bars two inches thick, the inner courses bolted lengthwise of the ship and the outer ones up and down. On the sides the casemate extended below the water to cover the "knuckle" where the shield joined the hull and at the ends the casemate was rounded to house pivot bow and stern chasers. An armored pyramidal structure pierced with narrow slits and standing atop the forward end of the casemate served as pilot house. That the gunners might have air a heavy iron grating was used, rather than a solid top, for the casemate. The armored gunshield rose at an angle of 35 degrees from the horizontal. Portholes were staggered on either side. Guns could not be mounted breech to breech, for inside the casemate behind the sloping side walls there was scant room for their recoil. Gunports were equipped with iron shutters manipulated by means of chains from within the casemate. Since the entire casemate occupied but 178 feet amidships of a vessel 263 feet in overall length, it was designed that when loaded the vessel's exposed decks should be just awash. The after deck or fantail was plated with boiler iron to give some protection to rudder and propeller against plunging shot. Bolted to her prow was a 1,500-pound cast-iron beak or ram that extended beyond the stem.

Procurement of sufficient iron for the armor, by far the most difficult job, was handled by Lieutenant John M. Brooke. The only iron-rolling mill in the South capable of rolling the necessary two-by-eight-inch bars was the Tredegar Iron Works in Richmond, a city not at all conveniently located with respect to coal and iron mines. The few iron foundries in Tennessee were unable to install rolling mill equipment and the foundry at Atlanta did not get such a mill into production before November, 1861. Paying inflationary prices, Brooke had to scour the country for any sort of iron to be rolled into armor. Brooke also designed and manufactured the two 7-inch rifles for the vessel's bow and stern armament. Her broadside guns included six 9-inch Dahlgren smoothbores from the *Merrimack's* former battery and two 6.4-inch rifles. At Richmond Lieutenant Brooke by practice firing at targets representing a section of the *Virginia's* casemate, determined the most favorable angle for the slope of the casemate.

Chief Engineer William P. Williamson's province was to so recondition the vessel's engines and boilers as to get every ounce of power out of them. Her engines and boilers, condemned by the navy yard authorities upon the *Merrimack's* return from her last cruise, had not since been improved by fire and sinking. "We could not depend upon them for six hours at a time,"[2] wrote Colonel John Taylor Wood; yet thanks to Williamson's persistence and industry these same engines would doggedly carry the novel craft, with her back-breaking casemate sinking her draft to 23 feet, into one of the most famous battles of history.

THE IRONCLAD BOARD'S DILEMMA

Neither the salvaging of the *Merrimack* nor the fact that the Confederate government ordered an ironclad warship to be improvised upon her old hull unduly disturbed Washington during the summer of 1861. On July 4—three weeks after Mallory's reconstruction order —when Secretary Welles requested the special session of Congress to authorize the appointment of a board to investigate the possibility of building ironclad warships and to make an appropriation for this purpose, there were two problems uppermost in his mind. Shallow-draft, iron-sheathed vessels were needed to beard the forts in shallow Southern rivers and harbors; and armored floating batteries for harbor

---

[2] *Battles and Leaders of the Civil War,* 1887, Vol. I, p. 694.

defense were deemed essential in view of the likelihood of European intervention in the war.

Congress took four weeks to consider the question. The mere mention of an appropriation for ironclads was sufficient to rattle a skeleton in the Federal closet. In 1842, Congress had first appropriated for the construction of the Stevens ironclad battery in Philadelphia. After 20 years this luckless craft was still on the stocks, a derelict in design whose cost had already run to the monumental figure of $500,000. For a time it looked as though political factions in the House would earmark part of the current appropriation to complete the Stevens battery, but this effort was frustrated by a compromise in the Senate. On August 3 Congress authorized the appointment of a board of naval officers to investigate armor-clad warships and appropriated $1,500,-000 "for the construction *or completing* of iron- or steel-clad steamships or steam batteries." (Italics added.) The three officers appointed to the Ironclad Board were Commodore Joseph Smith, Commodore Hiram Paulding, and Commander John A. Dahlgren. The last named, whose chief interest was the further development of ordnance at the Washington Navy Yard, requested to be relieved and his place was assigned to Commander Charles H. Davis. Commodore Smith, as Chief of the Bureau of Construction and Repair and the official to whom the supervision of any construction of ironclads would fall, was president of the board. He was a venerable gentleman, with 50 years in the Navy behind him and a vivid fear of blundering into another such mistake as the Stevens battery had proved to be. Commodore Paulding, as Chief of the new Office of Detail, was the individual primarily responsible for the assignment of officers to the various posts throughout the naval service, and Commander Davis was a scholarly officer who had served as a member and as secretary of Du Pont's Strategy Board.

"Distrustful of our ability to discharge this duty," the Ironclad Board recorded, "we approach the subject with diffidence, having no experience and but scanty knowledge in this branch of naval architecture." When the Department advertised for designs and offers to build ironclads, these documents flooded the Department and were turned over to the Ironclad Board. The latter reviewed published material on the iron-cased batteries which the British and French had used in the Crimea, and examined available information on the *Gloire* and the *Warrior,* the latest experimental armorclads built by France and England. A design which appealed to the Board, possibly because of its resemblance to the European ships, was submitted by Merrick & Sons, Philadelphia. This called for an ordinary wooden ship whose guns and vulnerable machinery would be protected by a heavy rectangular belt of armor amidships. Another favored design was that of an ordinary gunboat sheathed above the waterline with a double layer of wrought-iron plates, with a space left between the layers, the idea being that the outer plate would bend and check the force of a projectile before it hit the inner plate. This latter design was offered by Cornelius S. Bushnell of Connecticut, who also was responsible for persuading the inventor Ericsson to submit his model of a shallow-draft, turret ironclad.

On several principles the Ironclad Board reached general agreement. It decided that, while ironclads might prove to be "formidable adjuncts to fortifications," they could not "cope successfully with a properly constructed fortification of masonry." In other words they believed ironclads mainly useful for defense, preferably in conjunction with land fortifications. They were inclined to disparage the offensive value of ironclad ships on the open seas. Although "wooden ships may be said to be but coffins for their crews when brought in conflict with ironclad vessels," the superior speed of the former should enable them to "keep out of harm's way entirely."

Ericsson's model, a turret sitting on a raft, the raft superposed on a shallow iron hull, inspired the members of the board with conflicting emotions. Commodore Smith thought the idea quixotic and doubted that such a vessel would possess either buoyancy or stability. Commander Davis, perhaps more in seriousness than in jest, told Bushnell to "take the little thing [Ericsson's model] home and worship it, as it would not be idolatry, because it was in the image of nothing in the heavens above or on the earth beneath or in the waters under the earth."[3]

Ericsson himself, though he had sworn at the time of the *Princeton* disaster never to come to Washington again, appeared in person before the board. The irascible and not overly modest inventor found the air thick with croakings, yet he managed to check his ire and present a convincing argument for his vessel's stability.

On September 16 the Ironclad Board presented its momentous recommendation "that contracts be made with responsible parties for the construction of one or more ironclad vessels or batteries of as light

---

[3] W. C. Church, *Life of John Ericsson*, 1906, Vol. I, p. 250.

a draught of water as practicable consistent with the weight of their armor." Three contracts having the board's approval were made: (1) with Merrick & Sons, Philadelphia, for an armor-belted warship built on conventional lines, like England's *Warrior* (U.S.S. *New Iron-sides*); (2) with C. S. and H. L. Bushnell, Mystic, Connecticut, for an armor-plated gunboat (U.S.S. *Galena*); and (3) with John Erics-son, Green Point, L. I., for the historic first member of a new class of "monitors" (U. S. S. *Monitor*).

ERICSSON'S FOLLY

In a five-minute interview on Sunday September 15, Ericsson was instructed by the Secretary to go ahead with his plans at once, that the contract could be written latter. By October 4 when the contract was signed the dynamic inventor had already obtained financial back-ing and the plates for his novel vessel were going through the rolling-mill.

The vast disparity between North and South in industrial power is evidenced by the fact that Ericsson in a matter of 101 working days was able to build from the keel a complicated iron-hull, steam-driven, armor-clad warship. In the interest of speed he let out parts of the work to subcontractors. A burly Irishman, Thomas F. Rowland, built the vessel's scow-like metal hull at the shipyard-blacksmithy of the Continental Iron Works at Green Point, L. I. The Novelty Iron Works of New York, contractors for the turret, obtained the necessary one-inch, wrought-iron plates from a foundry near Baltimore. The engine, built by Delamater & Co. of New York, was of the double-trunk type, with power transmitted by rocking arms. Each of its two cylinders, bored in a single casting, was 36 inches in diameter, and the piston stroke 27 inches. The two return-tube "box" boilers were placed for-ward of the engine. Together with their furnaces they filled the nine feet of vertical space between the flat bottom and the raft-like deck overhead.

Ericsson himself divided his time between his office in lower Man-hattan and the shipyard. He designed each one of some 3,000 sep-arate parts of the mechanism as the work progressed, and never drafted a complete set of plans or constructed an accurate scale model.

As the work progressed Ericsson freely modified his own original plans and as freely forgot the terms to which Commodore Smith had bound him in the written contract. For example, because of the vessel's extremely small coal capacity, the Bureau of Construction and Repair had specified in the contract that she should be provided with "masts, spars, sails, and rigging of sufficient dimensions to drive the vessel at the rate of six knots per hour in a fair breeze."[4] Ericsson ignored this clause completely.

Reports on the rebuilding of the *Merrimack* at Norfolk disquieted Washington in January of 1862. Of the three ironclad vessels that had been ordered neither the armor-belted ship nor the double-plated gunboat could be ready for many months. Ericsson's small craft—"Ericsson's Folly," as she was now being named in the press—was the only hope of the Federal Navy Department in the way of an ironclad to match the Confederate threat to the blockade.

Ericsson launched the hull with engines and boilers in place on January 30. Upon this hull, which measured 124 feet in length, was quickly riveted a raft-like weather deck 172 feet long and 41½ feet wide. An armored "overhang," backed by seasoned oak, overlapped the hull to give resisting strength at the waterline. Indeed when the ship was fully loaded this overhang would be almost submerged to reduce its size as a target. For protection against plunging fire the weather deck was plated with one-inch iron. In the middle of the deck was inlaid a brass ring 20 feet in diameter, and upon this ring the cylindrical turret was placed.

The turret was 20 feet across and nine feet high. After the ship's two 11-inch Dahlgren guns had been mounted side by side on the turret floor, the laminated side wall was bolted together. Eight courses of one-inch, wrought-iron plates went into the cylindrical wall. Across the top was placed a grating of railroad rails. The turret's 140 tons of weight were borne by a central spindle which extended down inside the hull and connected with machinery for turning. The base of the turret wall was so arranged as to slide around as the device was turned, upon the brass ring inset in the deck, Ericsson's idea being to fire the guns "on the fly" while the turret was in motion and so minimize the enemy's chance of landing a direct hit on their muzzles. When the guns were withdrawn into the turret for sponging and loading, the gunports were closed by heavy blocks of iron that swung automatically into place like pendulums.

On Ericsson's suggestion his strange craft was named *Monitor*. "The impregnable and aggressive character of this structure," he wrote Assistant Secretary Fox, "will admonish the leaders of the Southern

---

[4] F. M. Bennett, *The Monitor and the Navy Under Steam*, 1900, p. 80.

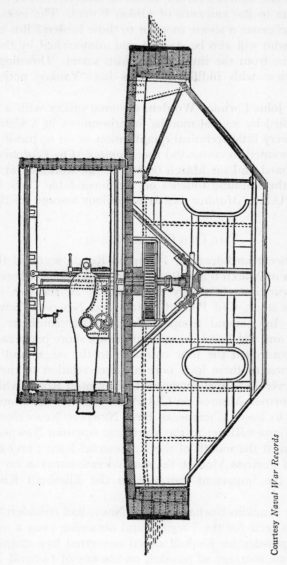

TRANSVERSE SECTION THROUGH TURRET OF ORIGINAL *Monitor.*

Rebellion that the batteries on the banks of their rivers will no longer present barriers to the entrance of Union Forces. The iron-clad intruder will thus prove a severe monitor to those leaders. But there are other leaders who will also be startled and admonished by the booming of the guns from the impregnable iron turret. 'Downing Street' will hardly view with indifference this last 'Yankee notion,' this monitor."[5]

Lieutenant John Lorimer Worden, a young officer with a zeal for service intensified by several months' imprisonment in a Confederate jail but with very little technical qualification as an operator of ironclads, was appointed to command the *Monitor*. On February 25 she was commissioned and on March 6, just as the workmen at Norfolk were putting the finishing touches on the formidable C. S. ironclad *Virginia*, the U.S.S. *Monitor* began a perilous voyage to Hampton Roads.

THE OLD ORDER PASSES

The magnificent anchorage of Hampton Roads, scene of the great two-act drama of March 8 and 9, 1862, formed a stage whose dimensions were approximately six by eight miles.[6] At the two northern corners of this stage, Old Point Comfort and Newport News, stood forts manned by Federal troops; while on the southern corners, Sewell's Point and Pig Point, were Confederate shore batteries. These fortifications controlled the four entrances to the stage, and the size and fearsomeness of these forts bore a direct relation to the importance of the several channel entrances to Hampton Roads which they dominated. Fortress Monroe on Old Point Comfort commanded the main channel to lower Chesapeake Bay; Newport News blocked the mouth of the James River; to the south and opposite Newport News stood Pig Point at the mouth of the Nansemond River; and six miles to the south of Fortress Monroe the Confederate batteries on Sewell's Point barred the important entrance to the Elizabeth River and Norfolk.

Flag Officer Franklin Buchanan, C. S. Navy, had considerable difficulty finding a crew for the *Virginia* and obtaining even a moderate supply of gunpowder for his half dozen converted bay steamers and tugs. A desperate shortage of powder, on the eve of General McClel-

---

[5] Church, *op. cit.*, Vol. I, p. 255.
[6] The chief source for the story of the *Monitor* and the *Virginia* is *Official Records . . . Navies*, Series I, Vol. 7.

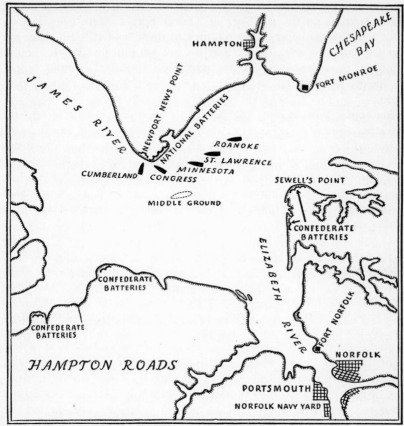

From *The United States Navy: A History* by Alden and Westcott.

lan's push toward Richmond, led the Confederate Secretary of the
Navy to caution Buchanan to make as great a use of the *Virginia's*
ram as possible in order to conserve gunpowder.

At 11 A.M. on March 8 the *Virginia,* accompanied by the tugs
Raleigh and *Beaufort,* left the Norfolk Navy Yard and descended the
Elizabeth River. "Up to the hour of sailing she was crowded with
workmen. Not a gun had been fired, hardly a revolution of the engines
had been made." Buchanan's plan was to proceed to Newport News
and ram the two old Federal sailing vessels *Cumberland* and *Congress* which for several months had been blockading the James
River; to release the remainder of his James River Squadron and with
their help proceed against the other wooden blockade ships in Hamp-

ton Roads. The threefold mission of his small wooden vessels was to screen the ironclad against any attempt of light vessels to ram her, to serve as tugs if necessary, and to hamper enemy vessels with their fire.

The *Virginia* headed south around the Middle Ground shoal and diagonally across the "stage" toward Newport News. The sailing frigate *Congress,* 50 guns, with sailors' laundry fluttering on her lines, rode at anchor about a mile east of the Newport News shore batteries. Half a mile west of her, in the mouth of the James River, lay the 24-gun sailing sloop *Cumberland.* About 1:30 P.M., as she came within range of the *Congress,* the *Virginia* opened fire with her bow pivot gun. An answering hail of metal hit, and glanced from, her tallow-slushed casemate. The Confederate "novelty in naval architecture" ignored this Federal fire and stood single-mindedly upon her course toward the *Cumberland.* Fifteen minutes later the ironclad plunged her beak through the wooden *Cumberland's* starboard bow; "the crash below the water was distinctly heard," reported the Confederate flag officer, who was himself only a few feet away at this moment, "and she commenced sinking, gallantly fighting her guns as long as they were above water. She went down with colors flying." The *Virginia* had some difficulty wrenching herself free of the wreck—some observers on the *Congress* believed she rammed the *Cumberland* twice—and when she did succeed in backing off she left her cast-iron ram to be carried down with her victim.

When the Confederate ironclad first rounded Sewell's Point all the Federal blockade ships off Fortress Monroe had hoisted anchor and cleared for action. Two of the original *Merrimack's* large sister ships, the *Minnesota* and *Roanoke,* got up steam and attempted to come to the *Cumberland's* rescue. The *Minnesota,* after steaming through Confederate fire from Sewell's Point, ran hard aground several miles west of Fortress Monroe. The *Roanoke,* her main drive shaft ailing from an old break that had not yet been repaired, took lines from two tugs and set her spanker and jib. She too was only moderately damaged in her shrouds by fire from Sewell's Point, but was unable to make sufficient speed to affect the battle that was in progress eight miles away.

Meanwhile the *Virginia* turned about in the wide mouth of the James and headed for the *Congress.* With her came several of the James River units which were now freed from the blockade—*Patrick Henry,* 10 guns, *Jamestown,* 2, and the tug *Teaser,* 1. As these frail craft ran the gauntlet of Newport News shore batteries the *Patrick*

Henry received a shot through the boiler which scalded to death four men. The invulnerable *Virginia,* on the other hand, in passing these batteries, blew to bits a large United States Army transport steamer that lay alongside the wharf at Newport News.

While the *Virginia* was sinking the *Cumberland,* the *Congress* slipped her cable, set jib and topsails, and with the aid of the tugboat *Zouave* ran aground in shallow water above Signal Point. By 3:30 P.M. the *Virginia* had taken up a raking position 150 yards astern, while several Confederate wooden gunboats had stationed themselves off the grounded *Congress's* starboard quarter. In this melancholy position the *Congress* could reply to the *Virginia* only with two guns run out through her stern ports. Two smashing broadsides from the *Virginia* shattered the muzzle of one of these two guns, dismounted the other, and swept down the length of the ship "with great rapidity and slaughter." Lieutenant J. B. Smith, son of Commodore Smith of the Ironclad Board, in temporary command of the *Congress,* was killed. His successor in command, to avoid useless slaughter, hauled down the colors and hoisted white flags of surrender.

Flag Officer Buchanan sent the tugs *Beaufort* and *Raleigh* alongside to receive the surrender, but while the Confederate boarding party was on the *Congress* two companies of United States infantry on shore, in disregard of the white flags flying at the gaff and the main, fired on the Confederate tugs. Incensed by a landlubberly error which he at the moment interpreted as "vile treachery," Buchanan now recalled his tugs and ordered the *Congress* to be destroyed with heated shot and explosive shell. In his excitement he leaped on top of the *Virginia's* casemate to better direct operations, when a Federal minie ball drilled his left thigh. The impetuous flag officer whose crowning achievement had been to mark the passing of the tradition of wood and sail thus lost the further honor of commanding an ironclad warship in the first battle of ironclads.

PANIC IN THE NORTH

Flag Officer L. M. Goldsborough, whose North Atlantic Blockading Squadron covered Hampton Roads, having known for a long time that the Confederate ironclad was practically completed, had planned a countermove. "My present purpose is," reads a confidential report to the Department, "to let her [the *Virginia*] get well over toward the *Congress* and the *Cumberland* off Newport News, and then to put at her with this ship [flagship *Minnesota*] and everything else that may be on hand at the time, with the view of bringing her between the fire of those ships and these, and cutting off all retreat on her part." Goldsborough himself was superintending operations down the coast on March 8, and his subordinates attempting to follow his plan of counteraction laid themselves open to being defeated in detail. Only the lateness of the hour and the receding tide, which compelled the deep-draft Confederate ironclad to retire early to an anchorage near Sewell's Point, saved the grounded *Minnesota,* the *Roanoke,* and the host of smaller wooden ships congregated in the vicinity on this black day.

On the day of the *Virginia's* sortie Assistant Secretary Gustavus Fox hurried to Hampton Roads, hoping to meet the *Monitor,* which had departed from New York two days before. Fox quickly appraised the situation of the now panicky blockaders and ordered them all to clear out of Hampton Roads as fast as they could. Tugboats pulled all night on the grounded *Minnesota* without being able to budge her.

In Washington and in seacoast cities of the North a near panic arose. In a doleful Cabinet meeting at the White House Lincoln and Secretary of War Stanton took turns going to the window to see whether the "Confederate terror" was yet coming up the Potomac. Secretary Welles, an old newspaper editor, thus described the scene: "The *Merrimack,* he [Stanton] said, would destroy every vessel in the service, could lay every city on the coast under contribution, could take Fortress Monroe; McClellan's mistaken purpose to advance by the Peninsula must be abandoned. . . . Likely the first movement of the *Merrimack* would be to come up the Potomac and disperse Congress, destroy the Capitol and public buildings; or she might go to New York and Boston and destroy those cities, or levy from them contributions sufficient to carry on the War."[7] Stanton telegraphed to several governors of seaboard states advising them to block their harbors with rafts or other obstructions.

VOYAGE OF THE CHEESE BOX

A wave "flows right across her deck; it looks to the sailor as if his ship was altogether under water, and it is only the man who has studied the philosophical laws which govern flotation and stability who feels exactly comfortable in her during a gale of wind." Thus Chief Engineer Alban C. Stimers could write with philosophical de-

---

[7] *Diary of Gideon Welles,* 1911, Vol. I, p. 63.

tachment a week *after* his trip down the coast in the untried and decidedly freakish looking "cheese box on a raft."

On Friday, March 7, however, when a gale caught her off Delaware Capes and blew water into the *Monitor's* ventilators, Stimers wished that Ericsson had made these blower pipes as tall as the turret instead of only four feet high. The inventor, intent on finding space inside the little ship to stow all tophamper during battle, had refused to follow Stimers' suggestion. Another bad feature was insufficient calking. Ericsson had insisted that packing about the base of the turret was unnecessary, that the mere weight of the turret would keep it seated on its brass ring. Ideally, perhaps the inventor was right. Practically, his cheese box was not a finely machined job, but the rough and ready product of a sort of overgrown blacksmith shop. Lieutenant S. Dana Greene, the *Monitor's* executive officer, wrote that "the water came down the turret like a waterfall. It would strike the pilot-house [a low iron box about 40 feet forward of the turret] and go over the turret in beautiful curves, and it came through the narrow eye-holes in the pilot-house with such force as to knock the helmsman completely round from the wheel. The waves also broke over the blower-pipes, and the water came down through them in such quantities that the belts of the blower-engines slipped, and the engines consequently stopped for lack of artificial draught, without which, in such a confined place, the fires could not get air for combustion." Asphyxiated firemen had to be handed up through two hatches to the grating on top of the turret, where the fresh air and water gradually revived them. "The steam-pumps could not be operated because the fires had been nearly extinguished. . . . The hand-pumps . . . had not enough force to throw water out through the top of the turret . . . and it was useless to bail, as we had to pass the buckets up through the turret, which made it a very long operation. Fortunately, toward evening the wind and the sea subsided, and, being again in smooth water, the engine was put in operation. But at midnight in passing over a shoal, rough water was again encountered, and our troubles were renewed, complicated this time with the jamming of the wheel-ropes, so that the safety of the ship depended entirely on the strength of the hawser which connected her with the tugboat. The hawser being new, held fast; but during the greater part of the night we were constantly engaged in fighting the leaks, until we reached smooth water again."[8]

---

[8] *Battles and Leaders,* Vol. I, pp. 720-721.

As the *Monitor* entered Chesapeake Bay around 4 P.M. on March 8, her commander Lieutenant Worden heard the roar of cannon in Hampton Roads and ordered the vessel stripped of her sea rig and her turret readied for action. At 9:00 P.M. the Senior Officer Present on board the *Roanoke* directed Worden to move up toward Newport News and give cover to the grounded *Minnesota*. The *Congress,* now burning fiercely on the water, lighted the last few miles as the *Monitor* took her place on the stage beside the hulking *Minnesota*. Shortly after midnight the *Congress* blew up, her powder tanks exploding in succession as they mounted into the sky.

THE MONITOR FIGHTS THE VIRGINIA
SUNDAY, MARCH 9, 1862

Peering through the early morning haze Lieutenant Catesby ap R. Jones, Buchanan's successor in command of the *Virginia,* assured himself that his intended victim the *Minnesota* was still grounded north of Middle Ground Shoal. But alongside of her lay a strange craft— "an immense shingle floating on the water, with a gigantic cheese box rising from its center; no sails, no wheels, no smokestack, no guns." As the day grew lighter it quickly became evident that this craft was neither watertank nor floating magazine. It could only be the Ericsson battery that Northern papers had been talking about. The *Virginia,* pouring black smoke through her riddled stack, steamed up the deep and narrow channel south of the Middle Ground and at the distance of a mile let fly a shell at the *Minnesota*. As she did so the Ericsson battery advanced to intercept her.

Lieutenant Worden directed the *Monitor's* movements from the pilot house. By crowding, three people were able to pack themselves into this tiny chamber: the captain, the pilot, and the helmsman. Only the armored top of the pilot house projected above the upper deck. This top, made of 9 by 12 inch cast-iron bars dovetailing at the corners, rose about four feet above the outside deck. A narrow eye-slit just under the topmost bar enabled the occupants to see how to navigate the ship, and the steering wheel was attached to the lowest of the iron bars. Through voice tubes Captain Worden was able at the outset of the battle to communicate with the turret and the engine room, although these tubes did not survive the first concussions and communication thereafter had to be carried on through messenger boys.

Lieutenant S. Dana Greene had charge of the *Monitor's* two guns and the 16 men in the gun crews. Since the *Monitor's* late model 11-

Top, ENGAGEMENT BETWEEN THE MONITOR AND THE VIRGINIA. From a contemporary engraving. *Bottom,* SURRENDER OF THE CONFEDERATE RAM TENNESSEE AT MOBILE BAY. From a painting by Xanthus Smith.

inch Dahlgren guns had not been completely tested, her gunners throughout this important day were limited by the Bureau of Ordnance to the use of only 15-pound charges of powder. The *Virginia's* ten guns gave her a margin of safety in case of bursting which the *Monitor* with only two guns did not have. Explosion of a gun on the *Monitor* would in all probability put the ship out of action. On board the little *Monitor,* moreover, there were no relief gunners to replace casualties, and these 16 irreplaceable men, like everyone else on board the ship, had scarcely slept for two days.

At 8:45 A.M. the *Monitor* yawed to jockey the pilot house out of the line of fire. Her turret commenced to screech and turn slowly. Lieutenant Greene peered out through the narrow clearance between gun and gunport and when the *Virginia* came in view pulled the lockstring. His shot bounced off the black sloping walls of the Confederate. Sooty exhaust gases from the gun billowed in through the grating across the top of the turret and blackened the *Monitor's* gunners. As the firing continued the direction markers, chalked on the stationary deck below the turret and visible through the open hatch in the floor, became too smudged to read.

For four hours the two iron champions sparred with one another. Twenty-two of the *Virginia's* shells landed on the *Monitor's* turret, pilot house, overhang, and deck in search of a weak spot. These shells either bounded off or were shattered against the *Monitor's* wrought-iron mail, leaving dents but inflicting no injury to the ship. The *Monitor* fired in all 41 solid cast-iron shot which cracked the *Virginia's* outer and inner layers of iron but lacked the punch to break through the thick wooden backing.

Because her projectiles had no more effect than "tossing pebbles" against the *Monitor,* the *Virginia* made an effort to run down her opponent. "Her bow passed over our deck," according to Chief Engineer Stimers who caught a glimpse of the affair from inside the revolving turret, "and our sharp upper edged side cut through the light iron shoe upon her stem and well into her oak. She will not try that again." As her already damaged stem began leaking, the *Virginia* made no further effort to ram. In maneuvering she once stuck on the Middle Ground Shoal, but pulled free in 15 minutes. Now and then her gunners on a side not engaged with the *Monitor* sent a shot into the stranded *Minnesota.* The tug *Dragon* which was trying to free the *Minnesota* from the mud was blown to bits.

Meanwhile, in the course of maneuvering, several casualties occurred on the *Monitor*. First Master L. N. Stodder, engaged on the lookout, braced his knee against the inside of the turret wall just at the instant a heavy missile hit on the outside. The concussion knocked him out for ten minutes. Peter Trescott, seaman, repeated the error and had also to be carried below insensible. At 11:30 while Captain Worden stood at his post in the pilot house a shell struck just outside of his lookout chink and within a few inches of his eyes. Blinded and bleeding, Worden turned over the command to Lieutenant Greene.

During the 20 minutes of confusion at this time the *Monitor* drifted into shallow water and firing ceased. Meanwhile, on board the *Virginia* a council of war concluded that the riddled *Minnesota* was no longer worth the *Virginia's* attention. The pilots also strenuously objected to remaining longer in this area on account of the receding of the tide. At 12:30 P.M., therefore, the *Virginia* retired toward Sewell's Point. The *Monitor* under Lieutenant Greene, after a token feint in the direction of the retiring enemy, returned to her station beside the *Minnesota*.

From a tactical point of view Hampton Roads was a drawn battle. Neither ironclad had seriously damaged the other and for some weeks after the battle the local situation was a stalemate. From a strategic point of view the *Virginia* failed to achieve her primary objective, which was to break open the Federal blockade. This failure, in combination with the disastrous loss of New Orleans in April, led the Confederates in May of 1862 to contract their military frontiers. The proud *Virginia* was destroyed by her own crew when the Confederate military forces evacuated Norfolk. The *Monitor* survived her late antagonist by seven months. At the end a victim of her own poor sea-keeping qualities, she foundered in a storm off Cape Hatteras while en route to Charleston.

☆ ☆ ☆ ☆ ☆

10
The New Orleans Campaign

BLOCKADE OFF THE DELTAS

EARLY IN JUNE of 1861 the first Federal blockade ships arrived off the deltas of the Mississippi.[1] Commander C. H. Poor in the screw-sloop *Brooklyn* anchored athwart Pass à l'Outre and 35 miles to the west of him Lieutenant David D. Porter in the side-wheeler *Powhatan* blocked the Southwest Pass. Each of the Federal officers sent a boat up-river to the nearest pilot town to announce formally the establishment of the blockade and to warn neutral ships that they might have 15 days in which to put to sea. In the ensuing stampede seaward many sailing vessels which attempted to navigate the passes without pilots or steam tugs, grounded inside the bars.

The blockading officers had to handle problems not covered in the regulations. Because of their Northern ownership a number of the stranded craft could not get tugs until the blockading officers granted the latter immunity from capture on condition that they haul foe as well as friend across the bar. Some Southern-owned vessels presented temporary foreign registers signed by the English or the French consul at New Orleans, an obvious subterfuge to avoid seizure. In the absence of instructions the blockaders searched these ships carefully before permitting them to leave to make certain that they were not outfitted as Confederate commerce raiders.

For more than a month the *Brooklyn* and the *Powhatan* were the only ships on this distant station of the blockade. They stoppered only the two most important entrances to New Orleans. Pass à l'Outre it-

---

[1] The chief source for this chapter is *Official Records . . . Navies*, Series I, Vols. 16-18.

self had two exits, Northeast and Southeast Passes, only one of which the *Brooklyn* could guard at a time. Further west were South Pass, available to shallow draft ships, and Southwest Pass. About ten miles above the Head of the Passes (where the Passes diverge on the final lap toward the Gulf) was another entrance into the lower river known as The Jump. In addition to these river outlets the great entrepôt of New Orleans, as Du Pont's Strategy Board pointed out, had lateral entrances through Barataria Bay, Lake Pontchartrain, Bayou Lafourche, and Atchafalaya Bayou.

With its limited number of ships all that the Navy Department expected to achieve in the early months of the war was a partial blockade. To the officers on the station, however, the unsatisfactory character of the blockade made it difficult to endure. Across the flat, miasmic delta on late afternoons the air was black with mosquitoes hanging in layers like mist. Sultry weather alternated with squalls and heavy rain. Nine inches of rain in 12 hours had been known to fall on the deltas. From the flow of comparatively cool muddy river water into the warm clear Gulf there sometimes arose a fog so dense that one could scarcely see the length of a ship. There being only 18 feet of water over the bar, the *Powhatan,* drawing 20, could not steam into the river to capture any of the Confederate ships which periodically came downstream looking for a chance to run the blockade. The Confederate side-wheeler *Ivy,* 5 guns, lookout for Commander Raphael Semmes's Confederate raider *Sumter,* came prospecting with such regularity that a boat party from the *Powhatan* was sent up to the Head of the Passes to ambush her. The Confederate telegraph operator was seized and his wires clipped, but the *Ivy* failed to appear during the next two days.

Instead the *Sumter* herself on June 30, 1861, sneaked down Pass à l'Outre at a moment when the *Brooklyn* was off station chasing a prize, and slipped through the blockade. Semmes's trim black-hulled raider, formerly the fast packet *Habana,* easily outran the *Brooklyn* and was off on a cruise that emphasized the necessity of an adequate blockading force for this wealthiest, largest, and most important port in the Confederacy.

AFFAIR AT THE HEAD OF THE PASSES

Complaints from shippers and insurance companies injured by the *Sumter's* maraudings were reaching the Navy Department by August 9, when Du Pont's board promised a plan not for the capture of New

Orleans but "for shutting it up, suspending its trade, and obstructing the freedom of its intercourse with the ocean and with the neighboring coasts." On September 19 the board proposed a threefold plan: occupation and fortification of Ship Island as a base at the outer entrance to Lake Pontchartrain; seizure of Fort Livingston in Barataria Bay; and in addition to these flanking operations, a frontal attack—the seizure inside the Mississippi River of the Head of the Passes. A few cannon on shore, they believed, with a "fieldwork for 2,000 men" would hermetically seal all of the passes in the lower delta.

New ships including shallow steamers for penetrating Confederate sounds and rivers now replaced the first cumbersome blockaders, and a new flag officer, William W. McKean, was appointed to command the Gulf Blockading Squadron. The retiring officer's request for a court of inquiry or a court-martial was denied on the score that the shift had been made "without the implication of crime or fault on your part," and that "neither the time nor the service in this crisis can be wasted in courts of inquiry or courts-martial growing out of the substitution of one officer for another on any duty. Mere forms and rank can not be permitted to control efficient and necessary action in an emergency like this."

Early in October the Head of the Passes was seized by a Federal force consisting of the screw steamer *Richmond,* the sailing sloops *Preble* and *Vincennes,* and the side-wheeler *Water Witch.* As the sailing vessels were being towed up Pass à l'Outre by the *Water Witch,* the Confederate *Ivy,* 5 guns, kept them under close surveillance and occasionally lobbed a shot in their direction.

So important was this threat to New Orleans that extraordinary countermeasures were at once undertaken to root out the Federals before they secured their lodgment at the Head of the Passes. By private subscription in New Orleans the propeller *Enoch Train* had been converted into a turtle-backed ironclad ram, which owing to its extreme simplicity—encased only in boiler iron and having only one hatch which served also as gunport for a carronade—was completed five months earlier than the C.S.S. *Virginia.*[2] This ram vessel, renamed the *Manassas,* on the black night of October 12 precipitated among the wooden sailing ships at the Head of the Passes a "Bull Run" panic in miniature. The *Richmond,* caught while loading coal, was dealt a blow abreast of her port fore channel that gouged a 5-inch hole below

---

[2] Scharf, *op. cit.,* p. 264.

her waterline. The Federal ships retreated down Southwest Pass, firing as they fled. In their hurry the *Richmond* and the *Vincennes* grounded on the bar. The signal "Retire from action" which flew from the *Richmond* was misunderstood by the *Vincennes'* captain to be "Abandon ship." Accordingly he heaved most of his guns overboard, sent off his crew to other ships, and before leaving the ship himself lighted a slow match to her magazine. As if to climax this comedy of errors, the match sputtered out, and long after the Confederates had retired upstream her crew returned to the *Vincennes* and the Head of the Passes expedition cleared out of the river to a region of greater safety.

A STRATEGY EMERGES

So far as the New Orleans area was concerned the Anaconda policy of a simple naval blockade was considered during the first summer of the war to be the only feasible policy, even though that blockade could be only partially effective with the ships that could then be spared. A departure from the Anaconda squeeze, a combined military and naval thrust against New Orleans for instance, was unthinkable at this time. Hatteras Inlet had not yet been fought. Seventy-five miles below the city of New Orleans and about 20 above the Head of the Passes stood two of the most substantially built masonry forts in the country, Forts Jackson and St. Philip. These, it was believed, would effectively bar the passage to wooden steamers. Du Pont's board, considering the military reduction of these forts a necessary preliminary to the conquest of the city, conjectured that the enterprise would require "the co-operation of a large number of vessels of war of a smaller class, but of formidable armament, a great many troops, and the conduct of sieges, and it will be accomplished with slow advances." Moreover, the fact that the level of water in the river reaches its highest stage from May to July automatically postponed for a year any major operations inside the river by ocean-going warships.

In September, after the first contracts for ironclads were awarded, the Du Pont board went on record as favoring ironclads for the New Orleans operation: "here, if anywhere, is the place for ironclad ships, which, unless a permanent obstruction (in our opinion impracticable) is placed across the river, could run the gauntlet of the forts above and attack New Orleans." No one of course knew when ironclads would be available; but this record, dated September 19, 1861, is the earliest indication of the strategic concept that ships *without first reducing* the forts might (1) run the gauntlet and (2) threaten to reduce the unarmed city with naval gunfire.

Continuing depredations of the New Orleans-outfitted raider, the C.S.S. *Sumter,* and the serio-comic ejection of the Federal ships from the Head of the Passes in October nettled the high command in Washington and kept their minds fixed upon the problem of capturing New Orleans. General McClellan when asked by the Navy Department for troops assumed that Forts Jackson and St. Philip would have to be reduced before wooden ships could proceed to New Orleans, and estimated that the operation would require 50,000 troops. So large a number, in view of his needs for the defense of Washington and for his forthcoming Peninsula Campaign, he felt that he could not spare.

Then in November came Du Pont's victory at Port Royal—a single-handed naval victory over forts. That the troops in this case had not been landed from their transports before the victory was won seemed to indicate that forts might be beaten by ships alone. If this were true, the Navy Department might be freed of its complete dependence upon the Army in certain offensive actions down the coast. Port Royal, moreover, had been won by *wooden* ships.

To these considerations Commander David D. Porter who returned to Washington in November added a suggestion that the Navy Department carry out its own siege operations against Forts Jackson and St. Philip, using 13-inch army siege mortars mounted on schooners. Porter, an old hand in navigating the lower Mississippi—during a year's leave in the early 1850's he had commanded the S.S. *Crescent City,* a coastal steamer whose home port was New Orleans—"knew every inch of the river."[3] Porter thought that an overwhelming bombardment for 48 hours would reduce the forts. His plan had at least one cardinal advantage to recommend it. With the Navy conducting its own siege operations, the co-operating army need only be large enough to garrison the forts and occupy the city of New Orleans.

The important strategic decision to undertake the capture of New Orleans as primarily a naval operation was made on the evening of November 12 by President Lincoln, Secretary Welles, Fox, Porter, and General McClellan, meeting at the latter's residence at 14th and H streets. A simple threefold plan was agreed upon: (1) A flotilla of

---

[3] R. S. West, Jr., *The Second Admiral, A Life of David Dixon Porter,* 1937, Ch. XII, ff.

mortar schooners would launch a preliminary bombardment of the forts; (2) a squadron of speedy naval steamers crowded with the heaviest guns would run the gauntlet past the forts and compel the city to surrender; and (3) the Army would furnish the Navy about 10,000 men under Major General B. F. Butler of Hatteras Inlet fame to garrison the forts and control the city of New Orleans.

The Selection of Farragut and Porter

To so shrewd a political analyst as Secretary Welles the applause that greeted Du Pont's victory at Port Royal was indication enough that the Government could not afford to fail in its New Orleans venture. The failure of Union arms to match the early successes of the Confederates had already bred discouragement at home, and stimulated abroad a desire to intervene to end the war. Ineffective as the blockade off New Orleans had been, it had nevertheless injured the textile manufacturing nations of Europe, who claimed a sort of vested interest in the extensive cotton warehouses of New Orleans. In planning to capture New Orleans, the "Queen City" of the South with a population larger than the combined population of all other Southern ports, Gideon Welles's chief task was to select the proper leaders.

The Secretary who admonished senior officers that considerations of rank should not stand in the way of the public interest was honest enough to impose the same rule upon himself. His acts as a public official he attempted to divorce completely from those personal prejudices he had acquired as a man. This unusual trait, evident in many of his decisions in personnel matters, is nowhere more strikingly illustrated than in his selection of Commander David D. Porter to command the Mortar Flotilla for the New Orleans Expedition. Porter was the officer whose connivance with Seward at the outbreak of the war had diverted the *Powhatan* from Fort Sumter to Fort Pickens. For Porter's part in that surreptitious exploit, Welles had sufficient personal cause to dislike him, yet he recognized the man's amazing energy and resource and harnessed that energy for the war effort.

Still more important was the selection of the flag officer and commander-in-chief of the naval expedition, the man whose part would be to lead the wooden steamers past the forts. Literally everything depended on choosing the right leader, who, in Welles's opinion, "required courage, audacity, tact, and fearless energy, with great self-reliance, decisive judgment, and ability to discriminate and act under trying and extraordinary circumstances."[4] With Assistant Secretary Fox at his elbow Welles went down the list of captains to pick such a leader. His bureau chiefs who were not too old for this strenuous command were needed in their present posts, as were the flag officers already on blockading stations. The New Orleans leader would have to be able to work with that difficult and troublesome spirit, General Ben Butler, who would command the army of occupation, a factor that eliminated many naval officers. Hitherto, Southern-born officers had not been considered for top commands, but the Department was now driven to consider them. Number 57 on the list of captains was David Glasgow Farragut.

Farragut, born in Tennessee in 1801, had entered the Navy as a protégé of the late Commodore David Porter, father of Commander David D. Porter. His wife was a Virginian, and for many years he had made his home in Norfolk. Though something of an ordnance expert, Farragut had as yet made no great name for himself. What "marked" him in Welles's mind was his unflinching and unwavering loyalty, certainly a controlling factor in the choice of any Southerner for this particular mission. Welles now learned that after Virginia seceded Farragut had "placed his wife, sister, and their children in a carriage, put his loaded pistols in his pocket, and within two hours from the reception of the news that Virginia had seceded," he had boarded a steamer for Baltimore and the North.[5] For the past few months, Farragut had served inconspicuously as a member of the Retiring Board. Welles had Fox and Porter sound him out and finally the Secretary called Farragut in for an interview and appointed him Flag Officer of the new Western Gulf Blockading Squadron.

In a jubilant note on December 21 Farragut enjoined his wife: "Keep your lips closed, and burn my letters; for perfect silence is to be observed—the first injunction of the Secretary. I am to have a flag in the Gulf, and the rest depends upon myself. Keep calm and silent. I shall sail in three weeks."

Farragut's sailing orders, dated January 20, 1862, read:

Sir: When the *Hartford* is in all respects ready for sea, you will proceed to the Gulf of Mexico with all possible dispatch, and communicate with Flag Officer W. W. McKean, who is directed by the enclosed dis-

---

[4] Welles's article in *Galaxy*, XII, p. 679, quoted in C. L. Lewis, *David Glasgow Farragut, Our First Admiral*, 1943, p. 8.

[5] West, *Gideon Welles*, p. 169.

patch to transfer to you the command of the Western Gulf Blockading Squadron. . . . There will be attached to your squadron a fleet of bomb vessels and armed steamers enough to manage them, all under command of Commander D. D. Porter, who will be directed to report to you. . . .

When these formidable mortars arrive, and you are completely ready, you will collect such vessels as can be spared from the blockade and proceed up the Mississippi River and reduce the defences which guard the approaches to New Orleans, when you will appear off that city and take possession of it under the guns of your squadron, and hoist the American flag thereon, keeping possession until troops can be sent to you. . . . The Department and the country will require of you success. . . . There are other operations of minor importance . . . which must not be allowed to interfere with the great object in view, the certain capture of the city of New Orleans. . . .

Very respectfully, etc.

Gideon Welles.

Organizing a New Squadron

A week before he sailed in the flagship *Hartford,* Farragut received instructions from the Department to maintain a "vigorous" blockade. "By cutting off all communication we not only distress and cripple the States in insurrection, but by an effective blockade we destroy any excuse or pretext on the part of foreign governments to aid and relieve those who are waging war upon the Government." But was it possible to interdict *all* commerce from the Southern States? At Havana on his way to the delta Farragut learned from the American Consul that small vessels loaded with cotton were continually running through the blockade. Indeed one had sprinted into Havana Harbor just a few hours ahead of the *Hartford.* "These vessels," explained Farragut, "are necessarily so small that it takes a great many of them to make one decent cargo. I am told that they come out through little places that it would not be supposed anything larger than a rowboat could pass." For sealing the many shallow inlets along the Gulf Coast Farragut urged the Department to send him shallow-draft steamers. Until New Orleans was taken, most of his largest and best steamers would have to operate inside the lower river, leaving blockade duty to be carried on largely by inefficient sailing vessels.

Ship Island, the new Federal base about 100 miles northeast of the delta, was "a low sand bank, nearly destitute of vegetation, with a little extemporized fort mounting two or three guns." It closed the entrance to Lake Pontchartrain and, according to Du Pont's Strategy

Board, formed "the key" to the blockade of Louisiana and Alabama. In the good anchorage which extended all around the island, there were, when Farragut arrived on February 20, a number of naval vessels under Flag Officer McKean, as well as transports and supply ships. Ashore on the white sands several hundred of General Butler's troops were busy drilling. Farragut and McKean divided the ships between them according to their instructions, with Farragut getting the lion's share of the steamers for his thrust against New Orleans. During the next few weeks, while the anchorage around Ship Island grew ever thicker with the funnels and masts of gunboats, mortar schooners, transports, tugs, colliers, etc., word was given out that the new Western Gulf Blockading Squadron might attack either Mobile or Galveston.

Farragut's real objective, however, could not long be concealed, as he immediately sent a party of coast surveyors to mark the channels through Pass à l'Outre and Southwest Pass and ordered Captain T. T. Craven of the *Brooklyn* to take possession of the Head of the Passes.

While his ships were gathering, Farragut gave attention to administrative details. His first needs were coal, hospital stores, and machinery to make emergency repairs. There were but 400 tons of coal at Ship Island, about the same amount at Key West, and several of his vessels needed replenishing. McKean's account of the "miserable" conditions of some ships led Farragut to request the Department to send down on the hospital ship, which was being prepared, some "tools for the repairs of engines." Farragut's fleet surgeon lamented the lack of muslin and other surgical supplies, above all, ether and chloroform. To patrol his 1,000-mile sector of the blockade, Farragut had only 30 vessels, 18 of which were sailing craft useful only as anchored gun platforms. The bulky administrative correspondence of the blockade absorbed much of Farragut's time while his offensive forces were assembling.

During a year of disuse the main Delta channels had so silted up that Farragut had great difficulty getting his larger ships into the river. For several days the *Brooklyn* was glued to the mud in Pass à l'Outre. Then after her guns had been removed she was heeled over and tugged across the bar at Southwest Pass. The side-wheeler *Mississippi,* on which young George Dewey was executive officer, could not be careened without crushing a wheel. After her coal bins had been swept, she was tugged by main force through several feet of mud, by the steamers attached to the Mortar Flotilla. The *Mississippi* required 11 days of tugging, the *Pensacola* 14. Much effort was expended to lighten the huge *Colorado,* a ship which Washington considered desirable to have in the line because her main top was so high that its howitzers could look down upon the Confederate forts. Every movable object was taken out of her at Ship Island. Twenty-four tons lightened the *Colorado* one inch. In the end Farragut gave up the futile attempt, but shifted her guns to other ships and slated her commander, Captain Theodorus Bailey, as one of his division leaders.

Inside the river the ships reloaded their ordnance and unshipped and stored at Pilot Town all useless encumbering spars and canvas. Farragut's instructions for preparing ships to run the gauntlet read in part as follows:

Send down the topgallant masts, rig in the flying jibboom, and land all the spars and rigging except what are necessary for the three topsails, foresail, jib, and spanker. Trice up to the topmast stays, or land the whiskers, and bring all the rigging into the bowsprit, so that there shall be nothing in the range of the direct fire ahead. . . . No vessel must withdraw from battle under any circumstances without the consent of the flag-officer. . . . Have light Jacob ladders made to throw over the side for the use of the carpenters in stopping shot holes. . . . Have many tubs of water about the decks, both for the purpose of extinguishing fire and for drinking. . . . I wish you to understand that the day is at hand when you will be called upon to meet the enemy in the worst form for our profession. . . . I expect every vessel's crew to be well exercised at their guns. . . . Hot and cold shot will no doubt be freely dealt to us, and there must be stout hearts and quick hands.

To his wife Farragut wrote, "I am up to my eyes in business. . . . Success is the only thing listened to in this war, and I know that I must sink or swim by that rule."[6]

From Confederate letters and newspapers which a boat party seized in Biloxi, Mississippi, Farragut learned that the Confederate defenders of New Orleans were worried over the advance of the Union Army down the Mississippi. The Confederates were confident that their two forts below the city could crush the threatening naval attack.

THE MORTAR BOMBARDMENT

To reduce Confederate fortifications on the vast river system above New Orleans, the Federal Army was using siege mortars mounted unsatisfactorily on scows. The punishing downward recoil from high-

---

[6] L. Farragut, *The Life of David Glasgow Farragut,* 1879, pp. 215-217.

angle fire sprang leaks in the scows. Even though powder charges were reduced, these miserable mortar platforms soon became water-logged and unmanageable. The depth of water below New Orleans, however, made feasible Commander Porter's idea of sea-going sailing schooners as platforms for the mortars. These schooners averaged in length 110 feet, beam 28, and depth ten. On each vessel there was installed amidships a solid pen of logs and stone as foundation for the thick-bodied, 13-inch mortars. Seven steamers, in addition to the 21 sailing schooners, comprised the Mortar Flotilla: the ex-revenue cutter *Harriet Lane,* Porter's flagship, two 90-day gunboats, *Owasco* and *Miami,* and four paddle wheel ex-ferryboats, whose sides had been built up to keep out the sea. One of the latter was wrecked off Nag's Head, but the others arrived in time to tow the mortar boats into the river and to help tow Farragut's heavy ships across the bar.

While the mortar schooners were being stripped at Pilot Town, a coast survey party triangulated the river, beginning about nine miles below the forts. Confederate sharpshooters in the swamps sniped at the surveyors and at night removed the markers they had affixed to trees along the banks. Farragut detailed a gunboat to protect the surveyors. Operations were further hampered on April 10 and 11 by a gale blowing down the river. This windstorm broke loose the Confederate barrier of logs and hulks below the forts, but the defenders restored it before the challengers learned that it had been broken. By April 17, as the surveyors completed their work by setting range markers for each of the bomb vessels, the crews of the latter had camouflaged the tops of their masts with branches of trees. "The 'bummers' think this is a holiday!" commented an onlooker in Farragut's fleet; while another predicted that "The bloody bottoms of the 'bummers' will drop out at the tenth fire!"

Forts Jackson and St. Philip dominated the river at its first turn, about 20 miles north of the Head of the Passes. Fort St. Philip on the east bank commanded a long view downstream. It mounted 42 guns in parapet. Fort Jackson, on the western bank on the inside of the elbow, had 58 guns. Under vaulted roofs beneath its parapet guns Fort Jackson had a tier of coast defense guns in casemate, and an additional battery near the water's edge to protect the log-hulk barrier. The garrison of Fort Jackson had felled the trees along the river as far as the lower limit of their casemate fire. Below this line the trees left standing on the west bank formed a natural screen for Porter's camouflaged vessels.

On April 18 two divisions of mortar vessels were towed up and anchored behind the trees some 2,850 yards below Fort Jackson; and a third division of seven ships was tugged along the east bank to a position within 3,680 yards of Fort St. Philip. The duel between the forts and the floating siege mortars began promptly, with the little 90-day gunboats "salvo chasing" in midstream to divert Confederate fire away from the bomb vessels. The sinking of one and damaging of another schooner led Porter to shift this exposed division to the west bank under the trees.

Fires that were started inside Fort Jackson were at first thought to be from fire rafts that the mortar shells had ignited beyond the fort. Reconnaissance after nightfall, however, revealed the fires to have consumed the barracks and other wooden structures inside of Fort Jackson. Thenceforth, Porter ordered the bombers to fire continuously night and day. On Saturday, April 19, Brigadier General J. K. Duncan, the Confederate commander in Fort Jackson, recorded: "Mortar Flotilla again opened at 6:00 A.M. . . . The enemy's fire was excellent, a large proportion of his shells falling within Fort Jackson. The terre-plein, parade plain, parapets, and platforms were very much cut up, as well as damage done to the casemates. The magazines were considerably threatened."

The bottoms of the bomb schooners did not drop out at the tenth round, nor, on the other hand, was Porter's prediction fulfilled that the forts would be reduced by 48 hours of bombardment.

Flag Officer Farragut, though he was not an advocate of mortar fire, permitted the Mortar Flotilla to continue its labors for the next three days. The heavy down-river wind was too favorable for the use of fire rafts against his fleet and he needed additional time to prepare his ships for running the gauntlet. On the 21st he explained to the Department: "I shall await a change of wind and a consequent less violent current before I attack the forts, as I find great difficulty in avoiding collision among the vessels. . . . [The Confederates] have sent down five fire rafts; none produced any effect on the fleet except the last, which only caused the collision of the *Sciota* and *Kineo,* both of which vessels dragged across the bows of the *Mississippi* and carried away the mainmast of the first and damaged them both very much otherwise."

Farragut's fleet captain, Captain H. H. Bell, broke open the barrier of hulks and logs on the night of April 20–21. The way was now clear for the thrust up the river. Before the wind subsided, however,

Farragut's captains had improvised partial coats of mail for their ships by hanging heavy anchor chains along their sides abreast the engines. Around vulnerable machinery they packed bags of wet sand and ashes. The rigging and guns of some ships were smeared with mud to render them less visible at night. The gun deck and gun carriages of another had been whitewashed so that side tackle falls, handspikes, and ammunition might be easily seen when the all-important moment came to serve, vent, and sponge.

Shortly after midnight on April 24, the fire of the Mortar Flotilla ominously slackened. Commander Porter with his 90-day gunboats and converted ferryboats moved up in the darkness to engage Fort Jackson's water battery; while downstream at 1:55 A.M. two dull red lanterns, hoisted perpendicularly at the peak of the *Hartford,* flashed the signal to the fleet to get under way.

RUNNING THE GAUNTLET

The Confederate States Government clung to their belief that ships could not stand up against forts, without realizing that Farragut's intention was not to engage in a protracted slugging match but simply to dash past the forts, cut their communications in the rear, and coerce the defenseless city into surrender. During the final weeks of Farragut's campaign, Richmond continued to believe that New Orleans was more seriously menaced by the Army's ironclad gunboats descending the upper river than by Farragut's wooden ships. Across the river at Carrollton, eight miles above New Orleans, the Confederates stretched a boom of chained logs each four feet across the butt and 30 feet long, and behind mounds of freshly dug earth they emplaced cannon pointing upstream. Confident that Forts Jackson and St. Philip were a sufficient defense in the lower river, the Confederates at New Orleans were pushing the construction of two casemated ironclads, the *Louisiana* and the *Mississippi,* similar to the *Virginia,* and looking forward eventually to bursting through the blockade at the Deltas. Upon the insistence of the commanders of the forts, about the time the mortar bombardment commenced, the uncompleted ironclad *Louisiana* was brought downstream and anchored near Fort St. Philip. The State Government also kept the ironclad ram *Manassas* below New Orleans and hastily improvised the River Defense Fleet, a motley assortment of about a dozen river boats, to operate as rams in case any of Farragut's vessels should survive the pounding of the forts.

Meanwhile, Farragut, to minimize damage to his ships during the

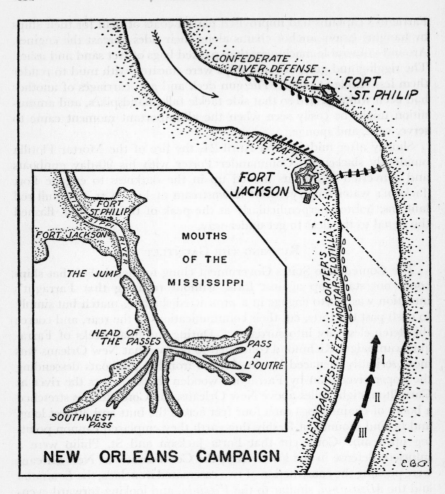

CONFEDERATE
RIVER DEFENSE
FLEET

FORT
ST. PHILIP

FIRE RAFTS

FORT
JACKSON

FORT
ST. PHILIP

MISSISSIPPI RIVER

FORT JACKSON

MOUTHS
OF THE
MISSISSIPPI

THE JUMP

HEAD OF
THE PASSES

PASS
A
L'OUTRE

SOUTHWEST
PASS

PORTER'S FLOTILLA

FARRAGUT'S FLEET. MORTAR

I

II

III

NEW ORLEANS CAMPAIGN

C.B.Q.

passage, at first planned for them to proceed in two columns abreast, with the column on the starboard hand engaging Fort St. Philip and the port column Fort Jackson. Because they would have to approach the forts bows on—in which position few of their own guns could operate while their decks could be freely raked by the enemy—the two columns were to be headed by battleships. Captain Theodorus Bailey was to lead the starboard column of gunboats and Captain H. H. Bell the port column. This initial plan had to be changed after April 21, since the narrowness of the opening in the log-hulk barrier below the forts dictated a single-file formation. In the final order of sailing the ships proceeded in three divisions. Captain Bailey, flying the red pennant on the swift gunboat *Cayuga,* led the first division of two battleships and six gunboats. Following after the divisional flag-gunboat the battleships *Pensacola* and *Mississippi,* "In reality the van," led the column of gunboats: *Oneida, Varuna, Katahdin, Kineo,* and *Wissahickon.* Farragut's blue-pennanted flagship *Hartford* and the battleships *Brooklyn* and *Richmond* constituted the center division. Then came the "Red and Blue" division, led by Captain Bell in the *Sciota,* divisional flag-gunboat, *Iroquois, Kennebec, Pinola, Itasca,* and *Winona.*

Although Farragut's signal was made at 1:55 A.M., the fleet did not get under way until 3:00, the *Pensacola* having had difficulty purchasing her anchor. At 3:15 Fort Jackson touched off a rocket and immediately afterward sent a rifle shot whistling over the *Cayuga,* as she sped through the barrier. On the west bank the mortars resumed their thunderous fire, crisscrossing the night sky with their comets' tails of burning fuzes. The mortar steamers, aided by the sailing sloop *Portsmouth,* which they had towed into position, began exchanging shots with Fort Jackson's water battery.

Although the leading gunboat *Cayuga* was struck 42 times during the half hour it took her to speed past the forts, she lost only six men wounded. Her crew lay flat on deck during the approach when her broadside guns could not be brought to bear. Abreast of St. Philip they leaped up for a brisk gunnery exercise that was over in ten minutes, when they were beyond the fort's line of fire. The *Cayuga* now pitched into the middle of the Confederate River Defense Fleet for a mad 30-minute tussle.

The *Pensacola* and the *Mississippi* followed their "pilot fish" only as far as the gap in the barrier. In the smoke-filled sector between the forts, with fire rafts being pushed downstream and the "pigmy monster" *Manassas* sideswiping the *Mississippi,* they both milled around a good deal. At times their navigators could scarcely tell which side of the river they were on.

With her bow guns the *Hartford* at 3:55 opened up against Fort Jackson and received a galling fire from both forts. Five minutes later, while attempting to clear a fire raft being pushed down upon her by a tug, she headed across the river and grounded on a shoal under Fort St. Philip. The firefangs enveloped the port side of the flagship. Her gunners beat off the fireraft and sank the tug, while her firefighters extinguished the blaze. In the blinding smoke astern of the *Hartford* the *Brooklyn* ran foul of a sunken hulk or raft. "For a few moments," reported Captain T. T. Craven:

I was entangled and fell athwart the stream, our bow grazing on the left bank of the river. Whilst in this situation I received a pretty severe fire from Fort St. Philip. Immediately after extricating my ship from the rafts, her head was turned upstream, and a few minutes thereafter she was feebly butted by the celebrated ram, *Manassas*. She came butting into our starboard gangway, first firing from her trapdoor when within about ten feet of the ship, directly toward our smokestack, her shot entering about five feet above the water line and lodging in the sandbags which protected our steam drum.

All save the last three of Farragut's gunboats succeeded in passing the forts. Caught by daylight and too far to the rear to be supported by the battleships, the *Pinola, Itasca,* and *Winona* dropped their crews flat on deck and drifted downstream out of action.

Above the forts the fragile matchboxes of the Confederate River Defense Fleet went down fighting. The broadsides from Farragut's battleships converted the once-dreaded *Manassas* into a sieve. Its crew rammed into the bank and escaped behind the levee. The cotton-clad C.S.S. *Governor Moore,* while at close quarters ramming the U.S.S. *Varuna,* depressed her gun and fired through her own bow in order to cripple her enemy. The merchant-built *Varuna,* unequal to such grim punishment, nosed into the west bank and sank by the stern, while in turn her stronger consorts destroyed the *Moore.* All told, about 11 Confederate vessels were annihilated in the "guerrilla" melee above the forts.

In his entire fleet Farragut's surprisingly small losses were 37 killed and 149 wounded. The Confederate casualties in the forts on this day were 11 killed and 37 wounded and on the ships, 74 killed and 72 wounded.[7]

The next day at noon Farragut dropped anchor off the wretched city. "The levee of New Orleans," Farragut reported, "was one scene of desolation; ships, steamers, cotton, coal, etc., were all in one common blaze, and our ingenuity much taxed to avoid the floating conflagration." Captain Bailey was sent ashore to demand that the city be surrendered. On the 28th Forts Jackson and St. Philip capitulated

---

[7] Lewis, *Farragut,* pp. 62-63.

and on the 29th officers from the fleet raised the United States flag over the public buildings in New Orleans, a pledge of nonresistance to United States authority having been accepted in lieu of a formal surrender. The first boatloads of General Butler's army of occupation arrived on May 1 off the charred and smoking levees of the once wealthy and still proud city.

To the Southern States the loss of New Orleans was a disaster of the first magnitude. In this great entrepôt the economic life of the Deep South had been concentrated. Its loss meant that Mobile and other lesser cities would have to expand their inadequate dock facilities despite critical shortages of manpower and material. For the Federal Government this first really major military achievement meant not only crippling the Confederacy economically but lessening the threat of diplomatic intervention and taking a giant stride toward opening the Mississippi to the normal flow of their own northwestern commerce.

II

The Vicksburg Campaign

IRONCLADS ON THE WESTERN WATERS

IMMEDIATELY after the Louisiana Convention had approved the Ordinance of Secession it hastened to declare that the navigation of the Mississippi should be free to all "friendly states," and the Confederate Congress at Montgomery similarly resolved, "That the peaceful navigation of the Mississippi River is hereby declared free to the citizens of any state upon its borders, or upon the borders of its navigable tributaries."[1] For the men of the Middle West the memory was still vivid of the old struggle with Spain over the free navigation of the Mississippi and the right of deposit at New Orleans. Northerners and Southerners alike depended for economic health upon the free and uninterrupted navigation of the Mississippi River. Despite the exuberant expansion in recent years of its railway mileage, the country north of the Ohio continued to load its heavy produce of farm and forest on steamboats to be sent to market. New Orleans was not merely the capital city of the "Cotton Kingdom," it was also a great entrepôt for the corn and livestock of the Northwest.

It was not surprising, therefore, that northwesterners immediately after Fort Sumter should take steps to build river ironclads. The Army as it slogged through canebrake and forest could often use impregnable floating artillery against river forts. In April of 1861 James B. Eads, a St. Louis engineer, submitted to the Navy Department a project for converting a heavy snag-boat into an ironclad battery. As operations in the West at this time were regarded as purely military, Eads's project was referred to, and accepted by, the War Department. During the

---

[1] Scharf, *op. cit.*, p. 239.

MISSOURI

KENTUCKY

CAIRO

FT. DONELSON

ISLAND NO. 10

FT. HENRY

CUMBERLAND R.

ARKANSAS

TENNESSEE

ARKANSAS RIVER

FT. PILLOW

MEMPHIS

LITTLE ROCK

TENNESSEE R.

ARKANSAS POST

YAZOO
DELTA

MISSISSIPPI RIVER

YAZOO R.

MISSISSIPPI

ALABAMA

SHREVEPORT

VICKSBURG

RED RIVER

ALEXANDRIA

MOBILE

PORT HUDSON

TEXAS

BATON ROUGE

LOUISIANA

NEW ORLEANS

FT. ST. PHILIP

FT. JACKSON

THE MISSISSIPPI

E. B. C.

ensuing months the Navy Department detailed naval officers and constructors to assist the Army in designing, building, arming, and fighting these novel ironclad steamboats.

Contracts for eight gunboats were awarded to Eads. Seven of these were designed by Naval Constructor S. M. Pook. The Pook gunboat was 175 feet long and 50 feet wide, its hull was divided into 15 watertight compartments, and it was driven by a paddlewheel in the stern. Sloping breastworks of oak across the bow and along the sides were overlaid with two and a half inches of iron. It was armed with 13 guns, chiefly 32- and 42-pounders. The Pook gunboats were christened for river cities: *St. Louis, Carondelet, Cincinnati, Louisville, Mound City, Cairo,* and *Pittsburg.* Two other ironclads improvised at this time were Eads's converted snag-boat, the *Benton,* and the ex-St. Louis ferryboat, *Essex,* an unusual and "gadgety" craft upon which every pump and winch was operated by steam.

In general these vessels were best adapted for fighting head-on and upstream, when if seriously injured by enemy fire they could simply drift downstream out of action. This was the situation in their first engagement, on February 6, 1862, against Fort Henry. In support of Grant's army advancing up the Tennessee River, Captain Andrew H. Foote, U.S.N., on this date led four ironclads (*Cincinnati,* flag, *Essex, Carondelet,* and *St. Louis*) up the Tennessee River against Fort Henry. Fort Henry stood in the center of the first line of Confederate defenses, along the northern border of Tennessee. Captain Foote's vessels, bucking a four-knot current with the river at flood stage, advanced in line abreast to within 600 yards of the fort, delivering a slow, well-aimed fire. During the approach a raking shot burst a boiler in the *Essex,* scalding 28 men and causing the vessel to drift downstream out of action. After a little more than an hour of duelling, Fort Henry surrendered to Captain Foote. The river ironclad thus got into action a month before the Battle of Hampton Roads, and despite its fragility it gained an exaggerated reputation for impregnability. Henceforth, no general, Union or Confederate, ever felt reasonably safe along these western rivers without a gunboat or two "in his pocket." Grant renamed the captured stronghold "Fort Foote" and shifted his army immediately to invest nearby Fort Donelson on the Cumberland River.

The vulnerability of the river ironclads to plunging shot became evident on February 14, when Captain Foote led four ironclads (*St. Louis,* flag, *Carondelet, Louisville,* and *Pittsburg*) against Fort Donelson. Situated on a high cliff at a bend in the river, Fort Donelson

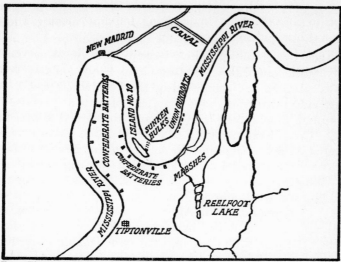

From *The United States Navy: A History* by Alden and Westcott.

could look down upon the unarmored topsides of the gunboats when they ventured up within 400 yards. Foote's vessel alone received 59 hits, four "between wind and water," and one in the pilot house, which mortally wounded her pilot. The other vessels suffered similar damages. Two days later Fort Donelson surrendered to General Grant.

Although these lightly armored river craft could not under all circumstances stand up to forts, they certainly had a valid tactical use in the fighting on the rivers. At Island No. 10, the corner where the states of Tennessee, Kentucky, and Missouri come together, the Confederates had lined the twisting river for many miles with shore batteries. In addition the so-called Pelican Dry Dock had been brought up from New Orleans and anchored off Island No. 10 as a gun platform. The series of fortifications was supplied from Tiptonville, a few miles south of Island No. 10. From the east the marshes of the Reelfoot Lake country rendered an overland approach impracticable. For several weeks the Federal forces tried a futile long range bombardment by gunboats and mortar scows. Finally on the night of April 4, Commander Henry Walke in the *Carondelet* boldly ran the gauntlet past the Confederate garrisons and made possible their capture.

Meanwhile the Confederate Government, aware of the naval axiom that like fights like, early took steps to build ironclad river steamboats to repel those of the Federals. On August 24, 1861, a contract was given to John T. Shirley to build two river ironclads at Memphis. At Cerro Gordo, Tennessee, another vessel was contracted for. But the Confederates were immeasureably handicapped for building ironclads in their industrially primitive western country. After the fall of Fort Henry the unfinished vessel at Cerro Cordo on the Tennessee River was captured and completed by the Federals. The *Eastport,* as this latter craft was called, saw two years of gruelling service on the rivers and had finally to be blown up and abandoned to avoid recapture by the Confederates on the Red River in 1864. Contractor Shirley encountered disheartening difficulties. The agents he sent to New Orleans and even Richmond could locate but few shipwrights and armorers willing to journey all the way to Memphis. The best armor he could find was used railroad iron, most of which he bought in driblets of 50 to 100 pounds each. After the fall of New Orleans, on Secretary Mallory's order Shirley burned one of his vessels on the stocks and hustled the partially plated ironclad ram *Arkansas,* together with his scanty supply of iron and his steam trip-hammer, to a point of safety up the Yazoo River north of Vicksburg. Here in the midst of a drowned forest he was feverishly at work in June of 1862, when news came that Captain C. H. Davis, Foote's successor, had won further victories against the River Defense Fleet at Fort Pillow and Memphis.

THE NAVAL ATTACK ON VICKSBURG

Following his clean-cut naval victory at New Orleans, Farragut pushed up the river for one of the most exasperating and unsatisfactory operations of the entire war. His orders of January 20 specified that in case the Mississippi expedition from Cairo had not descended the river he was to "take advantage of the panic to push a strong force up the river to take all their defenses in the rear." The Navy Department, gambling heavily on the political effect of such a move, thus concluded its instructions to Farragut: "Destroy the armed barriers which these deluded people have raised up against the power of the United States Government, and shoot down those who war against the Union, but cultivate with cordiality the first returning reason which is sure to follow your success."[2]

Although the move was not left to his discretion, Farragut had reason to doubt its feasibility. Above Baton Rouge, navigation was hazardous for large ships like the *Hartford,* the *Brooklyn,* and the

---

[2] The chief source for this chapter is *Official Records . . . Navies,* Series I, Vols. 18, 19, and 24.

Richmond, even when the river, as at present, stood at flood stage.
The deep channel, continually shifting beneath the muddy, drift-lit-
tered surface, defied the most skillful pilots, and the only good pilots
Farragut could find were secessionist and had to be coerced. Nor could
he leave the large ships behind and take only the gunboats. Along the
cliff-bound east bank of the river between Baton Rouge and Vicksburg
the Confederates were mounting guns to interrupt navigation. Hilltop
batteries that overlooked horseshoe turns in the river could rake vessels
both coming and going. The heavy bow chasers for head-on fighting
and the heavy broadsides of the large vessels were essential. Captain
Davis with the Eads ironclads was still above Memphis, and in the
vicinity of Vicksburg the Confederate ironclad ram *Arkansas* was
nearing completion.

Farragut sorely needed troops. There was little point in his simply
running to and fro beneath these river batteries unless they could be
seized and held, and General Butler could spare only a few hundred
soldiers for offensive action. By the end of May Farragut's gunboats
had ascended the river to a point just below Vicksburg. In the Louisiana lowlands Farragut had cut Vicksburg's railroad to the west, and
established a picket station. Repeated injunctions from the Navy Department, however, led him late in June to attempt a thrust past the
Confederate stronghold.

By this time two-thirds of his vessels had received injury from
grounding, snagging, and colliding. "The elements of destruction to the
Navy in this river are beyond anything I ever encountered," Farragut
reported.

More anchors have been lost and vessels ruined than I have seen in a
lifetime, and those vessels which do not run into others are themselves
run into and crushed in such a manner as to render them unseaworthy
. . . their sides are smashed in, their cutwaters entirely broomed up and
removed. . . . They all require more or less repairs to their machinery,
but the hulls all require docking—ribs broken, plank-sheer gone, stems
torn off to the wood ends. . . . I am worked beyond my physical ability
to keep up with my work.

The weather was hot and his seagoing crews, whose enlistments were
running out, were not acclimated to the malarial river valley. Many
were suffering from dysentery.

Farragut's plan for passing the Vicksburg batteries was a modifica-
tion of the one used below New Orleans. Sixteen of Porter's mortar

boats anchored below Vicksburg against the east bank would bombard the cliff-top batteries; six steamers of the Mortar Flotilla would shell Vicksburg's lower level "hospital" battery; while Farragut with three battleships and eight gunboats passed by the town. The battleships *Richmond, Hartford,* and *Brooklyn*—the leaders chosen because of their heavy bow chasers—were to move up in line ahead in the middle of the river; while the gunboats were to form a column to port of the battleships, so spacing themselves as to clear the battleships from their line of fire.

Before dawn on June 28 the mortar fleet opened fire and Farragut's ships got under way. In the darkness the slowly passing fleet aimed at the flashes from enemy guns, but in the opinion of Captain Bell they wasted much ammunition firing at the explosions of mortar shells. In the smoke and haze the *Brooklyn* and the two rearmost gunboats lost contact with the *Hartford*. Injuries to Porter's steamers about this time caused a certain amount of milling around before crippled ships could be righted. The *Hartford* with seven other ships succeeded in passing above Vicksburg.

"I passed up the river this morning, but to no purpose," Farragut reported to the Department. "The enemy leave their guns for the moment, but return to them as soon as we have passed and rake us. . . . I am satisfied that it is not possible for us to take Vicksburg without an army force of 12 or 15 thousand men."

On July 1 Captain Charles H. Davis, whose ironclads had won the battle of Memphis on June 6, came down to join forces with Farragut above Vicksburg. Farragut did not know quite what to do. "My orders are so peremptory," he told Davis, "that I must do all in my power to free the river of all impediments; that I must attack them, although I know it is useless. The river will soon be so low that we will not be able to get our ships down, so you see my position."

Farragut's dilemma was roughly solved on July 15 when the Confederate ironclad ram *Arkansas* came out of its lair in the Yazoo River and ran through the combined fleets of Farragut and Davis to sanctuary under the batteries of Vicksburg. None of the surprised Federals could get up steam in time to pursue her. The Confederate ironclad took the broadsides of the whole fleet, numbering nearly 40 vessels if Davis's wooden steamers are counted. Smarting with chagrin, Farragut passed back down below Vicksburg on the same night. While Davis bombarded to distract the Vicksburg batteries, Farragut's ships drifted in close to Vickburg's wharves hoping to sink the *Arkansas*.

Following this humiliation—in Secretary Welles's opinion "the most disreputable naval affair of the war"[3]—Farragut was ordered to take his battleships below New Orleans. The *Arkansas* after briefly threatening the wooden ships in the lower river was destroyed at Baton Rouge on August 6 by Commander W. D. Porter of the *Essex.*

THE NAVY'S MISSISSIPPI SQUADRON

Following Farragut's futile struggle against Vicksburg the Navy Department decided to postpone its naval offensive in the Vicksburg area until a sufficient military force should be available for a coordinated land attack. Too many troops for the time being were engaged in Virginia and most of the new levies in the West had not yet been recruited and trained. Both North and South used the last six months of 1862 as a period in which to recoup strength, to plan and prepare, and during this breathing space neither side was able appreciably to retard the other's preparations.

On the terraced hills of Vicksburg the Confederates built a "little Gibraltar." Additional guns, moved inland after the Confederates evacuated Pensacola and Norfolk, were placed at varying levels from the water's edge up to 260 feet on one hill back of the town. Under Vicksburg the river described a long horseshoe, down both shanks of which these cliff guns could range. Vicksburg was one of two key strongholds. The other, some 170 miles down the river, was Port Hudson, La. Port Hudson's hills, though not so lofty as Vicksburg's, offered the same defensive advantages and the Confederates fortified them well. Into the 170-mile segment of the Mississippi between these two fortifications flows the Red River, navigable most of the way to Texas. It was the Confederate plan by means of their two fortifications to shut out the Federals from a highly strategic water highway over which the cattle and grain of the Southwest could move to supply Confederate military forces east of the river.

For the Federal Government the opening of the Mississippi was a political as well as a military necessity. The products of two summers were now piling up in midwestern warehouses, and the Federals' failure to open the river to trade was being used by "Copperheads" and defeatists as an antiadministration argument, as ex-Congressman John A. McClernand pointed out to Lincoln. Lincoln commissioned McClernand as a major general of volunteers and sent him west to recruit

---

[3] Welles, *Diary,* Vol. I, p. 72.

men. On October 1, 1862, the Army rid itself of a long administrative headache by turning over to the Navy the gunboats of the Western Flotilla. Secretary Welles, rewarding Commander David D. Porter for his strenuous labors with the Mortar Flotilla and spurring him to even greater exertions in a new field, gave him a commission as an acting rear admiral and sent him west to command the Navy's new Mississippi Squadron.

Porter's first job was to repair and build up the squadron.[4] New ironclads on a number of patterns—one-turret, two-turret, single-casemate, double-casemate, etc.—were being built. A class of fast lightly armored dispatch vessels known as "tinclads," able to "float on a heavy dew," was built. The soft pine decks of the older gunboats had been scored by guntrucks and had to be replaced by oak planking. Heavier naval guns replaced makeshift army field pieces. A quantity of sodden gunpowder without water-proof casings had to be dumped. An extra inch and a half of armor was riveted on the older river ironclads. Porter purchased many light-draft vessels which were to be temporarily employed in his squadron but later, after the opening of the river, to be sent to Farragut in the Gulf.

Many of the recruits the Army had enlisted in its "Western Flotilla" had been given higher ratings and pay than Navy standards allowed, and had to be reduced to maintain the morale of the salt-water seamen who now joined the inland squadron. About 400 sick had to be discharged. A ten-acre tract at Mound City containing several supply sheds and docks was the navy yard for the squadron. Most of the machine shops, blacksmith shops, and living quarters were on barges. The headquarters of the squadron was in a hotel in Cairo at the junction of the Ohio and the Mississippi.

Grant met Porter in Cairo early in December and the two planned their first move against Vicksburg. North of the city lay a flat region of half-drowned forests and cotton plantations known as the Yazoo Delta, bounded by the Mississippi on the west and the Yazoo River on the east. Grant's Army was to move southward on the high ground east of the Yazoo Delta to the rear of Vicksburg; Porter's fleet was to convoy the transports of General William Tecumseh Sherman coming down from Memphis. Then while Porter bombarded and Sherman attempted to storm the fortress from the water front, Grant was to attack from its rear or landward front.

---

[4] West, *Porter*, Ch. XVIII, ff.

Unfortunately there was no means of communication between the two attack forces as they moved down along opposite sides of the Yazoo Delta. Porter and Sherman arrived above Vicksburg on December 24. Sherman's troops landed near the mouth of the Yazoo and slogged across marshy ground to the base of Vicksburg's Chickasaw Bluffs. Listening intently on the night of December 28, they believed that they could hear trains rumbling into Vicksburg. To the east of the town they observed rocket signals. On Monday, December 29, the day set for the two-pronged military assault, Porter's gunboats unleashed a heavy barrage while Sherman's troops time after time stormed the hills, only to be decimated by Confederate rifle fire. Sherman lost 1,500 in killed and wounded. Captain William Gwin, the "wood-and-sail" captain of the ironclad *Benton,* who refused to take cover because of his belief that a captain's place was on deck, was mortally wounded. From a dispatch sent down the river from Memphis, Porter and Sherman learned that Confederate General Van Dorn's cavalry had wheeled in behind Grant and destroyed his supply base at Holly Springs, while simultaneously Confederate General Bedford Forrest had cut Grant's rail communication to Columbus. Grant had been forced back to Memphis.

On New Year's Day Major General McClernand appeared on the scene and superseded Sherman. Together with Porter the two generals planned and executed a sure-fire victory over the Post of Arkansas, a diminutive cavalry station about 60 miles up the Arkansas River. Arkansas Post was defended by Fort Hindman, a square casemate structure scarcely larger than one of the Eads gunboats, and like them encased in railroad iron. Its armament, however, 11 guns of assorted sizes up to nine inches, was less. Fort Hindman was pounded in by a heavy naval barrage on January 11, 1863, and the Post was captured. The wide publicity given the event alleviated to some extent the sting of the disaster at Chickasaw Bluffs.

AMPHIBIOUS FLANKING MOVEMENTS

General Grant, frowning upon the Arkansas Post expedition as a "wild goose chase," brought the remainder of his Army of the Tennessee down from Memphis and reorganized the whole force, with McClernand, Sherman, and McPherson as corps commanders. For the next two months Grant's troops and the heaviest ironclads in Porter's squadron were concentrated just above Vicksburg—and vir-

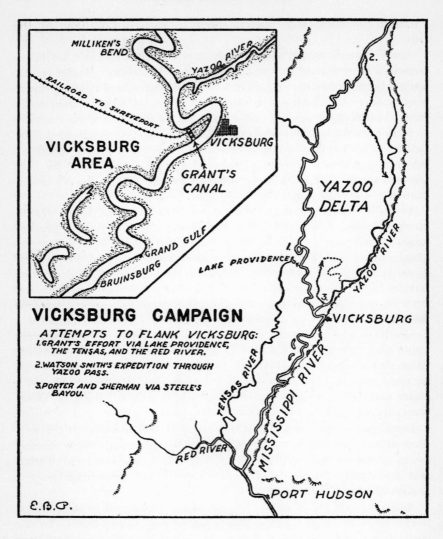

VICKSBURG CAMPAIGN

ATTEMPTS TO FLANK VICKSBURG:
1. GRANT'S EFFORT VIA LAKE PROVIDENCE, THE TENSAS, AND THE RED RIVER.

2. WATSON SMITH'S EXPEDITION THROUGH YAZOO PASS.

3. PORTER AND SHERMAN VIA STEELE'S BAYOU.

tually stalemated. Grant's plan now was to land his men on the east bank *below* Vicksburg, invest the city, and storm it from the rear, while the Navy bombarded it from the waterfront. To run his fragile army transports past Vicksburg would be suicide. Nor was it possible yet to march his men down the Louisiana shore to some ferrying point. The Mississippi was now flooding its banks. Men could not march through the backwater-covered forest of eastern Louisiana at this time.

Since Porter's moves were largely dependent on Grant's, his heavy ironclads were forced to remain idle above Vicksburg. These vessels having been greatly strengthened, were easily capable of running downstream past the Vicksburg batteries. As soon as Grant's men could march down the Louisiana shore the ironclad would descend the river to ferry the soldiers across the river. But until the waters subsided there was no point in their going downstream. Once below they could not get back against the four-knot current without being towed by light wooden steamers that could be smashed to splinters by the Vicksburg batteries.

In their frequent conferences aboard the flagship *Black Hawk,* Grant, Porter, and Sherman pondered the question of how to proceed against Vicksburg in spite of high water. Vicksburg's horseshoe curve almost surrounded a long tongue of land known as the "Peninsula." A canal across the neck of the Peninsula beyond reach of the Vicksburg batteries would enable the transports to by-pass the batteries and descend the river. Grant procured dredging equipment and set men to digging. Their hope of diverting the river into a new channel was presently dashed, however, when they encountered a stratum of very tough clay. Perhaps at some other point or points they might cut the levee and discover passages through the forests that were navigable by transports and lighter gunboats. In this way they might obtain a water highway to high ground on the right or the left flank of Vicksburg.

For Grant's first amphibian flanking effort, McPherson cut the west levee about 60 miles north of Vicksburg. It was hoped that a channel might be found through Lake Providence and thence via the Tensas and Red Rivers to the Mississippi. McPherson's expedition bogged down only a few miles inland.

A second and more ambitious expedition attempted to turn Vicksburg's right flank by forcing a way across the Yazoo Delta. In the early days, before the levee had been built, the Mississippi had been connected with the upper tributaries of the Yazoo through a bayou known as the Yazoo Pass. At this old pass, some 200 miles north of Vicksburg, the levee was blasted on February 3. For a week the river, nine feet higher than the swamps, poured into the gap, uplifting logs and trees and shoving them through the old pass. When the overflow approached the level in the river, Lieutenant Watson Smith with three ironclads and three light-drafts ran down the chute into the forest, followed by a miscellany of river transports bearing a force of 800 men under Brigadier General L. F. Ross.

Trees that had grown up in the pass had to be rammed and dragged clear, so that the expedition, which depended for success upon surprising the enemy, sometimes advanced scarcely a mile a day. By overhanging branches "vessels had their pipes knocked down, wheels carried away, and cabins swept off." It was March before the expedition reached *almost* to the Yazoo River, at a point 100 miles north of Vicksburg. Within a few yards of its goal the invaders were stopped by a Confederate cotton-bale fort. Here at short range the ironclads *Chillicothe* and *DeKalb* were perforated by conical steel-pointed shell and the expedition was blocked.

When Admiral Porter heard of the mishap he quickly organized with General Sherman a second and diversionary expedition to enter Steele's Bayou in the lower Yazoo Delta. Porter with five ironclads got approximately half way across the Delta when he ran into a narrow bayou filled with willows which caught under the metal overhang of the gunboats and slowed them down. Ahead and in the rear the Confederates now started felling trees across Porter's route. Only the timely arrival of General Sherman, whose troops in this region were able to march over dry land, saved the gunboats from being marooned. The rescued gunboats now bumped back out of the narrow bayou stern-first. A loaded coal barge that had sunk in their path was broken up and the coal spread out over the bottom so the gunboats could pass.

During the next few weeks there was much hammering and amateur blacksmithing in the mouth of the Yazoo River as the ironclads repaired their battered tophamper and prepared to run downstream past Vicksburg.

PASSING PORT HUDSON AND VICKSBURG

While these amphibian movements so mystifying to Washington were occurring, Admiral Porter was also sending various vessels down the river to interrupt the eastward flow of Confederate supplies from the Red River. The wooden ram *Queen of the West,* which ran the gauntlet on the night of February 2, destroyed a number of river freighters loaded with pork, sugar, molasses, and army supplies. The *Queen's* success persuaded Porter to gamble an ironclad. On February 13, 1863, he sent the new casemate ironclad *Indianola* with a coal barge lashed on either side. Then as a diversion from their monotonous routine Porter had his men outfit and drift down the river a dummy monitor. Porter wrote a friend:

Ericsson had saved the country with an iron one, why could I not save it with a wooden one? An old coal barge, picked up in the river, was the foundation to build on. It was built of old boards in 12 hours, with pork barrels on top of each other for smokestacks, and two old canoes for quarter-boats; her furnaces were built of mud, only intended to make black smoke and not steam. . . . When it was descried by the dim light of the morn, never did the batteries of Vicksburg open with such a din. . . . She was a much better looking vessel than the *Indianola*.[5]

Meanwhile below Vicksburg the *Queen* ran aground and was captured, and a Confederate force of three steamers, augmented by the *Queen,* now turned upon the *Indianola.* The slow ironclad, still mothering her coal barges, was rammed again and again and forced to surrender. At this moment news came down the river from Vicksburg that a "turret ironclad" was approaching. The conquerors, momentarily deceived by Porter's dummy and fearful of losing their prize, set off the *Indianola's* magazines and destroyed her.

When Admiral Farragut at New Orleans heard of the Confederate captures of the *Queen* and *Indianola,* he decided to pass up above Port Hudson at once, to destroy the Confederate vessels and to cut off enemy supplies from Red River. He planned to take four ships and three gunboats. To minimize damage from the forts he lashed a gunboat to the port side of each of his three leading ships: *Hartford, Richmond,* and *Monongahela.* The larger ships were to act as shields to the gunboats and in turn be aided in navigating the sharp-angle turn in the river under Port Hudson. The fourth ship, the venerable *Mississippi,* being a side-wheeler, was not provided with a consort. "I expect all to go by who are able," Farragut ordered, "and I think the best protection against the enemy's fire is a well directed fire from our own guns."

Farragut got under way at 10 P.M. on March 14. As his squadron moved upstream the defenders lighted rockets and bonfires of pitchpine to illumine the dark ships.[6] Under the enemy batteries the *Richmond's* steam line was severed, the *Monongahela* and her consort were both temporarily grounded, and the side-wheeler *Mississippi,* which nosed hard into the west bank, was set afire by enemy shells and destroyed.

---

[5] F. Moore (Ed.), *The Rebellion Record*, 1863, Vol. 6, Doc. 125, p. 427.
[6] Lewis, *Farragut*, p. 175.

Only the flagship *Hartford* with her accompanying gunboat *Albatross* succeeded in getting past the batteries.

For nearly a month Farragut remained in the no man's land between Port Hudson and Vicksburg, "blockading" the Red River and patrolling the Mississippi as far north as the Peninsula across from Vicksburg. Supplies and coal were drifted down to him on barges.

By mid-April, the backwaters having subsided over the eastern part of Louisiana, General Grant started his troops to marching down the west bank of the river past Vicksburg. Admiral Porter at 9 P.M. on April 16, 1863, showed two white lanterns on the *Benton* as signal to his line of seven ironclads to get under way (*Benton,* flag, *Lafayette, Louisville, Mound City, Pittsburg, Carondelet,* and *Tuscumbia*). For additional protection each ironclad had a tug or a coal barge lashed alongside, or logs triced up abreast its engines at the water line. Along with the ironclads went three empty transports to be used later in ferrying the Army across the river. The deck of the transport *Henry Clay* was packed with bales of hay and cotton. The ships slid out into the current with fireroom hatches covered. Steam was blown off through vents inside the paddleboxes as each vessel behind the flagship tried to maintain the prescribed distance of 50 yards from the vessel next ahead. At 10:30 P.M. Confederate pickets on the spit of the Peninsula sighted the *Benton* and fired several houses to spread the alarm. Flaming barrels of tar outlined the water front as Porter's vessels rounded the Peninsula.

At the horseshoe curve the current swept the stern of the *Benton* completely around, while from the bottom to the top the terraced Vicksburg amphitheater blossomed with explosions. The *Benton,* casting off her tug, righted herself and passed so close alongside the wharf that Porter, standing outside on top of her casemate, could hear the clatter of bricks falling as buildings collapsed under the fire of the squadron. A large calcium flare which was now ignited by the Confederates shed blinding white light down both shanks of the horseshoe. One after another the ironclads were roughly whirled by the current. Most of the barges had to be cast off before the heavy craft could right themselves. Confederate shell set fire to the highly inflammable *Henry Clay* and the transport had to be abandoned by its skeleton crew. Confederate troops, possibly believing that they had destroyed an ironclad, gave a rebel yell. The ironclad *Tuscumbia,* whipper-in of the fleet at the end of the line, ran aground under the Vicksburg batteries and in backing off was fouled by one of the transports.

As a pyrotechnical display the run past Vicksburg was one of the most colorful pageants of the war, but the danger to the ironclads, as Porter wrote later, "was more apparent than real." Only 14 men were wounded and no one was killed. The day after the spectacular passage Porter wrote to Assistant Secretary Fox:

It was a jolly scene throughout, and I reckon that the City of Vicksburg never got a better hammering. We all drifted by slowly, and opened on them with shell, shrapnel, and cannister, as hard as we could fire. . . . The scene along the river was beautiful—hundreds of little bunches of cotton all afire from the *Henry Clay* were floating down on the water, helping to light up what was already too light for us. These bunches of cotton followed us down the river, and when we anchored below Warrenton, it looked as if a thousand steamers were coming down. [7]

Unvexed to the Sea

Forty miles below Vicksburg at the village of Grand Gulf, Mississippi, Porter repeated the tactical error of the first naval assault on Vicksburg. Grant had picked Grand Gulf as his ferrying point, and as this village had now been fortified Porter made a single-handed effort to reduce it by naval bombardment. On April 29 seven of his ironclads engaged the enemy batteries in a five and a half hour artillery duel. Although he was able to silence the lower works he failed to drive the defenders back from the guns on the upper level. Grant now marched his men further down the west bank and ferried them across at Bruinsburg.

While Grant was crossing south of Vicksburg, Sherman with gunboat support was making a feint up the Yazoo River to the north of Vicksburg to distract the Confederates' attention. The ruse caused the defenders to shift a number of their reserve troops to Haynes's Bluff to oppose Sherman. Grant meanwhile, after landing 30,000 men on hard ground east of the river, headed boldly into the heart of Mississippi. With no supply train and only three days' cooked rations in his knapsacks, he depended on foraging from the country until he could establish contact with the Navy on the Yazoo above Vicksburg. After Grant's landing the Confederate garrison at Grand Gulf exploded their magazines and fell back upon Vicksburg.

Porter now descended to the Red River to relieve Farragut of the blockade at that point. The older admiral was glad to be able to return

[7] R. M. Thompson and R. Wainwright (Ed.), *Confidential Correspondence of Gustavus Vasa Fox*, 1919, II, p. 170.

to New Orleans where the work of the Western Gulf Blockade was demanding his attention. Porter organized a patrol force for the Red River and returned to Vicksburg. Sherman had now ferried his army across at Grand Gulf and with Grant was preparing to take Vicksburg by storm. By noon on May 18 the naval force above the city descried Sherman's blue-coated horsemen dashing along on the crest of the Chickasaw Hills where last December Sherman had made his disastrous assault. Grant had successfully interposed his army between Confederate Generals Joseph E. Johnston and John C. Pemberton, and was driving the latter into Vicksburg. Grant's men, after two weeks on foraged "hog and hominy," ate ravenously of the beef and the wheat bread sent up from the fleet.

On May 22 the combined naval bombardment and general army assault from the rear failed to force a surrender of the Confederate fortress. From this time on the tempo of Grant's attack slowed down to siege routine of ditch digging and tunneling, while Porter threw into the city a steady rain of mortar shells. The Navy assisted the Army in other ways than bombarding. Large naval guns with crews to man them were sent on shore to operate with the besieging army. On June 6 the gunboats repelled the effort of Confederate troops in Louisiana to wreck Grant's supply base above Vicksburg at Milliken's Bend. Throughout the siege the Army and the Navy under Grant and Porter co-operated "like the blades of a pair of shears."

Vicksburg fell on July 4, 1863, to the forces of Grant and Porter, and Port Hudson on July 9 to Farragut and Banks. As President Lincoln phrased it, the great Mississippi River now flowed "unvexed to the sea." "To the Army," wrote Porter, "do we owe immediate thanks for the capture of Vicksburg. . . . The conception [of the investment] originated solely with General Grant." And Grant returned the compliment: "The Navy under Porter was all it could be during the entire campaign. Without its assistance the campaign could not have been successfully made with twice the number of men engaged."

12

Later Amphibian Campaigns

FOUR JOINT military and naval campaigns were undertaken contemporaneously with and after the climactic Vicksburg Campaign, strenuous and costly ventures that racked the nerves of the nation for weeks and months. In chronological order these were the campaigns against Charleston, the Red River country, Mobile Bay, and Fort Fisher below Wilmington, N. C. None of these amphibian undertakings rivaled Vicksburg and New Orleans either in importance of the objective sought or in tactical efficiency with which the objective was pursued. Moreover, two of the campaigns, Red River and Charleston, were complete failures, and a third, Fort Fisher, was finally successful only after one of the worst fiascoes in the history of United States Army and Navy combined operations. Of the four, Mobile Bay alone— wherein Farragut arose magnificently to damn the torpedoes—has achieved fame; yet even the story of Mobile Bay leaves much to be desired from the exacting point of view of military strategy.

With the exception of Mobile Bay, a study of these campaigns is largely an examination into the causes of failure—a profitable study indeed for commanders and political leaders who seek to avoid mistakes of the past. Was the strategic conception faulty? Were the means of waging war—men and material—sufficient for the task blocked out? Was there a spirit of real co-operation between the military commander and the naval commander?

THE CHARLESTON CAMPAIGN

While retaliation upon Charleston, "the Cradle of Secession," had constituted a major political objective of the North ever since the

173

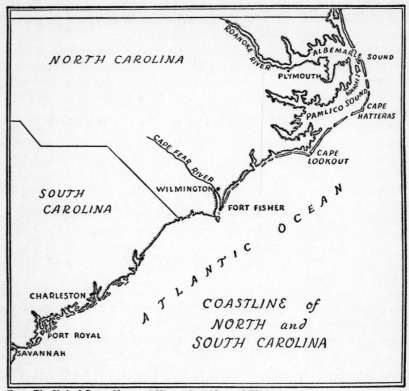

NORTH CAROLINA

ROANOKE RIVER

ALBEMARLE SOUND

PLYMOUTH

ROANOKE I.

PAMLICO SOUND

CAPE HATTERAS

SOUTH CAROLINA

CAPE FEAR RIVER

WILMINGTON

FORT FISHER

CAPE LOOKOUT

ATLANTIC OCEAN

CHARLESTON

PORT ROYAL

SAVANNAH

COASTLINE of NORTH and SOUTH CAROLINA

From *The United States Navy: A History* by Alden and Westcott.

evacuation of Fort Sumter, no offensive action in that quarter had been possible during the gloomy first year of the war. After Du Pont's seizure of his advanced base at Port Royal, the Federals attempted to block Charleston Harbor by sinking in its channels a number of New Bedford whalers loaded with granite, but the tides and currents readily swept new passageways around such obstructions.

Du Pont's South Atlantic Squadron did not have enough ships to seal the blockade completely at Charleston. The three practicable channels which converged to form the front entrance to the harbor had to be watched by as many vessels, and if, as often happened, sailing ships only were available for this locality, the chances of swift, steam-driven blockade-runners sneaking through were very good indeed. In addition to the front there were side entrances through Light House Inlet, Stono River, and North Edisto River, respectively about four, ten, and 40 miles south of the main entrance. For six months after Port Royal, Du Pont maintained as close a blockade as possible and waited for more ships to be sent to him.

In May of 1862, following the Confederates' evacuation of Norfolk, Assistant Secretary Fox offered to send Du Pont the *Monitor* and the ironclad *Galena* in the hope that he might be able to "finish Charleston" by a "purely Navy" attack. Should he succeed, wrote Fox, "the Country will rejoice above all other victories."

Du Pont replied that while he was ready for "do or die" work, the industry of the Confederate defenders of Charleston in preparing their defenses, "ceaseless day and night" for 13 months, had rendered the task difficult. Fort Sumter had been strengthened by a water battery; a formidable new earthwork, Battery Wagner, had been erected on Morris Island, at the southern side of the harbor entrance; and in addition to having its established forts—Johnson, Castle Pinckney, and Moultrie—strengthened Charleston Harbor itself had been obstructed by pilings and torpedoes. While waiting for the promised ironclads, Du Pont co-operated with Major General David Hunter in making two unsuccessful thrusts through river and swamp against the southern flank of the city.

Months before the new Federal ironclads reached Charleston, the Confederate defenders held a council of war in which Commodore D. N. Ingraham, C. S. Navy, foresaw the Union Navy Department's strategy. "The plan of naval attack apparently best for the enemy," Ingraham stated, "would be to dash with as many ironclads as he can command, say 15 or 20, past the [forts at the mouth of the harbor] without halting to reduce them."[1] Once past the forts Du Pont's powerful naval guns could control Charleston as Farragut's had controlled New Orleans. To fend off this dread contingency the Confederate defenders during the next few months installed various submarine obstructions, including pilings, rope entanglements, log and chain booms, and boiler iron torpedoes; and they rushed to completion two converted ironclads, *Chicora* and *Palmetto State,* built on the general plan of the *Virginia.*

Bad luck beset Du Pont in January of 1863. The veteran *Monitor,* while en route south to join his squadron, foundered in a storm off Cape Hatteras, and the Charleston ironclads *Chicora* and *Palmetto State* came outside their harbor on a dark night to cripple and drive

---

[1] *Official Records . . . Navies,* Series I, Vol. 13, p. 809.

off two wooden Union blockaders. The latter episode, heralded by the Confederate Secretary of State as a "breaking" of the Charleston blockade, was embarrassing to the State Department in Washington.

As his iron ships arrived in late winter and early spring, Du Pont sent them to try their new 15-inch guns against various Confederate outposts. The monitor *Montauk* under John L. Worden, now recovered from his injuries received in the *Monitor-Virginia* duel, exchanged shots at long range with Fort McAllister on the Ogeechee River, and on February 28 Worden ventured within pistol range of the fort in order to deliver the *coup de grâce* to the Confederate raider *Nashville* which had run aground near the fort.

It was April before Du Pont had finally assembled nine ironclads for his attack on Charleston. These were heterogeneous in type and, as the event was to prove, unsuited because of individual peculiarities to steam together in a battle line. The *New Ironsides,* which Du Pont selected as flagship, had a heavy rectangular iron casemate with a wooden bow structure projecting forward. She responded erratically to her helm, and if the situation ever required her to check her paltry three-knot speed the only way was to heave overboard an anchor. Du Pont had taken out the ship's antiquated masts and sails with which a conservative Bureau of Construction had sent her to Port Royal, and had sawed off her smokestack to clear the view forward of her pilot house. Seven monitors constituted his most maneuverable striking force: *Weehawken, Passaic, Montauk, Patapsco, Catskill, Nantucket,* and *Nahant.* The chief improvements built into these monitors as a result of the Battle of Hampton Roads were the location of the pilot house on top of the turret and the protection of the smokestack with heavy armor. Each of these later monitors carried one 11-inch rifle and one 15-inch smoothbore. The shift having been hastily made, Ericsson refused to cut out a port large enough for the 15-inch muzzle to protrude; instead he built a "gunport collar" to prevent the lateral escape of gases when the big gun was fired with muzzle inside the turret. For ease in signaling, Du Pont placed the flagship *New Ironsides* in the center of the line with four monitors ahead of him and three behind. Bringing up the rear was a third type of ironclad, the *Keokuk,* Commander A. C. Rhind, which had two rigid, non-turning, and only lightly protected casemates.

Disheartened by the many small technical defects that appeared in the preliminary trials of his ironclad novelties, Du Pont put aside the Department's "grand plan of sailing in silently" past the forts, and determined instead "to batter and pound beyond any precedent in history" against Fort Sumter.[2]

Early on the afternoon of April 7, 1863, his battle line rounded Morris Island to enter Charleston Harbor. On their somber black turrets the seamen had painted red "portholes." Drums and a strain of "Dixie" came from Fort Sumter. Inside the narrow channel the huge flagship turned out of line to avoid running down the monitors. For two hours the latter, milling around at ranges of 500 to 800 yards, loosed their fire on Fort Sumter. They fired slowly, only 139 shots in all, and their rate of fire declined as they suffered injuries to gun muzzles, port stoppers, and turret-turning mechanisms. Against them Forts Sumter and Moultrie hurled an estimated 2,200 projectiles. At 4:30 P.M., warned by his pilots, Du Pont ordered the squadron to withdraw from action. On her way out the flagship, which had devoted the afternoon to keeping clear of the monitors, fired her first and only salvo of the day, against Fort Moultrie.

Although the badly damaged *Keokuk* sank the next morning at her anchorage, the regular monitors survived the iron hail from the forts with only minor injuries. But these damages, trifling in themselves, were sufficient partially to disable them. After receiving the reports of his captains, Du Pont decided against a renewal of the assault, since to do so might convert a failure into a disaster.

Whether justly or not, Du Pont was relieved of his command and put on waiting orders. Admiral Dahlgren, the gun inventor, replaced him, while at the same time the Army substituted General Quincy A. Gillmore in place of General Hunter. Dahlgren and Gillmore in cooperation seized Morris Island at the south side of the harbor entrance, Dahlgren providing heavy naval support for the siege of Battery Wagner. Thereafter, until General William Tecumseh Sherman's march to the sea, the Federal operations against Charleston dragged through a succession of petty maneuvers around the mouth of the harbor, which succeeded in pulverizing by long range bombardment, but not in capturing, the incorrigible Fort Sumter. Nor was Charleston itself, citadel of secession, "chastened" until after Tecumseh Sherman had invested it from the rear.

THE RED RIVER FIASCO

After the opening of the Mississippi in midsummer of 1863 the Navy's river squadron was fully capable of "blockading" the impor-

[2] *Confidential Correspondence of Gustavus Vasa Fox,* 1918, Vol. I, p. 187.

tant military theater to the east and frustrating Confederate efforts to send grain, cattle, and blockade-run stores from Texas into the eastern half of the Confederacy. Captured letters revealed the chagrin of Confederates who, though they hid for days behind the western levee, were forced to give up hope of crossing "because the Yankee gunboats are thicker than fiddlers in hell." Such control over the great river dictated that henceforth Federal military operations should have been directed against objectives lying east of the river. With Admiral Porter dominating the river and keeping the two separated halves of the Confederacy from reuniting, General Banks and Admiral Farragut should have thrown their combined forces at once against Mobile Bay. In a strictly military view nothing west of the Mississippi mattered.

Yet it was difficult to consider the western country from the military viewpoint alone. Up the Red River on plantations as yet untouched by war lay a treasure-trove of cotton whose owners ignored the inducements of Union cotton factors in New Orleans. A joint military and naval expedition up the Red River might conceivably release this hoard of white gold. Moreover it was possible that such a move might justify itself in a political sense. General Banks, who had received his major-generalcy because of his political standing as Speaker of the House, had been enjoined by President Lincoln to administer the oath of allegiance and hold elections in Louisiana at the earliest moment, to elect a loyal (Carpetbagger) State government.

From the outset the expedition ran into unforeseen difficulties.[3] A late start was made, owing to the lowest level of water in 40 years, and all momentum was dissipated at Alexandria in the two weeks required to haul the river ironclads upstream across the Alexandria "falls" or rapids. During the delay the military and naval forces seized as prize of war several thousand bales of cotton from warehouses of the town and near-by plantations. A group of civilian cotton speculators following in the wake of the army further complicated the situation by their efforts to bribe army officers for the use of mules and naval officers for cargo space on coal barges. During this "cotton raid" expedition General Banks administered the oath of allegiance and held an election in Alexandria. By the first week in April, when the military and naval forces at length resumed their progress upstream, Confederate General E. Kirby Smith had given the order to apply the torch to all cotton in the path of the invaders.

[3] West, *Porter,* Chs. 24-25.

Under a sky overcast from the smouldering of cotton piles, Porter's vessels made their tortuous way upstream to an appointed rendezvous near Shreveport. So acute were the angles in the channel that tugs were required at both bow and stern of the ironclad *Eastport*.

General Banks was now caught in a trap at Sabine Crossroads and badly beaten, with the loss of 200 wagons of his supply train. Sending a courier to notify Admiral Porter, Banks ordered a precipitate and ill-considered retreat. Not waiting, as he should have, to effect his withdrawal along with the Navy, the general rushed ahead leaving the endlessly curving banks of the river in the control of the victorious Confederates. At Blair's Landing the river ironclads *Osage* and *Lexington* fended off an assault by 5,000 Confederate troops. The oversize transports repeatedly ran on snags and had to be towed. On the rocks at the village of Grand Echore the *Eastport* gouged a hole in her bottom. Porter himself in the shoal-draft tinclad *Cricket* raced down to Alexandria to procure pump boats. The *Eastport,* which had been captured by Foote's officers after Fort Henry, held a sentimental value for the squadron that exceeded her capabilities as a gunboat. After a flooded compartment had been sealed off, she was floated, but a few miles further down she ran on a torpedo, and this time had to be blown up by her crew. Banks's further retirement from Grand Echore to Alexandria in advance of the naval force again exposed the Admiral to needless hazards from the Confederates on shore. Near Cane River an artillery ambush riddled the *Cricket*. In less than five minutes Porter's little temporary flagship received 38 hits and lost 25 in killed and wounded out of a crew of 50.

"On our way down to Alexandria," Porter reported to Secretary Welles, "obstacles were overcome enough to appall the stoutest heart. Guns had to be taken out of vessels, and they jumped over sand bars and logs."[4]

The squadron reached the Alexandria rapids by April 28, only to find itself marooned by a water level lower than it had ever been. With his faith in General Banks completely destroyed, Porter implored the Navy Department: "I do not see why a fleet should not have the protection of an army as well as an army have the protection of a fleet. If we are left here aground, our communication will be cut off and we will have to destroy the vessels. . . . "

To his friend General Sherman the Admiral wrote bitterly: "You

---

[4] *Official Records . . . Navies,* Series I, Vol. 26, p. 26.

know my opinion of political generals. It is a crying sin to put the lives of thousands in the hands of such men, and the time has come when there should be a stop put to it."[5]

General Banks, however, did not desert the Navy at Alexandria. When Lieutenant Colonel Joseph Bailey proposed to build a series of wing dams to raise the water high enough to let the vessels pass over the falls, Banks at Porter's request assigned 3,000 men with 200 to 300 wagons and teams to do the work. Soldiers and sailors together built cribs of logs out from either side of the river and filled them with brick and stone. Hundreds of experienced lumberjacks felled pine trees and snaked them down to the river. Quarries were opened above the falls and stone was hauled down in barges. Porter, meanwhile, lightened the ironclads by taking out guns and stripping off armor. After two weeks the barges sunk in the sluiceway were removed and the "best part" of the Mississippi Squadron made a spectacular escape into the deep water below Alexandria.

The thrilling rescue diverted the press from the contemplation of one of the war's greatest fiascoes, and a year later the Joint Committee on the Conduct of the War, attempting to winnow the facts, found it impossible or inexpedient to get at the whole truth. The mistakes of the Red River Campaign are obvious. The purpose of the mission was poorly conceived by the statesmen in Washington. In order to test its real worth the objective should have been balanced against the risks involved and the cost estimated; natural hazards, like deficiency of water to float the ironclads, would have to be risked *if the objective was worth the cost.* But for the commanding general's military ineptitude and lack of frankness in conferring and co-operating with the commanding admiral there can be no excuse. General Banks merited the obscurity into which he was immediately retired after Red River. Admiral Porter emerged before the public as a hard-bitten commander, able to absorb exasperation and bad luck without buckling, able indeed when faced with possible loss of his fleet above Alexandria to toss off a pun. "If damning would get the fleet off," he remarked to General Banks, "I would have been afloat long ago!"

THE MOBILE CAMPAIGN

Because Mobile was the Confederacy's only Gulf port east of the Mississippi, Southern leaders throughout the war gave unstinted at-

---

[5] *Ibid.,* p. 56.

tention to its defenses. In addition to three lines of earthworks around the city itself, at various points down the bay batteries were so placed as to sweep the 30-mile channel up to the city. The principal barriers against attack by water were three forts that guarded the outer entrances to the bay. From east to west, and in order of descending importance, these were Forts Morgan, Gaines, and Powell, mounting respectively 45, 26, and eight guns.[6] Fort Morgan, a pentagonal brick structure, commanded the main ship channel, which ran close under its walls. Gaines lay across the channel four miles distant, and Powell, somewhat further to the northwest, guarded the difficult and shallow route plied by many scores of midget blockade-runners that darted into Mobile Bay via the shallows of Mississippi Sound.

As months dragged by and the Federal attack failed to materialize, the defenders developed new weapons of defense. With rows of pilings they partially closed the main entrance in such a way as to force any vessel entering the ship channel to proceed within very close range of Fort Morgan, the most powerful fort. These pilings in the spring of 1864 were supplemented by several rows of "torpedoes" or mines, about 200 in all, which further narrowed the free channel under Fort Morgan. To the conical powder demijohns were attached priming rods that projected upward to within a few feet of the surface and ropes that were left trailing in the water to foul propellers. Then, in May of 1864, the Confederates lifted their "greatest" ironclad, the C.S.S. *Tennessee*, across Dog River Bar into the bay. The *Tennessee* was 50 feet shorter than the *Virginia* and one-third shallower in draft. Her casemate of 5- and 6-inch armor resembled her predecessor's, but her engines, which had been salvaged from a Mississippi River steamer, were not as efficient even as the *Virginia's*. Her two 7-inch and four 6-inch rifles and her metal-sheathed ram rendered her a formidable antagonist. In addition to the *Tennessee* the Confederates had three light wooden gunboats: *Morgan, Selma,* and *Gaines.*

Had Mobile been a first-rate military objective it would have been worse than bad strategy to postpone the attack, since each month of delay increased the facilities for defense. Actually, however, in the broad strategic picture Mobile was insignificant. Its port facilities were scarcely a tenth the size of those of New Orleans, and its single deep-channel entrance could be, and was, effectively blockaded by a few ships outside. Most of the successful blockade-runners at Mobile were

---

[6] Lewis, *Farragut,* p. 224.

small craft of not over 50 tons burden, scarcely worth the cost in men and treasure of waging a great amphibian campaign.

Farragut returned to the Gulf in January of 1864 a few months before the new Confederate ironclad *Tennessee* was finished, and after the latter came down into the lower bay he saw at once that the honeymoon for his wooden blockaders was over. Farragut respected the fighting spirit of Admiral Franklin Buchanan, the South's senior naval officer who once had commanded the *Virginia* and was now the *Tennessee's* skipper. He believed that if given half a chance Buchanan would re-enact Hampton Roads, making *Cumberlands* and *Congresses* of the wooden blockade ships and breaking open the blockade at Mobile. Accordingly for six months Farragut, in the light of this new strategic situation, made urgent overtures to General Banks to obtain troops to co-operate in seizing the forts in the lower bay. He required a military force to land on Mobile Point and Dauphin Island to attack Forts Morgan and Gaines from the rear. He could not simply run the gauntlet with his ships as at New Orleans, because inside the lower bay there was only a narrow pocket of water deep enough for his sea-going ships to maneuver in, and much of this pocket was within range of one or more of the forts. Without an army to co-operate in seizing the forts it was useless for the Navy to make a move.

It was extremely fortunate for Farragut's plans that General Banks after Red River was replaced by a better soldier, General E. R. S. Canby, and that General William Tecumseh Sherman wanted Canby and Farragut to make a "demonstration" against Mobile in conjunction with his own descent upon Atlanta. In mid-June, 1864, Canby and Farragut arranged a schedule for troop landings back of Forts Morgan and Gaines early in August, and during the next six weeks Farragut received four monitors with which to outmatch the *Tennessee*. Two of his monitors were new double-turreted Mississippi River craft, the *Winnebago* and the *Chickasaw,* each 257 feet long, 57 in beam, and armed with four 11-inch guns. The other two monitors were new seagoing craft: the *Manhattan* and the *Tecumseh,* each 190 feet long, 37 feet in beam, and each mounting in her single turret two 15-inch guns. The *Tecumseh,* to Farragut's chagrin, did not join the fleet off Mobile Bay until the night of August 4, some hours after General Canby's men had been put ashore on Dauphin Island behind Fort Gaines.

For the naval participation in the campaign Farragut evolved a threefold plan. (1) While troops were landing on the beaches behind the forts, two groups of auxiliary vessels were to stand guard on the seaward sides of Dauphin Island and Mobile Point and flank the enemy land forces. (2) A main battle line of 14 wooden warships, lashed together in pairs with large ships to starboard and shielding the smaller from the fire of Fort Morgan, would then sail up the main ship channel into the bay. (3) The monitors' task was to be twofold: to draw Fort Morgan's fire away from the wooden ships by steaming in close to the fort in a column to starboard of the main battle line and after entering the bay to engage the ironclad *Tennessee*. All ships were directed to pass to the eastward of a certain black buoy, which it was assumed marked the end of the torpedo field. Farragut's General Order of July 12 reads:

Strip your vessels and prepare for the conflict. Send down all your superfluous spars and rigging. . . . Put up the splinter nets on the starboard side, and barricade the wheel and steersmen with sails and hammocks. Lay chains or sand bags on the deck over the machinery, to resist a plunging fire. Hang the sheet chains over the side, or make any other arrangement for security that your ingenuity may suggest.[7]

Since his wooden ships would have to steer bows-on toward Fort Morgan in approaching the entrance, Farragut mounted as many bow chasers as possible and hoped for a flood tide to speed his ships over this dangerous stretch of water. He also wanted a light southwest wind to waft the smoke of their guns back upon the defenders.

On the night of August 4-5 Farragut's ships had been stripped and were poised for their crucial run. During the night the admiral's steward brought word that light airs were commencing from the southwest. There would be a flood tide in the morning.

All hands were piped up at 3 A.M. Gunboats were made fast to the port sides of the larger ships by 5:30 and by 6:00 the columns of monitors and wooden ships were moving abreast toward the entrance.

Commander Tunis A. M. Craven in the *Tecumseh* led the ironclads, which were disposed in the following order: *Tecumseh, Manhattan, Winnebago,* and *Chickasaw.*

In deference to his captains, who insisted that the flag not risk itself, Farragut yielded the post of honor at the head of the battleship column. The positions in line of the pairs of wooden steamers were as follows: *Brooklyn* and *Octorara, Hartford* flag and *Metacomet, Richmond*

---

[7] *Official Records . . . Navies,* Series I, Vol. 21, p. 397.

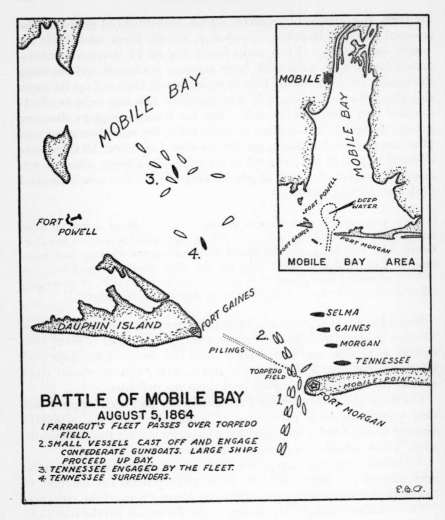

BATTLE OF MOBILE BAY
AUGUST 5, 1864
1. FARRAGUT'S FLEET PASSES OVER TORPEDO
      FIELD.
2. SMALL VESSELS CAST OFF AND ENGAGE
      CONFEDERATE GUNBOATS. LARGE SHIPS
      PROCEED UP BAY.
3. TENNESSEE ENGAGED BY THE FLEET.
4. TENNESSEE SURRENDERS.

and *Port Royal, Lackawanna* and *Seminole, Monongahela* and *Kennebec, Ossipee* and *Itasca,* and *Oneida* and *Galena.*

As at Charleston, the monitors proved difficult to manage, and so slow that the wooden ships were forced to make several stops to let them regain their station abreast the main column. Fort Morgan commenced firing at extreme range about 7:00 A.M. and the leading ships in the columns answered promptly. As they neared the narrow passage under Fort Morgan, the black, tallow-smeared C.S.S. *Tennessee* inside the bay moved out across their path into a ramming position.

As if drawn by a fatal attraction, the *Tecumseh* shifted slightly to port, so as to pass to westward of the channel buoy and over the torpedo field. Commander Craven's reasons for shifting course can never be known. He may have been momentarily confused as to the significance of the marker buoy, or, as seems likely, his entire attention may have been riveted on the movements of the Confederate ironclad. At 7:20 a torpedo exploded under her turret and the *Tecumseh* settled to the bottom in a matter of seconds. There was time for but one occupant of the pilot house to escape, and Craven, according to Pilot John Collins, declined that chance, with the gallant remark that has become a tradition of the service: "After you, pilot! I leave my ship last."

Farragut, who had climbed into the port main rigging of the *Hartford*, saw the *Tecumseh* disappear and immediately ordered Commander Jouett, who stood within shouting distance on the *Metacomet's* quarter-deck, to send a launch to rescue survivors. The most critical moment of the passage now arrived. Acting upon a report of torpedoes under his ship, the *Brooklyn's* captain ordered the leading pair of ships, *Brooklyn* and *Octorara*, to back water. Farragut instantly saw the danger of rear ships piling up behind a confused leader in the narrow passage and offering the most favorable targets for the gunners of Fort Morgan. "O God," he prayed, "direct me what to do." And an inner voice, Farragut later testified, counseled him to go on. Farragut ordered the *Hartford* and *Metacomet* to turn left around the stalled leaders, regardless of the Confederate torpedo field. As he did so the *Brooklyn's* captain messaged a warning of torpedoes.

"Damn the torpedoes!" Farragut shouted from his perch in the rigging. "Four bells! Captain Drayton, go ahead! Jouett, full speed!"

Farragut's bold acceptance of risk was equalled only by his extraordinary good fortune in getting his ships over the mine field with no further loss. As they entered the bay the gunboats were cast loose to give chase to the light Confederate gunboats, one of which was sunk and another captured. The ironclad *Tennessee*, proving unequal in nimbleness to the wooden ships, was unable to employ her ram during the passage.

Farragut steamed up into the deep water pocket about four miles beyond Fort Morgan and had all hands piped for breakfast. His chief problem now was how to deal with the *Tennessee*. Admiral

Buchanan had withdrawn the Confederate monster to a position of security under Fort Morgan. The Union admiral, however, had not long to ponder this problem. Before breakfast was finished "Old Buck," as Yankee seamen called the Confederate leader, was sighted coming up the bay, apparently intent on catching his prey in a huddle or at anchor.

Several of the Federal ships had been lightly plated with metal across their bows, and these were ordered to run down the enemy ironclad. *Monongahela,* nearest the enemy, was the first to crush her stem against the *Tennessee.* Next *Lackawanna* by a head-on blow against the portside amidships gave the ironclad a list. The *Hartford* now struck a glancing blow, just after the *Tennessee* had shifted her helm. As the ironclad rasped the hull of the towering *Hartford* the latter loosed her entire port broadside of 9-inch solid shot against the *Tennessee's* casemate. In further maneuvering for position the *Lackawanna* ran into the *Hartford,* striking forward of her mizzenmast and cutting her down to within two feet of the water's edge.

The finish was mainly left to the monitors, which clung tenaciously to the *Tennessee* and kept pounding her casemate with 11- and 15-inch shot. By this time, according to Farragut's report, "Her smokestack had been shot away, her steering chains were gone, compelling a resort to her relieving tackles, and several of her port shutters were jammed. Indeed from the time the *Hartford* struck her until her surrender she never fired a gun." At 10:00 the ram surrendered.

Within a few weeks all the forts at the mouths of the bay were in Federal hands, and the Navy's chief objectives had been achieved: countering the threat of the *Tennessee* and denying the use of the port even to light-draft blockade-runners. Once having started in the Mobile area, however, the Army continued its activity by laying siege to the earthworks around the city. The defenders held out until after Appomattox.

As a combined military and naval venture the Mobile Campaign was poorly planned and badly timed.[8] Forces were expended in operations on the coast of Texas and in the hinterland of Red River which might better have been utilized at an earlier date and against a *limited objective:* the forts at the mouths of the bay. Nor was it necessary to protract operations in the larger Mobile theater beyond the period when a demonstration might be useful to General Sherman in his

---

[8] West, *Gideon Welles,* Ch. 14, "Strategy and Mobile Bay."

Atlanta campaign. What lifts an otherwise unsatisfactory campaign above the commonplace is the fighting prowess of an outmoded wooden Navy led and inspired by a truly great admiral.

THE FORT FISHER CAMPAIGN

As one after another of their ports was lost, the Confederates paid increasing attention to running the blockade at Wilmington, N. C. For a blockade-running base, Wilmington, located about 20 miles up the Cape Fear River, enjoyed great natural and man-made advantages. The river had two good entrances, which, owing to the interposition between them of Smith Island and Frying Pan Shoals, were about 50 miles apart by sea. Specially built blockade-runners in the last year of the war were thus able to choose whichever entrance at the moment had the weaker force of blockade ships on guard. If they entered from the south through Lockwood's Folly Inlet, they quickly came under the protection of Confederate guns in Fort Caswell on the mainland and in the Bald Head Hill battery on Smith Island. Or they might enter through New Inlet, to the north of Smith Island, which was protected by Fort Fisher, a sprawling series of log-and-sand batteries that occupied the V-shaped peninsula known as Federal Point. The amount of goods run through Wilmington must have been substantial. J. T. Scharf in *The Confederate States Navy* rates the loss of Wilmington as "far more injurious than the capture of Charleston, and but for the moral effect, even more hurtful than the evacuation of Richmond."[9] The Confederate Secretary of the Treasury, to disparage and discredit the blockade, claimed that "8,632,000 lbs. of meat, 1,507,000 lbs. of lead, 1,933,000 lbs. of saltpeter, 546,000 pairs of shoes, 316,000 pairs of blankets, 520,000 pounds of coffee, 69,000 rifles, 97 packages of revolvers, 2,639 packages of medicine, 43 cannon" had been run through the blockade off Wilmington and Charleston in the period from October 26, 1864, to January, 1865. On the basis of these figures the Richmond *Dispatch* asserted that it was "a matter of absolute impossibility for the Federals to stop our blockade-running at the port of Wilmington. If the wind blows landward, they are compelled to haul off shore to a great distance to escape the terrible sea . . . supplies will be brought in despite the keenest vigilance."

Although the Federal Navy Department as early as 1862 began planning for a joint military and naval operation against Wilmington,

---

[9] Scharf, *op. cit.*, p. 427.

no troops were made available for this operation until the last year of the war. After the seizure of the Mobile Bay forts, this city was the only port remaining in Confederate hands. The sealing of Wilmington would destroy the South's credit abroad by shutting off its cotton export and it would doubtless shorten the war by denying access to foreign munitions and other essential supplies. Immediately after Mobile, therefore, the Navy Department in Washington set in motion a plan to transfer Admiral Farragut to the North Atlantic to capture Fort Fisher, and General-in-Chief Grant promised by October 1 to send 12,000 troops to co-operate. Farragut, however, declined the assignment because of health and Grant's armies in Virginia suffered a reverse. By October 15 Admiral D. D. Porter had been shifted to the North Atlantic and vast naval preparations had been made, but there were still no troops.

"Every other squadron," wrote Welles to Lincoln on October 28, "has been depleted and vessels detached from other duty to strengthen this expedition. The vessels are concentrated at Hampton Roads and Beaufort, where they remain, an immense force lying idle, awaiting the movements of the army. . . . If the expedition can not go forward for want of troops, I desire to be notified, so that the ships may be relieved and dispersed for other service."[10] At this point Stanton fell ill for a protracted period, and the public interest was absorbed by the presidential election of 1864.

The issue of troops for Fort Fisher had remained unsettled for another month, when Assistant Secretary Fox resorted to stratagem. General Butler, once commander of the troops occupying New Orleans and now commander of the Army of the James, suggested to Fox that a shipload of powder exploded close to Fort Fisher might so damage the fort as to ease the task of an assaulting army. Fox offered to try out Butler's plan if Butler would supply a co-operating army. The bargain was struck.

There was one monkey wrench which might clog the machinery of Army and Navy co-operation, and that was the personal animus between General Butler and Admiral Porter. On the occasion of the surrender of Forts Jackson and St. Philip *to the U.S. Naval Forces*, Commander Porter of the Mortar Flotilla had neglected to invite Major General Butler of the army of occupation to participate in the ceremony, although Butler at the time was in the immediate neighbor-

---

[10] *Official Records . . . Navies*, Series I, Vol. 21, p. 397.

hood. The omission had led to a good deal of name-calling which did not improve relations between the services.

Fox, as a boyhood friend of Butler and a correspondent to whom Porter had confided his innermost thoughts for the past several years, went to Hampton Roads to make arrangements with Porter. Butler, it was understood, would detach for this mission 6,500 troops under Brigadier General Godfrey Weitzel, a competent West Point engineer. Porter agreed to try out Butler's powder boat idea, and by doing so get the Fort Fisher expedition started. No one at this time had any idea that Butler himself might accompany the expedition.

Preparation of the powder boat went ahead at once, with both Army and Navy co-operating in furnishing the powder.[11] The "shaky" steamer *Louisiana,* hollowed out to become the shell of the mammoth torpedo, was loaded at Craney Island near Norfolk and at the advance blockade base, Beaufort, N. C., 70 miles north of Fort Fisher. The huge charge was placed in compartments above the water line so as to give the explosion its greatest lateral effect, and in order if possible to detonate the entire mass at the same instant a two-mile length of Gomez fuse was wound around the bags and over the open-headed barrels; clockworks were devised to ignite the fuse.

The first week in December, when Washington heard that the Confederates were withdrawing men from Wilmington for use against Sherman in his march across Georgia, General Grant tried to get the Fort Fisher expedition off "with or without" the powder boat. Like the ordnance experts whose opinions had been requested, Grant had no faith in the powder boat, and before the expedition sailed he caused entrenching tools to be loaded, and he clearly stipulated in an order to General Butler that "if the fort did not fall immediately upon their landing, then they were to entrench themselves and remain there and co-operate with the Navy until the fort did fall." Under cover of a naval bombardment troops were to land on Federal Point peninsula above Fort Fisher, as at Mobile they had landed on the peninsula back of Fort Morgan, and thus by entrenching themselves across the peninsula to cut the fort off from access to Wilmington by land and absolutely seal the port against blockade-runners.

On December 12 when the troops embarked for passage to Beaufort, General Butler embarked with them. Since Butler was Weitzel's military superior, it was his privilege to do as he wished; nevertheless

---

[11] West, *Porter,* Chs. 26-27.

in view of the grudge over New Orleans the circumstance of Butler's accompanying the expedition aroused suspicions and boded ill for the campaign.

After some delay due to storms the powder boat *Louisiana* was moved in to the beach near Fort Fisher on the night of December 23. The fleet, to prevent damage from the concussion, stood off about 12 miles with fires drawn. Commander A. C. Rhind, whose ironclad *Keokuk* had been sunk at Charleston, was in charge of the ship-torpedo. At midnight the *Louisiana* was anchored about 200 yards off shore and within 500 yards of the fort. A fire of pine knots was lighted in an after compartment in case the clockworks should fail. Rhind and his crew then steamed away in a fast tug. At 1:40 A.M., 22 minutes after the time set on the clockworks, a monster column of flame shot up from the *Louisiana* and four heavy explosions were heard. Only part of the cargo had exploded; most of it had merely burned. A few lookouts on the beach felt a slight tremor in the sand beneath them, but within the great log-and-sand fortress itself nothing out of the way was noticed.

Fort Fisher was shaped like an L with its angle pointing northeast. The long shank of the L, forming the seaward face of the fort, was a mile and a half long, and the short shank, which ran westward across the peninsula to form the land face, was half a mile. Near the southern end of the peninsula the L was anchored on the Mound Battery, a man-made hill of sand which afforded a platform 52 feet high for two heavy cannon. Fort Fisher's commander, Colonel William Lamb, C.S.A., had a force of about 1,500 men, including those on the sick list, to repel the attack.

At noon on December 24, following the explosion of the powder boat, Admiral Porter brought his fleet in close to shore and delivered a heavy bombardment. According to the admiral's lithographed instructions, the ironclads and monitors under Commodore Radford moved in within a thousand yards and shelled the land face of the fort, while divisions of wooden ships took positions on arcs of greater circles outside the monitors and extending below Fort Fisher's Mound Battery. Particular targets for each ship had been designated on the chart.

At 8:00 A.M. on Christmas day, with the bombardment at its height, Butler's troops began landing on the beach above the fort. About 2,300 of his 6,500 men were landed. Later in the afternoon, his scouts having reported that only one of the 17 Confederate cannon on the

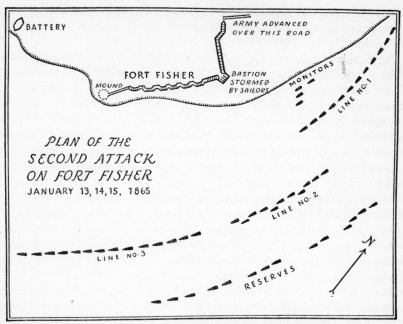

land face had been dismounted, General Butler re-embarked the troops and returned to Hampton Roads.

Porter's indignant dispatches sent via a special messenger to Washington were published by the Navy Department. "Admiral Porter writes as though even in his official capacity he remained a man," observed the New York *Evening Telegram* of December 30; "Admiral Porter's report has soul and life in it." Lincoln's first executive order of 1865 relieved Butler of his command and ordered him to return to his home in Lowell. Welles approved of Porter's dogged determination to continue the campaign against Fort Fisher. Grant, chagrined that his entrenching order should have been so patently disobeyed, wrote to Porter that he would send back the same troops under a different commander.

The new expedition, with General Alfred H. Terry in command, reached Fort Fisher and began landing through a rolling surf at 8:30 A.M. on January 13. All day the fleet, the largest concentration of naval strength the United States Navy had ever assembled for one operation, pounded against the fort. The next day a strong wind made it necessary for the wooden ships to haul off shore, but the low and heavy ironclads remained at their anchorages and kept up their pounding against the land face of Fort Fisher.

On Sunday, January 15, the fleet was again back at its task. The effect of the initial fiasco was to urge all hands in the fleet to extraordinary exertions in the second effort. At 10:30 A.M. landing parties of sailors and marines pulled ashore in small boats. Fleet Captain K. R. Breese commanded these "boarders," whose well-sharpened naval cutlasses flashed in the sunlight. While General Terry's men stormed the land face of the fort at its western end, Captain Breese and the seamen planned to dash up the beach against the northeastern corner of the fort.

At 3 P.M. General Terry signalled from shore. The fleet blew every whistle and shifted its fire away from the section under attack by the soldiers and sailors. The assault of the naval shore party was repulsed with heavy loss, but the sacrifice probably diverted the Confederates' attention from the attack of the soldiers which did succeed. Colonel Lamb and his gallant defenders, outnumbered by 5 to 1, fought hand to hand from traverse to traverse, until finally at 10 P.M. they were overpowered. General Terry sent up a rocket to announce the victory to the fleet. With the fall of Fort Fisher the work on the Navy's giant blockade was completed.

To the forbidding but very human Secretary Welles, as also to Porter, the success of the second expedition was doubly sweet. "The congratulations over the capture of Fort Fisher are hearty and earnest," Welles wrote in his diary on January 18, 1865. "Some few whom I have met are a little out of humor. General Butler [recently recalled from Lowell to testify before the Committee on the Conduct of the War] does not appear gladsome."

☆   ☆   ☆   ☆   ☆

13
The War on the Seas

THE OVERALL STRATEGY of the Confederate States Government for the war on the high seas was to loose a pack of wolves upon the fat geese of Northern commerce. This was the traditional strategy which America had employed in 1776 and 1812, and the only feasible policy which so weak a sea power as the Confederacy could employ. In Southern harbors at the outset of the war there were a number of merchant and passenger ships suitable for conversion into warships, vessels like the coastal side-wheeler *Nashville* and the fast packet *Habana*, which were immediately converted into serviceable commerce raiders. The South, however, could only *convert*, not *build*, steamers, owing to her complete lack of industries to produce marine engines. Necessity forced her by intrigue and subterfuge to obtain what ships she could from abroad.

On the other hand, the Federal Navy Department rightly considered the war on the high seas as secondary to the great blockade. By ever tightening their pressure around the Southern ports, the watchdogs of the blockade sought to prevent the Southern wolves from getting to sea. When an occasional raider managed to slip through, the temptation for blockade ships to give chase was very great, but as a general policy this temptation was resisted. Insurance companies, mayors of seaport cities, ship owners, and merchants protested vigorously against what appeared to them an official disinclination to afford their property adequate protection against the "rebel pirates." Without at all publicizing its policy the Navy Department in Washington sent out a number of ships to cruise in particular areas where the sea-wolves might be expected to appear, as in the English Channel and off Gibraltar. In 1863 a West India Squadron was improvised for

Commodore Charles Wilkes in the hope of capturing Semmes in the *Alabama*. The Union ships assigned to the war on the high seas, however, were those that were least useful for close-in blockading and for fighting in the sounds and rivers. Activity on the high seas was of secondary importance throughout the war, even though occasionally, as in the cases of the *Trent* affair and the *Alabama*, it made stirring headlines and threatened to embroil the North in war with Europe.

CONFEDERATE NAVAL AGENTS

In May of 1861 the Confederate States Congress appropriated $1,000,000 for six sail-steam cruisers and $2,000,000 for two ironclad warships. The cruisers for raiding enemy commerce and the ironclads for breaking the Federal blockade were to be purchased or built abroad. James D. Bulloch and Lieutenant James H. North were sent to England to manage procurement of the two types of ships.[1] Both men had been officers in the U.S. Navy, North having had 32 years of service and Bulloch 15. Bulloch, ten years junior to North, had resigned in 1854 to become a merchant, and was better fitted by training and temperament to manipulate the devious intrigues necessary to achieve his ends. North's assignment to procure ironclads was the more difficult owing to the novelty of this type of craft, the excessive demand for armored ships in Europe at this time, their relatively greater cost, and North's complete inability to cajole the Confederate authorities into sending him funds. It was not long before the younger man was carrying North's assignment as well as his own, a juggling feat of which he proved fully capable. An aggressive, dynamic individual, a precursor of Theodore Roosevelt whose uncle he was, Bulloch was able to inspire confidence and get things done. In July, 1861, within a month after his arrival in England, the keel of the first foreign-built Confederate raider (*Oreto*, later known as *Florida*) had been laid in Liverpool. On August 1 Bulloch signed the contract for the most famous of all the Confederate commerce destroyers (successively known as "the 290," *Enrica*, and *Alabama*).

The *Oreto-Florida* was completed and ready to sail in March, 1862. Her character as a prospective raider was "sufficiently indicated," as Bulloch admitted to Mallory, by her "hammock-nettings, ports, and general appearance"; yet Bulloch had prudently engaged an English advocate to help him keep his acts within the letter of British law.

---

[1] J. D. Bulloch, *The Secret Service of the Confederate States in Europe, or How the Confederate Cruisers were Equipped*. 2 Vols., 1884.

Though provided with port holes and bolts in the deck to secure the gun-mounts, the ship when she left port was technically not "fitted out." Bulloch planned for that to be done at sea. "Registered as an English ship, in the name of an Englishman, commanded by an Englishman, with a regular official number . . . she seems to be perfectly secure against capture, or even interference, until an attempt is made to arm her, or to change her flag."[2] Since arming her and signing on her crew at sea proved too difficult, she was taken to Nassau, where, after considerable indecision on the part of the colonial officials, she was permitted to put to sea under Commander John N. Maffitt, C.S. Navy.

The *290-Alabama* was admirably constructed as a raider. Her hull was 230 feet long, beam 32, and when provisioned and coaled for a cruise she drew 15 feet. Proud of her "perfect symmetry," her captain wrote that "she sat upon the water with the lightness and grace of a swan."[3] She was barkentine rigged, carrying large fore-and-aft sails on her extra tall lower masts. "Her sticks were of the best yellow pine, that would bend in a gale, like a willow wand, without breaking." The best of Swedish iron wire was used in her rigging. While engaged in a chase her 300 h.p. engine could drive her through the water at 13.5 knots; though most of the time she would proceed a few knots slower under sail, with propeller unshipped, to conserve coal.

Supervision of the *290's* construction as well as dodging the dragnet of Federal diplomacy in getting the ship safely to sea were to be Bulloch's most significant achievements for the Confederate cause abroad. He remained abroad for many months, let contracts for ironclad rams to be built by the Lairds, and took over the supervision of the "Thompson" ironclad that North had contracted for. When finally the Federal agents gained the upper hand in England, Bulloch with some assistance from John Slidell transferred his activities to France, whither he tried to shift the uncompleted rams. His efforts were stalemated, however, by lack of funds and Federal counter measures. When at long last he did manage to start one of his ironclad rams, the *Stonewall*, on its way across the Atlantic, the end of the war caught up with him and nullified his effort.

The *290's* escape from Liverpool was a close call. She was launched on May 15, 1862, as the British merchantman *Enrica*. On a tip apparently from a clerk in the Foreign Office, Bulloch got the *Enrica*

[2] *Ibid.*, Vol. I, p. 162.
[3] R. Semmes, *Memoirs of Service Afloat*. 1869, p. 402.

to sea early on July 28 for a "trial trip," even as the law officers of the Crown were pondering U.S. Minister Adams's incriminating documents and debating whether to detain the ship. Once clear of the harbor, the *Enrica* made a getaway to the Azores, whither she was followed by chartered vessels bearing her cannon, ammunition, coal, and her future officers.

THE TRENT CASE

In the fall of 1861 James M. Mason and John Slidell, ex-U.S. Senators and men of considerable prestige and influence, were appointed as special Confederate emissaries to Europe. So anxious was the North to prevent their getting abroad that a special watch was posted off Charleston to intercept them. When the Confederate cruiser *Nashville,* on which they were reported to have taken passage, slipped past the blockaders, the U.S.S. *James Adger* chased after her all the way to Europe.

Meanwhile Mason and Slidell escaped to Havana, together with their secretaries, George Eustis and James MacFarland, and their families. Here they engaged passage to Southampton on the British Royal Mail steam packet *Trent.* In a round of entertainments in Havana there was no attempt made to keep their plans hidden. At Cienfuegos on the south shore of Cuba these plans, as well as the sailing schedule of the *Trent,* came to the ear of Captain Charles Wilkes of the U.S.S. *San Jacinto,* and Wilkes decided to waylay the Confederates. Famous for his exploring expedition to the South Seas and known throughout the service for his willingness to take the bit in his teeth and make a quarter-deck decision when necessary, Wilkes took a station in the narrowest stretch of the Old Bahama Passage about 300 miles east of Havana. The *Trent* appeared before noon on November 8. When Wilkes fired a round shot across her bow she ran up British colors. Wilkes now fired a shell which exploded 100 yards from the vessel and the *Trent* hove to.

A boarding party, later reinforced by two boatloads of armed marines, went on board the *Trent.*[4] Mason, Slidell, and their secretaries yielded to a "gentle application of force" consisting of two seamen's laying their hands on Mr. Mason's coat collar. The wives of the Confederates having spurned Captain Wilkes's offer to permit them to accompany their husbands, Wilkes released the *Trent.* Although Captain

---

[4] *Official Records . . . Navies,* Series I, Vol. 1, p. 138.

Moir of the *Trent* by refusing to produce his passenger list had to some extent "resisted search" and possibly rendered his ship liable to capture, Wilkes forbore to seize her, "in consequence of my being so reduced in officers and crew, and the derangement it would cause inno- cent . . . passengers who would have been put to great loss and in- convenience."

Throughout the North the news of Wilkes's bold seizure of the Con- federate emissaries evoked a storm of applause. "Consecrate another 4th of July to him, load him down with services of plate and swords of the cunningest and costliest art," clamored a press fed up with inaction around the blockaded coast. Congressmen, smarting from indignities at Bull Run, introduced a resolution that Mason and Slidell be thrown into "the cell of a convicted felon." Fearful lest the prisoners prove to be "elephants on our hands, that we could not easily dispose of," Lincoln ordered Wilkes to lodge them for safekeeping in Fort Warren at Boston. Secretary Welles felt that Wilkes should have brought the *Trent* herself before an admiralty court; yet Wilkes's act presented so clear an object lesson in "decision and firmness" in the enforcement of belligerent rights that Welles tendered him "the emphatic approval" of the Department.

Meanwhile the *Trent's* arrival in England unleashed a "typhoon of fury" against the United States. Several thousand troops were sent to Canada, an embargo was placed on military stores being exported from the United Kingdom, and a vigorously worded diplomatic protest was sent to Washington. Happily by the time the protest reached the State Department American papers had had time to cool and Secretary Seward was able to avoid a foreign embroilment by releasing the prisoners. The *Trent* incident was the first and only Anglo-American difficulty growing out of the war between the States which might con- ceivably have led to a foreign war. There would be serious difficulties later on, the *Alabama* case for example; but these later matters would be capably handled by diplomacy without the angry popular frenzies that accompanied the *Trent* difficulty.

SCOURGE OF THE SEAS

Portuguese officials were allowed to believe that the *Enrica* at anchor in Porto Praya, in the Azores, was merely taking on coal from the tender *Agrippina*. Behind the screen of coal dust, however, a bat- tery of eight naval guns was also being shifted aboard the future raider. James D. Bulloch and Captain Raphael Semmes, C.S. Navy, now arrived in the *Bahama* from Liverpool. Having already violated Portuguese neutrality, Semmes took the ship out beyond the limit of territorial waters to muster the crew, read his orders, and raise the Confederate flag. The ceremony was performed at night under a starry sky auspiciously lit up by the fanlike tail of Swift's Comet. Eighty-three of the *Enrica's* seamen, chiefly Irish and English from the dives of Liverpool, succumbed to the lure of prize money and signed on as members of the crew of the C.S.S. *Alabama*—not a full crew, but enough to operate the ship until additional recruits from the crews of prize vessels could be persuaded to sign up with the raider. Bulloch, with a touch of envy, wished Captain Semmes good luck and returned to the *Bahama*. Possibly as he went over the side he read the new raider's gilded motto: *Aide toi et Dieu t' aidera.*

Captain Semmes well knew that on the high seas he would have to aid himself. As captain of the C.S.S. *Sumter,* Semmes in June of 1861 had dodged Federal blockaders off New Orleans and attained the open sea. Off Cuba he immediately had seized six prizes and had made the mistake of sending them in to Cienfuegos to be sold. He needed cash to maintain himself on a long cruise. In Cienfuegos, however, through intervention of the United States consul, his prizes were released to their former owners. Henceforth Captain Semmes released a few ships, those presenting the legal complications incident to friendly neutral cargoes, but for the most part he hastily stripped his prizes of whatever stores he needed and put them to the torch. Seven out of nine captures made by the *Sumter* after Cienfuegos were thus destroyed.

The active career of the *Alabama* was to last 22 months, from August 24, 1862 to June 19, 1864. Semmes's neat calculations of the time necessary for news of his whereabouts to travel to some United States consul and for an American cruiser then to overtake him, no doubt account for his remaining at large for so long; but important also was the fact that after Semmes had begun his operations near the American coast he thereafter worked in progressively more distant fields until he had touched French Indo-China. Had he not eventually been compelled to return to Europe for repairs, he might easily have remained at sea until after Appomattox.

Since most of his men were merchant seamen new to discipline, Semmes spent ten days stationing and drilling the crew, after which he descended like a plague upon the United States whaling barks near the Azores. Within a few weeks he made nine captures in this area.

The *Ocean Rover* from Massachusetts had a cargo of 1,100 barrels of oil. The *Alert* from New London was taken on September 9. "Supplied ourselves from her with some underclothing for the men, of which we stood in need, some tobacco, etc. About 9:00 A.M. [reads Semmes's journal] fired the *Starlight;* at 11:00 fired the *Ocean Rover,* and at 4:00 P.M. fired the *Alert.*"[5] From the Azores Semmes sailed northward to the latitude of Labrador to prey on eastward-bound grain ships. The burning of the great grain ship *Brilliant,* almost as large as the *Alabama,* made an "appalling" sight. Semmes was agitated by the master's entreaties, a one-third interest in the doomed ship representing his life savings; "but I was forced," writes Semmes, "to steel my heart."

According to rumor or propaganda, the "pirate" Semmes burned his prisoners with his prizes; and such canards account for the wartime rancor against him. Prisoners were a constant embarrassment to him, especially women, to whom the best cabins were assigned. Often the unwilling guests on board the raider had to put up with wet and crowded accommodations, but quarters were equally wet and crowded for the ship's company. To relieve the congestion Semmes would on occasion convert a prize into a cartel in order to free the *Alabama* of her burden of prisoners.

From the Banks of Newfoundland Semmes headed south. At Martinique, where he found his coal vessel *Agrippina,* he was blockaded by the Federal cruiser *San Jacinto.* Semmes sent out the coaler to a new rendezvous and successfully dodged "the old wagon," *San Jacinto,* as he called her, the following night. He refueled in an obscure shelter off the coast of Venezuela. "Finished coaling today," he wrote on November 24, "the bunkers are now all full, and we have on board at least 285 tons. Consuming at the rate of 16 tons per day, which will give us moderate steaming, we have on board, therefore, 18 days' fuel." Since the *Alabama* stoked furnaces only for chasing and did practically all of her cruising under sail, the full bunkers would last a much longer time.

Semmes cruised for several months in the relatively confined waters of the Gulf and Caribbean "looking for a California steamer." If he could intercept a treasure ship he might pay the overdue wages to his crew. He wrote:

"Many of my fellows no doubt thought they were shipping in a

---

[5] *Ibid.,* p. 789.

sort of privateer, where they would have a jolly good time and plenty of license. They have been woefully disappointed, for I have jerked them down with a strong hand, and now have a well disciplined ship of war. . . . It has taken me three or four months to accomplish this, but when it is considered that my little kingdom consisted of 110 of the most reckless sailors from the groggeries and brothels of Liverpool, that is not much."[6] With his crew under discipline Semmes began to consider striking a military blow, especially since merchant prizes were scarce in this area. "I am looking for a California steamer, and whilst I am looking for her perhaps I may find a fight."

Accordingly on January 11, about the time of General Banks's scheduled movement of troops down the Texas coast, Semmes ran the *Alabama* up to within sight of the blockade ships off Galveston. The U.S.S. *Hatteras* under Lieutenant Commander H. C. Blake was ordered out to investigate the stranger. So skillfully did Semmes lure the *Hatteras* away from the other blockaders that it was night before she came within speaking range.

"What steamer is that?" hailed the *Hatteras*.

"Her Britannic Majesty's ship *Vixen*," replied Semmes. The *Hatteras* sent off a boarding party, but almost immediately Semmes announced, "We are the Confederate steamer *Alabama*," and poured a raking fire into the smaller Federal ship. Blake recognized at once the hopelessness of his situation; yet he continued the unequal fight for some minutes in the hope of disabling the *Alabama* and attracting the attention of the blockade fleet. Finally with his walking-beam and boilers destroyed and several fires raging, he flooded his magazines and fired a gun to leeward to signify surrender. A few minutes after her crew had been transferred to the *Alabama*, the stricken ship lifted her stern in the air and plunged to the bottom. The "Scourge of the Seas," a naval victory added to her laurels as a raider, now raced to Jamaica to put her paroled prisoners on shore before the alarm had spread.

During the next 18 months Semmes's course ran to Capetown, Singapore, French Indo-China, and back to Europe. Along the busy traffic lanes of the South Atlantic the raider's wake was most often lighted by columns of flame. The Indian Ocean, where Semmes hoped to seize upon Yankee shipping from the Orient, proved his greatest disappointment. Fewer and fewer ships of American registry were encountered.

---

[6] *Ibid.*, p. 816.

Under the imperious necessity to save fuel he stopped overhauling ships that were not obviously "Yankee," and all too often a likely looking prize turned out to have been recently shifted to foreign ownership. Semmes's own efficiency as a raider now militated against him. He had scourged the seas so well that he found too few prizes to keep his larders and slop chests stocked. For a time he had to put his men on half rations of bread. In June, 1864, when the celebrated *Alabama* put into Cherbourg in need of a complete dockyard overhaul, her main work, the destruction of enemy commerce, lay behind her.

In 22 months she had sunk one warship and captured 63 merchant craft of all descriptions. Of her rich bag of prizes nine had been released on ransom bond, only one had been sold, 53 vessels had been burned.

THE FIGHT OFF CHERBOURG

The absence of oceanic cables had preserved the secret of Semmes's whereabouts when he put into Cape Town and Singapore, but now, as he well knew, his entry into Cherbourg would be ticked over the telegraphic wires of the continent in a matter of minutes. While Semmes's request to use the French government dock was being relayed to Emperor Napoleon III at Biarritz, a telegram from the United States minister was en route to Captain J. A. Winslow of the U.S.S. *Kearsarge,* anchored in the mouth of the Scheldt at Flushing. Winslow's first thought as he lifted his anchor was that there were two channels into Cherbourg. To make certain of catching this most dangerous of Southern raiders, Winslow telegraphed to Tangier and ordered the U.S.S. *St. Louis* to rendezvous with him off Cherbourg.

John Ancrum Winslow, whose duel with the *Alabama* was to be the envy of Farragut himself, was Raphael Semmes's contemporary in the Old Navy. In the Mexican War, in fact, the two had shared for a time the same stateroom on board the U.S.S. *Raritan.*[7] He was as sturdy and solemn as Semmes was facile and clever. "Quarter-deck Puritan" is the handle which one biographer attaches to him because of his earnest adherence to Calvinism and abolition. Up to the eve of his great fight his career had not been distinguished, and partly for that reason the Department had sent him out on the high seas as just another pawn that might win the thousand-to-one chance to trap the queen.

---

[7] J. D. Hill, *Sea Dogs of the Sixties,* 1935, p. 198.

In one particular at least Winslow exercised shrewd judgment. Instead of coiling his sheet cables neatly in the chain locker he had faked them up and down outside the ship abreast his engines and concealed them behind a sheathing of deal boards. Winslow came into Cherbourg on June 14. Without anchoring he communicated with the American consul and then took station outside the mole to blockade the *Alabama*.

The appearance of the *Kearsarge* afforded Semmes a way out of a difficult situation. American diplomacy, which had harried the Confederate agents out of England in 1863, was now stalemating their efforts in France. Some of the ironclads begun in France for the Confederacy had perforce been sold to Denmark. Official weaseling on the matter of docking was all too obvious to the sensitive and high-strung Semmes. Via a Confederate agent and the United States consul he sent word to Captain Winslow of his intention to come out and fight him in one or two days, as soon as he could make the "necessary arrangements." He now withdrew his embarrassing request to use the dockyard and received permission to take on a full load of coal.

Shortly after 10 A.M. on Sunday, June 19, 1864, Semmes headed out through the western channel. Winslow at the same time left his station outside the eastern channel and steamed out to sea to clear French territorial waters. The French ironclad *Couronne,* bent on enforcement of the technicality, trailed the *Alabama* and anchored at the three-mile limit. There was a slight haze, not enough to obscure the view of spectators who lined the French coast; "wind moderate from the westward, with little sea."

About seven miles from shore the *Kearsarge* turned short around and charged toward the *Alabama*. The latter sheered to present her starboard battery and slowed her engines. At "long range of about a mile" the *Alabama* opened with a full broadside. Seven of her eight guns (a rifled 100-pounder, a 68-pounder, and five of her six 32's) were in action in her starboard broadside. The first shots clipped some of the *Kearsarge's* rigging and splashed over and alongside of her. The *Kearsarge* put on a burst of speed to close the range. Within two minutes the *Alabama* fired her second broadside. "We had now arrived within 900 yards of her," reads Winslow's report, "and I was apprehensive that another broadside, nearly raking as it was, would prove disastrous. Accordingly, I ordered the *Kearsarge* sheered, and opened on the *Alabama*." For the next 60 minutes the two ships steamed in circles, each warily thwarting the other's efforts to sneak

Top, THE SINKING OF THE ALABAMA BY THE KEARSARGE. From a painting by Xanthus Smith in the collection of President Franklin D. Roosevelt. *Bottom*, ADMIRALS DUPONT, FARRAGUT, AND PORTER.

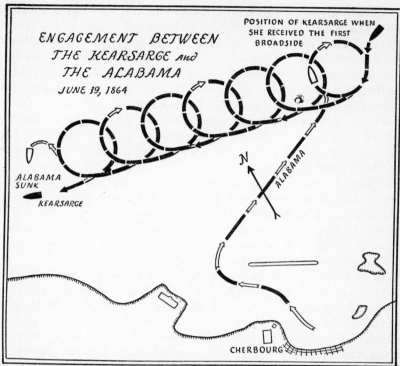

From *The United States Navy: A History* by Alden and Westcott.

in a raking blow. The tracks they described formed a series of circular loops, the centers of which drifted more or less in a straight line to the westward.

In their 65-minute gunnery duel the advantage lay entirely with the *Kearsarge*. The *Alabama's* powder had been stowed too long in the vicinity of her condenser; it no longer had the necessary punch. Too many of her shells, too, were duds. A 100-pounder dud which was planted in the stern post of the *Kearsarge* so jammed the helm that it took four men to operate it. One can imagine what damage would have been inflicted in this vital spot had the shell exploded properly! Without doubt the chain protection on the *Kearsarge* saved many of her crew. Shot after shot ripped through the outer planking and bounced off the chain armor.

The superiority of the Federal ammunition was immediately apparent on board the *Alabama*. While the *Kearsarge* had only five of her total of seven guns in action, these included two 11-inch Dahlgren guns, which gave her a superiority in broadside weight of at least six to five. Shot from the *Kearsarge* holed the Confederate raider through and through. The *Alabama's* bulwarks were shot away in sections, guns dismounted, decks splintered. The *Alabama* was filling rapidly. She became so dull in response to her helm that sail trimmers were ordered aloft to loose head-sails to pay her off. At length an 11-inch shell entering on the water line exploded in her engine room. The stricken ship trembled from stem to stern. Captain Semmes headed her southward in an effort to reach the French coast before sinking, but she refused to move.

Captain Winslow interposed between the enemy and the shore. After the *Alabama's* surrender and report that she was sinking Winslow sent his one undamaged lifeboat and requested a nearby English yacht, the *Deerhound,* also to pick up survivors. About 20 minutes after the *Alabama* was abandoned, her bow reared upright in the air and she plunged stern first to the bottom.

An incident unique in naval warfare was the escape of Semmes and forty of his men to England on board the fast neutral yacht *Deerhound*. Inevitably the aftermath of this only Civil War naval action fought on the traditional pattern—between approximately equal opponents who willingly accepted the gage of battle—was a bitter and anticlimactic battle of words, unprofitable now to rehearse. Semmes in the *Alabama* had already accomplished his mission as a commerce raider. His alternative to giving battle was to sit out the war blockaded in a neutral port where the Confederacy's welcome had already worn thin. Had he known beforehand that his opponent was partially armored, he might honorably have refused to give battle, or had he known how inferior was his own ammunition. The question he seems to have asked himself was not "Do I have a chance to be defeated?" but "Do I have a chance to win a victory?" Under the circumstances he deserves only praise. And the same can be said of Winslow. With better guns and a better ship he had fought competently and in the best naval tradition. "The victory of the *Kearsarge* over the *Alabama* raised me up," wrote Farragut. "I would sooner have fought that fight than any ever fought on the ocean."[8]

In addition to the *Alabama* the Confederates sent out 11 other commerce raiders, of which the most famous were *Shenandoah, Florida,*

---

[8] Lewis, *Farragut,* p. 255.

Tallahassee, Georgia, Chickamauga, Sumter, and *Nashville.* The *Shenandoah,* sailing from London in the fall of 1864, did not arrive in her chosen raiding ground, the North Pacific, until near the end of the war. News of Appomattox did not reach her until after she had destroyed 29 Yankee whaling vessels in the Okhotsk Sea, Bering Sea, and the Arctic. The total damage which all the raiders inflicted on American commerce was approximately $15,500,000. Of this total some $6,500,000 was credited to the *Alabama.* Nearly $6,000,000 was accounted for by the *Shenandoah* after the war had ended. The ten remaining raiders did but $3,500,000 worth of damage. However high their nuisance value, in the final analysis the raiders exerted only a negligible influence on the outcome of the war. And in the end the Federal Government's overall strategy to ignore the raiders and tighten the blockade appears to have justified itself.

☆　　　☆　　　☆　　　☆　　　☆

14
Between Wars: 1865–1898

THE 33-YEAR INTERVAL between the Civil War and the War with Spain can be treated in a single chapter. During this period there were but few unusual naval occurrences: disasters from hurricanes and tidal waves, a naval punitive expedition against Korea, voyages of exploration like the ill-fated *Jeannette* Expedition, the humanitarian Greely Relief Expedition; and there were a few international incidents which just missed involving the country in war such as the *Virginius* affair of 1873 and the *Baltimore* affair of 1891. The political reactions to certain of these naval events, as they reveal trends of popular thought on naval policy and naval strategy, are often more interesting and significant than the precipitating incidents.

Whether one considers the philosophical or the material aspects of the Navy, the period between the two wars is broken into two equal parts, with 1881 as the year of crucial change. Before 1881 the country was largely preoccupied with internal affairs: political reconstruction of the South, building transcontinental railroads, exploiting an ever expanding domestic market. So far as the outside world was concerned the country's policy was isolationist, and the deterioration of the Old Navy and the stagnation of naval thinking both seem of a piece with the general pattern set by the country as a whole. After 1881 the Navy experienced a renaissance which perhaps more than anything else was due to a change in the pattern of American thought. The disappearance of the frontier and the vast expansion of industrial production were potent inducements to America to emulate industrialized European states in the imperialistic field. The change in naval material, commencing with the naval bill of 1881, was supplemented by a change in strategic conceptions after the founding of the Naval

War College in 1885; and after the publication in 1890 of Alfred Thayer Mahan's *The Influence of Sea Power upon History, 1660– 1783,* new trends of popular thought on naval policy gained such momentum that in 1898 it required but a little shove by the yellow press to push the country into an imperialistic war.

Throughout the period from 1881 to 1898 a major scientific problem was not only to design the battleships of the New Navy but to master the many technological difficulties which beset the manufacturers of guns and armor. This significant and absorbing story is so highly technical that only an elementary treatment of it can be given.

THE NAVY GOES BACK TO CANVAS

The axman and the auctioneer fell upon the improvised blockade fleet and within nine months after Appomattox reduced its numbers from 471 ships to 29. The experimental ironclad fleet, numbering 65 vessels at the close of the war, including the now worthless river gunboats, was broken for scrap or moored in the fresh-water anchorage at League Island near Philadelphia, where the Navy Department planned to locate its new base for ironclads. Awake to the possibility of a "damage suit" war with England over the *Alabama* case or a war to eject Napoleon III from his conquest in Mexico, the Navy Department continued the construction of two seagoing monitors, *Miantonomah* and *Monadnock,* and in the face of discouraging metallurgical difficulties pushed ahead with the new *Wampanoag* class of speedy commerce raiders. These latter vessels, the first to embody the principle of superheated steam, developed the then phenomenal speed of 17 knots. They constituted "a race of Alabamas" that could harry an enemy's commerce and outrun any of his warships. Although the Civil War had taught several clear lessons in naval material—the superiority of steam over sail, of armor over wood, of rifle over smoothbore— there was no comparable evolution in strategy and tactics. The South with almost no navy had proved an inadequate tutor. The dominant American theory of waging naval war remained what it had been after the Revolution and after 1812: single-ship, commerce-raiding theory.

While strategic and tactical theory within the Navy had not changed, it was apparent that naval affairs at the policy making level were sooner or later due for a shake-up. This was the inescapable significance of the revolutionary changes in naval material. In the event of a maritime war America's speedy *Wampanoags* would require overseas bases. These long "ocean going canoes," in which both living quarters and coal bunkers had been sacrificed to make space for engines and boilers, were by their very nature restricted in operation to a comparatively short radius from their coaling docks. They needed for distant operations a chain of overseas bases. They could not makeshift under sail as had the *Alabama* without sacrificing their design and their only unique feature, speed under steam.

Need for a naval base and coaling station in the Caribbean led to an attempt in 1867 to purchase the Virgin Islands from Denmark. No sooner was the treaty signed than a hurricane and tidal wave swept the islands. The U.S.S. *Monongahela,* visiting the prospective new American harbor of Frederiksted, was by one wave lifted bodily ashore and by another returned to her natural element. The freakish circumstance at once soured the country on the merits of the deal with Denmark and it was not ratified by the Senate. Efforts of Secretary of State Seward to purchase a site on the Bay of Samaná from the bankrupt Dominican Republic fell through because of the political quarrel between Congress and Andrew Johnson. Later on President Grant tried to annex the whole Dominican Republic, but the idea of adding nearly a million West Indian Negroes and Creoles to our population, together with "nobody knows what debts and liabilities," again defeated the acquisition. Seward's purchase of Alaska, motivated by other than naval reasons, would carry immense strategic significance for the future. Seward, the most ardent post-Civil War expansionist, also wanted, but failed to obtain, strategic territory at the Isthmus of Panama. The problem of United States bases in the Caribbean, politically sidetracked for various reasons, would have to await the propitious opportunity of 1898.

Meanwhile the failure to acquire bases, as well as the long period of meager naval appropriations, imposed upon the Navy an ultraconservative routine and stultified the thinking of naval officers. United States naval ships now went back to canvas, an anachronism which prevailed to the eve of the War with Spain. The ultraslender *Wampanoags* were redesigned to become fatter and slower. New construction was stopped and funds were wasted in making excessive repairs on worn-out and out-dated wooden ships. The United States Navy fell behind European navies as a leader in armored ships and modern breech-loading rifled cannon.

After 1881 our interest in Caribbean bases passively persisted, owing to diplomatic questions raised in the area—the Isthmian canal, the

Venezuela boundary dispute, Cuba's revolt gainst Spain—but the Navy itself took no active steps to acquire bases here. In the Pacific, however, American naval officers were actively seeking to promote annexations of Hawaii and Samoa.

Showing the Flag

After 1865 the two issues most likely to involve the United States in war were the ousting of France's puppet emperor from Mexico and the settlement of the *Alabama* claims. Undoubtedly the existence of a victorious American fleet containing a handful of fast cruisers and seagoing monitors carried some influence with the European states, yet for both England and France the American Navy was but one factor in a complicated situation. The Mexican conquest had already proved too costly for France both in money and troops and France stood at this time on the brink of war with a rampantly nationalistic Germany. England delayed settling the *Alabama* claims until the agitation of the "Radical" Republicans had had time to cool; then evidently fearing that the precedent of the *Alabama* case might in the future be used against herself, she agreed in the Geneva negotiations to pay the United States $15,500,000 for the direct damages which American shipping had suffered at the hands of English-built commerce raiders.

The visit of the monitor *Miantonomah* to Russia in 1866 and the voyage of the monitor *Monadnock* around Cape Horn to join the Pacific fleet gave evidence of American mechanical skill, but such voyages, undertaken in good weather and in peacetime, since they really indicated nothing of the potentiality of these craft for use in a foreign war, could scarcely be interpreted as "saber rattling." Responsible American statesmen held little fear of Europe. In 1867–68 when Admiral Farragut was sent to fly in European ports the flag of the reunited America, he traveled in the old wooden U.S.S. *Franklin,* the most undistinguished flagship in the service. Built in 1815 as a ship of the line and rebuilt as a steamer in 1864, she was a fitting exponent of America's post-war policy to show the flag in the ports of the world but in so doing to stay out of trouble. The heart warming receptions for Farragut seemed to spring from an almost universal feeling of good will toward the United States.

Elsewhere in the world the situation was less cheerful. The disappearance of the American trading bark *General Sherman* in pirate-infested Korean waters caused Rear Admiral John Rodgers in 1871 to lead the Asiatic Squadron into the forbidden territorial waters of the

Hermit Kingdom to investigate. Rodgers found it almost impossible to communicate with the native ruler. While his vessels were at anchor in the Salee river below the capital city of Seoul he sent out several boat parties to survey the channel. These were fired on by batteries on shore and two Americans were wounded. Rodgers now sent several hundred seamen ashore with light artillery to destroy the native batteries. As the Korean troops were armed chiefly with spears and wooden cannon (cohorns), the fight was soon decided. The incident paved the way for the successful negotiation of a treaty with Korea by Commander R. W. Shufeldt, United States Navy, a decade later, by which Korea was opened to trade and provision was made for the safety of American seamen shipwrecked on her rocky coast.

That "showing the flag" had its ceremonial side was evident in the festivities abroad for Assistant Secretary Fox of the *Miantonomah* and for Admiral Farragut. Its main purpose was the protection of American life and property, as illustrated in Admiral Rodger's punitive expedition to Korea. To an increasing extent after 1881 the Navy promoted its new building program by advertising itself in visits to American home ports, to take part in public celebrations. Occasionally, as in the case of the Greely Relief Expedition, competently led by Commander Winfield Scott Schley, the Navy by a spectacular humanitarian mission won widespread acclaim which was shrewdly utilized by the Navy Department to win Congressional support for rebuilding the Navy. The assignment of naval personnel to man publisher James Gordon Bennett's steamer *Jeannette* for the ill-fated Arctic exploring expedition in the Pacific is an illustration of the Navy's two-fold desire to advance scientific knowledge and to win the support of the American people.

Unostentatiously and a step at a time the Navy in the Pacific was itself becoming an instrument for mobilizing public opinion. The Navy had lost the political battle for bases in the Caribbean. Naval officers, charged with maintaining America's first line of defense, were aware as few other Americans were of the issues of international competition in the Pacific. In August, 1867, Commander William Reynolds, U. S. Navy, took possession of Midway Islands, which were eventually to prove of inestimable strategic value in the defense of Hawaii and the Pacific coast. The reciprocity treaty of 1875 placed Hawaii under "an American sphere of influence"; and the renewal of this treaty in 1884 carried a clause granting to the United States the exclusive right to a fortified base at Pearl Harbor. The Samoan

Islands, on the main highway to Australia, a strategic area attractive to American naval officers ever since Captain Charles Wilkes's visit to Tutuila in 1839, was coveted in 1872 by Commander R. W. Meade, who negotiated a treaty granting the United States an exclusive naval station in the harbor of Pago Pago, Tutuila. Meade's treaty, though failing of ratification, was nevertheless a ground-breaker for a similar treaty which was ratified in 1878. Both Britain and Germany now became interested in Samoa, and for some years the islands were a scene of international intrigue. The great hurricane of 1889, which wrecked several American and German ships in Pago Pago harbor, suddenly broke up the tug of war over this "manger of potential international dispute," and a tripartite condominium was agreed upon.[1] During the hurricane American naval tradition was enriched by the heroic action of Naval Cadet R. H. Jackson, who led his men into the storm-whipped rigging of the *Trenton* to form a "human sail." While Jackson was not successful in saving the ship, his attempt had been, by heading the ship into the wind, to relieve the strain on her dragging anchors, and thus save her from being driven ashore to destruction.

The phenomenal growth of American imperialism in the 1890's—the desire for Pacific Ocean bases to support American trade in competition with the rest of the industrialized world, and an active interest in the strategic implications of an Isthmian canal—owes much to the stimulus of the newly established Naval War College and to the writings of Captain Mahan.

THE INTELLECTUAL RENAISSANCE

The most distinguished administrator of American naval education was Stephen Bleecker Luce. Four tours of duty at the Naval Academy, during the last of which he served as Commandant, gave him valuable experience in his twin specialties of school administration and teaching seamanship. During the naval decline of the 1870's Luce established and built up the Naval Apprentice Training System, the purpose of which was to train seamen for both the Navy and the languishing American Merchant Marine. In 1884 Luce finally gained acceptance for his idea that postgraduate study needed to be made available to junior officers of the Navy. The naval officer, Luce believed, could profit by a philosophic study of naval history, examining great battles "with the cold eye of professional criticism" to learn

---

[1] S. F. Bemis, *A Diplomatic History of the United States*, p. 458.

"where the principles of science have been illustrated, or where a disregard for the accepted rules of the art of war has led to defeat and disaster. Such studies might occupy the very best thoughts of the naval officer, for they belong to the very highest branch of his profession."

The Navy Department found temporary quarters for the new school in the old poor asylum on Coaster's Harbor Island, near Newport, and Commodore Luce, nearly sixty years of age, was detailed as its first superintendent. "Poor little poor house," the white-whiskered Commodore grasped the door knob and turned toward the group of Training Squadron officers who had escorted him ashore, "Poor little poor house, I christen thee the United States Naval War College!"[2] Luce spent a year laying plans and assembling a faculty, and then turned over the superintendency of the War College to Commander Mahan.

When Luce brought him to the War College to lecture on naval history and tactics, Alfred Thayer Mahan was already forty-five years old and looking forward to the day when he could retire from active duty in the line. A scholar by temperament, he had already published a slender volume on the Civil War entitled *The Gulf and Inland Waters*. Mahan found the profession of lecturer so thoroughly to his liking that when the enemies of the college sought to starve out the institution from lack of funds he and his wife had recourse to all sorts of expedients to keep the school alive.

In 1890 Mahan published his first lectures under the title *The Influence of Sea Power upon History, 1660–1783*. This epoch-making book is at once a history of British naval development in its most crucial period, a philosophical treatise on the art of naval war, and a great propaganda document justifying a big navy (whether British, German, Japanese, or American). What Jomini had done for military warfare, Mahan did for the art of naval warfare. In his analyses of naval actions he applied the well-known military principles in order to see whether the art of naval warfare parallels or differs from that of land warfare. The fact that his illustrations were drawn chiefly from English naval history and were quite flattering to English pride won for him immediate acclaim in England. England's new rival, Wilhelm II, also took up the book and placed a copy in each wardroom in the German Navy. Finally the book was seized upon by Theodore Roosevelt and Henry Cabot Lodge as a made-to-order American imperial-

---

[2] A. Gleaves, *The Life and Letters of Stephen Bleecker Luce,* p. 179.

ist's handbook. The book answers such questions as: What are the elements of sea power? What has been America's naval situation in the past? What of the future? At present, wrote Mahan, "an interest in sea power does not exist. . . . The motive, if any there be, which will give the United States a navy, is probably quickening in the Central American Isthmus. Let us hope it will not come to the birth too late."[3]

A cruise to Europe in 1893–94 as captain of the flagship *Chicago* became a triumphal procession for Mahan. Honorary degrees were conferred on him by Oxford and Cambridge. Naval men everywhere held banquets in his honor. After his cruise Mahan returned to his first love, the War College. His lectures and magazine articles on current strategic problems of the United States reached an ever-widening audience. America needed bases in the Caribbean and in the Pacific. After the Isthmian canal had been completed, Mahan predicted, the Caribbean Sea, "this now comparatively deserted nook of the ocean, will become, like the Red Sea, a great thoroughfare of shipping, and will attract, as never before in our day, the interest and ambition of maritime nations." Mahan presented to American business men a stimulating vision: "outside, beyond the broad seas, there are the markets of the world, that can be entered and controlled only by a vigorous contest."[4] With evangelical earnestness he pleaded that America build a Navy to compete for the world's trade and that American naval officers themselves devote some time to the philosophical study of their profession.

Sea power, according to Mahan, includes not only military strength afloat, but the fundamentals upon which that strength depends: commerce, industrial production, shipping, and colonies or foreign markets. A nation's sea power is affected by the spirit of the age, the will of its political rulers, and the natural conditions with which it is endowed: its geographical position, physical conformation, extent of territory, number of population, character of the people, and character of the government.

Under the stimulus of Mahan the Navy's leaders began a critical analysis of America's naval policies in the past. Mahan came to feel that the traditional "single ship, commerce raiding" theory was outmoded. In modern times a nation requires a seagoing fleet, an over-

---

[3] A. T. Mahan, *The Influence of Sea Power upon History, 1660–1783*, p. 88.
[4] A. T. Mahan, *The Interest of America in Sea Power, Present and Future*, pp. 4, 12.

bearing force, which can beat down an enemy's battle line. Mahan's theory of capital ships concentrated and maneuvering as units of a fleet was accepted by the Navy Department in the 1890's. The problems of building modern ships and weapons, however, required a rebirth of American industry comparable to the intellectual renaissance within the Navy.

BUILDING THE NEW NAVY

The years 1865 to 1898 witnessed fundamental changes in all branches of naval matériel. Muzzle-loading guns were replaced by vastly more destructive armament that required mechanized ammunition hoists and complex breech-loading gear. For some years armor—always behind guns in the race for supremacy—grew increasingly thicker. Improved armor-piercing projectiles of tremendous striking energy bored right through test plates of wrought-iron armor 24 inches thick. The new processes of steel manufacture, however, enabled ship constructors to build thinner and yet tougher armor plates of steel. In the 1890's American steel men developed a high-grade, nickel-steel alloy which, when "face hardened" by a carbonizing process invented by H. A. Harvey, became the best armor in the world.

New weapons appeared. The Civil War spar torpedo gave place to the automotive type, of which the British-built Whitehead torpedo was the first used in the United States Navy. The torpedo called for the construction of high-speed torpedo boats, which in turn led to the development of the modern destroyer, or "torpedo-boat destroyer" as it was at first called. The threat of underwater attack during fog or darkness caused grave concern in all navies, and led to the compartmentation of ships' hulls for greater security, and to adaptation of electric searchlights as detection equipment. Some new weapons, like the compressed-air dynamite-gun, were found to be impractical. The submarine, invented by the American John P. Holland, was partly perfected before 1898, but not used until 1914.

Of first importance was the development during the 1890's of the 4- to 6-inch quick-fire gun. This weapon, owing to the short battle ranges that prevailed in pre-range-finder days, was able to riddle all unarmored sections of "citadel" battleships. Henceforth to use wood as material for a ship's superstructure, as the Chinese discovered at the Yalu in 1894, was to invite disaster. The tremendous advancements in metallurgy, which revolutionized guns and armor, also made better engines possible. By 1890 a speed of 23 knots was not unusual for unarmored cruisers, while the trial speed of the best American battleships in 1898 was around 16.5 knots.

The first move to scrap the old wooden ships and start the long task of building a modern United States Navy was made by Secretary of the Navy W. H. Hunt, who in 1881 appointed naval boards to revise America's naval policy and recommend the number and types of ships to be constructed. Hunt's work was ably continued in later years by Secretary W. E. Chandler, an earnest political reformer; by B. F. Tracy, the first Secretary of the Navy to adopt and implement Mahan's imperialistic ideas; and by Secretary John D. Long, in office when the war broke out with Spain.

In 1883 Congress authorized the construction of the "protected cruisers" *Chicago, Boston, Atlanta,* and *Dolphin.* The "A.B.C.D.'s," as these first vessels of the New Navy were called, carried no armor but they had a steel deck up to three inches thick to give the interior of the ship some protection. They were constructed of steel, could be propelled either by their compound steam engines or by sails, and were armed with breech-loading rifles up to eight inches in diameter. From 1885 to 1889 Congress authorized 30 warships of different classes, aggregating nearly 100,000 tons. The *Maine,* the ship which was fated to be sunk at Havana, though rating at the time as a battleship, belonged to the type later identified as armored cruisers; she displaced 6,648 tons, carried an 11-inch belt of armor, was armed with four 10-inch and six 6-inch guns, and had a speed of 17 knots.

The earliest first class battleships authorized for the United States Navy, the *Indiana,* the *Massachusetts,* and the *Oregon,* had each a tonnage of 10,288, a speed of 16.7 knots, 18-inch armor, and an armament of four 13-inch, eight 8-inch, and four 6-inch guns. The *Iowa,* the most recently designed of the battleships that participated in the Spanish war, was 2,000 tons larger than the *Indiana* class, but by virtue of recent improvements in manufacture, the thickness of her armor was reduced to only 14 inches.

In 1891 the *Baltimore* incident, by raising the possibility of war, gave considerable impetus to the building of the New Navy. On October 16, 1891, a party of seamen from the U. S. cruiser *Baltimore* was permitted to go on shore leave in Valparaiso, Chile. The moment was ill chosen since Chile was in the midst of an insurrection. A seamen's brawl which started in the True Blue Saloon spread rapidly throughout the city and a number of Americans were stabbed and beaten. Two of the *Baltimore's* seamen were killed and 18 wounded.

Although a satisfactory settlement of the affair was finally negotiated by the State Department, the condition of our Navy at the time became a matter of vital public concern. When the incident occurred, none of our battleships had yet been launched, and the armored cruiser *Maine* was still waiting for some of her armor to be manufactured. To overcome the grave armor shortage the Navy Department detailed naval ordnance experts to co-operate closely with the steel men. New armor plants were built and new processes for treating armor devised. For the phenomenal success of the American armor production credit is due to such men as Captain W. T. Sampson, U.S.N., Lieutenant J. F. Meigs, U.S.N. (Ret.), and Professor P. R. Alger. American armor, face-hardened by the Harvey process, was found to be so tough that new techniques had to be devised for attaching it to the frame of a ship.

As the New Navy was materializing in the 1890's, increased attention was given to operation of ships in squadrons. At first only cruisers made up the so-called "Squadron of Evolution," but by the eve of the War with Spain the aggressive young Assistant Secretary of the Navy, Theodore Roosevelt, was reviewing from the bridge of the new *Iowa* the evolutions of a squadron of battleships.

In its test of battle in 1898 the new United States Navy was destined to surprise the world with the ease and cheapness of its victories. This overbearing naval force, which Mahan's new theories called for, was able literally and actually to "win the war in an afternoon." As we shall see, however, this seemingly perfect naval machine was in several respects inexperienced and handicapped by America's mistaken naval policies in the past.

Lacking a sufficient supply of the newly developed smokeless powder, the fleet had had too little firing practice with the 12- and 13-inch guns. As an expedient Springfield infantry rifles had been bolted inside the barrels of these great cannon and used in short-range gunnery practice. Not until Assistant Secretary Roosevelt boarded the *Iowa* to review the fleet on the eve of war had the men in the *Iowa's* turrets engaged in target practice with live ammunition! Little wonder the percentage of hits at Santiago was low!

Coaling bases should have been built in Florida long before the critical need arose in 1898. In the 1870's and again in the 1890's the United States Navy had striven to intercept the many anti-Spanish filibustering expeditions organized and launched from neutral United States soil. Only about a third of these had been caught or turned back. Enough had escaped our vigilance to exasperate Spain and contribute to the growing ill will between the two nations. With so much advance warning of naval warfare in the Caribbean it is remarkable that the officials in Washington responsible for our naval policy did not sooner develop adequate coaling facilities at Key West and Tampa. As we shall see, this failure to provide the Navy with adequate bases *on our own shores* complicated the logistical problem for Commodore Schley of the "Flying Squadron" at a crucial moment of the Santiago campaign.

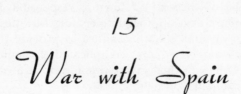

15

War with Spain

PROBABLY the battles and leaders of no conflict in our history have dwindled so rapidly in popular estimate as those of our war with Spain. The naval actions were almost bloodless for the victor and brought peace within a single summer. Yet, as the first foreign conflict in a half century, the war at the time engrossed the whole nation, uniting it in a wave of patriotic fervor. It provided also a most useful test for our new "White Squadron," and it had the lasting significance that it launched the nation into colonial empire and fuller participation in world affairs.

Even before the war, as pointed out in the preceding chapter, the nation was stirred toward a more adventurous foreign policy. It had felt the influence of the new imperialism, arousing among all the great maritime powers a renewed rivalry for colonies and world trade. It had accomplished an immense industrial and commercial expansion, creating increased interest in markets abroad. It had also extended its frontiers to the limits of the continent, and was now looking outward, with a greater concern in its naval defenses and other interests both in the Caribbean and in the Pacific, a concern further stimulated by the cogent and powerful writings of Mahan.

But, granted that the temper of the time was somewhat militant, it is hardly fair to accept the common later view that the conflict with Spain was a foolish and needless one, into which we were stampeded by the yellow journals and few ardent imperialists such as Theodore Roosevelt and Senator Lodge. The believer in democratic processes should at least bear in mind that popular and Congressional sentiment overwhelmingly favored intervention.

Spanish misrule in Cuba was in fact perennial, and the revolt which had continued since 1895 was but a recurrence of the "languid, desultory, ferocious, yet indecisive" conflicts of earlier years. The resultant suffering and starvation created conditions almost intolerable, and it mattered little that they could be attributed as much to the insurgent raids and depredations as to the Spanish Governor General Weyler's reconcentration policy, which herded the population into fortified towns. Inevitably the revolution caused loss of American lives and property as well as the ruin of our Cuban trade, amounting normally to nearly $100,000,000 a year. Inevitably, also, the juntas engineering the revolution made their headquarters in our coastal cities, and from these ports sent their filibustering expeditions to run men and arms to the island, though it is evidence of the good intentions of our government that out of 73 such expeditions in the years 1895–98, 33 were halted by our forces as compared with only five by Spain.

In view of the evil conditions in Cuba, even the anti-imperialist Cleveland, toward the close of his administration, had given warning that our respect for Spanish sovereignty might be "superseded by higher obligations, which we can hardly hesitate to recognize and discharge." President McKinley's subsequent offers of friendly intercession were declined. Indeed there appeared at the time no legal, peaceful solution of the problem which would not have left Cuba under Spanish rule, with the certainty of trouble later on. As admitted even by a severe critic of our Cuban policy, the war which followed "quickly ended the horrors and destitution of chronic insurrectionary hostilities and saved thereby the lives of hundreds of thousands, not only of Spanish soldiers, but of Cuban insurrectos and civilian population, men, women, and children It was in this sense a merciful war."[1]

Two developments early in 1898 made hostilities almost unavoidable. One was the publication in the *New York Journal* of a private letter written by the Spanish Ambassador at Washington, Dupuy de Lôme, in which he hinted at Spanish insincerity in certain recent trade concessions, and reflected also on President McKinley as "a small politician seeking the applause of the crowd." The Ambasador quickly resigned, forestalling an American demand for his recall.

Far more disastrous in its consequences was the sinking in Havana harbor of the American battleship *Maine*. At the suggestion of Consul General Lee, in view of disorders in Havana, the *Maine* had been held in readiness for sending thither, but her actual dispatch on Janu-

---

[1] S. F. Bemis, *A Diplomatic History of the United States,* p. 463.

ary 25 was without the Consul General's specific request and at a time which could hardly be regarded as opportune. Relations between Captain Sigsbee and the Spanish authorities nevertheless remained correct, if somewhat strained, and there was absolutely no forewarning of the terrific explosion, shortly before 10:00 o'clock on the night of February 15, which sank the warship with the loss of 266 of her 353 officers and men. The subsequent American naval court of inquiry declared the sinking due to "a heavy external explosion as by a mine, which drove the bowplates inward" and was followed by explosion of the forward magazines. This was further verified when the *Maine* was raised in 1911 and then sunk at sea. Neither at the time nor later was there the slightest clue to ultimate responsibility for the disaster, but the cry "Remember the *Maine*" echoed throughout the country and vastly increased the demand for the war.

Thereafter both nations, while continuing negotiations, hastened military preparations. In March the battleship *Oregon* began her famous cruise of nearly 15,000 miles from the West to the East Coast, a record engineering achievement completed in 66 days with an average speed at sea of 11.6 knots, and constituting at the same time a strong argument for an Isthmian canal. Congress appropriated $50,-000,000 for defense. In Spain the Liberal Ministry which had come into power in the preceding autumn realized the urgent necessity for concessions, and in early April indicated acceptance of practically all the American demands, including abandonment of reconcentration and proposals for an armistice with the insurgents.

But by this time the rebels would accept nothing short of freedom, and President McKinley had virtually given in to the popular clamor for intervention. His message of April 11, stressing the "cause of humanity" and the "constant menace to our peace," requested authorization to use the armed forces. It made only brief mention of Spanish concessions, of which he had received notice just the day before.

On April 19 Congress passed resolutions—311 to 6 in the House and 42 to 25 in the Senate—declaring Cuba free and independent, demanding the withdrawal of Spanish forces and authority, and directing the President "to use the entire land and naval forces . . . to carry these resolutions into effect." A fourth clause, the famous Teller Amendment, pledged the United States "to leave the government and control of the island to its people," thus expressing the unselfish sentiments which, whatever the later dreams of empire, swayed Congressional and popular feeling at the time. An American blockade of northern Cuba was proclaimed on the 22d, and on the 24th Spain declared a state of war.

Recognizing that the conflict would be primarily naval, hinging on control in the western Atlantic, foreign critics saw far less disparity between the fleets of the two antagonists than actual operations later revealed. They even prophesied "a long, desultory war," though Captain Mahan more accurately set its termination in "about three months." [2] The backbone of the American fleet consisted of the four new battleships *Iowa, Indiana, Massachusetts,* and *Oregon* of over 10,000 tons, the older *Texas,* and the two fast armored cruisers *Brooklyn* and *New York*. Against these Spain could oppose the four armored cruisers with which Admiral Cervera later crossed the Atlantic—the *Infanta Maria Teresa, Almirante Oquendo, Vizcaya,* each of about 7,000 tons, and the heavier, Italian-built *Cristóbal Colón,* which would have rated as a better ship than the *Brooklyn* if she had not had to sail without her two best 10-inch guns. Spain also had an older battleship *Pelayo* and another armored cruiser, neither of which was ready when the war began. In smaller cruisers the United States had an advantage of about 12 to 5 (actually available at the outbreak of war), and she had six double-turreted monitors which never proved of much value. In her 13 torpedo gunboats and destroyers, of which there were none in the American Navy, Spain possessed a possible menace, had these craft not been badly equipped and inexpertly handled. In fact no figures could reveal the corruption in supply service, the lack of training and engineering competence, the despondent inertia which, despite the high courage and devotion of its officers and men, vitiated the Spanish marine. Experience in later wars bore out Mahan's comment that we could not expect "ever again to have an enemy as inept as Spain."

Faults of equipment were matched by the pessimism of officers in command. From his squadron which had taken station in the Cape Verdes, Cervera deluged the Naval Ministry with complaints of the *Colón's* deficient armament, the bad boilers of the destroyers, the foulness of the *Vizcaya's* bottom which slowed her from 18 knots to less than 13, the lack of charts and lack of a plan of campaign. To this last reproach the Ministry made the extraordinary reply that "in these moments of an international crisis nothing can be formulated or decided." [3] "Nothing," declared Cervera, just before his departure,

[2] W. D. Puleston, *Life of Mahan,* p. 186.

[3] F. E. Chadwick, *Relations of the United States and Spain,* I, p. 108.

"can be expected . . . except the total destruction of the fleet or its hasty and demoralized return." On April 29 the Spanish squadron, comprised of the four cruisers already named and the destroyers *Pluton, Furor,* and *Terror,* sailed westward. The American consul cabled its departure, but during the ensuing 12 days, with no word of its whereabouts or destination, the American East Coast thrilled with the biggest war scare since the days of 1812.

THE PHILIPPINE CAMPAIGN

And within that same fortnight, the whole nation went wild over Dewey's victory at Manila Bay.

Probably most Americans of that period had only the vaguest notion of Spain's Pacific possessions. President McKinley himself acknowledged he could not have located the Philippines "within 1,000 miles." Fewer still dreamed that trouble with the Spanish would involve us in a Far Eastern campaign. But one official much alive to this possibility was the youthful and hotly belligerent Theodore Roosevelt, Assistant Secretary of the Navy under the staid and competent Secretary Long. Desiring Captain George Dewey for command of the Asiatic squadron, Roosevelt had induced the Captain to seek the influence of his home-state Senator in securing the assignment, and had pigeonholed a letter in favor of another candidate until Dewey's appointment went through. Then one February day when Secretary Long was absent from the office, Roosevelt, as the Secretary wrote in his diary, began issuing orders as if possessed by the "very devil." Among these was one to Dewey:

Keep full of coal. In the event of war your duty will be to see that the Spanish squadron does not leave the Asiatic coast, and then offensive operations in the Philippines.

Dewey needed little prompting. Before coming to the command he had read all the available literature on the Philippines and had seen to it that ample ammunition for his squadron was on its way. Prior to hostilities he moved the squadron to Hongkong, sold an old river gunboat, purchased two British supply ships, arranged to use the Chinese harbor of Mirs Bay where he would be less troubled by neutrality enforcement, and painted his white ships a war coat of slate-gray. Besides the *Baltimore,* which joined on April 22 with replenishment of ammunition, his force consisted of the flagship *Olympia* (5,870 tons), the smaller cruisers *Boston, Raleigh,* and *Concord,* the little gunboat *Petrel,* and the revenue cutter *McCulloch.*

On April 26 came this despatch:

War has commenced between the United States and Spain. Proceed at once to Philippine Islands. Commence operations at once, particularly against the Spanish fleet. You must capture vessels or destroy. Use utmost endeavors.

After awaiting the arrival of our consul from Manila with the latest news of conditions there, the squadron sailed on the 27th for the Philippines. During the two-day passage, furniture, wooden bulkheads, and other top hamper went overboard as a safeguard against fire. On the 30th, after vainly scouting Subic Bay, which the enemy fleet had left just the day before, Dewey assembled his captains and announced his intention to take the squadron that night into Manila Bay.

His decision was based on the belief that the entrance to the bay was too deep for mines and that "the more aggressive and prompt our action the smaller would be our losses." In fact Dewey's best claim to distinction lies in his thorough preparation, energetic action, and refusal to draw a false picture of the dangers he faced. A more cautious commander might well have hesitated to take his unarmored ships into a supposedly well fortified harbor, with no home base closer than 7,000 miles. It is significant that at this critical moment Dewey drew inspiration from his old leader Farragut, with whom he had fought years before on the Mississippi. In his *Autobiography* he wrote later:

Whenever I have been in a difficult situation, or in the midst of such a confusion of details that the simple and right thing to do seemed hazy, I have often asked myself, "What would Farragut do?" In the course of the preparations for Manila Bay I often asked myself this question, and I confess I was thinking of him that night when we entered the bay, and with the conviction that I was doing precisely what he would have done.

With the shores dimly outlined in the darkness, the fleet at midnight steamed through the wider Bocca Grande entrance. Sparks flew from the stack of the last ship, the *McCulloch,* and there were three shots from the 4.7-inch guns of the island fortress *El Fraile.* But the squadron was safely through, and slowed to four knots to arrive off

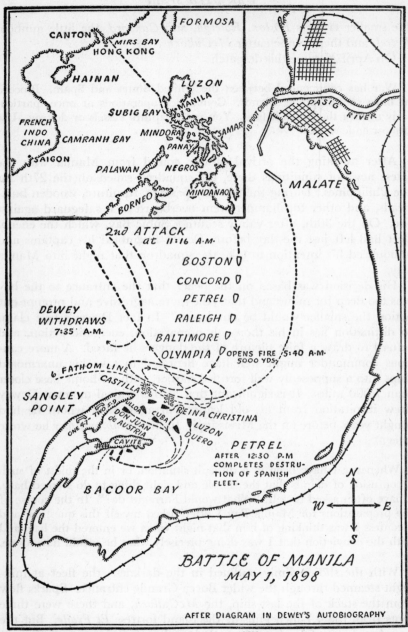

CANTON
MIRS BAY
HONG KONG
HAINAN
FORMOSA
FRENCH
INDO
CHINA
CAMRANH BAY
SAIGON
LUZON
MANILA
SUBIG BAY
MINDORA
PANAY
PALAWAN
NEGROS
BORNEO
MINDANAO
SAMAR

18 FOOT CHANNEL
PASIG RIVER
MALATE

2nd ATTACK
at 11:16 A.M.

BOSTON
CONCORD
PETREL
RALEIGH
BALTIMORE
OLYMPIA
OPENS FIRE 5:40 A.M.
5000 YDS.

DEWEY
WITHDRAWS
7:35 A.M.

6 FATHOM LINE
CASTILLA
2000 YDS.
4000 YDS.

SANGLEY
POINT
TWO 5.9
ULLOA
CUBA
DON JUAN
de AUSTRIA
ONE 4.7
CAVITE
LUZON
DUERO
REINA CHRISTINA

PETREL
AFTER 12:30 P.M.
COMPLETES DESTRUC-
TION OF SPANISH
FLEET.

BACOOR BAY

N
W   E
S

BATTLE OF MANILA
MAY 1, 1898

AFTER DIAGRAM IN DEWEY'S AUTOBIOGRAPHY

From *The United States Navy: A History* by Alden and Westcott.

Manila at dawn. Thus far resistance had been negligible. But there were 17 heavy guns guarding the entrance, six of which bore directly on the Bocca Grande. There were also launches and gunboats at Manila that might have been fitted out for torpedo attack. The ease of entry was due to the almost complete failure of the Spanish to utilize available means of defense.

As the spires and fortress walls of the city emerged through the five o'clock haze, the Spanish squadron was at first not in evidence, but was later seen drawn up some six miles to southward, between Sangley Point and Cavite Arsenal. Because of possible injury to the city, its commander, Admiral Montojo, had selected this position rather than a much stronger one directly under the Manila batteries. In the location chosen, guns of the Malata battery at Manila were in distant range of the American forces, and at least two 5.9-inch guns on Sangley Point bore more directly, but none of these had an effective part in the action.

The Spanish squadron itself was a motley collection of ships of all sizes in varying degrees of disrepair. The best were the flagship *Cristina* (3,500 tons), with six 6.3-inch guns, and the old wooden *Castilla,* moored and protected on her engaged side by sand bags and sand-filled lighters. The remaining five were small cruisers and gunboats of 1,100 to 500 tons, which proved little better than the auxiliary craft anchored further inshore. The Spanish mounted 31 guns (over 4-inch) afloat to the American 53, but they had nothing to match the combined battery of ten 8-inch guns in the *Olympia, Baltimore,* and *Boston.* Thus the ensuing fight, as described by the English historian H. W. Wilson in his *Downfall of Spain* (p. 152), became "a military execution rather than a real contest."

The well-known order, "You may fire when you are ready, Gridley," was given at 5:40 A.M. by the Commodore to his flagship captain when the leading ship *Olympia* had closed to about 5,000 yards. Thereafter, steaming at six knots close to the six-fathom line, the squadron, in the words of Dewey's report, "maintained a continuous and precise fire at ranges varying from 5,000 to 2,000 yards, countermarching in a line approximately parallel to that of the Spanish fleet. The enemy's fire was vigorous but generally ineffective. Three runs were made from the eastward and two from the westward, so that both broadsides were brought to bear." Early in the action the *Cristina* made a gallant advance as if to ram but was driven back under a heavy concentrated fire. Her magazines were flooded and the ship was afterward abandoned with a loss of over 200 killed and wounded. The *Castilla* was also abandoned and the fire of the little *Duero* was reduced to one gun.

The American squadron drew off at 7:35 A.M., partly because of a false report of ammunition shortage, and as the smoke cleared the damage to the enemy ships was more clearly revealed, some sunk and others on fire or retreating toward shore. The action was renewed shortly after 11:00 and ended an hour later with "every enemy ship sunk, burned, or deserted."

The Spanish loss was reported as 381 killed and wounded. The American ships were hit 15 times but suffered slight damage save from one 4.7-inch shell which exploded ammunition aboard the *Baltimore* and injured ten men. On threat of bombardment, the Manila authorities that afternoon agreed there should be no further firing from the shore and also promised surrender of the batteries at the entrance, which were dismantled two days later.

Though details reached this country slowly because of the cutting of the Manila cable, the full news of the victory aroused boundless enthusiasm. At Dewey's request troop transports with the cruiser *Charleston* were despatched from the West Coast, the *Charleston* on June 20 making the bloodless capture of Guam, whose governor had not yet been informed of the war. The monitors *Monterey* and *Monadnock* also labored slowly across the Pacific to reach Manila by mid-August.

Reinforcements were desirable, for Spain had scraped together the remnants of her navy, including the *Pelayo* and the armored cruiser *Carlos V*, to send to the Philippines under Admiral Camara. Camara, however, delayed at Suez and was recalled in early July, as a result of Washington's open mention of plans for a naval expedition to threaten the coast of Spain.

An even more serious problem was raised for Dewey by a concentration of no less than five German warships at Manila, with troops aboard, shortly after the battle. This was in a period, just after the seizure of Kiao-Chau in China, when Germany was eagerly seeking overseas expansion and ready to pick up scraps of the Spanish colonial empire, by purchase or otherwise, if opportunity arose. Through ignorance or for other motives, the German Vice-Admiral von Diederichs persistently disregarded Dewey's port regulations, landing troops for exercises, communicating with the Spanish, and even protesting when German ships were halted for identification on entering the harbor. To the officer who lodged this latter protest, Dewey declared warmly, as his words are commonly quoted, "If Germany wants war, all right, we are ready." British and Japanese ships in the harbor, following their national policies which preferred American to German occupation, supported Dewey's position; and later, at the time of an expected bombardment of Manila on August 9, some significance was rightly or wrongly attached to a movement by the British ships which placed them between the German and American squadrons.

At the final bombardment and occupation of Manila on August 13, Spanish resistance was by arrangement merely formal, to satisfy requirements of honor, and the chief problem of the American troops, now numbering nearly 11,000, was to keep the unruly insurgent army under Aguinaldo from getting into the city. Although the actual cession of the Philippines came later in the peace treaty, it was already fairly evident that the United States had gained a foothold in the Far East, and was to take over the rule of seven million Filipinos and the added problem of a lively insurrection, the suppression of which would extend over the next two years.

THE CUBAN CAMPAIGN

The panic fears aroused by Cervera's squadron, mentioned earlier, were in retrospect somewhat fantastic. The Admiral's sole hope was to get his ships safely to a Spanish West Indian port. His orders named San Juan, Puerto Rico, and only by stretching his coal supply could he have made even the briefest raid on American coasts or shipping on the way. Nevertheless guns were manned by Yale students on the Connecticut coast, the departure of New Hampshire militia from the state was halted, and Congressmen from seaboard states besieged the Navy Department with demands for protection. Clearly some form of press control, as well as popular education in naval problems, was desirable, for it was partly in response to popular pressure that our Atlantic forces were divided.

The "Flying Squadron" under Commodore Winfield S. Schley, including the flagship *Brooklyn,* battleships *Massachusetts* and *Texas,* and light cruiser *New Orleans,* was stationed at Norfolk, with a smaller patrol squadron, useless for defense or other purposes, guarding the coast from the Delaware Capes north. The bulk of the North Atlantic Fleet, including the flagship *New York* and the battleships *Iowa* and *Indiana,* was based at Key West. Rear Admiral Sicard, its commander, retired in March for physical disability and was succeeded by Captain William T. Sampson with the temporary rank of rear admiral. His promotion was clearly justified by his outstanding abilities and accomplishments in ordnance and all other developments of the new Navy, though some friction inevitably resulted from his advancement over seventeen officers senior on the Navy List.

A blockade of Havana and 100 miles of adjoining coast was established on April 22, but a bombardment of Havana, proposed by Sampson after careful study, was vetoed by the Department on the grounds that the enemy fleet was the primary objective and that our ships must not be risked against "strongly fortified ports" prior to establishment of sea control. At Washington, in recognition of the increasing need of sound central direction, an improvised "Strategy Board" was established, which included Admiral Sicard, Admiral Crowninshield in addition to his duties as Chief of the Bureau of Navigation, and, on May 9, after his return from Europe, Captain Mahan. For the brief duration of the war this board served reasonably well, though, aside from contacts of the civilian secretaries, no machinery was provided for joint planning and co-ordination of land and sea operations.

Eager for action, and convinced that Cervera's destination would be San Juan, Sampson on May 3, with the *New York, Indiana, Iowa,* and two monitors, lifted his guard on Havana and sailed for the Puerto Rican base. He was slowed down by the necessity of towing the monitors, and was eight days covering the 960 miles. At San Juan, there were no signs of Cervera. An hour's bombardment of the port next morning inflicted limited damage, and resulted in the loss of eight killed and wounded by hits from the guns on shore.

On this same morning, May 12, Washington received cables with the stirring news that Cervera had been sighted off Martinique, and that two of his destroyers had entered Fort de France the afternoon before. After a tedious crossing at an average speed of six to seven knots, the Spanish squadron had made its approach well to southward, thus avoiding the three American auxiliary cruisers, *Yale, Harvard,* and *St. Louis,* spread out as scouts to eastward of the Antilles. The entry of the *Pluton* and *Furor,* which sought news and applied vainly for coal for the squadron outside, was reported not only by the American consul but by officers of the *Harvard,* which had put in at the near-by Martinique port of St. Pierre.

At this time Washington had information, later proved erroneous, that Cervera carried essential munitions for Havana, and would try to reach either that port or Cienfuegos on the south coast of Cuba, connected with Havana by rail. From both these ports the two American

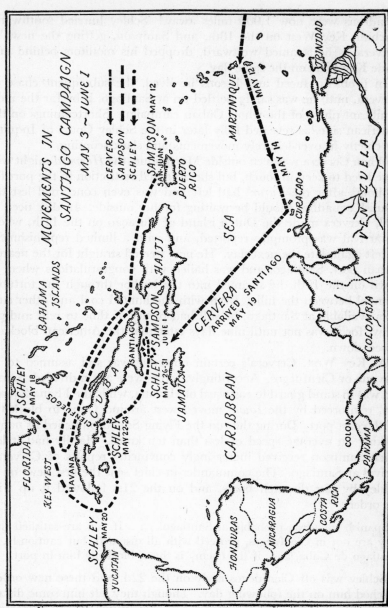

MOVEMENTS IN
SANTIAGO CAMPAIGN
MAY 3 ~ JUNE 1

CERVERA
SAMPSON
SCHLEY

TRINIDAD

MARTINIQUE
MAY 12

SAMPSON MAY 12

SAN JUAN
PUERTO
RICO

MAY 14

CURACAO

SEA

VENEZUELA

SAMPSON
MAY 19

HAITI

CERVERA
ARRIVED SANTIAGO
MAY 19

SCHLEY SAMPSON
JUNE 1
MAY 26-31

SANTIAGO

BAHAMA
ISLANDS

FLORIDA

SCHLEY
MAY 18

KEY WEST

HAVANA

SANTIAGO

C U B A

CIENFUEGOS

SCHLEY
MAY 22-24

SCHLEY
MAY 20

JAMAICA

CARIBBEAN

COLOMBIA

COLON
PANAMA

COSTA
RICA

NICARAGUA

HONDURAS

YUCATAN

From *The United States Navy: A History* by Alden and Westcott.

squadrons were now 1,000 miles away! Schley hurried southward, reaching Key West on the 18th, and Sampson, getting the news of Cervera as he steamed westward, dropped his monitors behind and made Key West on the same day.

In problems faced and lessons involved, the subsequent chase of Cervera, until he was safely bottled up at Santiago, is by far the most significant phase of the whole Cuban campaign. Shortcomings on the American side, as revealed fully later in the Schley Court of Inquiry, lay chiefly in over-leisurely movements and slack scouting.

When Cervera was seen outside Martinique, the *Harvard* might well have tried to keep in touch, but she accepted restriction in the port for 24 hours after the *Furor*[4] had left and was even concerned lest the Spanish squadron should be waiting for her outside. In dire need of coal, Cervera made the Dutch island of Curaçao on the 14th, where his arrival was promptly reported, and with a limited replenishment he left again late the next day. He now steered straight for the nearest Cuban port, Santiago, and was hailed with congratulations when, at dawn on the 19th, he steamed into the harbor through the tortuous channel between the hills. Even with the limited coal and other supplies available at Santiago, he still had plenty of time to refit and get away, for it was not until nine days later that the American blockade closed down.

At Key West, Cervera's certain objective was still assumed to be Havana or Cienfuegos. Accordingly, forces were again divided. Sampson was to stand guard to eastward of Havana, while the Flying Squadron, reinforced by the *Iowa*, moved west around Cuba to block the south coast port. During the run the Flying Squadron belied its name, making an average speed of less than ten knots. Hardly had it left when Sampson received increasingly convincing reports of Cervera's arrival at Santiago. The commander-in-chief sent the first news on to Schley by fast dispatch boats, and on the 21st followed it up with the order,

Spanish squadron probably at Santiago. . . . If you are satisfied that they are not in Cienfuegos, proceed with all dispatch, but cautiously, to Santiago de Cuba, and, if the enemy is there, blockade him in port.

Schley was off Cienfuegos early on the 22d, and these new orders reached him on the following day. Though they left him some discretion, neither at this time nor later did he show much energy in locating

---

[4] The *Terror* remained for repairs.

and pinning down the enemy. Low hills prevented a good view of Cienfuegos harbor, but the Commodore had seen smoke, and was at first convinced the Spanish were inside. Finally, after this was disproved by communications with the insurgents ashore (which should have been made two days sooner), he set out eastward on the evening of the 24th. In the prevailing heavy weather he kept for a while to the six-knot speed of the little gunboat *Eagle,* and it was not until the 26th that he completed the 315-mile run to Santiago. Still 20 miles distant, he made contact with three of our scout cruisers which had been near Santiago for several days but had still no positive evidence of the presence there of the Spanish squadron.

Schley, though he had a collier with him, was in constant worry over his coal supply and convinced that he could not coal at sea. That night came his extraordinary order to get under way, "destination Key West!" Fortunately, at this point the collier *Merrimac* had a chronic attack of engine trouble, delaying their departure, and next morning the *Harvard* came in with a sharp dispatch from Washington: "All Department's information indicates Spanish division still at Santiago. The Department looks to you to ascertain facts, and that the enemy, if therein, does not leave without a decisive action. . . ."

That afternoon Schley again got under way, sending by the *Harvard* a reply which read in part: "Much to be regretted, cannot obey orders of Department. Have striven earnestly; forced to proceed for coal to Key West by way of Yucatan Passage. . . ." Fortunately once more, the weather now cleared, and the squadron again halted, its commander considering that coaling at sea was now feasible, and considering also, no doubt, the consequences of a direct violation of orders. But it was not until the night of the 28th that his squadron actually took station off Santiago.[5]

Next morning the best of Cervera's ships, the *Cristóbal Colón,* was plainly to be seen, with awnings spread, lying athwart the entrance, where, as later ascertained, she had been anchored for the past four days. On the 31st, Schley shifted his flag to the *Massachusetts* and with the *Iowa* and cruiser *New Orleans* engaged the *Colón* and the shore defenses in a ten-minute bombardment at 7,000 yards, harmless

---

[5] Of Commodore Schley's movements up to this point Rear Admiral Sampson wrote, July 10, 1898, to the Secretary: "Had the commodore left his station at that time he probably would have been courtmartialed, so plain was his duty. . . . This reprehensible conduct I cannot separate from his subsequent conduct, and for this reason I ask you to do him ample justice on this occasion." (*Sampson-Schley Documents,* p. 236.) The later court of inquiry in 1899 pronounced Schley's service up to June as characterized by "vacillation, dilatoriness, and lack of enterprise."

to either side at that range. By June 1 Sampson was on the scene, and with the reinforcement of his own squadron quickly established a close blockade.

This blockade, as finally organized, consisted of an outer ring of battleships stationed three or four miles from the entrance, with cruisers and picket launches further in. At night the blockaders edged forward, and one of the battleships, still closer, kept its searchlight playing directly on the harbor mouth. In the month following there were frequent bombardments of the Morro and other shore defenses, and at night 200-lb. projectiles from the new-fangled pneumatic cannon of the gunboat *Vesuvius* dug deep dents in the hills. Coaling and other blockade operations were facilitated by the seizure of Guantanamo Bay, 37 miles to eastward, where Marines, landing on June 10, engaged in the first fighting on Cuban soil.

To prevent the escape of the Spanish squadron, in case a hurricane or other cause should force a temporary lifting of the blockade, Sampson early approved the project of sinking a hulk to block the channel into Santiago at its narrowest point. For this purpose Naval Constructor R. P. Hobson fitted out the old collier *Merrimac* and with a crew of seven picked men took her in on the night of June 3. A sharp fire from the batteries at the entrance carried away the *Merrimac's* steering gear, and as some of the powder charges intended to sink her failed to explode, she drifted beyond the point selected before going down and thus constituted only a minor obstacle. Hobson and his crew, escaping by a miracle, were picked up from a raft that morning by Admiral Cervera himself, who was out in a launch to investigate, and who courteously sent news of the rescue out to the American squadron under a flag of truce.

From the beginning, the danger from electric mines planted in the channel was regarded as an effective barrier to an American penetration into the harbor, since if a ship in mid-column were sunk, she would block those outside from those already in. In order to clear the passage, Sampson now called on Washington for an army force sufficient in strength to capture the Morro and other batteries at the entrance and thus permit sweeping up the mines. Eager for a share in the war, in which thus far the Navy had played a major role, the Army was quick to meet this call, and soon, in the steaming base at Tampa, already incredibly congested with troops and supplies, undertook to organize an expeditionary force of some 17,000 men. In 32 transports, with naval escort, the troops under General W. R. Shafter reached Santiago on June 20.

At this point occurred the only actual conference between the army and navy commanders which was to take place during the whole campaign. Though the objective of the operations was almost altogether naval—to get at Cervera's squadron, there was, it will be noted, no unity of direction and little or no co-ordination of the two commands. Shafter in this initial conference apparently fell in with the idea of capturing the isolated batteries at the harbor mouth, but all his later movements had the entirely different and much more difficult purpose of attacking the Spanish main forces and capturing the city itself, several miles distant at the head of the bay.

Though there were feints nearer the harbor mouth, the actual landing point was at Daiquiri, 16 miles to the eastward. The landings themselves, in the words of Lt. Col. Theodore Roosevelt who was there with his "Rough Riders," were handled "as we had done everything else—that is, in a scramble." As General Shafter later acknowledged, they could hardly have been accomplished at all but for the provision of 52 naval boats and steam launches and naval supervision under Captain Caspar F. Goodrich. Some 6,000 men were put ashore on the first day, the 22d, and the rest in four days following, despite the fact that the skippers of the chartered army transports insisted on keeping from two to five miles off shore.

In the subsequent arduous fighting at San Juan Hill and El Caney on July 1, the Army suffered heavy casualties, mounting to nearly ten per cent of the total force. General Shafter, who weighed over 300 pounds and was confined to his tent with the heat and illness, seriously considered "withdrawing about five miles," and now sent to the Navy an urgent call for help: "Terrible fight yesterday. . . . I urge that you make effort immediately to force the entrance to avoid future losses among my men. . . ." Thus the Army, which had been brought to Santiago to help solve a problem primarily naval, was placing itself in an opposite role.

It was in answer to this appeal that Sampson on Sunday, July 3, took his flagship some ten miles eastward of the entrance for a conference with the General on shore.

Fortunately at that very moment the difficulties of the Army and the problems of the Navy were both solved by an obliging foe. In the period preceding, Admiral Cervera had landed guns and men to support the defense of Santiago and had shown no intention of leaving port for a naval action, which he condemned as "a horrible and useless hecatomb . . . [of] lives sacrificed on the altar of vanity." But conditions of food and munitions supplies at Santiago were critical, and the fall of the city would mean the helpless surrender of the Spanish ships. From General Blanco, in authority though remote from the scene at Havana, came increasingly peremptory orders to quit the port. Thus, in obedience to higher command, the flagship *Maria Teresa* steamed out of the entrance that Sunday morning at 9:35, followed at about ten-minute intervals by the *Vizcaya, Colón,* and *Oquendo.*

By some American officers and neutral observers, it was held that Cervera would have fared better had he made a night exit, in which the resultant confusion would have enabled some at least of the Spanish ships to escape. But in Cervera's view this was rendered impossible by the blinding searchlights and the difficulties of navigation. For departure by day, this hot, quiet Sunday morning was a time well-chosen, for the *New York* was off station and the *Massachusetts* at Guantanamo for coal. The Spanish plan was to turn to starboard at the entrance, knock out if possible the fast *Brooklyn* on that side of the blockading line, and then break westward, with orders to each captain, as a last resort, to run his ship ashore.

As the *Teresa* emerged from the entrance and swung wide to starboard outside the Diamond shoal, the big blockaders almost simultaneously opened a hail of fire and pushed forward, lighting cold boilers and working frantically to get up steam. It was at this point that Schley's flagship the *Brooklyn,* with the *Teresa* heading toward her, swung away to open or perhaps to clear the range, and in doing so turned not to port but to starboard (see diagram of the battle), across the bow of the *Texas,* so that the latter had to back hard to prevent collision. During this period the *Teresa* suffered severely from the concentrated fire. In a few moments she was a mass of flames, hit 30 times, with her magazines flooded, her captain wounded, and most of her guns out of action. Shortly after 10:00 A.M. she ran ashore, about six miles west of the Morro.

The fire of the pursuers then centered on the last Spanish ship, the *Oquendo.* An American projectile detonated a 14-inch torpedo in her after compartment, which wrecked all that part of the ship. Burning fiercely, with only two 5.5 guns still firing, she ran ashore two miles further on. Under fire from the *Brooklyn* at 2,500 yards, the *Oregon* at 3,000 yards, and the *Texas* and *Iowa* at more distant ranges, the *Vizcaya* was the next to go. Like the other Spanish cruisers she suffered less from hits in vital parts than from flames which attacked the wooden decks and turned almost the whole ship into an inferno. In the words of one of the officers, "it seemed as if each shell

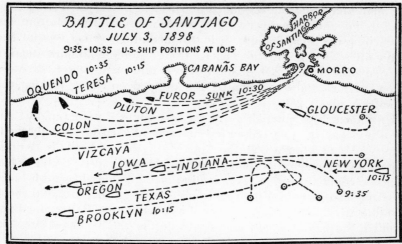

From *The United States Navy: A History* by Alden and Westcott.

started a new fire wherever it struck. Our men were driven from their guns by the rain of secondary battery projectiles, and by the flame and smoke of burning wood. . . . The decks and the joiner work in the officers' quarters and all along the berth-deck took fire." As she grounded shortly after 11:00 A.M. about 15 miles from the entrance, a great column of flames rose far above her stacks. Rescue boats sent in from the *Iowa* saw her captain lowered over the side in a chair, his body "covered with blood from three wounds."

By this time the *Colón*, steaming at better than 14 knots along the inner side of the line, was well out of range. Under pursuit by the *Brooklyn*, *Oregon*, and *Texas*, her speed slackened about noon and by 1:00 P.M. the *Oregon's* 13-inch shells at 9,000 yards were hitting near. A few minutes later, though scarcely damaged, the last Spanish cruiser hoisted the white flag and headed for shore. She had averaged 13.9 knots in her 55-mile run.

The destroyers *Pluton* and *Furor*, coming out astern of the cruisers, suffered from the secondary batteries of some of the American battleships and were hotly attacked by the converted yacht *Gloucester*, which dashed in to close range with her four 6-pounder and four 3-pounder quick-firing guns. Luckily she herself escaped a hit from either the destroyers or the shore batteries. The *Pluton* was struck by a 13-inch shell of the *Indiana* just as she ran on the rocks, and was almost broken in two. The *Furor* sank after surrender to the *Gloucester*, with a loss of 37 men. In the American squadron the total casualties were one man killed and one wounded aboard the *Brooklyn*. Perhaps the most daring and dangerous work of the Americans during the day was in rescuing the Spanish from their stranded and burning vessels, in a heavy surf, with the constant menace from explosions and fires nearing the magazines. Of 2,227 Spanish officers and men, over 1,800 were taken prisoner and an estimated 150 escaped on shore, making the actual loss about 260.

Until their ships suffered injury, the Spanish fired more rapidly than the Americans, but they scored few hits and inflicted surprisingly slight damage. As at Manila Bay, the American record of hits was also disappointingly low in proportion to ammunition expended. So far as hits could be counted from an examination of the battered Spanish hulls, the American guns of 4-inch and over scored 42 hits in 1,300 shots, or a little over three per cent. Even if as many more hits remained uncounted, the figures would abundantly justify the increased stress on gunnery practice which came in the post-war years.

With the destruction of the Spanish fleet the fighting on land lost much of its significance. In view of the food shortage, and after a long-range naval bombardment of the city, General Toral on July 14 consented to the surrender of his entire command in the Santiago area, numbering about 22,000, on pledge of their free transport to Spain. A week later the Spanish government initiated the first move toward peace negotiations, the protocol for which was signed on August 12. Meantime an expeditionary force under General Miles, with naval support, had landed on July 25 at Guanica on the southwest coast of Puerto Rico, and two days later at Ponce. Within the next fortnight a large part of the island was under American control.

In the final peace treaty signed at Paris in December Spain relinquished all title to Cuba, ceded Puerto Rico and Guam to the United States, and turned over also the Philippine Islands, receiving a payment of $20,000,000 in part compensation for public works and property. Most significant in the peace terms from the American standpoint were the new footholds afforded and the vastly increased responsibilities taken on in the eastern Pacific, and the strengthened means for defense of the Caribbean and the approaches to a projected Isthmian canal, a defense further aided by the grant from Cuba of a base at Guantanamo Bay. Our increased concern in the peace of the Pacific and Far East was undoubtedly welcomed by the British and by other colonial powers in that area, though at no later period was our policy backed up by the development of bases or other measures adequate to insure naval control.

☆   ☆   ☆   ☆   ☆

16

Geography and War Strategy

EDITOR'S NOTE: This and the two following chapters, dealing with certain general elements of naval strategy and logistics, are placed at this point because they apply with special emphasis to problems of twentieth-century warfare. The illustrative examples, it is believed, will be readily understood, even though they are drawn from periods both earlier and later than those covered thus far in the text.

INTRODUCTORY

ON FEBRUARY 13, 1935, General William Mitchell, testifying before the House Military Affairs Committee, said, "Alaska is the most central place in the world for aircraft. . . . He who holds Alaska will hold the world, and I think this is the most strategic place in the world. . . . If Japan seizes Alaska she can take New York. . . . They won't attack Panama." [1]

His warning went unheeded at the time. The air and other defenses of Alaska were not then enlarged as he advocated. But when the Japanese sent their major task force to Midway in June of 1942 and made a diversionary attack on Dutch Harbor at the same time, the American public overnight became aware of the strategic importance of Alaska and the Aleutian Islands. Fortunately for us, the Japanese were as ignorant of global geography as were we. Had they reversed the disposition of their task forces the whole course of the Pacific war might conceivably have been changed. Although we were belatedly

[1] *Chicago Herald-American,* August 2, 1942, pp. 1, 2, 6. Cited in Renner, *Global Geography,* p. 419.

rushing our Alaskan defenses in the spring of 1942, we were unprepared to stop a major assault there at the time of Midway. When that threat via the Aleutians had passed, we came to the realization that the Hawaiian Islands, long considered our first defense in the Pacific, might be regarded as a flank defense and not a main defense of our continent.

The Old Geography

The reasons for our misknowledge of geography are not hard to find. They lie in the methods of teaching by which generations of Americans have learned their geography. The older geography failed to develop that "geographic sense" which Napoleon described as the main prerequisite of strategy. We were taught to learn by rote the definitions of an isthmus and a peninsula, the names of the principal rivers of the world and even their lengths, the relative sizes of the continents, with perhaps a list of their principal products and manufactures. This method might give information; it did not make for understanding. The result was that we soon wearied of geography, and most of us forgot it as quickly as we could.

The fatal defect of this method of teaching geography was that it did not impress upon us that the world is round. "Never in all their history have men been able to conceive the world as one: a single sphere, a globe having the qualities of a globe, a round earth. . . ." [2] Rather, we have divided the world, in our minds, into continents and oceans and have lost sight of its oneness. If we are to acquire a proper geographic sense, if we are to understand the relations between geography and war strategy, we must learn to think literally in terms of the world as a *globe*. World War II, with its predominant emphasis upon air warfare, made this approach even more imperative.

We have not learned to think of the world in global terms because most of us have been brought up on the Mercator projection. It is generally known that the Mercator map distorts the globe; but the extent of the distortion is not so well known. On a Mercator map Greenland appears several times the size of Australia, whereas Australia is actually four times as large as Greenland. That the Afro-Eurasian continents are more than twice the size of North and South America combined is not apparent from a Mercator projection. For centuries the Mercator map with its distortions has colored man's thinking about

2 Archibald MacLeish, "The Image of Victory," in *Compass of the World: a Symposium of Political Geography,* p. 7.

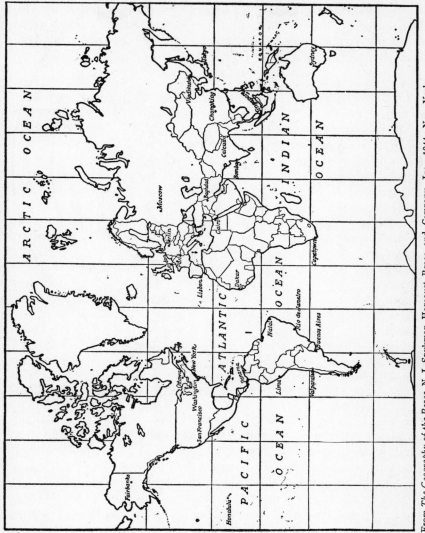

From *The Geography of the Peace*, N. J. Spykman, Harcourt, Brace and Company, Inc., 1944, New York.
MERCATOR PROJECTION MAP OF THE WORLD

From *The Geography of the Peace*, N. J. Spykman, Harcourt, Brace and Company, Inc., 1944.

POLAR-CENTERED AZIMUTHAL EQUIDISTANT MAP

the world. It has had its grip on the layman's study of geography, and until very recently has influenced the thinking of the professional military and naval strategists of all nations. Even Admiral Mahan, generally recognized by all writers on the subject as the first and foremost exponent of a global naval strategy, used only the Mercator projection for all the world maps in his books. And although the Germans have long led the world in cartographic excellence, their Mercatormindedness may account for some of their misconceptions regarding the relative strategic positions of the United States and Soviet Russia.

How misleading the Mercator projection is for a proper world view and for an understanding of war strategy may be illustrated by a few typical examples. No capital in Europe, not even Moscow, is as far from Chicago as is Buenos Aires. Salt Lake City is as close to Japan as Los Angeles. From San Francisco via Hawaii and the Philippines to Yokohama is 8,600 miles;[3] Seattle-Yokohama via Dutch Harbor is only 4,250 miles. Not many Americans realize that all of South America lies *east* of Savannah, Georgia. The significance of these facts for aerial warfare becomes strikingly apparent when it is recalled that Brigadier General Armstrong, Deputy Commander of the 20th Air Force, made a nonstop flight from Honshu to Washington, 6,540 air miles, in 27½ hours.

These are facts not revealed by the Mercator map. If we are to gain a true geographic perspective we must abandon our Mercator-mindedness. We must learn to use maps that teach us that the world is a globe, and that show the strategical importance of points upon the earth's surface for global warfare.

The New Geography

The conception of geography has been undergoing a profound change since World War I. A so-called new science of geography has been evolving. The Germans have a word for it—they call it *Geopolitik*.[4] In reality, *Geopolitik* is not a new term, nor is it exclusively a German product. The German geographer, Friedrich Ratzel, who lived and wrote between 1844 and 1904, has been called the "father of *Geopolitik*." But Kjellén and Mackinder, Swedish and English geographers respectively, have made valuable contributions to the study. Nevertheless, geopolitics went through an amazing development and transformation after World War I at the hands of German geographers, chief among them Professor Doctor Karl Haushofer, a Major General on the German General Staff. Yet it was only shortly before World War II that geopolitics made its appearance on the American horizon.[5]

After Germany was broken in 1918, Professor Haushofer sought to

---

[3] All distances are in nautical miles.

[4] *Geopolitik* has been defined as follows: "[It] is a political technique based on the findings of geography—in particular political geography—history, anthropology, geology, economics, sociology, psychology, and many other sciences which, combined, are able to explain a given political situation. These findings it 'activates'—it considers them as living dynamic forces out of which political developments evolve, and which, in turn, after careful analysis and evaluation, can be guided into definite directions." Andreas Dorpalen, *The World of General Haushofer: Geopolitics in Action*, p. 13 (New York, 1942.)

[5] Hans W. Weigert, *Generals and Geographers: The Twilight of Geopolitics*, p. 7. (New York: Oxford University Press. 1942.) See also Frederic Sondern, Jr., "The Thousand Scientists Behind Hitler," *Readers Digest*, June, 1941.

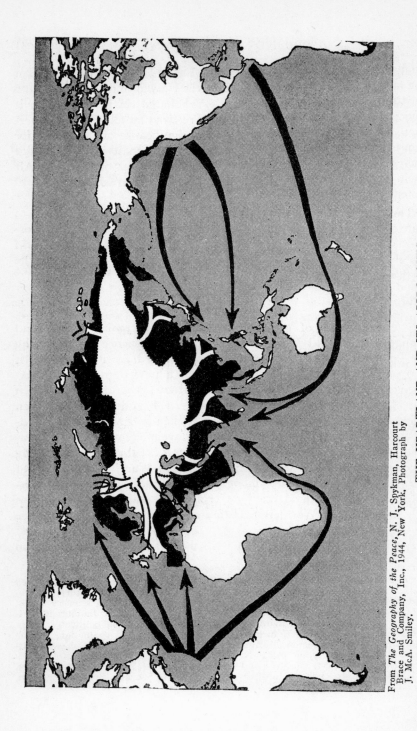

From *The Geography of the Peace*, N. J. Spykman, Harcourt
Brace and Company, Inc., 1944, New York, Photograph by
J. McA. Smiley.

THE HEARTLAND AND ITS APPROACHES

analyze the reasons for her defeat. The chief reason he believed to be the lack of awareness of the world political connotations of geography on the part of Germany's leaders. He then set out to overcome this deficiency. In 1922 he established the *Institut für Geopolitik* at Munich, and gathered about him an imposing array of geographers, economists and political scientists for the study of geopolitical problems and their relation to German war strategy. Beginning with the studies of their German predecessors in the field of political geography, Haushofer and his group also borrowed heavily from the Swede, Kjellén; the American, Mahan; and the Englishman, Mackinder.

From Mahan to Mackinder to Haushofer

The publication in 1890 of Alfred Thayer Mahan's *The Influence of Sea Power upon History, 1660–1783,* exerted a far-reaching effect upon the thinking of the naval powers of the world. Put briefly, Mahan's thesis was a restatement of the doctrine attributed to the Turkish leader at Prevesa, Barbarossa: "Sire, he who is master of the sea will very shortly become master on the land." Great Britain, Mahan believed, because of her insular position, and because of her control of the seas coupled with her outlying and easily defended bases, occupied a position of primacy in world power. Only the United States, because of her relative insularity by sea and her lack of a strong potential enemy on her borders, and with her own great internal resources, stood much chance of rivalling or succeeding Britain as the dominant world naval power.

Sir Halford J. Mackinder advanced a different thesis. In an article written in 1904, "The Geographic Pivot of History," and later, in a book published in 1919, he elaborated the view that "the facts of geography . . . the grouping of lands and seas, and of fertility and natural pathways, is such as to lend itself to the growth of empires and in the end to a simple world empire." [6] This world-empire he envisioned as located in what he called the Heartland of the World Island—the Triple Continent of Europe-Asia-Africa.

The World Island, Mackinder pointed out, is the only land mass bordered by all five oceans. Because of the vast area of the World Island, its Heartland is so situated as to be virtually inaccessible to sea power. The Western Hemisphere, England, Japan, and Australia are only smaller islands, lying on the periphery of the World Island.

[6] *Democratic Ideals and Reality,* p. 2. (New York: Henry Holt & Co., Reissue of 1942.)

Any great land power, bent on world conquest, by first controlling the Heartland would be in a position to bring the rimlands of the World Island into submission. By controlling the World Island such a nation could withstand any sea power or combination of sea powers that could be brought against it. With the resources of the World Island to draw upon, it could then develop such overwhelming naval strength as to conquer the sea power of the lesser, outlying islands. Mackinder epitomized these views as follows:

> Who rules East Europe commands the Heartland
> Who rules the Heartland commands the World-Island
> Who rules the World-Island commands the world.[7]

Mackinder wrote his book in 1919 as a warning to the victorious powers—a warning that Germany and Russia were so situated on the continent of Europe that, should a resurgent Germany conquer Russia and thus the Heartland, Germany would soon thereafter rule the world. Mackinder's warning, virtually unregarded by the English, made a deep impression upon Haushofer and his school of geopoliticians. Together with the theories of Mahan, Mackinder's work is the foundation of the modern *Geopolitik of* Haushofer. Under Haushofer, *Geopolitik* was elaborated and distorted into a pseudo-scientific philosophy of territorial expansion and world domination. Most of Hitler's ideas regarding *lebensraum* came from Haushofer.

Fortunately for the Allies, Hitler did not follow Haushofer's (and Mackinder's) blueprint for world conquest to the letter. Indeed, Hitler reversed the pattern and thereby made his fatal mistake. He did not conquer the Heartland of Russia first. Had he pushed on from Poland in 1939, meanwhile fighting a holding war in the West along the Maginot-Siegfried lines, the outcome of World War II might have been different. The Russian Army that fought the Germans in 1941 was an entirely different one from the Russian Army that fought the Finns in 1939; by attacking the rimlands first (Denmark, Norway, the Low Countries, and France), Germany gave the Russians precious time in which to overhaul their war machine and to exploit their war potential. History will probably record this deviation from the Mackinder-Haushofer strategy as Hitler's supreme blunder.

Haushofer, in line with the theories of Mahan and Mackinder, also advocated a strong navy. This policy likewise was not followed by

[7] *Op. cit.,* p. 150.

Hitler. In placing reliance on a lightning war on land, and in believing that the *Luftwaffe* could hold at bay the British Fleet, Hitler made a mistake similar to that made by the Germans in World War I—he demonstrated the truth of Admiral von Tirpitz' despairing cry, "The Germans do not understand the sea." [8]

The Importance of Geographic Study to the Naval Officer

The naval officer, no less than the statesman, must know the geographic facts of life if he is to become a master of his profession. The officers of all armies have long made the study of geography part of their professional training. This is but natural, since terrain plays such an important role in land warfare. The influence of geography has played a smaller part in the education of naval officers. It will be well to emphasize the importance of the study of geography to the naval officer, and how intimately connected it is with strategical and tactical naval operations.

An authority on military geography, writing in 1909, said,

In selecting a commander for a certain enterprise, it is no little recommendation that he should know the country . . . but no admiral would be selected because he knew a particular water, for the simple reason that fleets never engage but with ample room beneath their keels, and that it is no part of naval tactics to utilize shoals or rocks to the discomfiture of an opponent. . . .[9]

The history of naval warfare refutes this view. The Dutch admirals throughout three wars in the seventeenth century played tag with superior British fleets by taking advantage of the natural defenses afforded by their shoaling coasts. Nelson's foreknowledge of the shoal waters of Aboukir Bay enabled him to maneuver his fleet with confidence and precision to a smashing victory. Macdonough at Lake Champlain, on the other hand, in a very similar position to that of Brueys at Aboukir Bay, utilized his study of the position of Cumberland Head and of Crab Island, and his knowledge of the wind, to defeat the British.

Similar instances may be cited from World War II. One reason Admiral Helfrich of the Netherlands Navy was made commander of the Allied forces in the Western Pacific shortly after the outbreak of

---

[8] Admiral von Tirpitz, *My Memoirs,* Vol. II, p. 207.
[9] Brig. Gen. E. S. May, *Introduction to Military Geography,* pp. 5–6. (London, 1909.)

the war was his greater knowledge of the waters of the Dutch East Indies. Japanese superior knowledge of the waters of the Solomon Islands enabled them to navigate these waters freely at night, a feat which we at first believed improbable; the result was that on the second night of the invasion the Allies lost four cruisers and thereby imperiled the success of the Solomons Campaign. Had the landing at Okinawa been attempted at the southern tip of that island, the shoals and rocks there would have caused our amphibious operation to end in defeat and disaster.

Geopolitics may not be the "wave of the future," as some contend. But he who ignores the implications of politico-geography, be he statesman, professional naval officer, or plain citizen, will be lost in a world in which power politics and strategic security are based to a great extent on geography and natural resources. A knowledge of geography and an understanding of its politico-economic connotations for world peace and national security will be an important part of the mental equipment of the naval officer of the future.

It is the purpose of this and the two following chapters to inculcate a new "geographic sense" in the mind of the reader. Their aim is to impart a politico-geographic world view that will aid in comprehending history, past, present, and future, in terms of a *global* geography. By reference to specific examples the relation of geography to war strategy and to the military security of the United States will be emphasized.

THE GEOGRAPHIC FOUNDATIONS OF WAR STRATEGY

Geography has always played an important, if involuntary, role in warfare. For both strategy and tactics the earth interposes conditions which the commander must know and evaluate. Wars always have been, and always will be, fought in terms dictated by terrain, topography, space, climate, the relations of land and sea, and other earth conditions. Mountainous country held by a small force tends to offset the advantages that otherwise would accrue to a large attacking force. The nature of the coastline may prevent or facilitate the landing of an invading army. Natural defensive barriers, or their lack, go far toward determining the defensive and offensive potentialities of a nation.

During the centuries of recorded human history the physical facts of geography have remained substantially the same. But what man has done to, and upon, the earth, especially in the last century and a half, has greatly changed the strategical significance of geography to warfare. Inventions and discoveries have altered the relations between sea power and land power. The development of railways in the last century created a new threat to British sea power. The building of the Suez and Panama canals changed the geographic strategical positions of the British Empire, of the United States, and of the world. Motor transport and aviation in this century have wrought wholly new power-space relationships. A dozen minerals unknown or unused prior to 1900 have revolutionized ordnance and naval construction. Petroleum, first produced less than a century ago, proved perhaps the most decisive single economic resource in World War II. Jet propulsion, the rocket bomb, and atomic power will produce new strategic situations in the future.

The Physical Geography of Warfare

Physical geography must always form the basis of geography in general and of war strategy in particular. The basic factors of physical geography are location, or position, topography and other surface features, space, and climate. To these must be added the natural resources of the earth.

Location. The geographical position of a state determines its military security or insecurity in advance. Whether a state is insular, continental, or a combination of the two; whether it is bounded by few or by many other states, by large, powerful and aggressive nations or by small, weak and peace-loving ones; whether it possesses or lacks natural defensive boundaries: these, as well as other features of location, determine to some extent its ability to wage offensive or defensive warfare. Switzerland's interior position in the Alpine mountains and passes has long been an important factor in her military history. In World War II her position between Germany and Italy, controlling vital lines of communication between those Axis powers, kept her from being a possible battleground. The Low Countries, the "cockpit of Europe," have, on the other hand, been battlegrounds for centuries. It is interesting to speculate what might have been the military history of Great Britain had the coasts of Europe been bounded by the mountain ranges of our Pacific Coast states. The United States, because of her relative insularity and the presence of weak neighbors on her borders, has not been invaded for over a century.

Space. Mere space as such is a second geographic factor in warfare and in the security or insecurity of a nation. Large space favors the defense. If a country possesses a large area it may trade space for time, drawing the enemy deep into the interior where his lengthened

communication lines render him more vulnerable to counterattack
and to defeat. Furthermore, the conquest of space alone does not insure final victory; in a war against a country enjoying great spatial
advantages the destruction of her army must always be the paramount
objective. The Japanese spent eight years in China learning this lesson; Napoleon in 1812 and the Germans in 1943 learned it in Russia.
Small space, on the other hand, favors the aggressor. France furnishes
a good example. Because France's strategic industries, as well as her
capital, lie in a relatively small quadrilateral near her northeastern
frontiers, all that is necessary for an aggressor to subdue France is to
overrun this small area.

Space, or in this case more properly distance, is also important in
naval warfare. In World War II Britain had to let Singapore and her
possessions in the Far East go by default because it was simply too far
to send and maintain a large enough army. She nearly lost Egypt and
the Suez Canal because most of the supplies for Montgomery's army
had to be sent around Capetown, and the great distance presented an
almost insuperable difficulty until the Italian fleet was cleared from
the Mediterranean. The decision of the Allied High Command to
dispose of Germany before concentrating upon Japan was based in
part upon the fact that the Atlantic is much narrower than the Pacific.
And the vast reaches of the Pacific are such that our own supply problems were magnified as we got closer to Japan.

Topography. A third geographic factor in warfare is topography.
The impact of topography upon strategy has always been decisive in
land warfare. Flat country favors the offense, mountainous country
the defense. Large armies may be deployed upon the plain and battles
may be fought over a broad front. Mountain passes and peaks narrow
the points of engagement and tend to neutralize the superiority of sheer
numbers. The Germans were able to overrun Poland in six weeks
partly because the flat Polish plains are the ideal place in Europe for
mechanized *Blitzkrieg* tactics. Our armies in Italy, on the other hand,
failed to win a decision during almost three years of mountain warfare;
it was not until the mountain defenses of the Lombardy Plain were
breached that General Alexander's armies really began to roll.

Rivers and lakes likewise impose geographic considerations for strategy. They may or may not present defensive possibilities. The vast
network of the Mississippi-Tennessee river system enabled the Union
forces to penetrate deep into the heart of the Confederacy and to cut
off needed supplies from the trans-Mississippi basin. The Swedish geo-

politican, Kjellén, in his *Problem of the Three Rivers,* has pointed out how the military history of Central Europe has been inseparably tied up with the Rhine, the Danube, and the Vistula. Lake Champlain has twice proved a barrier to successful invasion from Canada.

An outstanding example of the disregard of topography was the British loss of Singapore. All of the defenses of Singapore were directed against sea-borne attack. The British mistakenly assumed that the jungles and swamps of the Malay Peninsula behind Singapore were impassable. The Japanese on the other hand realized that the island was vulnerable from the rear and secured it virtually without a struggle.

Climate. World War II, perhaps more than any previous one, demonstrated the importance of climate to warfare. "General Mud" aided the Russians against the Germans; but the lack of the usual autumn rains hastened the destruction of the Polish armies. The sirocco in North Africa immobilized both the British and Axis armies for long periods at a time. The fogs, cold, and heavy seas in the Aleutians affected alike our naval, air, and land operations. The monsoons in the Burma theater limited offensive operations to a few months of the year. The Germans are said to have feared the Russian cold more than Russian bullets; the cold destroyed more of Napoleon's Grande Armée than did the Russian guns. The scheduled landing in Normandy was delayed two days because of the weather; had it been delayed for very much longer the 70-mile-an-hour gales that swept the Channel at that time might have spelled the difference between success and failure. In the Battle for Leyte Gulf the carriers of the Seventh Fleet were unable to continue air operations after the Japanese cruiser line of the Imperial Second Fleet had come between them and the wind (see map, page 518). Six months later in the year the wind would have been inshore and our carriers might have turned *away from* the enemy cruisers in order to launch their planes. The wind, for the first time since the days of sail, has again become important as a determinant of naval strategy and tactics.

The Economic Geography of Warfare

In the twentieth century, the economics of war have played an even more important role than have the facts of physical geography. Major General J. F. C. Fuller, one of the foremost military writers of the world, in commenting on World War I, says: "The means of fighting were . . . revolutionary because, for the first time in the history of war, battles were as much tussles between competing factories as between contending armies. . . . God now marched with the biggest industries rather than with the biggest battalions. . . ."[1] And Hanson W. Baldwin, the military analyst of the New York *Times,* wrote of World War II:

> One major lesson—indeed, the major lesson—of this war is plain. . . . The war against Germany was won, the war against Japan is being won, because of the superiority of the industry of the United States. The industrial strength of America has been the dominating and decisive factor in this war. . . . This writer feels the war would have been lost had that industry failed in the tremendous demands put upon it.[11]

The economic geography of warfare is fundamentally a matter of natural resources and of the organization for putting those resources to military use. A country with relatively abundant natural resources has a much better chance of waging a successful and, if need be, long war than one not well endowed by nature. But no country is completely self-sufficient in war materials, as we learned when the Japanese seized the rubber of the East Indies. A developed economic organization and advanced technology are likewise important in utilizing available economic resources to their fullest; American "know how" is one of the chief weapons in our arsenal. Our combination of abundant raw materials and technical skill made it possible for us to produce toward the end of World War II as much steel in one month as Japan could produce in a year. This fact alone almost predetermined the outcome of the war with Japan.

The economics of war involves the employment of economic warfare against the enemy as well as the fullest utilization of available economic resources. The blockade is the foundation of all economic warfare. The Germans employed economic warfare at least to some degree in both World Wars. In their submarine campaign, however, the Germans in both wars were not successful in achieving the end-purpose of blockade—denial to the enemy of access to overseas foodstuffs and raw materials. England has long recognized the importance of effective blockade, against herself and against her enemies. Germany was almost literally starved out by the blockade in World War I, and starvation weakened the will of the German people to resist. Economic warfare utilizes other means in addition to the blockade at sea.

---

[10] *Army Ordnance,* June, 1945.
[11] *New York Times,* June 15. 1945. p. 3.

The United Nations, because of their greater financial strength and their ability actually to make payment, were able to make long-term contracts with certain countries for their entire output of strategic raw materials, thereby denying Germany access to those resources.

THE INFLUENCE OF GEOGRAPHY UPON NAVAL WARFARE

Admiral Mahan testifies to the value of historical illustration in the study of strategy. He also refers to the fact that the number of illustrations to be drawn from the history of land warfare is more extensive than those derived from naval warfare.[12] One reason for this obviously is that great battles have been fought again and again at the same points on land; less often have naval engagements taken place at the same spot upon the sea. Our primary interest here is with the influence of geography upon naval warfare; one example from the history of land warfare will therefore suffice.

Sedan in northeastern France has been a pathway of invasion and counter-invasion for centuries. Its location makes it the ideal invasion route between France and Germany. Situated in the valley of the Meuse River, it is also an important railroad junction. On the east it is flanked by the Ardennes Mountains with their heavy forests; on the west the terrain slopes gently down to the Straits of Dover. The Germans came through Sedan in 1870, in 1914, and in 1940. The famous Schlieffen Plan of World War I and its modified version in World War II utilized Sedan as a break-through and pivot point, with a wheeling movement to be executed over the lowlands to the Channel. When Pershing's army recaptured Sedan on November 7, 1918, the back of the German defenses was broken.

The Mediterranean Sea

The Mediterranean Sea, with its bordering lands, has been the seat of early as well as modern civilizations. Mahan wrote that it has "played a greater part in the history of the world, both in a commercial and a military point of view, than any other sheet of water of the same size."[13] Examples of its geographic influence may be drawn almost without number from the history of Mediterranean warfare.

Crete is the earliest example of an insular power exercising, by control of the sea, hegemony over nearby lands. Strategically situated to control the Eastern Mediterranean, on the basis of sea power Crete

[12] A. T. Mahan, *Naval Strategy*, pp. 9–13.
[13] *The Influence of Sea Power upon History, 1660–1783*, p. 33.

established and maintained a remarkable civilization that endured for centuries.[14] When her dominance on the sea declined, about 1400 B.C., the decay of Cretan civilization began. Crete's strategic situation was again emphasized in World War II. When the Germans took Crete by air-borne invasion in 1941, they denied the British the use of the excellent naval base at Suda Bay, stood athwart their lines of communication to Alexandria and Port Said, and posed the constant threat of air-borne invasion to Egypt.

The Battle of Salamis (480 B.C.) has its chief importance, from the standpoint of strategy, in its demonstration of the vital role of logistics in warfare. For the first time in history it showed how sea power, by severing the enemy's lines of communications and of supply, could defeat an overwhelming land power. When Xerxes' fleet was destroyed his armies were cut off from their means of retreat and from supplies, and were easily defeated the next summer at Plataea. A similar example of the same principle is afforded by the disaster that befell the Saracen fleet before Byzantium (Constantinople) in 718 A.D. In perhaps the most overwhelming defeat in all naval warfare, it is said that of an original fleet of 1,800 vessels only five reached Syria; because of this loss of its means of transport, of an army estimated at 180,000 only one-sixth survived the retreat to their homeland.

The three Punic Wars between Rome and Carthage were fought over a period of 123 years (264 B.C.-141 B.C.) They illustrate that when two nations are fairly evenly matched in both land and sea power, victory is difficult of attainment. At the outset, Carthage, because of her longer maritime history, had the greater sea power but lacked sufficient striking power on land; the Romans possessed larger armies but did not have the sea power to bring that superiority to bear. It was not until Rome had built up sufficient sea power to land her troops on the African shores that Cato's dictum, "Carthage must be destroyed," could be carried out.

The discovery of America was not in any sense a battle. It was nevertheless a turning point in the maritime history of the Mediterranean, of naval warfare, and of the world. The Commercial Revolu-

---

[14] Aristotle recognized the strategic geographical position of Crete. "Crete," he says, "appears to have been designed by nature for dominion over Greece, and to be well situated; it extends right across the sea, round which almost all the Greeks are settled. And while one end is not far from the Peloponnese, the other almost reaches to the region of Asia around Triopium and Rhodes. Hence Minos won the empire of the sea, and subdued some of the islands and settled colonies in others. . . ." *Politics*, Vol. II, p. 10.

tion of the sixteenth century opened up new trade routes, shifted the center of gravity of the commercial world from the Mediterranean to the Atlantic, marked the rise of the modern national state on the coasts of Europe, and in England created a new dominant sea power that was destined to rule the waves for centuries. The campaign of the Armada (1588), although fought between Spain and England in the Atlantic, indirectly sealed the doom of the maritime supremacy of Venice. It is interesting to recall that the victory at Lepanto (1573) was won by Venice and her allies only 15 years before the date of the Armada; although it checked the final attempt of the Turks to control the Mediterranean, it was a short-lived victory, because a new sea power had arisen in the West.

In modern times, Nelson was almost obsessed with the strategical importance of the Mediterranean. Who ruled the Mediterranean, he believed, held the key to Europe. Much of the admiral's career was spent in the Mediterranean, and many of his battles were fought in or near the approaches to that inland sea. Winston Churchill, like Nelson, also insisted upon the key position of the Mediterranean in the control of Europe and in safeguarding the Empire. The strategy of the Gallipoli campaign, fostered by Churchill when he was First Lord of the Admiralty in World War I, was based on these beliefs; in World War II he long preferred an attack on the "soft under-belly of Europe" to a cross-channel invasion.

The Atlantic Ocean

Illustrations of the geographic influence of the Atlantic Ocean may also be drawn from the history of naval warfare in that body of water. The Armada was the first outstanding example of an insular power defeating a combined land-and-sea power by sea power alone. Spain's superiority in land power went for naught because she did not command the sea. Against the Dutch in the seventeenth century the British Fleet again defeated a combined land and sea power; and it foiled Napoleon's invasion schemes in 1804-05. By their command of the sea the British, on the other hand, were enabled to land and to maintain for eight years Wellington's Peninsular Army in Spain, thus getting at the French through the back door and thereby eventually encompassing Napoleon's defeat.

But, as seen in American history, even a momentary lapse from command of the sea was to prove determinative in the War of the American Revolution. The Battle of the Virginia Capes sealed the doom of Cornwallis' army at Yorktown, a victory which led to the ultimate triumph of the colonies.

The British acquired the Falkland Islands in 1832. Not until 1914 were they called upon to make use of this strategic outpost. When the need arose, a squadron of battle cruisers was despatched in pursuit of Admiral von Spee with an established base from which to operate. The British in this instance were also favored by the fact that von Spee misconceived the function of his cruisers—in risking an attack upon the Falklands he did not utilize to the fullest the great value his cruisers might have rendered as commerce raiders. His defeat at the Falklands thus removed their nuisance value in tying up units of the British fleet in pursuit.

Jutland was a turning point in the war at sea in World War I. Volumes have been written about the meaning of Jutland. But if it may be said that the Germans won a tactical victory at Jutland, it remains equally clear that the British won the far more important strategic victory. Although Germany retained a sizable fleet in being after Jutland, the High Sea Fleet never again ventured to contest Britain's mastery of the sea.

The winning of the Battle of the Atlantic in World War II was one of the decisive factors in Germany's defeat. In failing to cut Britain's Atlantic life line by an all-out effort during the year following the fall of France, Hitler lost his last chance of bringing the war to a speedy conclusion. The Battle of the Atlantic, it should also be emphasized, was not merely a struggle upon the high seas; it was fought as well in the shipyards of the United States, again illustrating the vital role that economic resources play in modern warfare.

The Pacific Ocean

The sheer magnitude of the Pacific Ocean serves to point up the meaning of global warfare. In the Pacific, space or distance is as much a military phenomenon as it is on land.

In the Russo-Japanese War, that Rojdestvensky had to bring his Baltic Fleet over 18,000 miles to the point of engagement bore importantly on Togo's victory. Geography favored the Japanese in another respect. With three narrow straits—the Straits of Tsushima, Tsugaru Strait, and Soya Strait—barring his access to the Sea of Japan and Vladivostok, Rojdestvensky virtually had to fight on Togo's terms. Togo's defensive position was greatly strengthened because he could wait for Rojdestvensky to come to him; the element of surprise was denied to the Russians.

Few Americans had heard of the Solomon Islands before August, 1942. Fewer still were aware of their strategic value to Japan and to the United States. Our sea lanes to Australia had already been pushed far to the south by the loss of the British-owned Gilbert Islands. This life line was then protected on its northern flank only by New Caledonia (French), with its excellent harbor at Noumea. If the Japanese took the Solomons, New Caledonia would be threatened; if New Caledonia were lost, 1,500 miles would have been added to our supply line to Australia and we should have been deprived of the advantage of an advanced naval base at Noumea. If the Japanese, in turn, were to protect their own flank in their southward thrust toward Australia, it was just as imperative for them that they secure the Solomons before we did. It is no wonder that the Solomons campaign was a bloody and costly affair on both sides.

When the German possessions in the Pacific (the Caroline, Marshall, and Mariana islands) were mandated to Japan after World War I, the Japanese set out secretly and in violation of their mandate to fortify these strategically placed islands. Truk Island they made into a Japanese Pearl Harbor. We knew almost nothing of the defenses of Truk when war came. It was believed to be virtually impregnable. A frontal assault upon Truk promised at least to be a costly and long drawn out struggle. But the geography of the Pacific dictated a shorter and more direct route to the homeland of Japan—up the ladder of the Gilberts, the Marshalls, the Marianas, and the Bonin Islands. Truk was by-passed and neutralized. The Japanese fleet had to be withdrawn from Truk and stationed closer to home waters. Our leap-frog strategy, by taking advantage of the geography of the Pacific islands, thus brought us closer to Japan with less effort and in a much shorter time than if we had first attempted the reduction of Truk.

☆　　　☆　　　☆　　　☆　　　☆

17

Geography and Logistics

T̲HE SCIENCE OF WAR breaks down into three major compartments, each of which is subdivided into many minor ones. The major divisions are strategy, tactics, and logistics.

Strategy and tactics have long been familiar words in military terminology. The term logistics, on the other hand, came into widespread usage only during World War II. Despite the fact that the word is derived from the French (*logistique*), and although Napoleon gave classic expression to its meaning when he said "an army marches on its stomach," Napoleon himself never used the word logistics. Eight of the United States Navy's nine bureaus are directly or indirectly connected with problems of logistics, yet it was not until 1943 that a separate division of overall logistical planning was set up under the Vice Chief of Naval Operations.

Stated briefly, logistics is the science of transporting, supplying, and maintaining military strength in all its branches. A more comprehensive definition was provided by Secretary of the Navy Forrestal:[1]

Logistics is the process of providing what is needed when it is needed where it is needed. It embraces the supply and distribution of men and material. It involves forecasting requirements. It is the scheduling, production, assembly, storage, distribution, maintenance, repair, and replenishment of equipment. It is the procurement, training, billeting, feeding, distribution, staging, hospitalization, replenishment, and rehabilitation of personnel.

Logistics is used by writers on military subjects more or less inter-

[1] *Annual Report of the Secretary of the Navy, 1944,* p. 8.

changeably with the terms "communications" [2] and "supply," and will be so used here. Mahan throughout his writings prefers communications and supply rather than logistics; only once does he use the latter term logistics. Communications in Mahan's system refers to the "lines of movement between the force and its sources of supply." When we heard "too little and too late" applied to British efforts early in World War II it meant that their system of communications was not functioning properly; when we read that "our forces are advancing" we knew that the United States Army Service Forces were doing their part in rendering strategy and tactics effective—the logistics problems were being solved.

THE IMPORTANCE OF LOGISTICS IN GLOBAL WARFARE

The measure of success in modern war is the degree of co-ordination between Army, Navy, and Air Force, and this will depend finally upon the supremely important factor of supply. As the equipment of armies has increased in size and importance and as the battlefields have been enlarged to include the whole world, logistics has become the most vital problem in warfare. Admiral King said of World War II,[3] "The war has been variously termed a war of production and a war of machines. Whatever else it is, so far as the United States is concerned, it is a war of logistics." If one is to understand modern global warfare, he must have an appreciation of the importance of logistics.

Since about the turn of the century, writers on the science of war have emphasized the role of supply. "Communications dominate war," wrote Mahan; they "are the most important single element in strategy, political or military." The "eminence of sea power" lies "in its control over them. The power, therefore, to insure these communications to one's self, and interrupt them for an adversary, affects the very roots of a nation's vigor. . . . This is the prerogative of the sea powers; and this chiefly—if not, indeed, this alone—they have to set off against the disadvantage of position and of numbers. . . ."[4] Brevet Lt. Colonel G. C. Shaw, one of the few military authorities to devote an entire book to the subject, says that logistics "forms the basis

---

[2] Communications in this sense is not to be confused with the term Naval Communications, embracing the transmission of orders and information by visual signaling, voice telephone, radio, teletype machine, etc.; rather it is used in its military sense of "a system of routes for moving supplies, troops, etc., in military operations."

[3] First Official Report to the Secretary of the Navy, 1944, p. 22.

[4] Naval Strategy, p. 165; Problems of Asia, p. 124 ff; Influence of Sea Power upon the French Revolution and Empire, I, pp. 95–96, 184 and II, p. 106.

on which rests the whole structure of war; it is the very foundation of
tactics and strategy."[5]

Logistics has proved an important factor of success in battle since
early times. Alexander the Great was a master of logistics. He was
one of the first commanders to perfect a workable system of supply. In
the course of his campaigns his army marched a total distance of over
20,000 miles. Considering the crude means of transport and of supply
at the time, this ranks as one of the epoch-making feats in the annals
of war. Caesar's conquests likewise were logistic trumphs. He built up
the Roman fleet to insure his overseas communications; he recon-
structed the Roman ports and built new ones; he created the first
military highway system in the world; he established a commissary
system and set up granaries extending from Rome to the North Sea
so that his legionaries could be supplied by land or by sea.

Secretary Forrestal in his report for 1944 recognized the increasing
importance of logistics in modern war. He also emphasized the necessity for preserving an adequate logistical organization during peacetime. "The answer to this question," he said, "will modify the course
of study at the Naval Academy and the standards by which an officer's
qualifications for command are measured. . . . It is imperative that
the Navy in peace continue a first-rate logistical organization in which
men will be trained from the time they enter the Naval Academy."[6]

MAGNITUDE OF THE LOGISTICS PROBLEM

Two world wars have demonstrated that twentieth-century warfare
is a titanic struggle between opposing supply systems. The increase in
the magnitude of the supply problem in World War II over World
War I was an outstanding difference between them.

The flow of men and materials from the United States "arsenal of
democracy" had to be projected 3,000 miles across one ocean and
7,000 miles across another. The overseas communications of the
United Nations in World War II covered the globe and extended over
56,000 miles. The Naval Air Transport Service flew routes stretching
over 80,000 miles, covering three quarters of the earth. We delivered
to our Allies Lend-Lease equipment and materials having a value
greater than the total cost of World War I to the United States. The
great land campaigns of North Africa, Western Europe, and Russia,
despite the scale on which they were fought, were dwarfed by com-

[5] *Supply in Modern War,* p. 26. (London: Faber & Faber, Ltd. 1938.)
[6] *Annual Report,* 1944, p. 11.

parison with the war at sea. The Pacific Ocean alone covers 64,000,-000 square miles, an area 21 times that of the United States.

There had to be transported in World War II five times the equipment shipped per soldier in World War I. Twelve tons of supplies and equipment were landed for every soldier sent overseas; another ton was sent him each month in food, clothing, and ammunition. In the first ten days of the Okinawa campaign more than half a million tons were landed on the beaches—beaches where no landing facilities had existed before. The increase in firepower made possible by the Garand rifle, the tommy-gun, and antiaircraft weapons multiplied ammunition tonnage many fold. The Navy maintained a network of more than 700 depots and stations in which were kept stocks of over 4,000,-000 kinds of items. The Army Air Force alone kept in stock and regularly supplied to its units over 500,000 separate items of equipment and spare parts.

Lieut. Gen. Brehon B. Somervell described the Army Service Forces, the logistics branch of the Army, as "the biggest business in history, the most widespread, geographically. It employs more people, owns more land, spends more money, handles more merchandise than any other organization the world has ever known. . . . If all the land we have bought for camps and fields and target ranges and other installations were lumped, it would cover more than half of England."[7] Of a total of 6,500,000 men in the United States Army on June 15, 1943, more than 1,700,000 were Army Service Forces troops; an additional million civilians were employed in organizations directly under control of the Army Service Forces; one out of five of our armed forces overseas was in the services of supply. The Navy's Seabees, who proved to be one of our most potent "secret weapons" in the battle of supply, numbered at their peak more than the total enlisted personnel of the navy in June of 1941.

THE GEOGRAPHICAL FOUNDATIONS OF LOGISTICS

No branch of warfare, strategy and tactics not excepted, is more dependent upon geographical factors than logistics. Unless those in charge of logistical operations have a thorough comprehension of geographical concepts, the operations of military forces in the field will be hampered.

The initial scheduling of requirements and the procurement of sup-

---

[7] "The United States Army Services of Supply," in *Proceedings of the Academy of Political Science,* January, 1943, p. 61.

plies and equipment must take geographic factors into account at the outset. Different types and qualities of equipment are required for operations in Germany and North Africa, in Alaska and the South Pacific. Should our requirements schedule for the Pacific theater have called for deliveries from West Coast producers or from the Atlantic seaboard? If from the Atlantic, should the goods have gone by railroad across the Continent or by ship through the Panama Canal? Should we have built new factories here, or there? Such geographical considerations determined our building new steel plants in Utah and in California, nearer to the Pacific Coast shipyards.

The production of munitions of war is again a question of geography. The raw materials of war come from diverse parts of the globe —no country is self-sufficient either in war or in peace. The raw-material producing areas may be owned by the enemy or may be dominated by them, necessitating resort to alternative but poorer sources of supply or to the creation of substitutes. Should we draw upon sources that are closer, safer, but perhaps more expensive, or should we go to more distant countries where the initial cost may be lower but the goods must pass over enemy-menaced waters? These are questions of geography that must be decided by those in charge of logistical planning.

The movement of forces and supplies from the home front to advanced bases and staging areas, the moving and supplying of fleets and armies within and between battle areas, and the actual waging of campaigns are all governed almost entirely by geographical factors. War is movement all the way, and since movement is always dependent upon the properties of the earth's surface, logistics is therefore in the highest degree an affair of geography. This is especially true when sea powers, or combined land-and-sea powers, are arrayed against each other. Then distance becomes an even more controlling factor than in land warfare. When the whole face of the globe is the battlefield, the geographical character of logistical planning is clearly evident.

It will be useful to refer to a few specific campaigns to demonstrate the influence of geographic patterns upon logistical procedures. One illustration is drawn from ancient times, two from World War II.

In the Battle of Actium (31 B.C.), Octavius Caesar utilized the facts of geography to his own advantage and to the discomfiture of Mark Antony. With his navy in control of the Adriatic, Octavius could bring up his supplies across the narrow waters between the heel of Italy and Greece. Antony's communications stretched across the Mediterranean from Egypt; with his fleet bottled up in the Ambracian Gulf and his supply ships unable to break through the Roman blockade, the goods brought from Egypt had to be transported from Aegean ports over the wretched roads of mountainous Greece. When starvation-induced desertions depleted his crews and his garrisons, he was finally forced into a naval battle to try to make good his escape to Egypt. The geography of logistics caused Antony's defeat as much as the defection of Cleopatra's reserve squadron.

No more perfect examples of the influence of geography upon logistics exist than the campaigns in North Africa between the British and the Axis powers. Land, sea, and climate all contributed to the complexity of the logistics problems on both sides and also controlled the actual conduct of operations. The desert to the south rendered any large-scale encircling movement by either side impracticable; the combatants were limited to fighting back and forth along the narrow African coast, much as two professional fencers advance and retreat upon their strip. Because the Royal Navy did not at the time have mastery of the Mediterranean and because the Axis thereby occupied the interior position, the Eighth Army was at a disadvantage in the supply race. Matériel from the factories of Britain and America had to make the long journey around the Cape of Good Hope and up the Red Sea to Cairo, whereas Axis supplies had only to run the gauntlet of the Mediterranean narrows. The heat of the desert and the absence of adequate sources of supply created a monumental difficulty in the provisioning of water alone.

The campaign, or series of campaigns, swung back and forth like a pendulum for almost three years before either side could win the decision. Three times the Axis, first under Graziani and twice under Rommel, drove the British back; thrice the British launched counteroffensives. Prior to Montgomery's final successful assault neither army could advance beyond the limit of its inelastic supply lines. The attack stalled in each instance not because of the superiority of the defense but because the offense was unable to bring up supplies sufficient to maintain the momentum of the attack. And as the defense retired, its logistical position was automatically improved by the shortening of its lines of communication. Victory came finally for Montgomery only after he was able to build up matériel and supplies that would insure carrying him well beyond El Agheila, the farthest point of advance in the two previous British thrusts. His victorious sweep from El Alamein to Tunis, a total distance of 1,300 miles, was the longest sus-

tained drive in military history. The key to his success lay in his con-
quering the logistical problems set by geography.

Two and a half years elapsed after we entered the war before the
Allies could mount an offensive in Western Europe. For over two years
the Russians had clamored for a second front in the West. Our logistics
difficulties were so great, however, that they militated against an early
landing on the European coast. Our supply problems were doubly
complicated over those of World War I. We did not possess Continental ports in France, as in the earlier war; all of our troops, equipment,
and supplies had first to be shipped to the British Isles and then trans-
shipped across the Channel and landed on hostile shores. The "most
spectacular logistical achievement of this war" in overcoming the difficulties of geography was, according to Admiral King, the creation of
artificial harbors on the beaches during the Normandy landings.[8]
Secondly, the U-boat menace was greater than in World War I. The
Battle of the Atlantic had first to be won; supplies with the proper
margin of safety had to be built up in England before the landing
operations could be undertaken, and the U-boats throughout 1942 and
well into 1943 were taking a steadily mounting toll of precious ships
and even more precious cargoes. Until we overcame the submarine
threat we could not hope to launch and maintain an overseas invasion.

LOGISTICS AND STRATEGY

Logistics governs strategy at every turn. It is generally believed
that if our battle fleet had not sustained its damages at Pearl Harbor
we could have immediately assumed the offensive. Admiral King is
authority for the statement, however, that "Had we not suffered those
losses . . . our fleet could not have proceeded to Manila as many
people supposed and there relieved our hard pressed forces. Such
an undertaking, with the means at hand to carry it out *and support it,*
would have been disastrous."[9] Here we see geography governing
logistics, and logistics, in turn, determining strategy. Our logistical
position even more than the paralyzing blow against the bulk of our
Pacific fleet dictated our going on the defensive. It was with full
recognition of these logistical implications of strategy that Japan at the
very outset struck first at our fleet in the Harbor, then assailed outlying
bases beyond Hawaii and, by occupying those bases, made certain no
American fleet could engage in a grand-scale counteroffensive in the

[8] *Second Official Report to the Secretary of the Navy,* 1945, p. 45.
[9] *Our Navy At War: Official Report,* 1944, p. 24. Italics supplied.

Western Pacific unless the old bases were regained or new ones acquired.

The British High Command, forced in 1941 to choose between concentrating its scant available forces in the Middle East or in the Far East, decided to risk losing Singapore, Australia, and even India rather than take a chance on losing Egypt and the Suez, with their control of the oil fields of Mesopotamia, Iraq, and Iran. The region between the Eastern Mediterranean, the Red Sea, and the Persian Gulf has been described by Sir Halford J. Mackinder as the "geographical pivot of history." It is the bridge between Europe and Asia. He who holds this territory has a tight grip on the Eastern Hemisphere and conceivably upon the world. The British began the war in possession of this area and needed only to hold it. But to win, the Axis had to conquer this key region. The High Command's strategy to protect its Middle East position was almost entirely a logistical decision. The armies of the Middle East could be supplied, if only after a fashion; because of the distances involved and the lack of shipping space the forces in the Far East could not.

The United Nations' grand strategy to defeat Germany before concentrating upon Japan again turned upon logistics. The sea lanes across the Pacific are more than twice as long as the Atlantic routes. Our principal manufacturing centers are closer to Europe. We did not have in the Pacific a forward staging area at all comparable to the British Isles; the Asiatic coast was effectively closed to us. All of the logistical considerations resolved themselves in favor of an assault upon *Festung Europa* first.

The Borneo campaign illustrates the influence of logistics upon strategy in still another way. Borneo, the third largest island in the world, lies athwart what East Indian lines of communication then remained to the Japanese and therefore had strategic importance because of its central position; but Borneo lies away from, not toward the main objective of Japan, the Japanese had relatively few troops in the Indies, and since we controlled the Philippine and the South China seas, Japan was unable to exploit the resources of the Dutch East Indies. The key to the decision to recapture Borneo was oil. Borneo in Allied hands would be of great strategic value from the standpoint of oil alone. The wells of Balikpapan yield petroleum so pure that it can be used directly in ships' engines without refining. It was estimated at the time that Borneo's oil production, if restored to normal, could supply half the fuel needs of our Pacific Fleet. The recapture of the oil fields

of Borneo relieved the strain on our domestic oil resources and also
effected savings in time and in tanker space in fueling the fleet.

LOGISTICS AND TRANSPORT

The logistics of global warfare places a high premium upon transportation. The fact that the United States is in the most favored position production-wise is not enough. All of our production superiority
would go for naught unless supplies could be funneled through advanced communications zones and into the actual combat zones.
Without shipping sufficient to transport the greatly increased quantity
and complexity of equipment used in modern war, naval power can
be used only negatively.

In normal times our transport facilities, both land and sea, are adequate for our needs. In wartime, however, transportation is one of the
chief bottlenecks of the war effort and it is a major problem of logistics to overcome this difficulty. In most of the wars of the past there
has usually been only one major theater of operations (or at best two),
necessitating an open communications zone only for that theater.
Toward the end of World War II we had eight major fronts with perhaps an added dozen combat zones scattered all over the globe. This
first of total wars required transport facilities far in excess of any previous war. The speed and volume of movement required at critical
stages of a war make transport in many ways one of the supreme factors of victory. Lack of adequate transport in emergencies has many
times led to the defeat of well-trained, able armies, strategically disposed and capably led.

Means of transport from the most primitive to the most advanced
were pressed into the service of transport logistics in World War II.
Human porters, pack animals, dog sleds, horses and wagons, and the
cargo airplane all found their uses. The principal means of modern
transport, however, are motor trucks, railroads, steamships, and airplanes. Without these four means of locomotion war on a modern
scale would be utterly impossible. Of these four, the ocean-going
steamship is by far the cheapest and most efficient mode of transport;
the same number of tons that can be transported 500 miles by railroad
can be shipped for the same cost 5,000 miles by boat. The lowly tramp
steamer is a key weapon in the battle of transportation.

The dramatic achievements of the Army's Air Transport Command
and the Navy's Air Transport Service in moving strategic materials and
men in World War II caused over-enthusiastic supporters of airpower

to exaggerate the relative importance of the airplane as a cargo carrier. The limiting factor in air freighters is their fuel capacity in relation to their effective payload. A ton of fuel has to be sent by sea to enable cargo planes to deliver one ton of freight by air for even relatively short flights; a cargo vessel can carry enough fuel in its hold to get its load to its destination abroad and return home. The following theoretical calculation provides a comparison between movement of freight by air and by surface vessels. "Let us suppose that our problem is to move 100,000 long tons of supplies per month under present wartime conditions from San Francisco to Australia, a distance of approximately 6,500 nautical miles. How many planes of existing 4-engine cargo type will it take? How many cargo vessels? How much personnel? Will we need tankers? And so forth. The following simple comparison will give these answers."[10]

	Number	Crews	Fuel	Tankers
Surface Vessels ..... (EC Type)	44	3,200 (includes gun crews)	165,000 barrels	0
Cargo Planes .... (4-Engine C-87 Type)	10,022	120,765 (flight crews only)	8,996,600 barrels (overseas requirements)	85 (large size)

LOGISTICS AND COMBINED OPERATIONS

The science of logistics has reached its highest state of development in this age of amphibious warfare. The fundamental principles of strategy and tactics have changed but little over the centuries. Prior to World War II, technological developments in armaments always outstripped the technology of logistics. In the global warfare of the 1940's, however, logistics donned seven-league boots; the innovations in this field were as remarkable as those in armaments. The German invasion of Norway was the first great combined operation in modern warfare; it was as nothing, however, compared to our amphibious landings in the Pacific, where the great distances imposed the necessity of creating wholly new tools and techniques of warfare.

The technological innovations in our combined operations in the

[10] Assistant Secretary of War for Air Robert A. Lovett, "Airplanes for Men and Freight in Wartime," *Proceedings of the Academy of Political Science,* January, 1943, p. 40.

Pacific had no parallel in military history. New logistical measures of naval power were established, rendering traditional standards obsolete. The elements of which global warfare are compounded released American genius upon the logistical problems that confronted us, with results that astonished the world. Experts may argue whether the LCI or the LST was the greatest weapon of the war: the "alligator," the "duck," the "jeep" carrier, and the "bulldozer" in the hands of our Seabees, all shared their glory. As of July 1, 1945, the United States Navy had on hand a total of over 100,000 craft of all types. Of this number only 1,322 were combatant ships; the remainder were the supply ships, tenders, oilers, repair ships, ammunition ships, hospital ships, and transports that go to make up the fleet train, now called by the Navy the Service Force. The Service Force engaged in logistical support of the fighting fleet during World War II at distances and for periods of time formerly believed impossible. The Service Force maintained the fleet as much as 5,000 miles from a permanent base and was, according to Admiral Nimitz, "our greatest secret weapon."

From Pearl Harbor to control of the Marshalls required 26 months. Fourteen months later we had landed on Okinawa. This latter amphibious leap of over 3,000 miles was made possible by the Service Force that supplied our Fast Carrier Task Forces at sea. The Fast Carrier Task Force that struck out from the Marshalls in February, 1944, had not returned to a permanent base at war's end. The Service Force is a task force in itself, carrying with it its own surface screen and air cover. It is thus able to insure that no matter how long the fighting ships are at sea nor how great their expenditure of planes, ammunition, and fuel, they shall be able to stand to the attack with human endurance as their only limit. Some of the ships of the carrier task force that stood off Okinawa were in action for more than 60 days. Fleet support at sea for almost unlimited periods was the unique contribution of the United States Navy to the amphibious warfare of World War II.

The essence of combined operations overseas is timing. Proper timing requires meticulous planning to get the right number of the right men and ships to the right place with the right equipment at the right time. Some idea of the complexity of the logistical problem in amphibious operations may be gained from the Okinawa campaign.

For the Okinawa and related operations the planning started last September. . . . Exclusive of landing craft, some 1,400 ships took part at

Okinawa. Ships travel at different speeds. LST's cannot make much more than eight or nine knots; LSD's, 11 or 12; and attack transports, 15. Units moved from all areas of the Pacific. The northern attack group at Okinawa trained and staged and rehearsed in the Guadalcanal area. The southern attack group left from Leyte. The floating reserve staged from the Marianas and from Espiritu Santo in the New Hebrides. General Buckner's Tenth Army headquarters and service units embarked at Pearl Harbor, and certain garrison elements staged from the West Coast. All had to have surface screens and air cover. Some units had to be serviced on the way out; some had to be combat-loaded in forward anchorages. All had to arrive at a pin point on the charts after steaming anywhere from 1,200 to 8,000 miles. And they did.[11]

SUMMARY

Logistics, the supplying, transporting, and maintaining of military forces, occupies a role co-ordinate with strategy and tactics in the art of warfare. It has played its part in all the great wars in history, and the great military leaders of all times have been masters of logistics. Never was the part played by logistics so decisive as in World War II, for never before had war been fought on a truly world-wide battlefield. Successfully to cope with the problems of logistics, members of the supply force must have a sound understanding of geography. Logistical considerations underlie all decisions of strategy; they are equally important in land and naval warfare. In the combined amphibious operations of World War II the United States Navy brought its logistical organization to the highest state of perfection ever realized by any navy of the world. The aspiring naval officer of the future will have to be as well grounded in the study of logistics as he must be in geography.

---

[11] *Fortune* Magazine, July, 1945, p. 248.

18

Sea Power, Life Lines, and Bases

THE ACTIVE COMPONENTS of sea power are (1) combatant ships, (2) the auxiliary craft that comprise the fleet train or the service force, and (3) the merchant marine. Underlying and supporting these positive instruments of sea power are those elements of national wealth which combine to make up a nation's military potential—natural resources, manpower, industrial organization, financial resources, the state of technology, and the morale of the people. The geographic factors of location or position, the length and nature of the coastlines, the sea lanes that connect a nation with the trade centers of the world, and the bases that flank and guard these sea communications are still a third basic feature of sea power. Of these geographic factors, it is the sea life lines and bases that will concern us here. Certain other geographic factors have already been discussed in Chapter 16.

There is a popular tendency to confuse "sea power" with "fleet strength," and even further to measure comparative naval power only in terms of capital ships.[1] Capital ships alone are no more a measure of fleet strength than is the total number of fighting ships a true index of sea power. The service force is as much a part of a battle fleet as the fighting ships. As pointed out in a preceding chapter, our Navy as of July 1, 1945 had only 1,322 combatant ships out of a total of over 100,000 craft of all types. To look at it another way: at the end of World War I the Royal Navy had 444 destroyers in commission; it entered World War II with 184 destroyers in commission. It is needless to say how much difference 260 additional destroyers would have made in the defense against German U-boats. Our transfer of 50 over-

---

[1] Witness the 5-5-3-1.75-1.75 ratios, applied only to capital ships, in the Five-Power Naval Treaty of 1922.

age destroyers may have enhanced British fleet strength by more than
the addition of five battleships. World War II again demonstrated the
recognized rule of sea warfare that, at least after a point has been
reached, comparative naval strength becomes more a matter of multi-
plication than of addition; a superiority of eight to four is greater
tactically than six to three, simply because there are more total ships
available.[2]

The third major element of sea power, in addition to combatant
ships and the service force, is an adequate merchant marine. Although
not widely appreciated as such, the merchant marine is in many respects one of the most important components of sea power. "Men
live by exchanging," said Adam Smith, the father of political economy;
and maritime nations literally live by overseas trade. The whole history of sea power bears this out. The great maritime nations of all
ages—from Crete, Phoenicia, Greece, and Rome to Venice, England,
the United States, and Japan—have also been the great naval powers
of their time, and the strength of their merchant marine has been one
of the measures of their naval might. No naval power can long exist
without a steady flow of exports and imports. There is no instance in
military history of a maritime nation having won a war with its overseas trade cut off. Unless there is sufficient domestically-owned shipping to transport troops and supplies to the theaters of action, naval
power is nullified; reliance cannot be placed upon neutral shipping in
time of war. Twice in a generation we have engaged in a feverish
merchant-shipbuilding effort, and the winning of the battle of the shipyards contributed in no small measure to the winning of World War II.
Admiral Nimitz points out, on the other hand, that the pre-war Japanese merchant fleet of 8,250,000 tons was cut down by the end of the
war to about 750,000 tons, of which only about half could operate.[3]

The Functions of Sea Power: Command of the Sea

Broadly speaking, sea power has two major functions, which may be
classified as offensive and defensive. On the defensive side they include
the protection of one's own seaborne commerce and the prevention of
enemy invasion. Offensive functions include denying the use of the sea
to the enemy, transport and support of one's own overseas invasion
forces, and naval (and air) bombardment of enemy coastal installa-

[2] *New York Times,* October 8, 1945, p. 14.
[3] *New York Times,* October 7, 1945, p. 1.

tions.[4] The successful execution of all of these functions depends upon *command of the sea.*

The first aim of naval warfare, then, must always be to secure and to exercise command of the sea. Naval wars are not won exclusively by destroying the enemy's battle fleet—its annihilation is only a step in securing more complete command of the sea. The purpose of securing command of the sea is to control seaborne communications, both military and commercial. In its military aspect command of the sea connotes the ability to move men, supplies, and equipment into advanced bases, the supply of ships while they are at sea, the neutralization or destruction of enemy fleets and positions, and the furnishing of close cover for landing operations. Command of the sea also means freedom of movement of a nation's ocean-borne commerce and denial of that freedom to the enemy's merchant fleet. Naval power is worthless, or relatively worthless, unless it can protect the sea lanes over which travels the commerce that is vital to the nation's existence. Indeed, most authorities insist that this is the chief funcion of a navy— the *raison d'être* of sea power, the ultimate test by which command of the sea is to be judged.[5] As is well known, the first act of hostility in naval warfare is often directed against the enemy's merchant marine. A German U-boat sank the British merchant liner *Athenia* on the day England entered World War II, and our Navy's Communique No. 11, dated December 18, 1941, announced the sinking of a Japanese cargo vessel by one of our submarines.

Command of the sea, it should be noted, is a relative concept and not an absolute one. Rarely if ever in the history of naval warfare, even in such narrow seas as the Baltic, the North Sea, and the Mediterranean, has there been such a thing as undivided command of the sea; it may be general or local, temporary or relatively permanent, but it is almost never complete. What is important is that command be

---

[4] Bombardment of coastal objectives by ships of the fleet is as a rule an incidental use of sea power, but its importance at times is not to be disregarded. The British Navy during the Napoleonic wars repeatedly directed naval artillery against the coasts of France and Spain. Winston Churchill on February 22, 1944, announced that the Royal Navy had engaged in 716 separate coastal bombardments in the preceding year. In the month of July, 1945, Admiral Halsey's Third Fleet roamed at will off the shores of Japan and bombarded her "sacred soil" for days on end.

[5] Mahan in his earlier writing stated that "the necessity of a navy springs from the existence of a peaceful shipping." Cf. Corbett, *Some Principles of Maritime Strategy*, p. 143: ". . . over and above the duty of winning battles, fleets are charged with the duty of protecting commerce"; and Brodie, *A Guide to Naval Strategy*, p. 139: "There is really only one kind of command—the kind that enables one side or the other to control the movement of merchant ships."

established and maintained in the areas of chief importance. Even in those instances where the enemy's fleet has been swept from the seas altogether, so long as there remains to him "a fleet in being," even if bottled up in harbor, it cannot be said that the command is not in dispute. A fleet in being constitutes a potential threat which may contest command of the sea at any time it is believed the benefits may outweigh the risks involved. Although the United States and British navies held virtual command in the Atlantic and the Mediterranean in the later years of World War II, still their command was not absolute. The Germans and the Italians possessed sizable surface fleets and U-boats were operating off the American coast at V-E day.

THE STRATEGIC GEOGRAPHY OF LIFE LINES AND BASES

Foregoing paragraphs have discussed briefly the active ingredients of sea power together with some of the functions of sea power. The remainder of the chapter will be devoted to those two important geographic foundations of sea power, life lines and bases.

The term life line is not new. It has long been applied to Britain's Mediterranean-Suez route to India and the Far East. The need for a similar life line of our own across the Isthmus of Panama was dramatically emphasized in the Spanish-American War when it was necessary to send the *Oregon* from San Francisco around Cape Horn to Cuba. In World War II, however, the term took on a new and wider meaning for us; we learned that we have many life lines other than the Panama Canal. The sea lanes of the world link our nation with all the continents and with the great centers of world trade. They are the greatest highways of world commerce during peacetime; in war, they become veritable "life lines of victory." Inward along these routes pass materials vital to our industrial production; outward move the agricultural and manufactured products of the country in peace, and the troops, munitions, and supplies required in war. Whichever nation secures and maintains these life lines during wartime is in a fair way to attain ultimate victory; whichever loses control of its own vital sea communications has already taken a long step toward ultimate defeat.

It is in this matter of sea communications that the sea powers differ fundamentally from the land powers. In peace, the sea lanes of the world are open to all nations that possess even the semblance of a merchant marine. But both in peace and in war the ocean routes are vital to sea powers to a much greater degree than they are to land powers. Land powers may draw upon their hinterland, or upon contiguous or nearby countries, for foodstuffs and the raw materials of war, and may in some cases be able to wage war for years without access to the sea. France fought on under Napoleon for almost 22 years in the face of a virtual blockade. Japan choked off Chinese shipping, yet China held out against Japan from 1937 to 1945. Probably the outstanding example in recent military history is the Boer War; with no merchant shipping and with no outlet to the sea, the Boers nevertheless stood off the might of British arms for three long years.

In the matter of military operations the land powers are also less dependent upon the sea than are the naval powers. Land powers can carry out their concentrations of troops and can supply their armies by road and by rail relatively free from interference. In the closing months of the European war, even in the face of overwhelming Allied air superiority, General von Rundstedt was nevertheless able to mass his troops along his own interior lines of communications for the last big German offensive known as the Battle of the Bulge. For the sea powers, however, the oceans themselves must serve as the avenues for the deployment and concentration of their forces, and overseas troops must continuously be supplied by the same life lines.

The defense of a nation's life lines is conditioned principally by three factors: (1) the distances between the home ports and the overseas centers of trade or the overseas theaters of operations, (2) the number and position upon these routes of suitable and defensible naval bases, and (3) the number and location relative to (1) and (2) of enemy, or potential enemy, bases. The defense of these life lines requires a great number of strategically situated bases and fueling stations. The number, size, and defensive strength of these outlying bastions of sea power give range and mobility to the battle fleet. No nation can aspire to be a great sea power without adequate and properly situated bases. The long sway of British sea power in the nineteenth century rested as much upon her far-flung naval bases as upon the number of her warships. The mere possession of these bases, however, is not enough. They must be developed commensurately with their strategic location. The function of bases is to support the fleet, not the reverse. If the bases cannot defend themselves they lose their strategic value, for if the fleet has to be used to safeguard the bases then the fleet loses its value as an instrument of offensive warfare. When we lost Guam, Wake, and Manila Bay, and when the British and Dutch lost Singapore and Hong Kong, Soerabaja and Amboina, the range of operations of the Allies' fleets was thereby severely delimited. In consequence we were forced to go on the defensive in the Pacific. It was not until we had seized and secured new bases, notably Guadalcanal, Kwajalein, Tarawa, and Salamaua, that we could assume large-scale offensive operations.

Limitations of space necessarily preclude a complete description of all the naval bases of the world. Great Britain and the United States in 1946 were the only truly great naval powers. Their trade is also more world-wide in scope than that of other maritime nations, with sea communications extending over ocean routes whose combined length aggregates more than 80,000 miles. The Axis nations—Germany, Japan, and Italy—are no longer major naval powers. It is unlikely that they again will be allowed to build a fleet in the foreseeable future, their merchant marine is virtually destroyed, and it is probable that they will be stripped of their naval bases by the peace treaties. France may wish to rebuild her fleet, and Russia has given indications of wishing to become a great naval power; but the bases now owned by France and Russia have significance chiefly for their own home defense. It would appear, therefore, that the United States and Great Britain will own or control for a long time to come most of the major naval bases of the world. By limiting our survey of bases to those of the two greatest sea powers a sufficiently comprehensive coverage of the world's naval bases will be afforded for our purposes. The strategic geography of bases in relation to sea power and to command of the sea will thus be illustrated.

THE GEOGRAPHIC FOUNDATIONS OF BRITISH SEA POWER

British sea power in the nineteenth century is the classic example of the influence of geography upon sea power. Because of special and peculiar geographical conditions, Great Britain in that century arrived at a global command of the sea that has not been equalled before or since. By the end of the century she had become the first true world naval power in history; she was literally "Mistress of the Seas." So extensive was England's command of the sea between 1815 and 1914 and so far-reaching England's political and economic influence that historians have come to call that era the *Pax Britannica*—the British peace. This *Pax Britannica* was based upon a conjuncture of geographical, technological, economic, and political conditions unique in history. An analysis of the anatomy of British sea power will therefore be useful in revealing the pre-eminent part geography played in the rise and dominance of the Royal Navy's world-wide command of the sea.

The geographical location of Great Britain is the keystone of her naval strength. The discovery of America had revolutionized the geographical position of the British Isles. The opening of the new trade routes during the Commercial Revolution of the sixteenth century profoundly altered Britain's geographical importance, not only in regard to the New World but in relation to the Continent as well. From a spot on the fringe of the then known world Britain was shifted to a strategic power position almost at the exact center[6] of the new world of trade, a position from which by reason of geography she was enabled to exercise control over oceanic commerce.

Situated approximately midway between North Cape and Gibraltar, the British Isles are in what amounts to a central position vis-a-vis the nations of northern and western Europe. The ocean commerce of all northern and western Europe has to pass through narrow seas dominated by the Royal Navy. Northwestern Europe's overseas trade, as well as much of its coastal traffic, has either to go through Dover Strait and the Channel or undertake the longer and more difficult route to the north of Scotland. The naval base at Scapa Flow fronts the Skagerrack, within easy striking distance of the exit from the Baltic; the North Sea bottleneck between Scapa Flow and the Norwegian coast is only 200 miles wide. By concentrating superior forces in home waters, England is able to control the oceanic supply lines to and from the northern and western coasts of Europe. By employing the same strategy she is also able to prevent the junction of enemy forces that any coalition of northern and western naval powers can bring against her.

Geography also secures Britain's defensive position. Commanded by the Royal Navy, the narrow seas fronting directly upon Europe can be utilized offensively, thus realizing the ancient maxim that "the best defense is a good offense." The reaches of the Atlantic protect her rear; the same squadrons that control the exits from the inner seas are favorably situated to command the sea approaches from the north, west, and south.

---

[6] "A globe will show one outstanding fact about Great Britain. That is the sea centrality of these islands. It is upon this fact that we have been able to build up an Empire whose political and commercial dominion is world-wide. The island of England 'lies wholly in the sea and yet at the precise center of all the land of the earth. No other spot upon the globe either fulfils or can ever be made to fulfil these two conditions. Turn the globe as you will, contrive and consider as you please—in the end the hard geographical fact will remain that England, alone of all the communities of men, has the sea centrality of the world.' " A. G. Boycott, *The Elements of Imperial Defence,* p. 307.

In the course of the eighteenth and nineteenth centuries England also secured command of the southern portals of Europe. Gibraltar, acquired in 1704, dominates the western exit from the Mediterranean. The Suez Canal, completed in 1869, controls the eastern exit into the Red Sea. Malta, obtained during the Napoleonic wars, is strategically situated near the Sicilian narrows between the eastern and western Mediterranean basins. All commerce from this great inland sea, including even the hinterland of the Black Sea, must move through bottlenecks under the guns of the British fleet. The inner life line to India and the Far East is further protected by a naval station at Aden (1839), near the Red Sea exit into the Indian Ocean. Great Britain thus has a stranglehold on the four narrow seas—the English Channel, the North Sea, the Mediterranean, and the Red Sea—which constitute Europe's gateways to the outside world.

To almost the same degree, British sea power in the nineteenth century extended to the coasts of the Americas, commanded all the approaches to the Indian Ocean, and from colonies and bases in the Pacific was in a position to move at will over even that vast waterway. Admiral Lord Fisher once declared that "Five keys lock up the world." These he named as Dover Strait, the Strait of Gibraltar, the Suez Canal, the Cape of Good Hope sea passage, and Malacca Strait (Singapore). To these may be added the Panama Canal and the Straits of Magellan. Taken together they control the lines of communication that interconnect the great oceans of the world. During the course of the long war with Spain toward the end of the sixteenth century, the British Navy fought with only one of these keys, the Strait of Dover, in its control. By the end of the nineteenth century all but one—Panama—had passed into the hands of the British, and remained there as late as 1941. At or near these strategic passageways Britain possessed naval stations of great defensive strength as well as offensive potentialities. By controlling the bottlenecks through which seaborne commerce had to pass between the great centers of world trade, England could thus control the larger ocean areas of the world. In addition, a multitude of minor naval bases and fueling stations dotted the globe.

England's central position thus gave her command of all the ocean portals of Europe and her global network of bases gave her undisputed, if not incontestable, control of the sea lanes throughout the nineteenth century. No matter in what ocean they operated or over what route they travelled, British warships and British merchantmen were never very far from a British naval base. Out of the raw materials of geography Britain's Admiralty and her empire builders had fashioned the most comprehensive global command of the sea in history.

British Naval Bases in the Atlantic

After this brief survey of the broad geographical foundations of British sea power, we turn now to a more detailed description of her chief naval bases, beginning with the Atlantic ocean.

The Atlantic Ocean is roughly an S-shaped sea, covering approximately one-sixth of the surface of the globe, comprised of three main subdivisions—the North Atlantic, the Caribbean, and the South Atlantic. From the standpoint of commerce it is the greatest ocean highway of the world. In peacetime, approximately 75 per cent of all seaborne traffic moves over the Atlantic sea lanes. This is readily accounted for by the fact that the Atlantic lies between the two greatest industrialized areas of the world, Northwestern Europe and North America, while southward it connects those two manufacturing areas with the raw material producing and agricultural continents of Africa and South America.

The Atlantic is especially important to Great Britain because it connects the mother country with Canada, the leading Dominion in terms of manpower, industrial resources, and foodstuffs. Over the Atlantic arteries is also transported a large proportion (about 60 per cent in peacetime) of Britain's vital oil supplies. The principal British life lines in the Atlantic and the distances from Liverpool are as follows:

GREAT BRITAIN TO NORTH AMERICA

Liverpool to Halifax	2,490 miles
Liverpool to Quebec	2,630
Liverpool to Montreal	2,760
Liverpool to New York	3,219

GREAT BRITAIN TO SOUTH AMERICA

Liverpool to Colon	4,550
Liverpool to Rio de Janeiro	5,160
Liverpool to Buenos Aires	6,260

GREAT BRITAIN TO GIBRALTAR AND CAPETOWN

Liverpool to Gibraltar	1,343
Liverpool to Capetown	6,100

At the four corners of this S-shaped sea stand British naval bases. At the northeast corner is Scapa Flow, in the Orkney Islands just off the northern tip of Scotland, in which the British Home Fleet was based in both World Wars. It is the largest naval base in the British Isles, and provides an ideal naval anchorage. The Flow itself is surrounded by seven small islands, and its well-sheltered waters are large enough to anchor all the ships of the Home Fleet and at the same time furnish an excellent artillery and torpedo practice ground.

Almost directly across the Atlantic, at its northwest corner, is Halifax, in Nova Scotia. It is the only Canadian port that is ice-free in winter, and is the headquarters of the Royal Canadian Navy. Halifax harbor itself is about six miles long by one mile in width, and has excellent anchorage in all its parts; a still narrower passage connects the harbor with Bedford basin to the north, six miles by four miles, deep enough for the largest battleships. The harbor and its approaches have been fortified so that it has become the strongest position in Canada, and one of the strongest in the Empire.

Lying approximately 250 miles east of Cape Horn, guarding that passage between the Atlantic and the Pacific oceans, are the Falkland Islands, one of the most southerly colonies of the British Empire. There are over 100 islands in the group, but only two, which are separated by a narrow strait, are of importance. On one of these, East Falkland, the British have the naval base of Port William on land-locked Stanley harbor. Port William is little more than a fueling and radio station; nevertheless it proved the worth of its strategic position in 1914, when the Battle of the Falkland Islands marked the end of German cruiser warfare at sea.

The chief port in South Africa is Capetown, situated on Table Bay some miles up the west coast from Cape of Good Hope. The naval base protecting Capetown and guarding the Cape passage from the Atlantic to the Indian Ocean is Simonstown, about 22 miles south of Capetown on False Bay. The Bay has an anchorage that will accommodate men-of-war up to 30-foot draft; there are extensive dockyards, and the hill behind the town is heavily fortified. Simonstown completes the four strategic bastions that guard the inner reaches of the Atlantic Ocean.

British life lines in the Atlantic are further protected by a series of possessions, minor naval bases, and fueling stations. The Cape route is guarded all the way by British possessions; almost the entire eastern flank of the South Atlantic is British. There are bases at Bathurst (Gambia), Freetown (Sierra Leone), Accra (Gold Coast), Lagos (Nigeria), Walvis Bay (British Southwest Africa), and Port Nolloth

(Union of South Africa). Three small islands owned by Great Britain, Ascension, St. Helena, and Tristan da Cunha, lie slightly to the west of the route to Capetown. During World War II, Ascension Island was jointly developed by the United States and Great Britain into an important landing field and fueling stop for trans-Atlantic flights from Natal in Brazil. North of Ascension are the Cape Verde Islands, Madeira, and the Azores, owned by Portugal, a nation which has been friendly to Britain by virtue of centuries-old treaties. Portugal afforded use of these islands to Great Britain and the United States in the anti-submarine war.

The approaches to the West Indies and the Panama Canal are also well guarded by British bases and possessions. Nearest to Great Britain are the Bermuda Islands, which, by reason of their central position and isolation, are of strategic importance in the defense of the Atlantic. They are 750 miles from Halifax, 700 miles from New York, 600 miles east of Cape Hatteras, 1,700 miles from Panama, and 3,000 miles from London. This location makes the Bermudas a steppingstone on the routes from Europe to the West Indies, from Europe to the United States, from Canada to South America, and from the United States to Europe and to Africa. Port Hamilton on Ireland Island is the naval base and dockyard, and Bermuda has long been the home station for the British Fleet operating in American and West Indian waters. Beyond the Bermudas, on the way from England to the Caribbean, lie the Bahama Islands, strategically located to control both the Florida Straits and the Windward Passage which separates Cuba and Haiti. South of the eastern end of Cuba, near the Caribbean side of Windward Passage, is the island of Jamaica, with its naval base at Port Royal on Kingston Harbor, considered one of the best harbors in the West Indies.[7]

It remains but to enumerate the principal British home bases to conclude our survey of British sea power in the Atlantic. Their strategic importance for the defense of Britain is obvious enough; space does not permit description of each base in detail. These are, reading south from Scapa Flow, Invergordon on Cromarty Firth; Rosyth (where Beatty based his battle cruisers during World War I) on the Firth of Forth; Harwich at the mouth of the River Stour and Sheerness near the entrance to the Thames estuary; Portsmouth, Weymouth, Ply-

---

[7] Because the United States has taken the lead in developing bases on other British islands in the West Indies under the destroyer-base deal of 1940, their fuller recital will be reserved to the discussion of our own defense of the Panama Canal.

mouth, Devonport, and Chatham fronting the Channel to the south; and Pembroke in southwest Wales. Cobh, Berehaven, and Queenstown in southern Ireland and Lough Swilly in northwest Ireland were of immense value in World War I in protecting the entrances to the Irish Sea; but by an egregious blunder the British Government relinquished rights to these bases in 1938 and the Government of Eire, on the plea of neutrality, refused to allow the British to use them in World War II.

BRITAIN'S LIFE LINE TO INDIA

The Mediterranean-Suez route to India and the Far East is one of Britain's most important life lines. In normal times the bulk of her trade with India, British Malaya, Australia, and New Zealand passes through the Mediterranean, as does all her trade with Egypt, Palestine, the Anglo-Egyptian Sudan, and Iraq. Fully 70 per cent of the European trade of India, and 25 per cent of the import and 50 per cent of the export trade of Australia, passed through the Suez Canal before World War II, and the bulk of New Zealand trade used this route in preference to that via Panama. The distance from Liverpool to Gibraltar is 1,343 miles; from Gibraltar to Malta, 990 miles; from Malta to Port Said, 936 miles; Suez to Aden, 1,310 miles; Aden to Colombo, Ceylon, 2,170 miles. This route is heavily guarded by naval and air bases throughout its length; their number and their strategic location again attest to the perspicacity of Britain's Admiralty and her statesmen.

The Rock of Gibraltar is one of the most heavily fortified positions in the world. The fortress is a naval and air base, as well as a refueling station on the route to India. The Straits are only 15 miles wide at this point, and the big guns of the Rock can reach across to Ceuta, on the African mainland. A strategic canal, cut in 1940 across the low isthmus which joins the Rock to Spain, has transformed it into an island base. Malta, approximately midway between Gibraltar and the Suez Canal, is 60 miles from Sicily and 180 miles from the coast of Africa. Its strategic value was amply demonstrated in the North African campaigns, as shown by the tenacity with which the British held out against one of the heaviest air assaults of the war and the fury with which the Axis endeavored to reduce it. In the east, the Mediterranean Fleet is based on Alexandria near the mouths of the Nile and not far from Aboukir Bay. There are other bases at Port Said, near the Mediterranean entrance to the Canal, at Haifa in Palestine (the terminus of the pipe lines from the Iraq and Iran oil fields), and at Fumagusta on the British colony of Cyprus. In 1940 the British occupied the Greek island of Crete, and the fleet was enabled to use its fine harbor at Suda Bay until dislodged by the Germans in May of 1941.

The Red Sea is guarded by bases at Suez, the southern terminal port of the Canal; Port Sudan, about midway between Suez and the exit to the Indian Ocean; and by Perim Island, squarely in the middle of the Straits of Bab-el-Mandeb between Arabia and Africa. About 100 miles east of the Straits is Aden, in the Protectorate of Aden, in position to guard both the southern approaches to the Red Sea and the trade routes in the Arabian Sea. Aden is the most heavily fortified British naval and air base between Gibraltar and Bombay.

The Indian Ocean and its Approaches

The Indian Ocean is a roughly triangular-shaped sea, with the Arabian Sea and the Bay of Bengal at its twin apexes. It has frequently been called a British lake. The east coast of Africa, from Suez to Capetown, is almost entirely British; with the exception of French Madagascar and the Dutch East Indies, there are few islands or bases in the Indian Ocean that are not British. The principal entrances to the Indian Ocean are via the Cape of Good Hope, the Straits of Bab-el-Mandeb, Malacca Strait between Sumatra and the Malay Peninsula, the Torres Strait-Arafura Sea-Timor Sea route from the Coral Sea in the Southwest Pacific, and the Bass Strait-King George Sound route to the south of Australia. British bases are located at each of these strategic passages, as well as within the Indian Ocean itself.

The defensive pivot of the middle sea is Trincomalee, on the island of Ceylon. Trincomalee boasts one of the five or six greatest natural harbors in the world. Situated near the southern tip of India, midway between the Arabian Sea and the Bay of Bengal, it is in an excellent position to safeguard traffic within those narrow seas and is also athwart the trade routes from the Red Sea to British Malaya, Australia, and the Far East. Bombay guards the eastern side of the Arabian Sea, and Calcutta and Rangoon protect the Bay of Bengal. Singapore is the most important British naval and air base and trading port in the Far East, and before World War II had facilities for maintaining and repairing the biggest warships. The base is on an island near the southern entrance to the Straits of Malacca and is connected by a causeway with the mainland of British Malaya. Being almost equi-distant from India, Hong Kong, and Australia, it has strategic value in the defense of the Indian Ocean as well as the Pacific. Heavily fortified against sea attack, it nevertheless proved vulnerable to Japanese assault from the rear when they captured it in 1942; the British re-entered Singapore in September 1945, and it will no doubt again be the home base for the British Pacific Fleet. At the northern end of Malacca Strait, 375 miles from Singapore, the British have a small base on the island of Penang, thus controlling both entrances to this strategic bottleneck.

The easternmost entrance to the Indian Ocean, Torres Strait, be-tween Cape York on the Australian mainland and New Guinea, is guarded by a base on Thursday Island. This entrance is further bul-warked by a naval and air base at Port Darwin, approximately in the center of the northern Australia coast. After the Philippines, Singa-pore and the Dutch East Indies fell, Darwin became of even greater strategic importance and in consequence was heavily fortified. Ho-bart, on the island of Tasmania, guards Bass Strait, the southern ap-proach to the Indian Ocean from the east. The bases at Hobart, Thursday Island, and Port Darwin do double duty in the Empire's Pacific and Indian Ocean defenses. Near the southwestern corner of Australia is a base at Albany, on King George Sound, and not far up the west coast is Perth, completing Britain's defenses in the eastern Indian Ocean.

To the west, reference has already been made to Simonstown, Aden, and Perim Island. There is a minor base at Mombasa, in Britain's Kenya Colony. Approximately 550 miles due east of Madagascar is the island and British colony of Mauritius. There is no naval base here, because of the lack of adequate harbors; it has its importance chiefly as a fueling station and port of call on the route from Cape-town to Ceylon. The Bahrein Islands in the Persian Gulf complete the British bases in this area.

THE PACIFIC OCEAN

In the Pacific, the British have their weakest pattern of naval de-fenses. The principal bases in the Pacific, with the exception of Van-couver in British Columbia, are situated along its western side. Hong Kong, an island lying off the mouth of the Canton River, was, and again is, a focus of British interests in the Far East. Situated almost midway between Japan and Singapore, its location renders it a vital factor in the strategic geography of the Pacific, and before the war its naval base was the headquarters of the China Squadron. Captured by the Japanese early in 1942, it was reoccupied after the war. Sydney, Australia, located on a deep and sheltered harbor, is defensible yet easily accessible to the sea. After the battle of Java Sea, in February, 1942, Sydney became the main operating base for the Allied Nations' navies in the Western Pacific. Auckland, a naval and air base on North Island, New Zealand, is the headquarters of the New Zealand Division of the Royal Navy. Singapore and Hobart, the remaining major bases in far Western Pacific waters, have already been mentioned.

A double crescent of British and Australian island possessions guard the approaches to New Zealand, Australia, and the Indian Ocean from the north and east. Nauru, the Gilbert, Ellice, Phoenix, and Fiji islands comprise the concave outer arc. The Solomons, Santa Cruz, the New Hebrides, and Norfolk Islands make up the inner line of island defenses. The importance of these outer defenses was thoroughly understood by the Japanese; Nauru and the Gilberts were flanked by the Japanese-mandated Marshall Islands, and they were quickly overrun after the outbreak of World War II. It was to be anticipated that Japanese amphibious forces would then attempt to move down through the Solomons, the New Hebrides, the Fijis, and New Caledonia in an attempt to isolate Australia and New Zealand. By taking over New Caledonia from the Free French and utilizing its excellent harbor of Nouméa we were able to launch our own attack upon the Solomons, thus thwarting this plan and marking the turning point in the Pacific War.

THE ATLANTIC DEFENSE OF THE UNITED STATES

Turning from British to United States bases, we may note first that the Atlantic defense of the United States includes the two major problems of protecting our northeast coast, where much of our industrial strength is concentrated, and safeguarding the Panama Canal. Defense of the northeast sector hinges upon control of the North Atlantic "bridge" between Europe and the United States via Iceland, Greenland, Labrador, Newfoundland, and Nova Scotia. The Atlantic approaches to the Panama Canal are guarded by a dozen owned and leased bases that extend nearly 2,000 miles from Florida to the mainland of South America.

The North is the key to the defense of our Atlantic Coast. The shortest route from Europe to the United States is over the northern steppingstones mentioned above, and any invasion attempt on our northeast seaboard would presumably utilize this route. It was used by the Norsemen in their early voyages to this country, and the great French and English invasions moved through the Gulf of St. Lawrence and thence up the broad river highway to the heart of the continent. In this age of airpower the northern route has taken on new importance for our security. Between Trondheim in Norway and Scoresby Sund, Greenland, are a mere thousand miles of open flying water; from Bergen to Iceland the distance is even less.

When war broke out in Europe in 1939 we possessed no bases in these strategic areas of the North; after the invasion of Norway, however, we moved swiftly to ward off any possible threat from this direction. We took steps to maintain sea and air bases on the three most important islands between Europe and North America—Iceland, Greenland, and Newfoundland.

In September, 1940, we concluded negotiations with Great Britain by which we acquired rights to eight new naval and air bases in the Atlantic extending from Canada to South America, giving to the British in exchange 50 overage destroyers which they desperately needed in the antisubmarine war. On Newfoundland and Bermuda we obtained sites for bases for 99 years as outright gifts; six other sites, ranging from the Bahamas to British Guiana, we secured under rent-free leases for 99 years. President Roosevelt at the time informed Congress, "This is the most important action in the reinforcement of our national defense that has taken place since the Louisiana Purchase."

The strategic value of Newfoundland is obvious. It bars the St. Lawrence gateway to the interior of the continent, is only 1,100 miles from New York and 1,650 miles from Ireland. In football terms, it occupies the safety position behind Greenland and Iceland. During World War I naval and air facilities, as well as barracks for an army garrison, were developed on the Avalon Peninsula near St. John's, the capital, and at St. George Bay, in the western part of the island. St. John's harbor, which is ice-free for 11 months of the year, is deep enough for capital ships, and has a dry dock large enough for cruisers.

The next step in securing our North Atlantic defenses was the occupation of Greenland. It had been reported in early 1941 that there were German reconnaissance patrols and meteorological groups operating in this Danish colony. In April of that year the United States signed an agreement with the Danish minister in Washington permitting us to occupy the island for defensive purposes. Although her minister's action was disavowed by the Nazi-dominated Copenhagen government, we nevertheless proceeded to establish naval and air bases at Godthaab and Julianehaab, on the extreme southwest coast. Greenland is another important steppingstone on the North Atlantic route and constitutes a second line of defense to the northeast. It is only 1,200 miles from Maine, 900 miles from the bases in Newfoundland, and 700 miles from Iceland. Greenland is valuable not only for its naval and air defenses; its meteorological stations are also useful in forecasting weather conditions over the North Atlantic.

Iceland has been called the keystone to the control of the North Atlantic; it is the spearhead in the defense of our northeast seaboard. Situated almost squarely in the middle of the North Atlantic, it also lies between the Arctic and Atlantic oceans. Because the Gulf Stream passes close south of Iceland it has a number of good ice-free harbors and landing fields; the Bay of Whales is said to be large enough to accommodate all the navies of the world. In order to forestall possible Nazi invasion, the British occupied Iceland in May, 1940; as early as July, 1941, our forces landed there, to reinforce and eventually to replace the British. It became the key position in the Battle of the Atlantic, protecting our supply lines to England and to Murmansk.

A discussion of the defense of the Atlantic seaboard would not be complete without the inclusion of Bermuda, naval and air base rights on which were acquired in the destroyer deal. These islands have been termed the pivot of our Atlantic defense; they safeguard our Middle Atlantic states and are also an outpost sentinel in the defense of the Panama Canal. They are roughly midway between Newfoundland and Puerto Rico, 700 miles from New York, and only one day's fast steaming distance from the Norfolk and Charleston Navy Yards. From Bermuda, naval and air craft can patrol far out into the Middle Atlantic, north to Newfoundland, and south to our bases in the West Indies. In the war, Great Britain made available to our ships her docking and repair facilities at her base on Ireland Island in the Bermudas.

THE PANAMA CANAL AND THE CARIBBEAN AREA

The Panama Canal is one of the two most important strategic waterways in the world. It is as vital to our hemispheric defense as the Suez Canal is to the defense of the British Empire. The opening of the Canal wrought almost as much of a revolution in the commercial structure of the world as the discovery of America. The west coast of South

America moved nearer to New York than to San Francisco. The round trip from New York to Valparaiso, Chile was shortened by 10,000 miles, thus making possible a 50 per cent increase in the amount of Chilean copper and other raw materials that can be imported in a given number of vessels. By this shortening of the water route between the Pacific and the Atlantic, the whole of our naval forces may be brought into action in either ocean in comparatively short time.

On its Atlantic side, the Canal is protected by an island crescent of defensive positions 2,000 miles in extent, stretching from Florida to the South American mainland. These are the Greater and Lesser Antilles which ring the Caribbean, often referred to as the "American Mediterranean." There are but two narrow gateways to the true Mediterranean, whereas there are five major entrances as well as numerous narrower channels into the Caribbean. The most northerly of the wider passages is Florida Strait, leading directly into the Gulf of Mexico. South of the Florida channel, Cuba is a barrier for nearly a thousand miles, with Windward Passage separating Cuba from Haiti. Then come, in order, Mona Passage between the Dominican Republic and Puerto Rico, Anegada Passage between the Virgin Islands and St. Christopher, and lastly, the wide and easy passage north of Trinidad. Major United States naval and air bases dominate these five main waterways leading to the Caribbean and the Panama Canal; smaller bases in the Lesser Antilles guard the openings east and south of Puerto Rico.

Key West and the Florida Keys guard the entrance to the Gulf of Mexico. The main part of our Atlantic fleet was based at Key West under Sampson during the Spanish-American War; after the outbreak of World War II, Key West was expanded into one of our most important sea and air bases. The Florida passage is further screened by the six-hundred-mile stretch of the Bahamas, in which we have a leased base on Exuma Island, not far from Windward Passage. Three strategically situated bases stand guard over Windward—Exuma Island to the north, Guantanamo Bay near the eastern tip of Cuba, and Jamaica to the south. We have a lease for Guantanamo in perpetuity, concluded with Cuba in 1903, and have there developed our strongest position in the West Indies. The bay itself is large and deep enough to accommodate all the Atlantic Fleet with room to spare. Under our lease with Great Britain we have the privilege of sharing the facilities of the British base at Port Royal, Jamaica, and also have base rights at several other places on that island. It would prove a difficult feat for an invading force to pass the triple tier of bases guarding Windward Passage.

Naval and air bases on Puerto Rico overlook both Mona Passage and Anegada Passage. Fleet, air, and army bases are located at San Juan; Boriquen Field, in the western part of the island, is one of the largest air fields in the Caribbean. Some 40 miles east of Puerto Rico are the Virgin Islands, purchased from Denmark during World War I; our bases here further safeguard the Anegada entrance.

The opening that lies north of Trinidad is secured by three island bastions, and is flanked by two mainland bases to the south in British Guiana and Dutch Guiana (Surinam). Under the terms of the destroyer deal we secured base rights on the British-owned islands of Antigua, St. Lucia, and Trinidad, and in British Guiana. In November, 1941 we secured the consent of the Netherlands government to establish bases in Dutch Guiana. These mainland bases are especially valuable additions to our strategic security because the largest deposits of bauxite (aluminum ore) in the Western Hemisphere are found in British and Dutch Guiana; the two colonies together supply more than half our total supply of bauxite. Trinidad is important likewise, not only in protecting the southern gateway to the Canal but also for its oil wells and refineries and for its proximity to the rich Venezuelan oil fields. Trinidad is the most heavily defended of the West Indian bases secured from Britain.

Thus it is seen that the outer defense of the Panama Canal hinges upon a string of 11 bases that extend from Florida to South America. Four of these—Key West, Guantanamo, Puerto Rico, and the Virgin Islands—were bases developed prior to World War II; all were improved and strengthened after its outbreak. The remaining seven— the Bahamas, Jamaica, Antigua, St. Lucia, Trinidad, British Guiana, and Surinam—were leased in 1940. For an attacking force of surface vessels to break through this protective screen seems a remote possibility.

The Panama Canal Zone

The Panama Canal, completed at the outbreak of World War I, is 46 miles long and is in the center of a strip of territory leased in perpetuity from the Republic of Panama. The lease also includes rights in perpetuity to all islands within three miles of the entrance to the Canal.

The countries nearest to the Canal Zone—Panama, Costa Rica,

Nicaragua, and Colombia—are all within our "good neighbor" sphere of influence. Costa Rica and Colombia have signified their willingness to grant us base rights on either the Atlantic or Pacific coasts; Panama has agreed to grant additional sites outside the Canal Zone proper. Backing up our tier of defenses in the Antilles we have rights on several small islands in the Caribbean that can be used by submarines and patrol planes: Navassa Island, between Jamaica and Haiti, the Swan Islands, north of Honduras, and the Great and Little Corn Islands, near the entrance to the proposed Nicaraguan Canal.

We come finally to the immediate defenses of the Canal Zone itself. Shortly after the outbreak of World War II a heavy program of fortification was undertaken; secrecy still surrounds the nature and extent of these defenses, but it is known that numerous new air fields, anti-aircraft and other gun emplacements were built. A major submarine and air patrol base is located at Coco Solo near the Atlantic entrance to the Canal, and at Balboa, on the Pacific side, is a major naval operating base with a large dockyard.

The Pacific Defense of the United States

The greatest single factor in the strategic security of our Pacific Coast defense is distance. Distance, as a defense factor, is equivalent to a certain quantity of military force. The Pacific is an ocean of great distances; its area makes up almost one-third of the earth's surface. It is over 20 times the size of the United States, and is approximately as large as the Atlantic, Indian, and Arctic oceans combined. Although only a few miles separate North America and Asia at Bering Strait, the distance from Seattle to the Russian naval base of Petropavlovsk on the Kamchatka Peninsula is 2,900 miles and from Seattle to Yokohama, 4,250 miles. To the south, of course, the distances to any foreign power are even greater. Because of these facts the continental mainland of the United States (Puget Sound to San Diego) is relatively easy to defend against attack from the sea, provided the defense triangle of Alaska, Hawaii, and the Panama Canal is held.

The overall pattern of our Pacific defenses may be looked at from at least two points of view. Our major life lines that stretch across the Pacific, because they at the same time are the main lines of invasion from the west, constitute one approach. The shortest route from the United States to the Orient is the northern Great Circle "bridge" from Seattle via the Aleutian Islands to Yokohama and Manila, the distance between Seattle and Manila being 5,900 miles. The middle route goes from San Francisco to Hawaii, to Wake, to Guam, to Manila, a total distance of 6,900 miles. The third, and longest, life line extends 8,000 miles across the South Pacific from Panama via Samoa to Sydney, Australia. Secondly, our Pacific defenses may be regarded as consisting of a series of concentric arcs, beginning with our Continental mainland and working outward. They would be made up of (1) a strictly continental line from Puget Sound to San Diego,[8] (2) an inner defense arc stretching from the Aleutians to the Bay of Panama, a distance of approximately 5,200 miles, (3) an outer defense line of 6,700 miles, connecting Dutch Harbor, Pearl Harbor, and the Panama Canal, and finally (4) a series of outpost bases that swing out from Dutch Harbor to Guam, to Samoa, to Panama. The analysis that follows will, in general, begin with the Pacific Coast and work outward over the island steppingstones that mark our principal life lines in the Pacific.

PACIFIC DEFENSES OF THE PANAMA CANAL

On the Pacific side of the Panama Canal there are no major bases closer than our own Pearl Harbor, approximately 4,700 miles away. Two potential base sites exist in near proximity to the Canal, the Galapagos and Cocos Islands, owned by Ecuador and Costa Rica respectively; both of these nations are friendly to the United States. The Galapagos Islands lie about 800 miles southwest of the Canal, almost on the Equator; United States bases there would greatly extend the range of our patrol boats to the south and west. Closer at hand are the Cocos Islands; as already stated, Costa Rica has indicated her willingness to afford us base sites whenever and wherever needed. In the lap of the Bay of Panama is the Perlas Archipelago, an island group with an area of 450 square miles, which could be (and probably has been) made part of the immediate defenses of the Canal Zone. Immediately to the west of the southernmost tip of Panama are the islands of Coiba and Parida Grande, owned by that friendly republic; together with the Galapagos, Cocos, and the Perlas, they are the only island groups of consequence close to the approaches to the Canal from the west.

Looking at the west coast mainland in the vicinity of the Canal, we find no suitable anchorage sites in nearby Colombia. Above the Canal, however, are Montijo Bay in Panama, and the Gulf of Dulce and the

---

[8] As in our discussion of the Atlantic defenses of the United States, the familiar naval bases on the West Coast—Bremerton, Mare Island, San Pedro—are omitted.

Gulf of Nicoya in Costa Rica, large enough for seaplane, destroyer, and submarine bases. The United States has a renewable ninety-nine year lease with Nicaragua for establishing a naval base in one of the finest harbors on the west coast of North America, the Gulf of Fonseca, lying between Nicaragua and Honduras. Farther to the north is Acapulco in Mexico, another fine natural harbor, suitable for a large fleet anchorage.

ALASKA AND THE ALEUTIAN ISLANDS

Alaska and the Aleutians have belatedly been recognized as more and more important in the strategic geography of United States Pacific defenses. Except for the adversities of weather—the Aleutians are often referred to as the "weather factory" of the Northern Hemisphere —the route over the North Pacific "bridge" is the ideal invasion path between Asia and North America. Just as the Norsemen used the North Atlantic bridge to reach the East Coast, it has long been believed that the original settlers of this continent came from Asia over the North Pacific bridge. The Gulf of Alaska, the Alaskan Peninsula, and the Aleutians form a protective line that reaches to within 600 miles of the nearest Japanese possessions and less than 1,000 miles from the home islands of Japan.

After the outbreak of World War II we engaged in a feverish attempt to strengthen the defenses of Alaska and the Aleutians; at the time of Pearl Harbor they were far from complete. Sitka Sound, some 800 miles to the northwest of Seattle, is now a formidable submarine base and naval station. West 650 miles across the Gulf of Alaska is Kodiak Island with a commodious, almost landlocked harbor at Kizhuyak Bay. Here has been developed the Navy's biggest submarine base in Alaskan waters; drydocks and air bases supplement the defenses of Kodiak. Dutch Harbor on Unalaska Island, the largest of the Aleutian group, is the third leg on our northern defense line, 700 miles to the west of Kodiak. Unalaska has two good harbors in addition to Dutch Harbor. At Dutch Harbor we have our strongest naval base in the Aleutians, most of the defenses having been constructed after the outbreak of World War II. Continuing down this island chain we next come to Adak Island, about 500 miles west of Dutch Harbor. It contains two anchorages, the Bay of Islands and the Bay of Waterfalls, providing ample shelter for the entire fleet. The last two outposts in our Aleutian chain are Kiska Island, some 600 miles from Dutch Harbor, and Attu Island, 200 miles beyond Kiska. Even after the

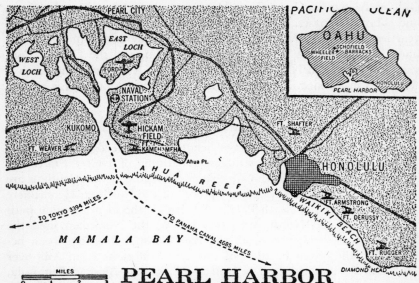

PEARL HARBOR

From *A Guide to Naval Strategy* by Bernard Brodie, Princeton University Press, Princeton, N. J.

United States entered World War II we neglected to construct bases on Kiska and Attu; the Japanese, recognizing their strategic significance, seized both at the time of their abortive attack on Midway in June of 1942, and we were forced into a bitter and long drawn out campaign to recover them.

The Hawaiian Islands

The Hawaiian Islands stretch 1,600 miles in a northwest-southeast direction in the center of the North Pacific. They lie at the crossroads of all trans-Pacific trade routes, and are the pivot of our defense triangle based on Panama and Alaska. Honolulu is 2,100 miles from Dutch Harbor, almost exactly the same distance from San Francisco, and 4,700 miles from the Panama Canal. Although in reality merely a flank defense to the shortest invasion route via Alaska, Hawaii has long been the keystone to our defenses in the Pacific. The naval base at Pearl Harbor on the island of Oahu is one of the two or three mightiest fortresses in the world and is the headquarters of the Pacific Fleet.

Vanguard Pacific Defenses

Approximately 1,150 miles to the northwest of Pearl Harbor, and 1,650 miles due south of Dutch Harbor, is the tiny coral atoll of Midway. Welles Harbor on Midway is too small to serve as a fleet anchorage, but it offers potentialities for a good submarine and seaplane base. The report of the Hepburn Board in 1938 advocated establishing a strong patrol base at Midway, and pointed out its significant position on the invasion route from Japan via the Bonin Islands; at the time of the Battle of Midway in June of 1942, however, the defenses of the island were far from adequate.

Even smaller than Midway is Wake Island, 1,034 miles to the southwest of Midway and 2,000 miles west of Honolulu. Like Midway, Wake is a coral atoll about four and a half by two miles in size; and like Midway, the Hepburn report stressed the importance of Wake in our Pacific defenses and recommended that its fortification be greatly strengthened. These recommendations were not carried out and Wake, hemmed in by Japanese-held Marcus and Marshall Islands, fell in December 1941 after a valorous defense which extended over three weeks.

The spearhead of our pre-Pearl Harbor outer defense line was Guam, ringed by a whole series of Japanese defense bases. The Japanese-mandated Marianas, with Saipan and Tinian as their main bases, were just to the north; the Carolines, with Ponape, Yap, and the great naval base at Truk, were less than 600 miles to the south; the line from Wake to Guam was flanked by the Marshalls and Marcus. Guam might have been made into a defensible position and possibly could have held out, at least for a considerable time, had the recommendations of various Navy boards regarding its defenses been heeded. Guam's Apra Harbor is a deep, protected anchorage that could have been developed into a second Pearl Harbor before the war. Congress, however, in 1940 declined to approve a requested five million dollar appropriation for the fortification of Guam on the grounds that it might "offend the sensibilities of the Japanese." After our recapture of Guam the Navy spent large sums on its defenses, and it now occupies its rightful role as our second strongest fortress in the strategic security of the Pacific.

The Samoan Islands, 2,260 miles to the south of Hawaii, complete our pre-war vanguard positions in the Pacific. Although Samoa is far distant from our mainland defenses—5,700 miles from Panama and 4,150 miles from San Francisco—the islands assumed major importance in World War II after the Japanese took Guam, Wake, and the British-owned Gilbert Islands. They will also figure in the future strategy of the Pacific.

The Philippine Islands

The United States had extensive installations in and near Manila Bay when the war with Japan began; as in the case of Wake and Guam, however, these defenses were wholly inadequate to withstand a determined assault. Our "too little and too late" policy in approaching the problems of Philippine defense again illustrate our pre-war lack of understanding of defense geography. Our main naval base there was at Cavite, well within the harbor and in the lee of Sangley Point; the island fortress of Corregidor stood at the entrance to the bay; and a submarine base at Olongapo, on the seaward side of the Bataan Peninsula, completed our Manila defenses. Our defenses on Bataan were little more than improvisations.

The future of the Philippines in our Pacific defense pattern is not clear at this time.[9] Under the terms of the Tydings-McDuffie Act of 1934 the Philippines were granted their independence in 1946. It seems fairly evident from the attitude of the Filipinos and from the expressed intentions of the Navy Department that the defenses of Manila Bay, one of the best natural harbors in the Orient, will be restored and strengthened by us, and that some of the archipelago's 7,100 islands will be made into United States air and naval bases.

The Future of the Navy in the Pacific

It is too early at this writing to appraise the future of our Pacific defense system. It is certain, however, that World War II forced upon us many new lessons regarding the strategic geography of the Pacific and our defenses in that ocean have been immeasurably strengthened. As reported in the summer of 1946, the Navy planned to maintain only three bases in full operating status—Hawaii, Guam, and Saipan. Four others—Adak in the Aleutians, Midway, and Leyte and Subic Bay in the Philippines—would be maintained at reduced strength. Still others, including Kodiak and Attu in the Aleutians, Okinawa, and the great sheltered anchorages of Eniwetok, Kwajalein, and Truk, would be kept on a "stand-by reserve" basis. Others, such as Dutch Harbor, Tinian, and Samoa, would have only a security watch.

Whatever the final disposition of Pacific island bases—whether under American sovereignty or supervision of the United Nations—it is evident that they constitute a highly important element in the security of the Pacific and in American continental defense.

---

9 October, 1946.

19

A Navy Second Only to Britain's

F ROM THE POINT OF VIEW of Theodore Roosevelt and the big navy
enthusiasts generally, the Spanish-American War was hardly an
important historical event—being merely the *coup de grâce* to a long-
tottering empire. The disparity in force was too marked for the professional Navy to be overimpressed with the results. Dewey's force
outclassed Montojo's in all respects; and the *Oregon* alone would
have been more than a match for Cervera's whole fleet in pitched
battle. As Mahan remarked, it was an "incident . . . something of a
side issue, though one most timely for the welfare of the nation." [1]

However, in publicizing the Navy, more particularly in demonstrating the validity of the Mahan school of thought—that insisted on an
ocean-going Navy designed to operate offensively far from American
ports—and in dramatizing the need of outlying bases and an Isthmian
canal, the Spanish-American War went a long way toward making the
modern American Navy a political possibility. And the acquisition of
a relatively insignificant colonial empire helped also to liberate American public opinion from the archaic view of the function of the American Navy to be coast-watching and commerce-raiding. Now at long
last a majority of the people and of Congress was prepared to accept
the idea of an offensive, line-of-battle fleet.

NAVAL POLICY

Significantly, the term *coast defense* battleship (which had been
applied to all the first-line vessels of the new Navy up to the time of
the Spanish-American War) disappeared from naval and congressional parlance after 1900. The last of the monitors was commissioned

---

[1] *Retrospect* and *Prospect*, p. 48.

in 1901. And naval appropriations continued at a record high level after the war—far higher, in fact, than in any earlier peace-time period.

It is conventional to say that with the Spanish-American War, America emerged from its long hibernation called "isolation," and began to exercise its power in world politics. The historian must label this an oversimplification; America wielded considerable influence throughout most of the nineteenth century. On the other hand, it is true that under the aggressive Theodore Roosevelt her voice was more strident, and more frequently raised among the nations. What is perhaps most important, the average American was increasingly aware of America's active importance in power politics, and more eager to support his country's "Manifest Destiny." In so far as naval might is quite likely to be the iron hand in the velvet glove of diplomacy, this altered popular temper is of significance in naval history. Through the first decade of the twentieth century, Roosevelt, Mahan, and the newly formed Navy League gave the literate voter no opportunity to forget the intimate relation of a strong navy and diplomatic victories. And throughout the period various international incidents in which the Navy figured with unvaried success were a more eloquent argument yet for the continued development of our sea arm.

In the early years of the twentieth century came a new consciousness, both to laymen and professional navy men, of the relative rank of the United States Navy among the navies of the world. Using the conventional yardstick of capital ship tonnage, the American Navy passed from fifth position in 1904 to second in 1907. The expression "a Navy second only to Britain's," which first appeared in congressional debate in 1904, came increasingly to represent an accepted national ideal in the same sense that (at that time) the "two-power standard" was a fixed tenet of British naval policy.

As it was Germany chiefly among the growing naval powers that seemed to challenge our aim, after 1906—incidental to her famous "naval race" with England—it became common to estimate our naval needs in terms of the Kaiser's building program. For various technical reasons, it is impossible to say whether the German or the American line was the stronger in the years immediately preceding World War I. The point is, it was regarded in America at the time as a question of very great importance.

It was not merely, of course, that the Germans were keeping pace with ourselves in building ships that made America in general and the Navy in particular suspicious of them. The rather hostile attitude of Von Diederichs' squadron in Manila Bay, the Second Venezuela Crisis (1902. See *infra*.), the precipitate eagerness with which the Germans undertook to develop their new Pacific possessions at Tsingtao and in the Carolines, added to the saber-rattling arrogance of Kaiser Wilhelm II, made the American government and the American people increasingly unfriendly to Germany.

Simultaneously there was developing a new sense of trust and confidence in Great Britain. It might not be literally true that Captain Chichester, R.N., thrust the *Iphegenia* and *Immortalité* between the German squadron and Dewey's force as a warning against interference at the time of the occupation of Manila, but it made a better story that way, and it was so accepted in the United States. Indeed the evidences of a new and positive friendliness on Britain's part were real enough. Not only had she undertaken to guard American interests in Spain during the war, she also had made possible our acquisition of two warships then building in English yards on Brazilian order, and she had permitted the transfer of revenue cutters from the Great Lakes via the St. Lawrence River. Above all, she had been our only friend in the councils of an unfriendly Europe. Her graceful concessions on the matter of fortifying the projected Panama Canal (Second Hay-Pauncefote Treaty, 1901), and the permanent withdrawal of the British West Indies Squadron (1904–1905) were further indications not only of a British policy of friendly co-operation but also of an awareness of America's new naval supremacy in the Caribbean.

The flowering of good feeling between the United States and Britain accounts in a large part for the fact that Americans at no time prior to World War I regarded the Anglo-Japanese Naval Agreement (1902) as an alarming alignment. The Japanese, as we have seen in preceding chapters, were, up to the early twentieth century, regarded by us as being in a measure our protégés—an amusing, childlike people to whose schooling in western ways we had gratuitously contributed. The professional toughness of Japan's Army and Navy in the Sino-Japanese War (1894) somewhat dispelled this naive notion, but Japan entered the Russo-Japanese War (1904–1905) with the full sympathy not only of President Roosevelt but also of American public opinion. Japan victor over mighty Russia was something else again. Almost overnight, along with a more just estimate of Nipponese strength, came a realization that some time this nation might seriously threaten our own oriental interests.

This sudden cooling of national sympathies was abetted by the fact that the Japanese felt President Roosevelt, who helped engineer the Treaty of Portsmouth (1905), had in a measure cheated them of a part of the fruits of their victory. The action of the San Francisco School Board in segregating oriental school children (1906), and the acerbity of the Japanese notes of protest made plainer still the wall of suspicion that had rapidly grown up between the two nations. After 1906, the big navy senators and representatives would refer not only to German fleet plans but also to the building program of the Japanese.

THE NAVY AND FOREIGN POLICY

It has been suggested that the American people were increasingly aware of the Navy's value in furthering American diplomatic ventures. What, then, were the objectives of American foreign policy in the period immediately following the Spanish-American War?

Apart from such obvious and general aims as protection of our territory, and furthering our commercial interests abroad, we were at the time mainly concerned in the international arena with: (1) constructing (and owning) an Isthmian Canal; (2) maintaining the Monroe Doctrine, with a new and particular emphasis on the Caribbean; (3) maintaining the "Open Door" in China; and (4) assisting in keeping the peace in Europe and the Far East, on the general theory that any upsetting of the balance of power would be likely to harm our own interests.

THE NAVY IN THE FAR EAST

The immediate task of the Navy after the Spanish-American War grew out of the acquisition of the Philippines. The *insurrectos* had expected independence, not an exchange of imperial masters, and our late allies soon became our enemies in the guerrilla fighting known as the Philippine Insurrection (1899–1901). Though not properly part of naval history in that there were no opposing naval forces, the campaigns were conducted in an archipelago, necessitating extensive naval operations both for transport and artillery support to the troops. Naval landing parties occupied important positions, and in some cases did extensive campaigning ashore.

In 1900, our Asiatic Squadron was suddenly called on to furnish a token force to march in the international army sent to relieve the beleaguered legations in Peking at the time of the Boxer Rebellion. The

Boxer movement was originally intended as a patriotic protest against Russian aggression in South Manchuria and the German occupation of Kiao-Chau, but it soon became a sort of oriental Ku Klux Klan, frantically hostile to "foreign devils" of whatever nationality. On May 31, the armored cruiser *Newark,* which had proceeded post-haste to Tientsin, sent a contingent of 53 marines and three bluejackets to reinforce the legation guard. These men joined the troops of the other western nations in the heroic defense of the Peking legations until the Allied Army reached the Chinese capital in August.

The first international relief column (2,078 men) under Vice Admiral Seymour, R.N., which in June tried unsuccessfully to fight its way to Peking, included 112 United States sailors under Captain McCalla of the *Newark.* This American officer, commanding the advance guard, performed with particular distinction.

The second "international army" (18,000 men) included 2,300 American Marines and soldiers. Our participation in this venture was related to Secretary of State John Hay's subsequent success in getting a qualified acceptance for his "Open Door" policy, by which the powers were to extend equal trading rights to all nations in their "spheres of influence," and to "preserve Chinese territorial and administrative integrity."

The before-mentioned San Francisco Board of Education incident (1906), and its consequent friction—aggravated as it was by yellow journalism in both the United States and Japan—was a sobering reminder to both the American people and the administration of how readily we might drift into a war with our quondam friends on the other side of the North Pacific. Earlier that same year, when there had been diplomatic friction over Japanese seal-poaching in the Aleutians, President Roosevelt had ordered all heavy ships of the Asiatic Squadron to stand prepared to leave for home ports at a moment's notice. Now the armored cruiser squadron on station in the Far East was, in accordance with the principle of fleet concentration, ordered replaced by less battle-worthy types. Fortunately, a diplomatic formula of compromise was discovered in Japan's "Gentlemen's Agreement" to restrict labor emigration. The objectionable segregation ordinance of the city of San Francisco was in turn rescinded.

Partly as a reminder to Japan that, though capable of speaking softly, the United States wielded a big stick, Roosevelt decided to send the battleships on a round-the-world cruise—including, on invitation, Yokohama as a port of call. This famous 46,000-mile voyage

(December, 1907–February, 1909) by 16 first-line fighting ships was
the most ambitious project of its kind till then attempted by any navy.
Its unqualified success had a number of important though unassessable
results: it served as an advertisement to the world of our naval might
and efficiency at the same time that it operated as a good will mission;
it benefited the personnel of the battle fleet in ways that normal training routines could not have approached; and it dramatized the Navy to
the American people as nothing else short of a war could have. Also
and incidentally, it demonstrated the need for more outlying bases and
coaling stations, and better collier and supply service.

The Navy in the Caribbean

The idea of a canal across the Isthmus of Panama was by no means
a new concept. The rather complex story of the French efforts to dig
it in the late nineteenth century, and the subsequent political intrigues
over sovereignty of the Canal Zone, cannot be recapitulated here in
detail. Suffice it to say that the events of the Spanish-American War,
notably the *Oregon's* flying trip around the Horn to reinforce our
Caribbean Fleet, constituted a striking lesson in the need of a means
of quickly shifting our naval strength from one coast to the other.
Furthermore, President Roosevelt, ever keenly aware of the Navy's
requirements, was eager to "make the dirt fly." When, in 1903, Colombia, which owned the canal route, held up the treaty conferring
it on the United States—presumably to exact a higher price—a revolt
started in Panama. By earlier treaty agreement, Colombia had ceded
to the United States the right to "keep the peace" on the Isthmus.
Opportunely, the U.S.S. *Nashville* arrived to give tacit support to the
revolutionary party, and incidentally to halt Colombian troops seeking
to land and cross to Panama City. Soon after, the *Dixie* appeared
with a force of United States Marines. Without bloodshed, Panama
at once proclaimed its independence from Colombia, and Roosevelt
recognized the new sovereign state promptly. With gratifying speed
a new treaty was signed by the United States and Panama, granting
us a ten-mile wide strip across the isthmus in return for a down payment of $10,000,000 and an annual rental of $250,000. The engineering skill of the U. S. Army Corps of Engineers and a decade's labor
by a small army of workmen enabled America to open the Panama
Canal to the ships of all nations in August, 1914. Subsequently, as a
means of restoring amity, Colombia was paid $20,000,000.

The prospect of a canal across the Isthmus gave particular point to the contention of Admiral Mahan and other naval strategists that the affairs of Caribbean Latin American countries were a matter of very particular concern to the United States Navy—and hence to the country as a whole. It was, for instance, of paramount importance that no potentially unfriendly foreign power establish itself within striking distance of Panama. In certain quite conceivable circumstances, the destruction of the locks of the Canal might well be the virtual equivalent of sinking half the United States Fleet. Hence, when in 1902 England, Italy, and Germany took concerted blockade measures against Venezuela to enforce debt payment, Roosevelt mobilized all available naval strength in Puerto Rico under Admiral Dewey. His intention to enforce the Monroe Doctrine was obvious, and his arbitration proposal was speedily accepted.

In view of the possibility of similar challenges from European powers, particularly in the Caribbean area, Roosevelt in 1904 proclaimed what has since been termed the "Roosevelt Corollary": the United States might be forced, "in flagrant cases of . . . wrongdoing or impotence [in Latin American countries], to the exercise of an international police power." In other words, in event of a debt default or maltreating of European nationals, the United States would do any "pacifying" or adjusting that might seem essential. Commonly, the Navy and the Marine Corps would be the military instrumentality of such a policy.

In fact, for the next 25 years, considerable desultory, small-scale campaigning in various Caribbean countries was carried out. Except in the Dominican Republic, Haiti, and Nicaragua, which were hotbeds of unrest and political maladministration, our occupations tended to be short-lived. In most cases, a show of naval strength was sufficient. Attacked as evidence of "Yankee Imperialism" by the outraged Latin Americans, and more lately replaced by the "good neighbor" policy, our "rough and ready" diplomacy south of the Rio Grande had at least the virtue of stemming from no basic hostile intent. And it did effectively prevent European involvement in the imbroglios of our neighbors to the South.

The most serious problem of American foreign policy in Latin America during the period under discussion was our chronically troubled relationship with Mexico. This came to a head in 1914. President Wilson had maintained sizable naval forces on both Mexican coasts for the protection of American lives and property, judged to be none too safe under the "unspeakable Huerta," head of the *de facto* government. Further, Wilson refused to recognize Huerta's as constituting a *de jure* government. It was the kind of tense situation in which a small incident can provoke war.

The spark was provided at Tampico on April 9: Mexican police arrested and jailed a Navy paymaster and his working party, legally engaged in "gassing up" a launch from Admiral Mayo's flagship *Dolphin*. The prisoners were promptly released, it is true, but the Admiral demanded a formal apology and a 21-gun flag salute. Huerta refused the salute. President Wilson, with Congressional approval, ordered the Navy to seize the Vera Cruz Customs House.

Evidently, the war was on! Eight hundred Marines and bluejackets landed on April 21. After considerable street fighting, with casualties on both sides, the landing party occupied the customs house and a number of other waterfront structures. The next day reinforcements were landed, supported by the fire of *Chester, Prairie,* and *San Francisco.* By noon, the city was completely occupied. Shore operations were presently turned over to the Army, but before a full-scale second Mexican War could develop, joint arbitration efforts by Argentina, Brazil, and Chile brought a cessation of hostilities. Huerta went into exile in July. The United States naval forces remained off the Mexican coasts until November.

An interesting sidelight is the fact that during the Vera Cruz operation United States naval aircaft made their first combat flights—as scouts over the city.

TECHNOLOGICAL ADVANCES

Like most of the second half of the nineteenth century, the period 1898–1914 was a time of very rapid technological advance in all major navies. Except for the emergence of carriers in the later period, it would be safe to say that more and greater change in ship types occurred during the decade 1900–1910 than in the ensuing 30 years. Furthermore such new devices as radio, the gyrocompass, and improved optical fire-control instruments made the typical fighting vessel on the eve of World War I a far cry from such a ship as the famous old *Oregon,* the last word in naval excellence at the time of the Battle of Santiago.

The most notable "revolution" in battleship construction was essentially a gunnery improvement; it came from the British, who in 1906 launched the secretly-constructed *Dreadnought,* after which all subsequent battleships in all navies were in a measure patterned. Typically, the pre-dreadnought line-of-battle ship had carried a main battery of four large-caliber guns, mounted in twin turrets fore and aft, an intermediate battery of 7- or 8-inch guns, and a secondary battery of quick firers, which in turn frequently ran to several different bores. In our own Navy, for instance, the five *Rhode Islands* (1904) carried no less than six different calibers, ranging from the four 12-inch rifles and eight 8-inch guns down to the small-bore, anti-torpedoboat weapons. The *Dreadnought* abandoned the intermediate batteries altogether, and mounted ten 12-inch guns in five turrets (three center-line, and one on each beam). This, in effect, gave her a main battery fire power on the broadside double that of any other existing ship (eight guns to four); and triple, on fore-and-aft fire (six guns to two). Her tonnage was somewhat greater than usual up to that time (18,200), though her offensive strength was disproportionately greater than her tonnage increase would ordinarily signify. She carried 11 inches of armor, slightly heavier than previously favored by most admiralties. Her designed speed was 21.5 knots. In a word, she was to all intents and purposes a modern battleship.

Almost at once naval constructors everywhere recognized her superiority, and every nation began the construction of "dreadnoughts." Though the pre-dreadnought vessels were by no means rendered useless (as some writers have suggested), they were relegated to a second-line status. Our own naval experts never agreed whether our *South Carolina* and *Michigan* (1908), carrying eight 12-inch guns on a 17,-900 ton displacement, or our *North Dakota* and *Delaware* (1908, 1909), mounting ten 12-inch guns on a 22,400 ton displacement, were our first "dreadnoughts." It is an academic point; the important thing is that we accepted at once the idea of the big-gun ship.

From 1898 to 1914, the tonnage of the average United States battleship went up from about 12,000 to about 30,000. Speed of the line increased from 16 knots to 20.5, at which latter point it remained until World War II. In both respects, American construction reflected worldwide trends.

In the United States Navy and in the Naval Affairs Committees of both the Senate and the House of Representatives, battleships were emphasized at the expense of cruisers and other lesser types. Since at the time it was generally four years after a battleship was projected that she was commissioned, and since smaller vessels could be built more quickly, it was easy to justify our increasingly unbalanced fleet.

In spite of the fact that the armored cruiser type had rapidly evolved into the battle cruiser in the navies of England, Germany, and Japan, none were authorized for our Navy until the 1916 program. (And none of those was finally completed as such.)

The destroyer first appeared about the turn of the century, as an anti-torpedo-boat weapon. In our Navy, the destroyer was from the beginning quite highly evolved. Those commissioned in 1900 displaced 500 tons, and had a speed of 28 knots. The destroyer almost at once superseded the type of vessel it was designed to combat, though we kept in commission a couple of dozen torpedo boats of the nineties vintage as coast-defense weapons. The destroyer also soon came to be regarded as a necessary adjunct of the scouting line. Consistent with the above-mentioned practice of concentrating on building battleships, the United States Navy had in 1914 fewer destroyers, proportionately to her line of battle, than any other major fleet.

The tactical concept of a "screen" of destroyers for capital ships was a logical development, and during this period became standard practice in all navies. Tsushima (1905) had seemingly demonstrated the battle superiority of the gun over the torpedo, but torpedoes were constantly being refined in the direction of greater speed and range, and no admiral could afford to overlook either the offensive possibilities of destroyer attack or the danger from enemy torpedoes.

The promising qualities of the torpedo as a means of "defeating" armor by striking below the armor belt were of course the impetus behind the development of the modern submarine. So much was learned in the course of construction of the *Plunger,* contracted for in 1895, that instead of accepting her, the Navy ordered an improved model. Our first submarine was the *Holland,* commissioned in 1900— the tiny prototype of the "fleet boats" of today. Her overall length was only 54 feet; her submerged displacement only 74 tons. She was of course single-screw, and was propelled on the surface by a gasoline engine. She had a single torpedo tube, and two dynamite guns, similar to those carried by the *Vesuvius.* Nevertheless she incorporated in less advanced form most of the devices used on submarines today, such as ballast and safety tanks, diving planes, periscope, and batteries for underwater propulsion. Her surface speed was seven knots and her range was 1,500 miles. Submerged, she could make nearly seven knots for short distances. Her submerged cruising range (at a low speed) was 50 miles. She could dive to 28 feet in eight seconds—faster than many of later date. Her performance prompted the authorities to order six more "Holland boats" of slightly larger size, and by 1914 the submarine was accepted as an important weapon. The substitution of Diesel engines for gasoline (1909–1910) was a very significant development, both for greater safety and for the fact that they provided much greater cruising range.

It is interesting that prior to World War I no admiralty correctly assessed the potential value of the submarine as a commerce destroyer —least of all the Germans, whose fleet was almost the last to adopt submarines (1906). The submarine was regarded as a valuable coast and harbor defense weapon—with potentialities as a fleet adjunct in certain types of tactical situations.

It is not possible to give more than cursory mention to the inventions and technical improvements that, viewed together, vastly increased the fighting efficiency of the Navy of 1914 as compared to that of 16 years earlier. As early as 1900, the service had experimented with and been favorably impressed by Marconi's "wireless." The self-evident merits of radio communication rapidly made it commonplace in the fleet. The gyrocompass was perfected (1908-1909)—an advance particularly valuable for submarines, magnetic compasses being virtually valueless for submerged cruising. Improved smokeless powder for our several calibers of naval rifles was developed by the Navy's organic chemists. With the *Texas* and *New York* (1914), the 14-inch gun first appeared. Oil-burning capital ships were projected and laid down. (*Nevada* and *Oklahoma,* commissioned in 1916, were the first oil-burning battleships in the United States Navy.) The electrical gear carried aboard ship increased phenomenally in extent, importance, and multiplicity of function.

Of special importance were the great strides made during this period in gunnery, intimately related to the many improvements in optical gunsights, rangefinders, and gunmounts. Under the stimulus of Sims in the American Navy and Percy Scott in the British, accuracy and rate of fire in target practice increased tremendously in a short time. In the Spanish-American War, the optimum battle range, even for heavy guns, was regarded to be in the neighborhood of 6,000 yards. And at the Battle of Santiago, fought generally at almost point-blank distance, our accuracy with heavy-caliber fire was only 3.2 per cent. Though the whole story of the improvement effected during the first decade of the twentieth century is too detailed to be developed here, suffice it to say that "continuous-aim," director-controlled, salvo fire made possible the extending of effective battle ranges for heavy rifles to over 20,000 yards in the World War I period. The guns themselves were not radically improved during this time; it was merely that optical

instruments and improved training methods made it at last possible
to exploit their full potentialities.

The Wright brothers made their first successful airplane flight in
1902, and the Navy early manifested an interest in this "weapon of the
future," which could self-evidently be invaluable for scouting purposes
if some means of making it usable at sea could be found. However,
though Glen H. Curtiss produced the first practicable hydroplane in
1911, the Navy had hardly more than begun its pioneering before
World War I. In November, 1910, Eugene Ely made the first experimental flight from the deck of the U.S.S. *Birmingham* at Norfolk;
two months later, he made a successful landing on the old *Pennsylvania*
in San Francisco. Ely landed his biplane on a temporary wooden platform, 130 by 50 feet in dimensions, sloping slightly aft; he was checked
by 100-lb. sandbags rigged to be caught by hooks in the lower frame-
work of the aircraft. Thus was demonstrated, for the first time in our
own or any other navy, the practicability of carrier aviation.

In 1911, the Navy contracted with Curtiss for two planes, and with
the Wrights for another. In 1912, Lieutenant T. G. Ellyson (the first
qualified naval aviator) demonstrated the workability of the newly
devised compressed-air catapult. He flew off a plane thus shot from a
barge in the Potomac. About this time, the fertile mind of Admiral
Bradley Fiske conceived the torpedo plane, and he sketched a practical torpedo release for such an aircraft.

The first naval aviation unit was organized at Greenbury Point,
Maryland, by Ellyson, John Rodgers, J. H. Towers, Victor Herbster,
and other pioneers. The Pensacola Naval Air Station was established
as a school for air personnel in 1913. The same year, Towers made the
first scouting flight with the fleet. As noted above, United States naval
planes were first employed operationally at Vera Cruz in 1914.

However forehanded we were in small-scale experimentation, our
development of aircraft in the fleet was to lag behind both the British
and the Japanese for a time. Until World War I showed the value of
planes as an auxiliary in the antisubmarine campaign, appropriations
even for further experimentation were woefully inadequate.

To summarize: the 16 years between 1898 and 1914 saw amazing
technological advances in the Navy. The depth charge, hydrophones,
the antenna mine, and the host of inventions that have since made carrier aviation so devastating in battle were yet unborn. Otherwise, nearly
every important mechanical feature of the fighting ships of the next
25 years had evolved by the end of this period. After 1939, of course,

World War II seemed to open a new Pandora's Box of radical devices, the concerns of a later chapter.

OTHER ASPECTS OF THE NAVY'S GROWTH

The matériel progress of the Navy was largely matched by other naval advances. Besides the improved gunnery training mentioned above, training in shore schools for the various specialized rates necessitated by the increasing complexities of the naval machine was very much expanded. During the nineteenth century, the Navy had relied on the merchant service to train its recruits as seamen. After 1900, it was increasingly the policy to recruit "landsmen," and let them serve their apprenticeship in the Navy. The long-term result was younger, and more alert and intelligent crews. The antiquated bureau system of administration was revised and improved. In 1909, large-scale improvements were made in the bases at Pearl Harbor and Guantanamo (Cuba).

On the other hand, the increase in number of ships was not adequately matched by a corresponding increase in personnel. The size of the enlisted force more than doubled between 1898 and 1914 (from about 25,000 to over 50,000), but our ships were still undermanned by European standards. Particularly were we short of trained officers. In 1912, for instance, the United States had 1,968 officers on the active list. Germany, with less tonnage, had 2,484, and Japan, with a considerably smaller navy, had over 2,700. Some of the important shore-based activities of the Navy found themselves severely handicapped by the absence of even one officer on leave.

President Theodore Roosevelt, who as a one-time Assistant Secretary of the Navy was personally acquainted with sound strategic doctrine, made a fetish of fleet concentration. He had no objection to shifting the battle line from the East Coast to the West from time to time, provided it made the move as a unit. His final advice to his successor (President Taft) in 1909 was an admonition never to divide the fleet. This policy, based on a fear of a recurrence of the situation in which the Russians found themselves in 1905, had the incidental valuable merit of furnishing abundant opportunity for full fleet maneuvers.

Taken all in all, and judged by the technical standards of the day, the United States Navy in 1914 was a formidable fighting machine. And as the dogs of war were unleashed overseas, the American people had good reason to feel secure under the protection of its mighty guns.

☆ ☆ ☆ ☆ ☆

20
The First World War

EUROPE'S LONG EXPECTED "GREAT WAR" finally broke out in August, 1914. After the first big German push towards Paris was stopped, the conflict on the Western Front settled down to immobile trench warfare with relatively little change in position for the remainder of the contest. On the sea England had a superiority of approximately eight to five over her chief rival, Germany, who did not intend to use her fleet in any decisive action against overwhelming odds. The naval war, therefore, almost immediately resolved itself into an economic struggle in the form of two opposing blockades.

AMERICAN APPROACH TOWARD WAR, 1914–1917

England, by the use of a "long-range" blockade, the doctrine of continuous voyage, and all the old familiar instruments for utilizing sea control to the utmost, sought to isolate Germany from the outside world and to cut off her importation of much needed supplies from abroad. The Germans, too, set up a form of blockade consisting of surface raiders and the increasing use of submarines to operate against British shipping and supply lines in order to starve England out of the war. Inevitably the United States became involved in this growing conflict because a great portion of the material to the warring powers was carried in American ships, and almost from the outset questions arose concerning American rights as a neutral shipper operating in the areas affected by the two blockades.

Our difficulties with England were concerned primarily with her evasions or broad extensions of accepted principles of international law. While condoning the English long-range blockade, the American State Department protested against any interference with our legal trade to continental neutrals. It was evident that much of this commerce found its ultimate destination in Germany since our exports to the Scandinavian countries were far greater in 1915 and 1916 than they had been before the war. We objected to Britain's use of the doctrine of continuous voyage because it was an extension of international law, and it caused vexatious delays for our ships to have to put in to British ports to be searched as well as to get directions for proceeding through the British mine fields in the North Sea. Furthermore, England greatly expanded the classes of contraband, and added another irritant by "black-listing" American merchants suspected of trading with the enemy. Despite the annoying British practices on the high seas, however, the fourfold increase in our exports to the Allied powers and the extension of over two billion dollars to finance these purchases tended to tie our interests to the Allied cause.

Nevertheless, President Wilson sent strong notes to the British protesting their interruptions to our free use of the ocean highways. In her diplomatic responses, England made full use of our natural pro-Allied sentiment and resorted to procrastination and vagueness so that the issue would be confined to the letter-writing stage. In this she was aided by our ambassador in London, a "hopeless Anglophile," and even by officials in our State Department. In our efforts to make a strong stand for our neutral rights against both Germany and England we were further handicapped by our patent unwillingness to back our protests with the threat of arms.

Germany, meanwhile, was complaining that the vastness of our trade with the Allied powers amounted to favoritism and therefore unneutrality. It is true that the war material we sold to the Allies was used to kill Germans, but we had the undeniable right to sell munitions to belligerents, so long as it was on an impartial basis. It was no fault of ours that Germany was too tightly blockaded by English sea power to obtain them, other than by submarines, or that England's control of the sea enabled her to trade freely with us. Yet this one-sided traffic soon brought us to diplomatic grips with Germany.

On February 4, 1915, Germany declared a war zone around Great Britain and Ireland, including the whole of the English Channel, wherein she would sink enemy ships without warning and would assume no responsibility for the destruction of neutral vessels. Though England replied with a more strict enforcement of her own blockade, the Germans had forced a crisis in their relations with the United States. Despite our sharply-worded note to Germany protesting her "unprecedented methods" and holding her to "strict accountability" for her submarine warfare and for the observance of recognized international law, sinkings of American ships and of Allied ships with American passengers soon followed. The torpedoing of the Cunard liner *Lusitania,* on May 7, 1915, off the Irish coast, with the loss of 1,198 persons, of whom 128 were Americans, was the climax of this first phase of Germany's new warfare. After renewed protests from us, we were finally given some assurance that liners would be spared if they did not attempt resistance or escape.

Our protests to Germany were particularly sharp and uncompromising primarily because her infractions of the recognized law of the sea entailed loss, not merely of property, but of lives. Furthermore, they involved not extension, as by England, but a growing disregard of the rules controlling sea warfare. There is a certain fundamental justice in the age-old principles governing the relations of neutrals and belligerents at sea. The high seas are a great common highway open to all, and at the same time an inevitable fighting arena of nations at war. The prime aim of each belligerent is to secure the free use of the sea for his own military movements and commerce, and to deny it to the enemy. As a compromise between the rights of the neutral trader and those of the belligerent, long custom had established the principle that the belligerent might use his naval strength against enemy and neutral trade in two ways: (1) to blockade enemy ports and coasts against all traffic, provided such blockade was clearly defined and effectively maintained; and (2) to cut off by seizure on the high seas any contraband—i.e., goods useful for war and destined for the enemy—whether in enemy or neutral ships, with the provision that the visit, search, and seizure should involve no injury to passengers or crew of the ship submitting to search. On the other hand, it was the right and also the duty of a neutral nation to oppose a "blockade" extending over great areas of the high seas, maintained not by continuously effective sea control but by a limited number of lurking submarines, which sank ships, belligerent or neutral, without warning.

International law, therefore, provides rights as well as obligations for both neutrals and belligerents, and each group is expected to protect its rights and maintain its obligations. In time of war, however, when a nation is fighting for its very existence, a belligerent will naturally expand its own rights and infringe upon those of neutrals, even to the point of violating law when it becomes of vital necessity. Moreover, in the 1915 period it was found that a submarine could not abide

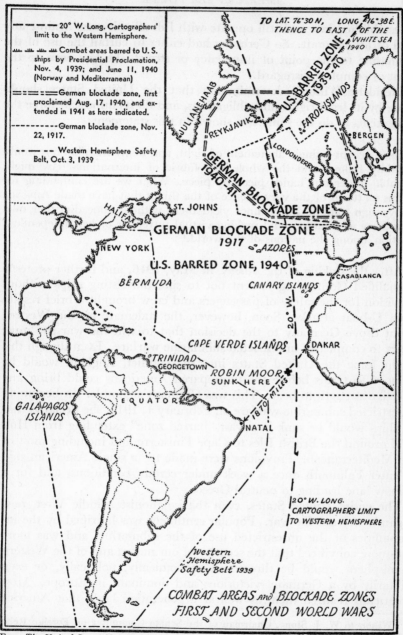

by established law and still operate with full effectiveness against any kind of armed craft. So Germany had either to curtail the use of the submarine to the point of impotency or stretch the law even to the point of complete disregard.

President Wilson's determination that the United States should abide by its legal rights and obligations, and do its utmost to force the belligerents to do the same was shown in this statement:

Once accept a single abatement of right, and many humiliations would certainly follow, and the whole fine fabric of international law might crumble under our hands piece by piece. What we are contending for in this matter is of the very essence of the things that have made America a sovereign nation. She cannot yield them without conceding her own impotency as a nation, and making virtual surrender of her independent position among the nations of the world.[1]

After the sinking of the *Sussex*, in May, 1916, and further protests, a qualified German agreement not to sink unresisting ships without provision for the safety of passengers and crew brought a brief respite from U-boat attacks. Soon, however, the stalemate on the Western Front drove Germany to the decision that to win the war she must resort to completely unrestricted submarine warfare. Even though this might force the United States into the conflict, England would be reduced to terms before the unprepared Americans could bring any effective strength to bear. This was Germany's gamble. In beginning unrestricted submarine warfare on February 1, 1917, she declared that all ships would be sunk in a vast "barred zone" extending from Holland around the British Isles to Cape Finisterre and including most of the Mediterranean. Provisions were made for a single American ship to enter Falmouth once a week under certain conditions, and for a narrow lane leading to neutral Greece.

The entire United States, even the isolationist Middle West, now began to cry out for war. Popular sentiment was horrified by the inhumanities of the unrestricted use of the submarine, and was more and more convinced that the security of our nation and of the Western Hemisphere would be threatened economically, politically, or even militarily by a Germany victorious and dominant in Europe. Most Americans realized then, as well as a generation later, that America

---

[1] Wilson to W. J. Stone, Chairman of the Senate Committee on Foreign Relations, February 24, 1916.

was no longer isolated but vitally concerned in an upset of the European and world balance of power.

With the nation now solidly behind it, the United States Government broke off diplomatic relations with Germany, armed American merchant vessels in March, and on April 6, 1917, with but seven Senators and 50 Representatives opposed, declared war. Thereafter, incidentally, it joined the Allies in putting into force most of the commercial restrictions—the extensions of contraband, black lists of neutral traders, and virtual rationing of supplies to northern neutrals—which it had hitherto opposed.

Moves for Naval Preparedness, 1914–1917

As the war in Europe progressed after 1914, it should have become increasingly clear that the United States would have to strengthen its military establishments, especially the Navy, so that our inevitable protests to the impositions on our free use of the seas might have more forceful backing, and so that we might be prepared to wage war in the event we were eventually drawn into the conflict. We had an excellent warning of the danger of such involvement from our experience in the Napoleonic wars.

Despite this precedent, despite the obvious fact that we were inextricably involved in European affairs and steadily approaching the precipice of war, our Navy was surprisingly unready for war in April, 1917. This fact was not known or probably even suspected by the general public either at the outbreak of hostilities or during the course of the war. After the armistice, however, Admiral William S. Sims, in 1920, wrote a letter to Secretary of the Navy Josephus Daniels, entitled "Certain Naval Lessons of the Great War," in which he outlined his conception of defects in our prosecution of the war at sea. He asserted that at the time of our entry the general unpreparedness of the Navy in personnel and material, the lack of definite plans for immediate and aggressive warfare, and the hesitancy with which we entered into whole-hearted co-operation with our British allies had produced unpardonable delays in throwing effective strength against our enemies and had probably prolonged the war by as much as four months.

In the detailed investigation of these charges by a subcommittee of the Senate Naval Affairs Committee the testimony of most of the many witnesses either openly substantiated or tacitly admitted the truthfulness of Sims's allegations. For a navy to be thoroughly efficient and ready for war it must have the requisite number of all classes of combatant and auxiliary vessels in good repair, an adequate number of properly trained officer and enlisted personnel, and a co-ordinated and efficient Navy Department. No one of these essentials was fully met by our Navy of April, 1917.[2]

At the time of our declaration of war only 33 per cent of the vessels of our fleet were reported materially fit; 67 per cent required an average of 56 days' repairs for war service. Only ten per cent of our vessels were fully manned, and the rest were manned to an average of only 57 per cent. Approximately two-thirds of our ships, therefore, were not materially ready for instant service and 90 per cent fell far short of the complement necessary for the efficient fighting of these ships. So critical was this personnel shortage that for the first six months of the conflict our chief problem was to train men rather than to fight. Moreover, we were woefully weak in the classes of light craft essential for antisubmarine warfare, despite the fact that for some time the German U-boats had become increasingly effective against vital supply lines and almost dominated the war at sea.

Furthermore, the Department's only war plan, the so-called "Black Plan," had been developed on the assumption that we would be fighting a naval campaign singlehanded with our major units against an enemy free to maneuver in the Atlantic and Caribbean. The actual European situation—the bottled-up German fleet and the devastating submarine warfare—was apparently ignored. Evidently the Navy Department intended to follow a "safety first" policy of staying on our side of the Atlantic and attending to our own special and immediate considerations. The combination of these factors necessarily resulted in a delay of several months before our naval strength began to be felt in the bolstering of our wartime associates.

Undoubtedly defective organization within the Navy Department, faulty naval administration, and the obstacles presented by the neutrality of a democratic and traditionally isolationist government contributed to our naval unreadiness and vacillating policy.

From the days of 1812 on, as we have seen from our earlier study, there had been discussion of the problem of obtaining more effective military organization within the Navy Department and more professional authority in control of war plans and fleet operations. In 1900 the General Board of the Navy was established to advise the Secretary

---

[2] See T. B. Kittridge, *Naval Lessons of the Great War;* E. E. Morison, *Admiral Sims and the Modern American Navy,* pp. 433–462.

of the Navy on questions involving policy and the preparing of war plans, but to have no actual authority over the activities of the fleet. Secretary George Meyer, in 1909, went further by organizing a system of officer aides to advise the Secretary on operations, material, personnel, and inspections. It was not until March 3, 1915, however, that as a result of the campaigning by Rear Admiral Bradley A. Fiske and the Navy League the Office of Chief of Naval Operations was created by Congress. This office, intended to function as a naval general staff, was to have control "under the direction of the Secretary" of the operation of the fleet and the preparation of plans for its use in time of war. Fiske, who had been Aide for Operations, 1913–1915, served as its acting chief until he resigned on the issue of more vigorous steps toward preparing the Navy for war. A graduate of the Naval War College and an advocate of the development of naval aviation, Fiske was a practical officer with vision and progressive ideas who accomplished much toward making the office an effective body. In May, 1915, Admiral William S. Benson, far more conservative and less inclined to what he scorned as being "theory," became the first actual Chief of Naval Operations, and continued to develop the office into an efficient organization during the war years, though at the time of our entry it was still inadequately staffed and too new for completely satisfactory work. One example, already mentioned, is the lack, in April, 1917, of a war plan which took into account the actual naval situation facing the Allies at that time; another is the failure of the Department to oppose a Congressional slash in the naval aeronautical appropriation in 1916 from $13,000,000 to $3,500,000, a sum which even in those days should have appeared absurdly inadequate for wartime aviation.

Any thoroughgoing strengthening of the Navy was retarded in part by our democratic form of government. The wishes of the leader of a totalitarian state are law and are final, but in a democracy any administration is guided and limited, to a great extent, by public opinion. During the period of our nonbelligerency public sentiment was undoubtedly divided. Despite a pro-German minority and a pro-Allied majority, the dominant and prevailing idea was to keep out of war. Wilson's Administration merely reflected these views; it was no more war-minded than the nation, nor could it afford to be. The Democratic party was traditionally isolationist, antimilitarist, and anti-imperialist, and at this time it favored only gradual and routine development of our military establishment, especially since the will of the people seemed to be opposed to belligerency and would have a chance to exert itself in the 1916 elections. It was also felt that any undue or strenuous preparations might savor of unneutrality to the already sensitive Germans. So the Navy Department requested of a Democratic Congress only the normal increases and upkeep of the Navy.

Secretary Daniels was thought of as being a "big navy" man, but actually he was probably more enthusiastic about the Navy's educational possibilities, its morals, and its social welfare than its use as an efficient war machine. Perhaps he was but reflecting the Administration's and the nation's state of mind—complete disinterest in war—when he evaded talking of war, and had difficulty in understanding that the Navy existed for the primary purpose of fighting and that the function of the Navy Department was to make the fleet ready for fighting. Unfortunately, in the Secretary's preoccupation with the relatively unimportant details of the naval establishment, vital military needs were sometimes neglected, postponed, or disregarded.

The decision for preparedness finally came largely from the country itself—from organizations and individuals interested in the Navy and national defense. Even President Wilson, who in general had followed a policy of pacifism and an extreme type of neutrality lest we offend Europe by any outward show of readying ourselves for war, was converted, by 1916, to the necessity of strengthening our defenses even to the extent of "incomparably the greatest navy in the world."[3] As a result of this aroused public demand and Administration leadership, Congress passed legislation which at last began the much needed program of making our nation ready for either strong diplomacy or war. The 1916 Naval Appropriation Act authorized a three-year building program to provide ten large battleships, six giant battle cruisers, ten scout cruisers, 50 destroyers, and 67 submarines. Increases were made in regular naval personnel; a naval reserve flying corps was created; the naval reserve was legally authorized and expanded; increased reserves in ammunition and supplies were provided for; and the functions of the Office of Naval Operations were enlarged. This progress in naval preparedness was of vital importance, but, even so, it fell short of making us ready for war in 1917. Much of the added personnel was at that time by no means properly trained; the Office of Naval Operations was still too new to its tasks; and the building program

[3] A statement made by Wilson in his St. Louis speech, February 3, 1916. Later the official version was changed to "the most adequate navy in the world."

was a long-range plan, inapplicable to the emergency of the actual naval situation. Fortunately it was wisely suspended in 1917 to permit concentration on the building of light craft for antisubmarine warfare, and in 1920 the original program was still three-fourths unfinished.

THE NAVAL SITUATION IN 1917

Three days after our declaration of war Rear Admiral Sims, who had been President of the Naval War College, arrived in England to study the naval situation, confer with the British Admiralty, and ascertain how American naval power could most effectively and expeditiously be used. The devastating effects of the U-boats on Allied supply and communication lines were not being revealed to the public, but in his talks with the First Sea Lord, Admiral Jellicoe, Sims was given full information on the actual status of the submarine war. British shipping was being sunk at an appalling rate, and approximately one-fourth of all available shipping was gone. A half a million tons had been sunk in February, and in April losses threatened to reach the unprecedented figure of 900,000 tons. Continued sinkings on this scale meant that England must starve or surrender within a few months' time, and already there was a grain supply on hand for only three weeks. Obviously Germany was winning the war; England must necessarily lose unless methods were devised for coping with the submarines. But Jellicoe saw little hope of this. Only 54 U-boats were known to have been sunk despite the concentration of British efforts against them, and Germany was building new underwater craft at the rate of three a week. The immediate dispatch from America of ships, and more ships, especially antisubmarine vessels, was needed to meet this threat to England's very existence.

In reporting to the Navy Department on the critical situation in Europe, Sims appealed for the prompt sending of the maximum number of destroyers and other antisubmarine craft, auxiliaries, and merchant tonnage, with continual augmentation of these vessels.

After conferring with French and British admirals who commanded squadrons off our coasts but who were not fully aware of the seriousness of the submarine campaign, the Navy Department had formulated general plans for using our fleet primarily in home waters to protect our shipping against possible submarine and surface raiders and for sending six destroyers to Europe as a mere gesture. Believing that Sims was extremely pro-English and that he was too quick to recommend

immediate aid for the Allies, the Navy Department hesitated to accept
his conception of the critical state of the war at sea. However, the
British and French missions soon convinced the Department that the
Allies were losing their fight against the U-boats. Finally, by July,
1917, Sims was advised that the policy would now be one of full co-
operation with the British and that ships, especially light craft, in any
number not incompatible with home needs and the adequate protection of our own waters would be sent overseas. Even with this change
of attitude Sims was hardly satisfied, for he contended that the crisis
of the naval war was in Europe, and that the best protection for the
United States was all-out participation and co-operation in attacking
the enemy where he was actually operating.

American Destroyers Overseas

On May 4, 1917, the inhabitants of Queenstown, Ireland witnessed
a historic event—"the return of the *Mayflower*" in the guise of six
American destroyers steaming up the swept channel amid the plaudits
of the people and the whistling of the harbor craft. The public was
greatly impressed with these strange destroyers, so unlike their British
counterparts in their general contour,[4] which had left Boston on April
24 in response to Sims's cabled appeal and which were arriving at
their destination at exactly the appointed time.

After the first greetings in the city, the American officers ascended
the hill to Admiralty House to meet their new commander, Vice Admiral Sir Lewis Bayly, R.N. Taut, taciturn, and exacting, Bayly was
one of Britain's most able and energetic officers, described in the British
official history as "the father of destroyer tactics and organization" in
the war. His primary interest was the immediate use of his American
support, and soon came his inquiry, "When will you be ready to go
to sea?" Commander Joseph K. Taussig, senior American officer, replied, "We are ready now, sir, that is, as soon as we finish refueling."

The Americans were given a more than ample four days for rest
and repairs and brief words of advice: no lights of any kind at night,
no steaming below 13 knots, constant zigzagging, only short signals,
no fixed system of patrol, careful watching of all fishing vessels lest
they be disguised submarines, and above all no underrating of an

---

[4] American destroyers were almost feminine in comparison with the more sturdy-
looking British ships. They were more slender and graceful with greater fuel capacity, but were less maneuverable and speedy. Different arrangement of stacks,
gun emplacements, torpedo tubes, depth charges, and machines contributed to the
generally contrasting profile.

enemy who had also shown skill, perseverance, and cleverness in the "art of irregularity." Bayly's orders on the duties of destroyers were, in order of importance, to destroy submarines, convoy and protect shipping, and save the lives of people from torpedoed ships. Now was the crisis of the submarine menace, and this experienced, war-weary Britisher was interested only in overcoming the threat to Britain's existence. Once the Americans had proved their worth and ability to perform their duties creditably, their relations with their British chief developed into understanding and affection. Something of this feeling was expressed in Bayly's message on the anniversary of their arrival in Queenstown: "To command you is an honour, to work with you is a pleasure, to know you is to know the best traits of the Anglo-Saxon race."

Admiral Bayly, as Commander-in-Chief of the coasts of Ireland, commanded the American destroyers at Queenstown during the entire war, even after most of the British units, save four or five, were withdrawn to strengthen the hard-pressed forces in other vital areas. To our first destroyer force others were soon added, almost a new division each week, until by July the number of American destroyers at Queenstown had reached 34, the approximate figure of our force there for the rest of the war. Eventually we had 79 destroyers in European waters, while the British increased theirs from 200 to some 400, which were deployed over many important areas including approximately 100 with the Grand Fleet.[5]

Because of the scarcity of naval vessels the British in the spring of 1917 were fighting the submarines mainly in two ways: by the constant laying of mines off the submarine bases and by the use of all possible light craft, especially destroyers, to patrol the sea lanes most commonly raided by the U-boats. The first method was unsuccessful because the mines were defective and easily swept; the latter succeeded only in driving the target underwater until the patrol passed on. The rigorous and highly ineffective routine, in which each destroyer patrolled about 900 square miles for six days and then spent two days in port, was soon replaced, in May, 1917, by the far more effective convoy system.

For some time the Admiralty had been discussing the possibility of using this age-old practice as a means of combating the submarine

---

[5] By this time the German High Sea Fleet was no real threat to the British and was used primarily as a fortress fleet and source of manpower for the U-boats. The criticism of the retention of American destroyers for protection of American waters might, therefore, apply equally to the British failure to use all their available destroyer force to protect shipping.

menace. Many naval officers were pessimistic because of its seeming impracticability, the 15 to 20 per cent delay to traffic, and the danger of losing stragglers to lurking submarines. The greatest hostility, however, came from the merchant captains, who feared their inability to maintain regular speed and to maneuver in close formation at night without lights. Above all else there was the obvious deficiency of destroyers for protecting the convoys in the danger zone and of cruisers for warding off surface raiders farther out.

The decision to adopt the convoy system came largely as a result of the emphatic insistence of Sims and Prime Minister Lloyd George, the hope that the United States could supply the necessary additional escort craft, and the realization that this would at least be a change to offensive warfare against the undersea raiders. Whereas the patrol system merely caused submarines to sink out of sight momentarily, the convoy system would force the U-boats to come within range of destroyer action or else operate only close inshore after the convoy was dispersed. When an experimental convoy from Gibraltar arrived in London without mishap on May 20, and another from Hampton Roads four days later, the matter was finally settled. It was evident to the Admiralty that one way of defeating the submarines had been found and that a turning point in the war at sea had arrived. From the first day of its adoption the convoy system was an "unqualified success," and immediately its effects were seen. The shipping loss of nearly 900,000 tons in April was gradually reduced to less than 300,-000 in November. Never again did the U-boat seriously threaten to win the war. The number of escort craft was gradually augmented, and finally about 92 per cent of Allied shipping was in convoy, with losses of vessels under escort less than half of one per cent.

The assembling, routing, and escorting of thousands of ships required an elaborate mechanism which would work with time-table accuracy. The control center for this vast traffic was located in a room in the Admiralty in London, where, under the charge of a single group of officers, the movements not only of convoys but also of the eight or nine German U-boats known to be at sea were plotted on a huge wall chart. Accurate and detailed information on the movements and activities of the submarines was obtained by direction finders which listened in on their almost daily communications with each other, and by reports from merchantmen which had made any kind of contact with them. Then it was possible, usually, to send wireless warnings to convoys and detour them around the submarines known to be lying in wait. Central headquarters in London was concerned with all Allied shipping throughout the world, but it became more acutely interested as the convoys began their trek toward Britain from the assembly ports of Sydney (Cape Breton), Halifax, New York, and Hampton Roads in North America; Dakar and Sierra Leone in Africa; and Gibraltar.

Allied cruisers escorted convoys from the assembly areas to the danger zone and protected them from possible attacks by surface raiders.[6] At a prearranged rendezvous, usually within about 200 miles from the British Isles, they were met by destroyers, which, with their speed and antisubmarine equipment, were a more effective escort in the submarine-infested danger zone. The opposite procedure was followed for outward bound convoys, for which safeguards were just as important, since the Germans were waging a war against the available shipping tonnage of the Allies. Convoys, consisting of from 20 to 30 ships, were arranged in several parallel columns, each containing about four ships in single file, and the whole covering several square miles. The speed of the convoy was necessarily the speed of the slowest vessel. Destroyers were stationed on each exposed flank, since those areas offered the best target for submarines, and usually one was detached as a rear guard and protection for stragglers.

At the first indication of a torpedo attack or of the presence of a submarine, speedy destroyers dashed to the suspected location of the submarine and bombarded this area with a pattern of depth charges. These "ash cans," loaded with 300 pounds of TNT and regulated to explode at any set depth, were run off the stern or tossed on either side from "Y" guns. As the supply of these bombs increased, they were used in greater numbers and created an unnerving barrage for the underwater quarry, if not inflicting actual damage. Among all the American escort forces in European waters there were 286 attacks, nearly 200 of which were on actual U-boats. As a result, there were four to six verified sinkings and 17 other encounters which caused damage necessitating the return of the submarine to its base or internment in a neutral port.

Convoy work amid the cold and foggy eastern Atlantic was dreary and wearisome work, with little to relieve the day-in day-out monotony of searching for an invisible foe. Occasionally, of course, there were moments of excitement, even of real drama, when contacts were made

---

[6] Actually the last raider even attempting to break into the Atlantic was sunk in the North Sea by the British Patrol Squadron in February, 1917.

with U-boats, or, better still, when a verified "kill" was made. One of the most striking instances occurred when the *Fanning,* with the co-operation of the *Nicholson,* damaged the *U-58,* causing her to surface, only to be scuttled by her skipper and sent to the bottom. Four officers and 35 men were rescued. This brought for the *Fanning* the congratulations of the Admiralty and Sims's inspiring words, "Go out and do it again."

CONTINENTAL BASES

The convoying of merchant shipping from North America was the primary duty of the American force based on Queenstown, and it escorted 40 per cent of all such tonnage. Brest, in 1918, was to be of equal importance and of larger size but concerned chiefly with the protection of troop movements. Gibraltar, however, was the "gateway for more traffic than any other port in the world,"[7] and in response to British appeals American ships, under Rear Admiral Henry B. Wilson, were ordered there. Rear Admiral Albert P. Niblack assumed command of our Gibraltar force for the remainder of the war when, in November, 1917, Admiral Wilson went to Brest as the Commander of American Naval Forces in France.

Though of tremendous importance because of the amount of traffic, the Gibraltar area was not so consistently visited by U-boats and was farther from the submarine-infested waters than were Queenstown and Brest. Accordingly, the major destroyer forces were sent to the more threatened areas, and the heterogeneous residue of all the Entente navies was based on Gibraltar. The American detachment here consisted of about 40 craft—scout cruisers, gunboats, converted yachts, Coast Guard cutters, and, later, seven submarine-chasers. This group included five antiquated 420-ton destroyers, which, under the command of Lieutenant Commander Harold R. Stark, had steamed 12,000 miles from Manila and then carried out 48,000 miles of convoy duty. The Gibraltar unit served gallantly in protecting some 562 convoys of 10,478 ships in the Mediterranean and its approaches. American yachts of this group were credited with sinking two submarines and damaging a third sufficiently to cause its internment in Spain.

Brest was more strategically located as a convoy base than even Queenstown, but an immediate concentration of forces here was impeded by its inadequate dock, tankage, and repair facilities. Beginning

[7] More than one-fourth of all the convoys to the Allies either assembled here or passed through these straits. W. S. Sims, *The Victory at Sea,* p. 161.

Top, UNITED STATES NAVY "BLIMP" AND CONVOY NEARING BREST,
JUNE, 1918. *Bottom,* EXPLODING A DEPTH CHARGE, FIRST WORLD WAR.

in July, 1917, American units under Rear Admiral William B. Fletcher, and later Admiral Wilson, were based here. A fourfold increase in tankage installations and great improvements in other facilities were undertaken in preparing Brest as our main continental base for the escort and reception of troop transports.

Our first forces ordered to Brest were armed yachts manned and officered primarily by reserves, who, with little training but with great spirit and ambition, performed exceptional service against submarines up and down the French coast. Duty aboard these light ships in the severe Biscay gales was exceedingly strenuous. As facilities were improved and enlarged, Brest gradually became the largest of all the 45 bases of varied types established by the United States during the war. Our naval strength on the Biscay coast was eventually comprised of 43 destroyers, 20 yachts, four tenders, 11 tugs, 12 submarine-chasers, and several minesweepers, as well as aircraft. Although the prime responsibility of the Brest establishment was the escort of American troops and supplies to the French coast, it nevertheless contributed significantly in escorting other Allied vessels, aiding torpedoed ships, sweeping mines, patrolling, and supervising port arrangements for the disembarkation of troops and stores. In addition to complete success, in 1918, in convoying 90 per cent of the convoys entering the Atlantic ports of France, these forces caused the gradual reduction of losses in other types of ships off the French coast—from 24 sunk in October, 1917, to none sunk in March, 1918.

SUBMARINE-CHASERS

Special mention must be made of one type of vessel, which, because of the shortage of destroyers, was developed for the sole purpose of fighting the submarine. The submarine-chasers—110-foot, 60-ton, wooden craft armed with 3-inch guns and depth charges—were well designed for taking the active offensive against U-boats. In 18 months the United States built nearly 400 of these small craft, and distributed 170 of them among Plymouth, Queenstown, Gibraltar, Brest, Corfu, Portsmouth, the Azores, and even Murmansk. This "splinter fleet" was manned by reserves[8]—college boys from practically every college in the United States—who, by their alertness and enthusiasm, learned sufficient seamanship to navigate these tiny ships across the icy, storm-swept Atlantic in the winter of 1917–1918.

---

[8] Less than one per cent were Naval Academy graduates. Only five per cent were experienced sailors.

The extensive success of German submarines in attacking ships after the dispersal of convoys in the restricted waters along the coast necessitated the immediate concentration of 36 sub-chasers at Plymouth for use in the English Channel. Operating in trios, these chasers would use their American-perfected hydrophones to spot their prey by a "triangulation fix," and then slowly close in, until at last they would dash in and bomb it with depth charges. So effective was the work of these boats off Plymouth that not a ship was sunk during their stay of six weeks, nor were any enemy mines laid. Immediately after their withdrawal, however, mines were laid and sinkings by submarines were resumed.

So successful were German and Austrian submarines against Allied shipping in the Mediterranean that an attempt was made to pen these undersea raiders in their Adriatic bases by a "barrage" across the 40 mile-wide Straits of Otranto. In the summer of 1918, 36 American sub-chasers, based on Corfu, added their tactical and listening qualities to the British and Italian destroyers, drifters, kite balloons, and net barrier defenses. Arranged to form a 35 mile-long gauntlet, this force made it almost impossible for submarines to pass into the Mediterranean hunting grounds. The effect upon enemy morale was so great that two weeks after the arrival of the chasers no Austrian crew could be forced to attempt the passage, and by November German crews went only when compelled at the point of a pistol.

In early October, 11 of the Corfu sub-chasers acted as an anti-submarine screen for six British and Italian cruisers in an attack on the Austrian supply port and naval base at Durazzo, on the Dalmatian coast. While the cruisers demolished port facilities, military buildings, and shipping, the chasers protected them from submarines and got credit for sinking two of them. "Their conduct," wrote the British commodore in charge of the operation, "was beyond praise. They all returned safely without casualties. They thoroughly enjoyed themselves." [9]

Until adequate destroyer forces were built up, the submarine-chasers were recognized as one of the most useful countermeasures against the submarine.

---

[9] Though there were almost unnumbered submarine contacts, this has not untruthfully been called "the only naval engagement participated in by the American Navy in the entire war." Ray Millholland, *The Splinter Fleet of the Otranto Barrage,* p. 239.

Submarine Against Submarine

In proportion to their numbers the Allied submarines were the most effective weapon against the U-boats.[10] The success realized in their fight against craft of their own kind in restricted waters completely reversed the pre-war opinion that "one submarine cannot fight another." In view of their value, a flotilla of small American coastal defense submarines was sent to the Azores, and later another of seven struggled through the wintry Atlantic gales to a base at Bantry Bay to protect shipping in the waters off eastern and southern Ireland. This was indeed arduous duty, involving eight-day patrols, dangers of mines, physical discomfort, fear of attack by even friendly surface vessels, and the necessity of remaining submerged as long as possible.

A submarine combat was short; the issue was determined in a few minutes either by an occasional ramming or, almost invariably, by torpedo, the ship being lost which revealed its position first. "We got used to your depth charges," said a captured German submarine commander, "and did not fear them; but we lived in constant dread of your submarines. We never knew what moment a torpedo was going to hit us." So great was this dread that U-boats avoided areas where enemy submarines were known to be operating.

Allied submarines accomplished three objectives: they reduced the effectiveness of U-boats by keeping them submerged more than was customary; they decreased the tactical value of the 300-foot, 3,000-ton "cruiser" submarine;[11] and they prevented the operation of U-boats in flotillas because of the inability to distinguish friend from foe.

Naval Aircraft: Fighting Submarines from the Air

World War I gave a tremendous impetus to the development of American naval aviation. Scant appropriations of earlier years caused us to enter the war with only 39 qualified pilots and 54 planes, useful only for training service, but this insignificant force grew until at the end of the war there were 1,300 officers (including 825 pilots), 1,500

---

[10] "The Allied destroyers, about 500 in number, sank 34 German submarines with gunfire and depth charges; auxiliary patrol craft, such as trawlers, yachts, and the like, about 3,000 in number, sank 31; while the Allied submarines, which were only about 100 in number, sank 20." W. S. Sims, *The Victory at Sea*, pp. 263–264.

[11] Construction of this new class was begun by Germany in the summer of 1917 as an answer to the Allied convoy system.

enlisted men, and 500 planes stationed in our 27 bases in Europe.[12] Naval reserve officers were primarily responsible for this remarkable growth and actually piloted the majority of the planes, though members of the regular Navy were in administrative authority. The first Yale University aviation unit, of 29 members, under Trubee Davison, formed the nucleus and training personnel of the Naval Reserve Flying Corps, which, in turn, was the nucleus from which grew the United States Aviation Forces, Foreign Service. Later recruits were primarily college men and civilian flyers.

A group of seven officers and 122 men of this corps, landing on June 7, 1917, were the first American forces, other than Army medical units, to reach France. This hitherto neglected branch of the service was tremendously expanded under Captain Hutch I. Cone, who had general charge of naval aviation overseas, and Captain T. T. Craven, who did outstanding work as Aide for Aviation in France. Americans took over a large seaplane base at Killingholme, on the east coast of England, where they operated with the British to escort convoys to the Scandinavian countries, act as an antisubmarine patrol, and make reconnaissances. In addition to this base, we had four seaplane stations, one kite balloon station, and one assembly and repair center in the British Isles. From two Italian seaplane stations, Americans bombed Austrian naval bases with good effect. In France, our Northern Bombing Group, operating from the large naval and marine station at Dunkirk, was intended to bomb German submarine bases at Zeebrugge and Ostend. As the retreating Germans began to abandon their bases in Flanders, this aviation unit worked with the British Army against military objectives. Elsewhere in France the United States had 11 naval air stations on the Atlantic coast, as well as a gunnery school and repair base. The enormous American naval aviation center at Pauillac, France, with its aircraft factory and accommodations for 20,000 men, was just approaching effective operation at the end of hostilities.

Air power as an adjunct to sea power was still in its infancy during this war; nevertheless it played an important part in combating the submarine menace. American airmen were credited with only one "kill," but of their 39 direct attacks on submarines ten were pronounced as being "successful" in varying degrees. This, however, by

---

[12] The entire Naval Air Corps was comprised of 2,500 officers (of whom 1,656 were pilots), 22,000 enlisted men, and 2,127 planes. Most of our planes overseas were of British and French make.

no means reveals the full effectiveness of naval air power in the anti-submarine campaign. The convoy system had caused submarines to seek their prey more and more in the coastal waters after the dispersal of the convoy. Patrol aircraft, with their speed, scope of visibility, and their own comparative invisibility, made these waters dangerous for submarine operations—either by direct air attacks or by acting as spotters for surface craft. Dirigibles added strength as escorts on the flanks of convoys; not infrequently aircraft formed the sole escort for coastal convoys. All in all, the combination of destroyers, submarines, and aircraft made U-boat operations, especially in coastal waters, "extremely hazardous and nerve-racking."

Naval aviators had their full share of thrilling action. Many examples of daring and skill might be given. As a single instance, Lieutenant Commander A. L. Gates,[13] at Dunkirk, received both British and American decorations for the heroic rescue of a British crew off Ostend, and for many flights over the enemy lines, in one of which he was finally shot down and made prisoner.

NORTH SEA MINE BARRAGE

The last of the Allied methods of combating German submarines was a weapon of an entirely different nature—a barrier of mines across the North Sea from Scotland to Norway. For some time naval authorities as well as laymen had discussed the feasibility of such a project, and there had been much criticism of the failure to adopt this obvious means of "shutting up the hornets in their nests." The Bureau of Ordnance of our Navy Department planned such an operation, but it was vetoed by the British Admiralty, in 1917, because of the seemingly insoluble problems involved. The Allies could spare neither the personnel nor the ships for patrolling and mining. Moreover, the British mines were easily swept, could not withstand strong tides and heavy weather, and had been far from effective off Helgoland Bight and in the narrow Straits of Dover. There seemed to be no possibility of producing the estimated 400,000 mines required for an area 230 miles wide with a depth ranging to 900 feet.

---

[13] Gates was a member of the First Yale Aviation Unit. He was made Assistant Secretary of the Navy for Air in 1941. Other distinguished members of this group were their leader, Davison, who was Assistant Secretary of War for Air, 1926–1932, and a colonel on the Army Staff in the Second World War; David S. Ingalls, spoken of by Admiral Sims as the "Naval Ace of the War," who was Assistant Secretary of the Navy for Air, 1929–1932; and Robert A. Lovett, who became Assistant Secretary of War for Air in 1940. See R. W. Paine. *The First Yale Unit.*

The American development of the new "antenna" mine to replace the old contact mine overcame most of the obstacles, however, and on November 2, 1917, the "Northern Barrage" project was officially adopted. This new mine was detonated by contact of any metal object not only with its projecting "horns," but also with a long copper wire antenna extending above the mine. Anchor, mine, and antenna could be dropped as a unit and set automatically at any desired depth. The antenna type extended the area protected by a single mine, and thereby reduced the required number of mines to 100,000, with a corresponding reduction also in the amount of shipping and personnel.

The Bureau of Ordnance, headed by Rear Admiral Ralph Earle, offered not only to produce the mines at the rate of 1,000 a day, but also to transport and lay them. Though there was practically no equipment or personnel available at the start, this enormous undertaking was successfully completed by American skill in organization and mass production. Ships were procured and converted for mine service; personnel was trained; contracts for mine parts were let to 500 different firms; bases were established in the United States and Scotland; and steamers were acquired to carry to Europe the mines which were being assembled at Norfolk at the rate of 1,000 a day—about one every two minutes. From the disembarkation ports in western Scotland the mines were transported by canal and by rail to the east coast bases on Moray Firth. By May, 1918, our mine-laying force of two old cruisers and eight converted coastal vessels, fitted with elevators and mine tracks for quick handling of mines, had arrived at the Scottish bases. Captain Reginald R. Belknap commanded the mine-laying force, and Rear Admiral Joseph Strauss was in overall command of the operation overseas.

The 230-mile barrage was a joint project, but the American part was by far the larger. The Americans mined the area for 150 miles eastward from the Orkneys; the British extended this to Norwegian waters. With a destroyer escort against submarines and a battleship screen against surface craft, the mine-laying units made their first "excursion" on June 7, and the ensuing 12 occurred at average ten-day intervals until late October. Though exciting and dangerous, the operations suffered no losses from accident or enemy action. Despite adverse weather the ships would keep station in line abreast at a speed of over 12 knots, laying mines at the rate of five a minute, and usually about 5,400 at every trip. Of approximately 70,000 mines laid, 56,-

571, or 80 per cent, were American mines, laid by the American force.[14]

Not every square foot in the North Sea barrage was mined, and there were unintentional gaps since about four per cent of the mines were defective. It was officially estimated that a submarine had about one chance in ten of threading its way through the thickest part. However, the barrage, with a width of from 15 to 35 miles—with ten lines of mines near the surface, four intermediate, and four lower-level lines—became a menace to the passage of submarines even before it had been completed. As early as July and August there were submarine damages and losses, including the *U-156* which was returning from American waters. The actual material damage caused by this barrier will probably never be known since there were often no traces left, but the barrage was credited with 17 U-boats sunk or seriously damaged.[15] It served further as a powerful deterrent by its effects on enemy morale, contributing to the decline of submarine activity in the final months of the war, and perhaps to the mutinous attitude of German crews. If the prosecution of the war cost $100,000,000 a day, the mine barrage was certainly worth its overall cost of $80,000,000.

BATTLESHIPS OVERSEAS

So far consideration has been given only to American co-operation in the efforts against the German submarine campaign, which was, of course, of acute and more immediate concern. However, had the German High Sea Fleet been allowed to operate against these escorts, convoys, and patrols, it undoubtedly would have driven them from the seas, and, combined with the U-boats, would have won the war for Germany. This was prevented by the British Grand Fleet, which was effectively blocking the German fleet and preventing its emergence.

Although no large scale fighting between heavy naval vessels occurred after our entry into the war, American battleships shared in the strategy adopted against the German fleet. At first there was no demand for their immediate use, and there was a scarcity of oil even for the British ships. As the transport of American troops increased, however, there was a growing danger that German surface raiders or even battle cruisers might elude the watchful British and perhaps destroy entire

[14] So successful was this venture felt to be that plans were made for other barriers, and the mine field laid in the North Irish Channel destroyed two German submarines.

[15] There were also some 40 to 50 lost U-boats that were unaccounted for either by German or Allied records.

convoys. Therefore, in December, 1917, five of our coal-burning battleships, *New York, Wyoming, Florida, Delaware,* and *Texas,* under the command of Rear Admiral Hugh Rodman, arrived to reinforce Admiral Sir David Beatty and to give the British even greater superiority over the Germans. These American dreadnoughts necessarily became an integral part of the Grand Fleet as the Sixth Battle Squadron. Using British signals, tactics, and fire control, they co-operated with the British in patrol, commerce protection, and ceaseless vigil in northern waters. Here was tangible evidence of Allied solidarity.

On the whole this was uneventful, though severe duty, despite attacks from U-boats on six occasions. In one instance the *New York* probably sank a U-boat by collision and later, while proceeding to dry dock, saw three torpedoes cross her bow.

Battleship protection against surface raiders was considered to be of great importance. Hence, as a further safeguard toward the end of the war, three of the faster and more powerful battleships, *Nevada, Oklahoma,* and *Utah,* under Rear Admiral Thomas S. Rodgers, were stationed on the extreme southwest coast of Ireland at Bantry Bay. The other major concentration of our battleships was based at Hampton Roads, under Admiral Henry T. Mayo, Commander-in-Chief of the Atlantic Fleet. These ships served as a reserve force in constant readiness for action as well as a training unit for more than 45,000 officers and men, most of whom were subsequently sent overseas.

The British containing of the German fleet allowed the Allies to have a surface control of the sea; at the same time, however, the presence of the German fleet helped prevent a close blockade, made the U-boat campaign possible, and, as a fleet in being, forced the British to concentrate at Scapa Flow vessels which were vitally needed in the antisubmarine campaign.

U-BOATS IN AMERICAN WATERS

Partly as an outcome of the success of the antisubmarine campaign in European waters, already covered, five large, long-range U-boats operated off the American east coast in the last summer of the war. Their purpose was primarily diversionary and propaganda—to show the American public that it was not safe from attack and to cause it to agitate for the withdrawal of antisubmarine forces from Europe for home defense. Such a campaign had been foreseen and by 1918 had little effect other than to indicate that the U-boats were hard-pressed in the waters nearer home. Usually not more than one or two of them operated in American waters at one time, and their attacks were sporadic. The *U-151* laid mines off the Delaware and the Chesapeake and in three months' activities between Hatteras and New York sank 23 vessels with an aggregate of 59,000 tons. Probably the most notable exploit of these submarines occurred when the *U-155,* the converted "merchant submarine" *Deutschland,* laid mines off Fire Island, near New York, one of which sank the old armored cruiser *San Diego,* of the Transport Service, with a loss of six men. In late September, the battleship *Minnesota* struck a mine off Fenwick Island Shoals but proceeded to Philadelphia under her own steam. U-boats off the American coast sank 79 vessels, totaling approximately 200,000 tons, but these were primarily sailing and coastal vessels and of little military significance.

The London "Flagship"

The necessary overall control of these American naval activities was centralized in two places, Washington and London. In our nation's capital, Secretary Daniels, Assistant Secretary of the Navy Franklin D. Roosevelt, and the Chief of Naval Operations, Admiral Benson, determined all the larger questions of American policy and strategy, and, with their bureau chiefs and vastly expanded staffs, supervised the furnishing of personnel, supplies, munitions, shipping, and repair for the far-flung operations. The London headquarters of Vice Admiral Sims[16] served as a central staff in the European theater. Here the rapid increase of American naval forces to 370 vessels, 5,000 officers, 75,000 enlisted men, and 45 bases, as well as the varied types of American activities, necessitated as much general control and co-ordination as possible. In April, 1917, Sims had one aide; at the armistice 1,200 officers, enlisted men, and clerks constituted his administrative and technical staff.

As Commander of United States Naval Forces Operating in European Waters, Sims was in general charge of American naval activities overseas. He adhered to the sound policy that his units should be closely integrated with the British under co-ordinated direction. As an example, Sims was in immediate command of our destroyers at Queenstown,[17] but they were under the operational orders of Vice Ad-

---

[16] He was promoted to this rank on May 26, 1917.

[17] His flag was flown from the tender *Melville* at Queenstown, and he was represented there by Captain Joel R. Poinsett Pringle, his Chief of Staff in Ireland.

miral Bayly. Elsewhere, American forces acted in close co-operation, and often as subordinate units, with the British. London was necessarily the headquarters of the naval war, and located here was the Allied Naval Council, of which Sims was a member. This body was an inter-allied conference for deciding questions on any phase of the naval war. The British Admiralty issued all general orders concerning the operations of British and American naval forces, although those affecting the Americans were first approved by the American staff. Needless to say, close co-operation and understanding necessarily existed between the British and Americans in London, and there was little valid criticism made of these arrangements. An innovation of Sims was his Planning Section, probably the first in any navy, which served as an advisory group and studied specific problems, planned operations, and analyzed all phases of the prosecution of the war.

In addition to reports from Sims and the commanders of our naval activities in Europe, the visits of Admiral Benson and Admiral Mayo, in the autumn of 1917, gave the authorities in Washington a clearer appreciation of the scope and exigencies of the naval war and a growing approval of Sims's organization and methods. It was unfortunate that during the war the exact position and authority of Sims was never clearly defined; nor was he allowed to choose the commanders of any of our major bases abroad. Only because he and these commanders agreed fundamentally on their objective and the means of attaining it were they able to succeed in their task.

THE BRIDGE TO FRANCE

The American naval forces used in combating the German U-boat undoubtedly added the strength necessary to prevent an inevitable German victory in 1917. It may also be said that American troops of the Western Front, aiding the Allies both materially and psychologically, proved the decisive factor in defeating Germany in 1918.

In 1917, Germany realized that her unrestricted submarine warfare might bring the United States into the war, but she was confident she could defeat the Allies before American forces in sufficient numbers could be brought to bear. Even the Entente powers were dubious of the ability of the United States to train soldiers, provide shipping tonnage, and transport troops and supplies in sufficient numbers to prevent a German victory. It is largely to the credit of the United States Navy that this seemingly insurmountable problem was solved.

In order to help relieve the grave situation on the Western Front it was imperative that merchant tonnage be accumulated in vast amounts and in quick time. The United States had only 1,000,000 tons available to help replace the 7,000,000 tons of Allied shipping sunk by the Germans up to the time of our entry. For some time, however, our Shipping Board had been trying to increase our merchant marine by a tremendous expansion of production. To spur this effort on, the Emergency Fleet Corporation was created on April 26, 1917, to procure shipping in great quantities immediately. By purchase, requisition, and construction of steel ships, wooden ships, prefabricated ships, and even concrete ships, our shipping increased finally to 10,000,000 tons. The Army had no troopships suitable for overseas service, and the Navy had only two, the *Hancock* and the *Henderson*. A partial answer to the immediate need of transports was found in 300,000 tons of idle Dutch ships and 600,000 tons of interned German ships lying in American ports. The latter had been expertly sabotaged by their crews, but in repairing the cylinders and boilers by the new electric welding process some 12 months' time was saved. Twenty of these German ships, including the *Leviathan,* were destined to carry over half a million American soldiers to France.

Ships from these sources, with about 20 American liners, brought the total available to 45. These troopships, manned by naval crews, together with 24 cruisers and other escort craft, formed the Cruiser and Transport Force, commanded by Rear Admiral Albert Gleaves. For supply ships, the Naval Overseas Transportation Service was established under the Navy Department late in 1917, with 72 vessels. At the time of the armistice it was operating a fleet of 453 ships, with a naval personnel of 5,000 officers and 45,000 men.

The convoy system, which had protected Allied shipping so well, was used even more effectively for the movement of American forces overseas. Despite General Ludendorff's assertion that the U-boats would prevent the transportation of American troops, not a single ship under American escort was torpedoed en route to France;[18] not a single man was lost by enemy action. This success was attained primarily by routing the fast-moving, well-guarded convoys directly to France on a course somewhat to the southward of the areas usually infested with submarines. The few German U-boats could not cover this route

---

[18] Westbound transports were not equally immune. They were less carefully guarded and routed, and the Germans were still anxious to sink tonnage. The *Antilles, President Lincoln,* and *Covington* were sunk by torpedoes but with little loss of life. The *Finland* and *Mt. Vernon* were torpedoed but managed to return to Brest.

in addition to the lanes more congested with shipping, and they chose to concentrate their attacks on the latter.

The transport of troops began in June, 1917, and continued with ever-increasing volume until the spring of 1918 when the situation on the Western Front demanded that more troops be sent as quickly as possible. Realizing that the submarines had failed, the Germans, in March, 1918, directed a tremendous drive into the Allied lines. England and France were now desperate for manpower. There were only 300,000 American troops in France, and it seemed impossible that others could be added in time. However, the transport of troops was speeded up to meet the crisis, and soon American troops were arriving in France at the rate of approximately 10,000 a day. They came in time to help stop the Germans and to share significantly in the final Allied offensive.

The records show that of the 2,079,880 soldiers sent abroad, over 46 per cent were carried in American ships (practically all naval transports), 48 per cent in British or British-leased ships, and the small remainder in ships of other allies. For the entire troop movement American naval vessels provided about 86 per cent of the escort protection.

NAVAL ACTIVITIES ASHORE

In recounting World War naval operations one must include some mention of the Navy's contributions to the conflict on land—particularly the employment of naval guns ashore and the work of the hard-fighting Marines. General Pershing requested the use of American naval guns and gun crews because the Allies had no other guns of such range available to use against the last German drive. The specific mission of the five 14-inch guns, originally intended for our new battle cruisers, was to destroy "Big Bertha"—a 75-mile-range gun which was dropping shells with demoralizing effect upon Paris—and to bombard specific points behind the German lines. Mounted on railway cars for mobility and with trains of 14 cars for each, these guns achieved full success. "Big Bertha" was withdrawn before it could be destroyed and was never heard from again. Firing in all about 782 shells at distances ranging from 18 to 23 miles, the naval batteries from several points on the Western Front rained destruction on German communication lines, bridges, railroad centers, and supply dumps well behind the lines.

Fighting with the well-known "spirit of the Corps," the Marines performed valiant service throughout the period of American participation. About 30,000 were sent overseas. In the critical areas of Chateau Thierry, Belleau Wood, St. Mihiel, the Meuse-Argonne, and elsewhere, they contributed immeasurably in stemming the tide of the last German drive and in pushing forward the "victory" offensive of the Allies. Casualties were severe, sometimes more than half of the force involved. It was at Belleau Wood that the typical courage and tenacity of the Marine Corps won from the dispirited Germans the appellation "Devil Dogs." [19]

The Surrender

American troops and equipment on the Western Front proved to be the margin necessary for victory, and, with the failure of the submarine campaign against Allied shipping, made the defeat of Germany inevitable. On October 21, 1918, as a result of preliminary negotiations with President Wilson, the German Government agreed to abandon submarine attacks on passenger ships, and this practically ended the U-boat campaign. A last desperate sortie of the High Sea Fleet was planned, but this was halted by mutinies among the seamen at Wilhelmshaven and Kiel. On November 21, in accordance with the armistice terms,[20] the bulk of the German fleet—nine dreadnoughts, five battle cruisers, six light cruisers, and 50 destroyers—steamed through the Grand Fleet, including the American Sixth Squadron, drawn up in two long lines at the entrance to the Firth of Forth. At sunset, from the masts of this great naval force intended as a potent instrument for world conquest, the German flag was lowered for the last time.

The task of our Navy in World War I, like that of navies in most wars, lay in maintaining sea control and sea communications; and its great achievements were its effective support for the British in combating the submarine and its major part in transporting our Army overseas. These activities were, of course, overlapping in many respects; success in only one of them would probably have been meaningless.

Admiral Sims was convinced that "without the co-operation of the American Navy the Allies could not have won the war." In estimating

---

[19] For full treatment of the Marine Corps in the war, see C. H. Metcalf, *A History of the United States Marine Corps*, 1939.

[20] The armistice terms called for surrender of ten battleships, six battle cruisers, eight light cruisers, 50 destroyers, and all submarines. The submarines and some of the larger craft were surrendered elsewhere.

our achievements, however, allowance must be made for the advantages we enjoyed—our remoteness from attack, time for preparation, participation with strong naval allies, and entry at a time when both sides had been worn down by nearly three years of exhausting conflict. It should be no cause for boasting or undue confidence that in these conditions our fresh forces turned the scales in favor of the Allies. But great credit may be taken for the energy, the spirit of co-operation, the magnitude of the effort with which, once the need was clearly realized, American resources and manpower were thrown into the war.

21
Between Two Wars, 1918–1941

NOVEMBER 11, 1918, found the fundamental power patterns of the world, which had developed gradually through a whole century, utterly upset. The empire of Wilhelm II and the other Central Powers were prostrate. At the time it seemed unthinkable that Germany would again be a major military or naval power. Italy and France were bled white and were nearly bankrupt. Russia was engulfed in a confused and bloody civil war. England, which had suffered three million casualties and strained every resource of empire in the war, faced a future in which both her economic and military security were infinitely less certain than would have seemed possible to Englishmen five years earlier.

In contrast, the ascendant power of Japan and the United States had been developed, rather than impaired, by the war. Though America's intervention was probably the decisive factor in the victory, our territory had not been invaded, nor our treasury reduced to bankruptcy. Our casualties, though painful, did not represent a serious drain on our manpower. The war altered our international credit position from that of perennial debtor nation to that of creditor nation; our industrialization was both speeded up and diversified under the goad of wartime necessity. To a lesser degree, the same might be said of Japan.

On November 11, 1918, though the British Grand Fleet was immeasurably the strongest in British history, Britannia had ceased to rule the waves—at least in the sense the phrase was used in the days of Nelson. Even before the war, back at the time of Theodore Roosevelt's administration, the primacy of the American Navy in Western Hemisphere waters had been tacitly recognized, and the British West

Indies squadron withdrawn. Now the destruction of both German and Russian power left Japan almost unchallengeable in eastern Asiatic waters, and there were already painful indications that the Japanese would not be slow in manipulating the lever of power suddenly within their grasp. Further, the technological development of both submarine and airplane gave Britain good cause to feel that sea power could no longer be statistically measured in dreadnought strength alone. In event of another European war, it already seemed likely that British capital ships might be unable to enter the "narrow seas" around Europe—close control of which had been for so long a basis of England's power.

The policy-makers of the United States Navy—well aware of the profound changes effected by the war—were eager to secure for their country the position formerly occupied by England, dominant world power based on a fleet "second to none."

This was a radical concept. As we have seen, from 1898 to World War I, the building policy had been a Navy second to Britain's, and our building competition had been with Germany, which also aspired to this position. Now, however, the United States was not merely a Great Power; it seemed that she was the greatest Great Power. And professional logic demanded that her Navy reflect this superiority.

After America's entrance into the war, the Allies' desperate need of small craft to implement the antisubmarine campaign had caused the heavy 1916 building program[1] to be shelved temporarily in favor of destroyers and sub-chasers. Now, however, with the war won, a newer and finer battle line, incorporating the lessons of Jutland, could be constructed. The General Board of the Navy pressed not merely for the completion of the 1916 building program, but in the 1919 program it presented to Congress a request for authorization to double the original 1916 schedule.

Bearing in mind that the United States had in commission at this time 16 first-line battleships, none older than 1910, and considering that technological advances would make the post-Jutland ships much more formidable than their predecessors, the reader will not wonder that the British Admiralty was shocked at the knowledge of the mere existence of such a plan. Though the British had in commission 42 capital ships, many were obsolescent, and the nine battle cruisers in

---

[1] As stated in the preceding chapter, Congress had authorized ten battleships and six battle cruisers in 1916. Of these, only 4 battleships (*Maryland, West Virginia, Colorado, Washington*) had been laid down by the time of the Armistice. The *Idaho, Tennessee,* and *California,* started earlier, were nearing completion.

Top, courtesy U.S. Naval Institute; *bottom,* official U.S. Navy photograph

Top, ADMIRALS SIMS AND RODMAN ON THE U.S.S. NEW YORK, 1918.
Bottom, CAPTURE OF THE U-53 BY THE U.S.S. FANNING. From a photograph taken aboard the *Fanning.*

this total had not proved particularly battleworthy at Jutland. Completion of the projected American program would relegate the traditional Mistress of the Seas not merely to a secondary position, but to a position of hopeless inferiority. England had but four capital ships building,[2] and the financial sacrifices of the war made her loath to undertake a building race with the United States.

It is probable that President Wilson, who supported the project of a big navy, was merely utilizing the program as one more means of coercing British support for the League of Nations. Be that as it may, the war-induced amity between the English-speaking nations cooled suddenly and perceptibly. Though there was, of course, no thought of war, the British were deeply concerned by a foreign naval construction program aimed so self-evidently at themselves, and the resolve to maintain superiority, whatever the cost, was common in official circles. The Japanese, also, who had no such limitless resources as the United States, could not fail to be fearful of the prospect of losing their newly won hegemony in Asiatic waters.

Meanwhile a widespread antimilitaristic feeling, common in all countries after wars, was growing among the American people. Disillusioned at the self-evident failure of World War I to make the world everywhere in fact "safe for democracy," and mindful of the historic benefits isolation had provided for the country in the past, public opinion revolted at the prospect of engaging in international power politics at all. The Wilsonian dream of American pre-eminence in the League of Nations was shattered by the Senate's rejection of the Versailles Treaty, and the forces of antinavalism, which sprang from the same fundamental attitude of mind as did opposition to the League, gathered strength in Congress—in which respect it probably accurately mirrored public opinion.

A postwar drive for national economy was politically in order also, and far from voting the tremendous sums which the Navy Department's full 1919 building program would have required, the Navy's "irreducible minimum" budget estimates were shaved, and Congress was slow even in voting funds for routine maintenance.

THE WASHINGTON CONFERENCE, 1921–1922

It is against this policy-background that the Washington Disarmament Conference of 1921–22 must be viewed. In fact, the whole ques-

---

[2] Only one of which, the huge battle cruiser *Hood,* was destined to be completed.

tion of disarmament and the relative size of the world's navies was so closely bound up with Far Eastern affairs and the political past and future of the world generally that it would be exceedingly difficult to isolate the purely naval aspects of the matter without leading to false conclusions.

This was recognized by the American State Department, and when Charles Evans Hughes, Harding's Secretary of State, opened the Conference, November 12, 1921, the scope had been defined to include a reaffirmation of international agreements on China, and a liquidation of the Anglo-Japanese Treaty of 1902, as well as naval disarmament.

In a dramatic speech in the first plenary session, Hughes, after outlining the basis of the discussion to be "existing strength of navies," [3] and advocating a building holiday for all capital ship construction, startled the delegates by not only offering to scrap all United States ships not actually completed and all 15 of its pre-dreadnought battleships, but also naming the specific concessions from Great Britain and Japan that the United States would regard as "fairly commensurate." The effect would be to reduce the battleline strength of the powers concerned to a 5:5:3 ratio. France and Italy were later included, each with a relative strength of 1.75.

This speech produced a sensation in the world press, and international acclaim hailed this fair and statesmanlike presentation of the American proposition. An auspicious beginning had been made.

Space is lacking for a full discussion of the elaborate compromises and technical discussions which followed. These lasted a full 12 weeks. Suffice it to say that agreement was reached on all conference issues then regarded as major. The Four Power Treaty, designed mainly as a "face-saver" for Japan, replaced the Anglo-Japanese Alliance with formal promises of the nations to respect each other's possessions in the Far East. The Nine Power Treaty[4] guaranteed the territorial integrity of China.

The provisions of the Naval Disarmament Treaty were more specific. Summarized, these were : (1) ultimate stabilization of capital ship tonnage at 500,000 each for Britain and United States: 300,000 for Japan; 175,000 each for France[5] and Italy; (2) the *status quo* with respect

---

[3] Defined by the American delegation as ships in commission *plus ships building* —a very important qualification.

[4] The United States, Great Britain, Japan, France, Italy, Holland, Belgium, Portugal, Italy, and China were the signatories.

[5] For the time being, France was allowed to retain tonnage considerably in excess of this displacement.

to fortification and naval bases in the "Pacific region" to be maintained; this provision applied to Hong Kong, Formosa, the Philippines, and the Aleutians; it did not apply to Singapore, Australia, New Zealand, Hawaii, Japan proper, or, of course, to the Pacific shores of the United States or Canada; (3) Japanese retention of the *Mutsu,* completed just before the conference. The United States might complete two more *Marylands;* Britain might complete two more capital ships, neither exceeding 35,000 tons; (4) a ten-year battleship building holiday otherwise to be observed; (5) carrier tonnage fixed at 135,000 for Great Britain and the United States, 81,000 for Japan, 60,000 for France and Italy; and (6) technical limitations, including—(*a*) no battleships above 35,000 tons, (*b*) no guns over 16 inches in caliber, (*c*) no carrier over 27,000 tons,[6] (*d*) no cruiser over 10,000 tons, and (*e*) no cruiser gun over 8 inches in bore.

Rules were also agreed to for scrapping procedure and replacement building. There were certain provisions regarding merchant shipping, and supplementary, necessarily rather ineffectual agreements binding the signatories to limit their use of submarines and forbidding poison gas altogether. The submarine and gas agreements, however, were never ratified by France.

World opinion was enthusiastic in its approbation. Indeed, in view of the failure of pre-war efforts at the Hague to reduce the mounting expense of competitive armaments, there seemed justification for satisfaction at the accomplishment as a long forward step toward true world order. The legislative bodies of the powers speedily ratified the main treaties.

From the point of view of the American delegation, the conference seemed a success in that: (1) it reached the goals which the American representatives originally put forward; (2) the Anglo-Japanese 1902 Treaty was abrogated; (3) Great Britain recognized our equality on the sea; (4) Japan, our most probable future enemy, acceded to a statistical inferiority; (5) our China policy was reaffirmed by the powers; and (6) the treaty obviated the tremendous expense of a full-scale naval race.

Perhaps the most controversial item in the treaty was the "non-fortification" clause, bitterly denounced by those who felt very heavy fortifications in the Philippines would be necessary if we were not to

---

[6] An escape clause allowed the United States to convert two battle cruiser hulls to the 33,000-ton *Lexington* and *Saratoga;* other powers enjoyed a similar privilege, providing they did not exceed their tonnage quotas.

allow them at some future date to fall prey to Japanese expansionism. On the other hand, we had held the Philippines for two decades and more without fortifying them, and there was little prospect that Congress would have voted funds for such a purpose.

Colonel Theodore Roosevelt, Jr., who as Assistant Secretary of the Navy was one of the guiding geniuses of the American delegation, wrote in his diary[7] that the fortifications agreement:

> . . . leaves us, in my opinion, in a slightly better position than Japan. We trade certain fortifications which we would never have completed, for fortifications which they [the Japanese] would unquestionably have completed. We retain one outpost of great importance [Hawaii] and they give up all but their mainland.

As it turned out, the Japanese did not comply with their pledged word in this particular.

Service opinion, with a handful of exceptions, was from the first overwhelmingly opposed to the treaty provisions. To most of the admirals, particularly, it seemed elementary that supremacy on the seas was a more trustworthy prop to national security than reliance on multilateral commitments. An articulate congressional minority seconded this view. But willy-nilly, they, and naval leadership elsewhere, settled down to a period of "treaty navies."

Later Naval Conferences and American Building Policy

After the scrapping provisions of the Washington Treaty were carried out, the United States attained an approximate parity with England in line-of-battle ships. And our destroyer strength, swollen by extensive wartime construction, was sufficient. In the cruiser category, however, the American fleet was woefully deficient. Ten 7,500-ton, 6-inch gun ships of the four-stack *Omaha-Marblehead* class were the only useful cruisers in commission. There was an extensive tonnage of seagoing antiques from the Spanish War period, but their slowness and general obsolescence gave little satisfaction to naval officers familiar with the vastly superior new construction abroad.

Failure to reach a successful compromise on the lesser warship types at Washington, moreover, left all the naval powers at once free to divert their building budgets to cruisers, and as the months passed, the American Navy found itself progressively more and more outclassed

---

[7] Quoted by H. and M. Sprout, *Toward a New Order of Sea Power*, p. 247. The diary is still unpublished.

both qualitatively and quantitatively in the very type of naval vessel in which it had once been traditional that America was supreme.

The United States government met this challenge by providing for cruiser construction[8], and by pressing for a new disarmament conference to extend the capital ship ratios to lesser types. The Geneva Conference assembled June 20, 1927, and broke up August 4. France and Italy refused to attend. Britain, Japan, and the United States were unable to reach a mutually satisfactory formula, and the net result of the conference was to stir up further distrust among the leading naval powers.

At Washington five years earlier, the United States had based its battleship ratio on "existing strength" rather than on what each nation might interpret for itself as its strategic requirements. At Geneva, however, had the United States delegation accepted this formula, it would have perpetuated a decisive inferiority not only to Great Britain, whose far-flung Empire "life lines" gave some excuse for a great cruiser force, but also to Japan, which had 213,955 tons of first-line cruiser strength built and building, compared to an American figure of 155,000 tons (including the eight unfinished *Northampton's*).

Great Britain, which at this conference was less conciliatory than Japan, was willing to accept the principle of cruiser strength parity with the United States, but the tonnage it demanded was well above the strategic requirements of the American fleet. Further, Britain, with its world-wide commerce and its global net of bases, favored small 6-inch gun ships, whereas the United States, whose strategic problems were very different, insisted on the right to build 10,000 ton ships, carrying an 8-inch main battery.

A renewed attempt to find a compromise to the points in dispute was made at the London Disarmament Conference in 1930. This time apparent success was achieved. Both Great Britain and the United States were allotted 339,000 tons of cruisers. The "heavy" versus "light" cruiser issue was compromised—each being allowed a slight superiority in the type it favored. Japan signed only after the United States and Britain had agreed to allow her a 10:10:7 ratio in the cruiser category, and full parity in submarines. The tonnage maximum for underseas craft was fixed at 52,700 tons. The naval holiday on capital ship construction was extended to December 31, 1936.

America had at last attained treaty confirmation of her aim of a

---

[8] The Naval Act of December 18, 1924, provided for the construction of eight 8-inch gun 10,000 ton "treaty cruisers"—the *Northampton-Chester* class.

navy "second to none" in all categories, and had at the same time been
the principal architect of an international naval structure that it was
hoped would preclude quantitative competitive building.

However, France and Italy refused adherence to the new "naval
system" in a number of important particulars, and the "escalator"
clause in the London Treaty provided a legal basis whereby expanded
building in every naval nation might result from the troubled Mediterranean situation.

Far more serious, moreover, was the fact that Japan had been able
to exact concessions that left her naval dominance in East Asian waters
even more unchallengeable. Benefited by a Class C mandate over the
former German Pacific islands north of the Equator, and possessing a
first class modern fleet, Japan could afford to disregard her statistical
inferiority in ships. Operating close to home bases, the Empire of the
Rising Sun could feel confidence in naval supremacy in the western
Pacific, unless the full strength of the United States and British navies
operated simultaneously against her. Italian Fascism's growing threat
to Britain's Mediterranean life lines, and the pacifistic leanings of the
MacDonald government, made such joint action immediately unlikely.

Unwittingly, the English-speaking powers, lost in the purely
academic question of the relative strength of their own fleets, had
strengthened immeasurably the power position of their inevitable
enemy in the Far East.

On September 18, 1931, came the notorious "Mukden Incident,"
and Japan was on the march—into China. The deteriorating European political situation during the 1930's tied the Grand Fleet increasingly to Scapa Flow, and the Japanese became more and more bold in
asserting their object of attaining a "Greater Eastern Asia Co-Prosper-
ity Sphere," which being translated meant a ruthless subjugation of
all East Asiatic peoples, and a thrusting out of all white men and all
American and European interests.

With Franklin Delano Roosevelt's inauguration as President in 1933,
the Navy gained a most powerful and sympathetic friend. Not only
did he possess a prophetic foresight as to the true seriousness of the
world political situation, he appreciated the fact that a navy cannot
be improvised overnight, that it takes years to complete modern fighting ships.

The Geneva General Disarmament Conference of 1932–1933 had
failed; the world was fully entered on a protracted period of tension;
a widespread need of unemployment relief demanded public works.

Section 202 of the administration-sponsored National Industrial Recovery Act of June 16, 1933 authorized naval building to full treaty strength as a relief measure. The Vinson-Trammell Act of March 27, 1934, provided for construction of replacement tonnage to the extent of 102 ships—a program to be completed by 1942.

The London Disarmament Conference of 1935-1936 represented the last effort at achieving treaty limitations. The active building policies of Italy, France, and Germany; the Anglo-German Naval Treaty of 1935 (which allowed the Germans 35 per cent of Britain's surface naval tonnage and substantial parity in submarines); and Japan's intransigent demand for equality in all lesser categories made its failure a foregone conclusion. On December 31, 1936, legal barriers to a naval building race expired.

The annual size of American naval expenditures constantly swelled from 1934 until in 1940 it reached the record peace-time figure of over $885,000,000. Building under the Vinson-Trammel Act of 1934 was supplemented by a second Vinson Act in 1938 which provided a further 20 per cent increase in tonnage. Modernization of a number of battleships, an increasing emphasis on the rapidly expanding naval air arm, and provision for numerous new bases were features of the appropriation act of 1939.

In 1940 and 1941, the frightening march of events in both Europe and the Far East made naval and military expansion on an unprecedented scale politically inevitable and set the stage for the astronomic expansion World War II would require.

As of December 1, 1941, the Navy's combatant ship strength was: (1) *battleships*, 17; building, 15; (2) *carriers*, 7; building, 11; (3) *cruisers*, 37; building, 54; (4) *destroyers*, 171; building, 191, and (5) *submarines*, 111; building, 73.

TECHNOLOGICAL PROGRESS

A sailor from Drake's *Revenge* at the time of the Armada (1588) could, with the aid of Mr. Wells' "Time Machine," have stepped on the deck of Nelson's *Victory* at the time of Trafalgar (1805), and have felt no great surprise at such changes as he would find. He would have understood the orders of the officers and could at once have done useful work. In contrast, a sailor from the *Olympia* of Spanish-American War fame would have been lost on a naval vessel in 1918. Technology had developed so many completely new devices that the nomenclature alone would baffle a seaman of an earlier day. One of the most impressive facts in naval history is that prior to about 1850, ships and weapons developed exceedingly slowly. After 1850, change came at such a reckless rate that ships were not infrequently obsolete by the time they were launched. This technological development proceeds fastest under the stimulus of war, of course, but the production of navy matériel is so closely integrated with peacetime industrial development that even peacetime progress is very rapid. This was notably true between 1918 and 1941.

The technological advance was most notable in submarines and naval aircraft. But the contrast between the fighting qualities of the *West Virginia,* commissioned in 1923, and the *North Carolina,* first of the "new" battleships, is impressive. Seven knots more speed; improved armor-protection; vastly heavier antiaircraft battery; superior fire control—all were features of the later ship. In every detail in all types of naval vessels, decisive qualitative improvement was effected.

In certain cases, technological change made for permanent changes in naval techniques. Complete conversion of the fleet to oil fuel, for instance, coupled with the development of the high speed naval tanker and of a technique of fueling at sea, made the traditional reliance on closely spaced coaling stations outdated, and vastly increased the Navy's effective range in Pacific operations. Similarly, rapid improvement in radio equipment made instant communication so positive that effective co-ordination of ships and fleets from shore stations could be expected. The carrier and the long range patrol bomber made exclusive reliance on cruisers for reconnaissance as unlikely in future naval warfare as a clash of galleys.

Within the naval organization itself, vastly improved submarine rescue methods were developed. New submarine-detection devices[9] were pioneered. The whole elaborate operational techniques of carrier war were developed to a high degree of efficiency. Throughout the period between the wars, the Navy aimed consistently at qualitative as well as quantitative superiority in any war to come.

NAVAL OPERATIONS

The immediate concern of the Navy after the Armistice of 1918 was the elaborate "tidying up" that modern wars require. The North Sea mine field was lifted; the A.E.F. was returned to the United States; naval support for the Archangel and eastern Siberian adventures of the

---

[9] Especially "Sonar"—duplicated by the British Navy's "Asdic."

United States Army was provided. Two cruisers and a destroyer force under Rear Admiral Mark L. Bristol evacuated refugees from newly sovietized Russia, and co-operated in moving 262,000 Greeks from Asia Minor after the Greek-Turkish War. The Navy itself was reduced in personnel from 497,000 in 1918 to 86,000 in 1922.

A tacit recognition of the new power relationships mentioned earlier in the chapter came in 1919, when a separate United States Pacific Fleet was created. In 1922, the ships of the Atlantic Fleet were shifted to the West Coast also, to constitute the unified United States Fleet. This operated as such in the Pacific until 1939, when four old battleships were brought through the canal, ultimately to form the nucleus of a new Atlantic Fleet.

China remaining unstable, the Yangtze River Patrol was reinforced in 1922 under flag command. Throughout the Chinese civil wars and during the long drawn-out "Chinese incident" (Japan's aggressive war), our gunboats were a necessary protection of American lives and property.

Acting apparently without authorization from their government, Japanese air units on December 12, 1937, bombed and sank the U.S.S. *Panay* in the Yangtze without warning. Two American sailors were killed and 14 injured. Apology and reparations by Japan were accepted by the American State Department. But the incident was not forgotten.

Extensive training exercises, culminating in annual fleet maneuvers, kept both the command and the rank-and-file at a high level of professional competency. The loss in training of four submarines, several dirigibles, and many aircraft was a part of the price for the vital "know how" that modern instruments of war demand.

The Merchant Marine

It is a basic naval axiom that a strong merchant marine is a vital naval need in time of war. And like the Navy itself, it cannot be improvised from scratch after hostilities have begun. Trained merchant seamen and experienced shipbuilding personnel must be developed in periods of peace if there is to be the necessary professional nucleus in a vast program of wartime expansion. World War I furnished an object lesson of this truth. The policy of Congress throughout this period was to foster United States shipbuilding and ship operation, at first by sale of government wartime construction at nominal prices, by subsidy disguised as mail contracts, and by a liberal loan policy.

The basic difficulty faced by American-operated shipping has been, and is, the greater construction and operating costs of American ships compared with those of foreign nations. Direct governmental aid given foreign shipping under the stimulus of renewed economic nationalism more than outbalanced the assistance of the United States government. Through the 1920's, American ships carried only about a third of our foreign commerce. Furthermore, after 1929 our foreign trade shrank very sharply in volume.

The unhealthy state of the American Merchant Marine was responsible for the highly significant Shipping Act of 1936, which established the Maritime Commission under the effective chairmanship of Rear Admiral Emory S. Land (Ret.). This superseded the old Shipping Board. For the first time in our history direct subsidy was resorted to, both for construction and operation. Ships constructed with government aid were designed with an eye to wartime auxiliary use; at least two-thirds of all crews were required to be United States citizens. In addition, the five-man Maritime Commission was granted certain investigatory and regulatory powers suggestive of the Interstate Commerce Commission's powers over the railroads.

In 1938, the Commission began a construction schedule to replace obsolete merchant vessels with faster ships at a rate of 50 units a year for ten years. In 1939 this program was stepped up. Under the stimulus of wartime needs merchant shipbuilding mushroomed, and by September, 1942, contracts had been let for 300 tankers and 2,000 "Liberty" and "Victory" ships—a total tonnage of 24,000,000, to be delivered in 1942 and 1943. At the time of the German surrender we controlled over 30,000,000 tons of merchant shipping.

NAVAL AVIATION

Naval aviation, though it had developed rapidly as an auxiliary weapon in the antisubmarine campaign in World War I, had still hardly progressed from the pioneering stage at the time of the Armistice. Unfortunately, the full story of how carrier aviation developed between World War I and World War II is much too detailed for more than the briefest outline here. The rapid evolution of the aircraft carrier is of course an obvious part of technical naval history. The evolvement of modern naval aircraft, on the other hand, is closely bound up with military and commercial aviation developments, and with the rapid progress made from 1918 to 1941 in electronics, metallurgy, oil chemistry, meteorology, and a dozen other fields. Space considerations thus preclude a full account of the development of this new weapon, which admittedly has altered the whole complexion of sea warfare.

How carrier-borne aviation was conceived and found practical before World War I has been told in an earlier chapter. It was not, however, until 1919 that authorization was given for the conversion of the collier *Jupiter,* which, as the *Langley,* became the United States Navy's first carrier, joining the fleet in 1922. Two unfinished battle cruiser hulls, in accordance with the Washington Naval Treaty, were converted to the 33,000-ton carriers *Lexington* and *Saratoga,* commissioned in 1928. It was on the flight decks of these three ships that the Navy's airmen first worked out the operational techniques and acquired the practical skill that made our naval air force the finest in the world during World War II. The *Ranger* (1934) was our first "from-the-keel-up" carrier. On December 7, 1941, the Navy List counted seven carriers, not including the old *Langley.*

In the years immediately following World War I, it was almost universally admitted that aircraft had materially affected the future of navies. The burning question was, How much? In a series of American tests (1921, 1923, 1924), air bombardment of ships to be scrapped focused attention on the question, Can bombs sink battleships? The journalistic field-day resulting from the court-martial of the late, posthumously-honored General "Billy" Mitchell—an exceptionally outspoken air enthusiast—resulted in a popular misconception that the above question, if answered affirmatively, spelled the doom of the surface ship. But the actual results were not conclusive. The *Ostfriesland,* a German battleship completed in 1909, a cruiser, a destroyer, and several American pre-dreadnoughts were in fact sunk by air bombing from a relatively low level. None of these ships, however, was equipped with the heavy deck armor which the long range, plunging fire of World War I had made standard in newer battleships. The uncompleted *Washington,* scrapped as part of our disarmament commitments, was able to withstand four 2,000-lb. bomb hits from an altitude of 4,000 feet, as well as two torpedoes. She was finally sunk by the main battery gunfire of the *Texas.*

On the other hand, the tests were sufficiently successful to dramatize the need of further large-scale experimentation and development. The Bureau of Aeronautics had been established in 1921, and five years later the post of Assistant Secretary of Navy for Air. Also in 1926, President Coolidge appointed the Morrow Board to consider the air power needs of the country. The report of this board resulted in a "Five Year Plan" for the Navy, looking toward a naval air force of 1,000 planes, the figure maintained until the Vinson-Trammell Bill (1934) lifted the sights of the service in this, as in other branches of the Navy. At the time of the Pearl Harbor attack, there were nearly 5,000 combatant aircraft in the naval service, and 6,900 accredited naval aviators.

Students of naval tactics have frequently commented on the fact that airplanes would have revolutionized war at sea even if they had never dropped a bomb or fired a gun. Very little reflection is necessary to appreciate the truth of this. Few, if any, of the sea fights of the pre-air age would have occurred exactly as they did if one or both of the opposing commanders had had the benefit of aerial reconnaisance. Many of them would not have taken place at all.

It was as a supplement to the scouting line that planes at sea were first assigned. In fair weather, under most tactical conditions, aircraft as "eyes" for the admiral are obviously superior to the most far-ranging cruiser or the speediest destroyer. So today, all battleships and cruisers carry seaplanes to extend their arc of visibility. Furthermore, the extensive use of planes in antisubmarine warfare in World War I gave special impetus to the development of the patrol type of plane—larger than other models, able to keep the air for much longer periods of time, and capable of much more extended flights.

Glenn Curtiss delivered the first four of these big flying boats—the famous NC planes—to the Navy just too late to be of use during World War I. These were large planes, even by modern standards, with a wingspread of 126 feet. The NC–4, flown by Lieutenant Commander A. C. Read, in 1919 made the first transatlantic flight of all time, stopping at Newfoundland, the Azores, Lisbon, and finally Plymouth, England.

The specialization of function represented by the relatively large, lumbering, long range patrol aircraft was matched by a differentiation of type leading ultimately to the dive bombers, torpedo planes, and fighters of today. Early in the twenties the archetypes of these were already appearing in every air force, army and navy, the world over. The United States Navy and Marine Corps are generally credited with the "invention" of dive bombing. And the time-honored insistence in these services on precision, "pinpoint" bombing of specific targets later paid big dividends in actual war.

Revolution after revolution in aircraft and engine manufacture was effected in the two decades between wars. All-metal construction replaced fabric, "dope," and wire of earlier days. The biplane gave way to the speedier monoplane. Much heavier armament, body armor, self-sealing fuel cells, slotted "diving flaps," and above all, vastly greater engine horsepower were just a few of the significant developments. Even the mighty NC's of 1918 were powered with Liberty engines of only 400 h.p. In World War II, 2,000 h.p. radial engines were the power plants of the Navy's single-engine fighters.[10]

The speed of fighter planes advanced from 132 m.p.h. in 1918 to the neighborhood of 400 m.p.h. in 1941. Furthermore, the service ceiling[11] went from 12,000 feet to over 35,000 feet, and rate of climb— a highly important feature in interceptor aircraft particularly—increased correspondingly. So, too, all the other performance statistics of military aircraft. Important above all else, perhaps, was the increase in *dependability*. During World War I, approximately one flight in three resulted in a forced landing because of engine failure. On the eve of World War II, such accidents as there were could in most cases be attributed to pilot error. Improved engineering and maintenance, and elaborate check-off lists and inspection forms insured a maximum of safety for the Navy's fliers.

The spectacular success of airplanes and other relatively recent technological innovations should not obscure for the student of naval history the fact that many, perhaps most, of the new ideas that are brought to the attention of the high ranking naval authorities do not develop into useful weapons in the long run. Most of them never progress beyond the blueprint stage. A few of them are tried experimentally, only to be abandoned.

One of the most promising new weapons of the twentieth century, in the eyes of a considerable group of aeronauts, was the rigid dirigible or zeppelin, named after Count Zeppelin, whose enthusiastic pioneering in the type resulted in Germany's possession of a number of them during World War I. They scouted for the High Sea Fleet, bombed London and other English cities, and in general were, at that stage of aeronautical development, a useful air and naval auxiliary. Their advantages were very long range, very high service ceiling, and great load capacity as compared with heavier-than-air craft. During World War I, and for a time thereafter, their obvious vulnerability was minimized by their being able to operate at heights to which no interceptor could fly.

---

[10] Both the F6F (Hellcat) and F4U (Corsair) were powered with the splendid P. & W. R-2800 engine, developing 2000 h.p.

[11] The altitude a plane can reach, maintaining a rate of climb of at least 100 feet per minute.

Impressed by their performance and apparent promise, an ardent minority in the United States Navy pressed successfully for their adoption in the fleet. America happens to enjoy the unique advantage of possessing natural helium gas, which, being noninflammable, renders American zeppelins and blimps much safer than their hydrogen-filled foreign counterparts. In spite of this safety feature, however, a series of dirigible disasters—the *Shenandoah,* 1925; the *Akron,* 1933;[12] and the *Macon,* 1935—helped to discourage the Navy's further work with the type. The *Los Angeles,* the sole surviving rigid dirigible, was soon afterwards put out of commission. It should be noted that the principal reason for abandoning experiment in this line has been the technical advance of the heavier-than-air plane, rather than the dangers involved—to minimize which, presumably, safety measures could have been found. Small, easily manufactured, nonrigid blimps continued to do useful work in the Navy as coastal patrol.

Immediately after the Pearl Harbor attack, rather widespread criticism of the Navy's tardiness in realizing the full significance of air power was the order of the day. In this connection, however, a few facts should be noted. Whereas it is true that the Japanese first employed the carrier task force as a main striking arm in war, this new tactical concept had been fully explored in fleet maneuvers by the United States Navy before World War II. Pearl Harbor in no way "rewrote the book" for the United States Naval Air Arm. Whereas it is true that many, perhaps most, of the flag officers in the fleet on December 7, 1941, did not yet appreciate the tremendous potentialities of carrier aviation, it is also true that there were many other admirals who had, as a result of their specialized naval training, been in a position to assess correctly the revolutionary nature of this new weapon. The professional abilities of such men as Towers, Halsey, Mitscher, and a dozen others whose names figure in the ensuing chapters, cannot be improvised overnight, any more than a fleet of ships can be.

The American Navy, between World War I and World War II, had fostered the construction of superior airframes and engines by such companies as Grumman, Douglas, Consolidated, Glenn Martin, Curtis, Pratt and Whitney, and Wright, so that its matériel in 1941 defied comparison with that of any other naval air force. Its naval aviators,

---

12 The loss of the *Akron,* with 15 men of her crew of 49, was the greater for the death of Rear Admiral W. A. Moffett, who as Chief of the Bureau of Aeronautics, 1921–1933, contributed as much as any other one man to the progress of naval aviation.

combat air crews, and maintenance men were probably as much superior as the planes they flew or worked on.

The Navy on the Eve

Despite the antinavalism of a large part of Congress and the American people after World War I, and despite the virtual suspension of new construction during the first half of the "Long Armistice," the Navy enjoyed the pride and confidence of the country. The four-year enlistment policy, coupled with the benefits of mechanical training valuable in civilian life, attracted a very high caliber of enlisted personnel. Every year the Navy recruited from 15,000 to 20,000 new "bluejackets" and returned a similar number to civil life—thereby building up a valuable reservoir of trained men to be called back to the colors in war.

Increased stress was put on postgraduate training for officers, in the Naval War College at Newport, in the Postgraduate School at Annapolis, and in civilian technical schools. The Naval Reserve Act of 1925 established the Merchant Marine Reserve, the Volunteer Reserve, and the Organized Reserve (Naval Militia). Naval R.O.T.C. units were established at six universities—a program vastly expanded when war threatened.

In spite of the Japanese achievement of tactical surprise in the attack on Pearl Harbor on December 7, 1941, in spite of certain matériel deficiencies (notably lack of adequate small bore, rapid-fire, antiaircraft weapons), and in spite of the hopeless inadequacy of the United States Asiatic Squadron for the task it faced in late 1941 and early 1942, the Navy entered World War II much better prepared for the trials ahead than the beginning of hostilities had ever found it in the past.

The solid core of the fleet that would support the final operations against both Germany and Japan was already in existence. The ships and planes which were to win the naval war were at least in the blueprint stage in 1941. And in spite of the debacle of Pearl Harbor the legacy of the peacetime Navy in high morale and gifted top echelon leaders has seldom been duplicated in world history.

It is well that this was so. For the Navy was on the eve of its supreme test, a test for which its 165 years of previous history were but an extended preparation.

22

Second World War: Peace to Pearl Harbor

WHEN JAPAN OVERRAN MANCHURIA in 1931, the United States Government took diplomatic steps to oppose the act of aggression, but in this it received no seconding by Britain and France, for neither was prepared to apply determined countermeasures. This unreadiness of the principal supporters of the League of Nations to uphold the rights of weaker states and to enforce treaty obligations proved immensely encouraging to those countries which, regarding themselves as "have-not" powers, were awaiting an opportunity to strengthen themselves on the international scene. In 1935 Italy invaded Ethiopia without arousing the League to effective action; in 1936 Germany, defying the Treaties of Versailles and Locarno, remilitarized the Rhineland; in 1937 Japan invaded China proper; and in 1938 Germany seized Austria, incorporating it as a province of her Third Reich. Already the lines were being drawn, and a European conflict in miniature was being fought in Spain. At the outbreak of the Spanish civil war in 1936, Germany and Italy actively supported the rebel Nationalist party, while Russia, France, and Britain directly or indirectly supported the more democratic Loyalist government.

American reaction to the troubled international situation expressed itself on the one hand, as we have seen, by a strengthening of the Navy, and on the other by legislation through which the United States hoped to avoid involvement in foreign wars by largely relinquishing her traditional rights as a neutral. This neutrality legislation culminated in the so-called Cash-and-Carry Act of 1937, which forbade sales of munitions or loans to warring nations and prohibited travel of United States citizens in belligerent vessels. Certain commodities designated by the President could be sold to belligerents but only if the goods were paid for before export and were carried away in other than American ships. It was obvious that the effects of such an act could not be entirely neutral. The measure, it was believed, would eliminate the major causes which had brought the United States into World War I, but in the event of a new outbreak in Europe, Britain would be favored. Having command of the seas, she could assure herself of nonmilitary supplies from America and deny them to her adversaries.

The bill thus correctly reflected the feelings of the American people, who desired to remain aloof from the approaching conflict but were becoming increasingly unneutral in sentiment. They were outraged by the persecution of minorities in Germany and the ruthless slaughter of Chinese civilians by Japan. Both the press and the Administration expressed indignation towards the aggressor nations. Of the harsh treatment of the Jews in Germany, President Roosevelt declared, "The news of the past few days from Germany has deeply shocked public opinion in the United States. . . . I myself could scarcely believe that such things could occur in a twentieth-century civilization."

The nadir of the appeasement policy which England and France felt constrained to pursue in their relations with Germany was reached in September, 1938, when at the Munich Conference they reluctantly consented to German seizure of the Sudeten region of Czechoslovakia. "It is peace in our time," said Britain's Prime Minister Chamberlain upon his return to London. But the following March the German dictator, flouting his pledges made at Munich, took over the remainder of Czechoslovakia and soon afterwards made impossible demands on Poland. In August, Germany announced a ten-year nonaggression pact with Russia. Hitler, thus freed of threats from the east, on September 1, 1939, marched his armies into Polish territory. Two days later Britain and France, in accordance with treaty pledges, declared war on Germany.

NEUTRAL TO NONBELLIGERENT

The American Government promptly took measures to insulate itself from the conflict and at the same time to make its resources available to the democracies. In co-operation with the Latin-American republics, the United States proclaimed an oceanic *safety belt* averaging 300 miles in width around the Americas south of Canada. Within the enclosed area the warring powers were warned to avoid belligerent action. Shortly afterwards the arms embargo was repealed. A new Neutrality Act, approved in November, 1939, permitted the sale of munitions on the same basis as free goods, cash and carry. This meant, of course, that France and Britain could now secure materials of warfare denied to blockaded Germany. The new act forbade travel of American citizens and ships into combat zones, and on this authority President Roosevelt issued a proclamation excluding United States vessels from the waters surrounding the British Isles and the coast of Western Europe from the Baltic Sea to the Bay of Biscay. Subsequent proclamations, keeping pace with the spread of hostilities, barred American ships from the seas adjacent to Norway and from the approaches to the Mediterranean.

In the spring of 1940, Germany, without declaring war and in disregard of nonaggression treaties, quickly overran Denmark and Norway. German mechanized divisions then plunged through the Low Countries into France, expelled the British army from European soil, and in six weeks forced prostrate France to seek an armistice. The American people were at last shocked into realization that their own position, despite the protecting oceans on either side, was not without peril. With Italy now in the war and Germany poised on the English Channel apparently on the verge of invading Britain, the United States was forced to contemplate the possibility of a defeated England and the consequent loss of the British fleet as an outer line of American naval defense.

Confronted with this situation, Congress voted funds for a two-ocean Navy and shortly afterwards passed the first peacetime conscription bill in United States history. During the same period, a Pan-American Conference, taking cognizance of the orphaned colonies of Denmark, Holland, and France, gave notice by the Act of Havana that western hemisphere territories in danger of being taken over by unfriendly powers might be seized and administered by the American republics. The United States then looked to her northern defenses by setting up with Canada a permanent board to consider measures for joint action in event of threats from overseas.

More important were steps taken to aid the countries in arms against aggression. England's most immediate need was escort vessels. A futile attempt to eject the Germans from Norway and the retreat of her army from European soil by way of Dunkirk had cost her heavily in destroyers. Her merchantmen, insufficiently escorted, were now being sunk faster than they could be replaced. In September, 1940, President Roosevelt and Prime Minister Churchill reached an agreement whereby in exchange for 50 over-age destroyers Great Britain leased to the

United States a number of sites suitable for a chain of naval bases or air stations extending from Newfoundland to British Guiana. The following March, Congress, at the urging of the President, passed the Lend-Lease Act. This bill permitted the transfer of implements of war on a loan basis directly to any nation whose defense was considered vital to that of the United States. "We must," said Roosevelt, "be the great arsenal of democracy." Munitions, tanks, planes, and foodstuffs soon began to flow to England and her allies, and later, when Germany invaded that country, to the Soviet Union. Nobody pretended that the act was neutral. It was America's reply to Germany's and Italy's abandonment of international law and their unofficial declaration of war on all democracies. Other unneutral acts soon followed—the seizure of Axis vessels interned in American ports, the freezing of German and Italian assets in the United States, the occupation of Greenland, and the taking over from Britain of the defense of Iceland.

As if to signalize the growing *entente* between their two countries, Roosevelt and Churchill met in August, 1941, at Placentia Bay, Newfoundland, to discuss problems of the common defense and aims for peace after victory. In an eight-point declaration known as the Atlantic Charter they set forth certain principles upon which they based "their hopes for a better future for the world." The eight points were: no territorial aggrandizement; no territorial changes contrary to the wishes of the people concerned; the right of all peoples to choose their own forms of government; access by all nations to trade and raw materials; international economic collaboration; freedom from fear and want; freedom of the seas; and abandonment of force for a permanent system of general security.

ACTIONS IN THE ATLANTIC

At the outbreak of war in Europe the United States Atlantic Squadron consisted of the battleships *New York, Arkansas, Texas,* and *Wyoming;* the aircraft carrier *Ranger;* nine cruisers; and some 30 destroyers. Soon afterwards 40 old destroyers, long retired from service, were recommissioned and added to the squadron to form a neutrality patrol whose range of activity and type of operations were delimited by the hemispheric safety belt proclaimed in October, 1939. Other ships were gradually added, notably the carrier *Wasp,* commissioned in 1940, and the 35,000-ton battleships *Washington* and *North Carolina,* put into service at the end of the following year.

During 1940 Atlantic patrol activities were facilitated and extended

by the establishment of a Caribbean Naval District under command
of Rear Admiral Raymond A. Spruance, with headquarters at San
Juan, Puerto Rico, and by the long line of new anchorages provided
by the destroyer-base deal. In 1941 the limit of the patrol was extended far beyond the safety belt by American occupation of Greenland and Iceland. By this time the Atlantic Squadron had become the
United States Atlantic Fleet, with Admiral Ernest J. King as Commander-in-Chief.

With the passage of the Lend-Lease Act the purely neutral or defensive aspect of the patrol ceased. "We cannot allow our goods to be
sunk in the Atlantic," said Secretary of the Navy Knox. "We must
make good our promise to Britain." Not long thereafter the fleet undertook escort duty, eventually convoying British as well as American
ships as far as Iceland. United States combat craft were not yet permitted to attack unfriendly vessels but they were directed to broadcast
the presence of any raiders discovered.

Such steps came none too early, for in the spring of 1941 England's
shipping situation had been made desperate by the new wolfpack
tactics of the Axis submarines. In April alone nearly 600,000 tons of
British-controlled vessels had been sunk, more than twice the combined capacity of Britain's and America's shipyards to build replacements. The increased integration of American and British patrols in
the Atlantic soon made itself felt. By midsummer the rate of sinkings
had dropped sharply.

On September 4, 1941, a German submarine commander lost
patience at being tracked and having his position broadcast by an
American patrol vessel. He opened fire and thus committed the first
act of hostility between United States and German naval units. The
patroller was the old four-stack destroyer *Greer*. Informed by a British
plane some 175 miles southwest of Iceland that a German submarine
had been seen to emerge ten miles directly ahead, the destroyer increased speed until she reached the point at which the U-boat had
been sighted. Here the *Greer* began a zigzagging search and, quickly
locating the submarine by her underwater sound equipment, trailed it
for three and a half hours. To escape from this persistent chase, the
U-boat, without raising its periscope, fired a torpedo by sound bearings.
The *Greer* sighted the impulse bubble formed by air rushing from the
submarine's torpedo tube and wheeled to attack as the torpedo passed
harmlessly a hundred yards astern. The destroyer dropped a pattern
of eight depth charges, whereupon the submarine fired a second tor-

pedo and missed again. The chase now proceeded in earnest. The *Greer,* no longer limited to advertising the presence of the submarine, was out for a kill. When a British destroyer hove into view she declined assistance and continued her tracking. In the early evening the U-boat succeeded in escaping, and the old flush-decker turned her nose again towards Iceland, her original destination.

The Navy now went on the offensive. Though this was the first shot fired at a United States naval vessel, American merchantmen had already been destroyed. In May the *Robin Moor* had been torpedoed in the South Atlantic by a German submarine and the ship allowed to sink without any attempt to provide for passengers and crew. No lives were lost, but survivors drifted nearly three weeks in open boats. In August another American-owned ship, the *Sessa,* of Panamanian registry, had been sunk near Greenland. Three days after the *Greer* incident the merchantman *Steel Seafarer* was sunk by German aircraft in the Red Sea. On September 11 the President issued his shoot-on-sight order. "Let this warning be clear," he said. "From now on, if German or Italian vessels of war enter the waters the protection of which is necessary for American defense they do so at their own peril." Navy patrollers were instructed henceforth to strike first at any submarine or other raider attacking merchant ships of any flag engaged in commerce inside American defense areas.

The new 1,630-ton destroyer *Kearny* was the first American warship in World War II to be damaged by the enemy. She was also to provide a shocked public with its first casualty list of men lost in action. In mid-October a convoy which she was escorting to Iceland was attacked by a U-boat pack. A tanker was torpedoed and began to blaze. The *Kearny,* coming to the rescue, dropped a pattern of depth charges and then wheeled to port as a spread of three torpedoes was seen coming her way. One of the torpedoes struck her starboard side just below the water line. Eleven men were killed and as many more wounded as the force of the explosion devastated the interior of the forward engine room, buckled the plates, and tore up through the main deck to smash the starboard wing of the bridge and knock back the forward funnel. Despite the heavy damage the engines still ran and the destroyer, navigating by makeshift means, was able to proceed to Iceland for temporary repairs.

Two weeks later the naval tanker *Salinas* and the destroyer *Reuben James* were torpedoed on succeeding nights. The *Salinas,* her compartments empty, absorbed three hits without sinking and was able to make port. The less fortunate *Reuben James,* struck amidships while steaming on the flank of a convoy, was torn apart by the force of the explosion. The forward section including the bridge sank at once, carrying to the bottom all the officers and a number of enlisted men. The remainder of the ship from the well deck aft kept afloat a few minutes longer but it quickly settled and then upended, going down stern last. Survivors, covered with heavy black fuel oil, swam to rafts or clung to wreckage. A number were killed when the vessel's depth charges went off, but the remaining 46 were soon cheered by the arrival of two American destroyers which had dropped behind to pick them up. In this first sinking in World War II of a United States warship, a hundred lives were lost.

This hostile act undoubtedly spurred Congress in removing those articles from the Neutrality Act of 1939 which hindered American defenses and restricted aid to Britain. Early in November the sections were repealed which forbade the arming of United States merchantmen and prohibited their travel in combat zones. American merchant ships were now able to carry lend-lease goods direct to British ports.

War Clouds in the Pacific

The Japanese, following their 1937 invasion, quickly overran the Chinese maritime provinces and set up a puppet regime with headquarters at Nanking. But the unconquered portions of China, rallying their forces under Generalissimo Chiang Kai-shek, put up a heroic resistance and at length the advance of the Japanese armies was slowed down to a virtual halt. The people of the United States, while generally sympathetic towards the Chinese, preferred at this stage to insulate themselves from the danger zones rather than to take positive measures against the aggressor. President Roosevelt, however, justifying his action on the technical grounds that no war had been declared in the East, supported China to the extent of not invoking the Neutrality Act. Japan's merchant marine and her command of the eastern seas gave her therefore none of the exclusive advantages England was to enjoy in the Atlantic. While the United States was not yet ready to declare an embargo on Japan, American ships could still carry munitions and other supplies to the Bay of Bengal for forwarding via the Burma Road to Chinese resistance forces. To assure the steady flow of such materials, Congress authorized a series of large loans to the Chinese government at Chungking.

By 1940 American public opinion was sufficiently mobilized against the aggressor to permit Roosevelt to clamp down an embargo on shipments of oil, aviation gasoline, scrap iron, and steel to all areas except Great Britain and the Western Hemisphere. This was a blow to Japan, especially since her relations with the Axis powers were temporarily strained. She had in 1936 signed an Anti-Comintern Pact with Germany and thereby had regarded herself as guaranteed against possible Russian interference. But the treaty of August, 1939, between Germany and Russia had left her isolated and exposed. Common interests, however, soon brought the aggressor nations into renewed alliance. In September, 1940, Japan joined Germany and Italy in a Tripartite Pact whereby the signatories pledged each other mutual support against any nonbelligerent who should enter the war against any of the three. Since Article 5 expressly exempted Russia from the terms of the agreement, the pact was obviously a warning to the United States to keep hands off. The following April this intent was underlined by a neutrality treaty signed between the Japanese and Soviet governments.

Provided now with powerful allies and freed from threats to her Manchurian border, Japan warned the United States against further interference in her "new order in Greater East Asia." She then proceeded to demand from the helpless French government bases in southern Indo-China in addition to some she had already extorted in the north. At this, the American government, condemning the new acts of aggression, froze Japanese assets in the United States and tightened the already rigid embargo restrictions. The two governments were already on the brink of war when, in October, 1941, the extreme militarist group headed by General Tojo took over the Japanese cabinet.

In the late fall of 1941 Japan was faced with a dilemma and an opportunity. The American embargo had cut off her source of gasoline and other war necessities. Most of her needs could be supplied by a push into Malaya and the East Indies, but the democratic powers and particularly the United States stood between her and further expansion. It was obvious that the only alternative to abandoning her plan of conquest was removal of that barrier. The time was now. The United States stood isolated among the great powers. The British army in Libya was backed up against the border of Egypt; Suez was in danger. Russia, with German forces at the gates of Moscow, appeared to be at the point of collapse. Above all, the United States Fleet, already cut down by arms-limitation pacts, pacifism, and the fallacy of isolationism, was divided—even as Russia's fleet had been divided in

1904. The necessity of maintaining the Atlantic patrol had drained away the major portion of America's warcraft to the East Coast. In the Atlantic were eight battleships, four aircraft carriers, 13 cruisers, and some 90 destroyers. In the Pacific the United States could muster only about a hundred combat surface vessels, Britain and the Netherlands together no more than 50. Japan had 170. The balance of sea power was thus on Japan's side, but time was not. The United States had launched upon the greatest naval construction program in history. Planes were coming off America's production lines in ever-increasing numbers.

The United States Pacific Fleet was heavily concentrated at Pearl Harbor—just as in 1904 Russia's had been concentrated at Port Arthur. At that time, by a surprise raid, Japan had weakened the Russian squadron to the extent of one battleship and two cruisers. In 1941 there were new weapons to implement a similar attack—the air arm and the undersea arm. A successful blow might give Japan the time requisite to fasten her hold on Malaya, the Philippines, and the Indies. It was worth a try.

As early as the preceding January Admiral Yamamoto, Commander-in-Chief of the Combined Japanese Fleet, had proposed a plan for a surprise attack on Pearl Harbor. In mid-September the details had been worked out and accepted. On November 5, 1941 (Tokyo time), the plans were promulgated to all fleet and task force commanders with the date for the raid set tentatively at December 8 (December 7, Hawaii time). The choice was based in part upon the procedure customary with the U. S. Pacific Fleet during maneuvers of coming into harbor on Friday and leaving on Monday. December 7, Hawaii time, was Sunday.

On November 22 at Hitokappu Bay in the Kurile Islands a fleet was assembled including a striking force of two battleships, the *Hiei* and *Kirishima;* six aircraft carriers, the *Kaga, Akagi, Hiryu, Soryu, Shokaku,* and *Zuikaku;* three cruisers; and 16 destroyers. Four days later the striking force departed on a circuitous path across the relatively untraveled north Pacific—with the understanding that it would be recalled if, prior to the date set for the attack, Japanese-American negotiations should reach an amicable settlement.

In the meantime, special envoy Saburo Kurusu had arrived in Washington to assist Japanese Ambassador Nomura in working out a basis of understanding with the United States. The State Department made its stand clear. It demanded that Japan withdraw from China and Indo-China and sign a nonaggression pact as a guarantee of future good behavior. "Fantastic!" said the Japanese Foreign Minister, but Kurusu and Nomura were directed to continue their discussions.

In the midst of the ensuing talks, information was received in Washington that large numbers of troops and huge supplies of war material were being moved into Indo-China. Their purpose obviously was further aggression. "It seems," said Ambassador Nomura on December 5, in response to State Department inquiries, "that an exaggerated report has been made of these movements." Dissatisfied with this reply, President Roosevelt appealed directly to the Emperor of Japan. "A withdrawal of the Japanese forces from Indo-China," said he, "would result in the assurance of peace throughout the whole of the South Pacific area."

A conciliatory reply was scarcely expected. Army and Navy Intelligence by cryptanalysis had discovered the nature of the ciphering machine used by the Japanese and had built a corresponding device which could decode their most secret messages. From this source Washington authorities knew that war was imminent but had deduced from information gleaned that Japan would strike only in the south. In late November and early December war warnings were sent to American bases in the Pacific, but the character of these warnings reflected the belief generally held in the State, War, and Navy Departments that the Japanese attacks would not include Pearl Harbor. Neither Lieutenant General Walter C. Short of the Hawaiian Department nor Admiral Husband E. Kimmel, Commander-in-Chief of the Pacific Fleet,[1] was supplied with the full data made available to army and navy commands in the Philippines. A message to Kimmel on November 27 stated that "Japan is expected to make an aggressive move within the next few days," but added that the attack would probably be in the form of "an amphibious expedition against either the Philippines, Thai or Kra Peninsula, or possibly Borneo." A message to Short on the same date said that hostile Japanese action was "possible at any moment" and ordered him to take reconnaissance and other measures but not to carry them out in such manner as to "alarm the civilian population or disclose intent." He was ordered to report measures taken. Short replied that his department had been alerted "to prevent sabotage." Though such action clearly did not carry out the intention

---

[1] In accordance with the rotation plan then in effect (see p. 317), Admiral Kimmel was also acting Commander-in-Chief of the United States Fleet. His headquarters were at Pearl Harbor.

of the warning message, neither the Army Chief of Staff nor his subordinates in Washington took steps to rectify this state of limited preparedness.

The answer to Roosevelt's appeal to the Japanese Emperor began to come in by radio during the night of December 6–7. The long 14-part message was intercepted by American stations and broken down faster than it could be decoded by the Japanese embassy. It was an extraordinary document accusing the United States of scheming to prolong the war and concluding with the statement that the Japanese Government "cannot but consider that it is impossible to reach an agreement through further negotiations." Kurusu and Nomura were instructed to hand the note to Hull at 1 P.M. That it was to be delivered on Sunday and that a definite hour had been assigned was significant. Copies of the text were rushed to the Secretary of State; and General George C. Marshall, Army Chief of Staff, proposed to Admiral Harold R. Stark, Chief of Naval Operations, that warnings be sent at once to Pacific commanders. Stark was of the opinion that further warnings would "only confuse them," but he acceded to Marshall's insistence and asked him to add a line to the Army warnings directing the addressees to pass the information to naval commands. Marshall then sent out a series of dispatches, giving top priority to General Douglas MacArthur in the Philippines. The message to Hawaii went by ordinary commercial radio. It reached General Short seven hours after the Pearl Harbor attack.

When the 1 P.M. deadline, December 7, arrived, the Japanese embassy had not completed decoding. Kurusu and Nomura did not present the text to Secretary Hull until 2:20 P.M., Washington time, an hour after the raid on Pearl Harbor had begun. Hull had, of course, already read the text and had some inkling of what was taking place in the Pacific. But, assuming a straight countenance, he accepted the note and made a pretense of reading it. His anger was smoldering, however, and as he reread the concluding lines breaking off negotiations he turned to the Japanese representatives and exploded with indignation. "In all my 50 years of public service," he said, "I have never seen a document that was more crowded with infamous falsehoods and distortions—infamous falsehoods and distortions on a scale so huge that I never imagined until today that any government on this planet was capable of uttering them!"

The ambassador and the envoy rose without comment and hastened back to the Japanese embassy to burn their papers.

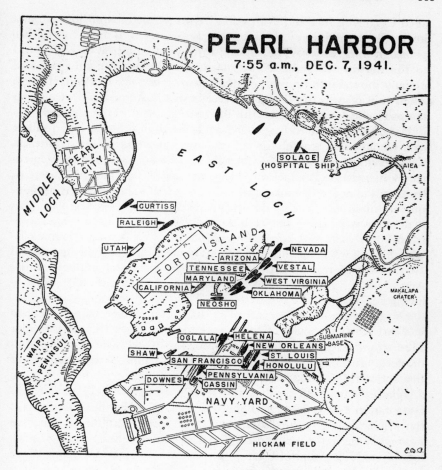

PEARL HARBOR
7:55 a.m., DEC. 7, 1941.

EAST LOCH

MIDDLE LOCH

PEARL CITY

SOLACE (HOSPITAL SHIP)

AIEA

CURTISS

RALEIGH

UTAH

FORD ISLAND

NEVADA

ARIZONA

TENNESSEE

VESTAL

MARYLAND

WEST VIRGINIA

CALIFORNIA

OKLAHOMA

NEOSHO

MAKALAPA CRATER

WAIPIO PENINSULA

KUAHUA

OGLALA

HELENA

SUBMARINE BASE

SHAW

NEW ORLEANS

ST. LOUIS

SAN FRANCISCO

HONOLULU

DOWNES

PENNSYLVANIA

CASSIN

NAVY YARD

HICKAM FIELD

ATTACK ON PEARL HARBOR

At dawn on December 7 (Hawaii time) the Japanese striking force stood 200 miles north of Oahu, the Hawaiian island whose southern coast is deeply indented by Pearl Harbor. The signal for attack, the phrase "Climb Mount Niitaka," had been received from Japan the day before. Carrier pilots had been accurately briefed regarding location of all ships and facilities at the base, for espionage had been thorough. A major portion of the population of Oahu is Japanese, and the large consular staff had made use of the cables to the last. Japanese announcers at the Honolulu broadcast station had managed to convey further information by pre-arranged wording of news items. Between 6 and 7:15 A.M. the six aircraft carriers launched 361 planes in three waves. The striking force then withdrew at high speed to the northwest. Japanese submarines, including five midgets, had already moved into position off the narrow entrance to Pearl Harbor. Their mission was to prevent the escape of the American fleet and attempt to close the harbor mouth by sinking a ship in the channel.

Hawaiian army and navy bases and the United States Pacific Fleet as a whole could scarcely have been more ill-prepared for the attack. The Services on Oahu had not achieved co-ordination regarding security measures. For lack of planes neither the inshore air patrol of the Army nor the distant reconnaissance of the Navy was being adequately maintained. The Army had recently been supplied with limited radar equipment but thus far only a training watch, operating from 4 to 7 A.M., was being kept. Aircraft were lined up on the fields wing tip to wing tip "to prevent sabotage." There was no general alert. Back of this condition was the general unpreparedness of the Army and Navy, and back of it all was the unpreparedness of a peace-loving nation.

On the morning of December 7, 1941, there were eight battleships in Pearl Harbor. Seven of them were moored along the south side of Ford Island in what is known as Battleship Row. The eighth was in drydock. In the area also were nine cruisers, some 28 destroyers, and five submarines, besides supply and repair ships, tenders, and other auxiliaries—in all 86 combat and service ships of the Fleet. No aircraft carriers were present. Four were operating in the Atlantic. Of the Pacific carriers, the *Saratoga* was at San Diego for repairs, the *Lexington* was on maneuvers southeast of Midway, and the *Enterprise,* flagship of Vice Admiral William F. Halsey, was returning from Wake Island whither it had gone to deliver 12 Wildcat fighter planes with Marine pilots. The *Enterprise,* with its escorting cruisers and destroyers, had been due in Pearl Harbor before Saturday night, but bad weather delayed its arrival until after the attack.

Shortly before 7 A.M. a destroyer on patrol duty off the harbor mouth radioed the base: "We have attacked, fired upon, and dropped depth charges upon submarine operating in defensive area." Though the message got through to the highest echelons, no alert was sounded. Such reports had come in before and had proved to be inaccurate. By the time the story was confirmed the air raid had begun.

That morning the army radar was working overtime. The operator, a private, continued instructing a new man past the usual hour for securing, and at 7:02 A.M. he had detected a large number of planes 132 miles away approaching from the north. He reported his findings to an inexperienced junior officer who told him to "forget it," apparently supposing the aircraft were a flight of Flying Fortresses expected from the mainland. To some extent the Pearl Harbor debacle may thus be attributed to an officer's hazy knowledge of geography, for planes from the United States approach Oahu from the northeast.

The Japanese struck first at Kaneohe Naval Air Station on the eastern side of the island. At 7:50 nine planes swooped low over Kaneohe Bay pouring incendiary bullets into seaplanes on the ramp or moored in the water. A second wave added to the destruction. These and other enemy aircraft then penetrated the clouds which at this season hover over the Koolau Range and swept down upon the air stations in the valley beyond—the Army's Hickam and Wheeler Fields, the Navy's Ford Island base, and the Marine Corps station at Ewa. Everywhere American aircraft were lined up, forming easy targets. In the midst of the melee dive bombers from the *Enterprise,* now only 200 miles away, began to arrive. Three or four were shot down by antiaircraft, which by this time was putting up a tremendous barrage, shooting at everything that flew. During the attack also the Flying Fortresses came in from the mainland. Unarmed, they were not able to defend themselves and several were shot down by the Japanese. At the beginning of the raid there were 202 serviceable naval planes in the Oahu area. When the attack was over, only 52 of these were sufficiently undamaged to take to the air.

Immediately following the initial attack on the airfields, Japanese torpedo planes, dive bombers, and high-level bombers came in, concentrating their attention on the heavy ships in Pearl Harbor. The pilots had been given precise instructions, not only as to targets which they were to attack and their location, but even regarding the points of greatest vulnerability in each ship. The careful planning of the Japanese extended also to armament. Their large torpedoes, for example, were fitted with wooden fins to insure shallow runs for a harbor attack.

Torpedo planes converged from two directions upon the ships moored in Battleship Row. Within a few minutes each of the outboard battleships had received one or more hits. The suddenness and swiftness of the attack was decisive, for whereas all the craft in the harbor were quickly alerted and soon put up a heavy screen of antiaircraft fire, there was no opportunity to provide for watertight integrity of

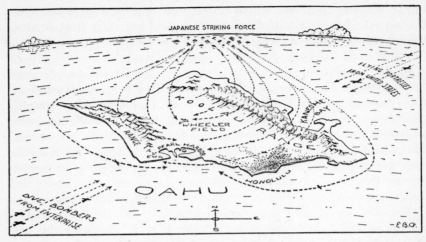

From *A Guide to Naval Strategy,* Bernard Brodie, Princeton University Press, Princeton, N. J.

JAPANESE ATTACK ON PEARL HARBOR

compartments. The *Oklahoma,* having taken four torpedoes in the first minute of the attack, listed to port and soon rolled over, thrusting her masts into the mud at the bottom of the harbor. No fewer than six torpedoes penetrated the hull of the *West Virginia.* Burning furiously, she began to settle, pinning the adjacent *Tennessee* against a concrete quay. Meanwhile, the *California,* two gaping holes torn in her hull by torpedoes, was almost completely encircled by blazing oil from her ruptured tanks. She too listed and began to settle into the harbor mud.

The torpedo planes were followed closely by enemy dive bombers and high level bombers. It was from this wave that other battleships received their severest damage. The *Pennsylvania,* in drydock, quickly put up such a heavy curtain of antiaircraft fire that she sustained comparatively little injury. Somewhat more heavily damaged was the *Maryland,* which was hit by two bombs, one of which, blasting a hole in the side of the hull, caused the ship to settle several feet by the bow. The *Arizona* was the victim of an almost incredible freak hit when a dive bomber succeeded in dropping a bomb into one of her stacks. The forward boilers and magazine blew up, throwing debris high into the air in one mighty burst of flame. The ship was virtually torn apart by the force of the blast, which sprayed the surrounding water with blazing oil. Eleven hundred officers and men lost their lives in that holocaust, among them Captain Franklin Van Valkenburgh and Rear Admiral Isaac C. Kidd.

As the flaming oil from the *Arizona* spread, it began to surround the stern of the *Tennessee*. Unable to escape from her wedged position, the *Tennessee* caught fire. Flames roared through the after officers' quarters and might have engulfed the ship had not the threatened vessel started her engines and repelled the burning fuel with her screws. The *California* received further and devastating damage from a 15-inch, armor-piercing shell equipped with fins and used as an aerial bomb. This device penetrated the main deck and, exploding inside the hull, killed many of the ship's company and set new fires raging.

The only one of the battleships to get under way during the attack was the *Nevada*. With a hole torn in her side by a torpedo and her quarter-deck wrecked by a bomb, she backed out of the burning oil from the *Arizona* and headed for the harbor entrance. As she neared the narrow channel, the Japanese pilots perceived that here was a chance to sink a battleship in the harbor mouth and so bottle up the fleet inside. Numerous planes switched their attention from the stationary ships and pounded away at her. Five more bombs hit and two more holes were torn in her sides. Sinking and unable to make good her escape, she was purposely run aground in shallow water inside the harbor.

The Japanese did not limit their attention to their primary objectives, the capital ships. In the first wave a single plane released a torpedo at the cruiser *Helena* and the minelayer *Oglala* tied up together at Ten Ten Dock. The torpedo passed beneath the minelayer and exploded against the cruiser. Both ships were damaged, and the *Oglala* began to capsize. Similarly a torpedo aimed at the repair ship *Vestal* passed under her keel and struck the *Arizona* tied alongside. When the *Arizona* blew up, a number of officers and men manning guns aboard the *Vestal* were blasted into the water. Among these was Commander Cassin Young, who swam back to his ship through burning oil, climbed aboard, and again took command. To escape the flames of the *Arizona* he weighed anchor and grounded his ship some distance away. Another wave of torpedo planes struck at the ships tied up on the north side of Ford Island. The *Raleigh* took one torpedo, the *Utah* two. The old target ship *Utah*, covered with a timber deck and lying at a berth customarily reserved for aircraft carriers, was probably mistaken for the *Saratoga* and received attention befitting that identification. After the first attack she quietly turned keel upward.

Most of the damage to ships other than those in Battleship Row was done by bombers. Both the destroyer *Shaw* and the floating drydock in which she stood were severely blasted by a quick succession of aerial bombs. The *Shaw's* magazine exploded, tearing her bow almost completely away. The destroyers *Cassin* and *Downes,* in drydock with the *Pennsylvania,* were practically melted down when an incendiary bomb passed completely through the *Downes,* rupturing her fuel tanks and causing burning oil to pour out on the floor of the drydock beneath both destroyers. As the heat increased, the oil reached the flash point and exploded with a spectacular force that sent great swirling sheets of flame high into the air. The torpedoes on the deck of the *Downes* now began to go off, as the *Cassin,* her supporting blocks burned from beneath her, fell over crazily against the other destroyer. The fire was brought under control only by flooding the dock. Meanwhile, the seaplane tender *Curtiss,* moored north of Ford Island, was struck by a flaming Japanese plane which doused her decks with burning gasoline. After this harsh initiation the *Curtiss* was strafed and then hit by two bombs, the second of which penetrated the boat deck and exploded at the main deck level.

The raid had lasted less than two hours. When it was over the Navy and Marine Corps had suffered a loss of 3,077 officers and men dead or missing and 876 wounded. In the midst of the universal shock at this disaster the nation took comfort in the efficiency, initiative, and invincible spirit shown by all personnel. Fourteen Congressional Medals of Honor were awarded, ten of them posthumously, for outstanding bravery.

Nineteen ships had been hit. In the months that followed most of those which had capsized or were resting on the shallow bottom of the harbor were righted and raised. All except two of the damaged vessels were repaired and made into more efficient craft than before the attack. Only the *Arizona* was beyond salvage. The *Oklahoma,* after a monumental engineering job which required more than two years, was at last brought to an even keel, but her hull was found unsuitable for further use as a man-of-war and she was decommissioned.

Following an investigation into the lack of preparedness in the Hawaiian area at the time of the attack General Short and Admiral Kimmel were relieved of their commands. Because of the danger of exposing America's prime military secret, her ability to break enemy codes, a complete public inquiry could not be carried out until after victory. Post-war Congressional hearings, while not absolving Short and Kimmel of negligence, brought out the fact that higher echelons were not without blame. General Marshall publicly acknowledged his fault in not checking on General Short's unsatisfactory reply to the November 27 warning, and it was announced that Admiral Stark would not again be assigned to a position of major responsibility.

War Declared

What had Japan achieved by her surprise attack on Pearl Harbor? She had temporarily weakened the United States Pacific Fleet, but the damage was not irreparable. The attack did not force a revision of the basic American strategy. Even had the Pacific Fleet not been damaged, it still would not have been strong enough to force its way through the fortified Japanese-held islands to the rescue of the Philippines. Until America had outbuilt the combined forces of her enemies, the Navy was necessarily committed to a policy of attrition. The Pearl Harbor raid did not change that.

Nor had Japan any reason to fear the arrival of reinforcements. With the forces of the European Axis rampaging across Russia and North Africa and their submarines sinking more ships than ever before, the United States could not afford to bring sufficient units from the Atlantic Fleet to take aggressive action in the Pacific. Here precisely the parallel between Port Arthur and Pearl Harbor falls down, for in 1904 Russia could and did move her Baltic Fleet bodily into the Orient, and here the Japanese met and destroyed it.

It would appear then that Japan gained little by her surprise raid. Had she, instead of attacking Pearl Harbor, merely continued her aggressive moves southward into Malaya and the Dutch East Indies, she would have strengthened her position by tapping sources of supplies now denied her by the United States. Meanwhile, it is conceivable that in the face of American disunity Congress would have delayed a declaration of war, perhaps indefinitely, while the "arsenal of democracy" would have continued in low gear, competing with "business as usual." But the Pearl Harbor attack brought the United States into instant unity, creating a moral potential which far outweighed the loss in ships and planes.

Some three hours after the raid on Pearl Harbor, Japanese Imperial Headquarters in Tokyo issued a rescript declaring war on the United States and the British Empire. The next day the United States and

Great Britain formally acknowledged themselves at war with Japan. On December 11 Germany and Italy, in conformity with the Tripartite Pact, declared war on the United States. Congress on the same day by joint resolution issued its declaration against the remaining Axis powers.

China, the long-suffering victim of an undeclared war, now issued declarations against Germany, Italy, and Japan. All the Central American states and the island republics of the Caribbean immediately took similar action. A basis was thus laid for formal world-wide collaboration. On January 1, 1942, representatives of the 26 governments at war with some or all of the Axis powers joined in a declaration of the United Nations, subscribing to the aims set forth in the Atlantic Charter and pledging full co-operation in the prosecution of the war and the making of the peace to follow.

23

The Fighting Retreat

REORGANIZATION OF THE NAVY

DURING THE PRE-WAR EMERGENCY PERIOD United States naval forces had been divided into the Atlantic, the Pacific, and the Asiatic Fleets, with the three Commanders-in-Chief rotating the overall command among themselves. In December, 1941, following the Pearl Harbor attack, the President separated the overall from the individual fleet commands, appointing Admiral Ernest J. King Commander-in-Chief of the United States Fleet with headquarters in Washington. In order further to unify the naval organization, Admiral King the following March was appointed also Chief of Naval Operations. Vice Admiral Royal E. Ingersoll was appointed to command the Atlantic Fleet, Admiral Chester W. Nimitz relieved Admiral Kimmel as Commander-in-Chief of the Pacific Fleet, and Admiral Thomas C. Hart remained in command of the Asiatic Fleet.

After February, 1942, when the Asiatic Fleet ceased to exist as such, the two remaining major fleet divisions were further divided into numbered fleets—even numbers in the Atlantic, odd numbers in the Pacific.[1] The two major fleets retained type organization, with type commanders as Commander Battleships, Commander Cruisers, etc., for administrative purposes, but for operations the numbered fleets were broken down into task forces comprising various types. The task forces might be subdivided into task groups and the task groups into task units. Thus Task Unit 56.2.11 would be a component of Task Group

---

[1] A "fleet" in the administrative sense is not an aggregation of fighting ships and support; it is a command. Vessels thus passed readily from fleet to fleet, and major forces sometimes changed fleet numbers with shifts in commanders and their staffs.

56.2, Task Group 56.2 would be a component of Task Force 56, Task Force 56 would be a component of the Fifth Fleet, and the Fifth Fleet would be a component of the Pacific Fleet. The task force and its sub-divisions were not standardized fleet elements. Their size and makeup depended upon the mission to be carried out.

It became clear at the very beginning of the war that civilians could not be safely employed for construction at advanced bases. In forward areas they would be in danger of being killed or captured, yet would have neither the training nor the legal right to defend themselves. The Navy therefore took advanced base construction under its direct control and began recruiting for a contingent of Construction Battalions (generally known as Seabees). Such battalions, organized and indoctrinated along naval lines and taught the use of weapons, regularly landed with assault troops. In both repairs and construction they soon proved their ability to outbuild the Japanese.

In order better to co-ordinate the activities of the Army and the Navy, work out a unified grand strategy, and promote more direct liaison between the services and the President, the Joint Chiefs of Staff was set up in supreme command of operations. The senior member, presiding over the meetings, was Admiral William D. Leahy, Chief of Staff to the President. Other members were General Marshall, Admiral King, and Lieutenant General H. H. Arnold, Chief of the Army Air Corps. Integration of the operations of the armed forces of the United States with those of the United Nations was achieved by the Combined Chiefs of Staff. Command thus could be organized to cut not only through the lines of the several services but through international lines as well. The military strength of the United Nations was thereby unified. A designated senior commander in any given theater, regardless of nationality or type of service, would command all the Allied forces in that area.

Loss of Wake and Guam

The Japanese surprise raid of December 7 (December 8 in the western Pacific) was not confined to Pearl Harbor. Wake Island, Guam, the Philippines, and the Malay Peninsula were all under attack within a few hours and all were sooner or later overwhelmed by enemy forces superior in numbers and equipment.

The siege of Wake lasted 16 days. Beginning with a 27-plane raid on December 8, Japanese bombers from Kwajalein in the Marshall Islands came over daily to pound at defenses. The military garrison on

Wake, commanded by Commander Winfield Scott Cunningham, numbered only 535, mostly Marines, under Major James Devereux, with 69 naval personnel, and an army communication unit of one officer and six men. There were on the island, however, some 1,200 civilian construction workers — noncombatants by international law. For ground defenses the garrison was provided with six 5-inch naval guns, twelve 3-inch antiaircraft guns, and about 50 machine guns. The only planes on Wake were the 12 Wildcat fighters flown in from the *Enterprise* on December 4. The Japanese destroyed seven of these in the first raid.

The enemy gave the island defenders three days of aerial bombardment by way of softening up. Then at dawn on December 11 surface ships moved in for a landing. For this amphibious operation the Japanese employed three light cruisers, six destroyers, two transports carrying 450 invasion troops, and an advance reconnaissance force of two submarines. Within a few hours this armada, smaller by two destroyers lost, was hauling out to sea again in some disorder. High winds which whipped up the waves and upset landing craft had helped, but the principal cause was the determined defense put up by the Wake Island forces. The Marines had held their fire until the enemy ships had closed to 4,500 yards. They had then turned on them their 3- and 5-inch guns and had sunk the first destroyer. Four Wildcats, all that were left, sank the other, strafed the cruisers, and bombed and set fire to one of the transports.[2] At the end of the attack the American planes were cut down to two.

The siege then continued for 12 more days, culminating in a raid by planes from the carriers *Hiryu* and *Soryu,* detached for that purpose from the Pearl Harbor striking force then en route back to Japan. On December 22 the last of the Wildcats was destroyed. That night the enemy invasion force returned, with the lost destroyers replaced by two others and with four heavy cruisers added. This time the gunnery ships remained out of range as a reserve while two transports moved in under cover of darkness, launched four 50-man barges, and then, after beaching themselves, disembarked 200 more troops. The Marines, exhausted by their ordeal, reduced in numbers, and scattered over the

---

[2] Because of the loss of important naval records in the Tokyo fires resulting from American air attacks, Japan's side of the story has necessarily been gleaned largely from United States Army and Navy interrogations of high-ranking Japanese officers. Information from this source, where it has appeared reliable, has been incorporated into the accounts of World War II actions given in this book. Other sources used were captured documents and ship casualty lists and other data submitted by the Japanese at the request of Allied authorities.

three islands which make up Wake Atoll, could not quickly assemble
in strength around the enemy beachhead. Those who did, put up a
desperate fight, machine-gunning many of the invaders, but at dawn
the bombardment ships had begun to move in and an hour later it was
clear that Wake was lost. By sunset the atoll was in the hands of the
Japanese and all the Americans were prisoners.

Guam fell more quickly. Virtually without defenses and within easy
striking distance of the enemy naval base at Saipan, its position was
untenable. When the Japanese struck on December 8, Guam time, its
defenders consisted of fewer than 400 naval personnel and 166 Marines. After two days of heavy aerial bombardment and strafing, the
Japanese forces landed at 3:30 on the morning of December 10. The
firing ceased at dawn, and the flag of the Rising Sun was raised over
the government headquarters at Agaña. Scattered resistance in the
interior continued until December 22.

SITUATION IN THE FAR EAST

It was in the southwest Pacific and in British Malaya that Japan
was expected to strike first. If, as was generally believed, the Japanese
contemplated moving into the Netherlands Indies, they must necessarily protect their flanks by seizing both Singapore and the Philippines. But extension of Philippine fortifications, prohibited by treaty
commitments with Japan, had been neglected for 20 years. Belatedly,
in July, 1941, General Douglas MacArthur was recalled from retirement and placed in command of all the United States Army Forces
in the Far East. A trickle of new armament—planes, tanks, artillery—
now began to arrive from America. The Navy set to work to make a
fortress of the naval base at Cavite. It further fortified Corregidor
Island at the entrance to Manila Bay. It began construction on a supplementary base on Mariveles Bay at the tip of Bataan. But all these
preparations came too late. The most that could be hoped was that
the Philippine defenders would be able to fight a delaying action until
major reinforcements could be sent to their relief.

Admiral Hart established headquarters at Manila and set about preparing his inadequate fighting strength and base facilities for the blow,
which by late November he regarded as inevitable. His fleet at that
time consisted of two cruisers, the *Houston* and the *Marblehead*,[3] 13
over-age destroyers, 29 submarines, a limited number of auxiliary ves-

---

[3] A third cruiser, the *Boise*, arriving at Manila with a convoy on December 4,
was immediately refueled and sent south to Cebu.

Top, U.S.S. HOUSTON AT HONOLULU. *Bottom,* FORMATION OF MOTOR TORPEDO BOATS.

sels, and the 30 slow and vulnerable PBY's, Catalina flying boats, of Patrol Wing 10. The Navy planes, based in lakes, bays, and swamps throughout the islands, joined the Army scouts in an extensive patrol of the Philippine coastline and the South China, Sulu, and Celebes Seas. Admiral Hart, in the meantime, held discussions with British and Dutch naval staffs for the purpose of achieving closer co-operation.

Early in December, while Washington was warning that negotiations with Japan were breaking down, naval planes patrolling the South China Sea sighted a heavy concentration of Japanese shipping, including men-of-war, in Camranh Bay on the east coast of French Indo-China. On the 4th these ships disappeared and, because of bad weather, were not discovered again until the 6th, at which time the armada was in the Gulf of Thailand headed west. The Japanese landed on the Malay Peninsula on December 8. At Singapore, 400 miles south of the invasion point, were Britain's most powerful battleship, the *Prince of Wales,* and the battle cruiser *Repulse,* but there were only four destroyers present to serve as escorts. Nevertheless, inadequately screened and with no fighter aircraft protection, the heavy ships set out to attack the enemy transports. Shortly before noon on the 10th Japanese torpedo planes and bombers converged upon the force and within an hour sank both the battleship and the battle cruiser. Neither America nor her allies had now a single capital ship in the Far East.

INVASION OF THE PHILIPPINES

News of the raid on Pearl Harbor reached Manila shortly after 3 A.M. on December 8 (8:30 A.M., December 7, in the Hawaiian Islands). Military forces in the Philippines were immediately alerted. By dawn both Army and Navy planes were on patrol or were dispersed to prevent the sort of attack on concentrated masses of aircraft that had occurred on Oahu landing fields. Enemy forces operating out of the Palau Islands made a minor sea-air assault on Davao Bay, Mindanao Island, far to the south, but hours passed without the expected attack on Luzon. The delay was not a part of Japanese planning. The strikes were to have been co-ordinated, but bad weather over Formosa, 240 miles north of Luzon, kept the enemy aircraft grounded all night and part of the morning. This postponement was to prove fortunate for the attackers but tragic for the Philippine defenders. By noon most of the United States Army planes on Luzon had returned from patrol. Bombers and fighters were being refueled or were parked in neat rows while the pilots awaited further orders.

It was then that the enemy struck. Japanese naval aircraft winging down from Formosa appeared over the Army's Clark and Iba Fields, blasting hangars, runways, and the lined-up planes. In the course of the afternoon landing strips on the northern and eastern coasts of Luzon were similarly treated, and at midnight Japanese bombers arrived to strike at Nichols Field south of Manila.

By December 10 United States air forces in the Philippines had been effectively crushed. In the early afternoon two waves of Japanese bombers, some 50 in all, with fighter planes above them, appeared over Manila at about 20,000 feet. In perfect V formation each wave circled the city. One proceeded to Nichols Field and gave it a final neutralizing bombing, while the other blasted at the shipping in the harbor. Both then converged over Cavite naval base. This they crossed and recrossed in leisurely fashion, picking their targets with ease and accuracy. The few remaining serviceable planes which rose to meet them were quickly shot down. The nine 3-inch antiaircraft guns, principal protection for the base, were useless, for they could put up a barrage no higher than 15,000 feet. The Japanese struck at oil tanks, docks, radio equipment, machine shops, and storehouses—everything, in fact, except the ammunition depot, which they unaccountably missed. When the two initial waves of planes had expended their bombs, they left in the same precise formation in which they had arrived. A third formation then appeared from the north and continued the pounding. At the end of four hours, when the last enemy plane had departed, the naval base was a shambles of twisted steel and powdered concrete lying under a pall of smoke towering thousands of feet into the air.[4]

Damage to shipping in the harbor was relatively light. One merchantman had been sunk; a submarine, the *Sealion,* had been destroyed by two direct hits; a minesweeper was so severely battered that it was later scuttled. Some 40 deep-sea ships and most of the naval craft in the harbor were untouched. Aware that such luck could not continue, Admiral Hart ordered most of his auxiliaries and small craft and all but two destroyers to proceed to the south. At the same time he advised owners and agents of the commercial vessels to leave under escort of the departing naval units. Over 20,000 tons of merchant shipping thus escaped undamaged.

---

[4] It was for some time believed that American aircraft striking at Japanese shipping on December 10 had sunk the battleship *Haruna.* Post-war investigation revealed that the *Haruna* was not in the Philippines area at that date. The vessel attacked was the heavy cruiser *Ashigara.* No hits were made. Nearly a year would pass before the first Japanese battleship would be sunk.

THEATER OF PHILIPPINES AND
NETHERLANDS INDIES CAMPAIGNS
DECEMBER, 1941-MARCH, 1942
1. ACTION IN MAKASSAR STRAIT   3. ACTION OFF BALI
2. ACTION OFF MADOERA STRAIT   4. BATTLE OF JAVA SEA

Japanese Tactics. Meanwhile, Japanese forces were making landings at Aparri and at Vigan in the northern part of Luzon. Within 48 hours a third landing was made to the south at Legaspi. These landings in general followed a carefully worked out pattern which served as a model not only for the Japanese themselves in subsequent amphibious operations but to some extent for the Allies. Bombers first pounded the landing area, shooting down any intercepting planes and silencing coastal batteries. Heavy surface craft then stood about five miles offshore blasting the area at long range. When the coastline and the im-

mediate interior had been sufficiently neutralized, destroyers and gunboats approached to within a mile of the shore for a final raking. Small
transports next moved in between the line of heavy ships and the light
craft. Here through side hatches they slid power-driven landing boats
loaded with men. The use of small, shallow-draft transports was particularly important in the Philippines operations, where American submarines were the principal remaining defense. This type of troop-
carrying craft was hard to hit, and whether one or many were sunk the
loss to the Japanese in men, materials, and shipping was generally
slight.

Both in the initial and later amphibious operations the key to Japanese success was air power co-ordinated with sea power. As soon as
the landings were established, airstrips were repaired and planes were
concentrated for the next move. Fighters from the new fields would
crush what was left of air opposition at the next landing point, while
bombers smashed the coastal defenses. Enemy men-of-war and transports would then move in. Thus, step by step, the Japanese proceeded
down the Philippines and deployed their forces through the islands of
the Netherlands Indies.

Retreat from Manila. Through most of December United States
forces held on stubbornly to Manila and the adjacent waters. American submarines hovered about the sea lanes or patrolled the coasts of
Luzon, slithering over the shallow bottoms of the harbors to strike at
Japanese transports and their escorts. But the underwater craft were
hampered by poor ammunition. Their torpedoes made easily detected
wakes; some ran erratically, broached, or blew up prematurely; those
which hit the target often failed to explode. A most disturbing demonstration of this weakness in weapons occurred on December 21, when
the Japanese made their main landing at Lingayan Gulf. Though
American submarines were stationed in an intercepting position, they
succeeded in sinking only one transport out of more than 80 ships of
varied types, including cruisers.[5]

When it became apparent that enemy air superiority was so over-
whelming that it was useless to retain good planes on Luzon, the 11
Catalinas that could still fly proceeded south to Mindanao. But the
Navy in the northern Philippines did not long remain entirely without

---

[5] The Japanese torpedo was superior to any developed by the Allies. It carried
almost twice the explosive charge of the American torpedo, had greater speed, and
left less wake. But the American weapon was gradually improved, with a resulting
sharp increase in sinkings by United States submarines. Toward the end of the
war the Allies were using a nearly wakeless electric torpedo.

wings. Technicians of Patrol Wing 10 pooled the engines and parts of six wrecks left behind and assembled four precarious but serviceable aircraft. In one of these Major General Lewis H. Brereton was flown south on December 24. Admiral Hart was to fly to Java on Christmas Day, but shortly before the hour planned for his departure the hiding place of the patched-together Catalinas was discovered by Japanese airmen who destroyed the planes in the water. The admiral there-fore left by submarine, as did President Manuel Quezon, who took up residence on the island of Negros.

Rear Admiral Francis W. Rockwell, now senior naval officer in the Manila area, had shifted his headquarters to Corregidor a week earlier. By the end of December he had ordered the last remaining destroyers, the *Peary* and *Pillsbury*, as well as all the submarines, to proceed to the south. Meanwhile, General MacArthur had begun his long-planned wheeling movement, whereby the Filipino-American land forces were to withdraw into the Bataan Peninsula to hold off the enemy until reinforcements could arrive. To prevent further slaughter of civilians in the now militarily useless capital, Manila on December 26 was declared an open city. On January 2 the Japanese took possession.

Defense of Bataan. Among the few naval craft now left in the Luzon area were six motor torpedo (PT) boats under the command of Lieutenant John Bulkeley. The 77-foot plywood boats, armed with torpedo tubes and machine guns and operating on adulterated gasoline, made a remarkable record. Until late January, when the land forces under the immediate command of General Jonathan M. Wainwright had established a defense line 20 miles above the tip of Bataan, the PT's had been used principally for courier duty. Thereafter, they went on a brief but stirring offensive. Striking always at night, they damaged several Japanese vessels, probably sank a tanker, and helped break up a landing behind Wainwright's lines by sinking two invasion barges, one filled with troops.[6] As additional duties they guided submarines through the minefields to Mariveles and Corregidor to bring in ammunition and take out key personnel.

By March the PT squadron had been reduced to four somewhat battered craft. On the night of March 11 these four boats headed south

---

[6] It may never be possible to determine how many ships were hit by the PT boats. The above, based in part upon Japanese statements of overall damage received during the landings, is perhaps as near as we shall come to an exact estimate. Despite optimistic claims made at the time, it is now known that no Japanese major fleet types were sunk in Philippine waters during the enemy invasion. No Japanese cruiser was sunk before the Battle of Midway in June, 1942.

carrying General MacArthur, Admiral Rockwell, and other high officers. One PT had to be abandoned in the Cuyo Islands, but at dawn on the 13th the three remaining boats, with all passengers somewhat shaken but safe, arrived at Cagayan on the island of Mindanao. The next evening, two PT's slipped over to Negros through a cordon of Japanese destroyers and brought out President Quezon. From Mindanao the PT boat passengers thus assembled were flown to Australia.

There were about 1,500 Marines and 2,500 naval officers and enlisted men among the last-stand defenders of Bataan. Many of the navy personnel together with about 100 Marines formed a Naval Defense Battalion under Commander Francis J. Bridget to assist in the defense of the west coast of Bataan. The sailor-infantrymen carried such rifles as they could beg or borrow and wore white uniforms which they had dyed with coffee grounds to cut down their visibility in the jungle. To this hastily-drilled outfit fell the task in late January of repulsing a landing made by picked Japanese troops in an attempt to cut off the front lines. For five days, using unorthodox tactics of their own devising, the Defense Battalion held off the enemy. At last they were relieved by strong units of Filipino Scouts, whose marksmanship, together with Corregidor's guns, drove the surviving Japanese over the cliffs.

Early in April it became evident that the Bataan defenders, short of food, ammunition, and medical supplies, and diminished in numbers by starvation, battle casualties, and disease, could no longer hold out against the Japanese pressing against their lines. In the southern Philippines preparations were being made to come to their relief. Two submarines loaded with food and supplies had been dispatched northward. Seven inter-island steamers were loaded and ready to depart. Flying Fortresses and B-25 medium bombers, on their way up from Australia, together with a number of P-35's locally available, would provide cover. But the planes from the south did not arrive in the Philippines until April 10. Bataan had surrendered the day before. Corregidor held out a month longer.

NETHERLANDS INDIES CAMPAIGN

Japan's objective in her drive to the south was to seize and hold British Malaya and the Netherlands Indies. Here she would be able to obtain the petroleum products she so sorely needed. Here she would acquire 90 per cent of the world's rubber and nearly all its quinine, at the same time denying these vital commodities to her enemies. Here also she would find tin and ample supplies of cotton, hemp, tea, spices, and rice—and sufficient slave labor to produce them.

Japanese strategy envisaged a three-prong drive. The western prong would follow the coast of China and proceed via French Indo-China and Malaya to Sumatra. The central prong would thrust down the South China Sea to Borneo and Celebes, taking the Philippines on its flank and forming with the push through Sumatra a pincers attack on Java. The eastern thrust would be via New Guinea to Rabaul in the Bismarck Archipelago. The East Indies, extended by bases on New Guinea, New Britain, and New Ireland, would then serve as a series of unsinkable aircraft carriers, forming a continuous fence against Allied attack from the south. Seizure of Wake and the British Gilbert Islands would buttress Japanese defenses in the east.

It was apparent from the beginning that the Allies were not prepared to halt Japan's all-out drive. Hong Kong fell on Christmas Day, 1941, and Manila, as we have seen, a few days later. And though parts of the Philippines held out for several months, the Japanese merely by-passed and contained such pockets of resistance. By the end of December they were establishing bases in southern Mindanao and at Jolo in the Sulu Archipelago.

During this advance a Dutch submarine patrolling along the west coast of Borneo sank a Japanese destroyer which had ventured prematurely into the area. Three days later six Catalinas flew up from Ambon to strike at the Japanese surface force at Jolo, but fighter planes intercepted them and shot down four. Army Flying Fortresses attacking enemy shipping off Davao in early January had better luck. They made a hit on the bow of a heavy cruiser and forced it to withdraw to Japan for repairs. All the Fortresses returned to base.

But the Japanese, undeterred by such relatively minor resistance, struck across the Celebes Sea and seized Tarakan and Menado preparatory to advancing through Makassar and Molucca Straits. The Allied forces, reduced to a fighting retreat, prepared to make a stand in order to gain time. While the Japanese drive was being delayed in Malaya and in the Netherlands Indies, the United States and her allies would be building up their armament and deploying their growing strength to put a halt to the advance and at length to enter upon an offensive which would push the enemy forces back.

The ABDA Fleet. From Luzon Admiral Hart transferred to Soerabaja[7] on the north coast of Java, and there, upon his arrival on January 1, he set up provisional headquarters for the Asiatic Fleet. In the conference which followed, British General Sir Archibald Wavell, in supreme command of all Allied forces in that theater, appointed Hart to the operational command of the ABDA (American-British-Dutch-Australian) combined fleet. In this post he would have the invaluable advice of the hard-hitting Dutch Commander-in-Chief, Vice Admiral Conrad Helfrich, whose knowledge of Indonesian waters was unsurpassed.

The combined fleet, in addition to Admiral Hart's three cruisers and 13 destroyers, comprised the Dutch light cruisers *Java, De Ruyter,* and *Tromp* and six destroyers; the British heavy cruiser *Exeter;* and the Australian light cruisers *Hobart* and *Perth* and seven destroyers. Thirty-nine submarines operated with the ABDA force; 27 were American, three were British, and nine were Dutch. Admiral Helfrich, who opposed the concept of a fighting retreat, is said to have pounded the table and demanded more cruisers, but his allies in that uncertain period were unwilling to risk their limited surface reserves in an area where the odds overwhelmingly favored the Japanese.

The first task of the combined naval command was to integrate the heterogeneous forces at their disposal. To overcome the difficulties imposed by two different languages and four different systems of fleet tactics and signals required the invention on the spot of a special plan of communications. Exchanging signalmen among the flagships facilitated execution of the plan to some extent, but never throughout the campaign which followed did the function of command operate with dependable smoothness.

Action in Makassar Strait. Throughout January the Dutch and British surface warships were busy escorting troop transports for the defense of Singapore. The American fleet remained on guard about eastern Java, while Dutch and American submarines and planes patrolled the straits flanking Celebes. On the 20th Netherlands planes sighted a large Japanese convoy in the Celebes Sea headed towards Makassar Strait. Submarines then took up the trail and reported the progress of the enemy force as it proceeded south. After midnight on the 24th four American destroyers, the *John D. Ford, Pope, Parrott,* and *Paul*

---

[7] Dutch spellings for Netherlands Indies geographical names have generally been used in this chapter. The following rules, giving Dutch spellings and their equivalents, should make pronunciation clear: oe=ōō, u=German ü, j=y, tj resembles English ch. Hence Soerabaja is sometimes Anglicized to Surabaya and Tjilatjap to Chilachap.

Jones, under Commander Paul H. Talbot, came in for an attack as the convoy lay off the oil port of Balikpapan. The destroyers had originally been supported by the *Boise* and *Marblehead,* but neither cruiser reached the scene of action. The *Boise* had ripped open her hull on a pinnacle rock and was out of the campaign for good. Shortly afterwards the *Marblehead* had developed turbine trouble and had fallen behind.

The enemy ships, including men-of-war and armed transports, were clearly silhouetted against fires on the shore, for the retreating Dutch had blown up oil wells, storage tanks, and everything else of possible use to the invader. Traveling at better than 30 knots, the destroyers, with the *Ford* in the van, penetrated the screen and made a series of runs through the line of transports, firing torpedoes on both sides. The Americans, though heavily outnumbered, had the element of surprise in their favor. In the flickering lights, with oil smoke covering the surface of the water, the Japanese were thrown into a state of bewilderment. They at first mistook the darting United States destroyers for their own and attributed the torpedo attack to submarines or planes. When at the end of half an hour two of the American vessels had fired all their torpedoes, they turned their 4-inch guns on the transports. The enemy, now aware that the attack was from surface craft, opened fire—but only intermittently, for in the smoke and confusion there was danger of hitting their own ships. Among the attacking destroyers only the *Ford* was struck; a shell wrecked her after deck-house and wounded four men. The Japanese lost four transports and had one patrol vessel severely damaged. By daybreak the American destroyers had reassembled and cleared the area. Later they sighted the *Marblehead,* formed a screen around her, and proceeded back to port.

Action off Madoera Strait. By the end of January, while repairs were being rushed on the *Marblehead* and *Ford,* the Japanese were pushing into Burma and had laid Singapore under siege. Other enemy forces moved almost without opposition down the west coast of Borneo; as far east as Rabaul; and southward through Molucca Strait to seize the Dutch base at Ambon, thereby bringing northern Australia within range of their bombers. On February 3, Japanese planes, operating from their new landing strips in southwestern Borneo, made the first of a series of bombing raids on Java. They gave the Soerabaja naval base scant attention; that could wait till later. As on Oahu and Luzon their initial targets were airfields. In this first raid the Japanese damaged or destroyed nearly every land-based plane on the island.

Early the following morning a striking force commanded by Dutch Rear Admiral Karel Doorman stood out from Madoera Strait off Soerabaja to tackle the now-reinforced Japanese convoy at Balikpapan. Under Doorman were his flagship, the *De Ruyter,* the *Houston, Marblehead,* and *Tromp,* and seven destroyers. There was, of course, no fighter plane protection, for none was available. The attack planned by Doorman was frustrated when in mid-morning several formations of Japanese bombers appeared overhead and struck at the cruisers. For more than two hours these vessels dodged and twisted and put up a heavy antiaircraft barrage that brought down several enemy planes. A bomb struck the mainmast of the *Houston,* glanced off, and smashed into the deck. Bomb fragments, penetrating the after turret, set off the ready powder inside, and there followed a blast which killed or mortally wounded 60 men and put the turret out of commission for the rest of the campaign.

The *Marblehead* was more severely damaged. A bomb landed on her fantail and, piercing the main deck, wrecked the steering gear and ruptured fuel tanks, starting several fires. Another penetrated the main deck and demolished the officers' quarters and the sick bay below. At the same time a near hit blasted a hole in the hull below the water line. The cruiser, out of control, took a sharp list to starboard and settled by the head. Steering with engines and kept afloat only by constant pumping and bucket bailing brigades, she limped into Tjilatjap on the southern coast of Java for a temporary patch on her hull, received additional repairs at Ceylon and at Durban, South Africa, and thence rounded the Cape of Good Hope, reaching the United States in May.

By mid-February the Japanese pincers had begun to close. The enemy, now secure in Borneo, Celebes, and the Moluccas, threatened eastern Java and the islands extending towards Australia. To the west they had by-passed doomed Singapore and begun landings on Sumatra. The Allied fleet was thus in danger of being trapped in the Java Sea. With four cruisers and ten destroyers, Admiral Doorman rushed to Bangka Strait to repulse an enemy convoy reported there, but Japanese aircraft attacked in such numbers that he was forced to withdraw. On the 15th Singapore fell, and the invader pushed unmolested towards Sunda Strait.

Admiral Hart, meanwhile, had been recalled by Washington, and Vice Admiral Helfrich was in command of the ABDA fleet, with Vice Admiral William O. Glassford heading the American naval component. Since Soerabaja was now subject to daily bombings, Glassford transferred his forward headquarters to Tjilatjap and selected Exmouth Gulf on the west coast of Australia as his main fleet base. The wisdom of not basing the fleet on nearer Darwin was demonstrated on February 19, when Japanese bombers appeared over that port, smashing airfields, warehouses, and docks, and sinking nearly every ship in the harbor, including the American destroyer *Peary*.

Action off Bali. No sooner had Doorman been repulsed from Sumatra than he had to turn his attention to an equally serious threat at the opposite end of Java. On February 18, after a three-day aerial bombardment, Japanese forces landed on the island of Bali and seized the airfield. On the following night, shortly after the invasion convoy of two transports and six destroyers had left the beachhead and was proceeding back through Badoeng Strait towards the Java Sea, it was overtaken and engaged by an Allied surface force attacking in two waves.

The first wave, comprising the *De Ruyter, Java,* and three destroyers, the *Piet Hein, Ford,* and *Pope,* came up from the south and made contact with the Japanese ships at 10:30 P.M. In the first exchange of gunfire the *Java* was slightly damaged at the stern. The destroyers, now arriving, at once went into action, the *Ford* and *Pope* launching spreads of torpedoes and apparently making a hit on an enemy vessel. At this point the *Piet Hein* turned out of line, burst into flames, and began to sink—it is not certain whether as a result of enemy shellfire or because she had run into the path of a torpedo from one of the American destroyers. The *De Ruyter* and *Java* continued northwest out of action and so on around Bali back to base, but the *Ford* and *Pope,* caught in intense cross-fire, were forced to turn back to the southeast. They were thus again obliged to run a gauntlet of Japanese vessels, but by dodging in and out of their own smoke screen and firing torpedoes they managed to escape undamaged to the open sea. Behind them the enemy ships were still firing away—evidently at each other.

The second wave consisted of the American destroyers *Stewart, Parrott, John D. Edwards,* and *Pillsbury,* with the Dutch cruiser *Tromp* following five miles astern to pick off with her guns any vessels disabled by the torpedoes of the smaller craft. This force, also approaching from the south, found the enemy shortly after 1:30 A.M. and promptly opened fire. In the engagement which followed, a shell passed completely through the *Stewart* without exploding. The *Tromp,* arriving at the scene of action, set fire to an enemy ship and then joined the destroyers in a run to the northeast through the Japanese formation. The *Pillsbury's* guns scored four direct hits on a destroyer, but the *Tromp,* now subjected to crossfire, was seriously damaged. All five Allied vessels, however, slipped away to the relative safety of the Java Sea.

Two of the Japanese destroyers were seriously damaged and were forced to return to Makassar. One of the battered vessels had to be towed and the other could make no more than eight knots. The injury done the ABDA fleet, which could less well afford it, was more severe—one destroyer lost, two cruisers laid up for repairs. This may be considered the price for failure to observe the military principle of concentration of forces. The *Stewart* never left drydock. In their haste the dock workers placed her improperly on her blocks. She rolled off and was later demolished to prevent her capture by the Japanese. But out of the action off Bali there came also a freakish bit of good luck. In the midst of the battle the *Ford's* motor whaleboat was shot away. It struck the water right side up and in it 33 survivors of the *Piet Hein* made their way back to Java.

The enemy troops on Bali were considerably strengthened by the arrival of reinforcements on February 25. On the same day another hostile force made landings on Bawean Island 100 miles north of Soerabaja, and reconnaissance revealed that Japanese fleets were approaching Java. Admiral Doorman continuously patrolled the Java Sea in the hope of meeting and repulsing the invader, but he was still hampered by lack of aircraft. Available to him at this time there were no more than 15 planes of all types.

Help was on the way. Two aircraft tenders, the American *Langley* and the British *Seawitch,* were approaching Java with 59 fighter planes, together with pilots and ground crews. One never arrived and the other arrived too late. The *Langley,* first of the two tenders to make the run to Java, was sighted by an enemy scout plane a hundred miles out of Tjilatjap. Not long afterwards nine Japanese bombers came over and so damaged the tender with five direct hits that one of her escorting destroyers was obliged to sink her. Two days later the naval tanker *Pecos,* with the *Langley's* survivors aboard, was sunk, also by enemy bombers.

Battle of the Java Sea. Admiral Doorman in the afternoon of February 27 led his striking force through the minefields into Soerabaja to refuel his destroyers and give his exhausted crews a chance to relax. While still in the channel he at last received definite information re-

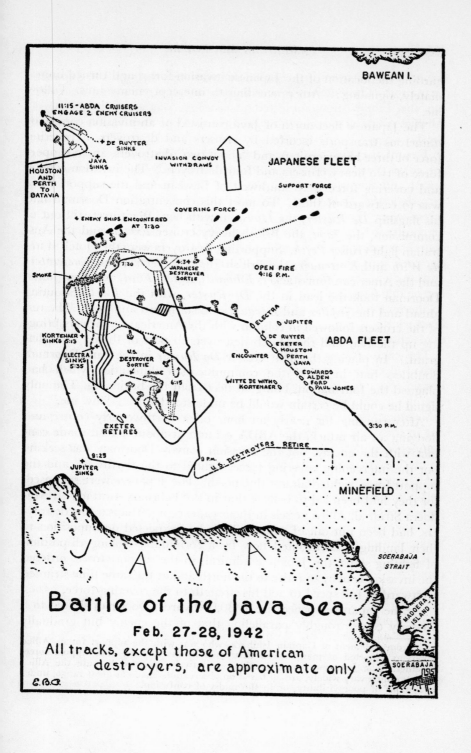

BAWEAN I.

11:15 - ABDA CRUISERS
ENGAGE 2 ENEMY CRUISERS

+ DE RUYTER
SINKS

JAVA
SINKS

HOUSTON
AND
PERTH
TO
BATAVIA

INVASION CONVOY
WITHDRAWS

JAPANESE FLEET

SUPPORT FORCE

COVERING FORCE

+ ENEMY SHIPS ENCOUNTERED
AT 7:30

7:30

4:34
JAPANESE
DESTROYER
SORTIE

OPEN FIRE
4:16 P.M.

SMOKE

ELECTRA O JUPITER
DE RUYTER
EXETER
HOUSTON
ENCOUNTER   PERTH
JAVA

ABDA FLEET

KORTENAER +
SINKS 5:13

ELECTRA
SINKS
5:35

U.S.
DESTROYER
SORTIE

SMOKE

6:15

WITTE DE WITH O
KORTENAER O

EDWARDS
ALDEN
FORD
PAUL JONES

EXETER
RETIRES

3:30 P.M.

9:25

JUPITER
SINKS

9 P.M. U.S. DESTROYERS RETIRE

MINEFIELD

J A V A

SOERABAJA
STRAIT

Battle of the Java Sea
Feb. 27-28, 1942
All tracks, except those of American destroyers, are approximate only

MADOERA
ISLAND

SOERABAJA

E.B.Q.

garding the location of the Japanese invasion forces and turned immediately, signaling: "Am proceeding to intercept enemy unit. Follow me."

The Japanese fleet north of Java consisted of an invasion convoy of numerous transports escorted by cruisers and destroyers, a covering force of three heavy cruisers and "about two" destroyers, and a support force of two heavy cruisers and four destroyers.[8] The invasion convoy and covering force were southwest of Bawean and the support force was to eastward of these. To meet this concentration Doorman had his flagship *De Ruyter*, the *Houston*, with her after turret still out of commission, the *Java*, the British heavy cruiser *Exeter*, and the Australian light cruiser *Perth*. Supporting destroyers were the Dutch *Witte de With* and *Kortenaer*; the British *Jupiter*, *Electra*, and *Encounter*; and the American four-stackers *Edwards*, *Alden*, *Ford*, and *Paul Jones*. Doorman took the lead in the *De Ruyter*, with the *Electra* scouting ahead and the *Jupiter* and *Encounter* to starboard and port. The rest of the cruisers followed in column with the American destroyers bringing up the rear and the Dutch destroyers to port of these. (See diagram.) In placing the light cruiser *De Ruyter* in the van, Doorman doubtless had in mind the communication difficulties which had plagued the four-nation, bilingual fleet from the beginning. The only signal he could be certain would be understood was "Follow me."

After running for nearly an hour on a northwesterly course and dodging an air attack, the ABDA column at about 4 P.M. made contact with the enemy, not the invasion convoy Doorman was seeking but the intervening covering force, sighted to the northwest, and the support force, sighted almost due north. The Japanese were surprised, for they had been led to believe that in the February 4 attack off Madoera Strait all Allied vessels in the area, except perhaps a few destroyers, had been put out of action. They had expected no opposition to their landings. Confronted now by a formidable-looking disposition of fighting ships, the Japanese admiral, in the support force, ordered the invasion convoy to retire to the north and at the same time steamed westward at full speed to add his strength to the covering force.

As the Japanese opened fire at 30,000 yards, Doorman shifted to a westerly course roughly paralleling that of the enemy but gradually

[8] From statement of Captain Ishihara, who was with the support force. Allied observers reported as many as 13 destroyers in the striking and support forces together. The Japanese figures are here tentatively accepted because the Allied reports which vary widely, are all based on observations made at great range, under conditions of poor visibility, or in the midst of confusion.

closed the range so that the 5.9- and 6-inch guns of his light cruisers could be brought to bear. At the same time the Allied destroyers moved to the disengaged side of the cruiser column. The Japanese, aided by a spotter plane overhead to correct their aim, made a hit on the *De Ruyter* and soon after on the *Java*. At 4:34 the enemy destroyers moved in for a torpedo attack, forcing the Allied cruisers to swing away briefly to the southwest. At the same time planes from Java passed over the enemy column dropping bombs but making no hits.

When the enemy destroyers retired, Doorman shifted to a north-westerly course and again began closing the enemy. During this phase the *Houston* was struck by an 8-inch shell which penetrated her engine room but failed to explode. Shortly after 5 P.M. the Japanese destroyers again swung in between the lines to fire torpedoes and make smoke, behind which the enemy cruisers made a turn to port and came in for a close-range attack. At this point the *Exeter*, disabled by a shell hit in her boiler room, swung to left out of line. The *Houston, Perth,* and *Java*, apparently not perceiving the cause of this maneuver, also turned left by individual movements and so broke up the formation. There followed a period of confused milling about and dodging of torpedoes, one of which struck the *Kortenaer*. The little destroyer burst apart, her bow and stern sinking separately.

The *De Ruyter* steamed ahead briefly and then turned back to re-form the Allied cruiser column behind a smoke screen laid by the American destroyers. At the same time the British vessels braved the enemy fire by moving in to cover the crippled *Exeter* with smoke. While thus engaged, the *Electra*, coming under simultaneous attack by three destroyers at close range, was sunk by multiple shell hits.

Doorman, ordering the *Witte de With* to escort the *Exeter* back to Soerabaja, left the southeasterly course on which he had re-formed his cruisers and moved northeast until the opposing forces were again moving parallel to each other at a range of 18,000 yards—this time on a bearing opposite to that of the first phase. In this run both sides fired steadily but ineffectively. Doorman, however, was anxious to disengage and go in search of his original objective, the invasion convoy. To cover his retirement and that of the *Exeter* he ordered in the American destroyers, which made smoke, fired their starboard torpedo broadsides, and then turned by column movement and fired their port torpedoes. Thus threatened, the enemy force broke off action and at about 6:15 headed north.

Doorman now led his formation in a wide sweep west and north—presumably in search of the convoy. At 7:30 the Allied column encountered four enemy ships and engaged in a brisk exchange of fire. But the Dutch admiral, evidently believing that the invasion force had now got between him and the coast of Java, soon turned away, moving first east and then south.

As the ABDA force approached the Java coast at nine o'clock, the four American destroyers, their torpedoes expended and almost out of fuel, left the column and retired to Soerabaja, whither the *Exeter* and *Witte de With* had already preceded them. Doorman with the remainder of the striking force now turned west to sweep along the coast. Twenty minutes later the *Jupiter* was torpedoed, evidently by a submarine, and began to sink. But the Allied force, without pausing, headed north and soon passed the spot where the *Kortenaer* had gone down. Admiral Doorman detached the *Encounter* to pick up survivors and the four cruisers pressed on without destroyer escort. At 11:15 these made a fresh contact with Japanese warships and opened fire at 9,000 yards. The Allied ships got in several hits, putting two destroyers out of action. This, according to Japanese accounts, was the only damage done by the ABDA force during the entire battle. The enemy now fired star shells between the lines to blind the Allies and conceal their own movements. Soon afterwards, the *De Ruyter* and *Java* were hit by torpedoes and began to sink. Even while his ship was going down, Admiral Doorman sent out a final command to the *Houston* and *Perth*: "Do not stand by for survivors. Proceed Batavia." Thereupon, the two remaining cruisers broke off action and headed west.

Retreat from Java. Though the Japanese invasion was delayed 24 hours, the enemy was in strength on Bali and Sumatra and was thus in a position to close the sea gates to the Indian Ocean. Admiral Helfrich, determined to make a last stand, ordered his remaining ships to leave the Java Sea on the evening of February 28. Only the four American destroyers *Edwards, Alden, Ford,* and *Paul Jones* made good their escape. They slipped through the Bali Strait and after a brief night skirmish with enemy vessels proceeded to the southeast. Because they were out of torpedoes and were therefore of little use as fighting ships, they continued to Australia.

The crippled *Exeter,* escorted by the *Encounter* and *Pope,* left Soerabaja at about the same time. Since the strait south of Madoera Island was too shallow for the cruiser, these ships were ordered to run north, then west along the southern coast of Borneo, and so through Sunda

Strait. In the Java Sea the next day they ran into a hostile force of five cruisers and 12 destroyers. The *Exeter,* opening fire, damaged one of the destroyers, but the other enemy vessels closed in and with gunfire and torpedoes quickly sank both her and the *Encounter.* The *Pope* escaped, only to be bombed later by a seaplane. Thus slowed down, she was overtaken and sunk by Japanese surface vessels.

The *Houston* and *Perth,* running along the Java coast under cover of darkness, reached Sunda Strait in safety. Here, however, they steamed directly into a Japanese invasion force of some five cruisers, 11 destroyers, and numerous troop transports. Under concentrated fire the *Perth* soon went down, but the *Houston* fought on for an hour longer, sometimes at such close range that her crew turned machine guns on the attackers. Though the American cruiser made numerous hits and sank two loaded transports, she was at length overwhelmed. Torpedoes had ruptured her steam lines, bringing her almost to a standstill; shells had ripped her topside decks into a shambles, reduced her fire to one main battery, and started blazes fore and aft. As her supply of ammunition began to run out, her commanding officer, Captain A. H. Rooks, gave the order to abandon ship, but he was killed by enemy fire before it could be executed. The *Houston* sank a few minutes later. Of her crew of 882, only 368 survived; 76 of these later died in prison camp.

That night the Japanese made landings on both the western tip and the north coast of Java. The next morning, March 1, the ABDA fleet was dissolved, and Admiral Glassford ordered all American ships in East Indies waters to proceed to Australia. Though a Japanase surface force and numerous submarines were patrolling in an intercepting position southeast of Tjilatjap, all the United States vessels except the destroyers *Pillsbury* and *Edsall* and the gunboat *Asheville* got safely through. After the *Asheville* had been sunk, two Japanese destroyers approached the survivors struggling in the water and rescued one man, apparently for questioning. They then steamed away, leaving the others to drown. The rescued man died later in prison camp.

Among the last Americans to leave Java were the wounded of the *Houston* and *Marblehead.* Their physician, Lieutenant Commander Corydon Wassell, requisitioned automobiles and drivers and succeeded in transporting his patients from the hospital across a hundred miles of rough mountain country to Tjilatjap, whence they were evacuated to Australia in a small inter-island steamer. Admiral Glassford and his chief of staff, Rear Admiral William R. Purnell, left in one of the last patched-up planes of Patrol Wing 10. With them was Admiral Helfrich, determined to carry on with the remnants of the Dutch Navy.

JAPANESE GRAND STRATEGY

Japan had now secured an inexhaustible source of raw materials and had drawn a defense line eastward from Singapore to Rabaul and northward through the Gilberts to Wake. She had thus in three months completed the first phase of the strategic plan drawn up by Imperial General Headquarters. The second phase would be a period of stabilization and development of the perimeter islands, including building of airfields and fortifications. This would have to be completed before the United States could build sufficient new ships to form powerful task forces. The third phase was planned as one of defense, with Japan secure behind her wall of island outposts, thrusting back any Allied attempts to penetrate towards the homeland and sending out her naval forces to wear down and perhaps destroy the United States Fleet. Every resource would be strained to maintain this defensive campaign until the American people, realizing that they were taking heavy losses in ships and men without hope of compensatory gains, would force their government into a compromise peace which would leave Japan a major portion of her conquests. Great Britain would then have no choice but to follow suit.

But it soon became apparent that to hold the bases already seized, Japan would be obliged to occupy neighboring islands as well. Rabaul, for example, could be secured from attack only by a further advance into the Solomon Islands and to Port Moresby on the southern coast of New Guinea. Thus each conquest would demand further conquests for its protection. The Japanese, despite themselves, were committed to a policy either of constant expansion or of constant retreat. There could be no static defense.

Some aggressive-minded officers urged immediate capture of bases in northern Australia and a thrust into the New Hebrides to cut the Australian-American supply line. To this proposal the General Staff, taking cognizance of the already critical supply problem, would not agree. A plan advocated by the popular and colorful Admiral Yamamoto, however, received more serious attention. Yamamoto recommended that the Gilberts-Wake defense line be extended east and north by seizure of Midway and the western Aleutians. Headquarters, while not denying the merit of the idea, chose to postpone its decision and let events decide whether these risky invasions should be attempted.

24

Holding the Line

I N THE LAST DAYS of 1941 Allied leaders assembled in Washington
drew up a broad, strategic plan for combined warfare. They were
obliged to consider with ruthless realism what could and could not be
done with the limited forces at their disposal. It was obvious that any
attempt to press the war with equal vigor against the European Axis
and against Japan would mean only a disastrous dispersal of strength.
The High Command therefore decided to stress the war in Europe,
while restricting the war in the Pacific for the time being to a gigantic
holding campaign. The Philippines and the East Indies region would
have to be sacrificed to the primary necessity of maintaining the supply
line between the United States and Australia. Japan must not be permitted to spread east through the equatorial islands or expand in the
central Pacific, nor must she be allowed to advance in the north via
the Aleutians or southward into Australia. Thus the first frontier was
drawn against Japanese aggression: Dutch Harbor to Midway, to
Samoa, to New Caledonia, to Australia. An order went out from
Washington that this line must at all costs be held. The United Nations had now set up a battle frontier which closely paralleled the Japanese perimeter as extended by the Yamamoto proposal. Time was to
prove, however, that America and her allies could no more maintain
a static defense than could the enemy. Eventually the line was certain
to give way in one direction or the other.

To carry out the Washington order, General MacArthur was placed
in supreme command of the Australian area, while Admiral Nimitz
undertook to hold the line in the central and south Pacific. To offset
Japanese expansion into the Bismarck Archipelago and the Gilberts
and to serve as springboards for future offensive action, the United

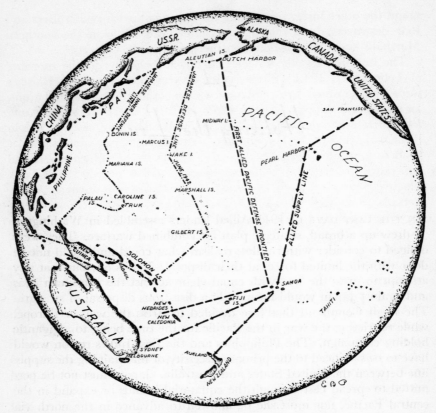

States established bases at Efate and Espíritu Santo in the New Hebrides, at Nouméa on New Caledonia, and on certain islands in the Fijis.

RAIDS ON JAPANESE POSITIONS

The earliest menace to the United States-Australian supply line appeared in the central Pacific, where in December the Japanese had pushed from their bases in the Marshalls into the nearby British Gilbert Group. To check this advance, Admiral Nimitz ordered Vice Admiral William L. Halsey to utilize two carrier task forces then available in a simultaneous strike against a number of fortified atolls on the eastern edge of Japan's expanded island empire. Halsey in the *Enterprise,* supported by three cruisers and six destroyers, would personally direct the attack on Kwajalein, Wotje and Maloelap in the central Marshalls, while Rear Admiral Frank J. Fletcher would command the other force, comprising the *Yorktown* with two cruisers and four destroyers, in a raid against Jaluit and Mille in the southern Marshalls and against Makin, northernmost of the Gilberts.

The multiple assault was carried out successfully on the morning of February 1, 1942. While cruiser-destroyer groups from Halsey's force went in under fighter plane cover to bombard shore installations, air strips, and shipping at Wotje and at Taroa in the Maloelap Atoll, *Enterprise* dive bombers smashed buildings at the air base on Roi in the Kwajalein Atoll. The bombers then sped 40 miles across the lagoon to join torpedo planes attacking structures on Kwajalein Island and naval craft in the adjacent anchorage. The enemy struck back effectively at Roi, where Nakajima-97's and Zeros[1] shot down six American planes, and off Taroa, where a bomb hit the cruiser *Chester,* tearing a large hole in the deck and killing eight men. About 30 Japanese planes were destroyed, half of them on the ground; hangars, fuel tanks, warehouses, and an ammunition dump were bombed and set afire; and off Kwajalein and Wotje numerous ships, including a cruiser, two submarines, and three tankers, were damaged, and several auxiliaries and small craft were sunk.

Aircraft from Fletcher's force, attacking to the south, struck through bad weather at targets which proved to be of little value. Electric storms, with erratic winds and heavy rain, destroyed six American planes and forced one to make a water landing, but enough reached their objectives to bomb buildings, damage two auxiliary vessels, and set fire to two seaplanes.

In the latter part of February, Halsey's task force shelled and bombed Wake Island and then continued 700 miles farther to the northwest to launch planes against the uncompleted Japanese air base on Marcus. On both islands shore installations were heavily damaged and fuel storage tanks set afire. Only two American planes were lost in these two raids.

Some weeks later the *Enterprise* force was assigned a still more hazardous mission in conducting the carrier *Hornet* to within 700 miles of Japan. From the *Hornet's* flight deck on April 18, rose 16 Army B-25 medium bombers under command of Lieutenant Colonel James H. Doolittle. Halsey's force had supported the first aerial attack on Japan.

[1] Japanese planes took their numbers from the year in which their design was adopted. The "Zero" fighter, or Navy-00, was adopted in the Japanese calendar year 2600 (1940 A.D.), the Nakajima three years earlier.

Meanwhile, a serious threat had developed in the southwest Pacific with the establishment of enemy bases in the New Guinea-New Britain area. From these points the Japanese could move into northern Australia or proceed by easy steps down the Solomons and beyond. To delay such an advance Vice Admiral Wilson Brown set out in mid-February with a task force built around the carrier *Lexington* for a raid on Rabaul, but enemy patrol planes sighted the force while it was still 350 miles northeast of the target, and a few hours later twin-engine bombers attacked in two waves of nine each. Five of the bombers were shot down by a single American pilot, Lieutenant Edward H. O'Hare, and most of the rest were destroyed by other fighter pilots or by antiaircraft. Only two of the carrier planes were downed and no ships were damaged, but Admiral Brown, having lost the advantage of surprise and expended his fuel in high-speed maneuvering, was obliged to call off his attack.

In the Coral Sea a few days later Brown was joined by Fletcher's *Yorktown* force and two additional heavy cruisers. Thus reinforced, he returned to the New Guinea area, approaching this time from the south. Since the thwarted attack on Rabaul, reconnaissance revealed that the Japanese had seized Lae and Salamaua on the New Guinea north coast. To attack these new bases, the carriers took a position in the Gulf of Papua and sent more than a hundred planes over a pass in the towering Owen Stanley mountain range. This time the surprise of the Japanese was complete. Before the enemy could put up an effective antiaircraft barrage, the American bombers had bombed and strafed landing strips, buildings, and batteries, and the torpedo planes had launched torpedoes at ships offshore. Several transports and small craft appear to have been sunk and two cruisers, a destroyer, and a seaplane tender damaged. The two Japanese aircraft which rose to meet the attackers were quickly blasted out of the way. Only one American plane was lost.

Compared to the great raids of 1944 and 1945 these attacks were small-scale affairs, and certainly they did not remove the threat of further enemy aggression, for the Japanese quickly replaced losses and built up their bases to as great strength as before. The raids had gained a little time, and they had a morale value which helped in some measure to offset the news of continued Japanese successes in the Far East; but their principal value lay in the lessons the Navy learned. Enemy fighter planes, for example, had proved superior to the American Wildcat. The Zero could climb 4,000 feet a minute and rise above the highest altitude of any military plane thus far produced by the Allies. Only concentration in numbers and superiority of training had enabled American pilots to achieve success over what were obviously Japan's second-best air teams. Thus challenged, United States technicians set to work to provide the Navy with planes of superior speed, greater maneuverability, and heavier fire power. The reports of carrier task force commanders led to other improvements. Planes were provided with leak-proof gasoline tanks and armor for the protection of the crews. The ratio of fighters to other types of aircraft was increased, as was the complement of pilots in excess of planes. Thus the bombers were given adequate protection, and the dangers of flyer fatigue were in some measure surmounted.

The unique outcome of these early raids, however, was the trial under fire of a new type of naval warfare. With a major portion of America's battleship fleet lying damaged in Pearl Harbor, United States striking power had perforce to be organized around such capital ships as were still afloat—the aircraft carriers. The success of the experiment radically changed weapons and methods. The classical big gun in the big ship was thereafter limited to such specialized functions as night surface actions, support of carrier strikes, and close-in bombardment of shore positions. Only gradually did the new task force, by proving its efficiency in combat and in support of invasions, prevail over a school of military thought which pointed out the vulnerability of the carrier, particularly when used against well-equipped land bases and land-based aircraft. Vulnerable the carrier undoubtedly was, but its long-range striking power gave it advantages over the battleship, and its mobility permitted a quick concentration of decisive strength upon enemy-held points where attack by surface forces or land planes would be impractical or impossible.[2]

The respite provided by the American raids was brief. In the long run they actually accelerated the enemy advance by convincing the Japanese that their defense lines must be extended without delay. Imperial General Headquarters adopted Yamamoto's suggestion that Midway and bases in the Aleutians should be seized, and no objection was raised to his further proposal that, following the Midway occupation, the still relatively weak United States Fleet should be forced

---

[2] The four large American carriers lost in World War II were sunk as a result of attacks by carrier planes or submarines. Of the 20 carriers of all types lost by Japan, ten were sunk by carrier planes, eight by submarines, one by carrier planes and surface units combined, and one by carrier planes and a submarine combined.

into a decisive engagement in Hawaiian waters. A Japanese victory in such a contest, he pointed out, would leave all the American islands in that area open to assault.

But the most immediate threat to Japan's defense line was in the south. The attempted carrier raid on Rabaul and the successful naval attack on Lae and Salamaua were merely supplementary to a continuous campaign being waged by Allied army aircraft. To buttress their positions in this area, the Japanese early in April pushed into the upper Solomons and soon afterwards prepared to seize Port Moresby.

Preliminary to the Port Moresby operation the enemy occupied and set up a seaplane reconnaissance base at Tulagi Island, off the south shore of Florida Island in the eastern Solomons. At the same time elements of an invasion force were assembled at Rabaul and at Buin on Bougainville Island, and a striking force was assembled at Truk in the Carolines. The two sections of the invasion force—transports, tenders, and cargo ships supported by a group of three cruisers, two destroyers, and the small carrier *Shoho*—would rendezvous in the Solomon Sea, establish an additional seaplane base on Deboyne Island, off the southeast tip of New Guinea, and then proceed through Jomard Passage to Port Moresby. In support of the invasion, the striking force, which included the two large carriers *Shokaku* and *Zuikaku*, two cruisers, seven destroyers, and a tanker, would pass around the eastern end of the Solomons and sweep the Coral Sea to search out and destroy Allied surface forces, and also, if possible, make an air attack on Townsville, Australia, where planes and ships were being concentrated.

THE BATTLE OF THE CORAL SEA

The Allied High Command, kept informed of these invasion designs through the breaking of coded Japanese radio messages, made plans of their own. American and Australian forces available in the south and central Pacific were ordered to proceed at once to the Coral Sea, where for some time Fletcher's *Yorktown* force had been on patrol. The *Lexington* force, now commanded by Rear Admiral Aubrey W. Fitch, arrived on May 1, making contact with the *Yorktown* west of Espíritu Santo.

Action at Tulagi, May 4. While the *Lexington* and her escorts were being refueled, Fletcher took his task force north for an attack on the enemy's new base in the eastern Solomons. On May 4, while the *Yorktown* maintained a zigzag course in the waters south of Guadalcanal, air attack squadrons from the carrier went over the Guadalcanal

THE U.S. AIRCRAFT CARRIER LEXINGTON. *Insert,* BATTLE OF THE CORAL
SEA. JAPANESE CARRIER SHOHO BURNING FURIOUSLY AFTER ATTACK BY
UNITED STATES NAVY PLANES.

mountains to make three separate strikes at the ships in Tulagi Harbor. The results were disappointing, illustrating the extent to which efficiency is likely to fall off under battle conditions. Though the planes attacked persistently, dropping 22 torpedoes and seventy-six 1,000-pound bombs and firing more than 80,000 rounds of machine gun bullets, enemy losses amounted only to a few torpedo boats destroyed and a destroyer, a minelayer, and three seaplanes damaged. The destroyer beached itself but later sank when it was swept out to sea by the tide. American losses were three planes which came safely through the attack but later failed to find their carrier.

The *Yorktown* headed south through the night and on the morning of the 5th made rendezvous with the *Lexington* force and with additional units, including two Australian heavy cruisers. Fueling continued until the following afternoon, when reconnaissance by General MacArthur's flyers based at Port Moresby indicated that the enemy invasion force was on the move. Fletcher promptly ordered fueling discontinued and detached the tanker *Neosho* southward escorted by the destroyer *Sims*. The main body then proceeded northwest operating as a single task force, with an attack group of five cruisers and five destroyers, commanded by Rear Admiral Thomas C. Kinkaid; a support group of three cruisers and two destroyers, commanded by British Rear Admiral J. G. Crace; and an air group comprising the *Yorktown* and *Lexington* and four destroyers, under the command of Rear Admiral Fitch.

Action off Misima, May 7. At dawn on May 7 Admiral Fletcher detached the support group augmented by an additional destroyer to block the southern opening of Jomard Passage. While thus engaged, the group was repeatedly but unsuccessfully attacked by enemy planes from Rabaul. They were attacked also, it appears, by United States Army bombers which failed to identify the ships as friendly. Fortunately, no damage was done.

The carrier force at this time had the good luck to be riding a weather front which concealed its location but did not prevent air operations. At about 10 A.M., as a result of an incorrectly coded contact report from a scout plane, an attack wave of 92 aircraft was launched to the northwest by the *Lexington* and *Yorktown*. Subsequent information from land-based Australian planes correctly located the *Shoho* and her escorts in the vicinity of Misima Island, and the information was passed to the attack groups, which changed course and found the target at 11:30.

The American aircraft squadrons pounced upon the Japanese carrier just as she was turning into the wind to launch planes. A few Zero fighters were in the air, but these gave their attention chiefly to the bombers, attempting the impossible maneuver of riding down with them in their dives. In the steep descent the Zeros, unable to decelerate to dive bomber speed, shot past their targets and left themselves vulnerable to the cross fire of rear-seat gunners below and American fighters above, and so went blazing into the sea in rapid succession.

While the *Shoho* turned frantically in circles, the American dive bombers made numerous hits on her flight deck, starting huge fires. But it was the torpedo planes which finished her. Coming in low under the smoke of the burning carrier, they pumped torpedo after torpedo into her sides. Within a few minutes she went down in a cloud of steam. Of her crew of 800 a quarter lost their lives.

The carrier sank so swiftly that some of the attacking planes turned away to expend their ammunition in several near hits on the accompanying cruisers and destroyers. Three bombers failed to return to the American task force. The Japanese, in addition to the aircraft which had gone down with the *Shoho*, had lost at least nine planes in combat.

Attack on the Neosho *and* Sims. As a result of the sinking of the carrier and the presence of the Allied ships off Jomard Passage, the Japanese invasion force retired to the north. The striking force, however, had already rounded the eastern end of the Solomons and was now in the Coral Sea. The heavy overcast concealed this and Fletcher's force from each other's air scouts, but shortly after dawn on the 7th pilots of the Japanese aerial patrol had caught sight of the *Neosho* and *Sims* through breaks in the cloud cover and had excitedly flashed back word that they had found the American carriers. Some 70 planes from the *Shokaku* and *Zuikaku* hastened to the scene and, finding only a tanker and a destroyer, searched the area in some bewilderment for two hours. At length for want of better targets, they came in for an attack upon the auxiliary and her escort. The *Sims* took three hits, broke in two, and sank with a loss of all but 13 of her complement. Seven bombs and a burning plane smashed into the *Neosho*. Drifting and helpless, she remained afloat until the 11th when an American destroyer took off her survivors and sank the useless hulk with shells and torpedoes. The *Neosho's* loss of 176 men might have been lighter had not a large part of her crew abandoned ship without proper orders. Sixty-eight men had drifted away on four lashed-together life rafts. Ten days later rescue ships found only four of the men alive.

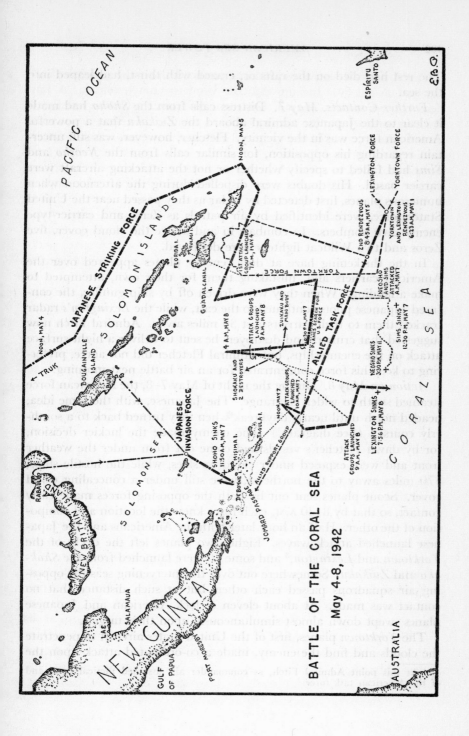

BATTLE OF THE CORAL SEA
May 4-8, 1942

The rest had died on the rafts or, crazed with thirst, had leaped into the sea.

Further Contacts, May 7. Distress calls from the *Shoho* had made it clear to the Japanese admiral aboard the *Zuikaku* that a powerful American force was in the vicinity. Fletcher, however, was still uncertain regarding his opposition, for similar calls from the *Neosho* and *Sims* had failed to specify whether or not the attacking aircraft were carrier based. His doubts were dispelled during the afternoon when numerous planes, first detected by radar as they passed near the United States force, were identified by air patrols as Zeros and carrier-type enemy dive bombers. In combats in and above the cloud cover, five Zeros and two Wildcat fighters were destroyed.

In the thickening haze at dusk, enemy planes appeared over the American carriers and, mistaking them for their own, attempted to make a landing. When they were driven off by ship gunfire, the confused Japanese pilots continued to the east, while the *Lexington's* radar tracked them to their carriers just 30 miles away. Admiral Fitch now suggested that cruisers and destroyers be sent to deliver a night surface attack on the enemy ships, but Admiral Fletcher did not agree, preferring to keep his force concentrated for an air battle next morning.

Action on May 8. During the night of May 7–8, the American force steamed south to widen the range. The Japanese, with the same idea, headed north until nearly daybreak when they turned back to a southerly course. (See diagram.) The enemy made the luckier decision, for by dawn Fletcher's vessels had come out from under the weather front and were exposed under cloudless skies, while the hostile ships, 170 miles away to the northeast, were still under a concealing cloud cover. Scout planes sent out by both the opposing forces made early contact, so that by 8:30 A.M. each force knew the location and composition of the other. Half an hour later both the Americans and the Japanese launched attack waves. Eighty-two planes left the decks of the *Yorktown* and *Lexington*,[3] and some 70 were launched from the *Shokaku* and *Zuikaku*. Somewhere out over the intervening seas the opposing air squadrons passed each other, but at such distance that no contact was made. At about eleven o'clock American and Japanese planes swept down almost simultaneously upon their targets.

The *Yorktown* planes, first of the United States aircraft to penetrate the clouds and find the enemy, made a co-ordinated attack upon the

---

[3] At this point Admiral Fitch, as commander air, assumed tactical command of the American task force.

Shokaku. While the Wildcats and Zeros were engaged in combat, the bombers dived upon the carrier, making two 1,000-pound bomb hits, which ripped up the flight deck and started gasoline fires. The torpedo planes, coming in at the same time, failed to score. According to the Japanese, they launched so far out that the wakes were seen in time and the torpedoes avoided. Of the *Lexington* aircraft, fewer than half were able to locate the enemy. Those that did, struck through a rift in the clouds at the *Zuikaku.* This carrier also avoided all torpedoes but may have been damaged by bombs.[4] The small *Lexington* attack group, as a result of its long search and the heavy opposition encountered, suffered serious losses. Three of the fighters were shot down and three of the bombers and one torpedo plane were destroyed by Zeros or ran out of fuel before they could get back to their carrier.

Radar aboard the American ships detected the oncoming Japanese air squadrons at a distance of 70 miles. Seventeen Wildcats, all the fighters that were available, went out to intercept; while 16 bombers remained near the carriers as an anti-torpedo plane patrol. The small and scattered intercepter groups proved less effective than antiaircraft fire and skillful ship handling in keeping damage to a minimum. Captain Elliott Buckmaster's adroit conning of the *Yorktown* carried that vessel through three torpedo attacks without a hit, but a dive bomber succeeded in striking the carrier with a bomb which tore downward through several decks and exploded in the aviation store room, killing 37 men. The *Yorktown* was able, nevertheless, to get her flight deck patched up in time to receive her returning planes.

Though the primary target of the Japanese planes was the larger *Lexington,* the greater number of cruiser escorts, in default of orders to the contrary, remained with the *Yorktown.* Thus, as rapid maneuvering caused the two carriers to draw apart, the *Lexington* was obliged to meet a superior offensive with an inferior defense. Captain F. C. Sherman met the first torpedo plane attack by ordering full left rudder in order to present as narrow a target as possible, but the planes swung with the ship and directed their torpedoes at the *Lexington's* port bow. Four subsequent waves, harassed by heavy antiaircraft fire, tended to

---

[4] At the time of writing it was impossible to ascertain definitely whether or not the *Zuikaku* was damaged. Captain Watanabe, of Admiral Yamamoto's investigation board, stated that this carrier was laid up one month for repairs. Captain Yamaoka, who was aboard the *Zuikaku* during the Coral Sea battle, claimed that the carrier was not damaged. In response to further questioning, however, Yamaoka made this contradictory statement: "These carriers [the *Shokaku* and *Zuikaku*] were to take part in the Midway occupation, but due to damage were unable to participate."

release too far out and from too great a height, so that some of the tor-pedoes, damaged by impact, ran erratically, broached, or dived under the carrier. Nevertheless, two struck the *Lexington* on her port side. In close co-ordination with these attacks, dive bombers came down at a 70-degree angle and made three hits and several near hits. A 1,000-pounder struck the port forward battery, destroying the guns and kill-ing the crews; a smaller bomb hit the gig boat pocket and another exploded inside the funnel.

Loss of the Lexington. Damage control parties soon extinguished the *Lexington's* fires and brought her to an even keel, but the heavy pound-ing which the carrier had received had sprung the gasoline pipes, caus-ing small leaks which evaporated into pockets of combustible vapor. Shortly before one o'clock one of these pockets exploded violently, starting fires which set off a series of subsequent explosions. Late in the afternoon, when the flames had got beyond control and were creeping towards the magazines, the order was given to abandon ship, and the men began sliding down lines into the water, whence they were picked up by boats from the escort vessels. That night Admiral Fletcher or-dered a destroyer to sink the flaming hulk. Of the *Lexington's* comple-ment of nearly 3,000 men, a little over 200 were lost, most of them as a result of the fires and explosions during the afternoon of the 8th.

The Battle of the Coral Sea, the first major naval action in history in which the opposing fleets remained out of sight of each other, has been claimed as a victory by both the Allies and the Japanese. When one compares the loss of the 33,000-ton *Lexington* with that of the 12,000-ton *Shoho;* the loss of the *Neosho* and *Sims* with the destroyer and torpedo boats which the Japanese admit losing at Tulagi; the loss of 543 American lives to perhaps 400 of the enemy killed; the destruc-tion of 66 United States planes to the 60 which the Japanese say they lost, the enemy claim would seem to be justified. But though Tulagi was retained and developed by Japan, the Imperial Navy was forced to abandon its primary aim, the occupation of Port Moresby by sea. The base remained in Allied hands, and subsequent attempts by Japanese troops to cross the Owen Stanley Mountains and seize it by land at-tack proved futile.

THE BATTLE OF MIDWAY

The Japanese, their operations to the south disrupted, pulled most of their fighting ships out of the Coral Sea area and assembled pow-erful forces for a two-prong invasion thrust at Midway and the

Aleutians. The time seemed ripe. They knew that they had hit the *Lexington* and *Yorktown* and believed that both carriers had sunk or at least been very seriously damaged. They knew also that the *Enterprise* and *Hornet* were in the South Pacific, where they had arrived just too late to take part in the Coral Sea battle. The *Saratoga*, they considered, must still be undergoing repairs for a damaging torpedo hit received earlier in the year. All American carriers in the Pacific were thus accounted for and none was in a position to interfere with the proposed new moves. These thrusts would leave the Solomons temporarily vulnerable, but quick and decisive blows farther north would restore the balance in Japan's favor and force Nimitz to spread his fleet dangerously thin.

Of one vital factor the Japanese were still ignorant, and that made all the difference. United States Army and Navy Intelligence was still breaking enemy codes and hence could state not only where and when the next offensives were to be launched but also approximately what forces would be employed. On the basis of this information, defenses on Midway and in the Alaska-Aleutians area were hastily strengthened, and the limited American air and surface strength was redeployed to best advantage. The *Enterprise* and *Hornet* turned back from the Coral Sea and sped north. The *Yorktown* was rushed to Pearl Harbor, where her damaged decks were repaired in record time. Before the end of May a fleet of sorts had been assembled in Hawaiian waters— three aircraft carriers, eight cruisers, 14 destroyers, and 25 submarines. At the same time a reserve force of old battleships with a small destroyer screen was sent to patrol the waters off the west coast of the American mainland.

Admiral Spruance took command of the *Enterprise-Hornet* force, replacing Admiral Halsey, who was ill, and on May 28 sailed from Pearl Harbor on a northwesterly course. Two days later the *Yorktown* and her escorting vessels set out in the same direction. On June 2 the two carrier forces made rendezvous and, under local command of Admiral Fletcher,[5] moved to a position north of Midway. The *Saratoga*, meanwhile, her repairs rushed to completion, had left the Puget Sound Navy Yard, picked up planes at San Diego, and was now speeding westward. She arrived at Midway too late to take part in the battle.

Japanese forces converging on Midway comprised more than a hun-

---

[5] Admiral Nimitz, at his Pearl Harbor headquarters, retained overall tactical command.

dred vessels, including 11 battleships and four aircraft carriers. The armada, under command of Admiral Yamamoto, was divided into three parts: a main body of battleships, cruisers, and destroyers; a striking force, which included similar types supporting the carriers *Kaga, Akagi, Hiryu,* and *Soryu,* all veterans of the Pearl Harbor surprise raid; and an occupation force centered about transports carrying 3,500 invasion troops. The transports were accompanied by supply vessels and screened by major combat craft. The striking force, sailing from southern Japan, would spearhead the attack, coming down from the northwest. The main body, with Yamamoto aboard the battleship *Yamato,* would follow at a distance and take a position west of Midway until the island base had been rendered impotent by a preliminary air attack. The occupation force, coming up from the Marianas, would make rendezvous with additional transports out of Eniwetok and approach the target from a little south of west. (See diagram.) Submarines were assigned to scout out ahead and take a line west of Pearl Harbor in an attempt to intercept any approaching American vessels.

Just at dawn on June 3, as the two American carrier forces were approaching Midway, a radio report reached Pearl Harbor that Japanese planes had struck at Dutch Harbor nearly 3,000 miles to the north. But Nimitz, well aware that the main show was to be in the central Pacific, issued no change of orders. Three hours later his judgment was confirmed. A navy Catalina patrol plane, quartering the seas 700 miles beyond Midway, sighted the enemy occupation force headed in an easterly direction.

The American carriers were too far away to send ship-borne planes, but from Midway nine army Flying Fortresses sped westward and dropped bombs, without, however, scoring any hits. That night four torpedo-rigged Catalinas sought out the enemy force and hit a tanker, killing 11 men and slowing the vessel down. Before the Catalinas got back to base, 15 more Flying Fortresses were headed towards the target. The Japanese were getting shuttle service.

Attack on Midway. Dawn of June 4 found Midway and the American carriers, now 200 miles away to the northeast, exposed under almost cloudless skies, while the enemy forces were moving in towards the objective under a concealing weather front. Navy patrol planes had been searching the seas since before daybreak, but not until nearly six o'clock were first contacts made. A Catalina pilot, flying the edge of the overcast 150 miles northwest of Midway, reported several large

Top, THE BATTLE OF MIDWAY. A Japanese bomber scores a direct hit on the U.S. Aircraft Carrier *Yorktown,* despite a tornado of anti-aircraft fire. *Center,* U.S. HEAVY CRUISER SALT LAKE CITY. *Bottom,* JAPANESE HEAVY CRUISER MOGAMI AFTER BOMBING BY UNITED STATES CARRIER-BASED AIRCRAFT IN THE BATLE OF MIDWAY.

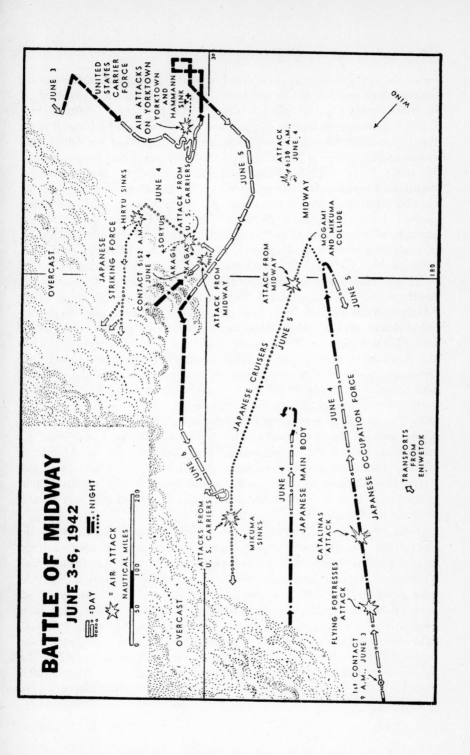

BATTLE OF MIDWAY
JUNE 3-6, 1942

formations of Japanese bombers and fighters heading out of the cloud-covered area towards the island base. A few minutes later word came in from another patrol pilot farther to the northwest. After flying through rain squalls he had popped out of a cloud to find himself over the Japanese striking force. This was the information for which the commanding officer of the Midway naval air station had been waiting. He radioed the 15 Flying Fortresses, already far out to sea, to change course and go after the enemy carriers. At the same time every plane capable of flying cleared the runways. Twenty-seven marine fighter planes—mostly old, slow Brewsters—headed for the Japanese air armada with its escort of swift and agile Zeros. All the other Midway aircraft—six navy torpedo planes, 27 marine dive bombers, and four torpedo-armed army B-26's—set out towards the enemy carrier force.

Thirty miles out the marine fighters met the Japanese air squadrons, nearly a hundred torpedo and dive bombers and some 50 Zeros. The Marines dived into the mass of enemy planes and succeeded in shooting down several bombers before the enemy escort groups could come into effective action. Then, while their fighters were occupied with the Americans, most of the Japanese bombers made a wide sweep to disengage and came in over Midway, crossing an arm of the circular reef to strike at the two tiny islands inside the lagoon. They avoided hitting the runways, which they expected to make use of later, but they dropped their bombs on most of the buildings, smashed a power plant, and set fire to oil tanks. Enemy losses in the raid amounted to more than 40 aircraft, all but one of them shot down by the American planes. Outnumbered and outmaneuvered by the fast and powerful Zeros, the Marines had put up a magnificent fight but most of their planes were lost. Fifteen of them had been destroyed and seven were severely damaged.

First attack on the Japanese carrier force. In order to carry on air operations the Japanese striking force maintained its southeasterly course into the wind. This soon brought the carriers from under the protective overcast into a relatively cloudless area. Here at a little past seven o'clock the navy torpedo planes and the torpedo-rigged army B-26's from Midway found them. The enemy ships were in a close, defensive formation with the surrounding air alive with Zeros. The American planes dived at once and came in, almost skimming the water. The Zeros immediately swarmed down upon them, while the heavy ships began firing shells to throw up a pattern of spray which could wreck a fast-moving plane. Most of the American aircraft were knocked down before they could approach the carriers close enough to release their torpedoes. Only three, badly shot up, managed to get back to Midway. No Japanese vessel had been damaged.

It was nearly eight o'clock when the first squadron of marine dive bombers arrived with their 1000-pound bombs. The Japanese force had now begun to deploy, seeking cover under the scattered cloud banks. The American planes, led by Marine Major Lofton Henderson, selected a carrier and came down in a glide rather than a dive. This was a hazardous approach which unduly exposed the bombers to enemy fighter attack, but there was no choice, for the Marines were untrained in the tricky technique of the steep dive and pullout. Henderson was hit. His left wing caught fire but he held his course for the carrier, narrowly missed it, and plunged into the sea alongside. The following planes passed over the target vessel, releasing their bombs at 500 feet or less, but made no hits. Half the 16 bombers were shot down, and those which made it back to Midway were riddled with bullets. In one plane 210 holes were counted. The second echelon of 11 bombers, arriving near the enemy force a few minutes after the first, struck at the escort vessels, also without success. Meanwhile, the 15 Flying Fortresses, originally assigned to attack the Japanese occupation force, had swung north and now came over at 20,000 feet. The Fortresses dropped more than a hundred bombs, but all missed.

Midway forces thus expended 15 planes without doing any injury to the approaching enemy force. Virtually stripped of defenses, the garrison with anxiety awaited another air attack and possibly a bombardment from surface ships. But at this point the attention of the Japanese was attracted elsewhere. One of their search planes had sighted the American carrier forces and flashed back their location by radio. Upon receiving this report, the striking force shortly after nine o'clock turned away and headed northeast to give battle. In preparation, crews began disarming torpedo bombers poised for a second Midway strike, substituting torpedoes for bombs. This caused a delay which proved fortunate for the Americans but disastrous for the Japanese.

Second attack on the Japanese carrier force. The American task forces had been closing the enemy since before six o'clock, when radio operators had intercepted the first contact reports of the Midway air patrol. *Yorktown* aircraft were being held in reserve awaiting further information, but as soon as the Japanese force was brought within attack range the *Enterprise* and *Hornet* had launched more than a hundred planes. Before eight o'clock the air squadrons were streaking southwest towards the supposed location of the enemy fleet.

But the pilots did not know of the Japanese change of course. That lack of information was to break up the American aerial concentration and prove fatal to many of its planes. The squadrons arrived over the designated spot, the point which the hostile striking force would have reached had it continued to the southeast, and found the seas empty. There were various reactions. The bombers and fighters from the *Hornet* turned south and searched along the enemy's extended track until their fuel ran low. Most of the bombers reached Midway on their last drops of gasoline, but all of the fighters were forced down at sea. The *Enterprise* dive bombers, led by Lieutenant Commander Clarence W. McClusky, continued to the west. All the rest of the planes after a brief search turned north. At about this time the *Yorktown* began to launch. Her fighter planes, flying at a high altitude, sighted the enemy without difficulty and led the bomber and torpedo squadrons directly to the objective.

The 15 aircraft of the *Hornet's* Torpedo Squadron 8, which had become separated from the others, were the first to reach the Japanese striking force—four carriers, with destroyers close in and battleships and cruisers in position to put up a screen of intercepting fire. It was 9:20 and the planes were almost out of gasoline but, following the squadron leader, Lieutenant Commander John C. Waldron, they dived at once and came in low, to be met almost immediately by Japanese fighters, which shot overhead and then turned and trailed them in, strafing at will. Several of the enemy aircraft took hits from rear seat gunners and dropped into the water, but the Torpedo 8 planes were shot down one by one until only a small remnant was left to face the full impact of concentrated antiaircraft fire and to dodge the impenetrable walls of spray cast up about the carriers by heavy shells. Some of the attacking squadron launched torpedoes. None hit, and all 15 planes were destroyed. The lone survivor was Ensign George H. Gay, who managed to fight free from his sinking craft. Clinging to a rubber life raft, which he dared not inflate and so reveal his presence to the enemy, he was a witness to what followed.

The *Enterprise* fighters came in soon afterwards. At 20,000 feet, high above cloud masses which permitted only intermittent views of the enemy fleet below, they were undetected,[6] for the Zeros, intent on

[6] The Japanese did not begin installing radar in their ships until the following August.

intercepting another torpedo attack, remained at low altitude. The American fighter aircraft patrolled for nearly half an hour and then, since no more of their planes appeared and fuel was running low, they returned to their carrier.

McClusky led his bombers far beyond the estimated position of the Japanese force. Finding nothing but empty seas, he had then swung about and headed north to backtrack up the enemy course. "One of the most important decisions of the battle," was the official comment. He arrived over the Japanese striking force a little after ten o'clock, at almost the precise moment that the *Enterprise* torpedo squadron and the planes from the *Yorktown* reached the same area. Here at last was an opportunity for the sort of concentrated attack which had been lacking thus far in assaults on the Japanese force.

But the timing was not perfect and full co-ordination was not achieved. The American bombers were a little behind the torpedo planes, and the fighters were not in position to make a simultaneous attack. It is not certain, however, that any advantage would have been gained by better timing, for the Japanese concentrated their attention upon the torpedo planes, considering them the major menace, and neglected to guard themselves adequately against the approaching dive bombers. More Zeros had been brought to the decks of the carriers and were beginning to take off. Of those already in the air some were engaged by the *Yorktown* fighters, but most spread out to meet the *Enterprise* and *Yorktown* torpedo squadrons heading in from opposite directions. Ten of the 12 *Yorktown* planes were quickly shot down and of the 14 from the *Enterprise* only four escaped. None had been able to put its torpedo into an enemy ship. This time it was the dive bombers, virtually unmolested, which turned the tide. McClusky's bombing squadrons divided, taking on two carriers close together, apparently the *Kaga* and the *Soryu,* while the *Yorktown* bombers dived on another carrier farther to the east. This appears to have been the *Akagi.*

The *Kaga* took four hits. The first shattered the island; the second fell among planes parked near the stern, causing huge fires; the next two, penetrating to the hanger deck, set off ammunition. The midships section of the flight deck ripped upward, throwing debris high into the air and leaving a gaping hole. Soon the carrier, burning from bow to stern, was dead in the water. Then more ammunition exploded and a burst of flame spiraled up through the low-hanging clouds. There were few survivors and these abandoned ship almost at once.

The two other carriers under attack also took hits, the *Akagi* two and the *Soryu* three. Ordinarily so few bomb hits would not have been sufficient to damage the vessels fatally, but it happened that both were caught at a particularly vulnerable moment. Their planes were being prepared for a sortie against the American task force. Many were on the flight deck ready to take off. In the hangar below, others were being refueled and loaded. The hits started planes burning. Then bombs and torpedo warheads went off one by one by induced explosion. Gasoline fires raged and the ships lay helpless.

So quickly were the three carriers disabled that several American planes turned away to drop their bombs on the escort craft but scored no hits. Then all the attacking aircraft, their loads expended, turned back towards their own task forces. Not all made it. Several of the *Enterprise* dive bombers, running out of fuel, were forced down on the water.

Ensign Gay, still clinging to his life raft, saw the enemy ships wreathed in smoke. Overhead, Zeros zoomed helplessly about. Their landing decks were smashed and there was only the sea in which to alight. But in the distance the *Hiryu*, undamaged, was slipping away with her escorts to the northeast.

The rest of the Japanese force drifted off on various courses to the northwest. In mid-afternoon the American submarine *Nautilus*, which had been trailing the enemy since early in the day, slipped in and fired all her torpedoes at the *Soryu*, making three hits. The carrier sank at dusk. Shortly afterwards the *Kaga* went down. The *Akagi*, gutted, its fires beyond control, lasted a little longer. At length Japanese destroyers approached and fired torpedoes into her glowing hull until she too slipped beneath the surface.

Attacks on the Yorktown. Shortly after noon 18 Japanese dive bombers supported by an equal number of fighters found the *Yorktown* and came in for an attack. Warned by radar of the approaching enemy aircraft, 12 American fighter planes went out to meet them. In the ensuing melee more than half of the attacking bombers plummeted down in flames, and all the rest were subsequently shot down over the *Yorktown* task force by antiaircraft or by American planes which pursued them through the gunfire from their own ships. The *Yorktown*, however, had taken three hits. Two bombs landed squarely on the flight deck, one penetrating to the hangar deck, where it set fire to planes. The third went through the side of a funnel, the concussion extinguishing boiler fires so that the carrier began to lose way. But the decks and uptakes were soon mended and the blaze in the hangar was quickly put out, for Captain Buckmaster, mindful of the fate of the *Lexington,* had ordered carbon dioxide introduced into the gasoline pipes at the first warning. By 2 P.M. the *Yorktown* was doing 19 knots.

Half an hour later radar detected more planes approaching and again the combat air patrol went out to intercept the attackers—torpedo planes this time, a dozen or more, accompanied by fighters. Only five of the Japanese torpedo planes were able to elude the American air attack and survive the heavy fire of the *Yorktown* screen. But these succeeded in dropping torpedoes before they too were destroyed.

Three of the torpedoes shot harmlessly past the big carrier but two struck, both amidships on the port side. The great hull surged upward, the bow almost leaving the water, the engines stopped, and the carrier began to list to port as clouds of smoke poured from her stacks. When it appeared that she might capsize, Buckmaster gave the order to abandon ship. All of her planes then in the air sought refuge on the decks of the *Enterprise* and *Hornet* as they drew away to the southwest.

Attack on the Hiryu. Scouts sent out earlier from the *Yorktown* had now located the source of the attacking planes. To the northwest, 175 miles away, they had found the undamaged *Hiryu* with a screen of two battleships, three cruisers, and four destroyers. Upon receipt of a radio report of this contact, the *Enterprise* began to launch dive bombers, more than half of which were refugee *Yorktown* planes. More bombers took off from the *Hornet.* All squadrons were away shortly after four o'clock. The scout planes, meanwhile, continued shadowing the retreating *Hiryu,* a worthwhile precaution, for presently the carrier and her escort turned sharply to port and headed northwest. A few minutes before six the *Enterprise* bombers found the target. Fewer than a dozen Zeros rose to meet them. These were the forlorn remnant of the morning's beehive of Japanese fighters. There was a brief skirmish in which one American plane went down, but most of the others dived and made six direct hits on the carrier. When the *Hornet* aircraft arrived, the *Hiryu* was blazing so furiously and was so obviously doomed that this group turned its attention to the escorts, achieving damaging near hits on the stern of the battleship *Haruna.* The *Hiryu* burned through the night and sank next morning. Her captain and the division commander remained aboard and went down with her, unwilling to survive the last of the carriers. ·

During the afternoon of June 4, Flying Fortresses from Midway and from the Hawaiian Islands attacked segments of the enemy fleet. Japanese witnesses state that, though the Fortresses caused some casualties by strafing, not a single bomb hit was made. It was becoming clear that high level bombing was ineffective against moving surface targets.

Pursuit of the Japanese fleet. Yamamoto, appalled by the loss of the four carriers, abandoned his invasion plans and ordered a general retirement to the west. As a final by-blow, however, he sent in four heavy cruisers from the occupation force to bombard the Midway airstrips and thus prevent further land-based air sorties against his retreating forces. The attack did not succeed. The Japanese bombardment group ran into the Midway submarine screen and, in maneuvering to avoid the American submarine *Tambor,* the cruisers *Mogami* and *Mikuma* collided. The bow of the *Mogami* was shattered and she began to leak oil. Thereupon, the cruisers and their accompanying destroyers abandoned the raid and turned westward. A lone Japanese submarine went in to fire a few shells at the island base. During the following day marine and army bombers from Midway tracked the cruisers by the *Mogami's* trailing oil slick. Near hits made by dive bombers punctured holes in the bridge and stack of the crippled ship. The *Mikuma* was more seriously damaged. A scout bomber, evidently that flown by Marine Captain Richard E. Fleming, crashed into her after turret, starting fires.[7]

In the early evening of June 4, Admiral Spruance, who had assumed local tactical command of the American task forces after the disabling of the *Yorktown,* ordered a retirement to the east. "I did not feel justified in risking a night encounter with possibly superior enemy forces," he stated in his official report, "but on the other hand, I did not want to be too far away from Midway in the morning. I wished to have a position from which either to follow up retreating enemy forces or to break up a landing attack on Midway. At this time the possibility of the enemy having a fifth carrier somewhere in the area . . . still existed."

Upon receipt of the *Tambor's* report in the early hours of June 5, he turned back and steamed southwest at 25 knots until at 10 A.M. his force stood directly north of Midway. By then it was clear that the enemy night attack had been frustrated. Accordingly, Spruance shifted course and headed northwest in a stern chase, hoping to reach a point

---

[7] This account is based upon a statement made by Rear Admiral Soji, who commanded the *Mogami* at the Battle of Midway. American flyers with Fleming reported that he made a near hit and then plunged into the sea in flames.

before evening from which he could launch an aerial attack on the scattered enemy striking force to the north. But bomber patrols sent out in that direction during the afternoon encountered only a few detached vessels half hidden by the overcast. The planes dropped bombs but made no hits. Thus disappointed, Spruance changed to a westerly course, which he maintained during the night, and at dawn, June 6, sent out scouts from the *Enterprise* for a broad search to north, west, and south. This time the search planes had better luck, picking up the *Mogami* and *Mikuma* accompanied by two destroyers almost due south and a little later sighting the other two cruisers with three destroyers forty miles west of the first group. Upon receiving word of these contacts, Spruance ordered another change of course, this time to the southwest, and during the morning and early afternoon launched two attack waves from the *Hornet* and one from the *Enterprise*. Planes of the first two waves made repeated hits on the *Mikuma* and the *Mogami*. The third wave found both cruisers afire. A bomb dropped during this attack penetrated the deck of the *Mogami,* wiping out damage control parties and so buckling the engine room doors that crews could not escape the flames. More than 90 men were killed. Another bomb exploded on the stern of a near-by destroyer. Several more hits were made on the *Mikuma,* whose torpedoes began to detonate. Battered, her hull perforated, she rolled over and sank. The *Mogami* was left listing to port, her plates sprung, a turret smashed, her after mast and half her funnel gone, her torpedo tubes knocked loose and trailing in the water, and her midships section a shambles of jagged metal. By a miracle of damage control she was able to limp as far as Truk.

Further pursuit by the American task force was not possible. Fast running out of fuel, it was obliged to turn away.

Loss of the Yorktown. Contrary to expectations the *Yorktown* did not capsize. All through June 5 and the morning of June 6, salvage crews labored to bring her to an even keel. But early in the afternoon of June 6 a lurking Japanese submarine came in close and fired a broadside of torpedoes, two of which hit the *Hammann,* made fast alongside the carrier, and sent her down in three minutes. As the destroyer sank, her depth charges went off, killing many of her crew in the water. Two of the remaining torpedoes struck the *Yorktown.* This time she began in reality to capsize. Before dawn on June 7 her port deck rail was under water. At 5 A.M. she rolled over and submerged.

Results and conclusions. The Japanese had tasted overwhelming defeat for the first time since 1592, when Admiral Hideyoshi lost his fleet to the Koreans. The battle was costly to the United States, but the cost to Japan was far greater. In the American force 307 lives were lost; the Japanese lost some 4,500. A hundred and fifty American planes were destroyed or damaged beyond repair; the enemy lost 258. And as against the sinking of the *Hammann* and the *Yorktown*, four Japanese carriers and a heavy cruiser were sunk, and another heavy cruiser was so thoroughly wrecked that she required almost complete rebuilding. At least three other enemy ships received moderate damage. Not again during the war would a hostile fleet venture into the central Pacific. It is clear that a turning point in the conflict had been reached.

Critics, studying the Battle of Midway in calm retrospect, have found flaws in the handling of the American forces. Reconnaissance they say, was inadequate, and they point out that had the enemy been shadowed continuously, a better coordinated carrier-based attack might have been effected, with smaller losses in planes and crews. Had the American carrier force not turned away to the east in the evening of June 4, they argue, a greater part of the Japanese fleet might have been overtaken and destroyed. Had the *Yorktown* not been prematurely abandoned and salvage operations suspended, the carrier might have been saved. But one may reply that such criticisms do not take into account the stress and confusion of battle, and certainly they are not based upon a full knowledge of the facts. Not until after the war was it learned, for example, that during the evening of Spruance's retirement a powerful surface force was on the prowl seeking American ships.

But, if it be acknowledged that the Americans made mistakes, it can be stated definitely that the Japanese made more serious ones, not the least fatal of which were their unwary approach to Midway; their inefficient reconnaissance, which failed to locate the American task force until part of their air strength had been expended; and their single-track concentration upon the torpedo planes while leaving their carrier decks open to destruction by dive bombers. Or to consider their failures in strategy, it may be said that Japan's decision to send her fleet across an ocean which she did not command and to fight in American waters was daring but certainly injudicious. Such errors on the part of the enemy, plus the fact that the United States had almost complete information of their plans, cost them the battle and left their navy seriously weak in air power during the ensuing operations.

The Aleutian Islands Campaign

In preparation for the expected attack in the north, fighting ships from Pearl Harbor and aircraft from as far away as California were ordered to the Aleutians-Alaska area. Towards the end of May Admiral Nimitz appointed Rear Admiral Robert A. Theobald to command all United States army and navy and all Canadian forces in the northern theater. These elements, organized as a single task force, comprised 169 planes, mostly army types, and 52 vessels, including five cruisers, 11 destroyers, and six submarines. Theobald, not knowing where the enemy would strike, ordered his main surface force to take a central intercepting position in the Gulf of Alaska and divided his planes among several airfields. On June 1 all bases and coastal positions from Seattle to Nome went on a 24-hour alert, with aircraft making continuous daytime searches to the limit of fuel endurance. Japanese submarines, meanwhile, were reconnoitering the area, sending in seaplanes to scout Seattle and Dutch Harbor and making surface and periscope observations off Kiska, Kodiak, and Cold Bay.

At the end of May a Japanese striking force comprising the carriers *Ryujo* and the *Hayataka,*[8] two heavy cruisers, and three destroyers set out from Japan on a great circle route with the double mission of striking at Dutch Harbor as a diversionary move preceding the attack on Midway and of supporting landing operations in the western Aleutians. At the same time two small occupation forces, one bound for Kiska and the other for Adak and Attu, departed from the Japanese homeland on a more southerly course.

On June 2 American air scouts sighted the striking force and notified headquarters. Admiral Theobald at once ordered all available 11th Air Force planes to Cold Harbor and to the secret advanced base at Fort Glenn on Umnak Island. The following day, while bad weather kept Allied army planes grounded, the Japanese force approached within 150 miles of Unalaska and launched two attack waves several hours apart. Most of the enemy planes, unable to navigate in the heavy mists, turned back to their ships, but nine bombers and four cruiser seaplanes penetrated to the comparatively clear area over Dutch Harbor. One of the seaplanes was shot down and another damaged by antiaircraft fire from two old destroyers and several auxiliary vessels offshore, but the bombers strafed naval installations and riddled a Catalina flying boat in the water. They then proceeded to the nearby

---

[8] Also known as the *Junyo*.

army base at Fort Mears, where they hit warehouses, barracks, and a radio station and started several fires. In a final and heavier attack on the 4th, enemy bombers made hits on Dutch Harbor naval structures, set fire to oil tanks, and partly destroyed the old station ship *Northwestern*. While returning from this raid the planes discovered the Fort Glenn airfield and went in for strafing runs, but were repulsed with a loss of two fighters and two bombers. The improved weather on the 4th enabled Allied planes to find the Japanese carriers. These they attacked persistently but did no damage. That night the striking force retired westward and took up a patrol south of Attu and Kiska.

Meanwhile, Admiral Yamamoto, depressed by his defeat at Midway, had ordered the Aleutian occupation forces to turn back. At the urging of his staff, however, he consented to let the northern invasion be carried out, but on a more limited scale—Adak would not be seized. The occupation forces, directed to head again towards the Aleutians, landed troops on Kiska and Attu on June 6 and 7.

United States and Canadian aircraft almost at once struck at these islands in a series of raids which so seriously complicated the enemy supply problem that additional units, including the carriers *Zuiho* and *Zuikaku* and two battleships, were added to the distant patrol. From the protection of this augmented force cargo vessels and transports would dart out to the bases at dusk, unload by night, and be away before dawn. Allied bombers nevertheless succeeded in sinking a number of them. American submarines were equally successful. Early in July the *Triton* sank a Japanese destroyer off Agattu, and on the same day the *Growler* fired torpedoes at three destroyers outside of Kiska Harbor and made a hit on each. One of the destroyers sank; the other two were so badly damaged that they had to be towed back to Japan. Of the *Growler's* exploit a Japanese officer afterwards said: "This was a daring and skillful attack by the American submarine and was admirably executed."

Throughout the year in which the enemy remained on the two bleak and dreary islands, the Allies continued their air raids and made occasional surface attacks. At last, following the United States occupation of Adak at the end of August, 1942, and of Amchitka the following January, the Japanese supply was reduced to a trickle and the bases became untenable.

☆ ☆ ☆ ☆ ☆

25
Guadalcanal Campaign

B Y REPULSING THE JAPANESE in the Coral Sea, defeating them at
Midway, and isolating them in the Aleutians, the Allies had, for
a time at least, secured the United States-Australian supply line and
established the battle frontier as required by the High Command. The
situation now invited the United Nations to shift to an offensive against
Japan. But top priority was assigned to the invasion of North Africa,
then being planned by British and American staffs. Operations in the
Pacific could be allotted only such men, munitions, ships, and aircraft
as could be spared from the European theater.

In view of these limitations, the obvious point at which to launch an
offensive was in the Solomons. Here the enemy's communication and
supply lines were stretched to the utmost, and in this area the United
States and her allies had bases—in the Samoa Islands, in the Fijis, in
New Caledonia, in New Zealand, and in Australia. Conversely, the
Japanese bases under construction in the Solomons presented the most
serious threat to Allied positions.

The initial attack, as planned, would be an amphibious operation,
America's first in World War II. Troops would be placed ashore on
Guadalcanal and on nearby Florida, Tulagi, and Gavutu Islands. The
ensuing campaign, it was realized, would necessarily be a war of attrition, the cruelest and most grinding sort of contest, but the sort which
America, with her superior industrial machine, could better afford than
could Japan.

INVASION OF GUADALCANAL

In July, 1942, the Japanese had landed troops and labor battalions
on Guadalcanal and had begun to construct an airfield on Lunga

Plain on the north coast. They thereby set the date for the Allied invasion. The island must be seized before the second week in August, for by that time, it was estimated, the airfield would be completed. It would then serve as a base from which planes could be flown to meet and turn back an approaching fleet.

The overall plan for the attack was worked out under the direction of Vice Admiral R. L. Ghormley, Commander South Pacific Forces, with headquarters at Aukland, New Zealand. An augmented First Marine Division (19,500 troops), designated to land and occupy the islands, would be carried to the invasion point in 23 transports supported by eight cruisers (three Australian) and 15 destroyers. Local air cover would be supplied by a force including the carriers *Saratoga,* *Enterprise,* and *Wasp,* the new fast battleship *North Carolina,* and a screen of cruisers and destroyers. Command of the various elements involved was assigned as follows:

Assault Forces . . . . Vice Admiral Frank J. Fletcher
Amphibious Force . . . . Rear Admiral Richmond K. Turner
Marine Landing Force . . Major General A. A. Vandegrift
Carrier Air Support . . . . . . Rear Admiral Leigh Noyes
Land-Based Air Support . . . . Rear Admiral John S. McCain

McCain's land-based air arm, operating from New Caledonia, the New Hebrides, the Fijis, the Tongas, and Samoa, would co-operate with the carriers and with General MacArthur's planes based on New Guinea and Australia.

Surface forces from New Zealand made rendezvous at sea with combat units, and the armada proceeded to the Fiji Islands for a realistic rehearsal. From here the fleet moved west into the Coral Sea and then, concealed by a heavy overcast, crept up the 159th east meridian towards the west coast of Guadalcanal. During the evening of August 6 the skies cleared. Before dawn next morning the carrier force took position south of Guadalcanal, while the occupation force slipped around the western end of the island and entered the sound[1] between Guadalcanal and Florida Islands.

The bombardment began a little after 6 A.M., August 7. Heavy guns of the invasion screen sank the single enemy vessel present and smashed a number of Japanese seaplanes. At the same time, in co-ordination with Admiral Noyes' carrier aircraft they proceeded to silence the bat-

---

[1] Savo Sound. In memory of the many ships sunk here, this body of water was later called Ironbottom Bay.

Top, U.S. Marine Corps photograph; bottom, official U.S. Navy photograph

Top, HENDERSON FIELD. Showing steel mat (removable in small sections) laid to facilitate the landing of large planes such as the Army B-17 shown here. *Bottom*, LANDING BEACH AT GUADALCANAL. Taken several weeks after the occupation.

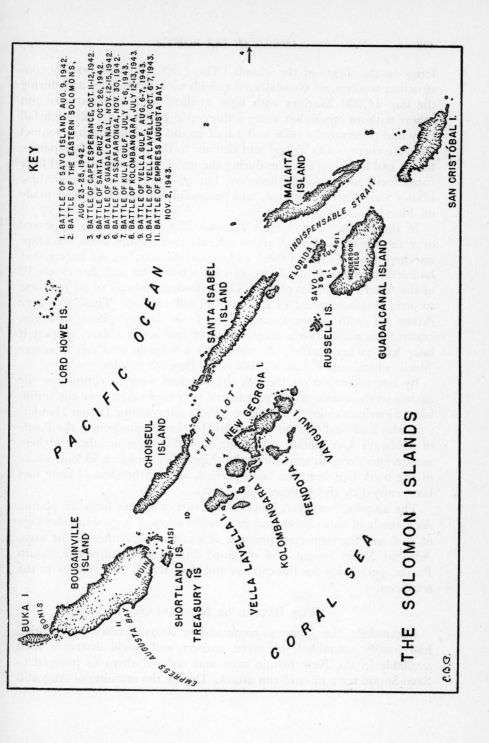

teries on the shores of the islands. The 2,500 Japanese, mostly construction workers, on Guadalcanal quickly took to the hills, and during the day 11,000 Marines with light artillery and supplies were put ashore without opposition along a three-mile beach front. By nightfall they had penetrated a mile and a half inland without making contact with the enemy. On Tulagi and Gavutu to the north, 1,500 Japanese troops had holed up in caves during the initial bombardment and later came forth to harass the invaders, but by the end of the day these islands were almost subdued, and successful landings had been made on Florida.

In the afternoon of August 7, some 32 enemy bombers appeared over the invasion area. Carrier aircraft and gunfire from the ships knocked down a score of them and routed the rest, but not before they had severely damaged a destroyer with a bomb hit and shot down 12 of the American carrier planes. The following noon 30 to 40 Japanese torpedo bombers swept in low over Florida Island. These too were driven off with heavy losses. One of the enemy pilots, however, crashed his plane into a large transport and set it ablaze, so that it later had to be scuttled. Another sent a torpedo into the destroyer *Jarvis,* which sank before it could reach base for repairs.

By late afternoon on the 8th the Marines were in control on the islands to the north. On Guadalcanal they had taken over the unfinished airstrip, naming it Henderson Field after Major Loften Henderson, who had died leading the marine bombing squadron at the Battle of Midway. Occupation was going according to schedule, but there was serious delay in unloading the ships. Organization in that phase of the work had been less than perfect, and further loss of time had been caused by the Japanese air attacks.

The attacks, moreover, had cost the carrier fighter force 21 planes. As a result of these losses and in consideration of a growing shortage of fuel and the suspected presence of enemy submarines in the area, Admiral Noyes sought and obtained from the Commander, South Pacific, permission for the carriers and their screen to withdraw to the southeast.

THE BATTLE OF SAVO ISLAND

Meanwhile, the Japanese command at Rabaul, taken by surprise, had hastily assembled the seven cruisers and single destroyer then available in the New Britain area and ordered them to proceed to Savo Sound for a hit-and-run attack. During the morning of August 8

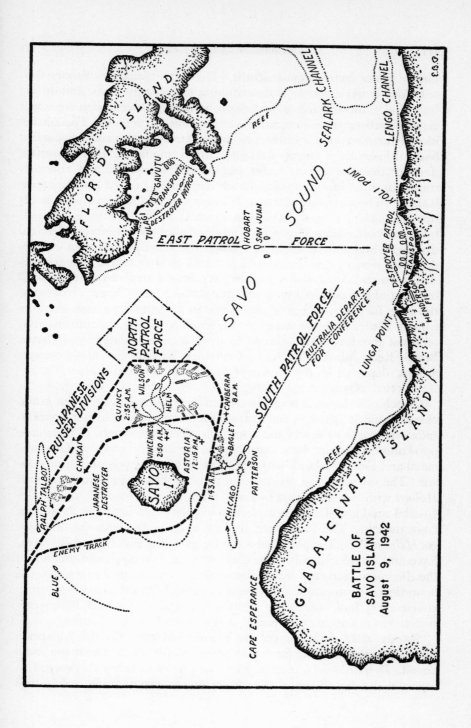

BATTLE OF
SAVO ISLAND
August 9, 1942

United States Army aircraft sighted this enemy force, once off Bougainville Island and again as it was entering the passage—later known as "the Slot"—through the major Solomons. Reports based upon the army air observations were inaccurate in two vital particulars. The pilots, identifying some of the cruisers as destroyers and others as auxiliaries, had misjudged the enemy strength. More important, they failed to discover that the Japanese, for purposes of deception, had reversed course after the first contact and had temporarily headed back towards Rabaul. The time and distance between the two known positions of the enemy ships caused Allied commands to underestimate their speed by about half. Since it was thus assumed that the approaching force was light and that it could not reach the Guadalcanal area before dawn the next day, no immediate precautions were taken. Aboard the American and Australian vessels in Savo Sound crews were exhausted, for most of the men had been at battle stations for 36 hours. Now was the time for them to rest if they were to be in fighting trim for the coming battle. All ships were held in second condition of readiness, and men not standing watch turned in early in the evening. At 10 P.M. British Rear Admiral V. A. C. Crutchley, commander of the escort groups, departed in the *Australia* to consult Admiral Turner in the transport *McCawley*.

Crutchley's disposition of his cruisers and destroyers has been criticized in that it failed to concentrate the defense and did not provide sufficient scouts to detect the approach of enemy vessels. The transports and cargo ships were assembled in the landing areas off Guadalcanal and Florida Islands with light screens of destroyers and mine vessels. The cruisers were divided into three groups. The *San Juan* and *Hobart* with two destroyers patrolled a north-south course between the Guadalcanal and Tulagi beachheads, in position to intercept an attack from the east. The *Vincennes, Astoria,* and *Quincy* with the destroyers *Helm* and *Wilson* patrolled a square guarding the channel between Savo and Florida Islands. The *Canberra,* the *Chicago* (and originally the *Australia*), screened by the destroyers *Patterson* and *Bagley,* steered a northwest-southeast line between Savo and Guadalcanal, reversing course every half hour. The destroyers *Ralph Talbot* and *Blue* were directed to maintain radar patrol west of Savo Island. (See diagram.)

Shortly after midnight on the morning of the 9th, the Japanese force, now approaching Savo, catapulted seaplanes to search the area ahead. Despite the darkness and heavy overcast these aircraft correctly reported the disposition of the cruiser and transport forces inside the sound and then withdrew to await the surface attack. Lookouts on at least four Allied vessels noted the planes, and one ship sounded a radio warning, which, however, did not get through to the senior commands. An hour and a half later the Japanese surface force sighted the *Ralph Talbot* and *Blue* and passed between them with all guns trained. The United States destroyers had detected nothing. The explanation appears to lie in the limitations of the radar then in use, the exhaustion of the watch, and the failure of American naval forces to rival the enemy in emphasis upon training for night maneuvers. The Japanese admiral, puzzled that the *Blue,* just 500 yards away, had failed to open fire, detached his destroyer to watch it and the *Ralph Talbot* and engage them if they should attempt to follow him. He then led his cruisers south of Savo into the sound.

The *Patterson,* on the port bow of the *Canberra,* was the first Allied vessel to sight the enemy. She flashed the word by TBS:[2] "Warning! Warning! Strange ships entering the harbor!" But the alarm was not received by all commands, for one of the cruisers was jamming the circuit with a discussion of course changes. The *Patterson* opened fire and was immediately illuminated by searchlights of the enemy force, which concentrated salvos upon her, making a number of hits. The *Bagley* now came about to fire torpedoes, but the torpedomen, taken by surprise, did not get the primers inserted until after the Japanese had passed out of range.

In the meantime, the seaplanes had again passed overhead, this time dropping parachute flares. In the eerie brilliance the south patrol cruisers were clearly silhouetted, and the enemy shifted fire to these heavier targets. Before the *Canberra* could train her guns she was struck by a score of shells and had taken one or two torpedo hits. Completely disabled, she drifted burning out of line. The *Chicago* received a torpedo hit and then, without firing her main battery, turned to port and sped westward towards the open sea. Later she turned back east and exchanged shots with the *Patterson* until the destroyer established her identity.

Having effectively knocked out the south patrol force, the Japanese cruisers changed course to port and split, four steaming across the rear of the Allied north force and three passing between it and Savo Island. Though topside personnel aboard the American ships in this group had seen lights and heard gunfire, no one had any clear idea of what

---

[2] High-frequency voice radio.

was going on. General quarters had been sounded, but stations were not yet fully manned when the approaching Japanese turned their searchlights upon the *Vincennes, Astoria,* and *Quincy* and opened fire with shells and torpedoes. Within a few minutes all three American cruisers, hit repeatedly, were put out of action. A salvo from one, however, had hit the enemy flagship *Chokai,* killing 30 men. This was the only notable injury done the enemy force during the action.

The Japanese ships ceased fire at 2:15 and passed out of the sound north of Savo. Here they again encountered the *Ralph Talbot,* which they illuminuated and took under fire, causing severe damage to guns, torpedo tubes, and superstructure, and killing 23 men.

Before 3 A.M. the *Quincy* and *Vincennes,* which had been struck by torpedoes as well as shellfire, had gone down. A few hours later the burned-out hulk of the *Canberra* was sunk by American destroyers. The *Astoria,* despite heroic efforts to bring her fires under control, finally sank at noon. Of about 3,500 men aboard the four cruisers, nearly half were lost. The heaviest losses were among the personnel of the *Quincy,* whose magazines appear to have exploded before she went down. The enemy ships slipped away unopposed, for with the American carriers gone there were no planes to pursue them up the Slot. On the morning of the 10th, however, as one division was approaching Kavieng Harbor, the 850-ton American submarine *S-44* came in for an attack and sank the heavy cruiser *Kako.*

BEGINNING THE FIGHT FOR GUADALCANAL

With his carrier air support withdrawn and his surface support seriously weakened, Admiral Turner had no alternative but to unload what he could on August 9 and pull his transports out of the Guadalcanal area. Much of the heavy material, including guns and some tanks, had been put ashore, but the land forces were left without adequate food and ammunition. The Marines and Seabees immediately went on iron rations and prepared with what supplies they had to make good their position.

For several days Guadalcanal, lying precariously between the major enemy base at Rabaul, 600 miles to the northwest, and the American base at Espíritu Santo, 600 miles to the southeast, was left relatively isolated. The Japanese, not knowing how much damage they had done in the Savo Island raid, were unwilling to hazard their limited southwest Pacific forces in anything more ambitious than small-scale air and surface bombardments; and the Allies, having felt the effectiveness of enemy sea and air power in the Solomons, hesitated to risk major surface units in running in reinforcements and supplies.

The Japanese, however, were determined to retake the lost islands. While the Marines on Guadalcanal were fighting skirmishes and extending their lines, and the Seabees were completing the airstrip, powerful forces were assembling at Rabaul and Truk. The enemy planned first to put enough troops ashore to destroy the American occupation force and seize Henderson Field, then to fly planes in from carriers, and lastly to reinforce the island with additional troops while the land-based aircraft kept Allied surface forces at bay. The plan might have worked had not the Japanese made the double mistake of assuming that only a few hundred Marines had been put ashore on the islands and that Allied land forces, when opposed by battle-hardened Imperial Army soldiers, would prove no more effective than the ill-trained, ill-equipped divisions of Chiang Kai-shek. It was thus with a sort of contempt for their opposition that about a thousand crack Japanese troops were sent to Guadalcanal to seize the airfield. Destroyers entered Savo Sound during the nights of August 18 and 19 and landed them east of American positions. Probably a thousand more were held in reserve at Rabaul to be sent in later if it should prove necessary.

In the meantime, Admiral Ghormley, aware of the enemy designs, had sent his three carrier task forces to operate southwest of the Solomons and requested that the remaining Pacific force, built around the *Hornet,* be dispatched forthwith from Pearl Harbor. Disregarding the risks of overseas transit, he now rushed necessities to the beleaguered Marines—32 aircraft for Henderson Field and transports carrying food and ammunition. The planes and convoy reached Guadalcanal on August 20 and were welcomed with shouts of relief. That evening the newly-landed Japanese troops began their attack, but the Marines in an 18-hour battle killed more than 700 of them, whereupon the enemy commander, in despair at his failure, burned his colors and shot himself. American casualties were 34 killed and 75 wounded.

THE BATTLE OF THE EASTERN SOLOMONS

While the enemy advance battalion was being annihilated on Guadalcanal, a powerful Japanese armada was moving southward beneath an overcast. Included were an occupation force of four transports screened by four destroyers and a cruiser, and a striking force built around the large carriers *Shokaku* and *Zuikaku* and the small (7,100-ton) carrier *Ryujo,* with a number of submarines scouting out ahead.

On the morning of August 23 these forces had reached the edge of the weather front some 200 miles north of Guadalcanal. The failure of their troops to seize Henderson Field had somewhat disrupted their plans, but the Japanese believed that the airstrip might yet be taken by sending in the reserves. The fleet therefore withdrew into the overcast but was again heading south by dawn of the 24th.

Preliminary contacts. At this time the *Enterprise-North Carolina* and *Saratoga* forces, under command of Admiral Fletcher, were operating 200 miles east of Guadalcanal. During the preceding day search planes from Espíritu Santo had sighted the Japanese occupation force, and *Enterprise* planes had unsuccessfully attacked enemy submarines, but Fletcher had been unable to obtain any clear idea of the strength opposing him. In the evening of the 23rd he had been obliged to weaken his striking power by detaching the *Wasp* and her escorts for refueling to the south. He was thus left with two carriers to meet the enemy's three, for the *Hornet* force, en route from Pearl Harbor, was not due for several days.

By noon of the 24th the opposing fleets had made air contact, so that each knew the strength and disposition of the other. The Japanese forces were spread out in an arc 70 miles wide along the edge of the overcast, the *Skokaku-Zuikaku* group farthest east, the *Ryujo* group in the middle, and the occupation force directly north of Guadalcanal. In the early afternoon the carriers of the eastern group launched on attack at the American task force; at the same time planes took off from the *Ryujo* for a strike at Henderson Field.

Attacks on the Japanese striking force. Shortly after 3 P.M. search planes from the *Enterprise* found the *Shokaku* and *Zuikaku* with only a light fighter patrol above them. Though they were not on an attack mission, two of the *Enterprise* bomber pilots could not resist diving into the antiaircraft fire and making a pair of near hits on the *Shokaku*. An hour later 36 aircraft from the *Saratoga* searched out the group centered about the *Ryujo* and, with only light aerial opposition, delivered a well-co-ordinated attack. The first bomber squadron to dive made a series of near hits which started fires aboard the carrier. Planes of the second squadron then holed her flight deck with three precisely placed 1,000-pounders. Just as the last bombers began their dives, the torpedo planes came in from two directions. One, possibly two, torpedoes struck the *Ryujo* amidships. Another missed its mark but sped on into the side of a Japanese destroyer, which burst into flames.

The *Ryujo* squadrons, meanwhile, were making a poor showing over

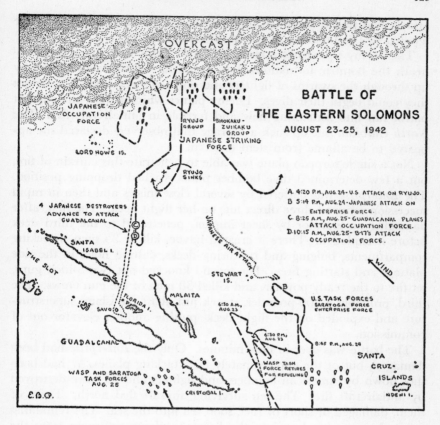

BATTLE OF
THE EASTERN SOLOMONS
AUGUST 23-25, 1942

A. 4:20 P.M., AUG. 24 - U.S ATTACK ON RYUJO.
B 5:14 P.M., AUG. 24 - JAPANESE ATTACK ON
ENTERPRISE FORCE.
C. 8:25 A.M., AUG. 25 - GUADALCANAL PLANES
ATTACK OCCUPATION FORCE.
D. 10:15 A.M., AUG. 25 - B-17's ATTACK
OCCUPATION FORCE.

Guadalcanal. The attack cost them 21 aircraft against three United States marine fighters shot down. The remaining Japanese planes, returning to their carrier in the late afternoon, found her ablaze and dead in the water and were obliged to hunt for other flight decks on which to land. The *Ryujo* sank during the night.

Attack on the American carrier force. Planes from the *Zuikaku* and *Shokaku* wandered about for some time without finding the American carriers. It was nearly 5 P.M. when they caught sight of the returning *Enterprise* search squadron and followed it in. The United States task forces, which had moved north to close the enemy and now stood 25 miles east of the Stewart Islands, made early radar contact with the approaching planes and launched a combat patrol of 53 fighters. At the first contact the *Saratoga* force, in order to divide the impending attack, had pulled away ten miles to the southeast. These ships were ignored by the Japanese planes in the ensuing battle.

The enemy squadrons approached with Zeros flying in a layer beneath the bomber formations, but American aircraft shot their way up through the swarms of fighters and downed several bombers before they could begin their dives. Enemy planes which eluded the combat patrol ran into something new and terrible in antiaircraft fire. The *North Carolina* put up such a barrage that observers declared she appeared to be aflame from stem to stern.

Not a single torpedo plane was able to penetrate this curtain of fire, but a few determined dive bomber pilots reached dropping position. The *Enterprise* was battered by several close misses and then in rapid succession received three direct hits on her flight deck. The first, after damaging an elevator by sheer impact, penetrated to the third deck before it exploded. There it created havoc, killing 35 men, wrecking compartments, bulging and rupturing decks, cutting holes in the side plating, and starting fires. The second knocked out two 5-inch guns, set fire to the ready powder, and killed 38 men of the gun crews. The third, probably a 500-pounder, struck just abaft the island superstructure and exploded on the flight deck, putting another elevator out of commission.

The battle was over in nine minutes. Only the *Enterprise* had been damaged, but of the approximately 80 attacking planes, 47 had been shot down by American bombers and fighters and 23 were destroyed by antiaircraft fire. The ten surviving aircraft fled north. Three of them, damaged or short of fuel, soon fell into the sea. The remaining seven then ran head-on into the *Saratoga* planes returning from the *Ryujo* strike and were reduced by four more. Three enemy aircraft presumably reached their carrier decks.

A second wave of Japanese planes was already approaching the United States task forces to deliver another attack on the heels of the first, but in the deepening twilight they were unable to locate their objective. Radar operators in the *Enterprise* force tracked them as they continued far to the south and then reversed course. Hours later the pilots were heard by radio desperately trying to home their carriers in the darkness.

Aboard the *Enterprise,* meanwhile, damage control parties had fought fires and made repairs with such efficiency that within an hour the carrier was steaming at 24 knots and landing aircraft. During the night the *Enterprise* and *Saratoga* task forces withdrew to the south and were replaced by the *Wasp* and her escorts, which took position southeast of Guadalcanal to repel further Japanese attacks. Here they were later joined by the *Saratoga* force, which had escorted the damaged carrier to safer waters.

Final contacts, August 25. During the evening of the 24th the four destroyers of the Japanese occupation force left their transports and headed south. After midnight they entered Savo Sound and began bombarding marine positions on Guadalcanal but were driven away by Henderson Field planes before any serious damage was done.

Just before dawn eight bombers from Guadalcanal took off to search for enemy carriers. They found instead the occupation force with the four destroyers now back in formation. The attacking planes hit the light cruiser *Jintsu* and a large transport with 1,000-pound bombs. The cruiser, severely damaged, was obliged to withdraw to Japan for repairs, and the transport was so gutted by fire that it had to be scuttled. Two hours later eight Flying Fortresses from Espíritu Santo also discovered the occupation force and sank one of the destroyers.

The Japanese made their final strike at noon when 21 planes dropped bombs from high altitude on Henderson Field, killing four Marines and wounding five. But the enemy surface forces were already beginning to retire to the north. It was evident that the Imperial Army had failed in its attempt to seize Guadalcanal and that, with American land-based and carrier air power concentrated in the area, no more troops could be landed there. Without army support the Japanese fleet was helpless, for it was running short of fuel and its losses were crippling—a carrier, a destroyer, and a transport sunk and, most serious, nearly half the carrier planes destroyed.

Reinforcing Guadalcanal

During the next six weeks the Japanese sent few major fleet units into the Guadalcanal area, generally preferring to risk nothing larger than destroyers or ocean-going landing craft. Small groups of such vessels came down the Slot with a nightly regularity which caused the Marines to refer to them as the "Tokyo Express." They would unload men and equipment west of American positions after midnight and be away before dawn. But planes from Henderson Field, though hampered by darkness, dispersed many such operations and damaged or destroyed a number of enemy craft.

The night sinkings in late August and early September of the American destroyer *Blue* and the destroyer transports *Little* and *Gregory* by

enemy fleet units in Savo Sound caused Allied supply ships thereafter
to avoid the area except during daylight. Even so, they were frequently
the targets of Japanese air raids, in one of which another American destroyer transport, the *Colhoun,* was sunk. But marine planes generally
frustrated such attacks, taking a toll of five or six enemy aircraft for
each of their own destroyed.

The regularity of the Toyko Express was not at first matched by
American reinforcements, for the seas to the south and east of Guadalcanal were infested with enemy submarines, and convoys were difficult
to protect. At the end of August a United States force scouting the
area east of San Cristobal was attacked by submarines which succeeded
in torpedoing the *Saratoga,* without, however, causing severe structural damage. A few days later the *Hornet,* operating with a force
farther to the south, narrowly avoided being hit by a torpedo. Through
these dangerous waters it was necessary to move men and supplies with
increasing speed, for the Japanese on Guadalcanal were soon numbered in the thousands. On the night of September 12–13 the enemy,
heavily reinforced, attacked United States shore positions near Henderson Field from three directions and killed or captured more than
100 Marines and wounded nearly 300. American artillery at length
beat off the attackers, who left 500 of their dead behind.

Major reinforcements for Vandegrift's garrison were soon on the
way. On the morning of September 14 the Seventh Marine Regiment
together with ample supplies, including 150,000 gallons of much-
needed aviation gasoline, departed from Espíritu Santo in a large convoy. To maintain an aerial anti-submarine patrol over the waters
which the troop and supply ships must traverse, two task forces including the *Wasp,* the *Hornet,* and the *North Carolina* had set out in advance. In the afternoon of September 15 the *Wasp,* the *North Carolina,* and the screening destroyer *O'Brien* were all struck within ten
minutes by torpedoes from enemy submarines. The carrier received
three torpedoes in her most vulnerable spot, the magazine and gasoline
storage areas forward, and in her most vulnerable condition, while she
was refueling planes. Gasoline lines were ruptured and planes tossed
into the air by the first two explosions. The third torpedo ignited
gasoline already pouring from the storage tanks and sent sheets of
flame 150 feet into the air. Then ready ammunition began to go off,
and there followed a series of increasingly heavy explosions. Though
heroic efforts were made to arrest the flames, her commanding officer,
Captain Forrest P. Sherman, was obliged within an hour to order the

ship abandoned. Of about 2,200 officers and men aboard her, nearly 200 were lost. That evening an American destroyer approached and with three torpedoes sent the flaming derelict to the bottom.

The single torpedo which struck the *North Carolina* killed five men and tore a huge underwater hole in her hull. She was able nevertheless to make port under her own power. The torpedoed *O'Brien* likewise made port, but soon afterwards her damaged plates gave way and she broke up and sank.

The convoy meanwhile had reached Guadalcanal safely on September 18. There, as a result of careful planning, the ships were able to disembark all troops and unload supplies in a single day and slip away through Lengo Channel in the early evening.

☆　　　　☆　　　　☆　　　　☆　　　　☆

26
Guadalcanal Campaign

(CONTINUED)

AMERICAN REINFORCEMENTS to the Guadalcanal garrison were soon offset by the Tokyo Express, which, despite occasional ship losses to Henderson Field planes, continued regularly to deliver men, tanks, and artillery to the island, until by the end of September, 1942, an entire new division, fully equipped, had been put ashore. Meanwhile, in the upper Solomons enemy forces were again assembling. It was apparent that another full-scale attempt to seize Guadalcanal was in the offing. This time, however, the Japanese were determined not to repeat the fiasco of the Battle of the Eastern Solomons. They would have troops on the island in overwhelming numbers before again risking their fleet in supporting operations.[1]

The race was on. Admiral Ghormley assembled at Espírito Santo 6,000 United States Army troops to reinforce Vandegrift's Marines and then set about to insure their safe arrival. First, to delay enemy operations, the *Hornet* task force made a daring sortie in the direction of the upper Solomons, sending in planes to bombard shipping and airfields at Buin and Faisi. The *Hornet* and her escorts then returned to a position westward of Guadalcanal, while another force built around the battleship *Washington* cruised the waters east of Malaita. A third force, comprising the heavy cruisers *San Francisco* and *Salt Lake City*, the light cruisers *Boise* and *Helena*, and five destroyers, was stationed south of Guadalcanal. The mission of these cruisers and destroyers, under command of Rear Admiral Norman Scott, was partly to protect the left flank of the approaching Army convoy, but their

---

[1] Captain Ohmae, Japanese planning and operations officer in the Solomons at this time, stated that in October, 1942, there were on Guadalcanal 26,000 Imperial Army troops and a special naval landing force of 3,500.

434

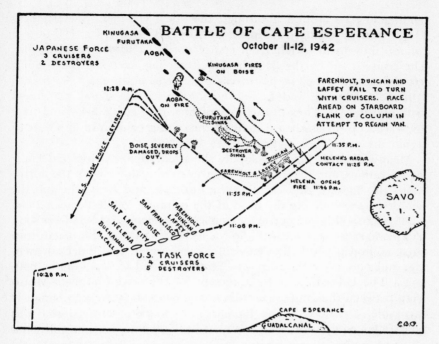

BATTLE OF CAPE ESPERANCE
October 11-12, 1942

KINUGASA
FURUTAKA
AOBA

JAPANESE FORCE
3 CRUISERS
2 DESTROYERS

KINUGASA FIRES
ON BOISE

12:28 A.M.

FARENHOLT, DUNCAN AND
LAFFEY FAIL TO TURN
WITH CRUISERS. RACE
AHEAD ON STARBOARD
FLANK OF COLUMN IN
ATTEMPT TO REGAIN VAN.

U.S. TASK FORCE RETIRES

AOBA
ON FIRE

FURUTAKA
SINKS

BOISE, SEVERELY
DAMAGED, DROPS
OUT.

DESTROYER
SINKS

DUNCAN

11:35 P.M.

HELENA'S RADAR
CONTACT 11:25 P.M.

FARENHOLT & LAFFEY

HELENA OPENS
FIRE 11:46 P.M.

11:55 P.M.

FARENHOLT
DUNCAN
LAFFEY

SALT LAKE CITY

SAN FRANCISCO

BOISE

HELENA

BUCHANAN

McCALL

SAVO I.

11:08 P.M.

U.S. TASK FORCE
4 CRUISERS
5 DESTROYERS

10:28 P.M.

CAPE ESPERANCE

GUADALCANAL

G.O.O.

main function was to prevent offshore bombardment of the Henderson Field area or reinforcement of the enemy island garrison. When notified by search planes that Japanese units were approaching Guadalcanal, they would move to an intercepting position near Savo Island.

THE BATTLE OF CAPE ESPERANCE

On the morning of October 11 the Tokyo Express started down the Slot in two divisions. The first, a supply force consisting of a tender and two destroyers, would reach Guadalcanal after dark, put troops and matériel ashore at Tassafaronga before midnight, and then retire to the northwest. The second, a striking force of three heavy cruisers and two destroyers, would arrive in time to cover the retirement of the supply ships and then proceed to bombard Henderson Field. In the early afternoon American search planes sighted the approaching enemy vessels, and shortly afterwards 75 Japanese aircraft attacked the island air base. Informed of these evidences of an impending assault, Admiral Scott brought his force up the west coast of Guadalcanal and late in the evening headed towards Savo Island, intending to pass around it through the north channel. Shortly after 11:30 P.M. he changed his plans and by TBS ordered a 180-degree column movement to left from course northeast to course southwest. The cruisers, led by the flagship *San Francisco,* executed the column left about, as did the two destroyers in the rear, but the van destroyers, *Farenholt, Duncan,* and *Laffey,* having missed the signal, continued to the northeast. Thus thrown out of line, they made a belated turn and raced up the starboard flank of the cruiser column in an effort to regain the van. (See diagram.)

Meanwhile, the Japanese supply ships had almost completed landing operations, and the striking force was coming down from the northwest—the flagship *Aoba* leading the *Furutaka* and *Kinugasa* and the two destroyers flanking the head of the column. While the American vessels were still in the northeast course, the *Helena* and *Salt Lake City* had made radar contact with the enemy striking force. The *San Francisco,* equipped with a less efficient type of radar, had detected nothing, and only after the turn was Scott informed by TBS of the contacts. The United States force, except for the three destroyers which were between the American cruisers and the enemy, was in the most favorable of positions. The Japanese, in complete darkness and with poor radar equipment, were running head-on into a column of ships all of whose big guns were in a position to bear. "It was one of those things that naval officers wait 20 years to see," said Captain Ernest G. Small, commanding the *Salt Lake City.* "We capped their 'T.'"

When the *Helena* had tracked the enemy formation to within 4,000 yards almost on her starboard beam, she opened fire. The other American cruisers joined almost instantly, the *Salt Lake City* illuminating with starshells from her 5-inch battery. For several minutes the Japanese, supposing that they were being fired on by their own supply force, failed to reply. Instead, all the enemy ships reversed course, the *Kinugasa* and the port destroyer to the left, the others to the right. During the turn the starboard destroyer, set afire by shells, blew up and sank. Convinced at last that the attacking force was American, the *Furutaka* opened fire, making three damaging hits on the *Boise,* which had turned on searchlights. The other United States cruisers then concentrated on the *Furutaka,* which quickly took a sharp list and began to sink. The *Aoba* escaped but not before she had been reduced almost to wreckage by 40 hits, one of which killed the Japanese admiral. Thus far, the *Kinugasa* and the port destroyer had not come under fire.

Meanwhile, the American destroyers caught between the opposing forces had been struck by shells from their own cruisers. The *Farenholt*, hit in the rigging and holed twice near the waterline, managed to retire from action, but the *Duncan*, set afire and almost out of control, came under heavy attack by the *Kinugasa*. She burned through the night and sank the next day.

Having lost the enemy, Admiral Scott shortly before midnight shifted to a northwesterly course, and after a brief lull the American force made new contacts with the retreating Japanese vessels. At this point the *Boise* again turned on her searchlights. She immediately came under fire from the *Kinugasa*, this time receiving seven hits which put most of her heavy guns out of action and opened her hull below the water line. Listing to starboard and ablaze, the *Boise* was obliged to withdraw to the south. Presently one of her magazines exploded, silhouetting the *Salt Lake City*, which at once became the target of heavy fire and took three hits. The American task force concentrated upon the *Kinugasa*, damaging her with shellfire, and forcing her into a final retreat.

The battle was over in 40 minutes, but the Japanese had not taken their last punishment. As the striking and supply forces were moving up the Slot next morning, they were overtaken by Henderson Field planes, which bombed the two remaining cruisers and sank two destroyers. On the American side, only the *Duncan* had been sunk. The *Salt Lake City* and the *Farenholt* were moderately damaged, and the *Boise*, which had lost 107 of her complement and at first appeared beyond salvage, was saved by a miracle of damage control and limped into Philadelphia five weeks later for repairs.

Following the battle there was a 48-hour lull in the Japanese campaign, during which time the American army convoy arrived at Guadalcanal, disembarked the reinforcing troops, and got safely away. Then, on the night of October 13–14, the pressure was resumed. Two battleships, a cruiser, and eight destroyers entered Savo Sound and shelled Henderson Field until nearly every plane there was destroyed. More enemy warships came in the next night to complete the destruction. As a result, only one bomber was left to oppose a Japanese invasion force which arrived on the morning of the 15th and landed several thousand troops with equipment west of American positions. On the same day Japanese dive bombers operating from carriers attacked an American convoy en route to Guadalcanal and sank the destroyer *Meredith*.

Attacks against American positions on the island continued from

land, air, and sea almost without interruption. This campaign, however, was merely preliminary to a major assault which began on the
night of October 23–24 with a full-scale offensive by enemy troops in
a renewed attempt to seize Henderson Field. Before dawn, cruisers and
destroyers came into the sound and joined aircraft in a furious bombardment of the American forces. Already a powerful Japanese fleet,
including four carriers and four battleships, was maneuvering off to
the north awaiting the outcome of the land battle. Three times the
Imperial Army command on Guadalcanal set the hour for the carriers
to approach and send in planes, but repeated postponements bespoke
the tenacity of the American defense. The defense extended to sea as
well, for in the afternoon of the 25th four Douglas dive bombers from
Henderson attacked and routed an approaching bombardment surface
force, sinking the light cruiser *Yura*. That night, however, the soldiers and Marines, exhausted by the incessant attack, fell back, and the
Japanese reached the edge of the airfield.

THE BATTLE OF SANTA CRUZ ISLANDS

It was obvious that the Japanese were repeating on a grander scale
their plan of two months before. But reconnaissance and analysis of
coded messages had kept Allied commands aware of enemy moves,
and countermeasures were being taken. Admiral Halsey, who had replaced Admiral Ghormley as Commander, South Pacific, sent the
Washington force to the vicinity of Guadalcanal, while two other
forces, one built around the *Hornet* and the other around the hastily-
repaired *Enterprise* and the new battleship *South Dakota,* proceeded
under command of Rear Admiral Thomas C. Kinkaid to a position
north of the Santa Cruz Islands. Again the American carrier forces
were going in against heavy odds, for, whereas Kinkaid had a few
more cruisers and destroyers than Fletcher had taken into the Battle
of the Eastern Solomons, the enemy fleet was now considerably more
powerful. The Japanese carrier forces were at some disadvantage,
however, for they had been maneuvering for several days while their
troops struggled vainly to seize Henderson Field. In the early morning
of the 26th, running low in fuel and food, they had been obliged to
begin a withdrawal to the north. It was on this retirement course that
Enterprise search planes found the enemy ships at 8 A.M. (see diagram)
and dropped two 500-pound bombs on the stern of the carrier *Zuiho*.
At about the same time that the *Enterprise* patrol was reporting contact, Japanese scouts over the American forces were making a similar

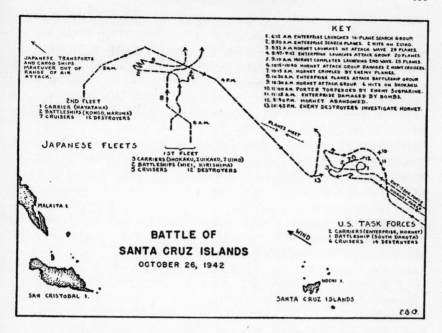

KEY
1. 6:12 A.M. ENTERPRISE LAUNCHES 16-PLANE SEARCH GROUP.
2. 8:30 A.M. ENTERPRISE SEARCH PLANES. 2 HITS ON ZUIHO.
3. 8:52 A.M. HORNET LAUNCHES 1ST ATTACK WAVE 29 PLANES.
4. 8:47-9:02 ENTERPRISE LAUNCHES ATTACK GROUP. 20 PLANES.
5. 9:10 A.M. HORNET COMPLETES LAUNCHING 2ND WAVE. 25 PLANES.
6. 10:15-10:40 HORNET ATTACK GROUP DAMAGES 2 HEAVY CRUISERS.
7. 10:15 A.M. HORNET CRIPPLED BY ENEMY PLANES.
8. 10:30 A.M. ENTERPRISE PLANES ATTACK BATTLESHIP GROUP
9. 10:30 A.M. HORNET ATTACK GROUP. 6 HITS ON SHOKAKU.
10. 11:00 A.M. PORTER TORPEDOED BY ENEMY SUBMARINE.
11. 11:15 A.M. ENTERPRISE DAMAGED BY BOMBS.
12. 9:40 P.M. HORNET ABANDONED.
13. 10:45 P.M. ENEMY DESTROYERS INVESTIGATE HORNET.

JAPANESE TRANSPORTS AND CARGO SHIPS MANEUVER OUT OF RANGE OF AIR ATTACK.

2ND FLEET
1 CARRIER (HAYATAKA)
2 BATTLESHIPS (KONGO, HARUNA)
7 CRUISERS (12 DESTROYERS)

JAPANESE FLEETS

1ST FLEET
3 CARRIERS (SHOKAKU, ZUIKAKU, ZUIHO)
2 BATTLESHIPS (HIEI, KIRISHIMA)
5 CRUISERS (12 DESTROYERS)

PLANES MEET

MALAITA I.

BATTLE OF
SANTA CRUZ ISLANDS
OCTOBER 26, 1942

WIND

U.S. TASK FORCES
2 CARRIERS (ENTERPRISE, HORNET)
1 BATTLESHIP (SOUTH DAKOTA)
6 CRUISERS 14 DESTROYERS

SAN CRISTOBAL I.

NDENI I.

SANTA CRUZ ISLANDS

report. The result was that the opposing fleets launched attack waves almost simultaneously. The *Enterprise* air group when 60 miles out ran head-on into one of the Japanese waves and engaged it in a short, sharp battle in which eight American planes and several Zeros were shot down. The remaining *Enterprise* aircraft, somewhat disorganized, then found a battleship-cruiser group on which they made an unsuccessful attack. The *Hornet* squadrons had better luck. Dive bombers of the first wave searched out a two-carrier group and bored through fighter interception to thump six 1000-pound bombs into the *Shokaku*, setting her afire and putting her out of action for several months. The second wave attacked a cruiser-destroyer group and made three bomb hits and two damaging near hits on the heavy cruiser *Chikuma* and several near hits on the heavy cruiser *Tone*.

Meanwhile, the *Hornet* task force was undergoing attack by enemy dive bombers and torpedo planes. One of the Japanese bombers deliberately dived into the carrier. The plane struck the smokestack, slammed against the signal bridge, dousing it with burning gasoline, and crashed into the flight deck. Its 500-pound bomb penetrated four decks without exploding, but two 100-pounders went off, one starting a fire among the parked planes on the hangar deck. At this moment seven torpedo planes came in and made two hits which severed water mains and electric cables and left the carrier dead in the water and ablaze amidships. While in this condition, the *Hornet* received three more direct bomb hits, and another suicide plane crashed into her side beneath the flight deck. Of the estimated 27 Japanese planes engaged in this first attack about 20 were shot down, most of them while they were withdrawing.

Not long afterwards 24 dive bombers struck at the *Enterprise-South Dakota* force. The carrier and the battleship put up an antiaircraft barrage which downed seven of the attacking planes and forced others to turn away, but enough got through to make three hits on the *Enterprise,* killing a number of men but causing no severe structural damage. Torpedo planes came in next, followed by more dive bombers. One of the torpedo aircraft crashed into the foredeck of the destroyer *Smith,* which, when other methods failed, put out the fire by plowing her bow under the wake of the *South Dakota.* The dive bombers made hits on the light cruiser *San Juan* and on the *South Dakota* without causing extensive damage to either. The enemy attack on this force was not confined to aircraft, for just as the first wave of planes came over, a submarine fired a torpedo into the destroyer *Porter,* causing such severe damage that the ship had to be abandoned and sunk.

During the late afternoon while the *Hornet,* her fires extinguished, was under tow by the cruiser *Northampton,* Japanese torpedo planes and dive bombers made a new series of attacks, hitting the carrier with two torpedoes and two bombs. Again the *Hornet* began to blaze and the order was given to abandon ship. Though listing 20 degrees to port, she did not sink. Destroyers left behind to sink her expended all their torpedoes and more than four hundred 5-inch shells without producing any noticeable effect. After dark they abandoned the hulk, none too soon, for presently Japanese light units approached to make a check. The *Hornet* went down during the night.

Though the Battle of Santa Cruz Islands had cost the Americans 74 planes and 316 men and reduced their carrier strength in the South Pacific to one damaged vessel, the results were not entirely unfavorable to the United States, for the enemy had lost about 100 planes, two-thirds of those used in the attacks, and had two carriers and a cruiser put out of action. The loss of Japanese flight decks and experienced pilots was to have its effect in the reduced air coverage which the enemy was able to supply in decisive actions three weeks later. But the real victory which saved American positions in the Solomons took place on Guadalcanal. The Henderson Field area, though partly in enemy hands on October 26, was regained by the United States army and marine forces, which in a bloody counterattack killed more than 2,000 Japanese troops and drove the rest back into the hills. After that there were no more serious threats from enemy land forces on Guadalcanal.

In the following weeks the opposing commands in the South Pacific continued to run in supplies and reinforcements for their garrisons on the island. To the Japanese it was soon apparent that the Tokyo Express, continually harassed by American planes, submarines, and torpedo boats, could not alone transport sufficient troops and supplies to retake Guadalcanal. They again, therefore, began concentrating surface forces at Truk, Rabaul, and in the upper Solomons for a decisive invasion attempt.

THE BATTLE OF GUADALCANAL

To meet the impending threat 6,000 additional United States army and marine troops were rushed under escort to Guadalcanal. During November 11 and 12, as parts of the convoy lay off the north shore of the island, unloading was frequently interrupted and some ships were damaged by a series of enemy air attacks. But the Japanese paid a heavy price for the delays they caused. Of some 25 bombers and torpedo planes which came over in the afternoon of November 12, nearly all were shot down by antiaircraft fire or by American fighter aircraft. One enemy plane, ablaze and disabled, made a suicide crash into the superstructure of the *San Francisco,* spraying the decks with burning gasoline and killing 30 of the ship's crew.

As in earlier actions, this aerial assault heralded the approach of surface forces. Coming down from Truk and elsewhere were the battleships *Hiei* and *Kirishima,* a light cruiser, and 14 destroyers for a night bombardment of Henderson Field. Transports would afterwards bring in Japanese troops. When sighted by scout planes before noon on the 12th, the main body of the bombardment force stood 300 miles north of Guadalcanal. Accordingly, the American convoy withdrew at sunset to the east. At that time the *Enterprise* force, including the *Washington* and *South Dakota,* was approaching from the south but was still more than a day's steaming away. As soon, therefore, as the United States transports had been escorted to a position of relative safety, five cruisers and eight destroyers, under command of Rear Ad-

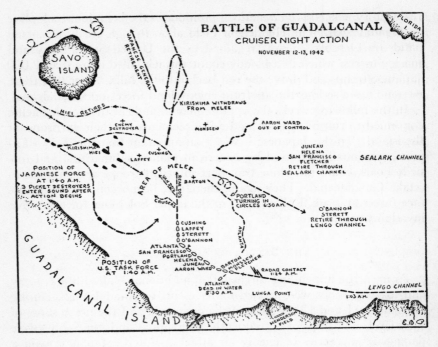

miral Daniel J. Callaghan, turned back toward Savo Sound in order to give what protection they could to the airfield.

Cruiser night action of November 12–13. An hour after midnight, in almost total darkness, Callaghan's ships re-entered the sound through Lengo Channel and continued westward along the coast of Guadal-canal—four destroyers ahead, followed by the *Atlanta, San Francisco* (flagship), *Portland, Helena,* and *Juneau,* in that order, with the re-maining four destroyers bringing up the rear. At the same time the enemy bombardment force, having skirted the southeast tip of Santa Isabel Island, was entering the sound from the opposite direction. Three destroyers, assigned to picket duty, remained outside until the battle began; the rest of the Japanese ships passed through the channel south of Savo. (See diagram.)

The two forces thus approached each other rapidly, almost on a collision course. Neither was in maximum trim for an engagement. The American flagship had lost its only radar detector in the after-noon suicide-plane attack. None of the Japanese vessels was radar-equipped, and all were armed chiefly with bombardment instead of armor-piercing shells. That last fact probably saved the United States force from complete annihilation.

The *Helena's* radar at 1:24 A.M. detected the enemy 28,000 yards ahead, but this information did not get through to Callaghan for six minutes. In the meantime, other ships in the American force had made contacts and were on the TBS circuit trying to communicate with the flagship. The result was chaos. The admiral ordered a turn to northwest, then to north, then again to northwest, and the column became disorganized. By this time the enemy, having made visual contact, had become similarly confused, and one group of ships intermingled with the American van. Suddenly the Japanese turned on searchlights and began firing. Admiral Callaghan immediately ordered, "Odd ships fire to starboard, even to port," and the guns of his cruisers and destroyers opened up.

What followed was no battle of maneuver. The formations broke completely, and the engagement became a series of ship-to-ship duels with both sides at one time or another firing at their own vessels.[2] The *Kirishima* made a left turn and withdrew to the north, lobbing shells indiscriminately into the melee behind her; but the *Hiei* bore down into the midst of the fracas. Here she became the chief target of American gunfire and torpedoes. The *Cushing, Laffey,* and *O'Bannon,* destroyers of Callaghan's van, attacked individually, damaging her bridge and starting fires. Later hits on the battleship were made by the *Portland* and *San Francisco* and by the destroyers *Aaron Ward, Sterett,* and *Monssen.* But at 2 A.M. the *Hiei* joined the Japanese cruiser and a destroyer in a concentrated attack on the *San Francisco* and scored numerous hits on her bridge and conning tower. Admiral Callaghan and all his immediate staff were killed, as was Captain Cassin Young, the commanding officer. Lieutenant Commander Bruce McCandless took command of the vessel and ordered a withdrawal to the east. At the same time, the *Hiei,* battered by more than 80 shell hits and steering with difficulty, drew away through the south channel and spent the rest of the night turning in circles.

By 2:12 most of the Japanese force was retiring in disorder, heading for the channel north of Savo. Several units were severely damaged and on fire but only one enemy ship, a destroyer, had been sunk. The

[2] The *Atlanta,* for example, was hit 19 times by 8-inch *armor-piercing* shells. The shell holes showed green dye splashes. This was the color used in the *San Francisco's* heavy ammunition to identify her hits. It should be emphasized, however, that, since the Japanese also used dye-loaded shells, it is possible that these hits were made by enemy vessels.

American retirement was equally piecemeal. The *Juneau,* put out of action by torpedoes, had already limped away to the east. At 2:30 the *Helena* led the *San Francisco* and the destroyer *Fletcher* out through Sealark Channel, while the *O'Bannon* and *Sterett* retired through Lengo Channel. All other ships of the American force had been either disabled or sunk. The battle, one of the most furious in naval history, had lasted 24 minutes.

At dawn one hapless enemy destroyer lay crippled off Savo Island. The *Portland,* herself a cripple, fired six salvos into the vessel and sank it. The *Hiei,* which soon went dead in the water northwest of Savo, became the day-long target of American planes. That evening, holed by three torpedoes and battered into a shambles, she was abandoned and scuttled. Three hundred of her crew had been killed.

The American force was in a worse case than the Japanese. Four destroyers, the *Laffey, Barton, Cushing,* and *Monssen,* went down during the battle or the next day. The *Atlanta,* gutted by fire and beyond repair, had to be scuttled. Among her dead was Rear Admiral Norman Scott. The *Portland* and *Aaron Ward* were unnavigable. Of the remaining ships only the *Fletcher* had come through undamaged. But the last of the American ship casualties, the one costing by far the most lives, was yet to come. As the remnants of the force headed south towards Espíritu Santo, a Japanese submarine fired a spread of torpedoes into the *Juneau.* She split in two and went down in less than a minute. Of her crew of nearly 700, only ten were rescued.

The American force, despite its heavy losses, had successfully carried out its mission. The bombardment ships had been turned back, and a large reinforcement group, which was to have landed troops following the shelling of the airfield, had reversed course and was now moving northwest up the Slot.

But the Japanese had by no means abandoned their plans. Three cruisers and four destroyers from Rabaul entered Savo Sound the following night, November 13–14, and finally carried out the bombardment, shelling Henderson Field for nearly an hour. They caused only moderate damage—less, certainly, than the battleships of the night before would have achieved with their 14-inch guns had they been allowed to accomplish their mission. The cruisers and destroyers were at length repulsed by PT boats, which made a valiant attack, firing 17 torpedoes.

Air operations of November 14. Though none of the ships of the Rabaul bombardment force was hit by the PT boats, they were not to escape unscathed. Next morning, planes from Guadalcanal and from the *Enterprise,* which had arrived in the area during the night, located them in company with other enemy vessels south of New Georgia Island and in a series of attacks bombed and sank the cruiser *Kinugasa,* seriously damaged another cruiser, and moderately damaged two others.

By now the Japanese reinforcement group, ten transports escorted by 12 destroyers, had again reversed course and was once more moving down the Slot towards Guadalcanal. Throughout the 14th, as these ships maneuvered in the vicinity of the Russell Islands, American planes bored in through a light and inadequate fighter aircraft cover to concentrate on the transports. Six of them, averaging 7,200 tons and carrying about 1,000 troops each, were sunk during the attack or were so battered by bombs and torpedoes that they went down later. The four remaining transports, all heavily damaged, continued on towards their objective.

Battleship action of November 14–15. The Truk bombardment force, which had been maneuvering in groups north of Florida Island during the attack on the reinforcement ships, closed formation towards evening and likewise headed toward Guadalcanal. But American planes had sighted them and reported their approach. Admiral Halsey, therefore, from his headquarters at Nouméa ordered the *Washington,* the *South Dakota,* and four destroyers to detach themselves from the *Enterprise* screen and proceed to an intercepting position in Savo Sound. This force, under command of Rear Admiral W. A. Lee in the *Washington,* reached the area west of Cape Esperance after dark and made a clockwise circuit of Savo Island without detecting any enemy units. The Truk force, however, had sighted Lee's vessels while they were north of Savo, and a sweeping group of a light cruiser and two destroyers followed the American ships into the sound. At the same time, a bombardment screen of a light cruiser and seven destroyers[3] proceeded southward on a heading which would carry it

---

[3] As originally organized by the Japanese, there were three destroyers in the sweeping group and six in the bombardment screen, but after the visual contact the destroyer *Ayanami* was detached from the sweeping vessels and operated with the screen until she was fatally damaged. Further complexities were introduced when, at about 12:40 A.M., two destroyers were shifted from the screen to the bombardment group. Towards the end of the battle two destroyers of the reinforcement group joined in firing torpedoes at the *Washington.* Of the other reinforcement destroyers, six remained near the Russell Islands to pick up survivors of the sunken transports and the rest accompanied the four damaged but navigable transports to Guadalcanal.

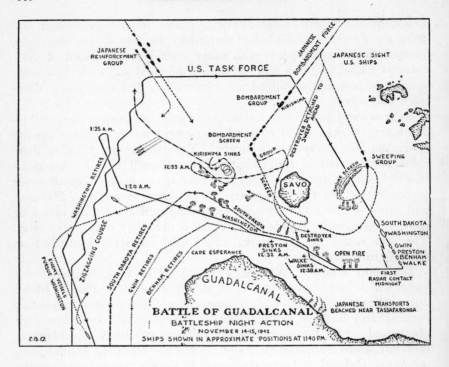

U.S. TASK FORCE

JAPANESE SIGHT
U.S. SHIPS

BOMBARDMENT
GROUP

DESTROYER DETACHED TO
SWEEP AHEAD

KIRISHIMA

1:35 A.M.

BOMBARDMENT
SCREEN

SWEEPING
GROUP

KIRISHIMA SINKS

12:55 A.M.

SAVO
I.

SMOKE SCREEN

1:20 A.M.

WASHINGTON RETIRES

SOUTH
DAKOTA

WASHINGTON

SOUTH DAKOTA

WASHINGTON

ZIGZAGGING COURSE

SOUTH DAKOTA RETIRES

GWIN RETIRES

BENHAM RETIRES

CAPE ESPERANCE

PRESTON
SINKS
12:32 A.M.

DESTROYER
SINKS

OPEN FIRE

GWIN
PRESTON
BENHAM
WALKE

ENEMY VESSELS PURSUE WASHINGTON

WALKE
SINKS
12:38 A.M.

FIRST
RADAR CONTACT
MIDNIGHT

GUADALCANAL

JAPANESE TRANSPORTS
BEACHED NEAR TASSAFARONGA

BATTLE OF GUADALCANAL
BATTLESHIP NIGHT ACTION
NOVEMBER 14-15, 1942
SHIPS SHOWN IN APPROXIMATE POSITIONS AT 11:40 P.M.

C.B.C.

along the west side of Savo Island and so through the south channel.
Behind these ships was a bombardment group consisting of the *Kirishima* and two heavy cruisers.

At midnight, as the two United States battleships, with the destroyers
in column 5,000 yards ahead, turned west towards Cape Esperance,
they made radar contact with the enemy sweeping group then east
of Savo, and opened fire at 15,000 yards with their 16-inch guns. One
of the Japanese destroyers, hit by one or more salvos, burst into flames,
whereupon the whole group turned away to the north under a smoke
screen. (See diagram.)

Admiral Lee chose not to pursue. He merely shifted to a northwesterly course and followed the Guadalcanal shoreline. This brought his
van within range of the enemy bombardment screen, now rounding
the southwestern side of Savo and hugging the shadows (radar as well
as visual) of the island. The vessels of this group, apparently failing to
detect the American battleships, made a sortie at the destroyers, attacking furiously with gunfire and torpedoes. The *Preston,* repeatedly

Top, THE 35,000-TON U.S.S. WASHINGTON STEAMS THROUGH HEAVY SEAS. Six of the battleship's nine 16-inch guns are visible. *Bottom,* ANTI-AIRCRAFT PROTECTION ON A MODERN BATTLESHIP. Dual purpose 5-inch 38's firing.

holed, on fire, her quarterdeck smashed, rolled over and sank stern first. A minute later the *Walke,* hit almost simultaneously by a torpedo and by a salvo from the cruiser, wrenched in two. Only her detached bow remained afloat. The *Benham,* also struck by a torpedo, managed to retire but in such condition that she was later scuttled. Only the *Gwin* continued firing, but she had been damaged so severely by shells that Lee ordered her to withdraw. The American destroyers, though knocked out of action, had served a useful purpose in drawing the fire of the enemy's surprise attack. The *Washington* and *South Dakota,* unscathed, dropped life rafts for the survivors and continued on to the northwest, firing salvos which started fires on three vessels of the bombardment screen and so wrecked one destroyer that the Japanese afterwards scuttled her.

In the waters west of Savo the *Washington* made radar contact with the *Kirishima* and her two attendant cruisers, now on a westerly course to the north of the American disposition. Admiral Lee ordered a slight turn to port to open range and so take better advantage of his excellent radar fire control, but the *South Dakota,* her surface search radar temporarily inoperative, was unable to keep station on the *Washington* and soon shifted to starboard. This unfortunate move brought her within 6,000 yards of the *Kirishima* group, which had come about to close the range. At this point two destroyers, detached from the screening group, turned searchlights upon the *South Dakota,* and the three heavy bombardment vessels concentrated their guns upon her, damaging her number 3 turret, knocking out her sky control, starting fires, and killing 30 of her crew. But the *Washington* quickly joined her fire to that of her consort and the enemy battleship-cruiser column drew away. The Japanese cruisers had been hit but not badly damaged. The *Kirishima,* however, battered by some nine heavy shells and forty 5-inch hits, soon lost control and began turning in circles. When it was clear that she would be unable to withdraw from the area, the Japanese commanding officer ordered the engineers to scuttle the ship by opening the sea valves. Of her crew, 250 had been killed. The survivors were transferred to destroyers.

Meanwhile, the *South Dakota* had retired southwards, while the *Washington,* still undamaged, continued alone to the northwest. Presently the flagship made radar contact with a column of cruisers and destroyers headed in the same direction. The Japanese vessels put up a smoke screen and fired torpedoes, whereupon Admiral Lee, convinced that the enemy bombardment attempt had been broken up and that it was therefore unnecessary to expose his ship to further hazard, ordered the *Washington* to withdraw to the south. A cruiser and several destroyers trailed her down the Guadalcanal west coast until shortage of fuel forced them to turn back.

Before morning the four damaged transports, all that remained of the original ten in the Japanese reinforcement group, beached themselves near Tassafaronga west of American positions on Guadalcanal. Here after dawn they were found unprotected and were battered to pieces by bombs from Henderson Field planes and by American ship and shore artillery.

THE BATTLE OF TASSAFARONGA

At the end of November Admiral Halsey, acting on evidence that the Japanese were about to make still another attempt to reinforce their garrison on Guadalcanal, sent up from Espíritu Santo under command of Rear Admiral C. H. Wright a force of five cruisers, the *Minneapolis* (flagship), *New Orleans, Pensacola, Honolulu,* and *Northampton,* together with four destroyers. At about 10 P.M. on November 30 this force, augmented by two additional destroyers, passed through Lengo Channel into Savo Sound. With the four original destroyers in column in the van and the two added destroyers in the rear, the cruisers then formed a line of bearing and swept the waters north of Lunga Point. At this time eight Japanese destroyers, carrying supplies and a few troops, were entering the sound from the opposite direction by way of the channel south of Savo.

When, shortly after 11 P.M., the United States force made radar contact with the enemy ships, Admiral Wright re-formed his column, closed for action, and ordered a torpedo attack. His van destroyers launched 20 torpedoes without making any hits; they then sped through the south channel and continued on around Savo Island. The Japanese commander, upon sighting the American vessels, signaled his own force not to use guns unless necessary. One of his destroyers, failing to get the order, opened with gunfire and was quickly sunk by a hail of shells from the United States cruisers. Except for shell fragments in the stack of the flagship, the enemy received no other damage.

The Japanese column, reversing course by divisions from southeast to northwest, swung out from the dark shoreline for a torpedo attack of its own. Two torpedoes struck the *Minneapolis,* tearing away her bow. Another hit the *New Orleans,* setting off her magazine so that her bow also was ripped away. The *Pensacola* took a torpedo which

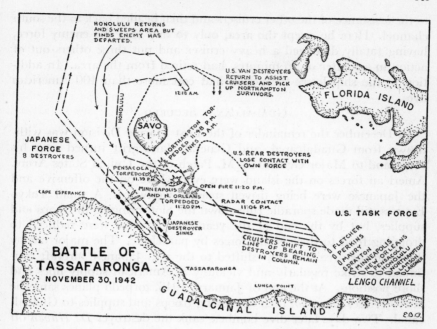

BATTLE OF TASSAFARONGA
NOVEMBER 30, 1942

started fires and flooded one engine room. The *Honolulu,* next in line, sheered out to starboard to pass on the disengaged side of the damaged vessels. The *Northampton* followed, but the two American rear destroyers, losing contact at this point with their own force and coming under fire from the American cruisers, turned away to the north and then headed back towards Lengo Channel to await further orders. Ten minutes later the *Northampton,* back on course, was struck by two torpedoes which tore a great hole in her port side and, rupturing her fuel tanks, caused her boat deck to be drenched with blazing oil. At 1:30 A.M., when the cruiser had attained a 30-degree list, the order was given to abandon ship. An hour later the captain and salvage crew were removed and shortly afterwards the *Northampton* heeled over, turned on her beam ends, and sank stern first.

In the meantime, Rear Admiral M. S. Tisdale, who had assumed command of the force, proceeded in the *Honolulu*[4] to the north of Savo Island in pursuit of four unidentified ships. When these revealed themselves as the American van destroyers, Tisdale ordered them to go

---

[4] The *Honolulu,* the only cruiser to remain undamaged, was also the only cruiser to adopt zigzagging tactics.

to the assistance of the other cruisers and then headed back to the south channel. Here he swept the area, only to find that the enemy force, having fatally damaged a heavy cruiser and put three others out of action in a matter of 16 minutes, had retired from the area. In addition to the ship losses the action had cost more than 400 American lives.

GUADALCANAL SECURED

In December the remainder of the First Marine Division was withdrawn from Guadalcanal, and General Vandegrift turned over his command to Major General A. M. Patch of the United States Army. American forces on the island were everywhere on the offensive and the Japanese were being driven steadily westward. A small Tokyo Express still made sporadic runs down the Slot, bringing in troops and supplies, but by the end of the year the Japanese were reduced to dropping food to their island forces by parachute. The major enemy threat in the area had now shifted to the air. Japanese aircraft continued to strike regularly and viciously at American supply lines and shore positions. At the end of January, 1943, torpedo planes sank the heavy cruiser *Chicago,* then convoying troops and supplies to Guadalcanal. Two days later dive bombers sank the destroyer *De Haven* off Savo Island.

But by February the Japanese knew that Guadalcanal was lost. The Tokyo Express, instead of bringing in reinforcements, had begun to evacuate the remnant of the Imperial Army garrison. On February 8 American troops, recently landed on the west coast, pushed eastward and met other troops thrusting westward from the Lunga area. Except for the cleaning out of a few scattered pockets of resistance, the Guadalcanal campaign was ended.

As had been expected, attrition on both sides had been grim. The following table compares losses in major combat craft of the American and Japanese fleets:

MAJOR COMBAT CRAFT SUNK IN THE GUADALCANAL CAMPAIGN
AUG. 7, 1942 TO FEB. 7, 1943

	UNITED STATES	JAPAN
Battleships	0	2
Aircraft Carriers	2	1
Heavy Cruisers	5	2
Light Cruisers	2	2
Destroyers	15	12
TOTAL	24	19

Though the United States suffered the heavier losses in surface warships, Japanese losses were greater in every other category: in submarines and auxiliary vessels, particularly in aircraft, and most notably in human lives. The decisive naval achievement in the campaign, however—the achievement upon which all the others were based—was America's victory in the six-month's race of supply and reinforcement.

"I look upon the Guadalcanal and Tulagi Operations," said Japanese Fleet Admiral Nagano after the war, "as the turning point from offense to defense, and the cause of our setback there was our inability to increase our forces at the same speed that . . . [the Americans] did."

27

Limited Offensive, 1943

T HE SIX MONTHS' CAMPAIGN to occupy and hold Guadalcanal had
done more than remove the chief threat to the United States-
Australian supply line and to Allied South Pacific bases; it had also
cut down Japanese fighting strength, particularly in the air, had provided a base from which to launch future offensives, and had kept
the enemy fleet occupied during a period when Allied positions in
the Pacific were dangerously vulnerable. Between December 7, 1941,
and the end of the Guadalcanal campaign, four new battleships, an
additional large carrier, 11 escort carriers, 12 cruisers, nearly 50 destroyers, and more than 40 submarines had been added to the United
States Fleet; four of the battleships damaged at Pearl Harbor had
been repaired and put back into service, and two more would soon
be added; and the fleet air arm had been increased to about 5,000
planes.

Many of the new ships were still undergoing shakedown, however,
and large numbers were required for convoying and antisubmarine
warfare in the Atlantic and for the Mediterranean campaign, then
in progress. Several months would elapse before sufficient strength
could be concentrated for the great push across the central Pacific
which Admiral Nimitz and his staff were already planning. In the
meantime, the Pacific offensive would necessarily be limited in scope.
The Navy, operating in close conjunction with the Army and Marine
Corps, would begin a program of "island hopping," of seizing bases
which threatened Allied positions and turning the threat back upon
the enemy. This slow eating away at the far-flung Japanese perimeter
was to be achieved by a series of amphibious operations involving sea,
air, and ground forces, acting under the overall command of General

MacArthur in the southwest Pacific and of Admiral Nimitz elsewhere. The immediate Allied objective was threefold: (1) to expel the Japanese from the Aleutians, (2) to advance up the Solomons, and (3) to clear the enemy from bases in northeastern New Guinea.

America's experiences in the first year of warfare led to important changes in naval construction schedules. An order placed in late 1940 for five *Montana* class superbattleships (58,000 tons) would be canceled in mid-1943. Already the emphasis had shifted to carriers, escort vessels, and amphibious craft. The Japanese also had been forced to change their schedules. The loss of six carriers in 1942, coupled with the relatively slow speed at which their shipyards operated, had driven them to experiment and improvisation. The heavy cruiser *Mogami*, now in process of rebuilding, would carry a flight deck aft; the battleships *Ise* and *Hyuga* were being similarly converted. In addition, a number of Imperial Navy seaplane tenders and other types were being rebuilt as fleet or escort carriers.

EXPELLING THE JAPANESE FROM THE ALEUTIANS

The occupation by American forces of Amchitka Island in January, 1943, permitted construction of an airfield only 65 miles from Japanese-held Kiska. By mid-February fighter aircraft from the new landing strip were providing excellent reconnaissance and were joining American and Canadian planes based on Adak and other islands to the east in almost daily raids on the two enemy bases in the Aleutians. This intensified air campaign quickly succeeded in cutting off Kiska from all surface communication with Japan. As a step towards isolating the more westerly base in like fashion, Rear Admiral C. H. McMorris on February 19 led a cruiser-destroyer striking group in a bombardment of shore installations on Attu; the striking group then proceeded to the southwest where it met and sank an enemy transport with shellfire. Following this double attack, the Japanese greatly increased the number of escort vessels screening their supply ships. A convoy thus augmented made one successful run from Paramushiru in the northern Kurile Islands to Attu and back. On March 24 the same convoy, composed of two transports escorted by two heavy and two light cruisers and four destroyers, set out from Paramushiru in a second attempt to carry troops and supplies to the beleaguered base. This time, however, McMorris' task group, comprising the light cruiser *Richmond* (flagship), the heavy cruiser *Salt*

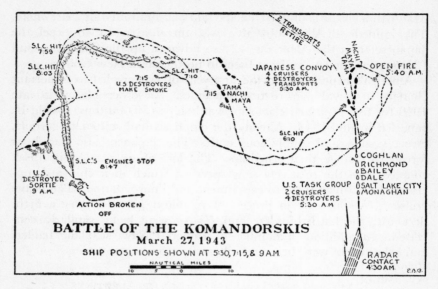

BATTLE OF THE KOMANDORSKIS
March 27, 1943
SHIP POSITIONS SHOWN AT 5:30, 7:15, & 9 A.M.

Lake City, and four destroyers, was patrolling the waters southeast of the Russian Komandorski Islands in a position to intercept.

Battle of the Komandorskis. At 4:30 in the morning of March 27[1] the American task group, steaming northeast in line of bearing, made radar contact with the Japanese convoy, which was then several miles to the north turning in column from an easterly to a northerly course. McMorris, uncertain of the enemy strength but determined to break up the convoy, ordered his group to form in column on the flagship and set out in pursuit. (See diagram.) In the first light of dawn the Japanese sighted masts of the United States force, and Admiral Hosogaya, supposing he had made contact with a pair of friendly vessels expected in this area, led his formation around to the right. Before the turn was completed, he was able to see that the approaching ships were American fighting craft—in numbers inferior to his own force. He therefore ordered the two transports to retire to the northwest and disposed his remaining units for combat in two divisions on parallel courses. At 5:40 both sides opened fire at 20,000 yards, the

---

[1] Local (zone −11) time. Official United States Navy accounts are expressed in Alaska (zone +10) time; most Japanese accounts use Tokyo (zone −9) time. Hence, American narratives state that fire was opened at 0840, 26 March, while Japanese statements give the time as 0340, 27 March. This book, in order to express operations with normal relation to sunrise and sunset, uses local time throughout.

Japanese cruisers quickly laying several straddles across the *Richmond*. Up to this point the American task group had continued closing on the transports as the primary target. When at last the Japanese ships became clearly visible and McMorris realized how heavily he was outnumbered and outgunned, retreat had become impossible, for the enemy cruisers and destroyers had slipped between him and the American bases to the east. He therefore headed southwest with the hostile force in pursuit. There followed a three-hour gun duel which was, in fact, a withdrawing action for the United States ships. It was chiefly remarkable for what the Japanese failed to accomplish with their superior fire power.

The flagship *Nachi* launched a seaplane, which spotted for the Japanese ships throughout the engagement, but the enemy force quickly lost some of its advantage when the *Nachi's* main battery became temporarily inoperative as a result of electric power failure. Further difficulties were caused aboard the flagship by hits from the *Richmond* which damaged the bridge and severed the leads from the sky control. The other Japanese cruisers, however, maintaining a range of from 16,000 to 22,000 yards, kept up an almost continuous fire, which was as steadily returned by the United States task group. Both sides were using a certain proportion of dye-loaded shells, a device which kicked up brilliantly-colored geysers and thereby enabled individual ships to correct their gunnery by identifying their splashes. But whereas the American vessels, especially the destroyers, made numerous hits on their pursuers, the Japanese caused no damage whatever during the first half hour. The success of McMorris' group in avoiding hits is attributable chiefly to expert salvo chasing— heading for the latest salvo splash, so that the enemy, in correcting for a miss, would miss again. During this first run the Japanese cruisers supplemented their gunfire with torpedoes; these likewise failed to score.

A little after six o'clock the *Salt Lake City*, then at the rear of the American formation, received a hit which tore a hole in her hull beneath the water line. After a second damaging hit on the same cruiser an hour later, McMorris ordered the destroyers to drop behind and make smoke. Thus concealed, the United States vessels presently made a turn to left and headed south. On this course the *Salt Lake City*, spotted by the *Nachi's* seaplane, was hit twice again in rapid succession. She began to lose way and just before nine o'clock went temporarily dead in the water. In this critical situation, McMor-

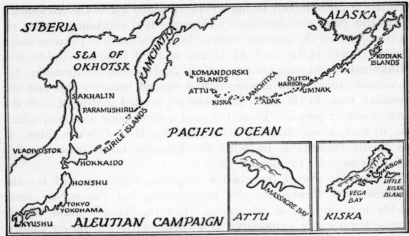

From *The United States Navy: A History* by Alden and Westcott.

ris ordered three destroyers in for a torpedo attack. These, heading northwest towards the enemy formation, came under such a hail of fire that it seemed impossible that they could survive. The van destroyer *Bailey*, severely damaged by two 8-inch shells and numerous near hits, launched five torpedoes at extreme range and reversed course. The two others followed without launching.

Though none of the *Bailey's* torpedoes scored, the destroyer sortie had forced the Japanese to turn away. They did not resume action, for Hosogaya estimated that planes from American bases, alerted at the beginning of the engagement, would soon be arriving in the area. Besides, his cruisers were running low in ammunition and three of them were damaged, the *Nachi* heavily, the *Tama* moderately, and the *Maya* slightly. The entire convoy, including the transports, returned to Paramushiru. Thereafter the Japanese were to rely solely upon submarines to supply their garrisons on Attu and Kiska.

Capture of Attu. By the end of April, 1943, Allied forces were ready to clear the enemy out of the Aleutians. There were at that time 5,400 Japanese on Kiska and 2,200 on Attu. Original plans called for an early assault on Kiska, but shortages, particularly of armed cargo vessels, made it necessary to shift the attack to the less strongly-held island. The substitution had an additional advantage in that Attu, lying nearer Paramushiru, would provide an airfield from which Kiska's final trickle of supplies could be cut off and its defenses softened up by shuttle bombing.

The entire operation was under the direction of Rear Admiral Kinkaid. An attack force consisting of the battleships *Pennsylvania, Idaho,* and *Nevada,* the escort carrier *Nassau,* and destroyers and transports was commanded by Rear Admiral F. W. Rockwell. Cruiser-destroyer covering groups were under command of Rear Admirals McMorris and R. C. Giffin. The fleet arrived off Attu in the morning of May 11 and under cover of a heavy mist put 1,000 army assault troops ashore at Holtz Bay on the northern coast and 2,000 more at Massacre Bay on the southern coast. The plan was for the smaller north force to hold and extend its position to the west of Japanese encampments in the Holtz Bay area, while the main assault force pushed its way across the mountains from the south for a juncture with the extended northern beachhead. The enemy would then be forced into the eastern end of the island where they could be bombarded into submission.

But the Japanese were not to be pushed into the eastern peninsula. Most of them withdrew instead into the mountain passes and there, by firing from concealed gun emplacements, delayed the juncture of United States forces for a week. Then for two more weeks, entrenched in the heights and generally protected from air and fleet bombardment by the continuous fog, the defenders repulsed attack after attack. At length it became necessary for the Americans to bring in reserves until ultimately about 12,000 troops were committed to the operation.

At the end of May, the Japanese, their ammunition almost exhausted, staked their last hopes on a bold attempt to rush the United States lines and capture the heavy artillery. The plan came perilously near success. Before dawn on the 29th the Imperial Army troops, many armed only with knives or bayonets, struck at the American advance positions, achieving complete surprise. They then continued down the valley without stopping to mop up and were finally halted just short of the artillery line. Of the Japanese who survived this final attack, most committed suicide by pressing armed grenades against their heads or chests.

By June 2, when Attu was declared secure, 550 Americans had been killed and 1,100 wounded. Nearly 1,500 more had been put out of action by unsuitable footgear and other equipment ill-adapted to the cold, wet climate. Except for 24 prisoners, the entire enemy garrison had been wiped out. The only Japanese attempt to come to the support of their troops appeared in the form of long-range bombers flown from Paramushiru. These achieved some slight strafing damage on American vessels and shot down two army fighter planes.

Occupation of Kiska. Lessons learned in the Attu operation were rigorously applied to the assault against Kiska, scheduled for mid-August. The pre-invasion bombardment from air and sea was far heavier than that brought against Attu. An expeditionary force of nearly 100 vessels was assembled at Adak, and 34,000 occupation troops, including 5,000 Canadians, all provided with tested arctic equipment, were put through final training in the Aleutian area. This huge force left Adak August 12. At dawn three days later it lay off Kiska and landing craft started moving in, while battleships, cruisers, and destroyers heavily bombarded shore positions. There followed one of the most complete anticlimaxes in military history. There was not a Japanese on the island! Sixteen days before, under cover of fog, cruisers and destroyers had evacuated the entire garrison.

Air reconnaissance had noted the waning and final absence of opposition, but it had been believed that the Japanese were merely withdrawing into the hills to await the expected invasion. There were some jibes in the press and embarrassed explanations from army and navy leaders, but there was also general relief at the saving of Allied lives. The Aleutians were now cleared of the enemy and the United States had bases within striking range of the Kuriles.

Upper Solomons Campaign

With the securing of Guadalcanal in February, 1943, the initiative in the Pacific war definitely shifted to the United States and her allies and was never thereafter regained by Japan. In the Solomons the new American offensive would be aimed at airfields in the New Georgia group and at bases on and about Bougainville. Occupation of these islands would remove the last serious threat to Guadalcanal and enable Admiral Halsey's forces effectively to co-ordinate with those of General MacArthur in a drive on the major Japanese base at Rabaul.

Throughout the first half of 1943 aircraft from Guadalcanal repeatedly bombed the newly-constructed Japanese air strips at Munda Point on New Georgia Island and at the mouth of the Vila River on nearby Kolombangara. During the same period American surface forces five times approached these fields by night and submitted them to prolonged bombardments, on one occasion sinking a pair of destroyers as a sort of by-product of the raid. But, though the Munda and Vila bases on several occasions were heavily damaged, the enemy made quick repairs and sent planes regularly the 200 miles to Guadalcanal to bomb Henderson Field and attack shipping in Savo Sound. At first the raids were small, for the Japanese had lost more than a thousand planes in the period from August, 1942, to February, 1943, and required time to furnish replacements. By spring of 1943, however, enemy aircraft began to appear in greater numbers. Early in April some 50 bombers and as many Zero fighters, striking at Allied vessels off Guadalcanal, sank the destroyer *Aaron Ward,* a New Zealand corvette, and a tanker. About a third of the attacking planes were shot down with a loss of only seven Wildcat fighters.[2] In a still heavier raid in mid-June the Japanese lost nearly all their planes while American aircraft losses were no more than six per cent. It was apparent that Japan had long since expended her first-line pilots, those who had given a good account of themselves in the sea-air battles of the preceding year, and that her planes were now manned by hastily-trained recruits.

Landings in the Central Solomons. The Allied "island hopping" campaign across the South Pacific began with the occupation in mid-February, 1943, of the Russell Islands, from which the Japanese had already fled. On these islands, 30 miles northwest of Guadalcanal, an advance staging base was set up and an airstrip was constructed to supplement Henderson Field and extend the reach of American planes up the Slot.

The next step was into the New Georgia group. For this move, which was to open an extended campaign, Rear Admirals Richmond K. Turner and T. S. Wilkinson would direct amphibious operations; air support would be under command of Vice Admiral Aubrey W. Fitch; while Admiral Halsey would retain direct control of surface support from his headquarters at Nouméa. The first major assault began at dawn June 30, when six transports, escorted by ten destroyers, arrived off Rendova Island, south of New Georgia, and put several thousand army troops ashore. While the troops routed the weak opposition on Rendova, the destroyers engaged in a gunnery duel with Japanese shore batteries five miles across the strait on Munda Point. The *Gwin* received a hit, but other destroyers kept the enemy guns

---

[2] A few days after this raid, a squadron of Army Lightning fighters from Henderson Field flew to Bougainville and there intercepted and shot down planes bearing Admiral Yamamoto and members of his staff. This well-timed attack was made possible by breaking of Japanese coded radio messages which gave the Commander-in-Chief's itinerary.

occupied until the landing party had set up shore batteries of its own to return the fire. Twice during the unloading operations, fighter planes from Guadalcanal and the Russells had driven off Japanese aircraft which threatened the invasion ships. But in mid-afternoon, as the convoy was withdrawing from the beachhead, an enemy plane got through and succeeded in putting a torpedo into Admiral Turner's flagship, the transport *McCawley*. That evening, after the ship was abandoned and was about to be scuttled, she was torpedoed and sunk by an American PT boat which had mistaken her for an enemy.

During the following week further amphibious operations were carried out in which soldiers and Marines were put ashore on New Georgia and on Vangunu Island to the southeast. On July 4 a striking force comprising the cruisers *Honolulu, Helena,* and *St. Louis* and the destroyers *Nicholas, O'Bannon, Strong,* and *Chevalier* set out from Savo Sound under command of Rear Admiral W. L. Ainsworth to bombard enemy positions on Kolombangara and New Georgia Islands in support of a daring landing inside Kula Gulf. Shortly after midnight the little column of cruisers and destroyers steamed boldly into the gulf and began to pound shore batteries. Japanese counterfire was steady but generally inaccurate. Shells, however, damaged the *Strong,* which soon afterwards was struck by a torpedo, evidently from a submarine, and began to settle. The *Chevalier,* coming alongside to remove survivors, crashed into the port bow of the sinking vessel and opened a large hole in her own bow. There was a tense moment as both destroyers, locked together, threatened to go down, but the *Chevalier,* though taking water forward, succeeded in backing free. Most of the *Strong's* crew were removed before she sank. Under cover of darkness the striking force at length pulled out of Kula Gulf and retired down the Slot. During the bombardment American transports had slipped in, hugging the shore, and landed troops north of Munda.

The striking force next morning steamed on past Guadalcanal and San Cristobal, and was headed for a fueling rendezvous with a tanker in the Coral Sea when new orders came in by radio from Admiral Halsey. An enemy surface force was coming down from Bougainville to the relief of New Georgia. Ainsworth's cruisers and destroyers were directed to reverse course and return to Kula Gulf. The damaged but still seaworthy *Chevalier* was thereupon ordered to proceed to base with the *Strong* survivors, while the remainder of the force, low in fuel and ammunition, executed a 180-degree turn and sped back to Guadalcanal. Here Ainsworth picked up two destroyer replacements,

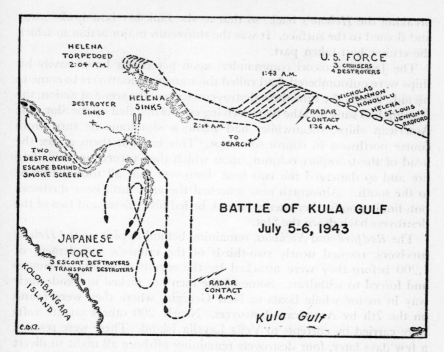

the *Jenkins* and *Radford,* and continued on up the Slot. It was evident that with the Tokyo Express running again the type of night battle which had characterized the Guadalcanal campaign was about to be resumed.

Battle of Kula Gulf. When the United States force reached the north tip of New Georgia at 1 A.M., July 6, seven enemy destroyers, four carrying troops and the others serving as escorts, had just entered Kula Gulf. The Japanese, making first radar contact, reversed course, the escorts moving north to attack, while the transports broke column to proceed with their troop-landing mission. At this point, American radars belatedly detected the enemy and Ainsworth's vessels promptly closed in, opening fire on the escorts at 7,000 yards. All three Japanese destroyers took damaging hits and the flagship blew apart with a spectacular explosion. The remaining escorts now launched torpedoes, taking as their target the *Helena,* which had expended most of her flashless powder the night before and was now using the smokeless type. Thus with each salvo the vessel was lighted up, providing a clear mark for enemy fire control. Three torpedoes struck, breaking the *Helena's* back, so that as she sank her bow broke away and floated to the surface. It was the thirteenth major action in which the cruiser had taken part.

The Japanese escort commander, upon perceiving how heavily his ships were outnumbered, had called the transport destroyers to come to his aid. But by the time these destroyers reached the scene of action, the flagship had sunk and the two surviving escorts had fled up the Slot. The American ships, meanwhile, had made a simultaneous turn from course northwest to course southeast. This brought them across the head of the transport column, upon which they turned an enfilading fire and so damaged the two lead destroyers that all four withdrew to the south.[3] Ainsworth now searched the area until near daybreak but, finding no further enemy targets, he led his cruisers and two of the destroyers back down the Slot.

The *Radford* and *Nicholas,* remaining behind to pick up the *Helena* survivors, rescued nearly two-thirds of the cruiser's complement of 1,200 before they were attacked by the surviving enemy destroyers and forced to withdraw. Some of the men not picked up made their way in motor whale boats to New Georgia, where they were found on the 7th by American destroyers. Nearly 200 others on life rafts were carried by currents to Vella Lavella Island. These were rescued a few days later, four destroyers remaining offshore all night to divert the attention of Japanese planes while two transports crept in close to the beach and sent in Higgins boats to bring the men away.

Battle of Kolombangara. The troops put ashore on New Georgia quickly consolidated forces and, aided by offshore bombardments from Third Fleet vessels,[4] moved towards Munda airfield and other Japanese positions. At the same time, Admiral Ainsworth's force, comprising now the *Honolulu* and *St. Louis,* with the New Zealand light cruiser *Leander* replacing the lost *Helena,* and a screen of ten destroyers, maintained a patrol to prevent landing of reinforcements and supplies by the still-busy Tokyo Express.

At midnight, July 12–13, this force, while passing the mouth of Kula Gulf on a westerly course, was notified by a night search plane that Japanese units were on their way down from Bougainville. Forming a column with five destroyers in the van and five aft, Ains-

---

[3] One of these destroyers ran aground that night and was destroyed the next day by American planes.

[4] Halsey's South Pacific forces were now generally referred to by their organizational title of Third Fleet to distinguish them from the Seventh Fleet, operating in New Guinea waters under the area command of General MacArthur.

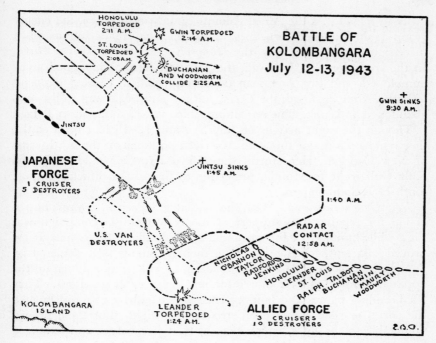

worth's force continued up the Slot and at 1 A.M. made radar contact north of Kolombangara Island with an enemy formation of a light cruiser, the *Jintsu*, and five destroyers. Swinging slightly to right and then to left, the Allied cruisers assumed a course across the starboard bows of the Japanese vessels and opened with an enfilading fire, concentrating principally upon the *Jintsu*. At the same time the American destroyers began launching torpedoes, releasing more than 50 in six minutes but making no hits. Shellfire, however, damaged one of the enemy destroyers and so wrecked the cruiser that she broke in two and sank. The Japanese had also launched torpedoes, and as Ainsworth's column reversed course to maintain the range, the *Leander* was hit and put out of action.

The American admiral now ordered his van destroyers to advance and finish off any crippled enemy ships they might find. Meanwhile, he led his cruisers out of the torpedo waters and then up the Slot. Once more north of Kolombangara, he made radar contact with units he at first took to be his own van destroyers. These, however, were the four undamaged Japanese vessels, which had withdrawn temporarily to reload. As the Allied column came within range, the enemy group again launched torpedoes. This time they made hits in quick succession on the *St. Louis,* the *Honolulu,* and the destroyer *Gwin.* In the confusion that followed, the Japanese formation slipped away unmolested, and two American destroyers collided, causing damages to both. After daybreak the *Gwin,* settling and beginning to list, was abandoned and sunk. The remaining Allied vessels returned to Tulagi.

Though the night actions of July 5–6 and 12–13 had been costly, they removed a major threat to American positions on the north coast of New Georgia. Henceforth, the Tokyo Express would avoid the Kula Gulf route to Munda, preferring to thread the difficult passage south of Kolombangara.

New Georgia secured. With the available American cruisers out of action for repairs, fleet support of the New Georgia campaign was for a while limited to PT boats and a small flotilla of destroyers. These proved sufficient, for the Japanese, their Solomons fleet depleted by damage and losses, had become loath to risk major units in the apparently hopeless task of reinforcing their island garrisons. They tried sending barges and landing craft which hid by day and hugged the coasts or sped across open stretches by night. But these proved vulnerable to the PT's, which sank at least five barges and damaged a number of others. Aircraft from Guadalcanal and the Russells, meanwhile, kept the enemy at bay during the daylight hours. In the last two weeks of July they sank a destroyer and several auxiliaries and small craft off Bougainville and two more destroyers in Vella Gulf. As a further aid to the land campaign they struck regularly at enemy strong points, dropping nearly 200 tons of bombs on Munda in one raid towards the end of the month. The troops on New Georgia, thus supported, converged rapidly on their main objective and on August 5 captured Munda airfield. This climaxed the central Solomons campaign and provided a base from which it was possible to neutralize the few remaining Japanese strongholds in the New Georgia group. The extent to which the balance of power had shifted may be measured by the fact that, whereas it had taken the Americans six months to secure Guadalcanal, New Georgia had been wrested from the enemy in less than six weeks.

Battle of Vella Gulf. It was soon apparent to the Japanese that the use of barges to replace the Tokyo Express was slow and costly. On August 6 they risked four destroyers in an attempt to rush much-needed reinforcements and supplies to their base at Vila. It proved

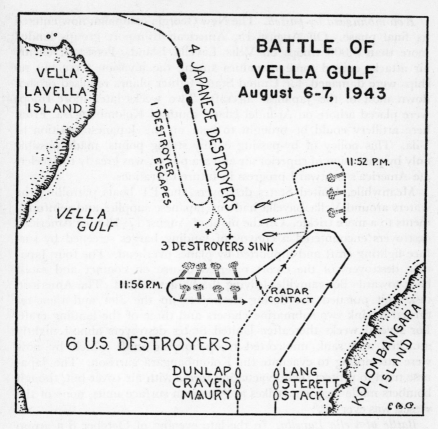

BATTLE OF VELLA GULF
August 6-7, 1943

VELLA LAVELLA ISLAND

4 JAPANESE DESTROYERS

1 DESTROYER ESCAPES

VELLA GULF

11:52 P.M.

3 DESTROYERS SINK

11:56 P.M.

RADAR CONTACT

6 U.S. DESTROYERS

DUNLAP
CRAVEN
MAURY

LANG
STERETT
STACK

KOLOMBANGARA ISLAND

C.B.O.

a bad risk. An American search plane reported the approach of the enemy units, whereupon a task group of six United States destroyers, under Commander Frederick Moosbrugger, proceeded to an intercepting position and attacked them at midnight as they entered Vella Gulf. In a brilliant use of radar, three of Moosbrugger's destroyers raced past the enemy on a parallel but opposite course launching torpedoes, while the other three, firing shells, crossed the van of the enemy column. Both American divisions then turned away briefly to avoid the expected torpedo counterattack and then, having reversed course, repeated their runs, all the vessels this time directing shellfire at the targets. Three of the Japanese destroyers were sunk and the fourth, seriously damaged, fled back up the Slot. The American ships were undamaged.

Kolombangara by-passed. The New Georgia campaign now entered its final phase. On August 15, American transport groups landed more than 5,000 troops on Vella Lavella Island. Persistant enemy air attacks caused some casualties among the invasion force but no ships were damaged, for United States fighter planes repulsed or shot down most of the Japanese aircraft. Two weeks later more troops were placed ashore on Arundel Island south of Kolombangara. From here artillery could be brought to bear on the Japanese position at Vila. This policy of by-passing enemy strong points, made possible only by possession of superior air and sea power, was greatly to accelerate America's westward progress in future operations.

Meanwhile, United States destroyers and PT boats patrolling the waters around Vella Lavella had cut Japanese supplies and reinforcements to a mere trickle. On the night of August 17–18 four American destroyers encountered a convoy of landing barges screened by surface fighting craft and supported by planes overhead. The four Japanese destroyers of the escort reversed course on contact and raced back towards Bougainville, leaving the barges behind. The American task unit pursued the fleeing destroyers up the Slot and then returned to sink two submarine chasers and three of the landing craft. For several weeks thereafter United States destroyers almost nightly attacked and sank unescorted troop-carrying craft which by now were attempting to evacuate the Kolombangara garrison. The Japanese tried to protect their evacuating forces with air cover but, though bombers made frequent strikes at American surface units, none of the vessels was ever hit.[5]

Battle of Vella Lavella. In the late evening of October 6 a group of three destroyers, the *Selfridge, O'Bannon,* and *Chevalier,* under command of Captain Frank R. Walker, encountered a considerable enemy force south of Choiseul Island. There was no surprise this time on either side. Captain Walker had been notified early in the day what he might expect and had attempted without success to strengthen his force with additional destroyers. The Japanese were also forewarned, for their planes had trailed the American vessels, marking their course up the Slot with flares. The enemy came down from the

---

[5] United States surface vessels were now protecting themselves by means of anti-aircraft shells provided with the new VT (proximity) fuze. This device, essentially a miniature radio transmitter-receiver, detonated the shell when radio waves sent out by it were reflected back from a plane or other object within 70 feet. The first VT-fuzed projectile to destroy a Japanese aircraft was fired from the *Helena* on January 5, 1943.

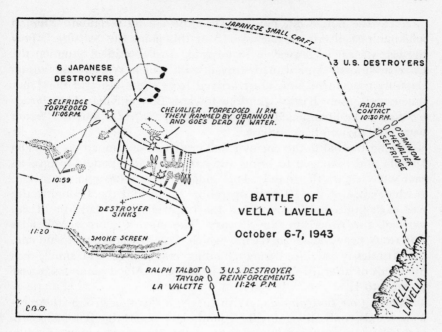

BATTLE OF
VELLA LAVELLA

October 6-7, 1943

northwest in three sections. Moving on a detached course was a group of submarine chasers and other small craft designated as transports to evacuate troops from Vella Lavella. Some distance from these were two groups of escorting destroyers, a main division of four and a secondary division of two.

As the opposing destroyer forces came within visible range of each other, the Japanese escorts turned away briefly. Then the main division swung south across the van of the American column. The Japanese, half convinced that Walker's destroyers were their own small craft, did not take advantage of this tactically favorable situation to open fire. Instead, the main division shifted to an easterly course, so that the opposing formations passed each other on opposite and nearly parallel courses. In this position the United States destroyers opened up with torpedoes and gunfire, sinking one Japanese vessel and severely damaging a second. The enemy replied in the same manner and a torpedo exploded against the *Chevalier* with such force that her bow was torn away. The *O'Bannon,* next in column, then rammed the *Chevalier,* causing further damages to the torpedoed destroyer and buckling her own bow. The American flagship *Selfridge,* proceeding alone to the northwest, now engaged the enemy secondary division and made shell hits on one vessel. At this point the *Selfridge's* bow likewise was sheared away by a torpedo. In this critical situation the three additional American destroyers with which Walker had unsuccessfully tried to make contact arrived from the south and the Japanese escort groups hastily withdrew towards Bougainville. The *Chevalier* had to be abandoned and sunk, but the *Selfridge* and *O'Bannon* were able to limp back to base.

During the battle the enemy small craft had continued on to Vella Lavella and managed to bring away nearly 600 Japanese troops, all that were left on the island. This ended the New Georgia campaign. In the course of the 10-week operation Japan and the United States had each lost a light crusier, but the Imperial Navy had lost 11 destroyers, the American Navy three. The enemy, moreover, besides suffering heavy losses in troops, which were considered expendable, had fruitlessly sacrificed many landing craft, large and small, and hundreds of aircraft. The ratio of Japanese to Allied plane losses was about 4 to 1.

Landing on Bougainville. With the New Georgia group in American hands, only Bougainville Island, largest of the Solomons, remained to be occupied in order to permit the construction of additional Allied airfields from which Rabaul could be regularly and methodically bombed. With this powerful base under continuous attack, the principal threat to MacArthur's forces in New Guinea would be removed.

But Bougainville was a formidable nest of enemy bases. For the assault Halsey had strengthened the Third Fleet, employing some newly-built units and some released from the North African-Italian invasion. Notable was a new powerful carrier force under Rear Admiral Frederick C. Sherman. This included the repaired and refitted *Saratoga* and the light carrier *Princeton*. Halsey had, moreover, built up his ground forces in numbers comparable to those then fighting in Italy. This was to be no shoestring campaign.

The assault began in mid-October, 1943, with a series of softening-up air attacks. Then, at dawn on October 27, New Zealand and American troops went ashore on two islands of the Treasury group south of Bougainville. That night United States Marines made a diversionary landing on Choiseul Island. The Japanese in something like a panic rushed barges to Choiseul to evacuate their garrison. While the enemy was thus occupied, further diversion was provided by a cruiser-destroyer force under Rear Admiral A. S. Merrill, which bombarded bases on Buka and at Bonis on opposite sides of the strait at the north tip of Bougainville and then raced back to strike at shore positions in the Shortland Islands to the south. At the same time Admiral Sherman's carrier force approached Bougainville from the east and sent in planes to continue the pounding of the Buka and Bonis airfields.

While the Japanese thus had their attention drawn this way and that, an occupation force under Admiral Wilkinson early in the morning of November 1 entered Empress Augusta Bay on the lightly-held west coast of Bougainville and, after preliminary air and surface bombardment of the beachhead, put 7,500 Marines ashore near Toro-kina Point. Though there were only about 300 Japanese in the area to oppose the landing, they put up a determined resistance. From well-concealed pillboxes along the beach they fired machine guns, mortars, and 77-mm. guns which took the lives of 70 of the assault force. A fighter plane cover repulsed several air attacks during the day but a number of enemy aircraft got through, causing minor bomb fragment damage on one transport and killing two men.

Battle of Empress Augusta Bay. That night, upon receiving information from spotter planes that surface units were en route from Rabaul to attack the Torokina beachhead, Halsey ordered Merrill's cruiser-destroyer force to return to the waters off the landing area to give cover. An hour and a half after midnight,[6] November 1–2, the American task force, then 45 miles off Empress Augusta Bay, made contact with enemy units coming down from the northwest. Merrill's formation, on a northerly course, included a van division of four destroyers followed by a division of four light cruisers, the *Montpelier* (flagship), *Cleveland, Columbia,* and *Denver,* with four more destroyers bringing up the rear. The enemy disposition included two heavy cruisers, the *Myoko* (flagship) and *Haguro,* in the center, with the light cruiser *Sendai* and three destroyers to port and the light cruiser *Agano* and three destroyers to starboard. (See diagram.) In the ensuing action, Merrill, mindful of the relative advantages of American radar-directed gunfire and the powerful and accurate Japanese torpedo, generally fought at extreme range, an arrangement which the enemy showed little inclination to change.

Immediately after contact, the van destroyers, led by Captain Ar-

---

[6] Zone —10 (local) time. American official accounts use zone —11 time; Japanese accounts use zone —9.

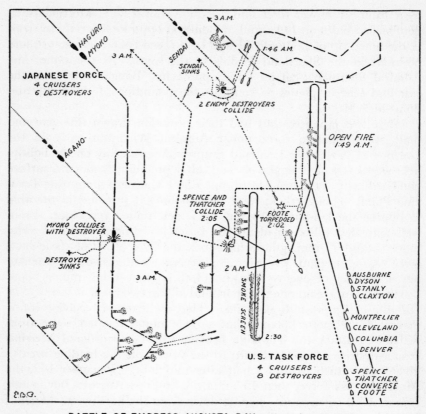

BATTLE OF EMPRESS AUGUSTA BAY, November 2, 1943

leigh A. Burke,[7] sped towards the *Sendai* division, fired half-salvos of torpedoes, and turned away. The enemy likewise launched torpedoes and turned away. The result was that American and Japanese missiles alike crossed the extended track of the opposing formation and did no damage. As the *Sendai* division changed course, the United States cruisers, now heading south, laid intense shellfire upon the knuckle. The *Sendai* was hit many times and went dead in the water, while two of the enemy destroyers, maneuvering to avoid hits, collided and were forced to limp out of action to the northwest.

At 2 A.M. Merrill's cruisers, having run far to the south, turned

[7] Known widely as "31-knot Burke" because of his predilection for high-speed maneuvers.

again to a northerly course and took the *Myoko* and *Agano* divisions under fire. In the ensuing maneuvers the *Haguro* took several hits and the *Myoko* collided with one of the *Agano* destroyers, cutting it in half and causing serious structural damage to herself. The rammed destroyer sank with loss of the entire crew. For a brief period now the Japanese cruisers, using starshells to illuminate their targets, fired on the American cruiser column, making hits on the *Denver* and *Columbia* but doing no important injury. Merrill's column quickly covered itself with smoke and was not struck again.

The American rear division, meanwhile, had headed west to engage the enemy, but one destroyer, the *Foote,* became separated from the others on the turn and soon ran into a Japanese torpedo which demolished her stern. At about the same time, two other destroyers of the rear, the *Spence* and *Thatcher,* sideswiped each other, and a few minutes later the *Spence* took a shell hit at the water line. The division, minus the *Foote,* continued on to the north, however, and fired ten torpedoes at the disabled *Sendai* without registering any hits.

The enemy was now in full flight. The Japanese commander, in explaining his decision to retire, paid the American task force a handsome compliment. Said he, "The analysis of reports indicated that there were at least seven heavy cruisers and 12 destroyers opposing us." All three United States divisions took up the chase, the van destroyers finishing off the *Sendai* with shellfire as they passed. Far to the northwest the same division overtook and made hits on one of the *Sendai* destroyers which had been slowed down by collision damage. Nothing else was accomplished, for the American divisions, widely separated and out of contact with one another, were hesitant to open fire lest they hit their own ships.

At 7 A.M. Merrill's task force, re-formed with the *Foote* in tow, was attacked by about 60 bombers and fighters from Rabaul. Two of the cruisers were slightly damaged, but the gunners, using VT-fuzed ammunition, shot down 17 of the enemy planes. Presently a wave of friendly aircraft arrived, whereupon the enemy squadrons broke off the attack and fled.

Offensive against Rabaul. There now occurred an extraordinary series of coincidences which were to have a profound effect upon the progress of the war. With the step-up of the Allied air offensive at the end of the New Georgia campaign, the command at Rabaul had urgently requested additional planes. Few land-based aircraft were available, but Tokyo, though unwilling to risk carriers in the threatened area, at the end of October ordered the 250 planes with Admiral Ozawa's Carrier Fleet, then at Truk, to be flown to the New Britain base "for a loan of ten days." While the air arm was en route on November 1, word came in that United States forces had landed on Bougainville. Headquarters at Truk thereupon directed Admiral Kurita's Imperial Second Fleet to assemble forces and proceed to the Solomons for an all-out attack. The fleet thus assembled entered Rabaul harbor at dawn on November 5 for refueling.

Meanwhile, Admiral Halsey, learning from reconnaissance planes of the concentration of air strength at the New Britain base, ordered Sherman's *Saratoga-Princeton* force to strike without delay. As the carriers on the morning of the 5th came within flying range of the enemy stronghold, fighters arrived from the Solomons to provide air cover for the ships. It was thus possible for the *Saratoga* and *Princeton* to strip their decks, launching nearly 100 planes against the target. In one of the most remarkable aerial exploits of the war, the American fighters destroyed about half the air force at Rabaul, while the bombers bored in through a steel curtain of antiaircraft fire to do crippling damage to the newly-arrived Second Fleet. Only eight American planes were lost.

Still, Halsey was not satisfied. He borrowed from Nimitz' new fast carrier task force, then poised to strike at the Gilberts, the carriers *Essex, Bunker Hill* and *Independence,* under command of Rear Admiral A. E. Montgomery, and sent them in on November 11 for a second attack. As before, United States land-based aircraft sortied to protect the task force, thereby releasing additional planes for the strike. The timing was perfect, for Imperial General Headquarters, appalled by the losses of the week before, had ordered the fleet air force to return to Truk that day. Before the planes could depart, however, Montgomery's squadrons arrived and, fighting through rain squalls, shot down 24 of them with a loss of seven of their own. American bombers then penetrated the overcast to strike at the shipping. Kurita's Second Fleet had prudently departed, but there were other targets. A dozen transports and a destroyer were sunk and several other ships were severely battered. The Japanese air arm this time struck back. In the afternoon 120 planes appeared over Montgomery's carriers. The enemy showed little teamwork. The battle that followed was a hopeless contest between well-trained pilots and hurriedly-instructed recruits. The attacking force was practically wiped out; not an American ship was damaged.

The Imperial Navy now possessed carriers but few pilots or planes. It would take months to build a new air arm and train replacements. As a consequence Japanese capital ships dared not again penetrate east of Truk, and in the following months American forces were able to sweep across the central Pacific virtually unmolested. It is perhaps no exaggeration to say that the timely strikes at Rabaul shortened the war by at least half a year.

The Solomons secured. With the main Japanese base thus weakened, American surface patrols dared to venture into the strait between Buka and New Ireland. In these waters on November 25 five destroyers under Captain Arleigh Burke attacked an equal number of Japanese destroyers and pursued them to within 60 miles of Rabaul, sinking three and damaging the other two without injury to themselves. During the month of December American surface vessels and land-based aircraft battered the enemy airfields on Buka and at Bonis into complete impotence. Thereafter, reinforcements and supplies moved into the new base at Torokina without opposition. With the construction of a landing strip in that area the 22,000 Japanese in the southern part of Bougainville were separated from the 5,000 to the north. It was not the purpose of United States forces now to back-track and expend time and men in wiping out the by-passed enemy garrisons. So long as these could be neutralized by aerial bombardment and their supplies cut off by increasingly tight Allied control of sea communications, they could do little harm. Many of the Japanese troops, in fact, took to gardening to keep body and soul together. At the end of the war they quietly surrendered, having long since literally beaten their swords into plowshares.

OPERATIONS ON NEW GUINEA

In 1942 the Japanese had seized very nearly the whole of New Guinea. The Dutch-controlled western half fell to them in its entirety. From here they had pushed along the north coast, setting up a chain of bases almost to the eastern end of the island. Milne Bay at the tip, however, they never seized, for the Allies, striking from their main base at Port Moresby, had established themselves there in force. In November, Australian and American troops under General Mac-Arthur pushed across the Owen Stanley Mountains, captured Buna and Gona, and began a drive northwestward towards the Japanese strong positions at Lae and Salamaua. This operation was to be coordinated with Admiral Halsey's advance in the Solomons, each supporting the other where necessary.

Throughout the double campaign, air forces under Lieutenant General George C. Kenney struck frequently at enemy bases in the Bismarck Archipelago and in the Bougainville region and maintained a vigilant watch over the Japanese supply line between Rabaul and the Lae-Salamaua area. It was on this supply line that Kenney's planes early in March, 1943, struck an important blow in a series of raids on an enemy convoy bound for Lae. For three days, in what is known as the Battle of the Bismarck Sea, American and Australian planes harried six transports and two freighters escorted by eight destroyers. In the course of the attack all the transports, both freighters, and four of the destroyers were sunk and about 50 enemy planes were shot down with a total loss of 3,600 Japanese lives.

On June 30, timed to coincide with landings on New Georgia and Rendova Islands, Army troops were put ashore almost without opposition on the Woodlark and Trobriand Island groups and at Nassau Bay on the New Guinea coast ten miles south of Salamaua. In the weeks that followed, as Allied forces in the severest kind of jungle campaigning pushed nearer the Japanese bases, Vice Admiral Kinkaid's Seventh Fleet lent support by bombarding enemy defenses and sending destroyers, PT boats, and planes against Japanese landing barges bringing reinforcements. Salamaua was captured on September 11 after air and sea bombardment of enemy coastal positions, and five days later Lae was occupied by Australian and American troops. Neither landing was contested. The Japanese merely withdrew to the westward, for Allied air interception of sea-borne supplies and reinforcements had long since rendered their positions untenable.

In the latter part of September, Seventh Fleet units, after a preliminary bombardment, put Australian troops ashore six miles north of Finschhafen. Here the Japanese elected to make a stand. There ensued two weeks of savage fighting in which 3,000 of the enemy were killed before the Allies were able to declare Finschhafen secured. It was during this campaign that American naval forces in the area suffered their first major loss when an enemy submarine sank the destroyer *Henley*. At the end of the year the Allies held the northeast coast of New Guinea from Milne Bay to the tip of the Huon Peninsula.

Landings on New Britain

When it became evident that progress of Allied forces along the northern coast of the Huon Peninsula was being severely hampered by Japanese planes from Rabaul, General MacArthur determined upon an invasion of New Britain itself in order to obtain airstrips from which the enemy citadel could be more readily neutralized. In mid-December, therefore, while diversionary strikes were made to east and west of the proposed landing point, a Seventh Fleet force under Rear Admiral D. E. Barbey approached Arawe on the New Britain south coast. Here, after a preparatory cruiser-destroyer and aerial bombardment, amphibious trucks (DUKW's) loaded with troops operating rocket-firing bazookas led landing craft ("buffaloes" and "alligators") to the beachhead.[8] Army forces landed with little opposition and in a six-day drive succeeded in taking the Arawe airstrip.

Similar in many ways was the landing of Marines on December 26 at Cape Gloucester on the New Britain north coast. Here the Allied amphibious force avoided the obvious beachheads near the enemy air base, selecting instead two points some miles away. The Japanese were thus thrown off balance, and planes and cruisers were able to reduce coastal defenses to impotence before the Marines went ashore. Enemy air squadrons, however, attacked promptly, damaging several vessels with near hits and sinking the American destroyer *Brownson* but losing 60 of their own planes. In the swampy interior the assault forces met hostile troops in increasing numbers, but by New Year's Day, 1944, they had captured both airstrips in the area.

Following the capture of Arawe and Cape Gloucester, Marines from the north and army forces from the south pushed forward rapidly to make a juncture and so secure the western tip of the island. It was becoming evident that the period of limited offensive had ended.

Submarine Operations

While surface operations in 1943 were restricted to a slow advance on the periphery of Japan's island empire, American and Allied submarines were patrolling the enemy's inside lines of communication, waylaying reinforcements and supplies bound for his threatened

---

[8] This invasion saw the first use of the LSD (landing ship, dock), which carried landing craft to a position near the beachhead and then flooded to permit them to move out under their own power.

areas and sinking foodstuffs, rubber, and petroleum products on their way from the East Indies to the imperial stockpiles. In 1943, submarines of the United States Pacific Fleet, under command of Vice Admiral C. A. Lockwood, sank 284 merchant ships totaling 1,341,968 tons. Of enemy fleet units, they destroyed one escort aircraft carrier, seven destroyers, and two submarines. Particularly noteworthy is the high score in enemy destroyers sunk, evidence of the courage with which American submarines turned upon and struck at their traditional hunters. Such courage paid dividends in cutting down the already-weakened Japanese screening forces, but it was perilous work. In the course of the year 17 United States submarines were lost in the Pacific. The Japanese lost 22.

☆   ☆   ☆   ☆   ☆

28
Across the Pacific

BEFORE THE END OF 1943 the war in the Pacific entered a new aggressive phase in which the United States Fleet swept the Japanese from the seas and built a highway of island bases across the ocean to the Philippines. This lightning war, contrasting sharply with the limited, costly offensive by which the Allies had moved up the ladder of the Solomons, was made possible by two developments which in their tremendous scope were new to naval warfare. These developments, entirely American in origin, were the fast carrier task force and the Service Force.

THE FAST CARRIER TASK FORCE

The fast carrier task force was essentially an expansion of the impromptu forces which raided the outlying Japanese-held islands early in 1942 and supported the invasion and reinforcement of Guadalcanal later in the same year. It was the American fleet of the Coral Sea and Midway battles enormously enlarged and, by the inclusion of new fast battleships, raised from the class of mere hit-and-run raider. Typically such a force included 12 or 15 carriers and light carriers, six to eight battleships, perhaps a dozen cruisers, and 30 to 60 destroyers. Its broad function, the traditional role of all naval forces, was to gain and hold command of the seas, assuring the safety of one's own lines of communication and rendering precarious those of the enemy, but its specific task in World War II was to pave the way for and then support amphibious operations. This task it carried out by pre-invasion and diversionary strikes, by serving as a floating fighter air base to screen the vulnerable craft of the amphibious forces, and by intercepting air or surface threats to the beachhead.

The creation of the new carrier task force was made possible by the American industrial machine, in which the shipyards and aircraft factories were but the points at which a multitude of complex parts were finally assembled. The United States Pacific Fleet, which at the end of 1942 was fighting with only a single aircraft carrier, saw the beginning of a resurgence of power when, at the end of May, 1943, the new 27,100-ton carrier *Essex* arrived at Pearl Harbor. In the following months others of her type arrived: the new *Yorktown, Hornet, Lexington,* and *Wasp,* and the *Intrepid, Franklin, Ticonderoga, Randolph, Bunker Hill, Hancock, Bennington, Bonhomme Richard,* and *Shangri-La.*[1] Still other major carriers were on the ways, including the 45,000-ton (CVB's) *Midway, Franklin D. Roosevelt,* and *Coral Sea.* Lighter carriers (CVL's), 11,000-ton craft, five of them built on hulls originally designed for cruisers, were likewise added to the fleet: the *Independence, Princeton, Belleau Wood, Cowpens, Monterey, Langley, Cabot, Bataan,* and *San Jacinto.* In addition, 1943 and 1944 saw the commissioning of fifty-seven 7,000 to 12,000-ton escort carriers (CVE's), which the public called "baby flat-tops" or "jeep carriers." A number of these were converted from fleet oilers and cargo ships.

To the new 35,000-ton fast battleships *North Carolina, Washington,* and *South Dakota* were added the *Indiana, Massachusetts,* and *Alabama* of similar displacement and the 45,000-ton *Iowa, New Jersey, Missouri,* and *Wisconsin.* Of lighter surface craft, 1944 saw the commissioning of 14 cruisers, including the large (27,500-ton) cruisers *Alaska* and *Guam,* and of 75 destroyers and 180 destroyer escorts. By the end of the year there had also been added to the fleet approximately 3,500 large landing craft (principally LST's, LCT's, and LCI's, ranging from 225 to 1,650 tons), 2,000 mine and patrol craft, and 1,200 fleet auxiliaries. By the end of 1944 the United States Fleet, comprising 60,000 vessels of all types and displacing 11,000,000 tons, was larger than the combined navies of the rest of the world. The following tables illustrate how, in major combat craft alone, America replaced her losses eightfold while the Japanese fleet fell farther and farther behind:

---

[1] Named from the mythical land in James Hilton's novel *Lost Horizon.* President Roosevelt had jokingly told the press that the "base" from which Doolittle's flyers raided Tokyo was "Shangri-La."

MAJOR UNITED STATES COMBAT CRAFT—LOSSES AND ADDITIONS

TYPES	Lost prior Jan. 1, 1943	Added Dec. 7, 1941, to Jan. 1, 1943	Lost 1943	Added 1943	Lost 1944	Added 1944	Total lost to end 1944	Total added Dec. 7, 1941, to end 1944
Battleships	2	4	0	2	0	2	2	8
Carriers	4	1	0	15	1	7	5	23
Escort Carriers	0	11	1	24	3	33	4	68
Heavy Cruisers	5	0	1	4	0	3	6	7
Light Cruisers	2	9	1	7	0	11	3	27
Destroyers	24	84	16	127	16	75	56	286
Destroyer Escorts	0	0	0	234	8	180	8	414
Submarines	8	37	17	55	19	80	44	172
TOTAL LOST	45		36		47		128	
TOTAL ADDED		146		468		391		1005

MAJOR JAPANESE COMBAT CRAFT—LOSSES AND ADDITIONS

TYPES	Lost prior Jan. 1, 1943	Added Dec. 7, 1941, to Jan. 1, 1943	Lost 1943	Added 1943	Lost 1944	Added 1944	Total lost to end 1944	Total added Dec. 7, 1941, to end 1944
Battleships	2	2	1	0	4	0	7	2
Carriers	6	4	0	1	9	6	15	11
Escort Carriers	0	3	1	2	3	0	4	5
Heavy Cruisers	4	0	0	0	8	0	12	0
Light Cruisers	2	1	2	2	14	1	18	4
Destroyers	22	10	34	11	61	22	117	43
Submarines	23	20	22	37	57	40	102	97
TOTAL LOST	59		60		156		275	
TOTAL ADDED		40		53		69		162

By the middle of 1943 the Navy's air arm comprised 18,000 planes; 18 months later the number had risen to 30,000. Carrier aircraft, meanwhile, showed steady increase in quality. For striking at enemy surface units and for bombardment of harbors and bases, the dive bomber and torpedo bomber remained the indispensables of the carrier task force. Newer types performing these functions were the Douglas Dauntless dive bomber, later replaced by the Curtiss Helldiver, and the Grumman Avenger torpedo plane. Both the Helldiver and the Avenger could carry 2,000 pounds of bombs. But in the year of decision, 1944, the major offensive weapon of the carrier force became the fighter plane, for as the conflict moved westward against bases of increasing power the primary problem became the quick destruction of the enemy's land-based air arm. The plane which carried out this task was the new Grumman Hellcat fighter. Equipped with leak-proof gasoline tanks, well armored, mounting six 50-caliber machine guns in its wings, able to carry 2,000 pounds of bombs on fighter-bomber missions, with a range of 1,500 miles, and capable of 400 miles an hour in level flight, the Hellcat was the answer to the Japanese Zero, outperforming it in every respect but maneuverability. In 1944, the United States was to destroy 3,500 Japanese aircraft with a loss of fewer than 400 of its own, evidence not only of the qualities of the new fighter plane but of the superior training of American pilots.

Service Force

The effectiveness of the fast carrier task force was a result not alone of its striking power but also of its amazing mobility. For the first time since sailship days entire fleets were able to remain at sea for weeks and months at a time. The secret of this new sea-keeping quality lay in the tremendous advances in the science of logistics which had begun with the establishment of a Fleet Train in World War I. The Train was later developed into the more closely co-ordinated Base Force and in 1941 had been reorganized, with an eye to the vast distances of the Pacific, into the Service Force.

The problem of such an organization is two-fold: the transport of troops and supplies to advanced shore bases, and the supply and servicing of ships at sea. The solution of this dual problem for World War II was essentially the responsibility of Vice Admiral F. J. Horne, Vice Chief of Naval Operations, and Vice Admiral W. L. Calhoun, Commander Service Force, United States Pacific Fleet. To work out the complexities of transportation they brought into the Navy men of experience in commercial shipping, teaming them with officers familiar with the problems of naval supply. Troops and stores were generally carried in commercial vessels furnished by the War Shipping Administration, but in order to cut the fleet free from its permanent bases it was necessary for the Navy to procure or to design and construct floating drydocks, repair ships, special fleet oilers, salvage vessels, hospital ships, ammunition ships, and tenders of various kinds. Means were devised for fueling and for transfer of ammunition and stores while under way; techniques, including special combat loading, were worked out for landing material along with the first waves of assault troops; a complex catalogue and time-table system was contrived in order to supply the right materials at the right time for setting up new advanced bases, new airfields, and new harbor facilities.

By late 1944, as the war in the Pacific approached its climax, the expeditious flow of supplies through West Coast ports became so critical and the problems so immense that Admiral R. E. Ingersoll, one of the ablest and most senior officers of the Navy, was transferred from command of the United States Atlantic Fleet and assigned the task, as Commander Western Sea Frontier, of assuring the steady outpouring of essential materials to the Pacific Fleet. By this time the Service Force, which at the outbreak of war controlled fewer than 100 auxiliary vessels, had expanded into a fleet larger than the entire pre-war Navy. It was this unglamorous fleet of auxiliaries and their screening ships which, bustling between the task force and its base, gave the new striking arm its endurance and its reach.

PRELIMINARY RAIDS

While the Solomons campaign was approaching its hard-won conclusion, Admiral Nimitz was planning the all-out offensive in the central Pacific. The principal weapon of the new aggressive movement was to be, of course, the fast carrier task force, but while this fleet was materializing it was necessary to build up island supply bases, to assemble troops at various staging areas, and to provide transports and landing craft. It was also necessary to test the new carriers against real targets—enemy bases powerful enough to provide genuine practice, yet sufficiently isolated from other bases that there would be little risk of overwhelming counterattack.

By August, 1943, the *Essex* and the new *Yorktown* and *Lexington* were in the Pacific, together with a number of light carriers, and a powerful screen of supporting vessels. A part of this force struck at Marcus Island early in September, achieving immense destruction with extremely light losses. A month later a similar force subjected Wake Island to a combined aircraft-cruiser bombardment. The enemy garrison had been forewarned and carrier aircraft losses were heavier this time, yet the score in planes destroyed was 5 to 1 in favor of the Americans. On the raided island more than 60 buildings were smashed or set afire and 300 personnel were killed.

In mid-September the *Lexington* and the smaller carriers *Princeton* and *Belleau Wood* sent 190 planes over Tarawa Atoll in the Gilbert Islands to drop 80 tons of bombs. This was part of a softening-up process already begun by army planes from Funafuti in the Ellice

Islands, for the Gilbert group was to be the first point of attack in the drive soon to be launched. Fifteen Japanese planes were destroyed on the ground, and the airstrip and installations appeared to have been thoroughly wrecked. Tarawa, it was thought, had been knocked out. But next day American army planes discovered the airfield there already repaired and in operation.

OCCUPATION OF THE GILBERT ISLANDS

The preliminaries now were over. In the third week of November, 1943, a force of 118 warships, including 19 carriers of all types and 13 battleships, together with dozens of transports, cargo ships, and other auxiliaries, converged upon the Gilbert Islands, easternmost stronghold of the expanded Japanese Empire. Overall command was vested in Vice Admiral R. A. Spruance, newly-appointed commander of the Central Pacific Forces, the operational strength of which was organized as the Fifth Fleet. Subsidiary commands were assigned as follows:

Assault Force..................Rear Admiral R. K. Turner
Carrier Force.................Rear Admiral C. A. Pownall
Shore-Based Air Force...........Rear Admiral J. H. Hoover

Nothing so huge had yet been seen in the Pacific and no operation thus far had been more carefully planned. After a thorough invasion rehearsal at an island base the armada moved with confidence towards the objective, prepared to put troops ashore simultaneously at three points on the morning of November 21.[2]

The careful plans were in some measure offset, however, by incomplete information regarding enemy fortifications and disposition of forces on the three target atolls. It was correctly estimated that Apamama at the southern extremity of the Gilbert group was lightly held, an estimate which was confirmed when a single company of marine scouts went ashore and seized it at the cost of one American life. But appraisal of the relative strength of Tarawa at the center and of Makin to the north was unfortunately less accurate. At least half the United States air and surface support and the personal attention of the senior commanders were devoted to the invasion of Makin, where, it developed, there were only about 400 Japanese soldiers and possibly as many Korean construction workers. After a tremendous

[2] East longitude time. Most published accounts of this invasion employ west longitude time and hence give November 20 as D-Day.

bombardment by heavy surface craft and carrier planes, 6,500 army troops were landed on the major island of this atoll. The enemy withdrew before the assault forces, harassing them with sniper fire and staging one night infiltration attack. At the end of the third day organized Japanese opposition ended and the commanding general of the invasion troops was able to report, "Makin taken." American casualties were 56 killed and something more than twice as many wounded. Except for about a hundred prisoners, all but three of them Korean laborers, the entire enemy garrison was wiped out or committed suicide.

Of the islands in Tarawa Atoll, only narrow, two-mile-long Betio was manned and fortified. Light resistance had been anticipated here, for during the weeks preceding the invasion land-based army and navy planes had systematically bombed the air strip and shore installations, and on September 19 and 20 carrier aircraft had flown a total of 445 sorties against the tiny island. By the date of the initial landings, the last enemy plane in the area had been shot down and all anti-aircraft fire had apparently been silenced. "There wasn't a square foot of the place that wasn't pockmarked with holes," said one pilot. "The place was a wreck," reported another.

But the fact, tragic in its consequences, was that Tarawa, pivot and stronghold of the Gilbert Island defenses, was far from crushed. Betio was protected by an intricate and only slightly-damaged system of concealed defenses which began with concrete blocks and barbed wire entanglements in the surrounding reef. The beaches were barricaded from the rest of the island by a wall of coral rocks and coconut logs, and beyond this at 20-yard intervals were pillboxes and machine-gun emplacements. About the perimeter of the island also were distributed a number of 8-inch guns trained to cover the lagoon and possible landing areas. In the interior were tank traps and barricades, and interconnected by trenches and tunnels there were steel, concrete, and coconut-log shelters and blockhouses, all carefully camouflaged with palm leaves. Into this complex defense network some 4,800 Japanese troops and Korean workmen had withdrawn to weather the preliminary bombardment and await the arrival of the American assault force.

Many factors, including mistakes resulting from inexperience, conspired to increase the hazards of seizing the island fortress. Before dawn on the 21st, transports loaded with Second Division Marines and accompanied by battleships, cruisers, and destroyers stood off the

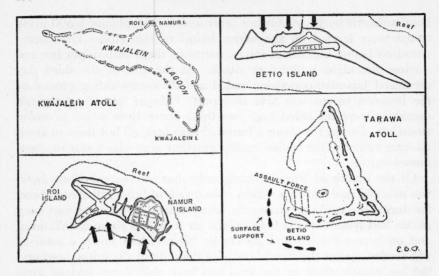

entrance to Tarawa lagoon, the support force exchanging heavy fire with Betio's shore batteries. Then, as later, communications were inadequate, so that the arrival of carrier planes was dangerously delayed. When at last air cover appeared, the support force moved in close to Betio's northern beachhead, firing bombardment ammunition directly at the target. In the opinion of some officers present, a plunging fire of armor-piercing shells propelled with a high trajectory by lighter charges, and hence with lower velocity, would have been more effective. As it was, the demolition shells tended to ricochet off the hard coral surface or to pass entirely over the low-lying island, endangering American ships on the other side.

Attempts to cover the landing approach with a smoke screen were frustrated by a strong breeze from the south. The breeze also blew the water away from the island, creating the effect of a low tide which caused landing boats to be grounded on the reef nearly half a mile offshore. Amphibious tractors were used to ferry the troops from this point onward, but, since the number of such tractors was limited, they could feed in reinforcements only slowly and were obliged to drop them several hundred yards from shore. From this point the Marines, loaded with equipment, had to wade to the beachhead in the face of withering fire. Three to four hundred men were killed in the water, and most of those who penetrated the hail of fire were quickly pinned down on the narrow north beach.

Though Marines of the center succeeded during the afternoon in penetrating as much as 150 yards inland, the greater part of the troops spent the night huddled with their dead and wounded under the seawall. But tanks had been landed and next day the rest of the Second Division was rushed down from Makin where they had been held in reserve and were not needed. Ultimately more than 15,000 troops were placed on Betio.

Landing casualties among the reinforcements were proportionately as heavy as those suffered by the first wave. Troops already ashore, however, were now beginning the dangerous work of eliminating the pillboxes and gun emplacements. This was in some ways the most difficult phase of the battle, requiring the use of sub-machine guns, flame throwers, satchel charges, and grenades at close range. By noon of the second day the battle for Betio, which until then had stood doubtful, reached a turning point, but the island was not considered secure until D-Day plus four. By then the Japanese garrison was practically annihilated. Nearly 150 prisoners were taken, all but 17 of whom were Koreans. Almost a thousand Americans had been killed and more than 2,000 were wounded.

Except for sporadic night attacks, carrier and land-based planes kept most Japanese aircraft away from the area, but one enemy torpedo bomber got through to fire three torpedoes into the light carrier *Independence*. Submarines proved a greater menace. One such prowler was rammed and sunk by the destroyer *Frazier*, but another put a torpedo into the escort carrier *Liscome Bay*, whose ammunition and gasoline storage tanks went off, causing her to disintegrate as internal explosions burst through her hull and upwards through the flight deck. Burning planes were tossed 200 feet into the air and these, falling back into the oil-covered water, started surface fires which engulfed many of the survivors. Within half an hour the little carrier, gutted and abandoned, went down. Of the thousand officers and men aboard, more than 700 lost their lives, among them Rear Admiral H. M. Mullinnix, commander of the escort carrier support group.

The cost of taking Tarawa was high and it seemed more so because all losses were compressed into a brief period. Actually the quick conquest, quickly exploited, ultimately saved many lives, for it opened the Gilberts to almost immediate occupation and thus shortened the campaign by providing the first stepping stone in the rapid march across the Pacific which followed. It may be taken as the second major turning point in the war against Japan, for as the victory at Midway

permitted the United States and her allies to abandon the purely
defensive phase of the conquest, so the capture of the Gilberts marks
the shift to an all-out offensive.

Capture of the Marshall Islands

The nearly-perfect invasion of the Japanese Marshall Islands northwest of the Gilberts is testimony to the care with which the Central
Pacific Command studied and applied the lessons of Tarawa. The
assault on the Marshalls set the standard and furnished the method
for all subsequent amphibious operations in the Pacific.

Original plans had called for an initial invasion of the eastern atolls
—Wotje, Maleolap, Mille, and Jaluit. This was the logical and
prudent approach. But air officers and others at Pearl Harbor convinced Admiral Nimitz that a successful assault could be made directly upon Kwajalein, largest atoll in the world and center and
pivot of the whole Marshalls defense system. Such a move would
bring American attacking forces within range of Japanese air and
surface craft based on Wake, Eniwetok, Nauru, and islands of the
Carolines mandate, but advocates of the plan believed that all surrounding enemy strong points could be neutralized by carefully-
worked-out and persistent raids.

Task forces including carriers and battleships struck effectively at
Nauru and at Kwajalein itself while the Fifth Fleet was still engaged
in the Gilberts campaign. Then, as the surface forces withdrew from
the area, Admiral Hoover's land-based planes took over and for six
weeks submitted every airfield in the Marshalls to raids of increasing
intensity. Early in January army and navy planes based on Tarawa,
Makin, and the Ellice Islands went on a one-a-day schedule, dropping
more than 2,000 tons of bombs on the hapless Japanese islands and
taking hundreds of reconnaissance photographs.

At the end of January the Fifth Fleet, now augmented to 2,000,000
tons of ships, was back in the Marshall-Gilberts area. The principal
divisions of the fleet into task forces (TF) and task groups (TG),
listed below, are of particular interest, for this was to be the basic
organization for central Pacific forces during the rest of the war.

Fifth Fleet (designated as TF 50)..Vice Admiral Spruance (flagship, *Indianapolis*)
    TG 50.15—Neutralization Group...Rear Admiral E. G. Small
    TF 51—Joint Expeditionary Force.....Rear Admiral R. K. Turner
        TG 51.2—Special Attack Group...Rear Admiral H. W. Hill
    TF 52—Southern Attack Force......Rear Admiral R. K. Turner

TF 53—Northern Attack Force......Rear Admiral R. L. Conolly
TF 56—Expeditionary Troops.......Major General H. M. Smith, U.S.M.C.
TF 57—Land-Based Aircraft.........Rear Admiral J. H. Hoover
TF 58—Fast Carrier Force...........Rear Admiral M. A. Mitscher
   TG 58.1⎫   ⎧Rear Admiral J. W. Reeves, Jr.
   TG 58.2⎪ Components of TF 58....⎨Rear Admiral A. E. Montgomery
   TG 58.3⎬   ⎪Rear Admiral F. C. Sherman
   TG 58.4⎭   ⎩Rear Admiral S. P. Ginder

Turner's force, consisting of 297 ships, carried 84,000 troops. Fifty-three thousand of these, Fourth Division Marines and soldiers of the Seventh Army Division in about equal numbers, composed the assault forces; the rest were garrison troops. The fast carrier task force, or Task Force 58, comprised six large carriers, five light carriers, eight new battleships, six cruisers, and 36 destroyers. Its air arm included more than 700 planes.

For 48 hours preceding D-Day, set for February 1, 1944 (east longitude time), this powerful armada set about flattening bases in the Kwajalein Atoll and neutralizing the surrounding islands.[3] Task Groups 58.1 and 58.2, assigned to the invasion target, gave special attention to Roi and Namur Islands at the northern end of the lagoon and to Kwajalein Island 40 miles to the south. Within a few hours every enemy plane on the atoll had been destroyed. During the next two days, the task groups, in addition to strafing from the air and firing rockets, hurled against Roi-Namur and Kwajalein 15,000 tons of aerial bombs and heavy shells, five times the weight Tarawa had received.[4] Virtually every mistake made in the Gilberts invasion was now corrected. Ships used both armor-piercing and bombardment ammunition, obtaining plunging fire by use of high-velocity charges at long ranges and shifting to lighter charges when the vessels came in close. Carrier planes picked their targets and bombed precisely and methodically. The earth was pitted and heaped in mounds; landmarks were wiped out; not a tree was left unfelled or unshattered— the "Spruance haircut," they called it. "The entire island," said an officer who visited Kwajalein afterwards, "looked as if it had been picked up to 20,000 feet and dropped." Of the 8,600 Japanese troops on Kwajalein Atoll, at least half, perhaps three-fourths, were killed before the first American set foot ashore. The rest were dazed and deafened.

---

[3] One atoll, Majuro, recently abandoned by the enemy, was occupied and soon developed into an important American base.
[4] Figures from Oliver Jensen, *Carrier Warfare,* p. 87.

On February 1, while planes and heavy guns continued their bombardment of the main targets, American troops occupied the adjacent islets and there set up artillery to protect the entry of surface forces into the lagoon and to cover landing beaches for the next day's invasion. That night underwater demolition teams penetrated by boat to within 50 yards of the main islands and swam among the reefs carrying explosive charges to blast out any obstructions or mines encountered. On the morning of the 2nd, landing boats approached the beachheads, transporting Marines to Roi and Namur and army troops to Kwajalein Island. Opposition to the landings was slight or nonexistent.

The Marines on Roi moved forward with such speed that they had to be restrained. One platoon charged completely across the island in 30 minutes. But Japanese were still there, hidden in shellholes or scrambling through the airfield drains to rise and snipe from the rear. Flame throwers cleared these out, and tanks, quickly brought ashore, blasted away the little resistance that remained. Roi was declared secure that afternoon. On Namur, just across a narrow causeway from Roi, enemy survivors held out longer, making two suicidal counterattacks from their hiding places in piles of empty oil drums and among the heaps of concrete rubble. But by the afternoon of the 3rd this island also was secure.

On Kwajalein Island the going was more rugged. Troops put ashore at the western end were obliged to march the entire length, crossing a terrain so plowed up by bombing and shellfire that maps and reconnaissance photographs were useless, for nothing could be identified. There were abundant holes in which the Japanese could hide, sniping by day and infiltrating American lines by night. For three days the invaders moved forward behind an aerial and surface barrage, finally pinning down 600 dazed but still-fighting enemy survivors in the northern tip. The island was declared secure in the afternoon of February 5.

Of 42,000 American troops put ashore in about equal numbers on Kwajalein and Roi-Namur, 368 were killed and 1,148 wounded. Except for 437 prisoners, of whom two-thirds were Koreans, the Japanese garrisons were wiped out.

Two weeks later the Fifth Fleet went beyond its original objective to invade the islands of Eniwetok Atoll 325 miles to the northwest. Here the Japanese had set up a rear base and aircraft staging point. The method of attack was much the same as at Kwajalein, but reconnaissance was not so thorough nor the preliminary bombardment so extensive. Marines invading the northern island of Engebi were obliged to clean out still-intact dugouts with grenades; the island was nevertheless overrun in a single day. Capture of Eniwetok Island to the south required two days.

Wotje, Maloelap, Mille, Jaluit, and other by-passed bases to the east were left, as Admiral Turner expressed it, to "wither on the vine." They did not precisely wither, but between spells of dodging bombs from neutralizing air raids the garrisons, like those on Bougainville, soon abandoned military activities and applied themselves to agriculture.

JAPAN'S INNER DEFENSE LINE

Japan had already abandoned her earlier defense perimeter in favor of an inner line stretching south through the Bonin and Volcano Islands; the Marianas; the eastern Carolines, including Truk; the Palau group; and New Guinea. Rabaul would be held merely as an observation post. It was assumed that all island bases east of the new defense line would fall to the Americans, but local forces were ordered to fight to the death to make their loss costly and time-consuming for the attackers. The Japanese hoped thus to weaken the United States Fleet and allow themselves time to build up their depleted air force.

Following the American air raids on Rabaul in early November, 1943, Admiral Ozawa's Carrier Fleet, now virtually without planes, retired to Japan, and Admiral Kurita's battered Imperial Second Fleet returned to Truk. From there Second Fleet cruisers and destroyers continued to Eniwetok but were hastily withdrawn when the power of United States central Pacific forces was revealed in the Gilberts attack. Kurita now realized the hopelessness of committing his surface forces to the defense of the mandate islands. He remained at Truk, however, until the fall of Kwajalein, when he withdrew his entire fleet to the Palau Islands. In the meantime, the sinking of tankers by American submarines had so reduced the fuel supply in the Japanese home islands that Ozawa's fleet was ordered to Singapore to complete training of a new carrier air arm. The flyers, it was estimated, would be ready for combat by June, 1944.

Pilots of land-based planes continued to be instructed in Japan. As they attained a moderate degree of skill they would be fed south to bases of the new inner defense chain, where their training would

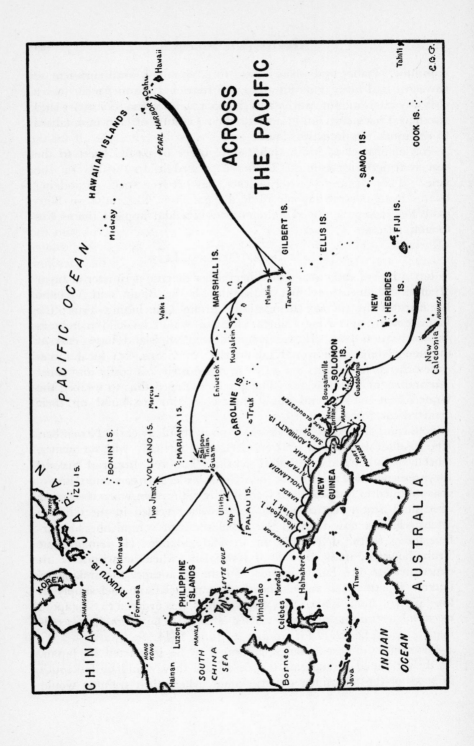

ACROSS THE PACIFIC

continue. Planes and pilots would thus be added until sufficient air strength had been built up along the restricted perimeter to hold at bay any attacking forces which might approach. By mid-February there were at Truk nearly 400 aircraft, three-quarters of them in condition for combat. In Japan 200 more planes were ready to take off for the aerial defense of the Marianas. The plan was not ill conceived, but timely American moves quickly threw it off schedule.

THE CRUISE OF TASK FORCE 58

While group 58.4 was engaged in supporting the invasion of Eni-wetok, the rest of Task Force 58 set out to neutralize Truk and the Marianas. On the morning of February 17, as the United States carriers and their screen stood 80 miles northeast of the Caroline base, Admiral Mitscher ordered off the first attack wave—some 80 Hellcat fighters. The enemy, belatedly warned, had a fair number of Zeros in the air over Truk to meet them, with more taking off by the minute. In the melee that followed, more than a hundred Japanese planes were shot down and almost as many were subsequently destroyed on the ground, against the loss of only a few Hellcats.[5] An hour after the first attack, American dive bombers and torpedo planes arrived shepherded by more fighters. The new arrivals sank or damaged nearly all the ships in the lagoon—mostly auxiliaries and small craft, while torpedo planes from the carriers *Bunker Hill* and *Cowpens,* scouting the surrounding seas in search of prey, found and sank the light cruiser *Naka.* Meanwhile, Spruance led a detachment of surface units, including three new battleships, in a circuit of the atoll in order to strike at enemy ships which were trying to escape through channels in the perimeter reef. North of Truk this group intercepted and sank a mine vessel, a destroyer, and the training cruiser *Katori.*

American torpedo planes made raids during the night, achieving excellent results by use of radar. The dozen or so enemy planes still available in the area also attacked, temporarily knocking out the steering control of the carrier *Intrepid* with a torpedo hit near the stern. This was the only damage done United States vessels during

---

[5] The Japanese state that in the course of the two-day raid 129 of their planes were shot down, 82 were destroyed on the ground, and 70 were damaged. The heavy losses were in part the result of a monumental blunder made by the atoll commander, Vice Admiral Kobayashi. The admiral, expecting an attack soon after the American invasion of Kwajalein, held the Japanese base at full alert for two weeks. At length, on February 16, assuming that the danger was past, he ordered most of the Japanese planes grounded, defueled, and disarmed. The Hellcats struck the next morning. Kobayashi was promptly recalled to Japan.

the operation. Next morning Task Force 58 launched at Truk, now completely stripped of air cover, a final carrier plane assault in which a Japanese destroyer was sent down. In the course of the two-day raid, 23 enemy ships—including two cruisers and three destroyers—had been sunk. American losses were 25 planes.

From Truk, Mitscher, after refueling, next led his force towards the Mariana Islands, less than 1,500 miles from Tokyo. This approach, he afterwards said, was for him the most anxious and exciting of the war up to that time. His anxiety was justified, for the 200 planes intended to augment the defense of the Marianas were just then beginning to take off from Japan. Fortunately for the carrier force, bad weather intervened, and many of the enemy aircraft were grounded on the Bonin and Volcano Islands en route. In the afternoon of February 22, a Japanese plane appeared briefly near the American fleet and then slipped away before it could be attacked. Mitscher at once alerted his ships. "We have been sighted by the enemy," he signaled. "Get ready to fight your way in." After dark, when the task groups had taken air defense dispositions, they became the target of a series of aircraft attacks that continued through the night. With a brisk following breeze, the force could not delay progress by turning back for the launching and recovery of night fighters. Defense, therefore, was left to the gunnery crews of the escorts. These, by use of radar, VT-fuzed ammunition, and expert fire control, kept the enemy at bay. During the night attacks no Japanese aircraft got within striking range of the carriers, though after daybreak the *Belleau Wood, Yorktown,* and *Essex* all had narrow escapes. As Admiral Montgomery's screen accounted for its eighth plane, the voice of the usually taciturn Mitscher came over the TBS, "That-a shootin', boys! Well done!"

Hellcats left the task force at dawn to strike through a layer of low-lying clouds at the islands of Saipan and Tinian. No more than half the reinforcement aircraft from Japan had now arrived and only 18 of these were fighters. Oddly enough, despite the warning they had had, most of the enemy planes were on the fields. The American squadrons pounced upon them, smashed large numbers on the ground, and shot down those which managed to take to the air. At the same time, bombers and torpedo aircraft from the carriers attacked cargo vessels and small craft in the island harbors, sinking two and damaging nine. American losses this time were six planes.

The raids on Truk and the Marianas left the Japanese inner defense line very nearly helpless. Had this been known to the United States Navy, assaults might have been carried out immediately at any point along the perimeter with an excellent chance of quick success and minimum losses. But General MacArthur, now preparing to make landings at Hollandia, asked for assistance from Admiral Nimitz, and the Fifth Fleet proceeded to the New Guinea area where, as events proved, it was not urgently needed after all. In the meantime, the Japanese in great alarm did what they could do to buttress their inner bastion. Thirty thousand troops were rushed to Truk; the garrisons at Palau and in the Marianas were augmented; Kurita's Second and Ozawa's Carrier Fleets were ordered to Tawi Tawi off the east coast of Borneo; defenses everywhere were strengthened. It was while on a tour of inspection of the new defenses at the end of March that Admiral Koga, successor to Yamamoto as Commander-in-Chief of the Combined Fleet, was killed. Caught in a storm while flying from Palau to the Philippines, planes bearing the admiral and most of his staff were forced down and lost. The command of the Imperial Fleet now passed to Admiral Toyoda.

When the United States Fifth Fleet, instead of striking at the center, appeared in the south, the Japanese were somewhat relieved, assuming that the Marianas were safe and that the Americans were henceforth committed to only one line of advance, that along the New Guinea north coast. But the assumption was incorrect, for before the middle of the year the big push across the central Pacific was to be resumed.

THE BATTLE OF THE PHILIPPINE SEA

Early in June, 1944, Mitscher, now promoted to vice admiral, led Task Force 58 out of Majuro to support a Fifth Fleet invasion of Saipan, Tinian, and Guam in the Mariana Archipelago. While occupation of these islands would provide American bases on the edge of the Japanese inner defense zone and cut the principal air line between the enemy home islands and the New Guinea area, their position, it was considered, also involved special hazards to the assault forces, for enemy planes could be flown up from airfields in the Carolines and down the stepping stones of the Bonin and Volcano Islands from Japan itself. A hostile fleet, moreover, could attack across the open spaces of the western Pacific. Actually the danger was not quite so great as the American command had been led to believe, for, though the Japanese had to some extent replaced their plane losses, many of their pilots were woefully unprepared for combat. Even Ozawa's

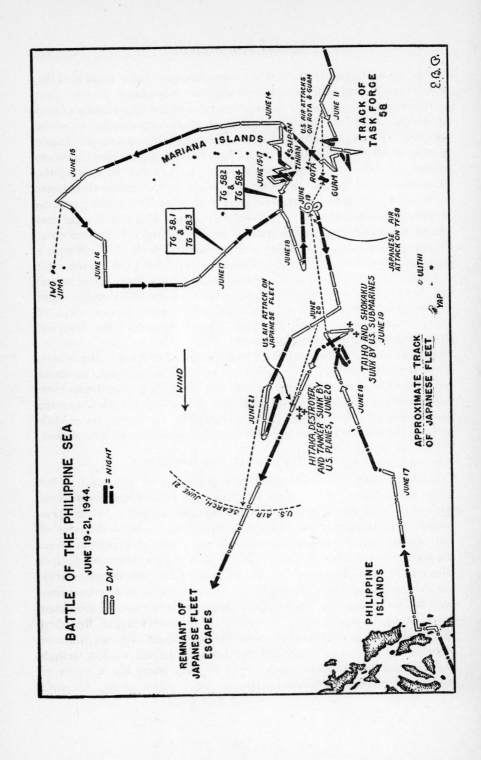

BATTLE OF THE PHILIPPINE SEA

JUNE 19-21, 1944.

= DAY

= NIGHT

carrier aircraft squadrons, under instruction now for several months, were unready for battle against well-trained air teams.

When, on June 11, the United States carriers were spotted by enemy air scouts, Mitscher decided to strike at once, though his force was still 200 miles east of Guam. That afternoon Hellcats raided the major Marianas landing fields, destroying more than a hundred Japanese planes. On the following day the Hellcats, together with bombers, smashed airfield installations and put holes in the runways. On the 14th, Task Groups 58.1 and 58.3 were detached and sent north to bombard landing strips in the Volcano and Bonin Islands, with particular attention to Iwo Jima, and to destroy any aircraft encountered. At the same time, land-based planes from General MacArthur's command began neutralizing Yap and Palau to the south. While the sources of possible enemy air reinforcements were thus being sealed off, fast battleships and destroyers moved in to bombard coastal defenses and airfields on Saipan and Tinian.

Information based upon submarine reconnaissance now revealed that the enemy fleet, so long in retirement, was once more on the move. From Tawi Tawi six battleships, nine carriers, 13 cruisers, 30 destroyers, and a train of auxiliaries were steaming across the Sulu Sea and filing through the straits of the Philippines. Spruance, now wearing the four stars of a full admiral, ordered all of Task Force 58, including the two raider groups cruising to the north, to concentrate west of Saipan, thereby interposing itself as a shield between the invasion operations and the approaching Japanese fleet. The juncture was made on June 18, three days after the first landings on Saipan. On that date the enemy ships stood 700 miles west of Guam.

On the evening of the 18th, information based on radio direction finding[6] confirmed an earlier report from the American submarine *Cavalla* that the Japanese fleet was then 355 miles west-southwest of Task Force 58. Mitscher at once proposed to close the enemy during the night to launching position, 150 to 200 miles from the target, and attack at dawn. To remain in the vicinity of the Marianas, he reasoned, would very nearly double the Japanese reach by permitting their planes to strike at the American fleet and then proceed to Guam for refueling before returning to their own flight decks. But Spruance would not agree to Mitscher's proposal. His orders were to cover the Saipan invasion. That was his primary responsibility and mission;

[6] The Japanese fleet had broken radio silence and thus permitted its detection and location by radio direction finders.

he would not risk giving the enemy an opportunity to pass around to the southward and come between the United States support force and the beachhead. During the night, therefore, on Spruance's order Task Force 58 moved east instead of west.

But the enemy commander, reflecting that in cutting off the American carrier force from the Marianas he would also be cutting himself off from his bases in the Philippines and Japan, attempted no end runs. He remained at long range to the west during the night, and next morning he struck. At 10 A.M. Task Force 58 detected Japanese planes approaching at a distance of 130 miles. Hellcats sped out to meet them, while bombers and torpedo planes proceeded in the opposite direction to blast the airfields on Rota and Guam. The Hellcats made contact with the enemy aircraft 60 miles out and there followed a fearful carnage. Japanese pilots plunged into the sea with astonishing regularity. Every enemy attack group was broken up and the few individual planes which succeeded in fighting their way through to the American fleet ran into VT-fuzed antiaircraft shells and got no farther. The Japanese tried every trick. They sent air squadrons in long curving courses to attack from new directions, but Task Force 58 intercepted the radioed instructions and had planes in position to meet them. Other enemy aircraft proceeded first to Guam before attacking, but here Hellcats pounced upon them and shot them down. Island-based Japanese planes joined the battle and suffered the same fate. At the same time, a conglomeration of miscellaneous aircraft, scrapings from the training fields of Japan, piloted for the most part by mere students, came down from the north to strike at the landing forces, but the United States carrier squadrons attacked these also and virtually obliterated them.

At the end of the day-long battle, which pilots afterwards referred to as the "Marianas turkey shoot," nearly 400 Japanese planes had been destroyed. The Americans had lost 27 aircraft, but nine of the pilots were rescued. Among the surface ships, the *Indiana* received minor damage when an enemy plane crashed into her side. More severe structural injury, but not of a nature to impair her military efficiency, was suffered by the *South Dakota,* on which the Japanese made their sole direct bomb hit of the attack.

Now that the enemy's wings were clipped, Spruance at last ordered a run to the west to close the hostile ships. But the Japanese were already in flight. Disaster upon disaster had befallen them. Even while their planes were being destroyed by the Hellcats, the *Cavalla* had fired six torpedoes at the carrier *Shokaku* and made three hits. Another American submarine, the *Albacore,* had pumped a torpedo into the new 40,000-ton carrier *Taiho.* Since neither submarine had remained to observe the full effect of its marksmanship, Spruance and Mitscher had no way of knowing that both Japanese carriers had gone down before midnight.[7] They suspected only that the Japanese fleet was hampered by cripples and thus underestimated its speed. With the coming of daylight, the westward progress of Task Force 58 was impeded by the necessity of frequently reversing course in order to head into the prevailing east wind for air operations. Thus it was that, though American scout planes quartered the seas all day on February 20, it was not until nearly 4 P.M. that a pilot 280 miles away at the extreme edge of his search sector at length descried the enemy fleet and flashed back his report.

"Well," said Mitscher, "can we make it?"

"We can make it," replied a member of his staff, "but it's going to be tough."

"Launch 'em," said Mitscher, grimly realizing that at this range his pilots would have to attack at twilight and, after returning from the long flight with nearly empty tanks, attempt to alight on their own carriers in darkness. But here was a chance, not to be ignored, to strike a crippling blow at the reclusive Japanese fleet.

"Get the carriers," was the order, and a wave of fighters, bombers, and torpedo planes was away at 4:23, two and a half hours before sunset. It was nearly seven, and the brief tropical dusk was setting in when the carrier planes came upon the Japanese fleet in several groups spread out over 200 square miles. No more than 30 or 40 enemy fighters rose to meet them but the antiaircraft fire was intense. The American aircraft nevertheless made numerous hits, sinking the carrier *Hitaka,* a destroyer, and a tanker, and damaging three additional carriers, a battleship, three cruisers, and three tankers.

Their strike made, the planes of Task Force 58 turned back into the growing darkness to face a steady head wind. Mitscher's carriers had continued to the northwest to close the distance, but several planes, their fuel exhausted, were forced to make water landings. It was nearly 9 P.M. when the first of the returning pilots began to orbit over

---

[7] The end of the *Taiho* resembled that of the first *Lexington.* The single torpedo which struck the Japanese carrier caused only superficial damage but loosed gasoline fumes which spread through many compartments. Hours later the fumes ignited with a violent explosion which caused the *Taiho* to disintegrate and go down in a few minutes with almost her entire crew.

the American flight decks. Few were trained in night landings and there was no moon. Mitscher was confronted with a dilemma. In the darkness most of the pilots would surely be lost, but if he turned on the lights, which included projecting searchlight beams straight upward, he would expose his entire task force, many thousands of men and a billion dollars' worth of ships, to attack by any enemy plane or submarine within a hundred miles. He went into flag plot, took a seat, and puffed thoughtfully on a cigarette.

"Turn on the lights," he said.

The pilots, ordered to land wherever they could find a flight deck, swarmed about the landing circles, each awaiting his opportunity to be waved in. Many, their gasoline exhausted, went down before their turn came. One desperate pilot without waiting for his signal crashed into the deck of the *Lexington* and rammed into six just-landed planes, killing two men and injuring four others. A total of 95 aircraft had been destroyed in action over the enemy fleet or were lost in subsequent water landings, but three-fourths of the pilots and crews were rescued.

It had been Mitscher's plan to detach a battleship group before turning into the wind to receive the returning planes. This detachment would then speed ahead to overtake and attack the crippled Japanese fleet next day. But Spruance countermanded the proposal, preferring to keep Task Force 58 concentrated for another air strike with reserve squadrons the following morning. Search planes early on the 21st, however, found the enemy 360 miles away making 20 knots. Since this was beyond air attack range, the American task force turned back east and abandoned pursuit.

This battle has inevitably been compared with the Battle of Jutland. With control of the sea at stake, the commander of the more powerful fleet preferred to avoid any aggressive move which might seriously weaken his forces or permit the enemy to come between his ships and the bases he was assigned to protect, while his subordinate was ready to take many chances in the hope of winning a decisive victory. And, as at Jutland, the full extent of the enemy's losses was unknown, was at first underestimated, and was clearly established only at the end of the war.

INVASION OF THE MARIANAS

Organization of the Fifth Fleet for occupation of the Marianas was essentially the same as for the Marshalls invasion. The sole

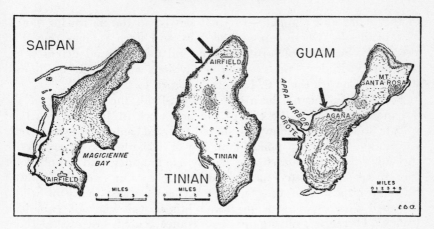

notable exception was the expansion of Rear Admiral Hoover's Task Force 57 into the overall forward area command, with responsibility of defending and developing the new bases after capture. Vice Admiral Turner's expeditionary force now comprised 535 vessels carrying 127,500 assault troops, two-thirds of them Marines, the rest army infantrymen. Saipan, Tinian, and Guam, the islands to be invaded, were garrisoned with some 50,000 Japanese, more than half of them on 14-mile-long Saipan.

After a four-day air and ship bombardment of Saipan, the veteran Second and Fourth Marine Divisions on the morning of June 15 went ashore on the west coast. The heavy bombing and shelling had cleared the beaches but no such general devastation was possible here as had been carried out on the tiny islands of the Kwajalein Atoll. The Japanese merely withdrew into the interior and directed heavy artillery and mortar fire at the coastal strip. Despite severe losses, the assault troops penetrated more than a mile inland during the afternoon, only to be forced back towards the beaches before morning.

With the landing of tanks and artillery the Marines thrust forward again, encountering everywhere carefully-prepared defense positions and gun emplacements. Losses among the invasion troops continued so high that Marine General Holland M. Smith ordered ashore the 27th Infantry Division, being held in reserve. The army troops, assigned to the southern end of the island, quickly seized the airstrip, later named Isely Field, while the Marines, thus relieved on their right flank, crossed to Magicienne Bay on the east coast. It was evident by now that the Japanese were abandoning the southern end of the island and planned to retreat slowly up the narrowing northeast peninsula, where among the hills and deep ravines they had prepared a network of fortified caves and underground defenses. As the enemy withdrew, the two marine divisions wheeled left and moved up the coasts with the 27th Infantry assigned to the center.

Forced into the northern tip of the island, the remnants of the Japanese garrison at the end of the first week in July made a final suicide attack. The enemy line surged forward some 1,800 yards, only to crumple under the point-blank fire of 105 mm. howitzers. With the failure of this attack the enemy commander and numbers of the officers and enlisted men killed themselves, an example followed by some hundreds of the Japanese civilian settlers, many of whom drowned themselves or leapt from cliffs in full view of American troops. Thereafter, all organized resistance ceased, but several thousands of the enemy still remained to be cleared out later from caves and ravines throughout the island.

It soon became evident that Tinian, two and a half miles south of Saipan, would have to be taken without delay, for artillery on the southern island was regularly shelling Isely Field. On July 24, while aircraft and heavy naval guns bombarded a southern beach of Tinian in demonstration of a mock landing, the Fourth Marine Division went ashore on the northwest coast. The Japanese, thrown off guard by the feint to the south, offered only light resistance at the beachhead. The following morning the Second Marines came ashore and took over the left or eastern sector. Thereupon the march down the island began. The invasion made rapid progress over the relatively flat plateau country, which contrasted agreeably with the rugged terrain of Saipan. The only serious Japanese resistance was encountered in the vicinity of their main base at Sunharon. That stronghold fell on July 30, and two days later the island was declared secure.

Thus far the invasion had cost 3,740 American lives, but more than four times as many Japanese had been killed. In addition to the damage to Task Force 58 received in the Philippine Sea Battle, 13 American vessels off the coasts of Saipan and Tinian had been struck by shellfire from shore batteries or by bombs or torpedoes dropped by enemy planes from bases in the Marianas and the Carolines. Torpedoes sank an LCI and ripped open the hull of the *Maryland*. Three other battleships, an escort carrier, three destroyers, an LST, and three auxiliary vessels received some damage, in no instance serious enough to compel immediate withdrawal from the invasion area.

Original plans had called for occupation of Guam directly following that of Saipan, but the necessity of pouring all reserve troops into the campaign on the northern island compelled drastic revisions. During the first critical days of the assault, the augmented Third Marine Division and elements of the 77th Infantry Division, assigned to invade Guam, remained at sea as an emergency reserve. They then proceeded to Eniwetok to be reinforced with additional troops from Hawaii. At the end of the first week in July intensive bombardment of Guam began. This island, 30 miles long and nearly eight miles in average width, was the largest yet to be invaded in the central Pacific. It required special treatment and got it. Before D-Day, July 21, more than 10,000 tons of shells had pounded its beachheads, airfields, and strong positions.

The landings, on the west coast to the north and south of Orote Peninsula and the adjacent Apra Harbor, were made against only sporadic mortar fire. A primary objective was Orote itself, but it required five days of hard fighting to seal off the end of the peninsula and three additional days to penetrate to its tip. This conquest, however, gave the Americans use of the harbor as well as the air strip. As on Saipan, the Japanese gradually withdrew to a hilly region in the north and the assault troops, wheeling left, followed them, keeping up a continuous pressure. Day attacks by the Americans were succeeded by night battles in which Japanese positions were illuminated by star shells fired from ships offshore. By August 1 the enemy had taken a stand at Mt. Santa Rosa near the northeast tip of the island. Here after a stiff defense they quite unpredictably abandoned their positions. The Americans then pushed forward rapidly to the north coast and on August 10 the island was declared secure, though as on Saipan and Tinian a great part of the Japanese garrison remained concealed in the hills and some did not surrender until the end of the war. Enemy killed on the three islands during the period of assault amounted to a few under 28,000 but by November this figure had risen to more than 50,000.

Capture of the southern Marianas, which broke the island chain guarding Japan's inner defense zone, was a necessary step preliminary to an American onslaught against that zone itself. Particularly important was the fact that the Army by this conquest was provided with unsinkable platforms from which its B-29 Superfortresses could strike directly at the Japanese homeland.

29

Philippines Campaign

The Approach from the Southeast

AS HAS BEEN RELATED, General MacArthur's forces, moving along the northeast coast of New Guinea, towards the end of 1943 seized Salamaua, Lae, and Finschhafen. Further progress was seriously hindered by air strikes from the Japanese stronghold of Rabaul on New Britain and to a lesser extent from Kavieng on New Ireland. Following December landings on the north and south coasts of New Britain, Marines and army troops pushed forward from opposite directions to make a juncture inland and by mid-March of 1944 had secured the western end of the island. Advance towards Rabaul was then discontinued, for neutralization of enemy strong points to the north had by this time been achieved by other means.

To the east of the Bismarck Archipelago, Admiral Halsey's Third Fleet in the middle of February, 1944, put a New Zealand assault force ashore on the Green Islands to kill off the hundred or so troops of the enemy garrison. There was then developed on the main island an airbase closer to Rabaul than any hitherto established. In the opposite direction, west of New Ireland, General MacArthur's forces two weeks later made landings on Los Negros in the Admiralty Islands. Here reconnaissance greatly underestimated the number of Japanese present, with the result that only about a thousand troops were put ashore to wrest the island from an enemy garrison of 5,000. There followed a period of desperate fighting and extreme uncertainty as reinforcements were rushed to the area. It required three weeks, and a far larger force than that originally committed, to render Los Negros secure. Meanwhile, the invasion of nearby Manus Island had begun.

With the conclusion of this operation the Allies gained not only ample area for neutralizing airfields but one of the finest harbors in the southwest Pacific. Manus, therefore, was quickly developed into a major base. The boxing in of Rabaul and Kavieng was completed in mid-March when Third Fleet units landed Marines on Emirau Island 75 miles northwest of New Ireland. The Japanese now withdrew most of their planes from the area, retaining Rabaul, as we have seen, merely as an observation post.

With the enemy bases to the north neutralized, Allied forces were ready for a major advance along the New Guinea coast. On New Year's Day, 1944, a United States Army division had been put ashore at Saidor to the west of Huon Peninsula. Here it was joined in February by Australian troops who had pushed along the coast from Finschhafen. Beyond this point, however, MacArthur's forces were stymied by the presence of almost the entire Japanese 18th Army, possibly 50,000 troops, centered about Wewak. Beyond lay Aitape and Hollandia, good potential bases for further advance and not too heavily defended. The possibility was now studied of by-passing the Wewak garrison in a leapfrog movement by sea. It would be a daring operation but in consideration of the weakened Japanese air power in the area, MacArthur thought it could be done without prohibitive risk. To prevent outflanking from enemy bases in the Carolines, however, he called on Admiral Nimitz for assistance from Task Force 58,[1] which had now completed supporting operations connected with the Marshalls invasion.

At the end of March, Task Force 58 began its new assignment with a strike at the Palau Islands, in which the carrier planes destroyed some 150 enemy aircraft and sank a destroyer and 22 auxiliary ships in the lagoon. Then, in withdrawing from the area, the carriers sent out air squadrons for raids on Yap, Ulithi, and Woleai. In mid-April Spruance and Mitscher had their force again in the Carolines. Here it patrolled for a week without being detected by the enemy. At last on April 21 it moved in close to Hollandia for offshore support of MacArthur's landing.

In the meantime, Seventh Fleet units had taken aboard two United States Army divisions at Saidor and then moved north to the Admiralty Islands. From here they set a course towards Palau to confuse the Japanese, but during the night they split into two groups and

[1] Task Force 58 and the Fifth Fleet were practically identical when organized as a striking, rather than as an invasion, force.

turned back southward towards New Guinea. On April 22 landings were made simultaneously at Aitape and Hollandia. Escort carriers provided air cover for the Aitape force, which went ashore with little opposition, finding no more than 1,000 Japanese in the area. There were nearly four times as many enemy troops in the vicinity of Hollandia, but so thoroughly had General Kenney's planes bombarded the adjacent airfields that on D-Day the invaders landed with comparative ease, while Task Force 58, standing by to give air cover, found little to do but send its planes against already pitted runways.

The Fifth Fleet force, released by General MacArthur on the 23rd, next headed east for refueling and further strikes at Truk, Satawan, and Panope. Meanwhile, the troops ashore set out to make good their positions. This was never completely accomplished for, though Hollandia became an important Allied base and neither it nor Aitape was ever in jeopardy, the by-passed Japanese 18th Army constituted a serious nuisance if not a menace, attacking and gaining ground whenever opportunity afforded but being in the end inexorably driven back into the jungle.

The great double leap from Saidor to Aitape and Hollandia set the style. Further looping advances were made during the following months to Wakde, to Biak and Noemfoor Islands athwart the mouth of Geelvink Bay, and finally at the end of July to Sansapor at the far western end of New Guinea. Many thousands more Japanese had thus been by-passed and were still to be reckoned with, but strategically the New Guinea campaign was completed. In 22 months MacArthur's forces had pushed 1,500 miles northwest from Milne Bay. Now only the islands of Halmahera, Morotai, and Talaud stood between them and the Philippines. Much of the credit for this triumphal march belongs to Admiral Kinkaid's Seventh Fleet, which provided surface support throughout, and particularly to Admiral Barbey's Seventh Amphibious Force, whose vessels brought the troops to the many successive beachheads.

In mid-September, while Halsey's Third Fleet neutralized enemy bases in the western Carolines and on Mindanao and Celebes, ships of the Seventh Fleet steamed past the great land-mass of Halmahera to the much-smaller Morotai beyond. This by-pass was to be MacArthur's final leapfrog move before the attack on the Philippines. Barbey's heavy ships first bombarded northern Halmahera airfields and then moved across to shell the beachheads on Morotai, which were already being bombed and strafed by planes from escort carriers.

When the barrage was lifted, army troops waded ashore with no opposition and within two hours secured the airfield. Only later did Japanese reinforcements begin crossing over by night from Halmahera until a formidable enemy garrison had been built up on the smaller island, and the battle which had begun as an easy triumph for the American forces quickly mounted in intensity as MacArthur poured in his reserves. Not until the middle of January, 1945, could Morotai be declared secure.

The Approach from the East

The war had long since moved out of the South Pacific and most of the Third Fleet vessels had been released for operations elsewhere, leaving little more than a patrol in that area. Admiral Halsey, ever ready for a fight, was not displeased therefore when, following the conclusion of the Marianas campaign, he was ordered to succeed to the command of the Central Pacific Forces. Admiral Spruance, who had held the command for a year and was understandably in need of a rest, would be temporarily relieved of combat duty. Since Halsey brought with him his staff and his old fleet title, the Fifth Fleet became the Third Fleet and the component task forces, in accordance with fleet tactical organization, assumed numbers from 31 to 39.[2] Under Halsey, Vice Admiral T. S. Wilkinson now commanded the joint expeditionary forces which conducted landing operations, Marine Major General J. C. Smith was Commander Expeditionary Troops, and Vice Admiral Mitscher remained in command of the fast carrier force, now designated as Task Force 38.

The first major project of the central Pacific fleet, thus restaffed, was seizure of the Palau Islands in anticipation of an early invasion of the Philippines.[3] In the first days of September, 1944, preliminary sweeps by task groups were carried out simultaneously against the

---

[2] The Seventh Fleet remained under command of Admiral Kinkaid, who in turn was responsible to General MacArthur, Commander-in-Chief, Southwest Pacific Forces. The other Pacific fleets were responsible to Admiral Nimitz, who, in addition to being Commander-in-Chief, United States Pacific Fleet and Pacific Ocean Areas, was also Commander, First and Ninth Fleets. The First Fleet now included the South Pacific Force, Amphibious Forces, Service Force, etc. The Ninth Fleet included the North Pacific Force, Forward Area Central Pacific, the Marshalls-Gilberts Force, etc. From this period on, the Central Pacific Force alternately carried the titles Third Fleet and Fifth Fleet. There was some attempt at the time to bemuse the Japanese, and incidentally the American public, by pretending in news releases that there actually were in the central Pacific two separate fleets of ships striking alternate blows against the enemy.

[3] Truk, twice raided by the Fifth Fleet, was now considered sufficiently neutralized to be safely by-passed.

Bonin and Volcano Islands in the north and against the Palaus themselves. In these attacks carrier aircraft squadrons damaged enemy installations and supply dumps, sank cargo and auxiliary vessels, and everywhere maintained their score of nine Japanese planes destroyed for each of their own lost. Then, while one group carried out a raid on Yap, the main body proceeded to pound airfields and shipping in the Philippines and on Celebes. Finally, in mid-September, timed to coincide with the landings on Morotai, the nearly 800 vessels of the Third Fleet approached Palau Atoll.

The largest island, Babelthuap, with its garrison of 25,000 Japanese, was bombarded but otherwise ignored. Peleliu and Angaur to the south would provide the needed airfields, and reef-surrounded Kossol Passage to the north would furnish a desirable anchorage. With these in their possession, the Americans could render the centrally-located Babelthuap impotent. Three days of the most intensive bombardment yet seen in the Pacific, followed by the firing of nearly 10,000 rockets from LCI's, preceded the landings of the First Marine Division on Peleliu. The Marines found the beach defenses heavily mined but mostly deserted. They pushed forward against sporadic artillery shelling and fairly heavy mortar fire, overrunning the southern end of the island including the airfield before the end of the second day. Thereafter, progress became more difficult. The enemy garrison, reinforced by night from Babelthuap and Angaur, took up positions in the natural fortress provided by a rough ridge running the length of the island. Here from interconnected caves, some fitted with steel doors, the enemy dominated the coastal road with fire from mortars and heavier weapons. From their hillside fastnesses also they counterattacked with tanks under support of a well-laid barrage. Though the Marines on Peleliu abandoned their usual rushing tactics for a policy of preliminary bombardment, tank attacks, and clearing out of caves before moving forward, their losses in proportion to the size of the objective and numbers involved exceeded those in any previous operation. Before the ten-weeks' campaign was ended, 60 per cent of the First Marines were casualties, and all reserves, including army troops rushed over from Angaur, had been committed. Not until the end of November was the Japanese garrison, numbering more than 12,000, wiped out.

In the meantime, other troops from Angaur—which had been captured without severe opposition—were transported to Ulithi Atoll 350 miles to the northeast. When it was discovered that the enemy had already withdrawn, the Third Fleet took possession and quickly developed the atoll into a major anchorage, fueling station, and forward base.

The Landings on Leyte

Original plans for invasion of the Philippines called for occupation of the Talaud Islands northwest of Morotai in mid-October, with landings on Mindanao to follow a month later. But results of the Third Fleet strikes in early September convinced Halsey that the Philippine middle islands were underdefended. Photo-reconnaissance and guerrilla reports confirmed his opinion. He therefore urged an immediate attack at the vulnerable center before the Japanese could rush in reinforcements. MacArthur agreed and at once ordered his staff to work out a new assault plan.[4] Then he radioed the Joint Chiefs of Staff, currently meeting with Roosevelt and Churchill at Quebec, that he was prepared to invade the island of Leyte on October 20. The Chiefs of Staff within a few hours sent back their acceptance of the proposed change, and Admiral Nimitz indicated his readiness to co-operate to the full extent of the resources at his command.

The invasion, it was clear, would require all the striking power that could be mustered. For land operations MacArthur had Lieutenant General Walter Krueger's Sixth Army. This Nimitz reinforced by making available the 24th Army Corps then in the Hawaiian Islands; he also temporarily transferred from the Third to the Seventh Fleet the Third Amphibious Force, comprising transports, escort carriers, and fire-support vessels, including the older battleships. The remainder of the Third Fleet, operating as Task Force 38, would first seek to cut communications between the Philippines and Japan by raids to the north; it would then take position off Leyte to furnish area support and general air cover to the invasion. Virtually the full striking and assault force of the Navy would thus be involved, for after the landings in Normandy the greater part of the Atlantic Fleet had been released to the Pacific.

While the expeditionary troops and invasion convoy were assembling at New Guinea bases and at Manus, Halsey and Mitscher set out on the first phase of the Third Fleet assignment. In the second week of October they struck at Okinawa, largest of the Ryukyu

---

[4] MacArthur's quick decision was doubtless influenced by information already in his possession. He had remained in contact with Filipino and American guerrillas in the Philippines, first by submarines, which had from time to time landed arms and supplies on isolated beaches, and later also by radio.

Islands. Here the carrier air squadrons damaged scores of cargo vessels, sinking many, and destroyed 82 Japanese planes against a loss of eight of their own. Then, after a fighter sweep against landing strips in northern Luzon, the fleet approached Formosa. Here American aircraft bombed warehouses, wharves, airfield installations, and coastal shipping and destroyed about 300 enemy planes. Here also the Japanese, beginning to recover from their initial shock, struck back. Large numbers of their aircraft carried out a series of determined counterattacks and succeeded in torpedoing the new United States cruisers *Canberra* and *Houston*. Both vessels were taken in tow, while American carrier squadrons struck repeatedly at bases on Luzon and Formosa to cover the retirement of the cripples. Japanese planes nevertheless continued their attacks by day and night and put another torpedo into the *Houston* before the two damaged cruisers reached Ulithi. For this moderate success the enemy paid a heavy price— more than a hundred additional planes destroyed, against an American loss of five.

The Japanese aviators, however, reported a great victory, and perhaps they really believed that in the confused night attacks they had done crippling damage to the carriers and their escorts. Encouraged by this comforting news, the Japanese high command broadcast by radio its intention to strike a knock-out blow at the American fleet and sent a respectable force out from the homeland to complete the supposed destruction. But enemy long-range search planes, probing out ahead, reported the Third Fleet not noticeably impaired, whereupon the Japanese surface units hastily withdrew. Halsey jubilantly reported to Nimitz that all the United States vessels which Tokyo had announced "sunk" had been quickly salvaged and that he was now "retiring at full speed towards the enemy." Then, leaving further neutralization of Formosa to army B-29 Superfortresses based in western China, he headed back to the seas east of Luzon and launched strikes against the northern and central Philippines in support of the Leyte landings.

Advance units of Kinkaid's augmented Seventh Fleet on October 17 put Rangers[5] ashore on the islands guarding the entrances to Leyte Gulf. The Ranger battalions quickly disposed of the few Japanese present and thus secured the flanks of the invasion forces. At the same time, minesweeping and underwater demolition activities

---

[5] Special assault troops usually assigned to dangerous missions. These were the American counterpart of the British Commandos.

were begun off the beachhead, while battleships, cruisers, destroyers, and escort carriers came in for a three-day bombardment of the coastal defenses.

On the morning of the 20th, after a final blasting of the landing areas by heavy guns, rocket fire, and aerial bombardment, the barrage was shifted inland and strongly escorted Seventh Fleet landing ships, coming in under the lee of a typhoon, put troops of the 10th and 24th Corps ashore at two points on the Leyte west coast. The landings were contested only by mortar fire, most of the enemy having already retired to defense positions in the hills. Early in the day the Japanese began a series of aerial counterattacks; but these, though increasing in intensity, never seriously threatened the invasion. A tug and an LCI were sunk and the light cruiser *Honolulu* was holed by an airborne torpedo. More ominous was the attack on the Australian cruiser *Australia*. This vessel was struck and heavily damaged by a Japanese suicide plane. Enemy aircraft had been deliberately flown into Allied vessels before, but in previous instances the planes were already on fire or beyond saving. The *Australia* was the first victim of a new *Kamikaze* Special Attack Corps, composed of pilots prepared to take their lives by crashing bomb-laden planes into their targets.[6] The *kamikazes* were to prove a growing menace, but a partial solution to this danger had already been found in the VT-fuzed antiaircraft shell.

A few hours after the first landings General MacArthur came ashore from the *Nashville*. He stepped up to a Signal Corps microphone and, in an emotional tone calculated to stir his Filipino listeners, broadcast by radio his speech of liberation. "People of the Philippines," he said, "I have returned. By the grace of Almighty God, our forces stand again on Philippine soil. . . . Rally to me. Let the indomitable spirit of Bataan and Corregidor lead on. As the lines of battle roll forward to bring you within the zone of operations, arise and strike! . . . For your homes and hearths, strike!"

THE BATTLE FOR LEYTE GULF

The timing of the American offensive caught the Japanese fleet

---

[6] *Kamikaze* means "divine wind." The term was first applied to a storm which in 1570 scattered a Mongol fleet en route to invade Japan. Though the idea of giving up one's life for emperor and country was an integral part of Bushido (Japanese code of chivalry), organized suicide air attacks were first carried out by naval pilots in the Philippines at the time of the American invasion. The effectiveness of the *kamikazes* is demonstrated by the fact that during the first three months of their use 121 crashed into their targets and 53 scored damaging near hits.

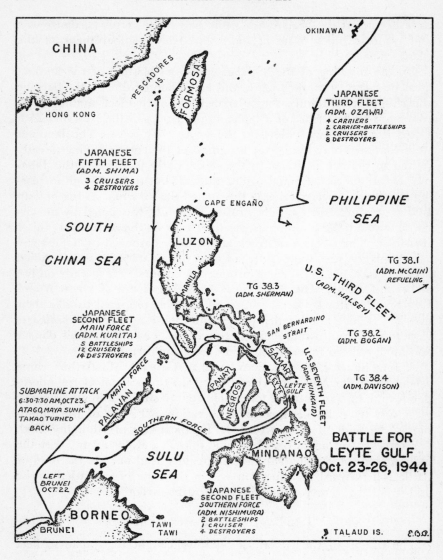

CHINA

OKINAWA

PESCADORES IS.

FORMOSA

HONG KONG

JAPANESE
THIRD FLEET
(ADM. OZAWA)
4 CARRIERS
2 CARRIER-BATTLESHIPS
2 CRUISERS
8 DESTROYERS

JAPANESE
FIFTH FLEET
(ADM. SHIMA)
3 CRUISERS
4 DESTROYERS

SOUTH

CHINA SEA

CAPE ENGAÑO

PHILIPPINE
SEA

LUZON

MANILA

TG 38.1
(ADM. McCAIN)
REFUELING

U.S. THIRD FLEET
(ADM. HALSEY)

TG 38.3
(ADM. SHERMAN)

JAPANESE
SECOND FLEET
MAIN FORCE
(ADM. KURITA)
5 BATTLESHIPS
12 CRUISERS
14 DESTROYERS

MINDORO

SAN BERNARDINO
STRAIT

TG 38.2
(ADM. BOGAN)

MAIN FORCE

SAMAR

U.S. SEVENTH FLEET
(ADM. KINKAID)

TG 38.4
(ADM. DAVISON)

SUBMARINE ATTACK
6:30-7:30 A.M, OCT 23.
ATAGO, MAYA SUNK.
TAKAO TURNED
BACK.

PALAWAN

PANAY

NEGROS

LEYTE

LEYTE
GULF

SOUTHERN FORCE

BATTLE FOR
LEYTE GULF
Oct. 23-26, 1944

LEFT
BRUNEI
OCT 22

SULU
SEA

MINDANAO

BORNEO

BRUNEI

TAWI
TAWI

JAPANESE
SECOND FLEET
SOUTHERN FORCE
(ADM. NISHIMURA)
2 BATTLESHIPS
1 CRUISER
4 DESTROYERS

TALAUD IS.

E.B.Q.

divided, with Admiral Kurita's Second Fleet, comprising most of the
heavy gunnery ships, in the Singapore area and Admiral Ozawa's
Third Fleet, including the four available carriers, in home waters. A
small Fifth Fleet, composed of cruisers and destroyers under command
of Admiral Shima, was in the Pescadores Islands, west of Formosa.

Early in October, when it appeared certain that United States forces were about to invade the Philippines, a plan was drawn up to unite these fleets in the East Indies and send them forth to stand off the expected assault; but there were delays. Most of Japan's carrier aircraft and practically all of her skilled naval pilots had been lost in the Battle of the Philippine Sea the preceding June. The planes had been replaced, but the training of pilots could not be rushed. A week or so more of instruction might weld the green recruits into something like a fighting team. Before the additional training was completed, however, Halsey had thrust his United States Third Fleet between Japan and the Indies and by destroying 300 navy and 200 army planes had cut down the supporting air forces based on China, Formosa, and Luzon to a dangerously low figure. Shortly afterwards came the invasion of Leyte.

The situation of the Japanese was desperate. It is useless to look for anything but the most superficial logic or foresight in their next moves. "We had to do something," as an officer of the Imperial Navy afterwards expressed it, "so we did our best. It was the last chance we had, although not a very good one." The fleet Commander-in-Chief, Admiral Toyoda, assuming overall tactical command, ordered the Japanese Second, Third, and Fifth Fleets to converge on Leyte Gulf. Ozawa's carriers, coming down from Japan, were assigned a double mission. Their aircraft pilots, for the most part untrained in deck landings, would strike at the American Third Fleet and then fly their planes to Luzon airfields. The carriers and their escorts would remain in the Philippine Sea as decoys to lure Halsey away to the north and possibly within range of Formosa-based aircraft. It was assumed that Ozawa's fleet, in accomplishing this task, would be destroyed. In the meantime, the Imperial Second and Fifth Fleets would penetrate the straits to the north and south of Leyte, break through Kinkaid's inshore support, and attack American transports inside the gulf.

Upon reaching Brunei on the northwest coast of Borneo, the Imperial Second Fleet split into a main attack force under the direct command of Kurita and a southern force under Vice Admiral Nishimura. The main force of five battleships, including the 73,000-ton[7]

[7] Full load displacement (standard displacement not available). These were the largest warships ever built. The largest battleships in the United States Navy, the *Iowa* class, have a full load displacement of 52,000 tons (standard displacement 45,000 tons). The main battery of the *Yamato* and *Musashi* consisted of nine 18.1-inch guns; the *Iowas* mount nine 16-inch guns. Design development of the

Yamato and *Musashi,* 12 cruisers, and 14 destroyers would proceed north of Palawan Island and through the Sibuyan Sea and San Bernardino Strait. The southern force, consisting of the over-age battleships *Yamashiro* and *Fuso,* the rebuilt heavy cruiser *Mogami,* and four destroyers, was to pass south of Palawan, cross the Sulu and Mindanao Seas, and penetrate to Leyte Gulf by way of Surigao Strait. Shima's Fifth Fleet, coming down from the Pescadores, was later ordered to join Nishimura's force in the Mindanao Sea.

Kurita's fleet quickly ran into trouble. At dawn on October 23, the main force was attacked off Palawan by the *Darter* and *Dace,* two of the numerous American submarines assigned to watch the approaches to the Philippines. The heavy cruisers *Atago* and *Maya* were sunk, and another heavy, the *Takao,* was so severely damaged that she was forced to return to Brunei. Halsey, apprised by this and other submarine contacts that enemy units were approaching from the west, redeployed his task groups. One, under Vice Admiral J. S. McCain, he sent east for refueling. Two others, under Rear Admirals G. F. Bogan and R. E. Davison, he stationed east of San Bernardino and Surigao Straits. The fourth, under Rear Admiral F. C. Sherman, he ordered to stand off Luzon, searching that area and the waters to the north. (See diagram, page 510.) In mid-morning of the 24th, planes from Davison's task group found Nishimura's southern force eastbound across the Sulu Sea and made bomb hits on the *Fuso* and one destroyer. At about the same time air squadrons from both Davison's and Bogan's groups discovered Kurita's main force off Mindoro Island advancing to enter the Sibuyan Sea and submitted it to a daylong series of air strikes. By dusk every battleship in this force had been hit by one or more bombs. The heavy cruiser *Myoko,* severely damaged, was limping away towards Singapore; a destroyer had been sunk; and the superbattleship *Musashi,* hit by 16 bombs and 19 torpedoes had capsized, carrying down 1,100 of her crew. Before dark Kurita reversed course and headed back west.

Sherman's carriers took no part in these attacks. Shortly after dawn on the 24th a Japanese search pilot, sighting this group, reported

---

Yamato and *Musashi* was begun in 1934 some time before Japan denounced the Washington Naval Treaty and a year before her withdrawal from the London Naval Conference. The *Yamato* was commissioned in December, 1941, and the *Musashi* was completed in August of the following year. A third unit of this class was converted during construction into a large aircraft carrier, the *Shinano.* Despite a highly complex underwater protection system, ships of the *Yamato* class proved vulnerable to torpedo attack.

back to headquarters that he had found the entire United States Third Fleet. Bombers promptly took off from landing fields all over Luzon and headed for a raid, in which they were soon joined by aircraft from Ozawa's carriers, now maneuvering east of Cape Engaño. The first of the enemy attack waves was luckily detected just as United States planes were about to be launched for a strike against Kurita's force. They took to the air instead to protect their own ships, forcing some of the attacking aircraft to turn away, and shooting down more than a hundred others. One Japanese pilot, however, bored through the American combat air patrol and anti-aircraft fire to plunge his bomb squarely amidships of the light carrier *Princeton*. The hit was in itself not serious but planes on the hangar deck caught fire and there followed a series of explosions which, blasting downwards, wrecked the firerooms and left the vessel dead in the water. As the fires spread, the order was given to abandon ship. The cruiser *Birmingham* and several lighter escorts approached to pump water into the flames, but the *Princeton*, rolling with the swell, lurched against and wrecked the superstructure of a destroyer. Shortly afterwards the carrier's magazines blew up. The *Birmingham*, close alongside, received the full force of the explosion, which killed more than 200 of her crew and injured nearly twice as many others.

Meanwhile, Ozawa's fleet to the north, bent on suicide, was doing its utmost to attract American attention—breaking radio silence on various frequencies, steaming back and forth, making smoke, and eventually sending the carrier-battleships *Ise* and *Hyuga* almost to within sight of Sherman's task group. At last in the late afternoon United States search planes spotted the enemy carriers and flashed back a warning, whereupon Mitscher ordered salvage operations on the *Princeton* abandoned and sent destroyers in to sink her.

Halsey now faced a problem similar in some respects to that which had confronted Spruance off Saipan. Not realizing that Ozawa's ships were intended as decoys, he conceived that they must by no means be allowed to approach the landing area. On the other hand, the Japanese surface forces to the west had to be taken into account. The approach of Shima's fleet had not been detected, but the progress and misfortunes of the Imperial Second Fleet were known. The small southern force did not present any great problem, for Kinkaid had battleships and cruisers to block its penetration through Surigao Strait. Kurita's main force was of a more respectable size, but it had been battered throughout the day and when last seen was headed back west. It was still powerful, however, and there was no certainty that it would not again reverse course and pass through San Bernardino Strait during the night, in which event it might find nothing more formidable than a few escort carriers and destroyers barring the way to Leyte Gulf. Halsey could, of course, have divided his strength and left some battleships and cruisers behind to help block the San Bernardino gateway. This alternative he rejected, believing that the destruction of the Japanese carrier fleet would require the full power he had at his disposal and that the Seventh Fleet forces off Leyte were ample to take care of any enemy threats which might develop in that area. He therefore ordered his task groups (less McCain's) to rendezvous at midnight and with his strength thus concentrated headed north towards the enemy carriers. Behind him in the Sibuyan Sea, Kurita had turned back east after dark and was at that moment threading his way through San Bernardino Strait.

Halsey's decision to run north has led to much discussion. His was certainly the bold choice, based upon a proper estimate of the enemy's confusion and weakness. He cannot, of course, be blamed for not realizing that Ozawa's fleet was a mere decoy; that was a fact not certainly known to the United States until after the victory. Less defensible, however, is the fact that he failed to notify Kinkaid of his departure. Had he done so, the limited Seventh Fleet strength might have been deployed to better advantage.

Battle of Surigao Strait. Oddly enough, though the Imperial Fifth Fleet and the southern force of the Second Fleet were both assigned to strike through Surigao Strait, they did not join forces or communicate in any way. One source has it that Nishimura deliberately refrained from co-operating to avoid coming under the command of the younger but senior Shima. The elder admiral also disregarded orders by speeding ahead to enter the strait hours before the time assigned. This permitted a night battle, which he preferred, but it rendered joint action with Kurita's main force impossible, even if the latter had not lost time by reversing course in the Sibuyan Sea. Nishimura's actions are an interesting indication of the low state of morale and discipline into which the Imperial Navy had fallen in the autumn of 1944.

As the two Japanese forces, 30 miles apart, headed for the southern end of Surigao Strait, a reception was being prepared for them. Rear Admiral Jesse B. Oldendorf, whose task group included the main striking power of the United States Seventh Fleet, considered the geographical factors and set his trap accordingly. In the late afternoon

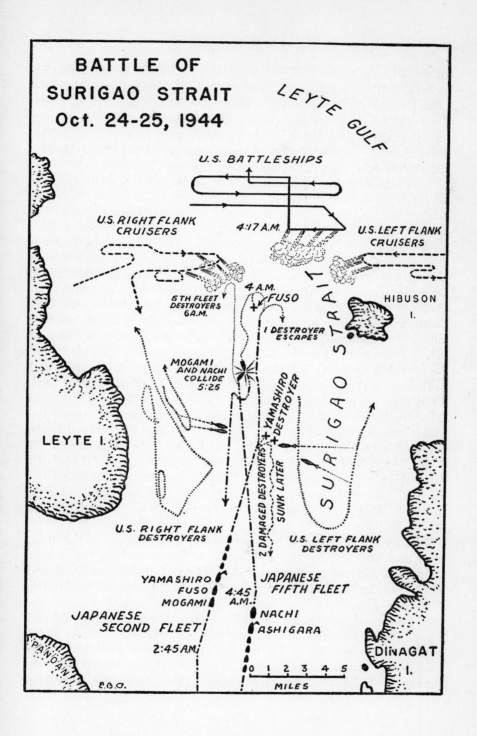

BATTLE OF
SURIGAO STRAIT
Oct. 24-25, 1944

LEYTE GULF

U.S. BATTLESHIPS

U.S. RIGHT FLANK
CRUISERS

4:17 A.M.

U.S. LEFT FLANK
CRUISERS

5 TH FLEET
DESTROYERS
6 A.M.

4 A.M.
FUSO

HIBUSON
I.

I DESTROYER
ESCAPES

MOGAMI
AND NACHI
COLLIDE
5:25

YAMASHIRO
DESTROYER

SURIGAO STRAIT

LEYTE I.

2 DAMAGED DESTROYERS
SUNK LATER

U.S. RIGHT FLANK
DESTROYERS

U.S. LEFT FLANK
DESTROYERS

YAMASHIRO
FUSO
MOGAMI

4:45
A.M.

JAPANESE
FIFTH FLEET

JAPANESE
SECOND FLEET

2:45 A.M.

NACHI
ASHIGARA

DINAGAT
I.

PANAON I.

E.B.J.

0 1 2 3 4 5

MILES

of October 24 he sent 30 PT boats down through the strait to take positions off the southern entrance. Within the strait he disposed two squadrons of destroyers, one on each side. At the northern or Leyte Gulf end he stationed his cruisers, five on the left (east) flank and three on the right. North of these, cruising on an east-west course, were six old battleships, five of them veterans of the Pearl Harbor attack but now modernized and more efficient than before.

Towards midnight Nishimura's force, in the lead, ran into the nest of PT boats outside the strait. There followed a brief battle in which one of the American boats was sunk, while the Japanese ships got away undamaged. At 3 A.M. they reached a position between the two waiting squadrons of American destroyers. The Japanese opened fire but without effect, for the nearby shore line prevented their getting dependable radar ranges. The United States vessels, their radar operating excellently, at once launched torpedoes from east and west. Brilliant flashes lit up the strait as the missiles hit their targets. The flagship *Yamashiro's* magazine exploded and she broke apart, her bow and stern sinking separately. One Japanese destroyer went down at once; two others, severely damaged, dropped out of line and were later sunk by gunfire. The fourth destroyer soon reversed course and withdrew to the south, her steering gear put out of order by a shell. Only the *Fuso* and *Mogami* continued to the north, firing to right and left. In this phase the Japanese cruiser hit and severely battered the American destroyer *Albert W. Grant*. This was the only damage received by a United States major vessel during the engagement. At four o'clock the *Fuso* and *Mogami* came within range of Oldendorf's battleships and cruisers and were subjected to furious shelling from three directions. The *Fuso* took numerous hits and began to sink, while the *Mogami,* on fire and almost out of control, limped away to the south.

Meanwhile, Shima's Fifth Fleet, entering the south end of the strait, was also attacked by the PT boats, which torpedoed the cruiser *Abukuma* and put her out of action. The rest of the fleet continued north, only to encounter the burning and sinking ships of Nishimura's force—evidence of an overwhelming Japanese defeat. Shima now sent his four destroyers on ahead for a torpedo attack, while the two remaining cruisers turned and launched torpedoes at a vague radar contact to the northeast. On the turn the Japanese Fifth Fleet flag-ship *Nachi* rammed the disabled *Mogami* and was herself seriously damaged. Shima had now had enough. He recalled his destroyers and his fleet retired to the south. The *Mogami* and *Abukuma* both eventually reached the Mindanao Sea, there to be finished off by American planes. Of Nishimura's force, only one battered destroyer was left.[8]

Battle off Samar. With the departure of Halsey's Third Fleet to the north, no American force was left specifically assigned to guard the exit from San Bernardino Strait. At dawn on October 25 Oldendorf's surface ships were at the southern end of Surigao Strait finishing off Nishimura's crippled destroyers. Off the landing area, furnishing air support to the troops ashore, were three Seventh Fleet task units built around escort carriers. The northernmost unit of six escort carriers, three destroyers, and four destroyer escorts, under command of Rear Admiral C. A. F. Sprague, was east of Samar. Southeast of Sprague's formation was the central unit, of similar composition, under Rear Admiral F. B. Stump. These were the only ships between San Bernardino Strait and Leyte Gulf.

Admiral Kurita's Second Fleet main force, now comprising four battleships, eight cruisers, and 11 destroyers, had passed through San Bernardino Strait during the evening of the 24th and at midnight, six hours behind schedule, had reached the Pacific end. During the early hours of the 25th it moved down the east coast of Samar until 6:45 A.M., when it made contact with Sprague's task unit at a distance of 17 miles and, opening fire, at once gave chase. While the American task unit, which had been on a northerly course, ran east into the

---

[8] A question naturally arises as to why Shima's Fifth Fleet should have crossed the track of the Japanese Second Fleet main force and proceeded south to attack through Surigao Strait. A more reasonable and fuel-conserving arrangement would have provided for sending Nishimura's force from Brunei in greater strength and adding Shima's vessels to Kurita's main force in the Sibuyan Sea. The answer is, of course, that the whole Philippine defense plan as carried out by the Japanese was impromptu and makeshift, with commanding officers having little knowledge of what was going on outside their immediate areas. Shima originally had been ordered merely to "co-operate" with Kurita. The decision to send him to Surigao Strait appears to have been made by the local naval command at Manila. Admiral Toyoda, Commander-in-Chief of the Imperial Fleet, first learned of the participation of his Fifth Fleet in the Leyte Gulf battle from American officers. This was in November, 1945. Upon being informed, he replied, "No, I still believe that the Fifth Fleet was not in those inland waters."

The PT boats stationed at the south end of Surigao Strait were the first United States units to note that two separate enemy forces were approaching the scene of action. Since, however, they did not get the information to Admiral Oldendorf until some time later, American vessels inside the strait concentrated upon Nishimura's force and were not even aware of the later arrival of Shima's fleet.

The account of Imperial Fifth Fleet movements given here is based chiefly upon the testimonies of Commander Mori, torpedo officer aboard Shima's flagship; and of Commander Nishino, commanding officer of one of Nishimura's destroyers. It is corroborated by other Japanese sources.

US THIRD
FLEET 200
MILES TO
NORTH

SECOND FLEET
ATTACKED BY
PLANES FROM
TG 38.1

**BATTLE
OFF
SAMAR**
OCTOBER 25, 1944

SAN BERNARDINO STRAIT

LUZON

IMPERIAL SECOND FLEET
(ADM KURITA)

TG 38.1
(ADM McCAIN)

SAMAR

JAPANESE
DESTROYERS
BATTLESHIPS
CRUISERS

6:45 A.M.
CONTACT

GAMBIER BAY
SINKS 8 A.M.

ST. LO SINKS
10:50 A.M.

8 A.M.

LEYTE

LEYTE
GULF

TU 77.4.3
(ADM C.A.F. SPRAGUE)

TU 77.4.2
(ADM STUMP)

SURIGAO STRAIT

DINAGAT I.

7:59 A.M.- SUWANEE
HIT BY SUICIDE
PLANE.

7:53 A.M.- SANTEE TORPEDOED
BY SUBMARINE.

BOHOL

TG 77.2
(ADM.
OLDENDORF)

7:40 A.M.- SANTEE HIT BY
SUICIDE PLANE.

TU 77.4.1
(ADM T.L. SPRAGUE)

MINDANAO

C.B.G.

wind, laying a smoke screen and launching planes, Sprague reported
his situation by radio in plain language. He urged that assistance be
rushed without delay, for nothing short of heavy reinforcements, he
believed, could save his ships from annihilation. But little help could
be sent at once. The Third Fleet was far to the north; Oldendorf's
surface force, even if it had not been practically out of fuel and ammunition, would be unable to reach the area before afternoon; the
southernmost escort carrier unit was off the northern tip of Mindanao
and was itself under aerial and submarine attack. Only Stump's
carriers were near enough to lend immediate air support.

When the greater part of his planes had taken to the air, Admiral Sprague turned south under cover of a rain squall and then gradually worked around to the southwest until he was headed for Leyte Gulf. The Japanese fleet, meanwhile, had split into three divisions, the fast cruisers speeding ahead of the main body and passing across the rear of the American formation before turning to starboard to resume the chase on the windward side. This failure of the enemy to cut across the angle gave the Americans a brief respite but it presented the Japanese with a greater advantage, for with the cruisers to the east of them, the carriers could no longer turn into the wind to carry out air operations. Sprague had no recourse but to order his planes already in the air to proceed to the unfinished landing field on Leyte and to launch others by catapult.

While the Japanese cruisers pressed ever closer on the port quarter of the United States formation, Kurita's heavy units took up a stern chase and his destroyers swung in to the west of the carrier unit. The American vessels thus found themselves menaced from three directions and in danger of being boxed in. That this did not occur is due chiefly to the effective work of Sprague's escort vessels. Beginning with a lone sortie by the destroyer *Johnston* at the time of the first contact, they made a series of courageous attacks on the pursuing ships, putting a torpedo into the cruiser *Kumano,* making shell hits on other vessels, and once forcing the enemy to turn away briefly. In these hazardous operations the *Johnston, Samuel B. Roberts,* and *Hoel* were sunk, and all but two of the remaining American destroyers and destroyer escorts were severely damaged. By eight o'clock the enemy divisions, having closed to within 20,000 yards, struck several of the American carriers with shells. The *Gambier Bay,* hit below the water line, one engine put out of commission, fell behind, whereupon two or three of the Japanese cruisers closed in and sank her at point-blank range.

Admiral Stump, whose task unit was just over the horizon to the east, decided against joining in the surface action, but planes from his carriers had for some time been coming over the enemy fleet, causing damage which, together with the destroyer sorties, had the effect of slowing down the pursuit. Other aircraft now began to arrive. Bombers from Sprague's own unit, after refueling and reloading on Leyte, were returning to the attack. More bombers came up from the southern unit off Mindanao. Under this concentration of air power the Japanese cruisers fired salvos of torpedoes, none of which reached the American disposition. Then the whole enemy fleet withdrew to the northwest.

Sprague's task unit was not further harassed by surface ships, but presently dive bombers from Luzon airfields appeared and made scattered attacks. A suicide plane struck the carrier *Kitkun Bay* without causing serious damage. Five minutes later another Japanese plane dropped a bomb on the carrier *Saint Lô* and then crashed in flames on her port beam. The bomb penetrated the flight deck and set off a series of explosions among the aircraft in the hangar, the blasts ripping back the upper deck and shooting flames and debris high into the air. The crew abandoned ship none too soon, for the carrier quickly rolled over and sank. Sprague left his remaining escort ships behind to pick up survivors and proceeded south with his carriers. "We had been through so much by then," he said afterwards, "that it didn't seem to matter whether we had escorts with us or not."[9]

Meanwhile, Admiral Kurita had reached a decision. He had withdrawn his Second Fleet from action because the American destroyer and aerial attacks had scattered his forces. At that time he had planned merely to close his formation and head again for Leyte Gulf. But a survey of his situation revealed its seriousness. The heavy cruiser *Suzuya,* struck near the bridge by a bomb, had caught fire; then her torpedoes blew up and she began to sink. Two other heavies, the *Chokai* and *Chikuma,* also struck by bombs, were unmaneuverable and helpless. There were other considerations. The Japanese vessels were running short of fuel; radio interception had given the impression that more American aircraft would soon arrive; no word had been received from the Imperial Second or Fifth Fleet forces in Surigao Strait. In these circumstances, Kurita felt that an assault upon American shipping in Leyte Gulf would be at best a hazardous operation and might well prove disastrous. But something might be accomplished, he decided, if he were to lend some protection to Ozawa's carriers by seeking out and attacking the American Third Fleet. He therefore ordered his destroyers to sink the *Chokai* and *Chikuma* and headed north in search of Halsey.

Admiral McCain, having intercepted Sprague's call for help, had left the fueling area and was now racing his task group back towards Samar. Planes from his big carriers found Kurita's Second Fleet at extreme range and slowed it down with a succession of attacks.

---

[9] Quoted in Gilbert Cant, *The Great Pacific Victory,* p. 307.

Though the American aircraft caused no disabling damage, they made hits and near hits which perforated the hulls of all the larger Japanese vessels so that they began to trail oil. Towards night Kurita abandoned his run to the north and retired through San Bernardino Strait.

Battle off Cape Engaño. Halsey and Mitscher, with the three task groups under Bogan, Davison, and Sherman, continued north through the early morning hours of October 25. At 2 A.M. a scout plane quartering the seas 85 miles ahead made radar contact with the enemy carrier fleet on a southeast course. Mitscher thereupon ordered aircraft readied for a strike, and as dawn was breaking search planes followed by attack groups took off from the American carriers. The Japanese fleet had turned away at the time of the first contact and was now headed northeast, on which course it was found by scouts from the *Essex.* Included were the large carrier *Zuikaku;* the light carriers *Chitose, Chiyoda,* and *Zuiho;* the carrier-battleships *Ise* and *Hyuga;* the light cruisers *Tama* and *Oyodo;* and eight destroyers.[10] To oppose this force Halsey had five large carriers, five light carriers, six fast battleships, eight cruisers, and 41 destroyers.

The *Essex* search planes, climbing steadily to elude expected fighter interception, remained nearly an hour over the enemy vessels, reporting their position and composition. Just before nine o'clock Mitscher's attack groups arrived. Most of the dozen Japanese fighter planes which came out to meet them were quickly shot down by Hellcats, and the American bombers and torpedo aircraft came in for a strike. The enemy ships put up a heavy curtain of fire but it was at once apparent that they were almost stripped of air cover. The attacking planes quickly sank a destroyer, made bomb hits on the *Chitose* and *Chiyoda,* and put a torpedo into the *Zuikaku.* The Japanese formation nevertheless continued to the north, albeit somewhat reduced in speed. A second and more severe American raid, an hour after the first, left all four Japanese carriers unnavigable and heavily damaged, so that in the early afternoon a third attack wave was able to put the finishing touches on three of them. The *Zuikaku,* hit repeatedly by 1,000- and 2,000-pound bombs, went down almost at once, to be followed within a brief period by two of the light carriers.

The remaining carrier, the *Chitose* or *Chiyoda,* lay dead in the water and listing. Most of the surviving Japanese vessels pushed on to the north, where they successfully evaded two final strikes by

---

[10] From testimony of Captain Ohmae, Chief of Staff to Vice Admiral Ozawa. American scout pilots reported more cruisers and fewer destroyers.

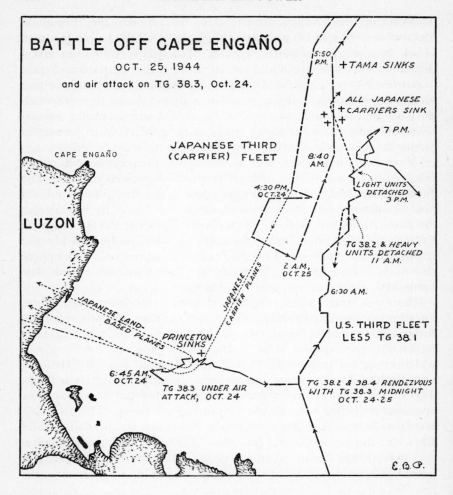

BATTLE OFF CAPE ENGAÑO
OCT. 25, 1944
and air attack on TG 38.3, Oct. 24.

5:50 P.M. +TAMA SINKS

ALL JAPANESE +CARRIERS SINK

7 P.M.

CAPE ENGAÑO

JAPANESE THIRD (CARRIER) FLEET

8:40 A.M.

4:30 P.M. OCT. 24

LIGHT UNITS DETACHED 3 P.M.

LUZON

TG 38.2 & HEAVY UNITS DETACHED 11 A.M.

2 A.M., OCT. 25

6:30 A.M.

JAPANESE CARRIER PLANES

JAPANESE LAND-BASED PLANES

PRINCETON SINKS

U.S. THIRD FLEET LESS TG 38.1

6:45 A.M. OCT. 24

TG 38.3 UNDER AIR ATTACK, OCT. 24

TG 38.2 & 38.4 RENDEZVOUS WITH TG 38.3 MIDNIGHT OCT. 24-25

E.B.Q.

United States aircraft, but the *Tama* and a pair of destroyers remained behind with the stricken vessel. Here was an opportunity for the American fleet to supplement its air strikes with surface action, but for this purpose only cruisers and destroyers were now available. Several hours earlier, when the call for help had come from Sprague off San Bernardino Strait, Bogan's task group, together with all the battleships, several cruisers, and a number of destroyers, had been detached and sent south. Such remaining escort units as could be spared from the screen, however, formed into a task group and sped north to finish off the cripple. Shortly after four o'clock they found the helpless carrier, now unattended, and fired shells at her until she sank. They then set out in pursuit of the cruiser and the two destroyers, which aircraft had spotted in the vicinity picking up survivors. The destroyers escaped, but the *Tama*, choosing to put up a fight, became the target not only of the task group but also of the American submarine *Jallao*, which was patrolling in the area. Heavy surface bombardment set the Japanese cruiser afire and torpedoes from the submarine caused her to explode and sink.

Meanwhile, Bogan's carriers and the battleship-cruiser force under Vice Admiral W. A. Lee had proceeded south, arriving off Samar several hours too late to be of assistance to Sprague's task unit, for the Japanese Second Fleet had already proceeded back through San Bernardino Strait. Gunners in the heavy ships, however, had the satisfaction of finishing off a crippled enemy vessel, evidently one of the disabled cruisers, which Kurita's destroyers had not succeeded in sinking. The next day, planes from Bogan's carriers joined those from McCain's group in a series of strikes on the Imperial Second Fleet as it retreated back across the Sibuyan and South China Seas. In these raids, and in other attacks carried out at the same time, United States aircraft succeeded in sinking the light cruisers *Noshiro* and *Kinu* and four destroyers.

In the Battle for Leyte Gulf American losses in combat ships were one light and two escort carriers, two destroyers, and a destroyer escort. Japanese losses were incomparably greater: three battleships, four carriers, ten cruisers, and nine destroyers. In all history no such weight of shipping had been sunk in so brief a period. Japan in three days had lost over 50 per cent more combat tonnage than was lost by the British and Germans together in the Battle of Jutland. It was a blow from which her Navy could not recover.

ADVANCE TO MANILA

The United States Third Fleet, its mission completed, now withdrew in order to co-operate with B-29 Superfortresses from the Marianas in an air raid on Tokyo. It was intended that General Kenney's planes should take over the responsibility of providing cover for the Leyte beachhead, but it soon became apparent that there were neither sufficient army aircraft nor sufficient landing strips for the purpose. Accordingly, the Tokyo raid was canceled and the Third Fleet returned to the Philippines, Admiral McCain replacing Admiral Mitscher in command of Task Force 38[11] During the month of November, Third Fleet planes, striking repeatedly at Luzon airfields and at enemy shipping, ran up an impressive score. They sank the heavy cruisers *Nachi* and *Kumano,* the light cruiser *Kiso,* eight destroyers, nine transports, eleven freighters, two tankers, and half a dozen small craft; damaged more than a hundred other ships; and destroyed nearly 700 enemy aircraft against a loss of 97 of their own.

Meanwhile, the land forces were being delayed in their conquest of Leyte by the monsoon rains and by Japanese reinforcements which continued to pour into the island. Early in December, after Halsey's carriers had withdrawn, a squadron of Seventh Fleet destroyers swept down through Surigao Strait and around to the western side of Leyte for a night attack on enemy shipping in Ormoc Bay. The result was a draw—one enemy destroyer sunk by shellfire and one American destroyer, the *Cooper,* sunk by a mine or an aerial torpedo. Four nights later a larger Seventh Fleet force, totaling about 80 ships, arrived in the same area and, after heavy bombardment and rocket fire directed against the beach, put ashore army assault troops. This operation and the subsequent protection of the beachhead cost the Navy two destroyers, the *Mahan* and *Reid,* and the destroyer transport *Ward,* all lost in enemy suicide air attacks; but it helped cut the Japanese overwater supply line and permitted an enveloping movement against hostile forces ashore. Before the end of the year Leyte was declared secure. Casualties were amazingly disproportionate— 74,261 Japanese killed to 3,135 Americans.

It had long been apparent that air strips must be obtained on one of the western islands of the Philippine archipelago, for the heavy rains on Leyte rendered that island useless as a base for neutralizing attacks against northern airfields. In mid-December, therefore, landings were made on Mindoro Island 300 miles northwest of Leyte. There was no opposition from the shore, but enemy planes from Luzon attacked and did some damage to the American invasion convoy during the approach, and three LST's were later sunk off the beachhead. The Japanese made one attempt to strike at the landing area with surface ships, but army aircraft and PT boats attacked and scattered the enemy force, sinking one destroyer.

Preceding and during the Mindoro invasion the Third Fleet again

[11] It should be clear that in such operations Task Force 38 and the Third Fleet were practically identical. The Commander Third Fleet, Halsey, held the over-all and tactical command. McCain was in command of air operations.

stood to eastward of the Philippines and sent in air attack squadrons over the Manila area. Large numbers of Japanese auxiliary vessels and small craft were sunk or damaged and more than 250 enemy planes were destroyed. Two days after the troops were put ashore, however, these supporting operations were cut short by a typhoon. The center of the storm, moving on an erratic course, missed the Third Fleet main body but sank the destroyers *Hull, Spence,* and *Monaghan* and damaged numerous other ships.

General MacArthur had already ordered General Krueger to proceed with the invasion of Luzon. This the Japanese expected, but they were taken by surprise[12] when Krueger by-passed the obvious landing point south of Manila and proceeded 300 miles north of Mindoro to Lingayan Gulf. For this operation Admiral Kinkaid, again augmenting his Seventh Fleet with many Third Fleet units, built up a formidable attack force of more than 850 ships. Krueger's Sixth Army Troops would be put ashore by amphibious groups under Vice Admirals Wilkinson and Barbey; Rear Admiral Conolly would command the reinforcement group; bombardment ships would be under Vice Admiral Oldendorf; surface cover would be provided by vessels under Rear Admiral R. S. Berkey; and inshore air support would be furnished by escort carrier units under Rear Admiral C. T. Durgin.

No large-scale surface opposition came out against the invasion forces, but persistent enemy air attacks including numerous *kamikaze* suicide planes struck at the Seventh Fleet en route to the beachheads and during supporting operations. The escort carrier *Ommaney Bay* and three minesweepers were sunk, and topside damage involving numerous casualties was done to the battleships *New Mexico, California,* and *Mississippi,* the light cruiser *Columbia,* and to smaller craft. Inside Lingayan Gulf power boats loaded with explosives came out on suicide missions and caused some damage among the slower transports and cargo ships. Less successful were individual Japanese who attempted to swim out to the American vessels with explosive charges strapped to their bodies. The fact that such desperate measures were being resorted to was in itself a cheering indication of the foe's extremity. After a thunderous and extended bombardment, landings were made on January 9, 1945, against only light resistance. In the next few days more than 200,000 troops of the 1st and 14th Army Corps were put ashore.

[12] Testimony of Vice Admiral Fukudome, then Commander Second Air Fleet with headquarters at Manila.

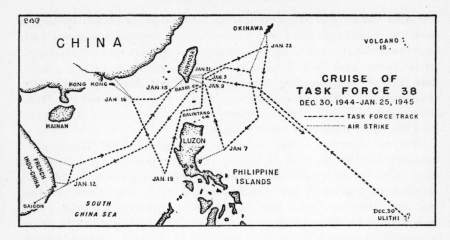

CRUISE OF
TASK FORCE 38
DEC. 30, 1944-JAN. 25, 1945

-------- TASK FORCE TRACK
.... AIR STRIKE

Meanwhile, to neutralize surrounding enemy bases and lend distant support to the Luzon invasion, Halsey and McCain with Task Force 38, its ships now repaired from their pounding by the typhoon, had set out on a record-breaking cruise.[13] Departing from Ulithi at the end of December, the force arrived north of the Philippines on January 3, attacked airfields and shipping at Formosa, Luzon, and Okinawa during the next six days, and then at Kinkaid's request made a daring sortie into the South China Sea west of the Philippines. The tanker group transited Balintang Channel north of Luzon but the main body made the passage by way of Bashi Channel just south of Formosa. "Almost unbelievably," wrote Halsey in his official report, "the force was not attacked or snooped." In 11 days it traversed 3,800 miles in this inner sea, so long denied to any but Japanese ships. No surface forces attempted to contest its movements and no enemy planes were able to approach its carriers within 20 miles. McCain sent air strikes against the coast of Indo-China on January 12, completely destroying one 17-ship convoy, including the cruiser *Kashii;* breaking up two others with heavy losses; and hitting docks, air facilities, and oil storage tanks. On the 15th and 16th, carrier squadrons did similar damage on the inner coast of Formosa and on the south China coast in the vicinity of Hong Kong. On the 21st, Task Force 38 was again in the Pacific, pounding the outer Formosa coastline. This time Japanese planes came over the carriers and made determined attacks.

[13] There were two Marine fighter squadrons aboard the *Essex*. This was the first use of Marine fighter pilots in Task Force 38.

The light carrier *Langley* was hit by a 100-pound bomb which caused moderate damage, but the vessel was able to continue operations. In the same raids the large carrier *Ticonderoga* was hit by two Japanese suicide planes and the destroyer *Maddox* was struck by another. Both ships were temporarily put out of action. After a final repeat strike at Okinawa on the 22nd, the force returned to Ulithi, having sunk or beached 114 large enemy ships with an estimated displacement of 300,000 tons and having destroyed more than 600 Japanese planes.

General Krueger's troops, in the meantime, had moved steadily down the central Luzon plain towards Manila. At the end of January, to prevent the Japanese from withdrawing into Bataan Peninsula, troops were put ashore without opposition northwest of Subic Bay, and two days later elements of the 11th Airborne Division were landed south of Manila Bay. On February 4, American troops entered the northern section of Manila, but three weeks of house-to-house fighting ensued before the enemy was cleared out. By then the southern half of the city was in ruins. Meanwhile, a combined paratroop and amphibious operation had been launched against the island fortress of Corregidor, which was taken in mid-February. The Japanese had lost control of the Philippines, but campaigns to subdue surviving forces were to continue to the end of the war and beyond.

American seizure of the Philippine Islands, by cutting off the East Indies fuel supply from the enemy war machine, made the defeat of Japan inevitable. The campaign, moreover, had reduced her fleet to decidedly fourth rate in terms of air or sea power. The following table, comparing numbers of United States and Japanese major fleet units available at the beginning of the war, during the war, and at the time of the fall of Manila, graphically portrays the situation:

TYPES	IN COMMISSION DEC. 7, 1941		TOTAL IN COMMISSION DURING WAR		IN COMMISSION OR AVAILABLE MAR. 1, 1945	
	U.S.	Japan	U.S.	Japan	U.S.	Japan
Battleships	17	10	23	12	23	5
Carriers	7	9	33	20	27	5
Escort Carriers ..	1	0	77	5	72	1
Cruisers	39	39	86	43	75	8
Destroyers	171	113	514*	177	455*	37
Submarines	111	63	312	193	264	41
TOTALS	346	234	1045	450	916	97

*Includes destroyers converted into other types during war. Does not include 414 destroyer escorts.

Submarine Operations

To American submarines, now using improved torpedoes, is due a large part of the credit for bringing Japan to the verge of defeat. Before the seizure of the Philippines the underwater craft in co-ordinated group attacks had so cut down the enemy merchant fleet that supplies from the East Indies were already reduced to a trickle. In 1944 alone they sank 492 large cargo vessels totaling more than 2,000,000 tons. In the same year they sank one-third of all the major enemy combat ships destroyed—one battleship, seven carriers, nine cruisers, 29 destroyers, and six submarines. The most spectacular submarine victories of the year were those of the *Sealion* (II) and the *Archerfish*. In the latter part of November the *Sealion,* in a daring attack on a Japanese force off Foochow, China, slipped in and sank the 29,330-ton battleship *Kongo*. A week later the *Archerfish*, patrolling the waters southwest of Honshu, with four expertly-placed torpedoes sank the world's largest carrier, the *Shinano,* recently launched and en route at the time to a safe port for fitting out.

30

Atlantic and Mediterranean

A PRIMARY CAUSE for Germany's defeat in the second World War, as in the first, was her neglect of her fleet. Such factors as her short and easily-blockaded coastline, the loss of her navy in 1918, and the subsequent restrictions imposed upon her warship construction, all served to place the nation at a disadvantage on the seas and to turn her attention towards the continent. Hitler wanted no naval warfare and believed he could avoid it. Convinced in pre-war days that England and the United States would not fight, he strained the German economy to make his army and air force the most powerful in the world, but gave scant attention to his fleet, rejecting the pleas of his naval officers for more ships, for better research facilities, and for aircraft and pilots specifically trained to operate with sea forces. His failure to provide a fleet air arm he afterwards conceded to have been a "historic mistake." Equally serious was his neglect of his primary sea weapon, the U-boat. Germany entered the war with only 64 submarines. That her navy nevertheless was at times able to imperil Allied communications may be attributed rather to the skill of her U-boat commanders and the belated but rapid building program of her shipyards than to any foresight on the part of Hitler's government.

Germany's conquests in 1940 secured for her the west coast of Europe from North Cape to the Pyrenees. The type of blockade which had stifled her in World War I could not again be applied; there was no longer any possibility of sealing her submarines and surface units in the North Sea by means of minefields; her fleet had ample harbors from which to operate. Despite these advantages, Germany was never quite able to cut British or American overseas troop and supply lines. Her lack of sea power, moreover, as German Naval Commander-in-Chief Grand Admiral Karl Doenitz later pointed out, resulted in four costly failures at crucial stages of the war. These were the failure to invade England, the failure to gain control of the Mediterranean, the failure to prevent the Allied invasion of North Africa, and the failure to stop the Allied invasion of Normandy.

In the summer of 1940, England, her army ejected from the European continent, was vulnerable and without allies. Hitler ordered preparations for invasion of the British Isles to be completed by mid-August, but Germany's land forces could not be trained in amphibious warfare by the assigned date, the *Luftwaffe* could never quite obtain air supremacy over the area of operations, and the German Navy lacked small craft to put troops ashore and fighting ships in numbers sufficient to screen the invasion from the British fleet. The attempt, therefore, was twice postponed. By spring of the following year, plans were under way for an attack on Russia and the proposed assault on England had to be abandoned. Thus, with the preservation of the United Kingdom, the Allied powers were left with an area for bases and airfields on the edge of the enemy homeland, a situation which was obtained in the Pacific only after three and a half years of fighting at sea.

In the Mediterranean, despite the strategic location of Italy, the Axis navies were not able to gain control. They never succeeded in cutting Britain's supply lines or in preventing interference with their own communications to North Africa. Malta remained in British hands throughout the war; Rommel's Afrika Korps was held west of Suez; and in November, 1942, Allied surface forces could not only put troops ashore on the Atlantic coast of Morocco but boldly steam through the Straits and seize points in Algeria. Allied preponderance of sea power then permitted the United States and Great Britain to place armies in Italy and later in France, whence they hammered their way into Germany from the west in co-ordination with Russia's drive from the east. German Fleet Commander-in-Chief Hermann Boehm in a post-war essay summed up the opinion of his colleagues. "The German Navy," he wrote, "knew quite well that a world war is in essence a sea war, and that no matter what great battles might occur on land, sea power is the deciding factor. Whether German statesmen and war leaders were equally clear about this I somewhat doubt. My view is rather, to quote Tirpitz, that 'They did not understand the sea.'"

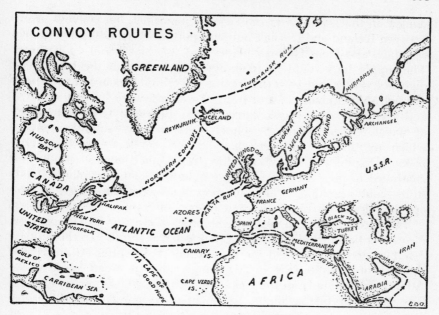

THE BATTLE OF THE ATLANTIC

The United States, upon entering the war, was faced in the Atlantic with the dual problem of maintaining transport lines to Europe and of keeping open the coastal shipping lanes through which passed cargo vessels supplying the industrial East with products of South and Central America and the Gulf states. The Atlantic fleet was already committed to trans-oceanic convoy duty, escorting ships as far as Iceland and protecting them in the run around the Cape of Good Hope to the Red Sea, whither they carried munitions and supplies to Britain's hard-pressed forces in North Africa. It was now necessary to extend the Iceland line to the United Kingdom. American and British sea and air forces combined in keeping losses on this route to a minimum. A United States naval base was established at Londonderry in Northern Ireland, thereby completing the North Atlantic chain, which already included the new bases on Newfoundland and Iceland. Along this sea lane large numbers of troops and vast quantities of equipment were soon moving in comparative security.

Getting Lend-Lease material to the Soviet Union was a far more difficult problem. Now that the Royal Air Force had spread an air cover over the approaches to England, almost the sole remaining danger on that route was from enemy submarines, but convoys plying between Iceland and Russia's northern port of Murmansk were subject to attack also from German planes and warships based on Norway. The supply lines could be maintained fairly well in the long arctic nights of winter, but with the coming of spring losses began to mount. Though ships moving to and from Murmansk were strongly escorted and even the cargo vessels carried extra guns and large contingents of naval Armed Guard personnel to man them, summer convoys which got through with less than 30 per cent loss were considered lucky. Despite the heavy casualties, the United States and Britain continued to pour into Russia large quantities of tanks, planes, food-stuffs, and munitions. The situation was eventually eased by the opening of a southern supply route by way of Iran.

To protect American coastwise shipping there was set up a system of sea frontiers including army as well as naval forces. To the Eastern Sea Frontier, commanded by Vice Admiral Adolphus Andrews, fell the task of guarding the earliest danger area, a broad band of the Atlantic stretching from the Canadian border to Jacksonville, Florida. The means at first available for such an assignment were meager, consisting only of about 30 small craft—sub-chasers, Coast Guard cutters, converted yachts, and Eagle boats—and four blimps. This small force understandably had little effect upon U-boat activities.

It required several weeks for Doenitz to prepare his special long-range submarines and get them into American waters, for the Japanese attack on Pearl Harbor was as much a surprise to Germany as it was to the United States, but before the end of January, 1944, they began to strike. American coastal ships were soon being sunk at the rate of one or more a day, sometimes in full view of the shore. Beaches from Maine to Florida became littered with wreckage and coated with fuel oil from torpedoed tankers and merchantmen. Harbors were often blocked by submarine-laid mines.

In time, naval aircraft became available for coastal defense, the Army's First Bomber Command was added to the sea frontier system, and civilians volunteered for scouting duty with privately owned planes. By such means enough U-boats were located and sunk to discourage further daylight attacks in American waters. At night, however, the submarines raised their periscopes or surfaced to strike at ships silhouetted against the glow of lights on shore. The entire seaboard was now blacked out, and merchant ships were ordered wherever possible to lie in harbors and bays by night, making their

Official U. S. Navy photographs

Top, AVENGER TORPEDO PLANES IN CLOSE ECHELON FORMATION. *Bottom*, U-BOAT FATALLY INJURED BY BOMBS DROPPED BY U.S. NAVY PLANES FROM ESCORT CARRIER.

runs up and down the coast only between sunrise and sunset. Such leapfrog passages were possible from Chesapeake Bay north, but to the south there were few havens into which deep sea vessels could retire. Accordingly, the U-boats concentrated around Cape Hatteras and the sinkings continued. This situation, anticipated by the Navy, was countered to some extent by a system of artificial retreats. Ship pens of mines and submarine nets were constructed at intervals of 125 miles from Virginia to Florida.

But it was evident that such makeshift means were insufficient. Fortunately, antisubmarine craft begun before the war were rapidly being completed and put into service. Other vessels were taken off the transatlantic convoys, and the British and Canadian Navies loaned additional craft. By May, 1942, Admiral Andrews was able to supply convoy escorts for the Eastern Sea Frontier and sinkings in those waters dropped sharply. The German submarines now shifted emphasis to areas around the Mona Passage west of Puerto Rico and off the northern coast of South America. The Navy thereupon acquired yachts and other privately owned seagoing craft and added them to the coastal patrol, thereby releasing larger vessels for service with the Gulf and Caribbean Sea Frontiers. Operating also in the Caribbean under United States command were a number of Netherlands vessels. Mexico, which declared war in June, and Brazil, which entered in August, added their forces to the patrols in that area. By the end of 1942, though U-boats still ventured into the western Atlantic, they had ceased to be a major menace.

Meanwhile, measures were going forward to remove the dangers to the transatlantic routes. Increase in numbers of planes available, together with improved techniques, enabled United States and Canadian long-range bombers in time to drive the submarine wolfpacks far out to sea. Air patrols were flown not only from North American coastal airfields but from Bermuda, from the West Indies, from Brazil, and from Ascension Island in the South Atlantic. In the north they flew from Newfoundland and Iceland. On the European side, British and American aircraft patrolled from the United Kingdom, from Gibraltar, and, later, by permission of Portugal, from the Azores. After the invasion of North Africa, other flights took off from Morocco and Dakar. This made the borders of the Atlantic exceedingly unhealthful for U-boats, for a plane could travel four miles while a submarine was crash-diving and drop depth bombs before it could reach a safe undersea level.

There remained, however, a large area in the middle Atlantic which was beyond air patrol range from either side of the ocean. Here the wolfpacks now congregated and continued their attacks on shipping. The answer to this situation was the destroyer escort and the escort carrier, both of which could be mass-produced at relatively low cost. The destroyer escort, averaging 1,300 tons, could do the work of a destroyer in ordinary convoy duty, and the escort carrier could bring planes to waters beyond the range of the shore-based air patrol. As the small carriers became available they were sent under escort to the danger zone. There they would pick up convoys as they reached the outer edge of one protected area and conduct them across to the air umbrella on the other side. When not engaged in convoy duty the escort carrier forces undertook independent "hunter-killer" missions against enemy undersea craft. The results were enormously successful. In the first six months of 1943, 150 U-boats were sunk. Admiral Doenitz called in his submarines and had them fitted with antiaircraft guns, but this proved a fatal mistake. When the submarines tried to fight it out with planes they usually lost.

The Battle of the Atlantic had from the beginning been fought to a large extent in the laboratories. Admiral King recognized this in adding to his Tenth Fleet—the co-ordinating agency for antisubmarine warfare—a Scientific Council made up of distinguished civilian scientists. Under the guidance of experimenters in both Axis and Allied countries a war of measures and countermeasures was soon raging. Axis scientists, for example, produced an acoustical torpedo which, when released into a convoy, headed for the screws of the biggest and noisest vessel. America's answer came in the form of towed and free noisemakers which attracted the torpedo away from the ships and out of the target area. When the Germans suspected that the Allies were aiming their guns by use of infra-red light rays, they spent frantic months developing a paint which would absorb such rays.

The chief battle was in the field of detection. The United States, like Great Britain, entered the war with two submarine detectors which they constantly improved—sonar, which bounced supersonic waves against the hulls of U-boats when they were submerged; and radar, which bounced radio waves against their hulls when they surfaced to charge their batteries. To offset sonar the Germans tried coating their submarines with rubber—a device which did not work, and firing noise-making chemical pills into the water—a device which did, but not well enough. Then the Allies invented an expendable Sonobuoy which enabled aircraft to find submerged submarines. When such a buoy was dropped into the water, its hydrophone would detect any nearby craft and its automatic radio sender would broadcast the sounds picked up.

But the terror of the U-boat was radar. After the German surrender Admiral Doenitz was to declare bitterly that plane-directing radar, "next to the atomic bomb, was the most decisive weapon of the war." Axis laboratories developed various weird countermeasures—submarine-borne helicopters; decoy balloons carrying tinfoil strips, which produced large pips on radar screens; "search receivers," which detected radar beams at great distances. But the Allies countered every move. Radar operators learned to differentiate between decoys and real targets, and scientists invented the S-radar, which could not be detected.

In the war of the laboratories the German Navy continued to be hampered by the fact that the best scientific brains were assigned to the other military services. It was not until the end of 1943 that Doenitz was able to set up a naval experimental staff which included top research men. To the head of this staff, Karl Kuepfmueller, he acknowledged that "for some months past, the enemy has rendered the U-boat war ineffective."

"He has achieved this object, not through superior tactics or strategy," Doenitz continued, "but through his superiority in the field of science; this finds its expression in the modern battle weapon, detection. By this means, he has torn our sole [naval] offensive weapon in the war against the Anglo-Saxons from our hands. It is essential to victory that we make good our scientific disparity and thereby restore to the U-boat its fighting qualities."

The German scientists at last found a partial answer, but it came too late. This was the *Schnorkel* tube, a breather device which permitted U-boats to charge their batteries under water and thus remain submerged for long periods. Then, just before the Allied victory, they brought out a submarine able to dive 700 feet beneath the surface and to move at 15 knots while submerged. Had these developments come earlier in the war, they might have proved a real threat, but by 1945 the Allies had long since won the Battle of the Atlantic.

One of the remarkable things about World War II is that while the Allies were rendering the U-boat innocuous in the Atlantic, American submarines were taking a steadily mounting toll of enemy shipping in the Pacific. Neither campaign was easy. In the Atlantic, for example, the U-boat ultimately destroyed some 3,000 vessels with a total displacement of more than 14,000,000 tons, or 62 per cent of all Allied shipping lost. But after the American Navy began to participate in the Atlantic patrol, the ratio of United Nations ships to German submarines sunk altered increasingly in favor of the Allies. In 1940, for each U-boat destroyed, about 26 Allied vessels went down; in 1941, this figure was cut to 16; in 1942, to 13; in 1943, to 2; in 1944, to .8; and in 1945, it was cut to .4. Until about the middle of 1942, the United Nations vessels were being sunk faster than they could be built, but in 1943 the United States and Great Britain replaced lost shipping fourfold. The U-boat was a tough craft, hard to knock out. In the summer of 1943 off Trinidad, seven planes and a blimp worked on a German submarine for 17 hours before they finished her off. Three months later the American destroyer *Borie* sank one U-boat with gunfire and depth charges and then sank herself in ramming another. Still, considering the dangers to which they were constantly exposed, United States fighting ships engaged in the Battle of the Atlantic took astonishingly few losses from enemy submarine torpedoes. American combatant vessels thus destroyed were the escort carrier *Block Island,* the destroyers *Jacob Jones* and *Leary,* the destroyer escorts *Fiske* and *Frederick C. Davis,* and five Coast Guard cutters. On the other hand, according to a definitive summary released by the United States Navy in April, 1946, the Germans lost 994 submarines and the Italians 116. By way of comparison, it may be noted that the United States lost 52 from all causes.

THE INVASION OF NORTH AFRICA

Long before the United States entered the war, British and Axis troops had been engaged in Egypt and Libya. In 1941 Great Britain laid plans for an invasion of French Morocco in order to keep German and Italian forces out of that area. With America's entry, these plans were expanded to include United States naval and military forces and to extend the proposed assault on Morocco by simultaneous landings on the Mediterranean coast of Algeria. The whole operation, as finally projected in the summer of 1942, was seen as a necessary prelude to the opening of a second front—to co-operate with the Russians, who held the first front—on the continent of Europe.

The major uncertainty in connection with this invasion was the question of how much opposition the French in North Africa would offer to the landings. Marshal Henri Pétain, head of the Government of occupied France, had ordered adherence to the armistice signed at Compiègne in 1940 with the Axis powers. It was not likely, therefore, that French army and naval forces, traditionally well disciplined, would permit an invasion without at least a show of resistance. As a final step in a series of exploratory contacts, Major General Mark W. Clark and a small group of Allied officers went ashore in Algeria from a British submarine three weeks before D-Day for a night conference with friendly French leaders. Two weeks later the same submarine slipped in to the coast of France and brought away pro-Ally General Henri Giraud, who was transported by seaplane to Gibraltar to employ his prestige in paving the way for the invasion.

To head the combined operation Lieutenant General Dwight D. Eisenhower of the United States Army was appointed Commander-in-Chief of the Allied force, with British Admiral Sir Andrew Cunningham as his chief naval subordinate. The plan, as finally worked out, called for assaults on Casablanca on the Atlantic coast of French Morocco, and on Oran and Algiers, on the Mediterranean coast of Algeria. For the Casablanca attack, United States naval forces under Rear Admiral H. K. Hewitt would put ashore American army troops commanded by Major General George S. Patton at points north and south of the target, while heavy ships contained the French fleet in Casablanca harbor. Simultaneously, forces consisting principally of British naval units would support landings by American and British troops at the Mediterranean invasion points.

The Casablanca invasion convoy, bearing 37,000 troops, set out in two sections from Hampton Roads, Virginia, in late October, 1942. At sea the sections joined and made contact with a covering group out of Casco Bay, Maine, and an air group which had been dispatched ahead to Bermuda. The groups thus brought together formed the Western Task Force, comprising 99 vessels of all types. Included were the battleships *Massachusetts, New York,* and *Texas;* the carrier *Ranger;* four escort carriers; seven cruisers; 28 transports and cargo vessels; and destroyers, mine vessels, and auxiliaries. After crossing the Atlantic by a circuitous route which carried it far to the south, the Western Force stood off Morocco on November 7. By this time the Center and Eastern Task Forces, 170 vessels carrying 49,000 American and 23,000 British troops, had left the United Kingdom, passed through the Straits of Gibraltar, and were approaching Oran and Algiers.

French Morocco. Towards dawn on November 8, landing operations began at Fedala, 14 miles northeast of Casablanca, with secondary landings at Port Lyautey, 50 miles farther up the coast, and at Safi, 140 miles to the southwest. The assault forces, after securing their immediate objectives, were to advance overland and converge on Casablanca from the rear. In the meantime, the covering group would watch the French ships in Casablanca harbor and attack at the first sign of resistance.

The landings at Fedala were made against only light opposition. After the first assault wave had gone ashore, coastal batteries opened fire on the beaches and at the boats closest in. The support ships *Augusta* and *Brooklyn* and a number of destroyers fired at the batteries, and rocket boats moved in to give direct cover. By 10 A.M. the heavy shore batteries were silenced, and early in the afternoon the garrison surrendered. French planes afterwards came over to strafe and drop bombs but did little damage. By the afternoon of the 10th more than 160,000 troops and about 70 tanks had been put ashore at Fedala, and American army troops were moving on Casablanca.

The secondary assaults were more hotly contested. To the north, near Lyautey, 18 assault waves of small, flat-bottomed landing boats had reached the shore at three points near the mouth of the Sebou River before the operation was detected by the defenders at nearby Mehdia. The French opened fire at the boats near the beach and later at vessels of the support group. The latter, consisting of the *Texas,* the *Savannah,* and three destroyers, replied with a series of salvos. Shortly afterwards, planes came over to strafe but were quickly driven off by 20 Wildcat fighters from the carriers off Casablanca. The forces ashore were now sharply engaged with French Foreign Legion troops. Both attackers and defenders were using tanks, but the Americans had the advantage of strong support from ships and aircraft. After two days of hard fighting the invaders succeeded in capturing the Mehdia fortress. In the meantime, the destroyer *Alexander Dallas,* after pushing nine miles up the shallow, winding Sebou, had put Rangers ashore to seize the airfield near Lyautey. When this was accomplished, army planes were flown in from the escort carrier *Chenango* and resistance in the area ceased.

At Safi, far to the south, the destroyer transports *Bernadou* and *Cole,* covered by the *New York,* the *Philadelphia,* and three destroyers, led the landing craft directly into the harbor. Though French batteries opened fire, the mole with its cranes and unloading facilities was seized intact. Heavy tanks could then be put ashore directly from the transports. Before noon on the 8th, the big ships with the aid of airplane spotting had silenced all batteries, and by nightfall the town was in American hands. The next day unloading of troops and supplies was completed, and on the 10th a military column of tanks and trucks began moving north, with the *Philadelphia* and two destroyers proceeding along the coast to lend support.

The United States covering group, consisting of the *Massachusetts, Wichita, Tuscaloosa,* and four destroyers, was assigned no inconsiderable task, for the Casablanca fleet which they were to oppose included the battleship *Jean Bart* with four serviceable 15-inch guns, a cruiser, ten destroyers and destroyer leaders, eleven submarines, and three sloops. But the defenders had grown careless and inefficient. Though they were equipped with aircraft and submarines, they allowed the American force to approach the harbor without being detected; and though they became aware of its presence shortly after midnight, they took no action until dawn. At daybreak on November 8, French planes attacked but were driven off by antiaircraft fire. Then shore batteries and ships in the harbor opened up. The covering group replied with a furious bombardment which sank three submarines, damaged a destroyer, and left the *Jean Bart* resting on the shallow bottom with her main battery temporarily knocked out.

During the bombardment the surviving Casablanca submarines sortied from the harbor, to be followed immediately by seven destroyers and a little later by the cruiser. The French surface vessels first engaged the Fedala support group at long range but broke off action after an hour, only to run into the covering group. The action quickly became a melee, with American carrier planes, now in complete control of the air, coming over to drop bombs. With the exception of one destroyer, which managed to slip away and return to the harbor intact, every one of the French surface ships was sunk or beached. The *Massachusetts* and *Brooklyn* were damaged slightly by shell hits.

On November 11, when the *Jean Bart* had been battered almost to wreckage by 1,000-pound aerial bombs, and American troops were nearing Casablanca, the French naval commandant at last requested a cessation of hostilities. That afternoon an armistice was signed. The French flag was left flying and the ships and shore batteries at Casablanca were allowed to remain in French hands.

After the armistice the Western Task Force took its first ship losses.

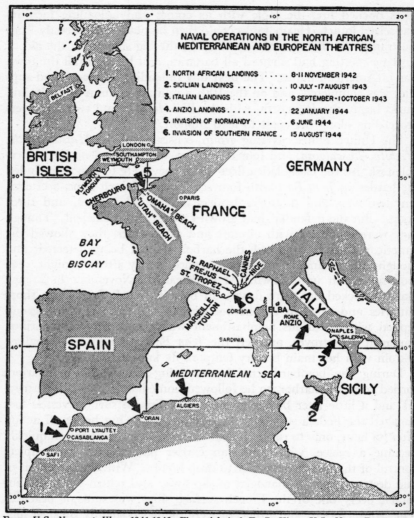

From *U.S. Navy at War, 1941-1945*, Fleet Admiral E. J. King, U.S. Navy Department, Washington, 1946.

During the two following nights seven American vessels in the Casablanca-Fedala area were struck by torpedoes. Four of them, all transports, went down—fortunately, after all the troops and most of the cargo had been disembarked. It has never been officially determined whether the torpedoes were fired by Axis submarines or by those which had sortied on the 8th from Casablanca harbor, but for reasons of diplomacy it was assumed that the attacking craft were not French. What is certain, however, is that the uncontrolled use of searchlights by the French ashore made the work of the attackers easier.

Algeria. To capture the well-fortified port of Oran, where resistance was expected, the Center Naval Task Force, composed mainly of British ships, was to put 39,000 United States troops ashore in the early hours of November 8 at positions flanking the target. The landings at Les Andalouses to the west were carried out without incident, but the occupation of Arzeu to the east was made notable by the exploits of two companies of Rangers and a raiding party of 12 Marines and two naval officers led by Captain Walter Ansel of the United States Navy. While the Rangers went ashore and seized the fort and beaches, Ansel's party in a landing boat entered the harbor and captured three ships without opposition. Fire continued from French batteries some distance inland, but American troops, landing under a smoke screen, quickly silenced the guns and occupied the town as a base for inland operations.

Meanwhile, a futile attempt was being made to seize the fort, harbor, and ships at Oran. To accomplish this task 500 United States combat troops, 30 United States naval engine-room personnel, and 52 British naval ratings and demolition experts crowded aboard two small Royal Navy vessels, former United States Coast Guard cutters, and approached the city. The cutters broke the boom guarding the harbor entrance but the French, already alerted, sank both vessels with heavy fire from ships and shore and killed or captured all the personnel. During the next two days French vessels made a series of sorties from the harbor. British men-of-war sank a destroyer and an escort vessel and made hits on four other destroyers. The defenders then re-closed the harbor by beaching one of their damaged craft in a position to block the entrance. On November 10, as armored columns from east and west were closing on the city and the battleship *Rodney* was bombarding shore positions, the French at Oran capitulated and hostilities ceased.

One section of the Eastern Task Force was attacked by an Axis submarine shortly after entering the Mediterranean. The American transport *Thomas Stone* was hit and forced to drop out of the convoy. The rest of the ships proceeded to the vicinity of Algiers and landed troops, mostly British, east and west of the city. There was some opposition from shore batteries, but this important port, whose garrison was commanded by General Juin, ardent admirer of Giraud, surrendered within a few hours. The chief resistance came from German bombers and torpedo planes in a series of raids in which one American transport was sunk. After the city was in Allied hands, troops from the *Thomas Stone* arrived. They had traveled 160 miles across the open sea in landing boats in order to join the assault.

It was well that the African landings were not opposed by forces genuinely determined to resist, for the Allied troops were new to the business and betrayed not a little ineptness. Naval personnel also revealed need of further training, for assault waves in several instances were landed far from the assigned beaches, and too many landing craft were wrecked in the surf or were sunk by backing off before the ramp was closed. Of the boats used in the Algiers assault 94 per cent were damaged or lost. But the invasion had provided invaluable experience and had revealed weaknesses that had to be overcome. The success of subsequent amphibious operations against more determined opposition indicated that the lessons of Casablanca, Oran, and Algiers had been well applied.

On November 10, Admiral Jean Darlan, Commander-in-Chief of all French forces, who was in Algiers at the time, went over to the Americans and British. Though Darlan had notoriously collaborated with the Axis, his friendship was accepted as an emergency measure. On the 11th, the Germans violated the Compiègne Armistice by overrunning the nominally unoccupied part of France, whereupon the French of North Africa promptly joined the Allies. A few days later the commander of the French Fleet at Toulon ordered his ships scuttled rather than let them be seized and used by the Axis. Allied fortunes were improving in other quarters. On October 24, while the United States troop convoys were steaming out of Hampton Roads, General Montgomery's British Eighth Army, freshly supplied with tanks, planes, and armament from America and Britain, had defeated Marshal Rommel's Afrika Korps at El Alamein, and the Germans and Italians were now speeding pell-mell in their historic 1,500-mile retreat westward along the Mediterranean coast. The newly landed Allied forces raced eastward from Algeria to close the pincers, but the Germans rushed thousands of troops from France, Italy, and Sicily, and a winter line was established in Tunisia running from Medjez-el-Bab northward to the sea. In January the tide of the battle for Russia was turned at Stalingrad with the annihilation of the German Sixth Army. Everywhere the Axis was on the defensive. Under these happy auspices, Roosevelt and Churchill early in 1943 met with Allied military leaders at Casablanca to plan future operations and formulate political policies. The next assaults would be against Sicily and Italy. The Allies would demand of the Axis powers nothing short of unconditional surrender.

The Invasion of Sicily

With the arrival of Rommel's battered Afrika Korps to reinforce Von Arnim's forces in Tunisia, the Germans felt strong enough to strike back at the Allies. In mid-February their offensive began. The untried United States Army, hard hit at Kasserine Pass, temporarily gave way. It appeared for a while that the Allied forces would be split in half, but two American infantry divisions raced in from Oran and joined in hammering at the bulge until the Axis troops were forced back through the pass. A month later the Allies went on the offensive and in six weeks pressed the Germans into the northeast corner of Tunisia. On May 7 the British smashed their way into Tunis and the Americans entered Bizerte. Four days later the Axis African army surrendered.

The Allies now had ports from which to stage and support an assault across the narrow waist of the Mediterranean against Sicily. The naval and military strength for such an invasion had long been assembling. By July, 2,500 vessels, 4,000 aircraft, and 250,000 troops were poised for the operation. The top command was the same as for the African landings: General Eisenhower was Allied Commander-in-Chief, Admiral Cunningham headed the combined fleet, Vice Admiral Hewitt commanded the United States naval task force, and Lieutenant General Patton led the American expeditionary troops. Army air forces were under Lieutenant General Carl Spaatz. Three United States attack forces would put Patton's soldiers ashore at Licata, Gela, and Scoglitti on Sicily's southwestern coast. British naval forces at the same time would land an army division on the east coast. D-Day was July 10, 1943.

The British task forces set out from England, the American from North Africa. On July 5 a group of large ships departed from Oran, picked up others at Algiers, and then proceeded past Tunis and Bizerte. Off these ports they were joined by LST's, LCI's, and LCT's, being used for the first time in amphibious operations. The new craft were to prove a valuable addition, for they could move in directly to the beach and put troops ashore without the necessity of loading them first into boats. After leaving Tunis the growing task force rounded Cape Bon and for a while headed south in order to mislead observers as to its destination. Hewitt's formation by this time stretched 60 miles and was more than a mile wide. After dark on the 8th it struck across the open sea to Malta, where all groups concentrated, and from which the three attack forces moved towards their separate beachheads.

Meanwhile, Allied planes had been bombing enemy airfields and strong points all over southern Europe and had virtually cut off communication in the Straits of Messina between Italy and Sicily. British submarines patrolled off all major Italian ports. Two forces including the heaviest Royal Navy vessels guarded the seas east and west of the target. Saboteurs had been parachuted into Sicily, and just before the landings paratroops were dropped behind the Axis lines.

Shortly after midnight, July 9–10, the three American attack forces reached their assigned target areas, and not long afterwards landing craft moved towards the beaches, while cruisers laid a heavy barrage inshore and rocket boats provided close support. The only notable opposition was in the immediate vicinity of Licata and Gela, where the enemy had coastal batteries. Fleet guns, however, gradually hammered these into silence, and the assault troops fanned out from the landing points. All went well on shore until 9 A.M. when German tanks came rumbling down the hills towards Gela. For a while it appeared that it would be impossible to prevent their driving a wedge through to the sea and splitting the beachheads, for American heavy artillery had not yet been unloaded. But the *Boise* and a number of destroyers moved in and smashed the enemy column when it had reached a point just 400 yards from the shore. By noon all beaches were secure, and a few hours later the three target towns had been captured. On the Sicilian east coast the British and Canadians were making equally good progress. They had seized Augusta and very nearly cleared the enemy out of Syracuse.

Beginning at dawn on D-Day, Axis planes directed at the fleet the first of a series of attacks which by the 11th were following each other at half-hour intervals. Several ships were damaged, the destroyer *Maddox* and a minelayer were sunk, an LST was wrecked, and an ammunition ship was blown up. Fighter plane support from Malta and North Africa and excellently-controlled antiaircraft fire prevented heavier losses. The expert gunnery, however, had one tragic consequence. During the night of July 10–11, air transports bearing

British paratroops took off from Tunisia. Someone made the fatal blunder of sending them on a different course from the one announced. As the aircraft came over Sicily, American batteries on ships and shore opened fire on them. Twenty-four were shot down. Though enemy artillery was also firing, it is believed that most of the planes were destroyed by shells from American-manned guns.

The Allied land forces now pushed inland and around the perimeter of the island, cruisers and destroyers remaining offshore to lend fire support, while PT boats patrolled the north coast to prevent the enemy from landing supplies and reinforcements. On August 17 the Sicilian campaign ended with the fall of Messina. Though determined attempts had been made to surround and capture the German forces in Sicily, 88,000 enemy troops escaped across the straits to Italy.

The Fascist regime was now tottering. Benito Mussolini had been dismissed from his dictatorship, and the Italians were trying to extricate themselves from the war. At the end of August the government at Rome agreed to unconditional surrender, but the announcement was held up until the Allies were ready to strike in force at the Italian peninsula.

THE INVASION OF ITALY

Before dawn on September 3, two divisions of the British Eighth Army began moving in small boats across the Straits of Messina into Italy under cover of aircraft and ship and shore artillery. The Italians, to whom the defense in that area had been entrusted, showed little fight, and the straits were secured by nightfall. During the following week the British made other landings near Pizzo, 50 miles northeast of the original invasion point, and at Taranto in the heel of the Italian boot. Fanning out from these points they quickly seized Brindisi and Bari on the Adriatic Sea, and then began pushing north, but in the mountains of the main peninsula they were slowed up by stiffening resistance.

Salerno. The main assault on Italy was to be on the Gulf of Salerno, 35 miles southwest of Naples. Lieutenant General Mark W. Clark's Fifth Army was to be put ashore at this point by an Anglo-American naval force under Admiral Hewitt. The Fifth Army troops, it was planned, would then push north to seize Naples and east to throw a barrier across the Italian peninsula, trapping all enemy forces between their positions and Montgomery's army to the south. On the evening of September 8, as the invasion force neared the landing area, General Eisenhower broadcast his announcement of Italy's surrender. This was expected to throw the Germans into confusion and serve as an invitation for the Italian forces to turn on their unpopular erstwhile allies and clear the way for the coming assault. No such happy results ensued. The Germans were not surprised by the surrender; it had been in the air for weeks. They had simply taken over all important communication and defense points and stripped the Italians of arms. Also, with a fairly good idea of where the Allies would strike next, they had set up strong defense positions around the expected beachhead and on the high ridges overlooking Salerno Gulf. Then they sat back and waited.

At 2:45 A.M. on September 9, Hewitt's force, five or six miles off the Italian shore, by army request began laying down only a light barrage, to which a few enemy batteries replied. Fifteen minutes later the first assault waves moved in, the British proceeding to the north, the Americans to the south. The second waves followed against light opposition. While these were disembarking, the third waves approached the shore. Then, when the beaches were crowded and the invasion was in its most vulnerable stage, the Germans opened a deadly cross-fire from pillboxes, batteries, and tanks. The landings very nearly came to disaster then and there. Some points along the shore had to be abandoned; at others the newly-arrived troops were literally wiped out. But the cruisers and destroyers came in close and began hurling salvo after salvo at the enemy. Under the shield of this barrage the assault forces began to move tentatively forward. At dawn, however, the invasion was again pinned down when the heavy batteries on the hills and ridges opened up. The Germans, said General Clark, were "looking down our throat." Then bombers of the *Luftwaffe* came over and began methodically blasting the beachhead to pieces. But Allied carrier planes and fighters from Sicily arrived and threw back the air attack, while the fleet, its fire directed by spotter planes, thundered at the enemy coastal and hill positions. Throughout the day additional troops were rushed ashore and tanks were landed under heavy shelling. By nightfall the invaders had secured a narrow beachhead and the next day they seized the port of Salerno.

On the evening of the 13th, when the assault forces had pushed as much as seven miles inland, the Germans, reinforced by fresh troops from northern Italy, launched a counteroffensive which for a second time threatened to push the invading army back into the sea. But the American and British lines held through the night, and before dawn the fleet had concentrated offshore to pound the Germans with a furious and sustained bombardment, supplemented after daybreak by clouds of planes from Sicily. The *Luftwaffe* at this critical stage made effective use of its new surprise weapon, the radio-directed glider bomb. The fleet held on, however, and at the end of the day the counteroffensive was smashed. Shortly afterwards the Germans began withdrawing to the north.

Aided regularly by naval gunfire, the Fifth Army now moved up the coast and after three weeks of hard fighting entered Naples. The Germans had already withdrawn, but they had left the harbor a wreck. Wharves had been blown up or blocked. Warehouses, dry-docks, and dockside installations had been demolished. The channels were obstructed by sunken ships, sometimes one on top of another. Allied salvage teams under Commodore William A. Sullivan of the United States Navy quickly set to work to clear the port. They floated or blasted most of the sunken ships out of the way and built causeways over others which had settled alongside wharves. In four months they had the port of Naples in full operation.

Anzio. Slogging through cold winter rains, the Fifth Army, joined by Italian units in December, slowly pushed the Germans up the peninsula, but in January, 1944, the advance ground to a halt before the Gustav Line, the enemy defense system south of Rome. In an attempt to turn the flank of this line, an Anglo-American naval force with a few French, Dutch, and Greek ships on January 22 carried out another landing operation. The beachhead this time was near Anzio, just south of Rome and 55 miles behind the German front. The assault troops, nominally three divisions, started going ashore at 2 A.M. The enemy, taken by surprise, at first offered almost no resistance, but at daybreak heavy shells began coming over, directed at the Allied fleet and land forces. The *Luftwaffe* soon appeared, but fighter aircraft from fields near Naples were able in most cases to keep the air attacks under control. In the afternoon the port towns of Anzio and nearby Nettuno fell, and throughout the day additional troops and supplies were rushed to the beachhead. Then bad weather set in and under increasing enemy opposition the Allied push came to a standstill. A long and difficult stalemate followed. General Clark could not strengthen the Anzio sector without dangerously weakening his position to the south, for by this time all available troops and equipment were being concentrated in the United Kingdom for a new and greater invasion. The Germans, for their part, preferred to launch no counteroffensive towards the sea, partly because they too lacked forces for major action on two fronts, and partly because they had learned at Salerno the folly of moving an army within range of fleet guns.

Throughout the winter and into spring the Anzio forces held on to a triangular beachhead about 15 miles deep, while German artillery emplaced on the heights inshore subjected them to unremitting bombardment. Meanwhile, United Nations vessels kept up a shuttle service of supplies and replacements, taking losses from air attacks and lending artillery support to their troops whenever possible. At last, in May, after the Allied Air Force had disrupted enemy communication lines as far north as Florence and had leveled the pivot of the German defense at Cassino, the Fifth and Eighth Armies again moved forward and soon made contact with the Anzio Beachhead. On June 4 American and British troops entered Rome.

THE INVASION OF FRANCE

Even as the Allied armies reached the Italian capital, the greatest invasion force in history was poised in the harbors of the United Kingdom for an assault on Western Europe. The decision had been made at the Casablanca meeting, and the plans had been completed by the Combined Chiefs of Staff and accepted by Roosevelt and Churchill at the first Quebec conference in August, 1943. At Teheran three months later the information was passed to Russia's Premier Stalin, who declared himself satisfied and promised that the Red Army would co-operate with an all-out drive from the east.

For nearly a year Americans, allotted the southwest quarter of England for the purpose, schooled and prepared themselves in amphibious operations. Meanwhile, United States and British air forces progressively weakened the *Luftwaffe,* and in methodical raids of increasing power cut down the enemy's manufacturing potential by striking at industrial centers throughout Germany and the occupied countries of Western Europe. In April, 1944, the Allied aircraft shifted their main emphasis to coastal landing fields and to channels of communication, tearing up railway lines, destroying trains, and blasting roads. By June not a bridge was left intact over the Seine between Paris and Rouen.

The Germans were well aware of what was in the offing, for such vast preparations could not be concealed. They built a formidable line of defenses along the French Channel coast, with particular attention to port areas, for they reasoned that an invasion of great magnitude could not be carried out without the use of harbors. Nazi propaganda now spoke much of the *Festung Europa,* the fortress of Europe, unassailable behind an "Atlantic Wall," and Hitler promised that if by some chance the Allies should succeed in making landings on the French coast, they would stay "exactly nine hours."

Normandy. The enemy had concluded that the main Allied landing attempts would be in the Pas de Calais area, the part of continental Europe nearest England. But the Combined Chiefs of Staff had decided otherwise. The initial landings would be made on the coast of Normandy, from a point some distance west of the Seine River mouth to the east side of the Cotentin Peninsula. A drive across the Cotentin would then seal off the port of Cherbourg, which could be taken later. Meanwhile, a temporary supply line would be run through artificial harbors which the Allies were prepared to set up. The whole operation was conceived as the climax of the amphibious assault on Europe, embodying all the principles learned in preceding invasions in the Atlantic, the Mediterranean, and the Pacific.

Since the assault would be over open beaches, D-Day was set for late May or early June, for the weather at that time was normally fair over the English Channel and the spring tides would present important advantages. Low water would permit the first attack waves of small craft to beach far out, beyond the line of enemy-emplaced underwater obstacles, and would expose such obstacles to destruction by demolition teams; the succeeding high tide would permit larger landing craft to move close inshore and discharge troops at points from which they would have only a narrow strip of sand to cross. After several days' delay because of strong winds and low clouds, the Supreme Commander of the Allied Expeditionary Force, General Eisenhower, set the machinery in motion for June 5. Four thousand ships bearing a million men prepared to leave port. A part of the armada, in fact, had reached the Channel when the invasion was postponed. A gale had sprung up which might imperil the landings. It is a tribute to the flexibility of the immense organization that no great confusion ensued.

In 24 hours the weather, though far from perfect, had improved. The starting signal was given again and the invasion got under way a second time. The heavy ships of the American fire support group came down from Belfast, Northern Ireland; American transports set

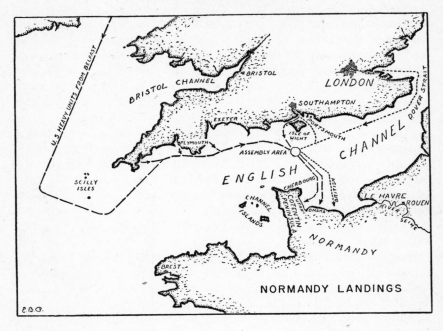

NORMANDY LANDINGS

out from harbors along the western sector of England's south coast; the British forces came from Southampton, Portsmouth, and ports as far east as the Thames. All these component parts by intricate scheduling made rendezvous at a single point south of the Isle of Wight and then headed towards France in predetermined order. Mine-sweepers had preceded them to clear wide channels, which they marked with lighted buoys. Four divisions of paratroops and glider-borne infantry were dropped behind the German coast positions to seize airfields and cut communication and supply lines.

Off Normandy the invasion armada split into sections. The British-Canadian task forces headed for the beaches to the east; the American task forces, under Rear Admiral Alan G. Kirk, for the west and center —designated as Utah Beach and Omaha Beach. Just as the dawn of June 6 was breaking, the guns of nearly 800 combat ships opened up, and Allied planes swept over for a thundering prelude to the assault. At first there was no reaction from the shore; the enemy had been caught off guard. Then flashes of light appeared along the dim coast as German guns began to reply. In some sectors a few enemy planes appeared—not enough to present a serious problem, for Allied control of the air was very nearly absolute. Now the first-wave landing craft were circling in the transport areas. When all were loaded, they moved to the line of departure, 3,000 yards offshore. Lights on the control vessels went on—five minutes to go. Then the lights went off and the boats started in.

At Utah Beach, on the Cotentin Peninsula, the enemy was least prepared to meet the assault. American demolition teams, going in with the first wave, soon cleared wide passages through the network of mined underwater obstacles. Fire from the *Nevada,* the *Quincy,* British and French cruisers, and numerous destroyers combined with aerial bombing to keep enemy opposition at a minimum. Now for the first time VT-fused ammunition, deadly to personnel, was used against land targets. During the first 12 hours 21,000 troops of General Omar Bradley's First Army, together with 1,700 vehicles and 1,700 tons of supplies, were put ashore at this beach. The British and Canadians, far to the east, likewise met only moderate opposition.

Omaha Beach, at the center, was the main assault point. It also proved the most difficult to take. A 20-knot southwest wind, from which other areas were somewhat shielded, here whipped up a choppy sea. Low-lying clouds and rain hampered air operations. Moreover, an entire German army division, which chanced to be nearby, quickly joined the Omaha coast defense. American demolition teams, under constant fire, lost nearly half their men and were able to cut only a few narrow channels through the unusually thick maze of offshore hedgehogs and tetrahedrons meshed together with barbed wire. The *Arkansas,* the *Texas,* and other United Nations combat ships poured a steady hail of shells at casemated gun positions which lined the beachhead, but enemy return fire continued heavy well into the day. Despite severe losses, First Army troops moved ashore steadily, only to be pinned down for hours at the water's edge. At four in the afternoon, when it appeared that the invasion in this area might be thrown back, Allied destroyers moved in until, as Admiral Kirk expressed it, "they had their bows against the bottom." From point-blank range they methodically blasted away gun positions near the beach and then stepped their fire inland as the assault troops began to advance. The heavy ships farther offshore, with the aid of air spotters and navy fire control parties attached to the army units, continued support, hitting tanks, vehicles, and concentration points several miles inland. Marshal Karl von Rundstedt afterwards gloomily gave credit to "the power of the Allies' naval guns, which reached deep inland in the time of the Normandy invasion, making impossible the bringing up of reserves needed to hurl Allied invasion forces into the Channel." Before the end of D-Day the follow-up force arrived with additional troops. These began going ashore against only intermittent fire.

After the beachheads were secured the problem of rapid supply had to be attended to. The answer was one of the most extraordinary engineering achievements of military history. Artificial harbors, long planned and prepared for, were built out from the Normandy coast. The first step was to sink numbers of old warships and merchant vessels in curved lines extending from the beaches. These provided small boat shelter. Then two of the blockship lines were extended by sinking huge concrete caissons. Outside of these, in order further to break the force of the waves, floating steel caissons were secured in line end-to-end and moored to buoys. Inside the harbors thus formed, pontoon causeways extended from the beach, ending in piers mounted on steel stilts but so constructed as to rise and fall with the tide.

The blockship shelters were ready by June 10, the two harbors a week later. Now LST's, which required 12 hours to unload at the beach, could be cleared of cargo in a single hour. Just as the harbors were coming into use, the English Channel was struck by the worst storm in 40 years. For three days high winds whipped up waves of destructive size. When at last the storm abated, more than 300 small craft had been destroyed or beached, and the harbor in the American sector had been battered to pieces. All heavy traffic now went through the British sector, which had not suffered so severely. Despite the difficulties thus imposed, the Navy in less than a month poured into France a million men, 650,000 tons of stores, and nearly 200,000 vehicles. Though the invasion had been costly in men and ships, it proved less so than had been expected. During the first 11 days, 3,283 Americans had been killed and 12,600 wounded; in the same period more than 30,000 of the enemy are estimated to have been killed or wounded and 15,000 had been taken prisoner. United States vessels sunk, mostly by mines, were the destroyers *Corry, Glennon,* and *Meredith;* the destroyer escort *Rich;* two transports; two minesweepers, and a submarine chaser. Major landing craft lost through enemy action were two LST's, three LCI's and six LCT's.

Cherbourg. With the destruction of one of the artificial harbors, it became imperative that Cherbourg be seized without delay. By the 18th, Bradley's First Army troops had cut across the Cotentin and began moving on the port from the landward side. On the 25th, when they

reached the outskirts of the city, a naval force under Rear Admiral M. L. Deyo came in to give direct support and to reduce the German forts and coastal defenses with shellfire. Included in Deyo's force were the battleships *Nevada, Texas,* and *Arkansas,* the American cruisers *Tuscaloosa* and *Quincy,* the British cruisers *Glasgow* and *Enterprise,* and 11 destroyers. When the ships had approached near enough to the shore to deliver call fire, enemy batteries, including casemated guns up to 280 mm., opened fire. The destroyers quickly laid a smoke screen, but the Allied vessels began to take hits. As the German bombardment increased in volume, the naval force broke up, each ship maneuvering independently. For three hours the vessels remained four to eight miles offshore, hurling salvo after salvo as requested by the American land forces or directed by spotter planes. When Deyo's force retired, more than half of his ships had been hit. The destroyer *O'Brien* had been heavily damaged and the *Texas* had been struck by at least ten shells. Personnel casualties, however, were remarkably light—14 dead and 28 wounded in the entire force. Two days later the 7th Army Corps occupied the city. Commodore Sullivan's salvage teams then went to work to clear the enemy's mines and obstructions from the harbor. Early in July Cherbourg was being used by the Allies as a major unloading point.

While the Americans were sealing off Cherbourg, the German Seventh Army was attempting to seal off the invasion area. In the vicinity of Caen, where the Germans were strongest, they and the British were locked in a stalemate. With the fall of Cherbourg the Americans turned south and on July 25, following a bombardment by 3,000 planes and massed artillery, broke through the enemy left flank at Saint Lô. They then shot forward in several columns. One sped south to the Bay of Biscay, blocking off 250,000 Germans in Brittany; two others raced for Paris; while a fourth encircled the enemy forces in Normandy, meeting the British, who had hammered their way inland to Falaise. In four days the trapped remnants of the Seventh Army were destroyed.

The frustrated Germans now belatedly commenced launching at Britain the first of a pair of weird devices which they had desperately tried to put into operation before the Allied invasion. One of these was the jet-propelled flying bomb, which, launched at the rate of 100 a day, damaged or destroyed more than a million houses, mostly in the London area. No sooner was the flying bomb got under partial control by planes and VT-fuzed shells, than a second type of missile, heavier and more deadly than the first, began coming over. This was a rocket which moved faster than sound. Only by seizing the enemy's launching areas in northern France and the Low Countries were the Allies able to halt the rocket barrage.

Southern France. The Allied strategy for the assault on Western Europe included putting an army ashore on the southern coast of France. Vice Admiral Hewitt would again command the naval invasion force, which would strike at three points east of Toulon while British and American parachutists and glider-borne troops were put down inland to cut communications and strike at German defense positions from the rear. Small craft for the expedition were staged from Naples and from ports in Corsica, which the Free French had seized. A fire support group, including battleships and cruisers brought from the Atlantic after the bombardment of Cherbourg, set out from North Africa. The Allied force when assembled comprised 515 United States, 283 British, 12 French, and seven Greek ships and major craft, together with 63 merchant vessels representing various of the United Nations.

For three months preceding the invasion the Mediterranean Allied Strategic Air Force had been intensively bombing targets in southern France, isolating the assault area by hitting at bridges, tunnels, and railroad lines. Then, in the hours preceding the landings, set for 8 A. M. August 15, more than 1,300 aircraft gave tactical support to the invasion by bombing and strafing along a 40-mile coastal front. Meanwhile, French Commandos and United States Special Service Battalions landed on the Hyères Islands and near Cape Nègre to secure the Allied western flank, and groups of small craft and destroyers drew enemy forces from the invasion area by staging mock assaults at points east and west of the proposed beachheads. At daybreak, as guns of the fire support group opened up, additional planes from nine escort carriers roared in towards the shore to furnish close cover and air spotting. The initial landings were virtually unopposed, but one assault team, scheduled to go ashore in the afternoon near Saint-Raphael on the east flank, met such heavy fire that it was obliged to shift to another beach.

Stunned by the preliminary bombardment and aware that no reinforcements were available, the Germans in many sectors abandoned their elaborate shore defenses and took to flight. Major General A. M. Patch's Allied Seventh Army, spearheaded by the newly-formed French Expeditionary Corps, was soon in hot pursuit up the Rhône Valley. Called up by General de Gaulle's National Committee of Liberation, the French Forces of the Interior—the underground movement which had harassed the Germans for four years—now broke into open warfare. Armed with weapons which the Allies had dropped from planes, they laid siege to Marseille and Toulon, while United Nations ships lent support by bombardment of enemy-held forts and strong points. By August 29 both southern ports were in French hands. Other forces of the underground struck at the fleeing Germans along the Rhône, materially aiding Patch's army, which entered Lyon within two weeks of the southern landings. Soon the French south of the Loire had cleared the enemy out of all positions except a few of the larger ports along the Atlantic.

Meanwhile, United States forces out of Normandy had swept upon Paris from two directions. In sight of the city the Americans stopped, permitting French troops under General Leclerc to advance and free their own capital. With the surrender of the Germans in Paris on August 25, Allied forces continued to the east and soon made contact with Patch's army coming up from the south.

THE GERMAN COLLAPSE

The great Allied thrust was now under way. Patton's Third Army advanced to Verdun; Bradley's First Army pushed through Luxembourg and was the first to stand on German soil; Montgomery's British and Canadian armies raced up the coast and crossed Belgium to the Dutch border. In mid-December, as the Allied Forces stood poised for an assault on the enemy's Siegfried Line, three German armies under von Rundstedt struck back along a 90-mile front through the forests of the Ardennes and advanced to within four miles of the Meuse River before they were halted by the Allies. In what is known as the "Battle of the Bulge," the United States armies forced back the counterattack.

By March, 1945, the Allies had reached the Rhine. One bridge, at Remagen, which the retreating Germans had failed to blow up in time, was left intact, and across it divisions of the First Army surged. But the narrow bridge collapsed in a few days; it could not in any event have carried the burden of an entire invasion. Other means of crossing the river were needed, and they were ready. Since October of the preceding year, naval landing craft units had been rehearsing, first in England, then in France and Belgium, for the task which they were to perform. Then, as the First, Third and Ninth American Armies approached the Rhine, the 37- and 50-foot craft had been hauled overland on trailers to the jumping-off points. Through the month of

March, in three separate invasion areas, they aided in ferrying troops and equipment across the river and assisted in the building of pontoon bridges.   It was dangerous business, for the crossings were generally made under enemy fire.   Numbers of the craft were destroyed, but they carried out a task which could have been accomplished by no other means.   The Navy had helped establish the last European beachheads.

In April, the Allied armies in Italy went on a final offensive, and in Germany the American and British armies pushed towards Berlin from the west while the Russians advanced from the east.   Everywhere German resistance was collapsing.   The careers of the Axis dictators had run their course.   On the 27th, Benito Mussolini, attempting to flee across the Alps, was caught and shot by Italian partisans, who hung his corpse up by the heels to be jeered at by the crowds.   Two days later Adolf Hitler disappeared, killing himself, it was reported, in his bombproof shelter beneath the Reich Chancellory.   On the left bank of the Elbe the Allies halted their headlong advance to allow the Russians the satisfaction of taking the Nazi capital.   This the Red Army accomplished on May 2.   The following day enemy resistance in Italy collapsed.   On all fronts Germany's armies were laying down their arms.   On May 7, representatives of the German high command arrived at General Eisenhower's headquarters in Rheims, France, to sign the instrument of surrender, a ceremony which was repeated the next day in Berlin.   "We the undersigned, acting on behalf of the German Supreme Command, agree to unconditional surrender of all our armed forces on land, on sea, and in the air, as well as all forces which at present are under German command . . ."

31

Victory in the Pacific

THE ALLIED PACIFIC OFFENSIVES of 1944, in which American forces played the dominant role, had demolished the restricted defense perimeter behind which the enemy had retreated following the Solomons campaign. There remained on Japan's ocean side only three chains of island positions from which she might a little longer limit United States air operations and hold off amphibious assaults against the homeland. These were the Ryukyus, extending southwest from Kyushu to Formosa, the Kuriles to the northeast of Hokkaido, and the Izu-Bonin-Volcano series south of Tokyo. All three island chains were made the target of repeated American raids. The Ryukus, as we have seen, were attacked by carrier planes, the Kuriles by air and surface forces based on the Aleutians, and the Bonin and Volcano Islands by central Pacific surface forces and by aircraft from the Marianas.

From Saipan, B-29 Superfortresses in late November, 1944, began striking directly at the Tokyo area.[1] But the big bombers operated under great difficulties. To make the 3,000-mile round trip they had to cut their bomb loads from a possible ten to something like three tons and, because the target was beyond the range of fighter aircraft cover, they were obliged to make fuel-consuming climbs to 25,000 or 30,000 feet, from which altitude precision bombing was impossible. Enemy bases on the Volcano and Bonin Islands, lying athwart the route to Japan, added special hazards by warning Tokyo of the approaching bombers and sending up interceptor planes to engage them

---

[1] As early as the preceding June, B-29's had raided Japan from Chengtu, China, but the difficulties of supply and the attrition caused by the long flights over enemy-held territory made such missions uneconomical. After the Mariana-based bombers went into full operation, flights from the Asiatic mainland were discontinued.

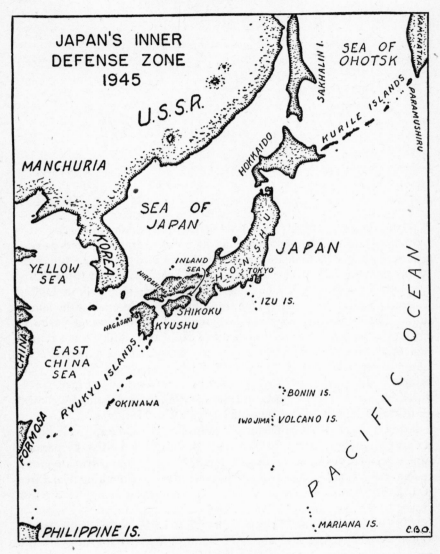

JAPAN'S INNER
DEFENSE ZONE
1945

in combat. Early plans had provided for support from carrier-based Hellcats, but, as has been noted, The Third Fleet was recalled to the Philippines following the Battle for Leyte Gulf and remained in those waters until near the end of January.

It was evident that a point nearer Japan would have to be seized before the big bombers could be employed with full effectiveness and minimum attrition. Okinawa in the Ryukyus was therefore selected as providing area for airfields within 400 miles of Japan, and numerous harbors as well, from which the United States could later stage an invasion of the Japanese home islands. Before the hazardous Okinawa operation could be attempted, however, the enemy striking power would have to be reduced by a series of telling bomber raids on aircraft and aircraft factories in Japan. To accomplish this it was necessary to capture one of the islands north of the Marianas in order to secure a fighter plane base for support of the B-29's. Iwo Jima, largest of the Volcano group, was chosen as the most readily assailable and providing the best terrain for airfields. Its seizure would permit emergency landings and refueling and would enable American planes to neutralize the remaining islands of the Volcano-Bonin chain, thereby ending air attacks on the Marianas and on the bombers en route to and from Japan. To direct the double operation at closer range, Fleet Admiral Nimitz at the end of January, 1945, moved from Pearl Harbor to advance headquarters on Guam. The task of carrying out the invasions was assigned to the Central Pacific Forces, now operating once more as the Fifth Fleet, with major commands designated as follows:

Fifth Fleet.........................Admiral Spruance
   TF 51—Joint Expeditionary Force....Vice Admiral R. K. Turner
     TF 52—Amphibious Support Force..Rear Admiral W. H. P. Blandy
     TF 56—Expeditionary {Iwo Jima...Lieut. Gen. H. M. Smith, U.S.M.C.
     Troops   {Okinawa....Lieut. Gen. S. B. Buckner, U.S.A.
   TF 58—Fast Carrier Force..........Vice Admiral M. A. Mitscher

With February 19 selected as D-Day for Iwo Jima and April 1 for the invasion of Okinawa, it was evident that the most precise timing and the utmost expedition would have to be exercised in order to free surface and carrier support from the first assault in time to begin the second.

THE CAPTURE OF IWO JIMA

Iwo Jima, eight square miles in area, roughly triangular, had been well fortified by General Kuribayashi, Japanese commander of the Bonin and Volcano Islands. He perceived that the only two possible landing beaches were along the sides of the tapering southwest peninsula. These were flanked by 556-foot Mt. Suribachi, a dormant volcano at the southern tip, and by a high plateau of broken rocks, cliffs, and gullies which occupied most of the broad northwest end. On the two heights, therefore, in well-concealed positions, Kuribayashi concentrated his mortars and larger guns where they could direct an enfilading fire upon either of the beaches or upon the ridge between. The northwest plateau he converted into an almost impregnable fortress of interconnected caves, blockhouses, and pillboxes. So complete were the defenses that, though the island was hammered regularly by carrier planes and surface ships for half a year and was bombed daily for nearly three months by Mariana-based Liberators, the 20,000 Japanese of the garrison continued strengthening their hill fortifications, at the same time maintaining two airfields and beginning construction on a third. When in mid-February it became obvious that an assault was imminent, they withdrew into their strongholds, vowing to take ten American lives for each of their own.

Following a series of intensified air attacks, Blandy's support force of old battleships, escort carriers, cruisers, and destroyers approached Iwo Jima on February 16 to begin the pre-invasion bombardment. At the same time, Spruance and Mitscher set out to isolate the target island by taking Task Force 58 boldly to the coast of Japan and sending planes over the Tokyo area, thereby, in the words of Admiral Nimitz' communiqué, fulfilling "the deeply cherished desire of every officer and man in the Pacific fleet." In attacks spread over two days, the carrier aircraft destroyed nearly 500 enemy planes with a loss of 49 of their own, sank a large tanker and several small craft, beached and severely damaged an aircraft transport ship, bombed three factories, and destroyed air base installations. At the conclusion of the raid the carrier force turned back to join in the bombardment of Iwo. Simultaneously, the expeditionary force approached with 50,000 assault troops of the Fourth and Fifth and 20,000 reserves of the Third Marine Division aboard. By the time the landing forces arrived off the target on the 19th, bombs, shells, and rockets had reduced all visible fortifications and apparently devastated every square yard of the island. Grim experience, however, had taught the invasion commanders to expect determined resistance. Their expectations were more than fulfilled.

The first wave of assault boats and amphibious trucks and tractors, going in under an intense artillery and aircraft barrage which kept enemy fire at a minimum, hit the southeast beach at 9 A.M. Here they ran into difficulties of an unexpected sort. The shore, rising so steeply from the water that the surf broke directly upon it, was composed of soft volcanic ash into which the bows of landing boats and the wheels of amphibious trucks sank without taking hold. Even the tractors in many instances floundered helplessly, unable to grip the soil with their treads. Craft of all sort were thrown broadside against the shoreline and swamped. "The resultant accumulation of wreckage," reported Admiral Turner, "piled progressively higher and extended seaward into the beach approaches to form underwater obstacles which damaged propellers and even gutted a few of the landing ships." As soon as the beachhead was secured, larger craft, LST's and LSM's, were sent in, but their anchors would not hold in the soft ash and a number of these collided and very nearly foundered. Fortunately, before the enemy opened heavy fire, tanks and armored bulldozers were put ashore. The bulldozers were able to flatten out the beach in the steepest places and cut segments into the terrace beyond to provide a few sloping roads to the higher ground inland.

The advancing Marines were soon harassed by machine gun fire and grenades directed at them from isolated pillboxes hidden among the sparse vegetation and the churned-up ash of the spinal ridge paralleling the beach. An hour after the first landings, the Japanese concealed in the high ground on their flanks opened up with intense mortar and artillery fire. American casualties began to mount, but the invading troops climbed a second and higher terrace and cleaned out individual enemy positions with flame throwers and 75 mm. tank guns. In the course of the day, the marine left wing crossed the narrowest neck of the island, cutting off Mt. Suribachi from the strong positions in the north, and the center reached the main airfield. The right wing, nearest the heavily-fortified plateau, remained pinned down by steady artillery fire. By nightfall 40,000 men had been landed on Iwo. Eighty-one had been killed and nearly 1,100 wounded.

On the second day, all of Airfield No. 1 was taken, and troops on the west shore began a gradual advance to the north. At the same time, Marines of the left wing undertook an assault on Suribachi. This involved blasting out scores of pillboxes, sealing up more than 100 caves one by one with explosive charges, and hand-to-hand encounters with the enemy, but on the 23rd a patrol reached the summit of the cone and raised the American flag. At the end of that day, casualties among the invading forces amounted to nearly 7,000. Particularly hard hit, then and later, were medical personnel attending to front line wounded; in one division 38 per cent of the corpsmen ultimately were lost, and several field hospitals were wiped out.

As the marine battalions which had been cut down most severely

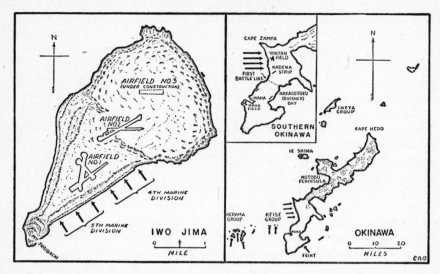

were relieved, Third Division reserves went ashore, moving in between the Fourth and Fifth Divisions. The American line stretching across the narrow part of the island now began slowly to move north, despite repeated Japanese counterattacks. On the right and left flanks the Marines could advance at no greater rate than 50 to 100 yards a day, but by the 24th the center had penetrated some 800 blockhouses and pillboxes to reach the middle of Airfield No. 2. Thereafter, the assault line entered the plateau area of rocks and gullies, where the Japanese were concealed in an extensive system of caves, many of which were reinforced with concrete and steel. The fleet, meanwhile, added call fire to the barrage from guns ashore and at night helped keep down Japanese infiltration attacks by illuminating with starshells and searchlights. Carrier planes were continuously overhead, striking at enemy gun emplacements. But most of the well-concealed strong points had to be taken the hard way by infantry action and by artillery at close range.

The only support provided the Japanese garrison was in the form of occasional air attacks on the American ships offshore. Most such raids were small and ineffective, but in a 50-plane raid on February 21 suicide aircraft hit five vessels. Four *kamikazes* smashed into the *Saratoga* and a fifth bounced against her side, tearing a hole in her hull as it exploded. One bomb penetrated several decks, demolishing living quarters. Fires blazed among the planes in the hangar. Total casualties were 110 killed and 180 wounded. Despite her heavy damages, the carrier was able to return to the United States for repairs. In the same attack another suicide plane, hitting the escort carrier *Bismarck Sea,* started fires which set off the vessel's torpedoes and caused her to capsize with a loss of 347 lives and all her aircraft.

Though five days had been the estimated time required for seizing Iwo Jima, it actually took 18 days of vicious fighting before the Marines reached the northeast coast, and another week before the island was officially declared secure. Even after that, enemy stragglers made one more organized counterattack which took a number of American lives. Ultimately the entire Japanese garrison, except for about 200 prisoners, was wiped out. Marine casualties on March 26 amounted to nearly 21,000 including 4,891 killed. To these must be added 726 killed and about as many wounded among naval shore parties and ship and boat crews. The casualty rate at Tarawa had been 8.6 per cent; at Saipan it had been 23.6 per cent; at Peleliu it had been about 25 per cent; the rate at Iwo Jima was 32.6 per cent.

With the capture of Iwo, the United States was provided with an air base only 750 miles from Tokyo. As early as March 3, a Superfortress, forced down while returning from a strike against Japan, made a successful landing on the island. Three days later Airfield No. 1 received its first fighter planes and by the middle of March Airfield No. 2 was operational. From this date it was possible for B-29's to proceed from the Marianas with full bomb loads, pick up an escort of Mustang fighters at Iwo, and proceed to attack Japanese manufacturing centers from levels which permitted precision bombing. On the return flight the big planes could, if necessary, land on Iwo airfields for refueling before returning to their home bases. Before the end of the war more than a thousand made emergency stops. Between the major raids medium bombers could strike from the Volcano Island base directly at Japan. Equally important, B-29 crews were assured of virtual immunity from attack during the long flights and of the probability of rescue by scouting seaplanes if they went down in the water. It is estimated that eventually as many American lives were saved by the capture of Iwo Jima as had been lost in the invasion.

Following the landings on February 19, most of Task Force 58 returned to Japanese waters and on the 25th co-operated with more than 200 B-29's in a raid on Tokyo. The big planes, bombing by radar through an overcast, burned out a square mile of the enemy capital. Fleet aircraft at the same time, despite the adverse weather conditions, destroyed about 150 planes, bombed two aircraft plants, and demolished two railroad trains. From the Tokyo area the carrier force proceeded to Okinawa for a strike on March 1 and then withdrew to Ulithi to prepare for the next invasion.

The Okinawa Campaign

By mid-March Task Force 58 was again on the prowl. Proceeding to a position 100 miles off Kyushu, southernmost of the Japanese home islands, the carriers on the 18th began launching a series of strikes which, at a cost of 116 American aircraft, destroyed more than 500 enemy planes. As a result of this blow the Japanese were unable to send any strong air attack against United States forces on Okinawa for nearly a week following the initial landings. In the course of the same raids Mitscher's carrier planes found remnants of the enemy fleet in the Inland Sea and damaged a number of units, including battleships and carriers.

On the morning of the 19th, while the task force stood 50 miles off the coast of Japan, an enemy bomber slipped through the combat air patrol and dropped two 500-pound bombs on the carrier *Franklin* just as she was launching planes. One hit near the bridge; the second penetrated the flight deck and exploded in the hangar. Aircraft on both decks caught fire and their bombs, rockets, and machine-gun ammunition began to go off. Forty thousand gallons of aviation gasoline, gushing from open lines, carried fire across the decks and far down into the bowels of the ship. A hundred tons of stored ammunition then began to go off in a series of rending blasts. The task group commander, Rear Admiral Davison, transferred to another vessel, as his duties required; but the carrier's commanding officer, Captain L. E. Gehres, determined to save his ship and mindful of the hundreds of men trapped below, would not order abandonment. For three hours the explosions continued with little interruption and the carrier went dead in the water. Davison sent the *Santa Fe* alongside to help fight the fires, but Gehres ordered her away when some of his crew, growing panicky, leapt from the flaming vessel to the cruiser. As the day wore on, the explosions became less frequent and the *Pittsburgh* took the carrier in tow. At last her fires burned themselves out. During the night her 13-degree list was corrected, and engineers, using rescue breathers, went below and restarted her engines. After temporary repairs at Ulithi, the *Franklin* steamed to Pearl Harbor and thence to New York Navy Yard for a major job of rebuilding. Of her crew of

Top, LSM'S(R) FIRING VOLLEYS OF ROCKETS AT OKINAWA PRIOR TO LANDINGS. *Bottom,* LANDING CRAFT PUTTING TROOPS ASHORE AT MORO-TAI ISLAND, SEPTEMBER, 1944.

about three thousand, 832 had been killed and 270 wounded. No ship had ever before taken such punishment and returned to port under her own power.

On March 24, Task Force 58 battleships, under command of Vice Admiral W. A. Lee, began bombarding the southeastern coast of Okinawa in support of minesweeping operations. This bombardment misled the Japanese commanding officer ashore, General Ushijima, regarding the location of the proposed landing point. He withdrew most of his nearly 120,000 garrison troops (originally estimated by the Americans at no more than half that number) from the rugged northern part of the 65-mile-long island and also from the southern tip, taking a position across the narrow neck five miles northeast of Naha, the capital city.

Six days prior to the main landings, United States forces seized the Kerama and Keise group of islands west of Naha, meeting only slight resistance. By this preliminary move the Americans obtained seaplane bases on the enemy's flank. They also unexpectedly removed a dangerous threat by capturing some 350 explosive-bearing suicide boats similar to those which the Japanese had used against the invasion ships in Lingayan Gulf the preceding January.

Before dawn on April 1, 318 combatant vessels and 1,139 major auxiliary craft with more than a half million men of the Army, Navy, and Marine Corps arrived at the scene of action. Aboard the ships of Turner's expeditionary force were 182,000 assault troops of the Tenth Army, comprising the 24th Army Corps and the First, Second, and Sixth Marine Divisions. Three European landings had been on a larger scale, but in those operations the communication lines had been incomparably shorter and the logistic problems far simpler than at Okinawa. Involved in the final preparatory bombing and bombardment of strong points in the area were the old battleships under Admiral Blandy, the new battleships under Admiral Lee, B-29's from the Marianas, and other planes from Luzon, from China, from Task Force 58, and from a formation of British ships, including a battleship and four carriers,[2] which was watching the chain of islands stretching southwest towards Formosa.

At 8:30 A.M., Turner began putting troops ashore on a six-mile

---

[2] All American carriers, previous to the construction of the 45,000-ton *Midway, Franklin D. Roosevelt,* and *Coral Sea,* had armored hangar decks but wooden flight decks. The British carriers, with armored flight decks, showed superior immunity to crippling damage by air attack.

stretch of beach on the southwest coast of Okinawa below Cape Zampa. At the same time a task group bearing the Second Marine Division, which was being held in reserve, made a feint at another beach to the southeast. By nightfall 50,000 soldiers and Marines were ashore, and the advance guards, pushing ahead against little opposition, had seized the valuable Yontan and Kadena airfields. By morning of the third day they had raced across the island and reached the east coast.

The Sixth Marine Division now began a march to the northeast, meeting only scattered resistance until it reached Motobu Peninsula on the 8th. Here in the hills and rough terrain the Japanese fought back for a week. The final mopping up of enemy troops in the area provided high positions from which guns could be trained on nearby Ie Shima, which American forces seized at once in order to make use of that island's airfield. By April 22 the Marines had advanced to Cape Hedo and the northern two-thirds of Okinawa was secured.

In the south the story was different. Here Ushijima had placed by far the greater part of his troops in the battle line north of Naha. The Japanese had now largely abandoned their blockhouse and pillbox system. Each hill and ridge was organized into a large-scale defense position by construction of tunnels and caves under 30 to 100 feet of earth and stone. From such strongholds, offshore and land artillery were unable to blast out the enemy. Against Ushijima's well-fortified line the American troops not committed to the north came on April 5. Here three United States divisions, forming a front only four miles long, were met by massed artillery, including howitzers, rifles, and large mortars and rockets. For two weeks the battle remained stalemated. Then the Japanese began slowly to give way under unrelenting pressure. But they maintained their line, permitting no flanking until the remnants of their original force had been compressed into the southern tip of the island. The Tenth Army's 14-mile push had required 11 weeks of intensive warfare. When the end came, General Ushijima had committed suicide in ceremonial fashion; and General Buckner, commanding the United States land forces, had been killed by a shell burst. Buckner's successor, Marine Major General Roy S. Geiger, completed the southward thrust. On June 21, after 82 days of some of the hardest fighting of the war, organized Japanese resistance ended, though General Joseph W. Stilwell, who relieved Geiger on the 23rd, was left the task of mopping up numerous small enemy pockets.

On Okinawa nearly 7,000 Americans had been killed and more

than 29,000 wounded. Except for some 10,000 prisoners—an unusually large number, indicating a decline in morale—most of the Japanese garrison was wiped out. In exchange for heavy losses, the United States had won a position vital for air raids against factories and aviation facilities in Japan and for staging the invasion of the enemy home islands, then being planned. Actually, when the ratio of Japanese to American casualties is taken into account, it becomes apparent that the capture of no major position in the central Pacific except the Marshalls had been more economical.

During the first two months of the Okinawa operation the Fifth Fleet, aggregating at one time as many as 1,600 ships, stood off the island giving support by shellfire and carrier plane raids and interception. During this period the surface forces went through an ordeal such as no fleet had ever been called upon to endure over such an extended period. For five days following the initial landings on Okinawa the ships were left almost unmolested. Then, on April 6, the enemy struck in force. Planes from Kyushu and the upper Ryukyus, mostly old crates rigged for suicide attacks, swept down upon the fleet and the beachhead. The majority of the oncoming planes were intercepted short of the target area by air groups from Task Force 58, and more than 200 were shot down, but an equal number came over the fleet, where another hundred were destroyed by fighters from escort carriers and by antiaircraft fire. Numerous American ships took damaging hits, however, and the destroyers *Bush* and *Colhoun* were sunk.

While this attack was in progress, the Japanese Second Fleet, comprising the remaining superbattleship *Yamato,* the cruiser *Yahagi,* and eight destroyers, departed from the Inland Sea to attack the United States Fifth Fleet. In view of the enormous disparity of the opposing forces, this sortie can be considered in no other wise than as a suicide mission, and so it proved.[3] American land-based planes reported the approach of the enemy ships that evening, whereupon Mitscher proceeded north with Task Force 58 to meet them. On the morning of the 7th, scout planes of Fleet Air Wing One, based in the Kerama Islands, made new contact with the Japanese force, then almost directly north of Okinawa. Like the *Prince of Wales* and the *Repulse,*

[3] Admiral Toyoda later said of this attempt: "We questioned whether there was a 50-50 chance. Even in assembling that squadron we had a difficult time getting the necessary 2,500 tons of fuel oil, but it was felt that, even if there was not a 50-50 chance, nothing was to be gained by letting those ships lie idle in home waters, and, besides, it would have been contrary to the tradition of the Japanese Navy not to have sent them."

sunk near Singapore at the outbreak of the war, the enemy ships were without air cover. Mitscher's carrier planes, in a series of strikes beginning at noon, sank the *Yamato,* the *Yahagi,* and a destroyer, and so damaged most of the other destroyers that two were scuttled and one was later decommissioned as beyond repair. This attack, which had cost Task Force 58 seven planes, ended the last sortie of fighting ships from Japanese home ports.

Following the first major air attack on United States forces off Okinawa, flights came down from the northeast at regular intervals, causing great damage, and killing or wounding so many navy personnel that for a while casualties at sea ran ahead of those on shore. To the *kamikazes* the Japanese now added another suicide weapon, the *Oka* (called by the Americans *Baka*—Japanese for idiot). This was a winged, jet-propelled, human-guided bomb carrying 1,135 pounds of explosive. Launched from a release gear attached to the belly of a medium bomber, it would be piloted at great speed into the ship selected as the target. As American ship losses and casualties mounted, a picket screen of destroyers and smaller craft was placed at distances varying from 20 to 90 miles around the fleet and battle area. The function of the picket ships was to give warning of approaching air attacks and handle fighter direction in the outlying areas. Since they were usually the first targets seen by enemy pilots coming in for a raid, they came under frequent attack. A great many were damaged and numbers were sunk, but they undoubtedly saved larger and more valuable ships near the beachhead.

In a particularly vicious raid early in May a suicide plane crashed among aircraft about to take off from the carrier *Bunker Hill,* starting a raging fire. A minute later another *kamikaze* dropped a 500-pound bomb through the flight deck and then smashed into the island superstructure, its motor bounding against the flag office and killing three officers and 11 men of Admiral Mitscher's personal staff. It was fortunate that Mitscher happened not to be on the flag bridge or in his quarters at the time, for both were demolished. He now transferred via destroyer to another carrier to direct defense tactics, while the *Bunker Hill* put up a fight for life reminiscent of that waged by the *Franklin* a few weeks before. The crew, risking destruction from a series of explosions, fought the fires for three hours until the decks were covered with tons of water on which floated burning gasoline and oil. As a measure of desperation, the navigator ordered a 70-degree turn. When the ship heeled, the flaming mixture spilled off the side into the sea. The

Bunker Hill was saved and was able to reach Puget Sound Navy Yard under her own power, but 392 of her crew had been killed and 264 wounded. Similarly hit at various times during the campaign, though less seriously damaged, were other big carriers—the *Intrepid, Hancock,* and *Enterprise.*

In order to destroy as many suicide and other planes as possible at their main point of origin, Task Force 58 three times approached Kyushu and sent in aircraft to raid landing fields. But the enemy attacks continued, albeit on a somewhat reduced scale. By June 1, when the major combatant ships were released from support duty, 30 American vessels had been sunk and more than 200 damaged, a fourth of them seriously. Nothing larger than destroyers had been lost, but 12 of these had gone down.[4] Among the units requiring repairs were ten battleships, 13 carriers, five cruisers, and 67 destroyers. No navy had ever before been hit so often in a single operation. About 80 per cent of the damage had been done by suicide planes. Casualties were extremely heavy—4,907 navy personnel killed and 4,824 wounded.[5]

OPERATIONS IN THE PHILLIPINES AND BORNEO

While the United States Fifth Fleet was engaged in the Iwo Jima and Okinawa operations, the Seventh Fleet co-operated with General of the Army MacArthur's land forces in the long, tedious process of clearing the enemy from the Philippines. It was necessary first to expel them from the key cities and air bases and to capture, destroy, or neutralize them in all areas where they might command supply routes, either Japanese or American.

At the end of February, just as the fight for Manila was being concluded, cruisers and destroyers supported an assault on Puerto Princesa on the east coast of Palawan Island. The harbor and nearby airfields, seized without opposition, provided bases from which United States forces could control the two straits leading from the South China to the Sulu Sea. A few days later, troops were put ashore on the western peninsula of Mindanao and subsequently on the Basilan, Jolo, and Tawi Tawi Islands. This cut the enemy supply route between the Sulu

[4] Destroyers lost: *Halligan, Bush, Colhoun (II), Mannert L. Abele, Pringle, Little (II), Luce, Morrison, Longshaw, Drexler, William D. Porter,* and *Twiggs.* The destroyer escort *Oberrender* also was sunk.

[5] American plane losses, including those destroyed aboard damaged carriers, amounted to about 900, though no more than 200 pilots and aircrewmen were killed. It is apparently impossible to determine enemy plane losses for the same period. American estimates have run as high as 4,200, Japanese estimates as low as 900.

and Celebes Seas and completed the isolation of the Japanese in the central Philippines. These moves also provided jumping off points for projected operations against Borneo, where some 30,000 of the enemy were in possession of petroleum wells and production facilities.

In March, assaults were made against Panay, Negros, Cebu, and smaller islands between Luzon and Mindanao. Opposition to the landings was generally light, but resistance tended to stiffen in the inland areas, notably on Cebu. By the end of May additional amphibious operations had been carried out on the north and south coasts of Mindanao. Troops from these beachheads advanced rapidly and joined forces, thereby splitting the enemy garrison and preventing a united front.

By this time the major units of the Seventh Fleet were committed to the invasion of Borneo, an operation which would cut off the rich storehouse of raw materials from the Japanese in South China, Burma, and the East Indies. The initial target was to be the island of Tarakan off the Borneo west coast. On May 1, after a three-day bombardment of enemy positions by Allied air and surface forces under Vice Admiral D. E. Barbey, Australian troops went ashore against only small arms opposition and quickly took possession. This conquest, besides returning important oil wells to the Allies, provided an airfield for close support of future operations.

In order to secure an advance fleet base, Barbey's force next struck at Brunei on the opposite coast. In preparation for this invasion, American and Australian planes came over regularly for ten days to hit shipping in Brunei Bay and fortifications and troop concentrations ashore. During the last three days a channel was cleared to the landing beaches by United States minesweepers, one of which struck a mine and went down with numerous casualties. On June 10, Australians went in under a heavy surface bombardment and seized three points in the target area. Fifty miles to the west, meanwhile, an interceptor patrol of Allied cruisers and destroyers steamed back and forth to prevent interference by enemy surface vessels. The precaution was unnecessary. A few weeks earlier the Japanese had had three cruisers in the East Indies. The light *Isuzu* had been sunk in April by American submarines. The heavy *Haguro* had been sunk in May by British aircraft and destroyers. Two days before the Brunei landings a British submarine patrolling south of Singapore had found the heavy *Ashigara* and sent her down. There were now no major enemy combat vessels in the area.

Both the Tarakan and Brunei invasions were in some measure preparatory to an assault set for July 1 on Balikpapan, richest source of oil in Borneo. Here the Japanese, assembled in considerable strength and barricaded behind formidable defenses, were determined to make a stand. To support the operation the Allies assembled in Makassar Strait the strongest cover force employed in the Seventh Fleet area since the Lingayan Gulf assault—nine cruisers, three escort carriers, and three destroyer escorts. For a month preceding D-Day clouds of Allied planes struck at the target, and for two weeks minesweepers and underwater demolition teams worked under cover of gunnery vessels to clear a passage to the beachhead. The task proved hazardous, for fire from well-placed enemy shore batteries was accurate and deadly; three of the minesweepers were sunk and three others were damaged by shells. Nevertheless, so intense was the Allied bombardment preceding the landings that a large Australian assault force was able to go ashore on the scheduled date without a single casualty. General MacArthur, who went in with the fourth wave, remarked: "I think today we settled the score of that Makassar Strait affair of three and a half years ago."

Once ashore, the troops established a beachhead a mile wide and a half mile deep before stiffening Japanese resistance began to slow down the advance. Cruisers remained offshore to provide fire support through the first week of bitter fighting. Two additional weeks of attack and counterattack followed before the enemy line broke and the Australians began to move up the coast towards other major oil-producing areas to the north. By this time the forces put ashore at Brunei had secured the northwestern part of Borneo, and at Tarakan oil was once more flowing from wells that had been set afire by the retreating Dutch in 1942 and again by the retreating Japanese in 1945.

PRE-INVASION OPERATIONS AGAINST JAPAN

The American capture of the Marianas and the subsequent bombing of Japanese cities had to some extent weakened the grip of military leaders on the government of Japan. The traditional ruling class, far better informed than the average citizen regarding the national peril, at length reasserted itself and forced the Tojo cabinet out of office. Total conquest of their country through invasion, they feared, would mean an end of the emperor system and their own prerogatives. Some way out, some formula short of unconditional surrender, must be sought without delay. At last in the early spring of 1945 a group of former premiers headed by Prince Konoye succeeded at considerable peril to themselves, for the military was still potent, in by-passing the Army and transmitting directly to the Emperor their conviction that negotiations should be opened with the United States and Great Britain. It had now become evident that, though Japan still had a large unbeaten army in China, her ability to fight was nearing an end. American submarines had gravely cut down the flow of food, fuel, and raw materials from the East Indies before the invasion of the Philippines had completed the blockade of supplies from that area. The capture of Iwo Jima had enabled the B-29's to increase the precision and power of their raids, with the result that production was rapidly falling off. Seizure of Okinawa by American forces would provide many airfields from which the attacks on Japanese manufacturing centers could be enormously stepped up. With the defeat of Germany, it was clear that the whole military power of the United States and Great Britain, and possibly also of the Soviet Union, would soon be concentrated against the home islands. In May, therefore, the Supreme War Guidance Council[6] in Tokyo began discussing ways to terminate the war.

Since the activities of the Konoye group and the deliberations of the Council were carried on in the strictest secrecy, the Allies had no way of knowing how much more punishment the enemy would take before acknowledging defeat. Certainly, the suicidal fury with which Japanese troops had fought to defend the farthest outposts of their empire gave little reason to believe that anything short of invasion and physical seizure would force Japan to surrender. The American high command therefore drew up plans for an amphibious assault on Kyushu, scheduled for the following November, and a subsequent invasion of Honshu in the Tokyo area. The Sixth Army, designated to carry out the land phase of these operations, withdrew from combat and began a program of special training on Luzon. Augmenting forces, troops released from the European theater, would be rushed to the Philippines as they became available. In the meantime, the planes of Fleet Air Wings One and Eighteen, based on Okinawa and the Kerama Islands, together with United States submarines, set out to make the blockade of Japan absolute by cutting her communication lines with the Asiatic continent. In this they were soon joined by army air-

---

[6] Members: The Prime Minister, the War Minister, the Navy Minister, the Foreign Minister, the Chief of the Army General Staff, and the Chief of the Naval General Staff. In May, 1945, Admiral Toyoda became Chief of the Naval General Staff, Admiral Ozawa succeeding him as Commander-in-Chief of the Combined Fleet.

craft, including B-29's, which not only attacked convoys but mined the straits leading into the Sea of Japan.

At the same time, the Superfortresses went on an ever-mounting campaign of destruction. They now shifted to night saturation attacks, using a new type of incendiary bomb which sprayed all objects surrounding the point of impact with blazing gasoline jelly. The task of destroying the Japanese manufacturing potential necessarily involved burning out great areas in the major cities, for under a remarkable system of decentralization much of Japan's industry, particularly in aircraft, was carried on in numerous small workshops and even in private homes, the factories serving principally as final assembly points. In a raid early in March the Superfortresses burned out 15 square miles of metropolitan Tokyo, and during the following week they destroyed an equal area divided among three other cities. By June the big bombers were arriving over Japan in waves of 500 or more. Tokyo had by then been bombed dozens of times and in all the larger towns of the home islands there were extensive flame-swept areas. By the end of July the B-29's, employing a terrifying psychological weapon, were dropping leaflets over their targets in advance of raids, warning the inhabitants to leave, and then following up the threats by hitting the cities indicated. The Japanese aircraft production rate had by this time been cut down to less than half that of the preceding year.

The United States Fleet had already joined the onslaught against the homeland. At the end of May, the Spruance-Mitscher-Turner team, which had just passed through its severest ordeal off Okinawa, was relieved; and the Halsey-McCain team went back in, with Vice Admiral H. W. Hill replacing Turner in command of the amphibious forces in the Ryukyus. At the same time, Admiral Nimitz took Hill's amphibious force and Buckner's Tenth Army under his direct control, thereby freeing the major central Pacific combatant ships, now once more designated as Third Fleet, to act as a striking team. On assuming command, Halsey ordered the big battleships to fire a few salvos at Japanese positions on Okinawa. "I just wanted to leave my calling card," he said. He then led his fleet against Kyushu, but bad weather cut down the effectiveness of Task Force 38 air strikes. In two days 16 American planes were lost and only 30 enemy aircraft were destroyed. The weather quickly worsened into a typhoon, in which mountainous waves driven by a 138-mile-an-hour wind knocked off a hundred feet of the cruiser *Pittsburgh's* bow and damaged at least 20 other ships, six of them seriously. Three days later the fleet resumed operations with additional strikes against Kyushu and the Ryukyus. It then retired to Leyte Gulf for replenishment and repairs.

On July 10 the Third Fleet was off Tokyo sending in planes to strike at airfields and industrial plants. Though enemy planes in large numbers were destroyed on the ground, the Japanese launched no counterattack. In an attempt to lure out the Imperial Air Force, Admiral Nimitz made public the names of many of the American ships present—big carriers, fast battleships, new cruisers and destroyers—but the results were negative. Japan was now carefully hoarding her limited air and fuel reserves for suicide use against the impending invasion. On the 14th, after refueling at sea, the fleet returned to the waters off Japan to strike beyond the range of B-29's at targets on northern Honshu and on Hokkaido. While the carrier planes hit vessels offshore and sank vital inter-island railroad ferries, divisions of battleships went in close to shell two coastal manufacturing towns. A pair of Japanese destroyers coming under American guns at this time were quickly sent down.

Halsey's 105 fighting ships, now turning back south, were joined on the 17th by 28 British men-of-war. This combined fleet, the most powerful striking force in history, paraded down the enemy coast to within 40 miles of Tokyo, the heavy gunnery ships bombarding shoreline targets, while the carrier planes in huge waves struck through foul weather at the Yokosuka naval base in Tokyo Bay. Despite unfavorable conditions, the Allied aircraft sank a destroyer, severely damaged the battleship *Nagato,* and battered shore installations and railroad facilities.

Between the 24th and 28th the combined British and American forces, moving to the southwest, sent planes across Shikoku and the Inland Sea to pound the key naval base at Kure. This time the Japanese tried aircraft interception in strength, only to lose about 150 planes, three times the Allied losses. The carrier aircraft achieved incredible destruction in this series of raids, sinking the *Kaiyo,* last of Japan's escort carriers; heavily damaging the *Amagi* and *Katsuragi,* last of her available major carriers; and leaving the *Haruna,* last of her usable battleships, burned out and beached. They also sank the carrier-battleship *Hyuga,* the cruisers *Kitagami* and *Oyodo,* and two destroyers, and put out of action the remaining carrier-battleship, *Ise,* the cruisers *Aoba* and *Tone,* and two destroyers. At the conclusion of these strikes, the Imperial Japanese Fleet, which at the beginning of the war had been the third largest in the world, was reduced to one light and one training cruiser, a dozen or so destroyers, and about 50 submarines.[7]

Halsey's ships now came back to Tokyo for further air blows and shore bombardment. While the fleet was en route to the target, the United States Navy suffered its last major loss of the war. A thousand miles to the south the heavy cruiser *Indianapolis,* approaching Leyte, was torpedoed by a Japanese submarine and sank in 15 minutes. Of her crew of 1,196, approximately 500 survived the sinking, but by a tragic blunder the fact that she was overdue was not noted at her port of destination. When the survivors were accidentally discovered and picked up after four days in the water, only 316 were left.

After striking at the Tokyo area on July 30, the Third Fleet gave Japan a brief respite while it rode out a typhoon. By August 9 it was on the prowl once more, blasting at airfields in Northern Honshu, where most of the remaining enemy planes had been sent. The carrier aircraft destroyed nearly 400 of them, mostly on the ground, and damaged almost as many more. Then, after another battleship bombardment of shore targets, the fleet returned on the 13th for a final blow at Tokyo.

THE JAPANESE SURRENDER

While all but the highest echelons of the Japanese Army and Navy, working on the assumption that the war would go on, were making preparations to meet the Allied invasion, the national leaders were

[7] The following table indicates the means by which Japanese warships were sunk:

TYPES SUNK	CAUSES					TOTALS
	SURFACE UNITS	SUB-MARINES	AIRCRAFT	COM-BINATION	OTHER CAUSES	
Battleships	3	1	3	1	1	9
Carriers	..	4	9	2	..	15
Escort Carriers	..	4	1	..	..	5
Cruisers	4	14	14	4	..	36
Destroyers	27	42	45	5	7	126
Submarines	64	26	12	4	19	125
TOTALS	98	91	84	16	27	316

seeking a face-saving formula which would bring hostilities to an end and yet permit the ruling class to remain in power. By early June the members of the Supreme War Guidance Council were unofficially agreed that peace feelers should be extended through Russia. Still, the Council temporized for another month, whereupon the Emperor, on June 10, peremptorily summoned the Foreign Minister and indicated his desire that negotiations via the Soviet Government be undertaken forthwith. The Japanese ambassador at Moscow then approached the Russian Vice Commissar on Foreign Affairs but was told that inasmuch as Premier Stalin and Foreign Commissar Molotov were about to depart for the conference of victorious powers at Potsdam, no official action could be taken until later. Unofficially, however, the Russians transmitted the Japanese request for terms to the Presidents of the United States and the Chinese National Government and the Prime Minister of Great Britain, who gave Japan her reply in the Potsdam Declaration of July 26: Japanese armed forces were to surrender unconditionally; Japanese sovereignty was to be limited to the four home islands; Japanese industry must be restricted to such enterprises as would sustain the national economy but not permit rearmament for war; stern justice was to be meted out to all war criminals, including those who had mistreated Allied prisoners; the Japanese Government was to "remove all obstacles to the revival and strengthening of democratic tendencies among the Japanese people"; a "peacefully inclined and responsible government" was to be established in accordance with the freely expressed will of the people; until these objectives were achieved, Allied forces would occupy points in Japanese territory.

The Allies, in guaranteeing Japanese sovereignty, were showing greater leniency towards Japan than they had shown the European Axis, which had been guaranteed nothing. But the Supreme Council found the terms too severe and considered how they might secure milder terms, meanwhile publicly announcing that they would ignore the Declaration. While these deliberations were in progress, the nation was subjected to a series of shocks which brought the discussion to an end and also provided the Japanese with a situation that was not without its face-saving value. A lone B-29 on August 6 dropped on Hiroshima an atomic bomb which exploded with the force of 20,000 tons of TNT and instantly destroyed the heart of the city. Two days later a second atomic bomb was dropped on Nagasaki. On the same day the Soviet Government declared war on Japan and sent its Red Army across the border into Manchuria.

News of these startling events appears to have been received by the Supreme Council with mingled feelings of horror and relief. One of their greatest problems had been how to present the fact of defeat to a citizenry, an army, and a navy from whom the nation's desperate state had been concealed and who had long been propagandized with stories of fictitious victories. There was even the possibility that the people and the military might rebel against an attempt to surrender. But the terrifying strangeness and power of the new bomb, resembling in its effects a cataclysm of nature, and the approach of Russia's armies provided convincing arguments. "I do not think it would be accurate to look upon the atomic bomb and the entry and participation of Soviet Russia as direct causes of the termination of the war," said Admiral Toyoda afterwards, "but I think that those two factors did enable us to bring the war to a termination without creating too great chaos in Japan."

On August 10 the Japanese Government declared its willingness to accept the terms of the Potsdam Declaration, subject to the condition that the Emperor's position would be in no way affected. The Allies agreed but stipulated that he should submit to the authority of the Supreme Allied Commander in Japan, and that his future status should be made the subject of free election by the Japanese people. The Imperial Government on the 14th announced its willingness to accept these terms.

When the "cease fire" order reached the Third Fleet off Tokyo the next day, one air attack wave was already over Honshu where it destroyed 30 enemy planes. A second wave of fighters and bombers had been launched, but these Admiral Halsey recalled, with the added order that if on the return they encountered any Japanese aircraft they were to shoot them down "not vindictively, but in a friendly sort of way." In a little over a month the Third Fleet had, in the words of Fleet Admiral King's report, "destroyed or damaged 2,804 enemy planes, sunk or damaged 148 Japanese combat ships, sunk or damaged 1,598 enemy merchant ships, destroyed 195 locomotives, and damaged 109 more."

On September 2, ships of the United States Pacific Fleet rode at anchor in Tokyo Bay. At 8:55 A.M. representatives of the defeated government came aboard the battleship *Missouri*. Here, in the presence of Allied military and naval leaders, the Japanese Foreign Minister and the Chief of the Imperial General Staff signed the instrument of surrender on behalf of the Emperor and the Imperial General Headquarters. General of the Army MacArthur signed the acceptance as Supreme Commander for the Allied Powers. He was followed by Fleet Admiral Nimitz, signing as Representative for the United States. Representatives of the United Kingdom, China, Russia, Australia, Canada, France, the Netherlands, and New Zealand then added their signatures.

It may be well to review briefly the contribution of sea power in the three and a half years of Pacific warfare thus ended, giving that term a legitimate extension to include the aerial, surface, and sub-surface weapons utilized to gain sea control. True, in this war, land, sea, and air forces were combined as never before on such scale, and, as in the whole history of warfare, the severest personnel losses were suffered in bitter fighting on shore—in the capture of island bases, in the difficult New Guinea, Philippine, and Okinawa campaigns. But the major factor in the Pacific war was the series of naval campaigns which deprived Japan of sea control. Midway marked the turning point. The immense naval construction program made possible the massing of combatant and transport craft and air power, which in turn made possible the advance up the Solomons, the capture of the Gilberts, and the steady advance across the Pacific in the following year, an advance which, it may be noted, was the principal means of bringing air power within striking distance of the Japanese homeland. In the destruction of Japan's merchant fleet, the primary means of supplying and drawing sustenance from her new-won insular empire, American submarines had a steady and outstanding share, sinking over 1,000 major vessels amounting to nearly 5,000,000 tons, or 63 per cent of all Japanese merchant ships destroyed. At the end, large Japanese armies remained undefeated in Asia and in the home islands. It was the loss of her cargo fleet and the blockade, depriving Japan of foodstuffs, oil, and strategic materials, which brought her to the verge of surrender before the atomic bomb and the advent of Russia into the war—even, in fact, before the Mariana-based bombers seriously crippled her industrial output.

Yet, it would be a mistake to assume that the victories over Japan and the European Axis were achieved predominantly by any one arm, land, sea, or air, as it would be a mistake to think of the plane

as a mere adjunct or weapon attached to land or sea forces. World War II was necessarily tri-elemental; armies, fleets, and aircraft were helpless except when operating in close co-ordination. Realization of this should not be obscured by the fact that in the Pacific all three elements were in many cases navy-controlled or that in Europe air power was generally army-controlled. Actually the strength of the Allied Powers lay to a large extent in the balance of their land, sea, and air forces and their ability to merge all three for the achievement of a single end. In the typical tri-elemental advance, ships and planes cleared the way by gaining command of the sea and then obtaining control around and above the target. Ground forces next went ashore under cover of sea and air forces to take control of the land. This once achieved, a base was provided for staging the next advance along the same lines. Throughout the process *balanced* power permitted operations which in former times would have been considered dangerous in the extreme, as when United States forces, dominant on the sea and in the air, safely by-passed strong Japanese garrisons, or when Allied ships, under air cover and using new techniques of fire control, engaged land forces and fought it out with coastal batteries. By the steps indicated, the conqueror approached the enemy's citadel. That the ultimate decision was attained in Europe by land and air and in the Pacific by sea and air was a result largely of the geographical factors involved.

Behind the success of the Allied sea-air-land forces lay, of course, the superiority of the United Nations in natural resources, in industrial output, in manpower reserves, and in scientific research, increasing the strength and effectiveness of all three branches. But in the concluding months of the long struggle, scientific discovery put an end to a way of warfare which it had done much to create. Developments in explosives and in means of delivering them to the target promised a new and more devastating character to future military operations. Armed might, in the old sense, lost much of its meaning. Russia, which had emerged from World War II as the world's greatest land power, and the United States, which had emerged as the leading sea power, were henceforth nearly as vulnerable as the weakest nations. Now, as never before, the hope of civilization lay in the creation of machinery to keep the peace.

Nevertheless, in the event of future armed conflict, the old means of waging war will probably not be altogether outmoded. So long as troops and supplies must be carried by sea, so long as it shall be necessary to seize and hold bases for operations, so long, in short, as the oceans and waterways of the world shall continue to serve either as paths for or barriers against conquest, fleets of ships and fleet-borne aircraft will have a vital function, and the basic concepts of sea power will remain.

☆   ☆   ☆   ☆   ☆

A Selected Bibliography

The following does not purport to be a full bibliography of American naval history or a complete list of sources consulted in the preparation of the present volume. It is intended primarily as a guide to useful books for further reading and study.

I.   BIBLIOGRAPHY AND REFERENCE

Brassey, T., *Naval and Shipping Annual,* 1886-1943.

Fahey, J. C., *The Ships and Aircraft of the United States Fleet,* 1942-1945.

Harbeck, C. T., *A Contribution to the Bibliography of the History of the United States Navy,* 1906.

Jane's Fighting Ships. Annual. 1898. . . .

Neeser, R. W., *Statistical and Chronological History of the United States Navy,* 1909.

Rimington, C., and Others, *Fighting Ships.* Annual. 1941. . . .

II.   GENERAL

Alden, C. S., and Westcott, A., *The United States Navy: A History,* 1945.

Chadwick, F. E., *The American Navy,* 1915.

Clark, G. R., and Others, *A Short History of the United States Navy,* 1927.

Cooper, J. F., *The History of the Navy of the United States of America,* 1839.

Knox, D. W., *A History of the United States Navy,* 1936.

Maclay, E. S., *A History of the United States Navy,* 1901.

Mahan, A. T., *The Influence of Sea Power Upon History*, 1943.
[Late ed.].
Mitchell, D. W., *History of the Modern American Navy*, 1946.
Pratt, F., *The Navy, a History*, 1941.
Vagts, A., *Landing Operations . . . From Antiquity to 1945*, 1946.
Westcott, A., ed., *Mahan on Naval Warfare*, 1942.

III.   THE REVOLUTION; QUASI-WAR WITH FRANCE; BARBARY WARS; WAR OF 1812

Albion, R. G., and Pope, J. B., *Sea Lanes in Wartime: the American Experience, 1775-1942*. 1942.
Allen, G. W., *A Naval History of the American Revolution*, 1913.
———, *Our Naval War With France*, 1909.
———, *Our Navy and the Barbary Corsairs*, 1905.
deKoven, Mrs. R., *Life and Letters of John Paul Jones*, 1913.
Goldsborough, C. W., ed., *The United States Naval Chronicle*, 1824.
Hollis, I. N., *The Frigate Constitution*, 1900.
Knox, D. W., ed., *Quasi-War Between the United States and France*, 7 vols., 1935-1938.
———, *United States Wars With the Barbary Powers*, 1939-41.
Lewis, C. L., *The Romantic Decatur*, 1937.
Maclay, E. S., *A History of American Privateers*, 1899.
Mahan, A. T., *Major Operations of the Navies in the War of American Independence*, 1913.
———, *Sea Power in its Relation to the War of 1812*, 1905.
Paullin, C. O., *The Navy of the American Revolution*, 1906.
Porter, D. D., *Memoir of Commodore David Porter*, 1875.
Roosevelt, T., *The Naval War of 1812*, 1882.

IV.   FROM THE WAR OF 1812 TO THE CIVIL WAR

Allen, G. W., *Our Navy and the West Indies Pirates*, 1929.
Baxter, J. P., *The Introduction of the Ironclad Warship*, 1933.
Benjamin, P., *The United States Naval Academy*, 1900.
Griffis, W. F., *Matthew Calbraith Perry*, 1887.
Narrative of the Expedition of an American Squadron to the China Seas and Japan, 3 vols., 1856. (The Perry expedition.)
Paullin, C. O., *Diplomatic Negotiations of American Naval Officers*, 1912.

V. The Civil War

Alden, C. S., *George Hamilton Perkins*, 1914.

Andrews, C. C., *Campaign of Mobile*, 1867.

Battles and Leaders of the Civil War, 4 vols., 1884-1887.

Bennett, F. M., *The Monitor and the Navy Under Steam*, 1900.

Church, W. C., *The Life of John Ericsson*, 2 vols., 1891.

Ellicott, J. M., *Life of John Ancrum Winslow*, 1902.

Farragut, L., *Life of David Glasgow Farragut*, 1879.

Hill, J. D., *Sea Dogs of the Sixties*, 1935.

Jeffries, W. W., "The Civil War Career of Charles Wilkes," *Journal of Southern History*, August, 1945.

Lewis, C. L., *David Glasgow Farragut*, 2 vols., 1941-1943.

———, *Admiral Franklin Buchanan*, 1929.

Mahan, A. T., *The Gulf and Inland Waters*, 1883.

———, *From Sail to Steam*, 1907.

Moore, F., ed., *The Rebellion Record*, 11 vols., 1861-1864.

Official Records of the Union and Confederate Navies in the War of the Rebellion, 30 vols., 1894-1922.

Porter, D. D., *Naval History of the Civil War*, 1886.

Scharf, J. T., *History of the Confederate States Navy*, 1887.

Semmes, R., *Memoirs of Service Afloat*, 1869.

Soley, J. R., *The Blockade and the Cruisers*, 1883.

Walke, H., *Naval Scenes and Reminiscences of the Civil War*, 1887.

Welles, G., *The Diary of Gideon Welles*, 3 vols., 1911.

West, R. S., Jr., *Gideon Welles: Lincoln's Navy Department*, 1943.

———, *The Second Admiral: A Life of David Dixon Porter*, 1937.

VI. The New Navy; the Spanish-American War

Bennett, F. M., *The Steam Navy of the United States*, 1896.

Brodie, B., *Sea Power in the Machine Age*, 1941.

Chadwick, F. E., *The Relations of the United States and Spain*, 2 vols. 1911.

Clark, C. E., *My Fifty Years in the Navy*, 1917.

Dahlgren, M. V., *Memoir of John A. Dahlgren*, 1882.

Davis, G. T., *A Navy Second to None*, 1941.

DeLong, E., ed., *The Voyage of the 'Jeannette,'* 2 vols., 1884.

Dewey, G., *Autobiography of George Dewey, Admiral of the Navy*, 1916.

Fiske, B. A., *From Midshipman to Rear Admiral*, 1919.

Goode, W. A. M., *With Sampson Through the War,* 1899.

Long, J. D., *The New American Navy,* 2 vols., 1903.

Mahan, A. T., *Lessons of the War with Spain and Other Articles,* 1899.

Millis, W., *The Martial Spirit,* 1931.

Morris, C. M., *The Nation's Navy,* 1898.

Puleston, W. D., *Mahan: The Life and Work of Captain Alfred Thayer Mahan,* 1939.

Sprout, Harold and Margaret, *The Rise of American Naval Power,* 1933.

Wilson, H. W., *The Downfall of Spain,* 1900.

———, *Ironclads in Action,* 2 vols., 1898.

VII.   Geography; Strategy; Logistics

Fairgrieve, J., *Geography and World Power,* 1941.

Geographical Foundations of National Power. Army Service Forces Manual M-103, 1944.

Harris, M. G., *Lifelines of Victory,* 1942.

Mackinder, H. J., *Democratic Ideals and Reality,* 1942. [Reissue.]

Mowrer, E. A. and Rajchman, M., *Global War,* 1942.

Spykman, N. J., *America's Strategy in World Politics,* 1942.

———, *The Geography of the Peace,* 1944.

Strausz-Hupe, R., *Geopolitics: The Struggle for Space and Power,* 1942.

Weigert, H. W., and Stefanson, V., eds., *Compass of the World: A Symposium on Political Geography,* 1944.

VIII.   Twentieth Century to World War II

Bailey, T. A., *Theodore Roosevelt and the Japanese-American Crises,* 1934.

Belknap, R. R., *The Yankee Mining Squadron,* 1920.

Buell, R. L., *The Washington Conference,* 1922.

Bywater, H. C., *Navies and Nations,* 1927.

Daniels, J., *Our Navy at War,* 1922.

———, *The Wilson Era, 1910-1917,* 1945.

Davis, F., *The Atlantic System: the Story of Anglo-American Control of the Seas,* 1941.

Dix, C. C., *The World's Navies in the Boxer Rebellion,* 1905.

Engely, G., *The Politics of Naval Disarmament,* 1932.

Evans, R. D., *An Admiral's Log,* 1910.

———, *A Sailor's Log,* 1901.

Fiske, B. A., *The Navy as a Fighting Machine,* 1916.

Frothingham, T. G., *The Naval History of the World War,* 3 vols., 1926.

Gleaves, A., *A History of the Transport Service,* 1921.

Johnstone, W. C., *The United States and Japan's New Order,* 1941.

Kittredge, T. B., *Naval Lessons of the Great War,* 1931.

Levine, I. D., *Mitchell, Pioneer of Air Power,* 1943.

Miller, H. B., *Navy Wings,* 1937.

Miller, R. J., *Around the World with the Battleships,* 1909.

Morison, E. E., *Admiral Sims and the Modern American Navy,* 1942.

O'Gara, G. C., *Theodore Roosevelt and the Rise of the Modern Navy,* 1943.

Roosevelt, T., *Autobiography,* 1913.

Sims, W. S., and Hendrick, B. J., *The Victory at Sea,* 1920.

Sprout, Harold and Margaret, *Toward a New Order of Sea Power,* 1943. [Covers period 1918-1922.]

IX. World War II

Bayler, W., and Gaines, C., *Last Man Off Wake Island,* 1943.

Bryan, J. and Reed, P., *Mission Beyond Darkness,* 1945. (Battle of the Philippine Sea.)

Burns, E., *Then There Was One,* 1944. (Story of the *Enterprise.*)

Cant, G., *America's Navy in World War II,* 1944. Revised ed.

———, *The Great Pacific Victory,* 1946.

Casey, R. L., *Battle Below,* 1945.

———, *Torpedo Junction,* 1942.

Coale, G. B., *North Atlantic Patrol,* 1942.

———, *Victory at Midway,* 1944.

Frank, A., and Horan, J. D., *U.S.S. Seawolf,* 1945. (Submarine.)

Hailey, F., *Pacific Battle Line,* 1944.

Horan, J. D., *Action Tonight,* 1945. (Story of the *O'Bannon* in the Solomons campaign.)

Jensen, O., *Carrier War,* 1945.

Johnston, S., *Queen of the Flat-tops,* 1942. (*The Lexington.*)

Karig, W. and Others, *Battle Report,* Vols. I and II. (Others in preparation.)

King, E. J., *U.S. Navy at War, 1941-1945,* 1946. (Admiral King's three reports to the Secretary of the Navy published as a single volume by the Navy Department.)

Merillat, H. L., *The Island,* 1944. (Guadalcanal campaign.)

Morris, C. G., and Cave, H. B., *The Fightin'est Ship,* 1944. (The *Helena.*)

Morris, F. D., *Pick Out the Biggest,* 1943. (The *Boise.*)

Pratt, F., *Fleet Against Japan,* 1946.

———, *The Navy's War,* 1944.

Shalett, S., *Old Nameless, the Epic of a U.S. Battlewagon,* 1943. (The *South Dakota.*)

Sherrod, R., *Tarawa: the Story of a Battle,* 1944.

Tregaskis, R., *Guadalcanal Diary,* 1943.

White, W. L., *They Were Expendable,* 1942.

Wilson, E. J., and Others, *Betio Beachhead,* 1945.

Wolfert, I., *Battle for the Solomons,* 1943.

Index